SIXTY YEARS OF EUROPEAN INTEGRATION AND GLOBAL POWER SHIFTS

This book focuses on a review of how sixty years of case-law and regulatory activity transformed the European continent and the world. It provides a critical analysis of the key features of EU integration and how this integration is perceived (internally and externally). In this context, this book also explores the EU's interactions with a number of other countries and organisations with the objective of assessing the EU's role in global governance.

Volume 97 in the Series Modern Studies in European Law

Modern Studies in European Law

Recent titles in this series:

Questioning EU Citizenship: Judges and the Limits of Free Movement and Solidarity in the EU
Edited by Daniel Thym

The European Union under Transnational Law: A Pluralist Appraisal
Matej Avbelj

Illegally Staying in the EU: An Analysis of Illegality in EU Migration Law
Benedita Menezes Queiroz

Social Legitimacy in the Internal Market: A Dialogue of Mutual Responsiveness
Jotte Mulder

The EU Better Regulation Agenda: A Critical Assessment
Edited by Sacha Garben and Inge Govaere

Administrative Regulation Beyond the Non-Delegation Doctrine: A Study on EU Agencies
Marta Simoncini

The Interface Between EU and International Law: Contemporary Reflections
Edited by Inge Govaere and Sacha Garben

The Rise and Decline of Fundamental Rights in EU Citizenship
Adrienne Yong

The Court of Justice and European Criminal Law: Leading Cases in a Contextual Analysis
Edited by Valsamis Mitsilegas, Alberto di Martino and Leandro Mancano

The EU as a Global Regulator for Environmental Protection: A Legitimacy Perspective
Ioanna Hadjiyianni

Citizenship, Crime and Community in the European Union
Stephen Coutts

Critical Reflections on Constitutional Democracy in the European Union
Edited by Sacha Garben and Inge Govaere

Constitutional Law of the EU's Common Foreign and Security Policy: Competence and Institutions in External Relations
Graham Butler

The Juridification of Individual Sanctions and the Politics of EU Law
Eva Nanopoulos

For the complete list of titles in this series, see 'Modern Studies in European Law' link at www.bloomsburyprofessional.com/uk/series/modern-studies-in-european-law

Sixty Years of European Integration and Global Power Shifts

Perceptions, Interactions and Lessons

Edited by
Julien Chaisse

•HART•
OXFORD • LONDON • NEW YORK • NEW DELHI • SYDNEY

HART PUBLISHING

Bloomsbury Publishing Plc

Kemp House, Chawley Park, Cumnor Hill, Oxford, OX2 9PH, UK

1385 Broadway, New York, NY 10018, USA

HART PUBLISHING, the Hart/Stag logo, BLOOMSBURY and the Diana logo are trademarks of Bloomsbury Publishing Plc

First published in Great Britain 2019

A catalogue record for this book is available from the British Library.

Library of Congress Cataloging-in-Publication data

Names: Chaisse, Julien, editor.

Title: Sixty years of European integration and global power shifts : perceptions, interactions and lessons / edited by Julien Chaisse.

Description: Oxford ; New York : Hart, 2019. | Series: Modern studies in European law; volume 97 | Includes bibliographical references and index.

Identifiers: LCCN 2019042002 (print) | LCCN 2019042003 (ebook) | ISBN 9781509933723 (hardback) | ISBN 9781509933730 (Epub)

Subjects: LCSH: Law—European Union countries. | European Union.

Classification: LCC KJE958 .S59 2019 (print) | LCC KJE958 (ebook) | DDC 341.242/209—dc23

LC record available at https://lccn.loc.gov/2019042002

LC ebook record available at https://lccn.loc.gov/2019042003

ISBN: HB: 978-1-50993-372-3
ePDF: 978-1-50993-374-7
ePub: 978-1-50993-373-0

Typeset by Compuscript Ltd, Shannon

CONTENTS

PART II
THE EUROPEAN UNION AS A GLOBAL ACTOR: ISSUES AND PARTNERS

PART III
EUROPEAN UNION'S TRADE POLICY: GLOBAL AND REGIONAL TRADE CHALLENGES

LIST OF CONTRIBUTORS

Nilanjan Banik has a degree in economics from Delhi School of Economics, India; and Utah State University, USA. His work focus on the application of econometrics in issues relating to international trade and development economics. Professor Banik has project experience with KPMG, India; Australian Department of Foreign Affairs and Trade, Australia; Laffer Associates, USA; Ministry of Commerce, Government of India; RIS and ICRIER, New Delhi; Center for Economic Policy Research, UK; Asian Development Bank Institute, Tokyo; Asian Development Bank, Manila; Copenhagen Consensus, Denmark; UNESCAP-ARTNeT, Thailand, Australia India Institute, University of Melbourne; and World Trade Organization, Geneva.

Nilanjan Banik has teaching experience with Utah State University, USA; University of Durham, UK; University of Greenland, Nuuk; Institute for Financial Management and Research, Chennai; Indian Institute of Management (campus at Indore, Rohtak, Nagpur, and Ranchi); Mahindra Ecole Centrale, Hyderabad; Madras School of Economics; and Reserve Bank Staff College, Chennai.

Nilanjan Banik has publication in reputed journals such as International Review of Economics and Finance, Empirical Economics, Review of Development Economics, etc. He also has the distinction of writing editorials for all major English dailies in India, and has written over 175 editorials including the ones at Wall Street Journal and Huffington Post.

Daniele Bianchi is Advisor-Senior Legal Expert of the Legal Service of the European Commission and contracting Professor of Food Law at Sorbonne University in Paris.

Olga Boltenko is a chairperson of the ICC Hong Kong Commercial Law and Practice Committee and a partner in the Hong Kong office of Fangda Partners. She specialises in international trade, investment protection, and investment arbitration. She acted as legal counsel in investor-state disputes under the auspices of the Permanent Court of Arbitration and as tribunal secretary in dozens of commercial disputes, both ad hoc and institutional (including SIAC, ICC, HKIAC, SCC), in a wide array of industries including oil and gas, infrastructure, construction, telecommunications and pharmaceuticals.

Olga Boltenko is listed as arbitrator on the Hong Kong International Arbitration Centre (HKIAC) list of arbitrators, and on the arbitrator panels of CIETAC, SIAC, and AIAC. She teaches international arbitration at The University of Hong Kong, and investment law at the Royal University for Law and Economics in Phnom Penh.

Julien Chaisse is Professor at the City University of Hong Kong, School of Law. He is an award-winning scholar of international law with a special focus on the regulation and development of economic globalisation. His teaching and research include international trade/investment law, international taxation, international arbitration, and Internet law. Before joining CityU, Dr Chaisse had over 15 years' teaching experience at universities mainly in Hong Kong and Europe. Prior to his academic career, he was a senior fellow at the World Trade Institute (Switzerland), and a diplomat at the Embassy of France in New Delhi (India). Dr Chaisse has constantly set up forward-looking interdisciplinary projects, and attracted major research grants for his universities. The former includes the series of 'Asia FDI Forum', one of the most prominent conferences on foreign investment law and economics in Asia, and the latter includes the Jean Monnet Network's 'The European Union at the Crossroads of Global Order' (EUCROSS), one of the biggest interdisciplinary research projects for the EU and its main international partners.

As one of the leading scholars in the field of international economic law, Dr Chaisse presently serves as an editorial board member for some high-impact international journals. He has also frequently been invited as a manuscript reviewer for top-notch journals in the field, including *European Journal of International Law*, *Journal of International Dispute Settlement*, *Melbourne Journal of International Law*, *Washington Journal of International Law*, *ICSID Review*, *Columbia FDI Perspectives*, *Journal of International Economic Law*, *TDM* and *Leiden Journal of International Law*.

In addition to his professorship, Dr Chaisse is a well-experienced arbitrator and a main consultant to international organisations, governments, multinational law firms, and private investors. Dr Chaisse is also very active in professional communities locally and internationally. In Hong Kong, he serves as Deputy Secretary-General of the Asian Academy of International Law (AAIL), Director of the Dot Trademark Policy Committee (DTPC), co-founder of the Internet Intellectual Property Institute (IIPI), and Member of the Hong Kong's Government Board of Review (Inland Revenue Ordinance). Dr Chaisse is also a member of some of the world's foremost organisations, including the World Economic Forum Tax and Globalization Working Group and the Internet Corporation for Assigned Names and Numbers (ICANN) Working Group on gTLDs' rights protection. He an Advisor and Partner to the United Nations ARTNET on FDI and a member of the Academic Forum on ISDS.

Debashis Chakraborty is an Associate Professor of Economics at the Indian Institute of Foreign Trade (IIFT), New Delhi. Previously he was associated with Rajiv Gandhi Institute for Contemporary Studies (RGICS), a policy think tank based in New Delhi. He has obtained his PhD degree from Jawaharlal Nehru University (JNU), with a focus on trade-environment linkage in the Indian context.

Debashis Chakraborty's research interests include international trade policy and WTO negotiations and environmental sustainability. His forthcoming co-edited volume entitled, *Environmental Challenges and Governance: Diverse Perspectives from Asia* will be published by Routledge, UK. He is also Associate Editor of *Foreign Trade Review*, Sage.

Panagiotis Delimatsis is Professor of European and International Trade Law at Tilburg University, the Netherlands. He is Director of the Tilburg Law and Economics Center (TILEC), an interdisciplinary Center of Excellence, the biggest of its kind in Europe, studying the governance of economic activity. Panos leads the research cluster 'Finance, Trade and Investment' within the TILEC Research Program and co-leads TILEC's work on standardisation, competition and innovation. Previously, he was a senior research fellow at the World Trade Institute, where he led the preparation of a comprehensive report on the fragmentation and coherence of international trade regulation and an interdisciplinary two-year project on financial innovation. In the academic year 2015–16, Panos was a visiting Scholar at Harvard Law School and a Fellow with the Program on International Financial Systems, on research leave from Tilburg University.

In December 2016, he was awarded a Consolidator Grant by the European Research Council (ERC), the most prestigious mid-level personal grant at the EU level. With his team, Panos conducts empirical research on the strategies and transformative abilities that enhance the resilience of non-State regulatory bodies in finance and manufacturing.

Panos' research focuses on the comparative regulation of services industries, issues of transnational governance and the regulation of international trade. More recently, he has worked on standardisation in services, including the financial sector, and on financial innovation. His work has appeared in top refereed international and European journals.

Panos is the author of *International Trade in Services and Domestic Regulations – Necessity, Transparency, and Regulatory Diversity* (International Economic Law Series, Oxford University Press, 2007). He also co-edited two collective volumes, the first on *The Prospects of International Trade Regulation* (Cambridge University Press, 2011) and the second on *Financial Services at the Crossroads – Implications for Supervision, Institutional Design and Trade* (Kluwer Law International, 2011). More recently, he edited a comprehensive book on *The Law, Economics and Politics of International Standardization*, published by Cambridge University Press in 2015, and a *Research Handbook on Climate Change and Trade Law*, published by Elgar Publishing in 2016. Panos studied law in Greece, Germany and Switzerland.

Fernando Dias Simões is Associate Professor at the Faculty of Law of the Chinese University of Hong Kong since January 2019. Before joining CUHK, Professor Dias Simões taught for 14 years in universities in Macau and Portugal; in addition, he practised in a major law firm and served as in-house counsel to a water concessionaire company in his native Portugal. His research interests include international adjudication (in particular, commercial and investment arbitration), investment law and comparative contract law.

Professor Dias Simões is fascinated by the idea of international arbitration as more than a simple dispute settlement mechanism: arbitrators are private service providers, and arbitration a market. However, this 'market' is undergoing profound changes, particularly in the field of investment arbitration. In his ongoing research projects Professor Dias Simões questions whether this phenomenon is evidence of simple growing pains or, more than that, of a true identity crisis.

Ian S Forrester is Judge at the General Court of the European Union. He was previously a Partner at White and Case where he advised companies, as well as sovereign states and other governmental authorities, industry associations and private individuals, on European Union law, especially competition law, trade law, customs, internal market rules, intellectual property and constitutional rights in a variety of sectors, including broadcasting, chemicals, information technology, pharmaceuticals, software and sport. Clients on whose behalf he has acted before national courts, national competition authorities, the European General Court and the European Court of Justice or the European Commission include the BBC, Canon, DuPont, the European Commission, GlaxoSmithKline, the Government of Gibraltar, the Liberal Democrat Party, Microsoft, Pfizer, Scottish Football Association, Toshiba, Toyota, UEFA and Union Carbide, as well as a number of private individuals. He has been involved in a number of leading cases, including *Magill*, *IMS* and *Microsoft* (compulsory licensing), *Bosman* (transfer of professional football players), *Syfait v GlaxoSmithKline* (parallel trade), *Pfizer Animal Health* (the precautionary principle) and *A v National Blood Authority* (whether blood transfusions causing hepatitis C were a 'defective' 'product'). He also practised trade law, having handled numerous customs and anti-dumping cases at both the administrative and appeal stages, as well as a number of WTO matters. He has served as an arbitrator in ICC and ICSID proceedings. Ian Forrester has particular experience representing individuals and companies on questions of human rights as recognised by the European Convention on Human Rights and Fundamental Freedoms. The Convention is respected both by the European Union courts in Luxembourg and the ECtHR in Strasbourg. Notable cases include defending an investigative journalist, Hans-Martin Tillack, against attempts to force him to reveal his sources, and a challenge to how the European Commission conducts competition cases. He has published a number of academic articles on the latter topic which has become increasingly important in light of the Lisbon Treaty, which from December 2009 made the case law of the Strasbourg court binding on the Luxembourg courts. He has acted in a number of other pro bono matters before the European courts on behalf of civil servants and their families. In 1981, Ian Forrester co-founded with Christopher Norall the Brussels EC law firm of Forrester & Norall, which subsequently became Forrester Norall & Sutton and merged with White & Case in 1998. Ian Forrester has written numerous articles and chapters on competition law, legal privilege, science and good regulatory practice, trade policy, customs and dumping.

Danny Friedmann is an award-winning researcher and lecturer of Intellectual Property Law, especially trademark law, geographical indications and patent law.

Professor Friedmann's monograph is titled *Trademarks and Social Media, Towards Algorithmic Justice* (Edward Elgar Publishing, September 2015). His peer-reviewed articles are published by *Journal of Intellectual Property Law and Practice* (Oxford University Press), *European Intellectual Property Review*, *Benelux Trade Marks and Design Rights (BMM) Bulletin* and *GRUR Int*. He also published in the *California Western International Law Journal*.

His book chapter on Google and China was quoted by the Advocate General of the Court of Justice of the European Union in *Google Spain* C-131/12 in 2013.

Professor Friedmann has been involved with WILMap of the Stanford Center for Internet and Society since 2014. His blog called IP Dragon, which he founded in 2005, is widely read. Friedmann also publishes in media, such as IP Kat, IP-Watch, SCMP and Hong Kong Free Press.

Professor Friedmann was invited as International Guest Speaker of the EU Centre for Global Affairs at the University of Adelaide in October 2016, and Castetter Visiting Scholar at California Western School of Law in San Diego, in July 2016. He is a Principal Commentator and External Examiner at the University of Macau since 2016. In October 2017 he was a Visiting Scholar at the University of Macau.

Professor Friedmann is member of the editorial board of the *Journal of Intellectual Property Law and Practice*.

Irene Sobrino Guijarro is an Associate Professor of Constitutional Law at the University of Seville, Spain. She holds a PhD from the European University Institute in Florence (Italy) and conducted postdoctoral research at Harvard Law School as a Fulbright scholar. Her research interests lie in the relationship between federalism and welfare state, the constitutional protection of social and economic rights, focusing in particular on the right to health care.

Shintaro Hamanaka is currently Overseas Fellow of Institute of Developing Economies of Japan External Trade Organization (IDE-JETRO), stationed as Washington DC. He is holding Visiting Fellowship at Reischauer Center for East Asian Studies at School of Advanced International Studies (SAIS), Johns Hopkins University. Before joining the IDE-JETRO in 2016, he worked for the Asian Development Bank (ADB) for eight years as Economist at Office of Regional Economic Integration. Between 2006 and 2008, he was involved in the Doha Round services trade negotiations at the Japanese Mission to World Trade Organization (WTO) in Geneva. Shintaro Hamanaka also worked for Bank of Japan for eight years and was involved in economic research and policy making on regional financial cooperation in Asia soon after the Asian financial crisis. His research interests include international political economy (IPE), regionalism, free trade agreements

(FTAs), bilateral investment treaties (BITs), international financial institutions, trade in services and trade facilitation. He authors several books and numerous journal articles in the field of international relations, political science, economics and international economic law.

Shintaro Hamanaka is the author of *Asian Regionalism and Japan: The Politics of Membership in Regional Diplomatic, Financial and Trade Groups* (Routledge, 2009), and *Asian Free Trade Agreements and WTO Compatibility: Goods, Services, Trade Facilitation and Economic Cooperation* (World Scientific, 2014). He has a PhD from the University of Sheffield.

Helen E Hartnell Emerita Professor Helen E. Hartnell, Juris Doctor (JD), was a faculty member at Golden Gate University School of Law in San Francisco from 1997 until 2013. She was DAAD Guest Professor of Anglo-American Law at Freie Universität Berlin, Fulbright Visiting Professor at the University of Helsinki, and Visiting Scholar at the University of Cologne. Professor Hartnell has also taught at numerous other universities, including Tulane Law School and Harvard Law School. She teaches international economic law, European law, private international law, arbitration, commercial law, and courses offering a socio-legal perspective on law.

Trygve Ben Holland is Project Expert and Permanent Lecturer for European and International legal affairs at University for Public Administration Bremen/Germany, Institute for Police and Security Research. Trygve Ben Holland also is legal advisor and practicing consultant for security and trade issues at public and private level, and Former Professor of European and International Law at University of New York Educational Group in Europe.

Kirstyn Inglis currently works as Visiting Professor at the Institute of International Relations (IRI) at the University of São Paulo (USP). She is Vice-Coordinator of the Brazil-C-EU project, a Jean Monnet Support to Institutions project (2015–18) and Co-financed by the Erasmus+ Programme of the European Union. Her research focus is on EU external relations law and policy generally, and more specifically focusing on Brazil's relations with the European Union in a broad range of subject spanning trade, food and the environment.

Sufian Jusoh is the Director and Professor of International Trade and Investment at the Institute of Malaysian and International Studies (IKMAS), Universiti Kebangsaan Malaysia, as well as the Chair for the ASEAN Integration Grand Challenge at the university. Sufian is a co-founder of the ASEAN Economic Integration Forum. He is an External Fellow of the World Trade Institute, University of Bern, Switzerland, a Distinguished Fellow at the Institute of Diplomacy and Foreign Relations, Ministry of Foreign Affairs, Malaysia, and a Member of the Pacific Economic Cooperation Council Malaysian Chapter. Sufian plays a key role in the reform of the investment laws in Myanmar, Timor Leste, Laos and the Federated States of Micronesia.

Sufian is a Barrister-at-Law (England and Wales) of Lincoln's Inn, London. Sufian holds an LLB from Cardiff Law School, an LLM (Merit), University College London and a Doctor in Law (summa Cum Laude) from University of Bern, Switzerland.

Katharina L Meissner holds a PhD in Political and Social Sciences from the European University Institute. After having defended her PhD thesis in 2016, she moved to the Institute for European Integration Research (EIF), University of Vienna, as Assistant Professor. Prior to her PhD research, she obtained a Diploma in Political Science (MA equivalent) from the Otto-Friedrich University of Bamberg, Germany, as well as a Postgraduate Diploma in Arts in Peace and Conflict Studies with distinction from the University of Otago, New Zealand.

In 2013, she was awarded a Master of Research by the European University Institute. Parts of her research has appeared in outlets such as the Journal of Common Market Studies, the Journal of European Public Policy, Public Administration, or the Review of International Political Economy. Working at the intersection of European Union Studies, International Relations, and International Political Economy, her research interests include European Union external relations and Regional Integration.

Rostam J Neuwirth is Professor at the Faculty of Law of University of Macau where he also serves as the Programme Coordinator of Master of International Business Law (IBL) in English Language. He received his PhD degree from the European University Institute (EUI) in Florence (Italy) and also holds a Master's degree in Law (LLM) from the Faculty of Law of McGill University in Montreal (Canada). His undergraduate studies he spent at the University of Graz (Austria) and the Université d'Auvergne (France). Previously, he taught at the West Bengal University of Juridical Sciences (NUJS) in Kolkata (India) and the Hidayatullah National Law University (HNLU) in Raipur (India). Prior to that, he worked for two years as a legal adviser in the Department of European Law in Department I.4 (European Law) of the Völkerrechtsbüro (International Law Bureau) of the Austrian Federal Ministry for Foreign Affairs before and during the Austrian EU Presidency.

Ernst-Ulrich Petersmann is Emeritus Professor for international and European law and former Head of the Law Department of the European University Institute (EUI), Florence. During 40 years, he has combined teaching of European and international law at numerous universities in Germany, Switzerland, Italy, the USA, South Africa, China and India with legal practice as legal advisor in the German Ministry of Economic Affairs, representative of Germany in UN, NATO and European institutions, legal counsellor in GATT, legal consultant for the EU, OECD, UNCTAD and the WTO, and secretary, member of chairman of numerous GATT/WTO dispute settlement panels.

Professor Petersmann was born in Hamburg and studied law and economics at the Universities of Berlin, Heidelberg, Freiburg (Germany), Geneva and the London School of Economics.

Ernst-Ulrich Petersmann received his Habilitation in 1989 for Swiss and German Public Law, European Law and International Law at the University of Fribourg (Switzerland). Petersmann has served as chairman of the International Trade Law Committee of the International Law Association (1999–2014) and has published 30 books and about 300 contributions to books and journals on international and European law.

Akhil Raina is Marie Curie Fellow and PhD candidate at the Leuven Centre for Global Governance Studies. He is an Indian lawyer specialising in international economic law and policy. After completing his bachelor studies in science and law, he attended the IELPO LL.M. (Uviversidad de Barcelona) as an ELSA (Europeans Law Students association) scholar. His Master's thesis, on Energy trade at the WTO, was supervised by Professor Pierre Sauvé.

Aside from doing his PhD, Akhil is a mentor associated with the TradeLab project, which provides pro bono economic law services. He has interned with the World Trade Organization (WTO) as well as with law firms and government institutions in India. He served as the Editor-in-Chief of the *Indian Journal of Arbitration Law*, and was a Teaching Assistant at National Law University, Jodhpur. His work has appeared in the *Global Trade and Customs Journal* and the *Indian Journal of International Economic Law*.

Akhil is fluent in English, Hindi and Kashmiri. He works to promote blood and stem-cell donation in India with Gene Bandhu Organization.

Susana de la Sierra is Administrative and EU Law Professor at the University of Castilla-La Mancha (Spain).Master in German and Comparative Law at the University of Bayreuth (Germany), she defended a PhD thesis at the European University Institute in Florence on judicial review in Europe. Her research has focused mainly on judicial review, comparative law and law on culture (film and audiovisual law). She is currently law clerk at the Spanish Supreme Court, Administrative Law Chamber.

Manfred Weiss started as a research fellow at the Center for the Study of Law and Society of the California University in Berkeley from 1965 to 1966. From 1970 to 1972 he was assistant professor and from 1972 to 1974 associate professor at the Law School of the J.W. Goethe University in Frankfurt. Since 1974 he has been full professor for labour law and civil law, first (from 1974 to 1977) at the Law School of the University in Hamburg and then (since 1977) at the Law School of the JW Goethe University in Frankfurt. Longer-term guest professorships brought him to universities in France, Belgium, the United States and still South Africa. He is also a consultant to different governments abroad (especially South Africa and Eastern Europe), consultant to the International Labour Organization and Consultant to the EU Commission since 1986.

Professor Weiss is the co-editor of the *International Labour Law Reports* and of several journals. He is author, co-author and editor of books and articles in the fields of labour law, industrial relations, civil law and sociology of law. He received honorary doctorates from universities in France, Peru, Hungary and South Africa. In 2015 He got the award for outstanding contribution to labour law.

Jan Wouters is Full Professor of International Law and International Organizations, Jean Monnet Chair ad personam EU and Global Governance, and founding Director of the Institute for International Law and of the Leuven Centre for Global Governance Studies, an interdisciplinary research centre with the status of both a Jean Monnet and KU Leuven Centre of Excellence, at KU Leuven. He is also President of KU Leuven's Council for International Policy.

He studied law and philosophy at Antwerp University, obtained an LLM at Yale University and was Visiting Researcher at Harvard University. As Visiting Professor at Sciences Po (Paris), Luiss University (Rome) and the College of Europe (Bruges) he teaches EU external relations law. As Adjunct Professor at Columbia University he teaches comparative EU-US perspectives on international human rights law. As Visiting Professor to the Universities of Ottawa and Trento in 2019, he teaches global and regional perspectives on international law. Prof. Wouters is a Member of the Royal Academy of Belgium for Sciences and Arts and practises law as Of Counsel at Linklaters, Brussels. He is Editor of the *International Encyclopedia of Intergovernmental Organizations*, Deputy Director of the *Revue Belge de Droit International*, and an editorial board member in 10 other international journals.

He has published widely on international and EU law, international organisations, global governance, and corporate and financial law, including 70 books, 130 journal articles and 200 chapters in international books. His most recent books include *Informal International Lawmaking* (2012), *Private Standards and Global Governance* (2012), *China, the European Union and Global Governance* (2012), *The EU's Role in Global Governance* (2013), *National Human Rights Institutions in Europe* (2013), *The Law of EU External Relations* (2nd edn 2015), *China, the EU and the Developing World* (2015), *Global Governance of Labour Rights* (2015), *Global Governance Through Trade* (2015), *The Contribution of International and Supranational Courts to the Rule of Law* (2015), *Global Governance and Democracy* (2015), *Armed Conflicts and the Law* (2016), *Judicial Decisions on the Law of International Organizations* (2016), *Internationaal Recht in Kort Bestek* (2nd edn 2017), *Research Handbook on EU Energy Law and Policy* (2017), *Commercial Uses of Space and Space Tourism* (2017), *The Commons and a New Global Governance* (2018), *EU Human Rights and Democratization Policies* (2018), *International Law: a European Perspective* (2018), and *The G7, Anti-Globalism and the Governance of Globalization* (2018).

Apart from his participation in international scientific networks, he advises various international organisations and governments, trains international officials and is often asked to comment international events in the media. He was coordinator of a large FP7 Programme FRAME, 'Fostering Human Rights Among European (External and Internal) Policies' (2013–17), and currently coordinates a large Horizon 2020 Project, RECONNECT ('Reconnecting Europe with its Citizens through Democracy and Rule of Law', 2018–22).

Chien-Huei Wu is currently Associate Research Professor in Academia Sinica, Taipei, Taiwan. He received his PhD degree in European University Institute, Florence in 2009. Since then, he worked as Assistant Professor in National Chung Cheng University, Chiayi, Taiwan for a short period. Before pursing his doctoral degree in Florence, he worked for the Ministry of Justice in Taiwan as a district attorney.

In 2011–12, Chien-Huei Wu advised the Ministry in drafting prisoner transfer legislation in Taiwan with a view to facilitating the prisoner transfer between Taiwan and China, and Taiwan and Germany. His research interests cover EU external relations law and international economic law. He follows closely EU-China and EU-ASEAN relations and pays particular attention to Asian regionalism and WTO-IMF linkage. He has just published a new book with Martinus Nijhoff entitled *WTO and the Greater China: Economic Integration and Dispute Resolution*.

1

The European Union: Achievements, Ongoing Challenges and Future Prospects

JULIEN CHAISSE

In recent years, crises have rocked the world, and the European Union (EU) has not been spared. While the EU was an exemplary model of prosperity and peace, seen as one of history's greatest successes in regional cooperation just a decade ago, it is now seen as being in decline, with its leaders and institutions unable to solve the economic crises or appease the mistrust of citizens.[1] Sixty years after the signing of the Treaty of Rome in 1957, the construction of Europe is going through a deep crisis which raises questions, criticisms, doubts and sometimes taunts.[2] The EU does not leave citizens and experts indifferent.

This book is about the 60 years of European integration which have transformed the European continent and the world. It provides a critical analysis of the key features of EU integration and how this integration is perceived (internally and externally). In this connection, this book also explores the EU's interactions with a number of other countries and organisations with the objective of assessing the EU role in global governance.

The EU has the capacity to turn diverging interests into common policies.[3] This observation can summarise in itself the relevance of the concept of 'governance' to analysis of the European political system.[4] In fact, it is possible to identify three basic features of the decision-making process in Europe. First, the actors involved

[1] See Marian Popa, 'How Deep Is the European Crisis' (2016) 8 *Cogito: Multidisciplinary Research Journal* 91–103.

[2] See generally Robert Schutze, 'Re-Reading Dassonville: Meaning and Understanding in the History of European Law' (2018) 24 *European Law Journal* 376–407; Evan G Hebert, 'Citizenship, Welfare, and National Sovereignty in Modern Europe' (2018) 6 *University of Baltimore Journal of International Law* 56–92; Daniel Davison-Vacchione, 'How is the EU like the Marvel Universe: Legal Experientialism and Law as a Shared Universe' (2018) 30 *Law & Literature* 185–220.

[3] See Philip Allott, 'The Concept of European Union' (2000) 2 *Cambridge Yearbook of European Legal Studies* 31–60.

[4] Dan Vataman, 'History of the European Union' (2010) 17 *Lex ET Scientia International Journal* 107–37.

are multiple. They are both European and national, public and private. Second, political negotiation and compromise are the key words in the decision-making process. Third, the decision at the EU level is framed by a whole set of procedures, control mechanisms and legal norms which, if they guarantee a certain effectiveness of public action, undeniably contribute to the complexity of the EU system.

This complexity can therefore be analysed and modelled using the concept of 'governance'.[5] Indeed, this notion and its different characteristics allow to explain the dynamism as well as the uncertain, multi-actor and multidimensional nature of the EU integration.[6] However, there is a great risk of seeing in the term 'governance' more a tool and technical procedures to respect rather than a utopia to achieve. To a certain extent, the use of the notion of governance could contribute to a certain depoliticisation of power in favour of technicality and the effectiveness of public action.[7] It is up to scholars, in particular, to ensure that the reform of 'European governance' is not limited to the introduction of procedural tools and instruments, but that it can also contribute to the further integration of a Europe founded by law and based on collective preferences close to the interests of European citizens (protection of the environment, basic social standards and a role in the maintenance and protection of peace).[8] It is only on this condition that the EU can fill its democratic deficit and move forward, in total harmony with the aspirations of its citizens.

I. The EU in Global Governance

The EU is a fantastic laboratory for building a new form of political unity. Despite its weaknesses, the EU has considerable value as an example to emulate. The EU is a true community of nations, dedicated to ensuring the security and prosperity of its members and projecting itself externally as a 'soft power', whose power is not expressed aggressively.[9] The EU addresses problem solving in new terms, ones which are not expressions of 'hard power'.[10] The EU integration is not an easy

[5] Anne Isla, 'For an Institutional and Organizational Economics of Law: Governance in the European Union' (2003) 54 *Droit et Societe* 353–76.

[6] See Kenneth A Armstrong, 'Rediscovering Civil Society: The European Union and the White Paper on Governance' (2002) 8 *European Law Journal* 102–32.

[7] See Diana-Ionela Anches, 'The Issue of the European Governance' (2016) 1 *Cross-Border Journal for International Studies* 7–26.

[8] See generally Roderic O'Gorman, 'EU Environmental Law and Policy Post-Brexit: Models for Engagement between the EU27 and the UK' (2018) 69 *Northern Ireland Legal Quarterly* 327–46; Tzehainesh Tekle, 'Labour Rights and the Case Law of the European Court of Justice: What Role for International Labour Standards' (2018) 9 *European Labour Law Journal* 236–62.

[9] See Jean-Yves Haine, 'The EU's Soft Power – Not Hard Enough' (2004) 5 *Georgetown Journal of International Affairs* 69–78; and Kristian L Nielsen and Maili Vilson, 'Eastern Partnership: Soft Power Strategy or Policy Failure' (2014) 19 *European Foreign Affairs Review* 243–62.

[10] Patryk Kugiel, 'End of European Soft Power: Implications for EU Foreign Policy' (2017) 26 *Polish Quarterly of International Affairs* 57–70.

project. In fact, it is undoubtedly a project constantly questioned, but it is a model of governance for the world. If things go well, global governance in a few decades may have achieved something on a planetary scale that looks like what the EU is trying to be. In this respect, the concept of the EU has a global vocation.

Despite its considerable economic weight, the EU plays a negligible role on the international scene. Often caricatured as an economic giant but a political dwarf, the EU seems to be struggling to turn its economic strength into diplomatic influence.[11] Indeed, there is no such thing as a European foreign policy, each EU Member State retaining full sovereignty in the conduct of its foreign policy.

This dichotomy between the economic weight of the EU and its place on the international political scene can largely be explained by its complex relationship with the very notion of power, which has its origins in the beginnings of European integration.[12]

When France proposed the creation of the European Coal and Steel Community (ECSC) on 9 May 1950, it did so in the name of peace and Franco-German reconciliation, but also with ulterior motives of power. For France, building a united Europe was a way to regain a role lost because of the two World Wars, and especially the second.[13] Behind the project, France hid its ambition to take the leadership of a Europe able to have weight in the world.[14] However, France's partners were not at all aligned with this objective. For the Federal Republic of Germany (FRG), the EU construction was a vector of rehabilitation.[15] But it was also a guard against power tendencies that could manifest themselves in the future. After the wars, Germany was afraid of itself, and a united Europe was a way to guard against its own demons. There is therefore distrust of power, which often leads to confrontation between nations. The Benelux countries share this feeling, as they have had to undergo the domination of their two great neighbours over the course of history. For them, Europe is a bulwark against the excesses of the French and German powers. They undoubtedly prefer American supervision, distant, less threatening and protective, than that of France and Germany in a political Europe. In fact, France is the only country for which Europe represents a vector of competition against the American superpower.[16] These ambiguities and mistrusts largely explain the failure of political Europe to this day.

[11] See Brigitte Leucht, 'The Policy Origins of the European Economic Constitution' (2018) 24 *European Law Journal* 191–205.

[12] See generally Mircea-Dorin Dobra, 'Towards a New European Paradigm' (2017) 9 *Cogito: Multidisciplinary Research Journal* 66–75 and William Phelan, 'Supremacy, Direct Effect, and Dairy Products in the Early History of European Law' (2016) 14 *International Journal of Constitutional Law* 6–25.

[13] See William I Hitchcock, 'France, the Western Alliance, and the Origins of the Schuman Plan, 1948–1950' (1997) 21 *Diplomatic History* 603–30. See also A W Lovett, 'The United States and the Schuman Plan. A Study in French Diplomacy 1950–1952' (1996) 39 *Historical Journal* 425–55.

[14] See Raymond Vernon, 'The Schuman Plan – Sovereign Powers of the European Coal and Steel Community' (1953) 47 *American Journal of International Law* 183–202 and W Friedmann, 'The European Coal and Steel Community' (1955) 10 *International Journal* 12–25.

[15] See Walter McDougall, 'Political Economy versus National Sovereignty: French Structures for German Economic Integration after Versailles' (1979) 51 *The Journal of Modern History* 4–23.

[16] See Hitchcock (n 13).

The end of the Cold War, however, marks a turning point. The threat posed by the Union of Soviet Socialist Republics (USSR) to Europe diverted the Europeans, French aside, from a desire for power. An organization of the 'Old Continent' based on a diplomatic and military agenda was likely to lead to an American disengagement in Europe. But no European defence could compete with Soviet power better than that of the US. The collapse of the Eastern bloc and its leader in 1989–91 instead raised doubts about maintaining a strong American commitment in Europe.[17] Moreover, at the end of the twentieth century, wars reappeared on the continent, making it necessary to reflect on the creation of a political Europe. This partly explains the birth of the EU's second pillar in the Maastricht Treaty (1992): the Common Foreign and Security Policy (CFSP).[18] Intergovernmental co-operation is planned in the fields of diplomacy and defence, in order to allow Europeans to react when a conflict such as that of Yugoslavia (1991–2001)[19] comes their way, and to be able to make their voice heard against the American hyper-power.

Since the entry into force of the Lisbon Treaty in 2009, the EU has exercised its diplomatic muscle, notably through the European External Action Service (EEAS), its 139 delegations around the world and its 17 civilian missions and three continents (Europe, Africa and Asia).[20] The EU deploys a range of instruments, from peacekeeping and support for security sector reform, to humanitarian assistance, support for the rule of law and reconstruction. Nevertheless, almost 30 years after the end of the Cold War, the EU has still not become a major international power at the diplomatic level. It was able to impose sanctions against Russia during the 2014 Ukrainian crisis[21] but remains divided on the Syrian issue and on the Israeli-Palestinian conflict.[22]

Yet, the EU has an opportunity to make its voice heard in the world through its multilateral approach, marked by its desire to uphold international law.[23] The EU was able to stand out from the United States during the presidency of

[17] Robert Schutze, 'On Federal Ground: The European Union as an (Inter)national Phenomenon' (2009) 46 *Common Market Law Review* 1069–106.

[18] See Sergio Baches Opi and Ryan Floyd, 'A Shaky Pillar of Global Stability: The Evolution of the European Union's Common Foreign and Security Policy' (2003) 9 *Columbia Journal of European Law* 299–332. See also Joachim Gruber, 'European Schools: A Subject of International Law Integrated into the European Union' (2011) 8 *International Organizations Law Review* 175–96.

[19] See Radovan D Vukadinovic, 'Dusko Lopandic: Trade Policy of the European Union and Yugoslavia' (1999) 1 *Review of European Law* 231–34.

[20] Simon Duke, 'The European External Action Service: Antidote Against Incoherence' (2012) 17 *European Foreign Affairs Review* 45–68.

[21] See James Headley, 'Perceptions of the Ukraine Crisis: A Clash between a Modern Russia and a Postmodern European Union' (2018) 23 *European Foreign Affairs Review* 101–18.

[22] See Pawel Turczynski, 'European Union Policy towards Ukraine' (2005) 14 *Polish Quarterly of International Affairs* 49–81. See also Stephan F H Ollick, 'The European Union in the Mediterranean Sea: Navigating the Political-Legal Shallows' (2018) 21 *Max Planck Yearbook of United Nations Law* 273–98.

[23] See Marise Cremona, 'Rhetoric and Reticence: EU External Commercial Policy in a Multilateral Context' (2001) 38 *Common Market Law Review* 359–96.

G W Bush (2000–08) and has continued to do so since the election of President Trump (2016).[24] The US withdrawal in 2017 from the Paris Climate Agreement signed in 2015 offers the EU a leadership position in this area.[25] In addition, the EU offers third countries a model, that of regional integration, which other parts of the world can try to replicate (such as Mercosur in Latin America, for example).[26]

The EU is a regional organisation with a unique integration model. With a solid institutional architecture, it benefits from significant transfers of sovereignty in a range of areas, particularly economic and commercial. Diplomacy and military affairs remain largely the preserve of the Member States. If the EU struggles to intervene in international crises (Syria, etc) and to carry weight in the international balance of power (for example against Russia), it is in fact not without influence. This is not exercised through coercion and military power but is based on the norms it promotes.[27] This particular form of integration into international relations is due to the very nature of the EU and its genesis.

II. The Evolution of a European Political Community

The current geopolitical context is conducive to a revival of European integration.[28] An exceptional opportunity is opening up for Europe to contribute to the international scene via its values of freedoms, the arts and sciences, and the economy, and its example of cooperation between States. Beyond Donald Trump and Xi Jinping, there is room for an alternative political and economic model which should bring European together. How can the integration of the continent be revived?

The dream of the founding fathers of the EU has been an 'ever closer' union, but also a 'bigger one'.[29] From the beginning, their vision was continental in scope. Building a 'community of law' based on treaties and institutions breaks with a past based on power relations.[30] Extending the borders of the EU therefore

[24] Richard O Cunningham, 'Leverage Is Everything: Understanding the Trump Administration's Linkage between Trade Agreements and Unilateral Import Restrictions' (2019) 51 *Case Western Reserve Journal of International Law* 49–76.

[25] See Timmons Roberts, 'One year since Trump's withdrawal from the Paris climate agreement', *Brookings Institute* (2018), available at www.brookings.edu/blog/planetpolicy/2018/06/01/one-year-since-trumps-withdrawal-from-the-paris-climate-agreement/.

[26] See Francois d'Arcy, 'Political Perspectives of Mercosur: Comparisons with the European Union' (2005) 59 *Droit et Societe* 19–38.

[27] Ilann Margalit Maazel, 'What is the European Union?' (2002) 16 *BYU Journal of Public Law* 243–60.

[28] See eg Maria Demertzis and Gustav Fredriksson, 'The EU Response to US Trade Tariffs' (2018) 53 *Intereconomics* 260–68.

[29] Ian Ward, 'An Ever Closer Union: The Continuing Travails of the Peoples of Europe' (2001) 15 Temple *International & Comparative Law Journal* 247–74.

[30] See R Daniel Kelemen, 'The Court of Justice of the European Union in the Twenty-First Century' (2016) 79 *Law and Contemporary Problems* 117–40.

denuclearization process. The United Nations (UN) is still waiting for the reform of its Security Council;[41] Africa is waiting for its time to mandate a permanent member (Senegal, South Africa or Nigeria?); some UN Security Council majority votes have no effect (recognition of Palestine); and the two muzzled powers – Germany and Japan – have not yet joined the Security Council. The International Monetary Fund (IMF) is slow to emerge from ambiguities (policies of adjustment and rigour) and is often seen as an instrument of constraint on the social consensus (eg Greece at the heart of the Troika's injunctions). Also, financing problems are urgent: military budgets are being revised upward, while budget deficits and the cost of sovereign debt are shifting government spending.

In any case, it is important to stress that the new global governance challenges are not naturally linked to statehood, and instead include the environment, health, human rights, women's rights, habitat protection, deforestation, the mafia, the fight against tax havens, migration, in short, broad areas but with the underlying problem of state transfers of power. In fact, globalisation is increasing and intensifying the level of interdependence between all States and international actors. In doing so, it multiplies the subjects for which the States, international organisations, NGOs and companies must set up 'international governance', understood as the capacity and the way to manage the transnational stakes by negotiation and compromise. In this respect, the EU should see opportunities in all these new challenges to contribute more stable global governance.

The EU attracts important migratory flows and provides and hosts the main tourist flows of the planet.[42] The same is true with respect to the external dimensions of environmental policies, agriculture and fisheries, transportation, energy, and research and development. The EU is a key player in combating climate change.

The EU also has a responsibility and role to play on climate issues, as illustrated by its positions and its diplomatic activism in this realm: as a leading economic and commercial player, it is indispensable on environmental issues.[43] Seasoned in the exercise of compromise and international co-operation, it has a special role and know-how which can be useful for the conclusion of complex international negotiations. Member States rely on it, both by virtue and by necessity.

The central role of the EU in international trade largely explains its position. Europe is the least protectionist trade zone in the world. It therefore constantly denounces the freedoms taken by its main partners with World Trade Organization (WTO) rules.[44] This is the case with the dumping of certain products such as

[41] See Karen E Smith, 'The European Union and the Politics of Legitimization at the United Nations' (2013) 18 *European Foreign Affairs Review* 63–80.

[42] Graham Butler and Gavin Barrett, 'Europe's Other Open-Border Zone: The Common Travel Area under the Shadow of Brexit' (2018) 20 *Cambridge Yearbook of European Legal Studies* 252–86.

[43] See Nuno S Lacasta and others, 'Consensus among Many Voices: Articulating the European Union's Position on Climate Change' (2002) 32 *Golden Gate University Law Review* 351–414.

[44] See Peter K Yu, 'Fair Use and Its Global Paradigm Evolution' [2019] *University of Illinois Law Review* 111–70.

solar panels made in China, the excessive subsidization of companies, especially Chinese, by their government, or the lack of reciprocity in the awarding of public contracts.[45] However, the European position is becoming increasingly difficult to meet in the context of growing trade tensions. This upheaval, begun under the previous US presidencies, intensified with the arrival of Donald Trump at the White House. It can be explained as much by the arrival of new players – the former emerging countries and mainly China – as by the change in the nature of trade. Services, technologies, patents and other intangible assets now constitute the bulk of the comparative advantages of countries like the US, exchanges for which the tax system is outdated. While China remains the prime target of US attacks, its historical partners, from Mexico to Canada to the EU, have not been spared. With renegotiation of trade treaties, tariff increases or even geopolitical pressures (as illustrated by the Huawei case),[46] the trade war is in full swing.[47] Europe has already paid the price with the cancellation of the European exemption for steel and aluminium exports to the US.

This clash has taken an eminently political turn. Beijing fights with its own weapons, reciprocal US tariff increases and actively supporting its businesses while the EU, for its part, leaves with a disability.[48] Europe is an economic power but not yet political. And this new context challenges its cohesion. Although it officially speaks with one voice, internally, the differences of interest are heard between the countries which, like Germany, are net exporters and those which, like France, are net importers. In the absence of a political union, and between the strategies deployed by Washington and Beijing, the EU wants to embody a third way. Alongside China, Europe can contain the unilateral instincts of American trade policy. And in partnership with the United States, it can push China to follow the rules of the WTO, especially by channelling Beijing's interventions on its economy.

The EU economic policy therefore associates the signing of strategic trade agreements with a well-understood protection of the interests of its members. In response to the US decision on steel and aluminium, the EU decided in June 2018 to apply additional tariffs on iconic US products, such as jeans and bourbon.[49]

[45] See Francais-Charles Laprevote and Sungjin Kang, 'Subsidies Issues in the WTO – An Update' [2011] European State Aid Law Quarterly 445–56. See also Raj Bhala, 'The WTO's Under-Capacity to Deal with Global Over-Capacity' (2019) 14 *Asian Journal of WTO and International Health Law and Policy* 1–32.

[46] 'Huawei faces US charges: The short, medium and long story', *BBC News* (2019), www.bbc.com/news/world-us-canada-47046264.

[47] See Ben White, 'Dark clouds hang over Trump's trade war', *Politico* (2019), www.politico.com/story/2019/05/20/trump-trade-war-2020-1455474.

[48] David J Lynch, 'Trump did something unusual on the trade front: He removed a tariff', *The Washington Post* (2019), www.washingtonpost.com/gdpr-consent/?destination=%2fbusiness%2fecon omy%2ftrump-delays-auto-tariff-threat-for-up-to-180-days%2f2019%2f05%2f17%2f95432e8e-78a7-11e9-b7ae-390de4259661_story.html%3f&utm_term=.559c5c51b4c4.

[49] Joe Raedle, 'EU's tit-for-tat tariffs on US goods come into force', *France24 News* (2019), www.france24.com/en/20180622-eu-tit-tat-tariffs-usa-goods-come-force-trump-bourbon-jeans.

At the same time, it introduced new anti-dumping and anti-subsidy trade defence tools to its market and, in November 2018, its Member States agreed to improve the screening of foreign direct investment (FDI).[50] The objective of these measures is to ensure that FDI does not pose a threat to critical infrastructures or key technologies or in terms of access to sensitive information. The EU's commitment to accompany the reform of the WTO is part of the same trend, that of imposing a third way. The major trade agreements currently being negotiated by the EU now envisage the establishment of an Investment Court System (ICS) in lieu of ad hoc arbitration tribunals.[51]

It is undeniable that the EU has many assets with which it can play a role in the affairs of the world. The first consideration is that it exists and carries weight on the international scene when it is united through its commercial policy, its competition policy and the standards that it defines for the largest single market in the world. As the world's leading economic power, it has the world's second-largest currency and a space where more than 500 million citizens globally hold a high standard of living and an envied social model worldwide. Demographically, if the European population stagnates and ages, it is not the only one. In 2050, the Union will still be more populated than the US, being, like today, the third largest in the world behind India and China.

The potentiality of all these tools available has so far been little exploited. The reasons are essentially political. If the EU appears to be a possible model in globalization, it will probably never be a classic power. European power is based not solely on coercion but also on persuasion, a method that calls for communication skills and international legitimacy. It is by nature destined to act in the medium and long term, to bring about profound changes in the countries concerned. Then, like the whole European construction, it is an original experience, progressing step by step, and one which, in this respect, cannot be compared to any other initiative.

This book delves into the EU integration process and discusses some of the key changes and pillars of the EU integration (Part I). The book then reviews the elements that allow us to assess the global role and influence of the EU (Part II), in particular with respect to the EU international trade policy (Part III).

[50] EU, 'Commission welcomes European Parliament's support for investment screening framework', *Press Release* (Brussels, 2019). See also Paulette Vander Schueren, 'EU Agrees on FDI Screening Framework', *Mayer Brown* (2018), www.mayerbrown.com/en/perspectives-events/publications/2018/12/eu-agrees-on-fdi-screening-framework.

[51] See Xavier Fernández-Pons and others, 'CETA on Investment: The Definitive Surrender of EU Law to GATS and NAFTA/BITS' (2017) 54 *Common Market Law Review* 1319–58. See also Julien Chaisse and Matteo Vaccaro-Incisa, 'The EU Investment Court: Challenges on the Path Ahead' (2018) 218 *Columbia FDI Perspectives* 1–3 and Julien Chaisse and Yves Renouf, 'Investor-state Dispute Settlement' in Jane Drake-Brockman and Patrick Messerlin (eds), *Potential Benefits of an Australia-EU Free Trade Agreement: Key Issues and Options* (Adelaide, University of Adelaide Press, 2018) 281–313.

A. Part I – European Legal Integration: Process, Difficulties and Achievements

Part I focuses on the historical EU integration process with respect to key features and dynamics of the EU as we know it today.

The process of European integration began without emphasis in Europe in the 1950s, tending, over time, to produce incisive or almost revolutionary effects in terms of the transformation of the lexicon and the cultural and training acquis of the jurists. The process of EU integration has gradually developed, albeit in a rather stratified and fragmented way, and remains a constantly evolving phenomenon. This process may have been situated, since the same period, in the more general context of the so-called globalization phenomenon, regarding its legal and institutional aspects.

In 1941, two political prisoners of Mussolini wrote a manifesto which is called the *Manifesto of Ventotene*.[52] One of these two prisoners can be considered one of the founding fathers of the European communities: it is indeed Spinelli. This *manifesto* proposed to bind the European countries in such a way that any war would be rendered impossible, so that there could no longer be any conflict. The President of the European Parliament, Pöttering, has expressly paid tribute to the foresight in this manifesto.[53]

Linking the European states was intended to be done through the establishment of an integration organisation, integration being simply the consequence of the awareness by sovereign states of their interdependence in the economic and social field. If the integration organisation is born it is because the States are aware of their interdependence. European integration is going to be done in a progressive way that has a name, ie 'functional integration'.[54] It is an integration that will be done step by step, Schuman said moreover 'Europe will not be made all at once, or according to a single plan. It will be built through concrete achievements which first create a *de facto* solidarity'.[55] The functional integration is connected to a current of thought and notably, among others, to two theorists: David Mitrany (close to the theory of functionalism)[56] and Ernst Haas

[52] Altiero Spinelli and Ernesto Rossi, *Il Manifesto di Ventotene/The Ventotene Manifesto, Editrice Ultima spiaggia* (Sand Grains 2016), www.cvce.eu/content/publication/1997/10/13/316aa96c-e7ff-4b9e-b43a-958e96afbecc/publishable_en.pdf.

[53] See Sharon Spiteri, 'Prodi manifesto creates political turmoil', *EU Observer* (2003), https://euobserver.com/institutional/13540.

[54] See Carl Lebeck, 'Implied Powers beyond Functional Integration – The Flexibility Clause in the Revised EU Treaties' (2008) 17 *Journal of Transnational Law & Policy* 303–58.

[55] The Schuman Declaration – 9 May 1950, https://europa.eu/european-union/about-eu/symbols/europe-day/schuman-declaration_en. See also Vernon (n 14) and Stuart A Scheingold, *The Rule of Law in European Integration: The Path of the Schuman Plan* (New Orleans, LA, Quid Pro Books, 2013).

[56] See David Mitrany, *The Functional Theory of Politics* (New York, NY, St Martin's Press, 1976).

(supporter of neo-functionalism).[57] The essential difference between the two theoreticians is that for David Mitrany, integration is the result of more and more developed technical cooperation between states, while for Haas integration is the result of a transfer of sovereignty. Haas will add socio-political elements in his analysis unlike Mitrany. If we go beyond this difference of approach, functional integration is based on the idea that sovereign states create an international organization with limited economic competence at the outset.

Given that there is an interaction between the economic and political domains, a 'spill over' movement is gradually being set up, meaning that the actions that have been transferred to the international organisation will develop and expand, in other words the organisation will progressively have more and more skills (initially limited in one sector and then in other areas of competence).[58] As a consequence, this increase in the organisation's competence is to the detriment of the nation state: the states will have less power. By developing, these common actions with economic effect will lead to an integration of the markets, which itself will lead to an integration of the economies, and as there is an interaction between the political and the economic, in the long run we end up with an organisation policy. That is the theory of functional integration. The EU competences have continued to grow since its creation.[59] Although these were essentially economic, they gradually spread to new areas. The Maastricht Treaty, signed in 1992, for example, gave the EU the power to legislate, under certain conditions, in the field of education, culture and consumer protection.[60]

Chapter two is written by Judge Ian Forrester and addresses the role of the rule of law in the EU integration. Judge Forrester's chapter notes that over the centuries in Europe, many treaties concluding international conflicts contained promises of eternal friendship but did not prevent future wars. The founders of what is now the EU were more successful. From 1951, a succession of treaties aimed to make war impossible by integrating economies and opening frontiers. The best known was the Treaty of Rome, which established the principle of an open economic area, free of hindrances to free movement of goods, people, services and capital. The Court of Justice of the EU (CJEU), to use the new label, was given several roles: a constitutional court which decides on disputes between the European Institutions and the Member States, and also replies to questions from national courts about the interpretation of EU law; a court of appeal which hears challenges to

[57] Ernst Haas, *Beyond the Nation-state: Functionalism and International Organization* (Stanford, CA, Stanford University Press, 1964).

[58] See Hugo Paemen, 'The European Union in International Affairs: Recent Developments' (1999) 22 *Fordham International Law Journal* 136–S148.

[59] Jeff Edmund Katcherian, 'Unraveling the Paradox: Competence and the Failure of Subsidiarity in the European Union' (2012) 35 *PoLAR: The Political and Legal Anthropology Review* 271–88. See also Julien Chaisse, 'Promises and Pitfalls of the European Union Policy on Foreign Investment – How Will the New EU Competence on FDI Affect the Emerging Global Regime' (2012) 15 *Journal of International Economic Law* 51–84.

[60] See Genevieve Helleringer and Anne-Lise Sibony, 'European Consumer Protection through the Behavioral Lens' (2017) 23 *Columbia Journal of European Law* 607–46.

the legality of actions taken by the EU agencies and institutions; and a source of advisory opinions. The Court in its early days took important decisions establishing basic doctrines: direct effect such that citizens could invoke EU law in national courts, and primacy, such that European law prevailed over inconsistent national law. The Court has produced some celebrated decisions in the field of free movement of persons, equality of pay for men and women, sport, environment, trade and competition, data protection and fundamental rights. It is evident that the European venture is passing through one of its worst crises now. The tank of enthusiasm for the European vehicle is quite empty for now, and indeed 'Europe's' great successes (eliminating war in Europe and bringing down the Iron Curtain) date from last century. We don't know what solution or adaptation the political leaders will adopt. But whatever these are, there will remain a need for resolution of legal controversies. The EU is the only place on Earth today where (almost) a continent of states has agreed to deliver to their citizens access to healthcare, equal treatment of men and women, freedom of speech, a pension, education and a minimum wage. There are assuredly imperfections and gaps and inconsistencies. The constitutional architecture of the EU is creaky. There is no 'government' and no 'opposition' in the European Parliament. But the achievement of delivering decent standards by exploiting the opportunities of cross-border commerce and an open labour market is real and difficult to deny. It is also fair to note that the common market, despite its curious constitutional architecture, has delivered increased prosperity, the elimination of military rivalry and the liberation of Eastern Europe from Communism. These achievements have been based on a multitude of detailed steps reached by cooperative regulation on matters which often seem obscure, in order to expand economic opportunity, competitive choice, and to deliver prosperity to those who wanted to work in a free (or less unfree) economy. It is of enormous importance to build into our democracy judicial review of public actions. And the European Courts have played a necessary role in that respect.

In chapter three, Rostam J Neuwirth argues that generally contradictions do not go well with the underlying educational and scientific paradigm prevalent in Europe of what is called 'the law of the excluded middle', which is usually expressed by the claim that 'everything must either be or not be'. In other words, the original idea underlying the EU is oxymoronic. As such, it was therefore already at its inception ahead of its time, given that still today the foundations of education as well as scientific and public discourse are largely based on a wide set of traditional lines of thinking expressed through numerous dichotomies, such as those of national versus international (or European) law, or public versus private (international) law, to mention but two examples from the field of law. Exemplified by selected essentially oxymoronic concepts coined and applied in the process of European integration, the chapter will try to identify the main causes for Euroscepticism translated into a stagnating progress towards an ever closer union in an era constantly accelerating change in order to find ways to bring the oxymoron of the EU alive (again).

In chapter four, Manfred Weiss provides a thorough analysis of the social dimension of the EU. In 1957 the Europeanisation of social policy and in particular of labour law was not on the agenda of the European Economic Community (EEC). This was left to the Member States. The goal was merely to establish a single market. Due to severe labour market problems in the 1970s, the first steps to elaborate European labour law were taken. In the 1980s and 1990s, the Treaties were amended. The powers to legislate on labour law were extended, the requirement of unanimous voting for legislation for many topics was modified to the requirement of qualified majority, and the social partners were integrated into the legislative machinery. All this is now contained in a consolidated version in the Treaty on the Functioning of the EU (TFEU). After a long and controversial discussion, a Charter of Fundamental Rights of the EU has been developed, first as a ceremonial declaration in 2000 and since 2009 integrated into the TEU as binding law. This Charter contains a whole set of fundamental social rights guaranteeing individual and collective social standards. The European legislature has passed quite a few Directives on individual and collective labour law, thereby establishing minimum standards throughout the EU. This legislation, however, is still fragmentary and unsystematic. It urgently needs to be extended. The EU needs a new push on social policy in order to overcome the present legitimacy crisis. Due to the enlargements of the originally small and rather homogeneous EEC, the EU has become not only big but very heterogeneous. This has led to an increasing diversity of interests which has made it more and more difficult to get the necessary majority for legislation. Therefore, the EU has chosen alternative strategies to promote social policy: the so-called Lisbon Strategy and the Strategy 2020. These strategies are meant not to establish hard law on the European level but merely to put soft pressure on the Member States. This has turned out to be insufficient. Recently a new initiative has been presented: a European Pillar of Social Rights. However, this pillar to a great extent remains soft law; only to a marginal extent does it strive for hard law on the EU level. In order to overcome the stagnation of hard law in the social field, two strategies are possible: either enhanced cooperation of some Member States, which would lead to an EU of different speeds, or an amendment of the Treaty to facilitate EU legislation on social topics. Whether in view of the Brexit shock this latter alternative is a realistic option remains an open question.

In chapter five, Trygve Ben Holland critically discusses the geographical scope and diversity of EU rules on public procurement. The EU and its Member States have developed detailed provisions on public procurement processes to ensure fair and transparent practices and application of impartial legal remedies. These provisions apply within the Single Market and to a great extent outside the EU. There is a multitude of agreements with third states, which, in their current or future effect, are aiming at market access for undertakings from the respective territory of one party within the territory of the other party. Some agreements are intensifying the integration of the Single Market, while others are of pre-accessional character or are an expression of political intention; some of the bilateral agreements extend the applicability of the Government Procurement Agreement (GPA).

This chapter addresses the territorial applicability of EU provisions of public procurement processes and outlines the major differences according to the State or region in question.

In chapter six, Irene Sobrino Guijarro focuses on cross-border health care in the context of spatial configurations of welfare in the EU. Despite the scarce explicit powers that the EU has over social areas, the EU law has a significant impact on the laws and practices of the Member States in the area of welfare broadly conceived. There are two main aspects to the claim that the EU has an important role in this field. The first relates to the 'transverse' impact that EU economic law and policy have on existing national laws and policies in the area of social welfare, and the second relates to the graduate emergence of elements, although still in a fragmented form, of a distinctive EU welfare dimension. The EU health care law provides an optimal case through which to explore the basic tensions and logic structurally linked to the 'welfare construction' in the EU. On the one hand, the TFEU explicitly states that health care is the responsibility of the Member States, which preserve their own national health policy as part of their unique social policy. On the other hand, as the health systems of Member States involve interactions with people, goods and services, all of which are granted freedom of movement across borders by the same Treaty, many national health systems are in fact subject to EU law and policy. Specifically, Irene Sobrino Guijarro focuses on the analysis of cross-border healthcare in the EU and on the tensions underlying its construction. Through case law, and by enforcing the internal market Treaty provisions on the fundamental principles of free movement of services, the European Court of Justice has created a procedure that fosters patient mobility in the EU, through the development of an interesting operation of translation of the internal free movement into a right for patients to access health care services outside their home state.

In chapter seven, Panagiotis Delimatsis offers an authoritative review of services regulation, a key aspect of the EU internal market. The Services Directive has been the EU's controversial reaction to the never-ending tale of completing the single market for services. An initially central piece of the Lisbon Strategy, the Directive ambitiously aims at the elimination of the remaining legal barriers to the achievement of the internal market for services, while ensuring legal certainty for service suppliers and consumers. The Directive operationalises Articles 49 and 56 of the TFEU and thus consolidates six decades of case law delivered by the CJEU. It is a dynamic legal instrument which includes various initiatives and additional measures to be undertaken in the wake of the implementation of the Directive, thereby calling for continuous communication and exchange of information among national authorities of Member States. In this communication network, the role of the European Commission is to monitor, and if necessary, launch infringement proceedings. Panagiotis Delimatsis reviews the first 10 years after the adoption of the Services Directive and its first enforcement period. In this respect, the chapter argues that the Directive constitutes, along with EU primary law, an additional legal instrument to be used by the CJEU judges with a view to further pursue the objectives of the fundamental freedoms of services and establishment. The second, arguably more important, level on which the Directive operates relates to the transparency-enhancing and mutual-trust-building benefits from the implementation of the Directive, which should lead to important compensatory measures of formal and informal nature alike. On a pessimistic tone, then, Panagiotis Delimatsis submits that the Directive will not serve as a vector for completing the single market in services anytime soon. In the end, its effectiveness will depend on the Member States' discretion and the capacity of regulators to build trust despite regulatory competition within the EU.

In chapter eight, Susana de la Sierra turns her attention to government, culture and movies to see whether there is a common understanding from a European perspective. Sixty years after the adoption of the Treaty of Rome, many conclusions can be drawn on the evolution of the European project. Clearly, social and economic developments are at stake daily in practical life and in the media. Yet one of the major achievements of the EU is precisely a legal one: the fact that what is now the EU is a 'Community of Law'. This was very soon stated by the European Court of Justice, together with the major features of EU law, namely direct effect and its legally binding character. Yet, this being so, there is a need for a guardian to be set. Whatever the features of EU law, unless there is a body controlling these features, the whole project remains a dead letter. Therefore, the role of the European Court of Justice (ECJ) has proved vital since the very beginning, as it started a bold case law designing the whole judicial architecture, on the basis, of course, of the guidelines provided by the Treaties. It strengthened the position of national judges, providing them with instruments in order to control the application of EU law and, therefore, its effectiveness. As a conclusion of the former, among the many stories that can be told, one is the story of the so-called judicial dialogue, a story that involves ups and downs, as any other story, but which can be qualified all in all as a story of success. The chapter by Susana de la Sierra is devoted to developing this idea, focusing on the following points: the system of preliminary rulings as the context for judicial dialogue; the role of national judges, and its strengths and its weaknesses; and in particular, the role of Supreme Courts and the trend towards the 'objective character' of justice before final or Supreme Courts.

B. Part II – The EU as a Global Actor: Issues and Partners

Part II looks at the role of the EU at the global level. While the EU certainly has developed robust integration, these foundations allow for ever-increasing action and influence at the global level.

The political models born in Europe have often influenced the rest of the world, either through colonisation or by positive inspiration drawn from the formulation of universal values.[61] But the growing difficulties of the EU experience, stumbling

[61] See Smith (n 41).

at the stage of 'politicization' at the supranational level, have made the beautiful innovation falter. Among the errors committed by the Member States, there are three irremediable ones: lack of unity, levelling down and lack of independence.

The lack of unity between Member States – both too numerous and still masters of a game that failed to reposition themselves on a common European democratic legitimacy – deprived the EU of a voice on the international scene, preventing strong positions on major international issues, economic ones as well as those of diplomatic or security.[62] The search for pure and perfect competition in order to create a perfect market has brought competition within the continent, which has led to a levelling down of standards (social, environmental, health, etc).[63]

In the last few years, the debt crisis, the fragility of its financial institutions, the fights for growth and against unemployment, and the rise of populism, have been hoarded by the EU, which has not been able to consolidate, much less to increase, its influence and role on the international scene. Can Europeans make the EU a real strategic player? Or can the EU, weakened by its internal divisions, its dependence on the United States and its risk aversion, aspire only to be a 'small power'?

This situation has made the old continent inexistent on major international issues, unable to assert itself and give birth to a technological giant even though many Europeans have played a major role in technological advances. On the question of the environment, the Paris agreement has made a lot of noise, but we already know that most commitments will not be respected.[64] In fact, the EU has difficulties in inaugurating an original economic model that can respond to the challenges of the twenty-first century and protect against crises and shortcomings in the current system. On the humanitarian and military issues of recent years, Europe has not been more present. Totally absent from the Syrian tragedy, the EU suffers the migration crisis by always reacting too late and still insufficiently.[65] More recently, the clash between India and Pakistan would require, according to some opinions, the intervention of a third party to bring the two parties to the negotiating table.[66] But here too, there are no traces of the EU that would be perfectly suited to this kind of mission even if it had the possibility to act in this area.

[62] Trevor Salmon, 'European Security and Defence Policy: Built on Rocks or Sand?' (2005) 10 *European Foreign Affairs Review* 359–80.

[63] See Anca D Chirita, 'Competition Policy's Social Paradox: Are We Losing Sight of the Wood for the Trees?' (2018) 14 *European Competition Journal* 367–416.

[64] See Gillian Nelson, 'EU and China Underscore "Highest Political Commitment" to Effective Implementation of Paris Agreement', *IISD News* (2018), https://sdg.iisd.org/news/eu-and-china-underscore-highest-political-commitment-to-effective-implementation-of-paris-agreement/.

[65] See Graham Butler, 'Legal Responses to the European Union's Migration Crisis' (2018) 19 *San Diego International Law Journal* 277–310.

[66] See Billy Perrigo, 'Tensions Between India and Pakistan Are at Their Highest Point in Decades. Here's What to Know', *Time* (2019) https://time.com/5538756/india-pakistan-kashmir-tensions-airstrikes/. See also Jonathan Landay, 'US remains concerned about India-Pakistan tensions', *Reuters* (2019), www.reuters.com/article/us-india-kashmir-crisis-usa/us-remains-concerned-about-india-pakistan-tensions-official-idUSKCN1R12HO.

In recent years, the difficulties of multilateralism have led to a return to the national level, the only way to return to politics. This trend carries dangers and hopes – the hope of relaunching dynamics of adaptation of the systems to the new realities mentioned above, but also, the danger of falling back into the previous century, with armed confrontations. It is this second pitfall, the reinvention of a new multilateralism that is at least temporarily under the responsibility of States, which must be avoided. With its present and past failures, the next European multilateralism must reaffirm democracy, independence and exemplarity.[67] It is by demonstrating the effectiveness of the method applied to its continent that it will be able to inspire the rest of the world in its adoption, allowing the world to emerge from this period of resurgence of the projects of global mono-state governance (American in particular), and validating the compatibility between political anchoring and the effectiveness of supra-national governance.

The EU has many attributes of power (economy, trade, technology, culture and money), a range of policies that cover the most important issues of contemporary international politics, including the military and strategic aspects, and a broad network of relations with all the countries of the world as well as with regional or international organisations. Therefore, the question is to know whether these assets, strategic and relational, allow it to project itself in the world, to play a substantive role, to be recognised as an actor in its own right and thus to have taken on this environment.

In chapter nine, Jan Wouters and Akhil Raina question the EU approach vis-à-vis global economic governance. The EU has shown and claimed great attachment to multilateralism but, in recent years, the EU did not hesitate to also pursue bilateral negotiations in apparent contradictions with the multilateral agenda. Jan Wouters and Akhil Raina consider the reasons and drivers for these seemingly conflicting policy choices while trying to assess whether any options lead to greater successes. The chapter demonstrates that the EU support for multilateralism (whether WTO, UN or G8) lacks the formulation of a clear and coordinated strategy (vis-à-vis its Member States) in economic bodies. In this respect, the EU will need to enhance its coordination with Member States to also gain greater influence (and more significant success) at most international economic governance bodies, which is an important direction for both the EU for the integration and the other architects of global governance.

In chapter 10, Ernst-Ulrich Petersmann draws the lessons from European constitutionalism for reforming multilevel governance of transnational public goods in Asia. *Constitutionalism* (as a normative conception for the input-legitimacy of public law, a sociological conception for its output legitimacy, and as a legal methodology for interpreting and developing public goods systems) has proven to be the most important 'political invention' for protecting public goods. The historical evolution from 'constitutionalism 1.0' to multilevel 'European

[67] Cremona (n 23).

constitutionalism 3.0' suggests that functionally limited 'multilevel constitutionalism 4.0' is both a necessary and politically realistic methodology for making multilevel governance of transnational public goods more legitimate and effective. Multilevel constitutionalism is required by the universal recognition of human rights; the transformation of *national* into *transnational public goods* due to globalisation; the need for limiting 'collective action problems'; and the greater effectiveness of citizen-driven 'network governance'. Ernst-Ulrich Petersmann demonstrates that European constitutional law offers six important lessons for extending 'republican' and 'cosmopolitan constitutionalism' beyond national borders: constitutional and 'cosmopolitan interpretations' of international law are legitimate because they support 'citizen struggles for justice' and 'democratic peace'; they strengthen the 'instrumental' and 'systemic functions' of law and the input and output legitimacy of intergovernmental law-making. As also shown by this chapter, empirical evidence confirms that '*cosmopolitan legal systems*' promote 'network governance' and public goods more effectively than 'inter-governmental chess-board governance', for instance by empowering citizens through 'countervailing rights', remedies and 'bottom-up constitutionalisation'.

In chapter 11, Helen E Hartnell concentrates on the EU's civil justice policy field. Signed in 1997, the Amsterdam Treaty added building an Area of Freedom, Security and Justice (AFSJ) as an integration goal. One piece of the AFSJ puzzle is the field that the European Commission calls *civil justice*. Initially based on a narrow conception of measures aimed at enhancing *judicial cooperation in civil matters*, civil justice now incorporates a wide array of issues relating to civil procedure, conflict of laws (private international law) and the administration of justice. After 15 years of rapid and at times even astonishing development, the EU's civil justice policy field has recently entered a slower and possibly more mature stage, thanks in large part to a changed institutional environment in Brussels. After providing a conceptual overview and identifying phases in its historical evolution, Helen E Hartnell surveys key legal instruments in the policy field. Next, the chapter turns to the changing institutional environment in Brussels and considers its impact on civil justice matters. Some current projects are noted. Finally, the chapter asks about the significance of developments in the civil justice policy field for the process of European integration.

In chapter 12, Katharina L Meissner analyses the EU's shift from interregional negotiations with Mercosur to a Bilateral Strategic Partnership with Brazil. In 2007, the EU launched a Strategic Partnership with Brazil despite the EU's commitment to multilateralism and despite the long-lasting interregional relationship between the EU and Mercosur since 1995. By singling out Brazil, the EU shifted from the EU–Mercosur interregional negotiations on an Association Agreement (1999–2004) to a bilateral track. In view of the EU's inconsistency in multilateral, interregional and bilateral approaches towards South America, the chapter analyses why the EU shifted to a Strategic Partnership, and it will compare the interregional negotiations (1999–2004) with the bilateral talks with Brazil (since 2007). The comparative analysis relies on original data from 29 semi-structured elite interviews conducted in Brussels, Belgium, and Montevideo, Uruguay, and on grey literature and the news portal Mercopress. Katharina L Meissner argues that the EU switched from interregional to bilateral talks because it feared losing Brazil to its competitors, the US and China. In its endeavour to prevent this loss, when interregional negotiations seemed fruitless because of Mercosur's increasing fragmentation, the EU privileged Brazil as a strategic partner. Although the EU has committed itself to supporting regional integration in South America, material interests have side-lined this commitment. This chapter looks at these – to date little studied – material interests that have rendered the EU's foreign policy towards developing regions vulnerable to international factors.

In chapter 13, Chien-Huei Wu looks at the EU-China Partnership and Cooperation Agreement. At the 9th EU–China Summit in 2006, the leaders of the EU and China recognised that the EU–China bilateral relationship was maturing into a comprehensive strategic partnership. The leaders further declared that

> [i]n order to reflect the full breadth and depth of today's comprehensive strategic partnership between the EU and China, the two sides agreed to launch negotiations on a new Partnership and Co-operation Agreement which will encompass the full scope of their bilateral relationship, including enhanced cooperation in political matters.

The EU–China Partnership and Cooperation Agreement (PCA) negotiations were regularly mentioned in subsequent joint statements of EU–China Summits, but since 2009, there has been no further reference to this. In fact, Chien-Huei Wu explains that since the launching of the negotiations with a view to upgrading the 1985 Trade and Economic Cooperation Agreement in 2007, little progress has been reported and the negotiations have been stalled since 2011 due to divergences between the mandates and expectations of the parties. Such a result is not surprising. In setting out the objective for launching the PCA negotiations, the leaders of the 9th EU–China mentioned several critical issues that anchor EU–China relations in general and EU–China PCA negotiations in particular. These issues include, from the China side, the One China policy, arms embargo and market economy status, and from the EU side, human rights and China's ratification of the International Covenant on Civil and Political Rights (ICCPR), China's accession to the Rome Statute and the International Criminal Court, climate change, complete and faithful implementation of China's WTO commitments, and the establishment of a transparent, open and predictable regulatory environment. Indeed, some of these issues still plague both the EU and China and prevent the PCA negotiation from breaking through the deadlock. This chapter traces the development of the EU–China PCA negotiations and looks at major challenges facing the two parties for its successful conclusion, with a focus on two dimensions: political and security; and trade and economy. In the context of the political and security dimension, this chapter address the 'One China' policy, market economy status, the arms embargo, human rights, China's accession to the Rome Statute and climate change. In the trade and economy dimension, Chien-Huei Wu examines China's implementation of its WTO commitments and the transparency, openness and predictability of China's trade regime. This chapter probes the future of EU–China PCA negotiations and explores possible ways to break the deadlock. This will be done in the broad context of the changing landscape of global economic governance, in particular in the wake of Brexit and Trump.

In chapter 14, Shintaro Hamanaka extends the reflection by looking at legalisation of international economic relations, and explores the questions of whether Asia is unique in terms of integration. It is not easy to conduct theoretically informed comparative studies of regional economic integration. Limited scholarly interactions between international economic lawyers and political scientists are one of the reasons for this. However, several important theoretical works that look into the legal aspects of economic integrations have been conducted by political scientists since 2000. The concept of legalisation of economic relations has been significantly developed, and political scientists are now studying specific questions regarding legalization of institutions, such as the impact of flexible language and the form of dispute settlement. Based on the latest developments of the political science literature on legal aspects of economic integration, Shintaro Hamanaka clarifies what we know about the difference between Europe and Asia with regard to legalisation of economic relations, and discusses what should be studied to deepen our knowledge on the difference with regard to specific form de jure integration.

C. Part III – EU's Trade Policy: Global and Regional Trade Challenges

Part III delves into international trade policy, which probably is the most important external policy of the EU and, as such, the main channel of EU influence at regional and global levels.

Since the EU's areas of competence are mainly economic and commercial, it is logically on these grounds that it has the most influence. With an internal market of half a billion inhabitants representing 20 per cent of global GDP and international trade, the EU is a major economic player in the contemporary world, particularly in bodies such as the WTO, where the EU Commissioner negotiates on trade for all Member States.[68] The EU is also a recognised interlocutor in areas where skills have been transferred at the Community level, such as in international climate negotiations. Finally, the EU provides more than half of the world's development aid (€ 76 billion in 2017), making it also a major player.

[68] See Mark Clough, 'The European Union and the WTO Dark Room' (1997) 2 *European Foreign Affairs Review* 287–90.

Logically speaking of this centrality in the commercial sector, the EU directly negotiates bilateral agreements with states (the US, China, etc) or regional groups (Mercosur [Southern Common Market], ASEAN [Association of Southeast Asia], etc), and has established institutional relations with most countries of the world and major international institutions.[69]

EU trade diplomacy has been further strengthened since 2010 in the framework of the Europe 2020 strategy. The new generation of trade agreements now extends to the protection of intellectual property, the liberalisation of investment, and public procurement or sustainable development. The latest agreement, which came into effect on 1 February 2019, is the Japan–EU free trade agreement, which is also the largest ever signed; trade in goods and services between the two economic zones is estimated at 36.9 per cent of world trade. Europeans expect this agreement to increase their exports to Japan by 25 per cent and to save € 1 billion in tariffs, in particular through the abolition of those on its food products.[70] In return, Japan gains facilitated access to the common market for its automotive industry.[71] By this treaty, the Europeans want to reaffirm loud and clear the principles that have guided them since the 1960s: refusal of protectionism and defence of free trade.[72]

In chapter 15, Fernando Dias Simões addresses the significant issue of transparency for the EU trade policy. The negotiation of international trade and investment agreements has been attracting ample controversy. There is a growing anti-trade rhetoric in political speeches and campaigns across Europe. A number of civil society organisations have been vigorously working to increase mobilisation against agreements such as the Comprehensive Economic and Trade Agreement (CETA) and the Transatlantic Trade and Investment Partnership (TTIP). One of the most prevalent critiques is the perceived lack of transparency of the negotiation process. The EU is represented in the negotiation process by officials from the European Commission Directorate-General for Trade who meet with officers from partner countries in private. According to some, the negotiation behind closed doors of an international agreement with tremendous economic and social impact goes against democratic values. This criticism is part of a larger, older debate about the perceived lack of transparency in EU decision-making processes. Designing and implementing a Common Commercial Policy (CCP) raises particular difficulties that need to be addressed by European institutions in order to promote the economic and social progress of the Union. Fernando Dias Simões discusses the specific political, economic and legal challenges that the Common Commercial

[69] See Ari Afilalo and Dennis Patterson, 'Global Economic Constitutionalism and the Future of Global Trade' (2019) 40 *University of Pennsylvania Journal of International Law* 323–82.

[70] See Emil Kirchner, 'EU-Japan trade deal comes into force to create world's biggest trade zone', *The Conversation* (2019), https://theconversation.com/eu-japan-trade-deal-comes-into-force-to-create-worlds-biggest-trade-zone-110729.

[71] ibid.

[72] See generally Emil J Kirchner and Han Dorussen (eds), *EU-Japan Security Cooperation Trends and Prospects* (Abingdon, Routledge, 2018) 222.

Policy raises for the European project, namely the need to involve a large variety of stakeholders, civil society organisations, and national parliaments in the decision-making process so as to ensure its democratic legitimacy.

In chapter 16, Kirstyn Inglis and Daniele Bianchi look at investor-to-state dispute settlement (ISDS) mechanisms and make a comparison of evolving legal approaches in Brazil and Latin America with the EU. The reform of ISDS and potential alternatives to it is a priority for the EU today. FDI by the EU in Brazil and Latin America is considerable, and vice versa. Various forms of settling disputes between investors and states are incorporated into agreements carrying FDI. Classical ISDS mechanisms have become increasingly contentious in recent years, and with the growth in the number of ISDS agreements, public fears that investors may gain control of sensitive areas of public policy have also grown in importance. Compared to state-to-state dispute settlement (SSDS) mechanisms, ISDS mechanisms are criticised for giving companies and multinationals the potential to undermine a country's public policy objectives with the threat to national sovereignty that this implies. Justifications for ISDS boil down to states' provision for protection of investors in order to progress toward their development goals. However, the core drivers of globalization are changing rapidly, and the rise of countries capable of exponential growth accentuates the negatives of ISDS, including the lack of democratic accountability of and scrutiny over third-country investors, the use of private arbitrators, the secrecy of proceedings and rulings, and no participatory rights for third parties holding a direct interest in the process. To date, investment protection has been confined to case-specific international agreements, rather than through overarching bilateral agreements. Legally speaking, these agreements span the public international law basis of the treaties and the public law nature of the relationship between the investor and sovereign state concerned, and asymmetry between states in international agreements further complicates multilateral approaches to reforming ISDS. At the EU level, FDI was included in the EU's powers under the Common Commercial Policy under the Treaty of Lisbon in 2009, but such initiatives when involving ISDS reform remain complex and must respect the EU Member States' competences. Thus, the entry into force of the CETA between the EU and Canada in September 2017 is preliminary: all the EU Member States must ratify it, raising again the spectre of political resistance to its ISDS clause as experienced in 2016, particularly in the Belgium State of Wallonia. The ISDS mechanisms in CETA must respect the delineation between EU and Member State competences established by the CJEU in May 2017, and Belgium raised important questions for the CJEU in September 2017 on the compatibility of CETA with EU law, even before the preliminary entry into force of CETA. Following EU Commission President Jean Claude Juncker's State of the Union Address in September 2017, the EU is committed to making ISDS fit for purpose both within the EU 28 Member States and also in the EU's external relations with third countries. The EU is abiding by its commitment to unprecedented transparency in all its trade and investment actions following the pathway set down by President Juncker. Improved democratic controls over ISDS to improve public trust at home and abroad will also be an important yardstick. Already the UNCITRAL working group began work in November 2017 on the topic of ISDS reform, and the EU has been advocating the Multilateral Investment Court (MIC) to this end. This contribution focuses on ISDS in EU external relations. The chapter also explores EU policy reform of ISDS – notably proposing a new, permanent, judge-based MIC for investor-state disputes – to set a level playing field at the global level for the protection of FDI while also guaranteeing states and society their democratic rights to shape public policy. Kirstyn Inglis and Daniele Bianchi then examine the experience of Latin America, revealing a long-established refusal of any transfer of sovereignty through bilateral agreements regarding ISDS, resorting more to experimental forms of mediation based on the willingness of the state concerned. Given that investor protection clauses have not been incorporated within the EU–Mercosur draft trade agreement, and the consistent refusal of Brazil's parliament to ratify agreements containing ISDS, would an MIC render ISDS more palatable to Brazil and other ISDS averse countries? Or is there indeed a sufficient critical mass of problem cases to justify the EU's bazooka approach in the form of the MIC? Is this solution proportionate as well as acceptable democratically and legally speaking, especially given the questions as to the compatibility of the MIC with EU law? While the European Commission can negotiate and ratify agreements containing provisions for the protection of direct foreign investments of third country nationals in the EU (and vice versa), the EU Member States must be involved in the negotiation of clauses on dispute settlement between investors and states, as well as in relation to non-direct foreign investment ('portfolio' investments made without any intention to influence the management and control of an undertaking). The Member States' national constitutional procedures must be respected in the ratification of such clauses in multilateral or bilateral agreements between the EU and third countries. All this said, the conclusions consider whether Latin American approaches present a viable alternative that the EU might emulate – even in part – in the modernisation of its ISDS system, or whether these approaches present more of a blank cartridge in addressing sovereignty and democracy concerns. Is there any intermediate solution in between the European legal bazooka and the Latin American blank cartridge?

In chapter 17, Olga Boltenko provides an interesting analysis of normative influence. Instead of only focusing on the EU–China investment negotiations in isolation of any other treaties, Olga Boltenko relates the Regional Comprehensive Economic Partnership (RCEP), a broad trade and investment pact involving China and 15 other Asia-Pacific countries, to the current investment negotiations between China and the EU. Having studied China's latest positions, in particular in the context of RCEP negotiations, a safer prediction appears to be that China will move away from its traditional treaty practice and negotiate a treaty that will inform a new generation of BITs. Olga Boltenko's more detailed textual predictions are that the China–EU BIT will contain at the very least: an RCEP-inspired expropriation provision that links the standard of expropriation to customary international law and carves out from the scope of the expropriation provision the parties' regulatory measures intended to protect matters of public policy such as environment, health and public safety and security; an RCEP- inspired fair and equitable treatment (FET) standard that is linked to customary international law and is described as limited to the obligation not to deny justice in criminal, civil or administrative adjudicatory proceedings in accordance with the principle of due process of law; and potentially a balancing provision that safeguards the states' regulatory space.

In chapter 18, Sufian Jusoh looks at the Comprehensive and Progressive Agreement for Trans-Pacific Partnership (CPTPP) to see whether some lessons can be drawn from the EU approach towards research in biotechnology and the price of medicines. ASEAN Member States have been actively engaged in negotiating and entering into the free trade agreements, including the CPTPP and the RCEP. Of the two major deals, only CPTPP, which involves four ASEAN Member States, ie Brunei Darussalam, Malaysia, Singapore and Vietnam, has been concluded and come into force. Of the four countries, Malaysia and Singapore have an established biotechnology industry and research and development activities. Biotechnology is important for these two countries' economic growth; and to address pressing domestic issues such as disease eradication, addressing environmental concerns and increasing food production. However, much of the biotechnology-related activities in these two countries are dominated by foreign investors, with foreign registered patents and domestic registration of foreign patents under the international Patent Cooperation Treaty and priority registration under the Paris Convention. These patents owned by foreigners may hinder the development of indigenous research and development activities involving local research institutions where their research activities may be subject to complying with foreign-owned patents. The chapter examines how the CPTPP Intellectual Property Chapter affects the research and development activities in the biotechnology sector in these two countries, and how these two countries can employ research exemption flexibility as provided in the WTO TRIPS Agreement and also the CPTPP Intellectual Property Chapter. Sufian Jusoh also argues that the research exemption flexibility in the IP chapter has a neutral effect on the price of medicine. The chapter makes comparisons with the similar research exemptions and biotechnology in the EU.

In chapter 19, Danny Friedmann compares the geographical indications in the EU, China and Australia. The EU is ferociously protecting its Geographical Indications (GIs) in the name of authenticity and rural development, not only in the countries of the EU, but internationally. Australia and most other New World countries protect geographical names via their trademark system, but also via a *sui generis* system. This chapter looks at the approaches to the protection of geographical names in the respective systems and on the strategies vintners use to exclude each other in the People's Republic of China (China), where there is a 'gold rush' to export as much wine as possible. The chapter first provides an introduction to the concept of GIs. Danny Friedmann also gives the Old-World approach: registration of appellations of origin and the New World approach: protection of wine GIs via trademarks and *sui generis* systems. The chapter then covers international GI treaties and deals with China's GI system. Finally, Danny Friedmann discusses the bilateral agreements on GIs between the EU and China and uses *prosecco* as a case study, where Italy and the EU try to 'transubstantiate' a grape into a GI.

Finally, in chapter 20, Debashis Chakraborty and Nilanjan Banik consider the lessons for India from negotiations with the EU and RCEP with respect to the Indian pharma sector. It has been observed that there exists a both-way causality between health and income in many regions across the world, creating room for possible policy interventions. India presently stands at a crucial juncture on this front. On one hand, as compared to its regional neighbours, the country performs modestly in terms of health sector indicators (eg, life expectancy and infant mortality rate). On the other hand, given the prominence of the Indian pharmaceutical sector, which is third largest in terms of volume and tenth largest in terms of value, the country is planning to turn itself in a global manufacturing hub through the 'Make-in-India' initiative launched in 2014. With this background, this chapter intends to analyse the intellectual property rights (IPR) protection scenario in India, the evolving policy orientations and competitiveness as reflected through emerging trade patterns, with respect to the pharmaceutical sector. Through an analysis of Indian data, the modest health achievements are underlined, and given the lower level of public expenditure on health, the increasing trend of out-of-pocket (OOP) expenses in household budgets is acknowledged. While these observations prima facie make a case for price controls in the pharma market, several other prevailing barriers at the border and behind borders pose far greater challenges to the pharma companies, namely unfinished reforms in ease of doing business, high logistics cost, unresolved questions in the tax framework, procedural bottlenecks, a poor productivity scenario, prevailing tariff and non-tariff barriers (NTBs) and so on. The Indian Patent Act (1970) lowered the IPR protection by introducing a process patent regime, with the premise that a stronger patent regime would increase the prices of medicines, providing excessive rights for corporations and hurting the poor as they spend a larger proportion of their disposable income towards OOP medical treatment. However, absence of a strong patent regime disincentivises and deters future innovative activity, discourages trade and FDI flows, and unduly forces firms to invest heavily in protecting their rights rather than invention. Although the process patent regime has enabled India to deepen its presence in the world market as an exporter of generic medicines, the poor R&D and innovation scenario has greatly limited India's competitiveness. The country has also adopted the compulsory licence route for controlling medicine prices, but in recent times refrains from granting the same excessively. Acknowledging the urgent need for securing innovation, appropriate policy measures have been introduced, namely Science and Technology Policy (STP) (2003), product patent regime in 2005, and Science, Technology and Innovation Policy (STIP) (2013), but the intended R&D intensity among Indian pharma majors has not yet emerged.

India is presently involved in RCEP negotiations involving ASEAN countries and its six FTA partners. As India's average tariff in the pharma sector is higher than other RCEP members, in coming days the onus of tariff reform will be more on India. RCEP also involves several Anti-Counterfeiting Trade Agreement (ACTA) members, namely Australia, Japan, New Zealand, Singapore and South Korea, who are quite keen to include several TRIPS-Plus provisions in the agreement, eg, rules on generic medicines in transit. India needs to carefully adopt policies, by learning from the experiences of the EU and other countries to facilitate firm-level innovations on one hand and protect public health interests on the other.

PART I

European Legal Integration: Process, Difficulties and Achievements

2

The Rule of Law and Integration in the EU

IAN FORRESTER QC

I. Introduction: History of the EU

Today's European Union (EU) of 28 Member States is the descendant of the first successful attempt at the European Union, the European Coal and Steel Community (ECSC), whose founding treaty was signed in 1951. The first purpose of the original entity was to end military rivalry in Western Europe.

The ECSC was the conception of Robert Schuman, born on 29 June 1886, in Luxembourg, of a Luxembourger mother and a French father. His family was from Alsace-Lorraine, on the eastern border of France, where my family spent summer holidays when our children were young and where in old cemeteries the language engraved on tombstones changed every few decades reflecting whether the cemetery was under French or German rule. Schuman went to university in Germany, passed the bar there, and then in 1912 set up a practice in Metz, a town that was at that time German, but later passed back to France. He served in the German army in the First World War, then was a French citizen reflecting the peace treaty, then a French politician then arrested by the Gestapo in World War II. A true European.

Schuman's idea was to make war in Europe fuelled by economic rivalry impossible: the coal- and steel-making capacities of France and Germany, the two historic combatants, were placed under the control of a High Authority.

There were six signatory states to the ECSC. These six countries then went further. The Treaty Establishing the European Economic Community (known as the Treaty of Rome or EEC Treaty), signed by them in 1957, established the European Economic Community (EEC). The EEC Treaty established a number of new substantive legal features that corresponded to the needs of the time. It moved integration from industry to the market, from goods to people, and it created the Four Freedoms: for goods, for workers, for services and for capital. It also included a painstakingly and elaborately drafted set of competition (or antitrust) rules which have been echoed or copied in at least 40 countries.

The Treaty of Rome was a bold venture to create a mutual interest in life without war, in a Europe rich with colour and with difference, a Europe composed of nation-states which not only promised to cooperate at the Member State level but also promised benefits to each other's citizens, a Europe of many languages and much familiarity with different cultures, foods, poets, painters, music, climates, wines and beers, and sports, a Europe where France is as French as Japan is Japanese. To those who suggest that it would be more efficient for Europe to have fewer languages and less diversity, I reply that it would be more efficient for there to be only 40 French cheeses, not 400, but it would also be more soul-less, less diverse, less rich and less European. There was an informal decision to adopt as the motto of the EU *in varietate concordia*, which was rendered in the unadopted European Constitution as 'United in diversity'.

Building a constitutional structure as successful as the EU Treaty was about defining the substantive principles to be pursued. The constitutional architecture of the EU is neither clear nor widely understood, nor is it firmly established because adaptations are virtually certain. Union law has flourished notwithstanding, often thanks to the creativity of practising lawyers.

II. Contribution of the Court of Justice to EU Integration

The ECSC and EEC Treaties each provided a role for a 'Court of Justice'. The six founding Member States chose to locate the European courts in the capital city of the Grand Duchy of Luxembourg. The judges still sit in Luxembourg: polyglot, remote from the political intrigue of Brussels, in a Grand Duchy historically marked by modern warfare. French was the national language for three of the founding Member States and was still the language of diplomacy, so it was the natural choice for the new court's working language. That choice has an impact which is important today, as French administrative law doctrines and style are a big influence on how judgments are drafted.

However, although the EEC Treaty provided for judicial review of the legality of Union acts, it did not decide on the question of primacy: would Union law prevail over inconsistent national law? Could private citizens invoke the rights established by the treaties before their national courts? How would it work in practice? Would private citizens be heard on the same footing as Member States?

The Treaty of Rome, drafted with that monumental brevity which is characteristic of constitutional documents, was agreed by diplomats who had very different notions of what they wanted. Exactly what the words meant was often not clear, as we can observe from just one part of the Treaty, dealing with competition (antitrust is the American term).

The Court of Justice of the European Union (CJEU) consists of two courts: the Court of Justice (ECJ) and the General Court (created in 1988). With the entry into force of the Treaty of Lisbon in 2009, the court system obtained its current name (Court of Justice of the European Union), while the original court itself (the former CJEC) was renamed 'Court of Justice'.

The Court is a *constitutional court*. It considers challenges by the Commission or a Member State to the constitutional propriety of actions by the Member States pursuant to article 258 and article 259 TFEU. The largest part of the case load of the Court is responding to questions referred by national courts (453 preliminary ruling proceedings out of 704 cases in 2016). A reference from a national judge to the Court under article 267 TFEU can give answers to questions presented to it by national judges who consider that in order to decide a pending case they require clarification on the principles of Union law at stake. It is the responses to some of these hundreds of questions which have most shaped popular perception of the Court of Justice and European law.

It is also a *court of appeal*. The competence most familiar to lawyers in private practice in Brussels is appeals against Council or Commission action in such fields as competition, foreign trade and technical regulations. Judgments of the Tribunal can, in due course, be reviewed on a point of law by the Court.

The Court also issues *advisory opinions*. Pursuant to article 218(11) TFEU, the Court can issue opinions upon the request of the Parliament, Council, Commission or a Member State concerning an international agreement and its compatibility with the Lisbon Treaty. In one celebrated opinion, the Court found there was no exclusive competence for the Union in the field of intellectual property; therefore, the World Trade Organization (WTO) Uruguay Round agreement had to be signed by the Member States *and* the EC (see Opinion 1/94, 1994 ECR I-5276, I-5282). In its recent Opinion 2/15 of 16 May 2017, the Court held that the free trade agreement with Singapore cannot, in its current form, be concluded by the EU alone.

The Courts' early cases were a mixture of precise, even formalist quite literal interpretations where the text was clear. Where the text was not clear and there were gaps, these were filled by common sense, *effet utile* and consistency. It was not clear whether the treaties had internal domestic effect or whether they conferred rights upon private parties of which national courts could take cognisance. The Court in its first 20 years laid down basic principles on direct effect, free movement, supremacy and probably went faster than Member States expected. During a period of political paralysis in the 1970s, the Court produced answers to questions which arose and was accused of/praised for being an engine of progress. These days are now over. The pressure of cases is immense, and there are far more decisions than any one person can read.

A. Landmark Judgments

The first case for the new Court of Justice, a French challenge to measures taken by the High Authority, was symbolically propitious and the outcome politically welcome.[1] France was successful; the Court finding that elements of the contested

[1] Judgment of the Court of 21 December 1954. *French Republic v High Authority of the European Coal and Steel Community*. Case 1-54.

decision infringed the EEC Treaty and should be annulled. The fact that a Member State successfully brought a case in order to challenge a measure under the new EEC Treaty was an encouraging start.

In its early years, the young European court took some bold steps, creating two fundamental doctrines: (1) direct effect, giving rights to individuals flowing directly from a treaty between states, in *van Gend & Loos v Netherlands*;[2] and (2) primacy of Community law over national law, in *Flaminio Costa v ENEL*.[3]

i. Van Gend & Loos v Netherland*s*

The EEC Treaty provided that Member States would progressively reduce to zero their customs duties on each other's produce. The Netherlands, usually one of the most diligent Member States, neglected to ensure that its tariff matched its EEC Treaty commitments. It was clear that the country should answer to its cosignatories for its breach of duty; it was less clear that the trader should be entitled to rely upon the EEC Treaty itself. In *Van Gend & Loos*, the imported product was urea-formaldehyde. Should the duty rate be eight per cent (the Dutch rate) or three per cent (the Treaty rate)? The Court said it gracefully:

> [T]he Community constitutes a new legal order of international law, for the benefit of which the states have limited their sovereign rights, albeit within limited fields, and the subjects of which comprise not only the Member States but also their nationals. Independently of the legislation of Member States, Community law therefore not only imposes obligations on individuals but is also intended to confer upon them rights which become part of their legal heritage.[4]

Inside a few years, this principle of direct effect was no longer controversial. Should a trader who imports some turkey tails have standing to argue that he is entitled to pay a lower duty rate? The Court settled the vexed question of whether the rumps of turkeys (the parson's nose when on British tables) should be classed as part of the turkey's back or as edible offal.[5] By confirming that such produce is to be classified as edible offal, the Court ensured that the importer was able to prevail over the Member State customs authorities, which wished to levy a different rate of duty. The cases confirmed the principle of direct effect and the propriety of verifying whether national law complies with Union law. National judges could thus ask if their domestic legal rules were consistent with Union law.

[2] Judgment of the Court of 5 February 1963, *NV Algemene Transport- en Expeditie Onderneming van Gend & Loos v Netherlands Inland Revenue Administration*, Case 26-62.

[3] Judgment of the Court of 15 July 1964, *Flaminio Costa v ENEL*, Case 6-64.

[4] Judgment of the Court of 5 February 1963, *NV Algemene Transport- en Expeditie Onderneming van Gend & Loos v Netherlands Inland Revenue Administration*, Case 26-62 at para B.

[5] Judgment of the Court (Tenth Chamber), 16 October 2014. *The Queen, on the application of: Newby Foods Ltd v Food Standards Agency*, Case C-453/13.

ii. Flaminio Costa v ENEL[6]

Mr Costa refused to pay his electricity bill of 1,925 Italian Lira (about $3.00), claiming that it had been contrary to the EEC Treaty to nationalise ENEL, the electricity company. He used the claim to elaborate his constitutional theory that membership in the Community limited the sovereignty of the Member States. The Court was faced with the proposition (not a foolish one, but not a felicitous one) that an Italian statute adopted after the entry into force of the Treaty of Rome prevailed over this treaty. The Court produced another rich statement:

> The integration into the laws of each Member State of provisions which derive from the Community, and more generally the terms and the spirit of the Treaty, make it impossible for the States, as a corollary, to accord precedence to a unilateral and subsequent measure over a legal system accepted by them on a basis of reciprocity…
>
> The obligations undertaken under the Treaty establishing the Community would not be unconditional … if they could be called in question by subsequent legislative acts of the signatories.[7]

The Court went a bit further in *Administration des finances de l'État v Société Simmenthal anonyme* (*Simmenthal*),[8] which concerned whether an Italian court had the power itself to annul a domestic measure or whether it needed higher judicial (Italian) authority to do so:

> [E]very national court must, in a case within its jurisdiction, apply Community law in its entirety and protect rights which the latter confers on individuals and must accordingly set aside any provision of national law which may conflict with it, whether prior or subsequent to the Community rule.[9]

iii. Gabrielle Defrenne v SABENA[10]

One classic example relates to sex discrimination. Article 141 TEC provided: 'Each Member State shall … ensure and … maintain the application of the principle that men and women should receive equal pay for equal work'. The goal of the drafters had not been to help women get equal pay, but to help those Member States which had legislation on sex discrimination to insist that other Member States adopt legislation which imposed an equally burdensome obligation on their industries. Gabrielle Defrenne worked as an air hostess for the now-sadly-defunct Belgian airline, SABENA. Female stewards had to stop working at 40, whereas no such age

[6] Judgment of the Court of 15 July 1964, *Flaminio Costa v ENEL*, Case 6-64.

[7] ibid, para 11.

[8] Judgment of the Court of 9 March 1978, *Amministrazione delle Finanze dello Stato v Simmenthal SpA*., Case 106/77, European Court reports 1978 Page 00629.

[9] ibid, paragraph 21.

[10] Judgment of the Court of 8 April 1976, *Gabrielle Defrenne v Société anonyme belge de navigation aérienne Sabena*, Case 43-75, European Court reports 1976 Page 00455.

limit was placed on male stewards. Was there an infringement of article 141? The Member States argued – accurately – that article 141 was not actually meant to give women a right to equal pay. They also pointed out that equal pay as between men and women did not necessarily address how long someone could work. Nevertheless, Mme Defrenne prevailed. The Court stated:

> [T]his provision forms part of the social objectives of the Community, which is not merely an economic union, but is at the same time intended, by common action, to ensure social progress and seek the constant improvement of the living and working conditions of their peoples, as is emphasized by the Preamble to the Treaty.[11]

iv. Marshall v Southampton & South-West Hampshire Area Health Authority[12]

In *Marshall v Southampton & South-West Hampshire Area Health Authority*, the Court confirmed that Member State entities, when employers, are obliged to respect directives which have not been implemented and must therefore give employees the rights conferred under the directive. Nevertheless, although the Court has confirmed that directives can be invoked by an individual against a Member State, it has not gone so far as to recognise 'horizontal direct effect', whereby one private individual can invoke against another private individual rights created by an unimplemented directive. So the employee of a public sector employer would be better placed in this respect at least than the employee of a private employer.

B. State Liability

The ECJ has been willing to look sympathetically at claims which have the effect of making Community law more efficient and remedies more effective – *effet utile* is an untranslatable phrase connoting teleological efficacy. One big problem involved Member State failures to obey their EEC Treaty commitments. In a number of cases, the ECJ was invited by the Commission to condemn, pursuant to article 169 (now article 258 TFEU), Member State failures to obey EEC Treaty obligations in the form of adopted legislation or respect for such legislation. Italy, which had a creaky and unsatisfactory legislative system, was judicially chastised on dozens of occasions, unsuccessfully pleading that its parliamentary system was overloaded, that it was doing its best, that everything was very difficult, and that in due course it would get round to addressing the problem. These cases seemed endless.

[11] ibid, para 10.

[12] Judgment of the Court of 26 February 1986, *M H Marshall v Southampton and South-West Hampshire Area Health Authority (Teaching)*, Case 152/84.

i. Andrea Francovich and Danila Bonifaci and others v Italian Republic[13]

Then things changed with *Francovich v Italian Republic*. Mr Francovich was the employee of an Italian company which went bankrupt. His employer had not provided enough social security contributions for its employees; indeed, Italy had not implemented the Community directive on protection of employees in the event of employer insolvency. As a result, Francovich and his co-workers did not get the benefit of its provisions and had no financial cushion. Their creative counsel sued the Italian state for damages before the *Pretura di Vicenza* and *Pretura di Bassano del Grappa*, which referred the matter to the Court. The case was of evidently huge importance. Could a Member State escape domestic consequences for those damaged by its failure to implement Community law? Should national failure to comply with EEC Treaty obligations be sanctioned by a duty, a potentially massive duty in some cases, to pay compensation? The timing for a constitutional explosion was propitious. There was massive neglect by Member States of their duty to implement their own promises. Italy (and not only Italy) was what might be called a recidivist scofflaw. The Court took a bold step. It found for Mr Francovich and his claim for damages against the Italian state.

The Court recalled the unique legal system created by the EEC Treaty which the Member State courts are bound to apply:

> Just as it imposes burdens on individuals, Community law is also intended to give rise to rights which become part of their legal patrimony …
>
> Furthermore, it has been consistently held that the national courts whose task it is to apply the provisions of Community law … must ensure that those rules take full effect and must protect the rights which they confer on individuals.
>
> …
>
> The possibility of obtaining redress from the Member State is particularly indispensable where … the full effectiveness of Community rules is subject to prior action on the part of the State and where, consequently, in the absence of such action, individuals cannot enforce before the national courts the rights conferred upon them by Community law.[14]

It follows that the principle whereby a State must be liable for loss and damage caused to individuals as a result of breaches of Union law for which the State can be held responsible is inherent in the system of the Treaty.

Francovich (dealing with damages) and the *Factortame* cases[15] (dealing with the need for adequate national *remedies* for breach of Union law in the case of

[13] Judgment of the Court of 19 November 1991, *Andrea Francovich and Danila Bonifaci and others v Italian Republic*, Joined cases C-6/90 and C-9/90.

[14] ibid, para 31.

[15] Judgment of the Court of 19 June 1990. *The Queen v Secretary of State for Transport, ex parte: Factortame Ltd and others*, Case C-213/89.

Spanish fishermen who were denied licences to fish in UK waters) have transformed Member State patterns of behaviour with respect to Union obligations.

Some of the questions put to the Court by national judges have been difficult, some rather easy, and in a number of celebrated cases the Court has had to change its mind. Advocacy, of course, helped it do so. Here are a couple of examples.

ii. Yvonne van Duyn v Home Office[16]

Mrs van Duyn, a Dutch citizen, was an active member of the Church of Scientology, a lawful institution regarded by the UK authorities as a socially undesirable cult. As a result, she was denied permission to live in the United Kingdom to work for the Church. Mrs van Duyn challenged the immigration officer's decision as being an unjustified restriction on the free movement of workers. The UK government invoked public policy for the restriction. The Court found that Mrs van Duyn's personal conduct did not in itself need to be unlawful. The United Kingdom was allowed to exclude her from entering the country.

The *van Duyn v Home Office* approach was departed from in *Adoui v Belgian State*,[17] the first of a number of interesting cases on free movement of persons from Belgium in which the Liège *avocat*, Luc Misson, was involved. Two French nationals, delicately referred to in the *European Court Reports* as 'waitresses', who attracted customers by sitting in the windows of establishments in the red-light area of the city of Liège, were threatened with deportation on morals charges. Prostitution was not illegal in Belgium. The clients of Maître Misson prevailed on the grounds that French citizens could be deported only if Belgian citizens, who could not be deported, were equally liable to repressive penalties intended to combat the same conduct.

iii. Dassonville[18], Cassis de Dijon,[19] *and* Keck & Mithouard[20]

Two seminal cases on free movement and their successors, the first being *Dassonville* about Scotch whisky imported into Belgium from France without a certificate attesting to the whisky's origin, and the second being *Cassis de Dijon*. Those liquor cases were of great importance.

In *Dassonville*, we learned that '[a]ll trading rules enacted by Member States which are capable of hindering, directly or indirectly, actually or potentially,

[16] Judgment of the Court of 4 December 1974. *Yvonne van Duyn v Home Office*. Case 41-74.

[17] Judgment of the Court of 18 May 1982. *Rezguia Adoui v Belgian State and City of Liège; Dominique Cornuaille v Belgian State*, Joined cases 115 and 116/81.

[18] Judgment of the Court of 11 July 1974. *Procureur du Roi v Benoît and Gustave Dassonville*, Case 8-74.

[19] Judgment of the Court of 20 February 1979. *Rewe-Zentral AG v Bundesmonopolverwaltung für Branntwein*, Case 120/78.

[20] Judgment of the Court of 24 November 1993. *Criminal proceedings against Bernard Keck and Daniel Mithouard*, Joined cases C-267/91 and C-268/91.

intra-community trade are to be considered as measures having an effect equivalent to quantitative restrictions'.[21]

Instead of the EEC Treaty's rules on free movement of goods being available to combat discriminatory national measures which deliberately hindered imports, they were held available to combat *any* measures which intentionally or accidentally hindered cross-border trade. Because national regulations in a multi-country market are very likely to affect cross-border flows of goods, the implications were startling. *Cassis de Dijon* went further. It was a very potent judgment and provoked a rush of attacks on a miscellany of measures that were 'indistinctly applicable' to domestic and imported products and which arguably fell within the *Cassis de Dijon* proscription.

So, if it could be sold lawfully in France, there was a Union law reason to say it was unlawful to block its sale in Germany. Pressing on that slightly open door, lawyers in the *Sunday Trading* cases argued that any sort of rule which constrained the flow of trade between Member States was challengeable.[22] Sunday market traders claimed that 'blue laws' constrained their handling of goods imported from other Member States. A flood of cases arrived, mainly from England (litigation funded, I suppose, by large retailers chafing at the law), but also cases challenging Dutch, German and Italian rules on various marketing questions.

The music stopped with *Keck & Mithouard*, which essentially held that further creative attacks on essentially domestic trading regulations would not be welcome judicially. The Court rather grudgingly acknowledged that its prior attempts to handle the progeny of *Cassis de Dijon* had been unsuccessful.

C. Right to Compensation

Could a tourist, Mr Cowan (not a migrant, not a worker, merely a solvent tourist), who had been attacked and robbed outside a Paris underground station, be denied criminal-injuries compensation, which was available to French nationals and others living in France? The Court, extending its rules on free movement, said that when Union law allows a person to move freely in another Member State, the corollary right is that the individual be protected on the same basis as nationals of that Member State.[23]

i. The Case of College Fees

In 1983, a French student, Françoise Gravier, went to Belgium to pursue a course in cartoon art in the city of Liège. She was charged an enrolment fee for the course,

[21] Judgment of the Court of 11 July 1974. *Procureur du Roi v Benoît and Gustave Dassonville*, Case 8-74 at para 5.

[22] Judgment of the Court (Sixth Chamber) of 23 November 1989. *Torfaen Borough Council v B & Q plc*, Case C-145/88.

[23] Judgment of the Court of 2 February 1989. *Ian William Cowan v Trésor public*, Case 186/87.

which her Belgian colleagues were not required to pay. The Treaty of Rome did not deal with education. Maître Luc Misson brought her case before the Belgian courts, arguing that although educational organisation and policy were not provided for within Community competence, these issues were nevertheless 'not unconnected' with Community law.[24] The EEC Treaty provided for general principles to be laid down in relation to a vocational training policy and in order for this training policy to be gradually established and extended, freedom to choose the place of training is important. He noted that freedom of movement of workers is a cornerstone of Community law. The Court, to which a preliminary reference was made, conceded that conditions of access to vocational training fell within the scope of the EEC Treaty. Article 7 of the EEC Treaty prohibited discrimination on grounds of nationality. The Court held that the imposition of an enrolment fee only on non-national students, as a condition of access to such training, was contrary to article 7.

I have mentioned a few of the questions which the Court had to decide during its early years. In the 1970s, the Community went through a period of political stagnation. But the simple and potent principles set forth in the EEC Treaty continued to present problems for national judges. During this fallow period, *the Court was the most dynamic of the institutions*. It produced a string of important judgments and was, predictably, criticised for following teleological interpretations and for being over-activist, mainly by commentators from the common law and Scandinavian countries. Walter van Gerven says, interestingly:

> Certainly, the Court has been 'active' in its desire to improve legal protection of individual rights. But that is the essence of any supreme court's task: in that field, every national legal system offers examples of so-called activism. However, at the same time it has been asserted, that the Court, if anything, has been more 'passive' than 'active' in its willingness to review Council or Commission decisions or regulations limiting the free market and free competition concepts, mainly by respecting the so-called discretionary powers of these institutions in, for example, the agricultural field, even when they are used for protectionist or over-regulatory purposes. Having said that, one should not forget, though, that judicial activism is, more often than not, the consequence of inability or unwillingness to act on the part of the legislative.[25]

A more accurate (and more court-friendly) version of the controversy would be that opinions of the Court do not consistently please Member States. The directives and regulations that constitute the bulk of European legislation are almost never perfectly clear in every feature. They are drafted by civil servants who are

[24] Judgment of the Court of 2 February 1988. *Vincent Blaizot v University of Liège and others*, Case 24/86 at para 30.

[25] Walter van Gerven, 'European Court of Justice Case Law as a Means of Unification of Private Law?' (1996) 20 *Fordham International Law Journal* 680–98 at 690.

responsible to different masters (the Commission, 28 Member States who are rarely unanimous, the Parliament, the parties affected, the public interest and other vocal causes). They are often drafted so as to please, or not to displease too much, those who disagree: reconciling divergent views by linguistic obfuscation delivers consensus on tersely worded principles today at the price of controversy or litigation tomorrow. The Court has the task of ensuring that the Member States adhere to what they promised, but not more than they promised. While some judgments provoke agitation for a number of Member States and while the press (and even ministers, who should know better) will present the matter in terms of a patriotic battle whose outcome is decided by foreign judges, my personal impression is that the Court's decisions do not consistently enhance Union power at the expense of the Member States. The Lisbon Treaty establishes broad duties of pro-Union behaviour for the Member States: for example, they 'shall abstain from any measure which could jeopardise the attainment of the objectives of this Treaty'. The judges have to decide, sometimes, important questions governed by imperfectly clear texts. No wonder their conclusions cause intermittent outrage. This is not new.

III. Constitutional Architecture

Most European lawyers know what the Treaty of Rome provided, and when. Few European lawyers could list accurately the series of Treaties which have altered matters from 1986 (Single European Act) to 2007 (Lisbon). This is a regrettable reflection of the fact that European Union structures do not match those of orthodox democracies, yet the government and political parties of the 28 Member States strongly favour democracy and transparency. During 20 years the European house got constitutional extensions, pillars and extra rooms, then improved them, then demolished the pillars and renamed the whole EU instead of EC. More precisely, the Treaty of Maastricht (1992) structured the EU into three pillars: the Community pillar (Euratom, European Coal and Steel Community and European Community, formerly known as the European Economic Community), the Common Foreign and Security Policy pillar (CFSP) and the cooperation in the field of Justice and Home Affairs pillar (JHA). The Treaty of Amsterdam (1997) transferred policies on judicial cooperation in civil matters, visas, immigration and asylum from the JHA pillar to the Community pillar; the police and judicial cooperation in criminal matters remaining the sole subject of intergovernmental cooperation. Finally, the Treaty of Lisbon (2007) demolished the pillar structure, since the Treaties now only provide for a specific regime for the Common Foreign and Security Policy (CFSP).

One of the sad consequences of this complexity has been the alienation of voters attracted by populist parties. In addition, that complexity makes effective judicial review all the more essential. And that brings me to the Courts where I sit.

IV. The Court of Justice Today

Since the first judgment in 1954, 33,764 judgments and orders have been delivered, 229 Members and 5,582 civil servants and temporary agents have served as officials. The Court comprises 28 Judges, 11 Advocates General and one Registrar. The General Court is composed of 44 Judges and one Registrar. I think I am the 69th member of the General Court and its predecessor the CFI. In 2016, 1604 cases have been brought to the Courts and 1628 cases were completed.

The average duration of proceedings is 14.7 months before the Court and 18.7 months before the general Court. In its line of case law *Gascogne*,[26] the Court found that the General Court breached Article 47 of the Charter of Fundamental Rights of the EU by failing to adjudicate these cases within a reasonable time and that an action for damages brought before the General Court would be an appropriate remedy.

The Court of Justice has grown into an institution with a strong identity and three buildings, operating in 24 languages and occupying a huge building on the Kirchberg in Luxembourg. Its judges come from 28 countries with a very wide range of legal and administrative traditions. It uses French as the lingua franca. Judgments must be accessible to the citizens of 28 countries in their national languages. Translation is of very high quality but that quality takes time. It is not surprising that about half of all the staff of the EU courts are engaged in translation. In 2016, 46 per cent of cases have been brought in English, just under 15 per cent have been in German, 10 per cent in Spanish and nearly 12 per cent have been in French.

A special challenge for those who appear regularly is that they may sometimes be called upon to speak in a foreign language. This means losing the native fluency which gives a lawyer distinctiveness and resourcefulness in the face of questions. Lawyers in the legal service of the European institutions are quite regularly required to speak in their second, or even third, language. Correspondingly, the advocate speaking his native tongue has an advantage albeit small to moderate.

There are other challenges to be borne in mind. In a court of 23 languages and judges from 28 countries, it is a statistical certainty that a majority of judges in a typical chamber of five judges will not speak the language of the case as a native language. The advocate's remarks will therefore be interpreted by the courts' team of simultaneous interpreters. The interpretation in my experience thus far is of extremely high quality. But if lawyers speak too fast, the interpreters must omit some phrases or ideas so as not to be left behind.

[26] Judgments of the Court, 26 November 2013, *P Gascogne Sack Deutschland GmbH, Kendrion NV and Groupe Gascogne SA v Commission*, Cases C-40/12 P, C-50/12 P and C-58/12.

V. Europe's Current Challenges

A. Case *Schrems*[27]

Directive 95/46/EC attempted to reconcile the interest of the individual in having data protected with the interests of businesses in sharing data for legitimate purposes. For many of the services that society needs to function, information must be collected and shared. For the efficient running of many businesses outside of the internet itself it is also necessary to share or move data from one entity to another, or at least from one jurisdiction to another even if it is under the control of the same entity. This is true in the banking sector, and insurance and health. Any large corporation with employees and customers around the world needs to transfer data, say the corporations.

Originally, data protection across the Atlantic was done through a 'safe-harbour' agreement between the US and the EU. This agreement allowed the transfer of data to the US so long as the entity controlling the data conformed to standards equivalent in their level of protection to what would be required in Europe. This was ensured in the case of US companies by the publication of a privacy policy and submission to the jurisdiction of the Federal Trade Commission Act §5 prohibiting application of 'unfair or deceptive acts or practices in or affecting commerce, or that of another statutory body that will effectively ensure compliance' which would make that privacy policy fully binding.

This regime became controversial after 2013 with the revelations of Edward Snowden concerning the intelligence collections efforts by the US government. The safe harbour agreement was applicable to private entities and did not take into account the 'lawful' seizure of information by government entities that might seem to contravene the publicly stated privacy policies of those entities.[28] In response to this, Max Schrems, an Austrian student privacy activist, brought a complaint against Facebook Ireland to the Irish Data Protection Commissioner ('IDPC'). Ultimately the issue made its way to the Court of Justice in Luxembourg, which among other things found that the safe harbour was not adequate for the protection of EU citizens' private data that was transferred into US jurisdiction. The decision provoked considerable excitement and gave rise to new agreements between the US and the EU with greater assurances of privacy protections for EU citizens. It also sparked the creation of a revamped directive.

[27] Judgment of the Court (Grand Chamber) of 6 October 2015. *Maximillian Schrems v Data Protection Commissioner*, Case C-362/14.

[28] ibid, para 89.

B. Trade Agreements

Far from being an intriguing set of hypothetical questions, trade threatens a real emergency with grave social, economic and political risks.

It should not be thought that trade sanctions are an invention of modern times. The first Queen Elizabeth was the object of excommunication pursuant to the Bull of Pope Pius V, Regnans in Excelsis proclaimed in 1570. That papal interdiction had a commercial consequence.

Good Catholic traders were expected to refrain from dealing with merchants in a country whose monarch was under such an interdiction. The English court accordingly explored new markets further afield, notably the Ottoman Empire. The BBC has discovered some charmingly obsequious letters to the Sultan, by which the Queen's ministers expressed respectful confidence that great trading opportunities would emerge in Turkey. England thus pursued export opportunities with the Ottoman Empire as an alternative to trading with geographically closer Catholic kingdoms in Continental Europe. The accession of the Queen's Scottish cousin King James VI of Scotland to the English throne in 1603 was remarkably smooth. James VI was a Stuart with a French mother and a sympathy for high church practices. He was more of an internationalist than Elizabeth. In March 1604, King James VI of Scotland and I of England spoke to the English parliament for the first time.

> I have ever, I praise God, yet kept peace and amity with all … for by peace abroad with their neighbours the towns flourish, the merchants become rich, the trade doth increase and the people of all sorts of the land enjoy free liberty to exercise themselves in their general vocations without peril or disturbance.

It would seem that King James's policy of seeking political peace had good mercantile consequences. In August 1604 came the signing of the Treaty of London with Spain. Local Catholic kingdoms became more accessible. Exports became immediately easier. English total exports in 1603 were £136,000 in value. By 1609 exports had reached £198,000, and by 1612 £275,000.

It is intriguing to note that after a period of alienation from continental Europe, a Scottish leader pursued a re-entry strategy, on the basis that domestic peace and international peace were good pre-conditions for prosperity, conditions within which citizens could pursue their respective interests freely. (For the avoidance of doubt, even if I believe the foregoing historical assertions are more or less correct, I doubt that reliable lessons can be drawn for the Brexit era from them.)

C. Brexit

For 44 years the UK has managed the regulation of the country's affairs in collective cooperation with its European partners.

Regulation is an ongoing process, dominated by expert advice. European Union law primarily aims at the construction of a functioning common market, a process which involves the reduction or removal of national rules which impede that goal. While most EU law is economic in nature, it is necessarily technical, prescriptive and precise. General principles are insufficient. It is easy to decree that farmers shall give healthy feed to their animals. It is difficult to decide which feed additive is good, bad or uncertain. The same idea roughly applies to cars, pharmaceuticals, pesticides, plastics and fire extinguishers.

Science and industry keep discovering new techniques and technologies and creating new products. It is not practical to decide each new inclusion on a white list or a black list via a Parliamentary vote, still less a vote by 28 parliaments. The answer to the democratic impossibility of parliamentary voting is expert advice, followed by the adoption of secondary legislation. There are scores, probably hundreds, of technical or advisory committees staffed by national experts. The purpose of these mechanisms is to help form and implement the language of the legislation – making it work in the real world. There are thousands of individual problems that arise on subjects such as safety, customs, health, environment, data security, privacy, child abduction, private international law and the rest. These debates are resolved within the technical committees. They may render an opinion on the basis of which the Commission will propose or adopt action. During the debates, it often happens that a state's scientific representative will plead for his state's view of the issue. A Swedish national expert may favour different environmental or animal welfare standards than a Portuguese expert. Neither is right or wrong, but they are different. Reaching consensus between them has helped the market which can be served by the product to grow to 500 million people.

The goal of these communings is the creation of a competitive market that will favour innovation, risk-taking, decent treatment, the expansion of choice to consumers through competition, prosperity and security. The process is largely unknown to the public, and is criticised for being opaque and undemocratic.

Sometimes the rule makers have been criticised for intruding into matters best left to local choice: the principle of subsidiarity. Often ministers chose to disown what they had agreed in Brussels, blaming the European bully instead of defending the merits of the action which they have helped to draft. In such conditions, truths and myths can flourish unverified so that 'Europe' implies interference with lawnmower design, votes for prisoners and straight bananas.

Professional organisations pursue – like mediaeval guilds – the goals of ensuring quality standards and the defence of the members' economic interests. Professional bodies are intrinsically conservative and have historically favoured classical candidacies from locally qualified people. Young people and newcomers have frequently done battle with professional bodies over the adequacy of their qualifications to enter the profession. In a previous incarnation, I challenged a New York State rule which refused admission to foreign lawyers who had passed the bar exam of the State of New York, but who did not have the right to reside permanently in the United States. In the legal profession as in others, international practice has since become entirely routine. A Scots lawyer is today quite likely to have studied or worked outside Scotland, and probably has considered working as a lawyer in England as an alternative to Scotland. The growth of large international law firms confirms that clients want multilingual cross-border advice, and that young lawyers do not stay in one place.

The Professional Qualifications Directive 2005/36/EC is intended to reinforce the opportunity for qualified persons to enter professions in other European countries. Architects, hairdressers, ski instructors and doctors are among the persons who are free to move to work in another Member State than the country where they trained and got qualified.

People travel and settle down in other countries far more than was the case 40 years ago. I am doubtful if the process is reversible, despite the Brexit vote. Students have for centuries travelled to study, to work and sometimes to settle down. Talent and opportunity attract candidacies and creativity. Talented people look to work in new places. Political frontiers in Western Europe are not what they were 40 years ago. That toothpaste cannot be squeezed back into the tube.

A different way of presenting these questions would be to note that the UK government has generally favoured the concept of the economic market and free movement of *workers*. After the Treaty of Lisbon, the European Union law concept has to an extent expanded to embrace the notion of rights of EU *citizens*, I may note that at the same time the decisions of the European Court on 'health tourism' have been robust. Freedom of movement is *not* an absolute right. It is impossible to predict for the moment what tendency would prevail in deciding a controversy in this area. It will also be necessary to consider judicial structures within which these matters can be raised: parallel competence? Appeals or references during a transitional phase? Consultation between judicial entities?

VI. Conclusion

The first thing to say is how astonishingly far European law has come in 50 years. Judges have delivered judgments which were bold, prudent, cautious, obscure, clear, widely praised or widely blamed. They have worked successfully across the barriers of language, different legal traditions, and governmental criticism, and lobbying (overt and, one must assume, covert), to build a coherent legal architecture. Many of their judgments have required them to choose between powerful opposing forces – security and safety versus freedom of choice or freedom of enterprise; residents versus immigrants; France versus Germany; consumer safety versus consumer choice; the familiar versus the foreign; protectionism versus free trade.

However, my anecdotal impression is that the judges of the United Kingdom do not feel that they are subject to the yoke of Luxembourg rulings which encroach on their independence. It is true that individual decisions are criticised by academics and judges; but debate about important judgments is wholly desirable.

Some of the judgments have been mocked, and some of the judges have been derided in their national press (one was pilloried for working more hours than the hours stipulated by the Working Time Directive). The judges' tenure is not secure; in some Member States replacement of judges (appointed for a six-year term) may ensue when national general elections lead to a change of governing party. So while we honour the advocates who have helped to develop the law by zealously defending their clients, we should also honour the judges who have built the law, not without occasional risks to their own security of tenure in their job.

It is evident that the European venture is passing through one of its worst crises at the moment. The tank of enthusiasm for the European vehicle is quite empty for now, and indeed 'Europe's' great successes (eliminating war in Europe and bringing down the Iron Curtain) date from last century. We don't know what solution or adaptation the political leaders will adopt. But whatever these are, there will remain a need for resolution of legal controversies.

I think that the EU is the only place on earth today where (almost) a continent of states have agreed to deliver to their citizens access to healthcare, equal treatment of men and women, freedom of speech, a pension, education and a minimum wage. There are assuredly imperfections and gaps and inconsistencies. The constitutional architecture of the EU is creaky. There is no government and no opposition in the European Parliament. But the achievement of delivering decent standards by exploiting the opportunities of cross-border commerce and an open labour market is real and difficult to deny. King James was not wrong to note that when merchants get rich the people prosper, and that peaceful conditions both at home and overseas are the best basis for achieving prosperity.

It is also fair to note that the common market, despite its curious constitutional architecture, has delivered increased prosperity, the elimination of military rivalry and the liberation of Eastern Europe from Communism. These achievements have been based on a multitude of detailed steps reached by cooperative regulation on matters which often seem obscure, in order to expand economic opportunity, competitive choice and to deliver prosperity to those who wanted to work in a free (or less unfree) economy.

In order for the rule of law to be credible, the public authority must accept that it will from time to time lose in its own courts. It will be obvious to this audience that the scruffiest legal practice in a grey industrial town has the power to challenge a government measure in court, and win; not often, but sometimes, frequently enough to make the government hesitate before taking a potentially important step. It is of enormous importance to build into our democracy judicial review of public actions. And the European Courts have played a necessary role in that respect.

There was a birthday celebration in March at the Court to remember the Treaty of Rome. Some 64 delegates came from the Supreme Courts of the 27, plus Scotland, and a delegate from England. The speeches were graceful. Every language of the Union was deployed: no less than 552 interpretation combinations could have been (Lithuanian-Greek; Portuguese-Swedish) available. Brexit was barely mentioned and the working sessions touched on such matters as the anonymisation of judgments for the protection of the privacy of the individual litigant, cooperation between national courts and EU courts, and the best means of exchanging information about legal developments. There is a constant dialogue between national courts and the EU Court about many topics.

Then spoke the sharp clear voice of history. The President of the Supreme Court of Lithuania, Mr Norkus, reminisced about where his country stood 60 years ago. He began by recollecting a melancholy anniversary which the Court honoured last year: the brutal suppression of the Hungarian uprising in 1956. And the less celebrated killing of Lithuanian partisans who aspired to freedom and independence.

He noted how in 1957:

> there were not many discussions about economy and markets in eastern and Central Europe. Or rather, at that time many countries of this region already had a kind of single market. A market of oppression, of ideology, fake news and alternative facts, such as stating many human, political and other rights in the Constitution, but recognizing almost none of them in reality. However, there were many citizens in those countries who still had a vision. A vision which very much also drove the founding fathers of the European Union.
>
> A vision of modern democratic state, based on the rule of law, which is able to live in peace with the neighbours without building walls against them.
>
> A vision of the State protecting human rights and liberty; able to prosper by trusting, not humiliating, its citizens and neighbours. Without these citizens I doubt I would stand here today in front of you. We – Eastern and Central Europeans first of all owe very much to our citizens, less to markets.
>
> I am not sure whether we – the newcomers – share the same memories about the start of our common journey in the Union. Now we sometimes hear voices – give us our rights back. But I am not sure whether they have ever been taken away. Especially when every member can participate in creation, implementation and enforcement of them. Such judge has competence and abilities, personal strength and courage to resist choosing the easiest path and reuses to close the eyes to the law when she feels that it's threatened. Even if later such judge is downgraded to 'so-called judge' and her judgment is described as ridiculous.[29]

Any diplomatic agreement will be better respected if it provides a mechanism for the resolution of controversies. The controversies can involve disagreements between States and a citizen's dispute with a public authority. In some cases, the

[29] Rimvydas Norkus, Speech given at the conference of the Network of the Presidents of the Supreme Judicial Courts of the European Union, 1 November 2015 (available at www.lat.lt/download/1369/introductory%20report%20-%20the%20filtering%20of%20appeals%20to%20supreme%20courts%20).

citizen will want to seek judicial review of the authority's action. Two kinds of controversy can be anticipated. One is whether the existing rules were correctly applied. Another is whether the rules match national obligations under the secession treaty. These matters are of immense complexity and importance. In some cases, these topics may present a tension between EU law as today established and the political or administrative goals of the UK government. Persons, workers, families, access to social benefits and rights to abide may well be such. Access to a profession, equivalence of qualification and related issues touching the capacity to work would be another. There is a huge difference between having a right and having a right to request in this area.

To be appointed to sit on such a court is a great honour. I have found my new role after that of advocate utterly fascinating. The institution is truly a place where we have been able to unite with all our differences intact.

3

The European Union as an Oxymoron

From Contest via Contradiction to Constitution?

ROSTAM J NEUWIRTH

I. Introduction

> An oxymoron ('dazzling darkness') is a paradox compressed into a single self-contradicting phrase, and is therefore the show-off among figures of speech.[1]

Since its inception around 60 years ago, the European Union and its law have been one of the most dynamic laboratories for the development of supranational law and a harbinger for trends in international law.[2] More still, the European Union has also proven to be a fertile ground for so-called 'essentially oxymoronic concepts', namely the rhetorical figures of oxymoron and paradox. As rooted in its etymological origin, 'oxymoron' is an oxymoron itself, because it combines, in one word, the Greek words '*oxus*', meaning 'sharp or pointed' and '*moros*', meaning 'dull or foolish'.[3] Thus, usually an oxymoron appears in only one word, whereas 'paradox' expresses a similar contradiction in more than just one or two words, as in the phrase 'I know that I know nothing' attributed to Socrates.[4] Both types of concepts share that they carry in essence the idea of an apparent contradiction between antagonistic concepts.

[1] Helen Vendler, *The Music of What Happens: Poems, Poets, Critics* (Cambridge MA, Harvard University Press, 1988) 242.

[2] See also Christiaan Timmermans, 'The EU and Public International Law' (1999) 4 *European Foreign Affairs Review* 181 and Rostam J Neuwirth, 'Global Governance and the Reform of the Global Legal Order: Insights from the European Union's Legal System' in Pascaline Winand and others (eds), *The External Relations of the European Union* (Brussels, PIE Peter Lang, 2015) 331.

[3] Catherine Soanes and Angus Stevenson (eds), *Concise Oxford English Dictionary* 11th edn (Oxford, Oxford University Press, 2008) 1024.

[4] Gail Fine, 'Does Socrates Claim to Know that He Knows Nothing?' (2008) 35 *Oxford Studies in Ancient Philosophy* 49, 49.

The relevance of essentially oxymoronic concepts for the development of the European Union may not be obvious at first sight but rather only reveal their close connection bit by bit. The fact is that the notion of so-called 'essentially oxymoronic concepts' was coined in 2013 to indicate an observable shift in language usage that had occurred since Walter B Gallie introduced the notion of 'essentially contested concepts' in 1956, ie those 'the proper use of which inevitably involves endless disputes about their proper uses on the part of their users'.[5] This shift marks the gradual replacement of contested concepts, like art,[6] the rule of law,[7] democracy,[8] development,[9] globalisation[10] or power,[11] by oxymoronic concepts like creative industry,[12] substantive due process,[13] representative democracy,[14] sustainable development,[15] glocalisation[16] or the paradox of power,[17] to mention but a few.[18]

This shift can be noticed not only in artistic, scientific, political, economic or legal discourses, but in daily chitchat as well. There has been hardly a day where new products (eg, '*frappuccino*' or 'SUV'), new movies (eg, 'True Lies' or 'Act Naturally') or songs (eg, 'Sound of Silence'), or new political controversies (eg, 'burkini', 'Soft Brexit', 'artificial intelligence' or 'alternative fact') have not made an appearance in the news or in our lives in the form of oxymoronic concepts. While this trend, which has also earned it the connotation of the 'Age of Paradox',[19] may be fun or a sign of an increasing creativity in the arts, the economy or in advertising, it may have more serious repercussions in science in general, as the latter is meant

[5] Walter B Gallie, 'Essentially Contested Concepts' (1956) 56 *Proceedings of the Aristotelian Society* 167, 169.

[6] Walter B Gallie, 'Art as an Essentially Contested Concept' (1956) 6(23) *The Philosophical Quarterly* 97, 97.

[7] Jeremy Waldron, 'Is the Rule of Law an Essentially Contested Concept (in Florida)?' (2002) 21(2) *Law and Philosophy* 137.

[8] Howard A Doughty, 'Democracy as an Essentially Contested Concept' (2014) 19(1) *The Innovation Journal* 1.

[9] Björn Hettne, *Thinking about Development: Development Matters* (London, Zed Books, 2009) 1.

[10] Jonathan R Strand and others, 'The Essentially Contested Concept of Globalization' (2005) 1(1) *Journal of International Political Theory* 45.

[11] KI MacDonald, 'Is "Power" Essentially Contested?' (1976) 6(3) *British Journal of Political Science* 380.

[12] Theodor W Adorno, *The Culture Industry* (London, Routledge, 1991) 98.

[13] James W Ely, Jr, 'The Oxymoron Reconsidered: Myth and Reality in the Origins of Substantive Due Process' (1999) 16 *Constitutional Commentary* 315, 315.

[14] Benjamin R Barber, *Strong Democracy: Participatory Politics for a New Age* (Berkeley CA, University of California Press, 2003) xxxiv.

[15] Esther Njiro, 'Introduction: Sustainable Development an Oxymoron?' (2002) 52 *Agenda* 3 and Michael Redclift, 'Sustainable Development (1987–2005): An Oxymoron Comes of Age' (2005) 13 *Sustainable Development* 212.

[16] Habibul H Khondker, 'Globalisation to Glocalisation: A Conceptual Exploration' (2005) 13 *Intellectual Discourse* 181, 187–88.

[17] George Kunz, *The Paradox of Power and Weakness: Levinas and an Alternative Paradigm for Psychology* (Albany NY, State University of New York Press, 1998).

[18] For more examples, see Rostam J Neuwirth, *Law in the Time of Oxymora: A Synaesthesia of Language, Logic and Law* (London, Routledge, 2018).

[19] Charles Handy, *The Age of Paradox* (Cambridge MA, Harvard Business School Press, 1995).

to clearly discern the true from the false, or scientifically proven and unproven. By the same token, it poses a serious challenge to law, where the judicial answer of someone being guilty or innocent is crucial for where the person affected will spend the next years of her or his life.

Given that the European Union is built on a vast body of laws, the so-called '*acquis communautaire*', and also constitutes an oxymoron, it is extremely important to understand better the lessons that the emergence and rise of essentially oxymoronic concepts try to convey for the management of the future of European governance in particular and global governance in general. This need is related to the observation that 'law changes as language changes – perhaps because language changes',[20] which also means that when the law changes due to changes in language, life changes as well – and often very drastically indeed.

Before the oxymoronic or apparently contradictory genetic code of the European Union is addressed, section II first addresses a dominant trait of European culture, namely the one of 'contest'. It shows how contest and contestation, regarded as the struggle between opposing forces, may be linked to a fragmentation in terms of policy coherence and ambivalence or confusion in EU citizens contributing to a rise in Euroscepticism. The strong reliance on contest and the aversion to apparent contradictions may also be directly linked to the failure of the European Constitution to materialise. Subsequently, section III contrasts contest with contradiction as rooted in various examples of paradoxes or oxymora that dominate the European political and legal discourses. In the end, the conclusion synthesises what the 'European Union' and other oxymora may signify in the present, and what lessons Europeans can learn from Asian philosophies for the future of the process of integration in Europe.

II. European Integration: From Contestation via Contradiction to Constitution

> Contest is a part of human life everywhere that human life is found. In war and in games, in work and in play, physically, intellectually, and morally, human beings match themselves with or against one another.[21]

In Europe, in particular, 'contest' seems to be put into everyone's cradle at birth. Some even go as far as to describe it as an innate feature of human nature.[22] Nature versus nurture, or innate versus learned, it is safe to contend that old habits die

[20] Adolph S Oko, 'Foreword' in Nathan S Isaacs, *The Law and the Change of Law* (Miami FL, Hardpress, 2012) 6.

[21] Walter Ong, *Fighting for Life: Contest, Sexuality, and Consciousness* (Ithaca NY, Cornell University Press, 1981) 15.

[22] ibid, 15.

hard, especially when it comes to cognitive modes of thinking.[23] This is why contest is a part of European life wherever we look. From kindergarten via school to university, from internship via various employments to retirement, or from city council via national assembly to European Parliament, and in the institutional balance between EU institutions, contest – exercised through a fierce competition – aimed at eliminating the other contestants so as to take home victory as the 'first prize' is usually hailed as the ultimate goal or success. Sports too are sold by the media as a brutal contest and no longer understood in the sense of 'sportsmanship' or persons playfully being 'good sports'. Even in music, Europeans seemingly succeeded in defying rather than supporting theories about the unifying power of music as a means for conflict transformation.[24] The oldest annual international TV song competition is not referred to as a 'concert' or 'festival' but rather as the 'Eurovision Song *Contest*'. The prevalence of 'contest' comes as no surprise given that for a long time dictionaries defined 'contest' as 'dispute, debate, quarrel' and even as 'dispute with arms (field, victory, issue, battle)'.[25] It comes as no surprise that when looking back at European history, one finds a history of war written in numerous bloody contests.[26] In other words, contest is what *is*, what we teach and what we are taught, it simply is what we do and how things are done.

Yet, what may surprise, is a look at the etymological origin of 'contest', where we learn that it derives from the Latin '*contestāri*' which has been translated as 'to bring together the witnesses for both parties'.[27] Literally it means thus to 'witness' ('*testare*') together ('con-'), a kind of different understanding which would better suit the founding letter and spirit of the law underlying the European Union. This letter and spirit of the EU is best characterised by the Preamble of the Treaty Establishing the European Coal and Steel Community, which aimed to create 'the basis for a broader and deeper community among peoples long divided by bloody conflicts; and to lay the foundations for institutions which will give direction to a destiny henceforward shared …'.[28] Later, the Rome Treaty also added the important objective of laying 'the foundations of an ever closer union among the peoples of Europe'.[29] Both preambles thus promote a different understanding of

[23] See Gabriel Segal, 'Poverty of Stimulus Arguments Concerning Language and Folk Psychology' in Peter Carruthers and others, *The Innate Mind: Foundations and the Future* (Oxford, Oxford University Press, 2008) 90, 101.

[24] See eg 'American Unity through Music' (1941) 27(5) *Music Educators Journal* 10 and Olivier Urbain (ed), *Music and Conflict Transformation: Harmonies and Dissonances in Geopolitics* (London, IB Tauris, 2014).

[25] Cf Noah Webster, *A Dictionary of the English Language* (New York NY, Huntington Savage, 1845) 98 and HW Fowler and FG Fowler (eds), *The Concise Oxford Dictionary of Current English* (Oxford, Clarendon Press, 1919) 179.

[26] See also Michael Howard, *War in European History* (Oxford, Oxford University Press, 1979).

[27] See Eric Partridge, *Origins: A Short Etymological Dictionary of Modern English* 4th edn (London, Routledge, 1966) 3426.

[28] Recital 5 of the Preamble of the Treaty Establishing the European Coal and Steel Community [1951] 261 UNTS 142.

[29] Treaty Establishing the European Economic Community [1957] 294 UNTS 5.

contest, as it was also recognised in the way the common market was supposed to be monitored by competition rules not trying to foster predatory practices but to restrain them instead.

Unfortunately, however, the European project itself was contested in its essence rather than the previous understanding of military contest and conquests.[30] This can be seen from the fact that at least two central institutions were created to foster European integration, one more political in the form of the Council of Europe, and the other having a more economic focus as reflected in the name of the European Economic Community which was created in 1958. Instead of securing greater coherence between politics and economics by entrusting a single institution with the future henceforward shared, two twins – separated at birth – were created to compete in a contest about human rights and the supreme rule of European law.[31] To summarise the past 60 years of European integration, the EU and its predecessors, their 'identities' all met or were infused with a culture of 'contest'" at birth.

Even more recently, the prevalence of 'contest' resurfaced and became reinvigorated rather than diffused in the context of the negotiation of a Constitution for Europe following the 2001 Laeken Declaration, which called for a 'Constitution for European citizens', which later resulted in the presentation of a Draft Treaty Establishing a Constitution for Europe in 2003.[32] The said Constitution, however, was never adopted, and only later resulted in the Lisbon Treaty entering into force on 1 December 2009 instead, which not only further undermined the equal rights of EU citizens and equal obligations of EU Member States by allowing an opt-out to the UK and Poland but also – as a further setback – introduced a so-called 'withdrawal clause' (Article 50 TEU).[33]

To cut a long and well-known story short, the time between the years 2000 and 2010 can be aptly termed a 'lost decade in EU integration history', because too many opportunities passed by unused and many projects or strategies ended in failure, like the EU Constitution itself or the Lisbon Strategy, which aimed to make Europe 'the most competitive and dynamic knowledge-based economy in the world, capable of sustainable economic growth with more and better jobs and greater social cohesion' by 2010.[34] As a result of an apparent standstill or

[30] See also Zenon Bańkowski and Emilios Christodoulidis, 'The European Union as an Essentially Contested Project' (1998) 4(4) *European Law Journal* 341.

[31] See G Quinn, 'The European Union and the Council of Europe on the Issue of Human Rights: Twins Separated at Birth?' (2001) 46 *McGill Law Journal* 849.

[32] *Draft Treaty Establishing a Constitution for Europe* (Office for Official Publications of the European Communities, 2003).

[33] Treaty on European Union (TEU) and The Treaty on the Functioning of the European Union [2008] OJ C115/01 (consolidated version) [Lisbon Treaty (LT)]; see also I Pernice, 'The Treaty of Lisbon and Fundamental Rights' in Stefan Griller and Jacques Ziller (eds), *The Lisbon Treaty: EU Constitutionalism without a Constitutional Treaty?* (New York NY, Springer, 2009) 235 and Hannes Hofmeister, '"Should I Stay or Should I Go?" – A Critical Analysis of the Right to Withdraw from the EU' (2010) 16(5) *European Law Journal* 589.

[34] 'Presidency Conclusions' (Lisbon European Council, 23 and 24 March 2000) www.europarl.europa.eu/summits/lis1_en.htm, accessed 8 September 2017.

the frequent divides among Member States, European scepticism or so-called 'Euroscepticism' continued to grow according to Eurobarometer surveys,[35] if it was not stirred up by incompetent news reporting by several media outlets as well as nationalist sentiments invoked by local politicians putting personal or party interests before European citizens' long-term interests.

In this last point, the inability to formulate a long-term vision and related strategies, like the vision laid down in the Schuman Declaration on 9 May 1950, may be directly linked to the current political system based on contests between ruling and opposing or left and right political parties. This system is the result of a culture of contest (which could also be regarded as an oxymoron) which does not favour coherent long-term planning. Like the name Europe, the culture of contest may have also originated from ancient Greece, the consequences of which the Indian poet Rabindranath Tagore aptly described as follows:

> The civilisation of ancient Greece was nurtured within city walls. In fact, all the modern civilisations have their cradles of brick and mortar. These walls leave their mark deep in the minds of men. They set up a principle of 'divide and rule' in our mental outlook, which begets in us a habit of securing all our conquests by fortifying them and separating them from one another. We divide nation and nation, knowledge and knowledge, man and nature.[36]

This paragraph sums up the principal dilemma found in the process of European integration, one caused by a mental outlook rooted in regarding boundaries as merely dividing lines and not possible points of contact between peoples, countries or other phenomena. As a result, there is a widespread ambivalence towards European integration, in the sense of simultaneous conflicting feelings expressed in a great uncertainty over its *finalité*, ie both its purpose and end.[37] This ambivalence usually translates into a strong and paralysing indifference, which then reinforces a nationalist focus in political participation or outright opposition to European integration.

Ultimately, it can be argued that the cause of this ambivalence is a confusion caused by an exclusive logic expressed in a culture of contest in view of apparently contradictory concepts, like those of oxymora and paradoxes. Yet, in view of their recent rise and an increasing complexity in global affairs too, it will be necessary to introduce a new layer of 'oxymoronic thinking' and fuzzy logic into the present educational methods, ie one which complements but does not replace dualistic

[35] On the support of Membership in the various EU Member States see EUROBAROMETER, 'Public Opinion in the European Union' (European Commission 2007) http://ec.europa.eu/public_opinion/archives/eb/eb67/eb_67_first_en.pdf, accessed 8 September 2017; see generally Aleks Szczerbiak and Paul Taggart (eds), *Opposing Europe? The Comparative Party Politics of Euroscepticism* (Oxford, Oxford University Press, 2008).

[36] Rabindranath Tagore, *Sadhana: The Realisation of Life* (New York NY, The MacMillan Company, 1925) 3.

[37] Rostam J Neuwirth, 'The European Union and the Ambivalence towards the Process of European Integration' (2008) 1 *NUJS Law Review* 33, 33.

thinking and exclusive logic.[38] Fortunately, however, such thinking in Europe has not been unknown but merely seems to have lain dormant for centuries. There are indeed numerous accounts of a more inclusive rather than exclusive logic in Europe too, one which places emphasis not only on the law of an excluded middle but one of an included middle as well.[39] Put differently, a more holistic and even oxymoronic mode of thinking, where opposites do not always contradict each other but may actually mutually enrich and enhance each other, was and is also known in Europe and is not the sole privilege of Eastern philosophies, where, however, it seems to have been cultivated and preserved better in recent centuries.[40] As a possible exception confirming the rule, such a complementary (and not alternative) mode of thinking emerges in many efforts related to the process of European integration. One may think of the term 'European Union' as well as its motto 'united in diversity', as well as wider tendencies surfacing in drastic changes in words, language and logic as manifest in the rise of rhetorical figures called 'essentially oxymoronic concepts'.[41] These rhetorical figures can be regarded as harbingers of imminent changes in the way we think, and when fully understood can also be used constructively for better governance modes in times of an accelerated pace of change. Eventually, these oxymoronic concepts may inaugurate a new way of thinking, one which will make the adoption of a European Constitution appear a logical step.

III. The 'European Union' and Other Oxymora

> People conceptualize their experiences in figurative terms via metaphor, metonomy, irony, oxymoron, and so on, and these principles underlie the way we think, reason, and imagine.[42]

The widespread ambivalence towards the European Union and its dynamic process of European integration may be caused by a cognitive clash deriving from a culture of contest with a reality of increasing contradictions. It may thus be related to a

[38] See also James L Eliason, 'Using Paradoxes to Teach Critical Thinking in Science' (1996) 25(5) *Journal of College Science Teaching* 341, 341; see also Marianne W Lewis and Gordon E Dehler, 'Learning through Paradox: A Pedagogical Strategy for Exploring Contradictions and Complexity' (2000) 24(6) *Journal of Management Education* 708 and Matthew Bryant, *Oxymoron? A Practical Guide to Fun and Effective Teaching* (Bloomington IN, iUniverse, 2006).

[39] On the law of an included middle, see Joseph E Brenner, *Logic in Reality* (Dordrecht, Springer Science + Business Media, 2008) 4.

[40] See Neuwirth (n 18) and Kaiping Peng and Richard E Nisbett, 'Culture, Dialectics, and Reasoning about Contradiction' (1999) 54(9) *American Psychologist* 741.

[41] See Rostam J Neuwirth, 'Essentially Oxymoronic Concepts' (2013) 2(2) *Global Journal of Comparative Law* 147.

[42] Raymond W Gibbs, *The Poetics of Mind: Figurative Thought Language and Understanding* (Cambridge, Cambridge University Press, 1994) 5.

frequent use and even rise of oxymoronic concepts in life in general and in the EU in particular. In this regard, the European Union and its law appears not only as one of the foremost and most dynamic laboratories for the development of supranational law and trends in international law.[43] The EU is also a fertile ground for the creation or usage of essentially oxymoronic concepts. This is no surprise given that the term 'European Union' can already be regarded as an oxymoron (or enantiosis to be precise),[44] because a union between sovereign territorial nation states is difficult to imagine. As a euphemism perhaps, the difficulty of such a union is being circumscribed by virtue of the oxymoronic term '*discordia concors*' (harmonious discord)[45] or its unofficially official motto 'united in diversity'.[46] More so, the term may even have evolved in line with the broader trend from an essentially contested to an oxymoronic concept, but the contestation of the project itself may have stayed the same.[47] The supranationalism advocated by the European Union and its predecessor, the European Economic Community, was also described as dualistic and, therefore, said to give rise to numerous contradictions.[48] Or else, described as 'European Polity', the EU was characterised as a paradox, which consists in various 'features of the process of European integration which suggest that the European Union is simultaneously both "near-state" and antithetical to stateness' and 'a parallel development of two dimensions: one institutional, the other theoretical'.[49]

Another EU law paradox was said to lie in the fact that 'European legal integration provides an enduring challenge to social scientists and lawyers, who have not yet been able to establish the integration processes as a coherent scientific object'.[50] This means that despite being multidisciplinary and cross-sectional in its scope and application, EU law is still largely divided along the traditional lines of various dichotomies, such as national versus international law, public versus private, or civil versus criminal law, to mention but a few. Only slowly does the overall legal

[43] See also Neuwirth (n 2) 331.

[44] For a definition of enantiosis (or *contradictio in adiecto*), see Samuel Neil, *The Elements of Rhetoric; A Manual of the Flaws of Taste, Including the Theory and Practice of Composition* (London, Walton and Maberly, 1854) 183–84, defining enantiosis as an 'expression of an opposition of meaning in such a manner that the words also stand opposed to each other'.

[45] See Werner Kaegi, 'Discordia Concors: Vom Mythos Basels und von der Europa-Idee Jacob Burckhardts' in Marc Sieber (ed), *Discordia Concors – Festgabe fur Egar Bonjour zu seinem siebzigsten Geburtstag am 21. August 1968* (Basel, Helbing & Lichtenhahn, 1968) 131 mainly at 136–52.

[46] See the Declaration No. 52 on the Symbols of the European Union [2010] OJ C83, 355.

[47] See also Bańkowski and Christodoulidis (n 30) 341.

[48] See Joseph Weiler, 'The Community System: the Dual Character of Supranationalism' (1981) 1(1) *Yearbook of European Law* 267, 267.

[49] See Jo Shaw and Antje Wiener, 'The Paradox of the "European Polity"' in Maria Green Cowles and Michael Smith (eds), *The State of the European Union: Risks, Reform, Resistance, and Revival* (Oxford, Oxford University Press, 2000) 64, 64.

[50] See Mikael Rask Madsen and others, 'General Introduction: Paradoxes of European Legal Integration' in Hanne Petersen and others (ed), *Paradoxes of European Legal Integration* (Farnham, Ashgate, 2008).

framework of the EU even overcome the fragmentations which derive from these dichotomies.[51] It suffices to mention here first, the institutional split or 'separation of twins at birth' between a political and economic process of integration, manifest in the original bifurcation of competences between the European Economic Community (EEC) on the one hand, and the Council of Europe on the other.[52] Or else, the birth as an ordinary organisation of international law and its gradual transformation into a *sui generis* supranational organisation by having 'limited their sovereign rights and hav[ing] thus created a body of law which binds both their nationals and themselves'.[53]

More paradoxes have been identified in what has been termed 'in practice a set of relative oppositions which are important drivers in the continuous making of Europe'.[54] In other words, the EU, in its present 'dynamic status quo', is driven by a great number of dichotomies, or apparently antagonistic forces, such as widening and deepening or negative and positive forms of integration.[55] Also, the method is controversial and combines elements of a constitutionalist and a functionalist method of integration.[56] Further dividing dichotomies in Europe are those of cooperation versus competition, or of centralisation versus decentralisation, which are perhaps not expressed in essentially oxymoronic but at least in essentially contested concepts or disguised in a plethora of technical terms or 'Eurospeak' (a kind of EU version of Orwell's 'doublethink'). Such technical terms include the open method of coordination or the principle of subsidiarity. The open method of coordination (OMC) is a kind of oxymoronic soft law mechanism of decision-making, notably in areas where the EU had no competence and was said to organise 'a learning process in order to promote the exchange of experiences and best practices', as a departure from the traditional forms of legislative procedures.[57] Interestingly, the open method of coordination was itself born out of a paradox, namely that this '"new" mode of governance was not originally recognised as such by the summit which launched it'.[58] Subsidiarity is defined as requiring a justification for any proposed actions in areas which do not fall within the EU's exclusive

[51] See also Marise Cremona, 'Coherence through Law: What Difference Will the Treaty of Lisbon Make?' (2008) 3(1) *Hamburg Review of Social Sciences* 11.

[52] See also Gerard Quinn, 'The European Union and the Council of Europe on the Issue of Human Rights: Twins Separated at Birth?' (2001) 46 *McGill Law Journal* 849.

[53] See Case 6/64, *Costa v ENEL* [1964] ECR 585 at pt. 3.

[54] See Rask Madsen and others (n 50) 1.

[55] See eg Markus Jachtenfuchs, 'Deepening and Widening Integration Theory' (2002) 9(4) *Journal of European Public Policy* 650; John Pinder, 'Positive Integration and Negative Integration: Some Problems of Economic Union in the EEC' (1968) 24(3) *The World Today* 88, and Fritz W Scharpf, 'Balancing Positive and Negative Integration: The Regulatory Options for Europe', *EUI Policy Paper 97/4* (1997).

[56] See eg Léontin -Jean Constantinesco, *Das Recht der Europäischen Gemeinschaften: Das institutionelle Recht* (Baden-Baden, Nomos, 1977) 113–22.

[57] See eg Sabrina Regent, 'The Open Method of Coordination: A New Supranational Form of Governance?' (2003) 9(2) *European Law Journal* 190, 190–91.

[58] See Claudio M Radaelli, *The Open Method of Coordination: A New Governance Architecture for the European Union?* (Stockholm, Swedish Institute for European Policy Studies, 2003) 14.

competence, and that the objectives of the proposed actions can be better achieved at the Union level.[59] It too has been referred to as a paradox, namely in the sense that its function and aim are antithetical because 'subsidiarity seeks to integrate nations and individuals while simultaneously sustaining the diversity of the EU's Member States and their regions by preserving their autonomy in certain fields of governance such as "culture"'.[60] Subsidiarity has also been found to be in a paradoxical relationship to democracy, because when subsidiarity is fully applied, the decision-making process becomes more complex and less transparent, which is the opposite of what democratic decision-making implies.[61]

Together, the problems tackled by the open method of coordination and subsidiarity were also discussed in the context of the oxymoron 'flexicurity', a portmanteau of flexibility and security, which historically tended to be seen as diametric opposites.[62] Gradually, the opposition has given way to their approach where flexibility and security are no longer contradictory to one another, but in many situations can be mutually supportive.[63] Later, flexicurity was defined as a policy strategy that

> attempts, synchronically and in a deliberate way, to enhance the flexibility of labour markets, work organisation and labour relations on the one hand, and to enhance security – employment and social security – notably for weaker groups in and outside the labour market, on the other hand.[64]

Even at a broader level, social policies in the context of the EU's new growth strategy for the next decade, termed 'Europe 2020', was described as a potential oxymoron.[65] This means that, still, economic and social policies are widely regarded as mutually incompatible or their goals as contradictory. The whole process was in fact also referred to by the paradox of the EU being in a state of just running to stand still.[66] This widely characteristic phenomenon may also be captured by the term 'dynamic

[59] Art 5(3) Treaty on European Union (TEU) in Consolidated Versions of the Treaty on European Union and the Treaty on the Functioning of the European Union (TFEU) [2010] OJ C83/1.

[60] See Jeff Edmund Katcherian, 'Unraveling the Paradox: Competence and the Failure of Subsidiarity in the European Union' (2012) 35(2) *Political and Legal Anthropology Review* 271, 271 (citing Chantal Millon-Delsol, *Le Principe de Subsidiarité* (Paris, Presses Universitaires de France, 1992).

[61] See Steven van Hecke, 'The Principle of Subsidiarity: Ten Years of Application in the European Union' (2003) 13(1) *Regional & Federal Studies* 55, 67.

[62] See Pascale Vielle and Jean-Michel Bonvin, 'Putting Security at the Heart of the European Social Pact – Proposals to Make Flexicurity More Balanced' (2008) 14(3) *Transfer: European Review of Labour and Research* 419, 421.

[63] See Per Kongshøj Madsen, '"Flexicurity" A New Perspective on Labour Markets and Welfare States in Europe' (2007) 14 *Tilburg Law Review* 57, 75.

[64] See Luigi Burroni and Maarten Keune, 'Flexicurity: A Conceptual Critique' (2011) 17(1) *European Journal of Industrial Relations* 75, 77 [references omitted].

[65] See Bart Vanhercke, 'Is the "Social Dimension of Europe 2020" an Oxymoron?' in Christophe Degryse and David Natali (eds), *Social Developments in the European Union* (Brussels, ETUI and Observatoire Social Européen 2010) 141.

[66] See David Natali and Bart Vanhercke, 'Foreword: European Paradox: is the EU running to stand still?' in David Natali and Bart Vanhercke (eds), *Social Developments in the European Union* (Brussels, ETUI and Observatoire Social Européen, 2011) 11.

status quo' or the Lampedusa paradox, in a sense that the EU keeps changing (and amending its treaties as well as reforming its institutions) only to keep things the same way. In 2011, Giuliano Amato and Yves Mény also referred to some of the institutional changes in the EU as paradoxes, or else even serious problems, which bring the EU back into the age of paralysis and inefficiency as the United Nations has done over the past half a century.[67] Among these problems, they mention the difficulty in taking decisions, the defence of national interests, and the supremacy of the larger countries, which also characterise the United Nations (as another oxymoron).[68] Amato and Mény see it as a broader trend, which is the result of more obvious contradictions, which they explain as follows:

> Firstly, while the intergovernmental approach seems to have the upper hand, we are at the same time seeing the emergence of an embryonic budgetary and fiscal federalism. Secondly, the EU has received greater economic powers, yet it is not able to offset these (by direct or indirect redistribution) through the EU budget, and nor has it been given any further powers in the area of social policy. There has, moreover, been no strengthening of the democratic legitimacy of the EU. The future, therefore, gives cause for concern: further integration does not seem to be a viable option, involving as it does the risk of serious popular protests against the European process.[69]

Clearly, there are many more apparent contradictions found along the lines of various dichotomies, such as between old and new Europe in different contexts, from security questions to the global banking system.[70] These various dichotomies can be summarised by the European integration process often proceeding in the form of 'agreements to disagree' or, stated in a more euphemistical term, 'happy compromises', both terms also being oxymora.

To cut a long and complex story short, the process of European integration as governed by EU law is both explicitly and implicitly replete of oxymora, contradictions and paradoxes. This is caused by many dichotomies, which, paradoxically, signify both its strength and weakness, bliss and curse, challenge and chance. In general, among such forces, EU law scholars and lawmakers oscillate nervously between the extreme poles of antagonistic concepts as much as EU citizens struggle to understand the dual nature of 'state citizenship' and 'union membership' as

[67] See Giuliano Amato and Yves Mény (with Cécile Barbier and David Natali), 'Is the EU becoming more like the UN? Paradoxes around EU Institutional Developments in 2011 and Risks for Future Integration' in David Natali and Bart Vanhercke (eds), *Social Developments in the European Union* (Brussels, ETUI and Observatoire Social Européen 2011) 25; see also Neuwirth (n 2) 331.

[68] Franz Baumann, 'United Nations Management – An Oxymoron?' (2016) 22 *Global Governance* 461. See eg United Nations High Level Panel on Coherence, *Delivering as One: Report of the High-level Panel on United Nations System-wide Coherence in the Areas of Development, Humanitarian Assistance and the Environment* (G.A. A/61/583, 9 November 2006).

[69] See Amato and Mény (with Barbier and Natali) (n 67) 25; see also Neuwirth (n 2) 331.

[70] See eg Jiri Sedivy and Marcin Zaborowski, 'Old Europe, New Europe and Transatlantic Relations' (2004) 13(3) *European Security* 187 and Allen N Berger, 'Obstacles to a Global Banking System: "Old Europe" versus "New Europe"' (2007) 31 *Journal of Banking & Finance* 1955.

printed on each EU Member State's passport.[71] European citizens must thus feel schizophrenic like Dr Jekyll and Mr Hyde,[72] wondering who is the 'evil personality', the national or the supranational (ie European) identity? Related to this issue is the question of whether European citizens feel alienated from the EU or, put simply, whether Europe is a democracy without a '*demos*'.[73] It also invites the question of whether the EU's dual federalism is cooperative, which sometimes appears as an oxymoron and at other times as a tautology.[74]

In all cases the answers appear clear, as European scepticism or 'Euroscepticism' have been on the rise, while support for European integration is waning.[75] Therefore, it can be wondered whether 'mainstream Euroscepticism' is a trend or an oxymoron.[76] In either case, the answer to this question is complex, as both the causes of the problems of Euroscepticism and their possible solutions may be found in paradoxes, as Joseph Weiler explained in the following paragraph:

> We come to understand here one of the profound paradoxes of European Integration. These very values, which find their legal and practical expression in, e.g., enhanced mobility, breakdown of local markets, and insertion of universal norms into domestic culture are also part of the deep modern and postmodern anxiety of European belongingness and part of the roots of European angst and alienation. A meaningful, legitimate and legitimating concept of Constitutionalism would have to face and mediate this paradox.[77]

Thus constitutionalism, or more concretely the adoption of a European Constitution, as a possibility to reconcile divergent forces or simply for people to disagree,[78] was also seen as a possible way out of the dilemma. Adopting a European Constitution was seen as a chance to finally put an end to the uncertainty and indeterminacy about the EU's legal status, which had been thus far approached merely by vague and contested concepts or paradoxical phrases like being 'less than a federation but more than a regime' or 'an international agreement but none the less constituting the constitutional charter of a Community based on the rule of law'.[79]

[71] See also Joseph HH Weiler, 'Does Europe Need a Constitution? Demos, Telos and the German Maastricht Decision' (1995) 3(1) *European Law Journal* 219, 250–56.

[72] See Robert L Stevenson, *The Strange Case of Dr Jekyll and Mr. Hyde* (London, Longmans & Green, 1886).

[73] See eg Mette Jolly, 'A Demos for the European Union?' (2005) 25(1) *Politics* 12.

[74] See Robert Schütze, *From Dual to Cooperative Federalism: The Changing Structure of European Law* (Oxford, Oxford University Press, 2009).

[75] See eg Eurobarometer, *Public Opinion on the European Union* (European Commission, 2007).

[76] See Leonard Ray, 'Mainstream Euroskepticism: Trend or Oxymoron?' (2007) 42 *Acta Politica* 153.

[77] See Joseph HH Weiler, 'Epilogue: The European Courts of Justice: Beyond "Beyond Doctrine" or the Legitimacy Crisis of European Constitutionalism' in Anne-Marie Slaughter and others (eds), *The European Court and National Courts – Doctrine and Jurisprudence: Legal Change in Its Social Context* (Oxford, Hart Publishing, 1998) 365, 371.

[78] Cf *Roe et al v Wade* (Supreme Court of the United States, 1973), 410 US 113, stating that '[The Constitution] is made for people of fundamentally differing views …'.

[79] See William Wallace, 'Less than a Federation. More than a Regime: The Community as a Political System' in Helen Wallace and William Wallace (eds), *Policy-Making in the European Community* (Oxford, Oxford University Press, 1983) 403 and Opinion 1/91, Draft agreement between the Community, on the one hand, and the countries of the European Free Trade Association, on the other, relating to the creation of the European Economic Area [1991] ECR I-6079, para 1.

In fact, it was the way chosen following the speech by Joschka Fischer on 12 May 2000, which turned a 'constitutional conversation'[80] or the EU's 'constitutional *Sonderweg*'[81] into concrete action.[82] To this end, the Laeken Declaration on the Future of the European Union was aimed to pave the way towards a Constitution for European citizens.[83] However, what ensued from the work of the European Convention on the Future of Europe was not a European Constitution but the birth of an oxymoron. The reason for such qualification as an oxymoron is given by Giuliano Amato, and retold by Jacques Ziller, as follows:

> 'È un maschio!', exclaimed Giuliano Amato (former Prime Minister of Italy and Vice-President of the Convention), referring to the text which the Convention had just ushered into the world in June 2003: 'It's a boy!' And this remark plays on the fact that, in Italian, the word for 'treaty' (*tratatto*) is masculine, whereas Amato would have preferred a 'girl', since the word *Costituzione* is feminine. The remark was thus a kind of gentle indictment of the Convention for its lack of boldness, ie, for its failure to go beyond the existing Treaties and transform them into a true Constitution. Amato also made reference to Neil Jordan's film The Crying Game, in which a militant of the IRA holding a British soldier captive falls in love with his prisoner's girlfriend, only to find in due course that this 'girlfriend' is in fact a transvestite.[84]

So the final result of the convention, the 2004 Treaty Establishing a Constitution for Europe, was, factually and legally speaking, an oxymoron, or, put differently, a legal 'transvestite'.[85] Technically speaking, it was considered 'a hybrid text reflecting hard-won compromises between opposing visions of the purpose and direction of European integration'.[86] The rest of the story is well-known, and the Constitutional Treaty failed to be ratified after negative referenda in France and the Netherlands.[87] The final result was also explained by essentially oxymoronic concepts, such as a 'successful failure' or the paradox of 'no' meaning 'yes'.[88]

[80] See Bruno de Witte, 'The Closest Thing to a Constitutional Conversation in Europe: The Semi-Permanent Treaty Revision Process' in Paul Beaumont and others (eds), *Convergence and Divergence in European Public Law* (Oxford, Hart Publishing, 2002) 39.

[81] See Joseph H.H. Weiler, 'In Defence of the Status Quo: Europe's Constitutional Sonderweg' in Joseph HH Weiler and Marlene Wind (eds), *European Constitutionalism Beyond the State* (Cambridge, Cambridge University Press, 2003) 7.

[82] See Joschka Fischer, 'From Confederacy to Federation: Thoughts on the Finality of European Integration' in Christian Joerges and others (eds), *What Kind of Constitution for What Kind of Polity? – Responses to Joschka Fischer* (Florence, European University Institute, 2000) 19.

[83] See *Laeken Declaration on the future of the European Union* [December 15, 2001] EC Bulletin 12-2001.

[84] See Jacques Ziller, *The European Constitution* (Alphen aan den Rijn, Kluwer, 2005) 29.

[85] See Treaty Establishing a Constitution for Europe [2004] OJ C310/1; see also Draft Treaty Establishing a Constitution for Europe [2003] OJ C169/7.

[86] See Ziller (n 85) 29.

[87] Giuliano Amato and Jacques Ziller, *The European Constitution Cases and Materials in EU and Member States' Law* (Cheltenham, Edward Elgar, 2007) 1–67.

[88] See Andreas Philippopoulos-Mihalopoulos, 'Moment of Stasis: The Successful Failure of a Constitution for Europe' (2009) 15(3) *European Law Journal* 309 and Andreas Philippopoulos-Mihalopoulos, 'When "No" Means "Yes": A Constitution for Europe and the Limits of Ignorance' in Maria Green Cowles and Michael Smith (eds), *The State of the European Union: Risks, Reform, Resistance, and Revival* (Oxford, Oxford University Press, 2000) 29.

In concrete terms, the 'successful failure' of the Constitutional Treaty led to the adoption of the so-called 'Lisbon Treaty' in 2007 instead. More recently, the ongoing negotiations of the United Kingdom with the EU about its withdrawal, possibly seeking a smooth continuation of bilateral relations, was termed 'Soft Brexit', and also called an oxymoron.[89] The reason for this is that either there is a Brexit or there is not. Moreover, Brexit or Grexit or any similar term used in the context of the withdrawal clause, all constitute, de iure, an oxymoron, since a 'withdrawal from the EU' is against its founding spirit, its basic norm (*Grundnorm*), and even now is still against the letter of the law when considering the rights conferred upon EU citizens both present and future. In the end we find that, since its origin, the EU continues its quest for a *finalité* by virtue of various essentially oxymoronic concepts, such as the aspiration for a 'constitution without a constitutional treaty',[90] a shift from 'dual to cooperative federalism',[91] or strong ambivalence towards the process of European integration altogether.[92]

IV. Conclusion

> This was some time a paradox, but now the time gives it proof.[93]

In retrospect, 60 years seems like a long time, but perception of time usually depends on the context. It seems like a long time when comparing times of peace against those of war in Europe. By contrast, it is a very short time when applied to 'old habits', which usually die hard. In this regard, changes in language may occur at a faster pace, but old language, reflecting old ways of thinking, is also reluctant to give way to neologisms or new meanings given to old terms. Even longer to change, it seems to take logic applied to our thinking, which in Europe appears still to be largely dominated by an Aristotelian approach called 'exclusive logic', or the 'law of an excluded middle' according to which 'everything must either be or not be'.[94] In following such an approach, the European Union and other oxymora inevitably create confusion and cause ambivalence towards the European integration project, as EU law is a veritable factory for the production of apparently contradictory concepts like oxymora and paradoxes. In law, however, reconciling

[89] See eg David Sweet, 'Understandable Confusion' (Letters to the Editor), *Financial Times* (27 September 2016), ('Sir, The term "soft Brexit" is an oxymoron ("May limbers up for a hard Brexit", September 21). We voted for the full sovereignty of leaving, not the no sovereignty of partially staying in. No wonder the Remainers are confused.') www.ft.com/content/b0c3a34c-7fed-11e6-8e50-8ec15fb462f4, accessed 8 September 2017.

[90] See the Treaty on European Union (TEU) and the Treaty on the Functioning of the European Union (TFEU) (consolidated version), [2010] OJ C83/01; see also Stefan Griller and Jacques Ziller (eds), *The Lisbon Treaty: EU Constitutionalism without a Constitutional Treaty?* (New York NY, Springer, 2009).

[91] See Schütze (n 75).

[92] See Neuwirth (n 37) 33.

[93] William Shakespeare, 'Hamlet' in John Dover Wilson (ed), *The Works of William Shakespeare* (Cambridge, Cambridge University Press, 2009) 62.

[94] Bertrand Russell, *The Problems of Philosophy* (London, Williams & Norgate, 1912) 113.

the irreconcilable, merging antitheses and synthesising opposites were singled out as constituting its central problems and main challenges.[95] For this reason, law may follow what language manages to achieve by using essentially oxymoronic concepts, which provide an umbrella for opposites to move from contest on to apparent contradictions and then further to a new understanding. The same will have to be achieved in the European Union, where the 'culture of contest' (possibly an oxymoron in the meantime) will move to one of contradiction and further on to a new understanding of a destiny henceforward shared. To achieve this, it will be necessary to seek a more consistent regulatory framework in the form of a European Constitution.

For the cognitive cycle from contest to contradiction to be completed, first a new philosophy and educational approach is required, one which is more 'oxymoronic' whereby apparent lines of distinctions are not taken only as lines of separation but of connection too. In this regard, (EU) law can learn from Eastern philosophies to reconsider its own traditions so to as be able to function as a social medicine.[96] The analogy between law and medicine also resonates in the medieval maxim "*solve et coagula*" (dissolve and coagulate), which – borrowing freely from Carl G Jung and applying it to the European integration process – means for EU citizens that they need to overcome the initial state in which opposite tendencies or forces appear in conflict and to initiate 'a procedure which would be capable of bringing the hostile elements and qualities, once they were separated, back to unity again'.[97] This is what the notion of the European Union and other essentially oxymoronic concepts seem to prepare us for after decades of contests and endless disputes about 'essentially contested concepts'.

To recap briefly, the EU was born as an oxymoronic concept but was perceived as a contested project. Since then, it has grown up and moved from contestation to contradiction. It is now time to take the next step, to complete what a majority of European citizens were already prepared to do not long ago, namely, to adopt a European Constitution in the sense of a Constitution for European citizens. The reason is that it is in a Constitution, like in an oxymoron – where opposite views can be voiced in a joint forum – that the apparently contradictory tensions become transformed and can mutually enhance each other to set off a mutually beneficial virtuous cycle toward a peaceful destiny not contested, but rather witnessed and shared together. Geographically, the European destiny has always been shared, and it is time to do this legally as well, as ultimately the best way to predict and to meet the challenges brought by the future, is to create it. Eventually, there will be a day when – borrowing from William Shakespeare – it is possible to say that '*the European Union was some time an oxymoron, but now the time has given it proof*.'

[95] Benjamin N. Cardozo, *The Paradoxes of Legal Science* (New York NY, Columbia University Press, 1928) 4.

[96] Pierre Lepaulle, 'The Function of Comparative Law with a Critique of Sociological Jurisprudence' (1922) 35 *Harvard Law Review* 838, 838.

[97] See Carl G Jung, *Mysterium Coniunctionis: An Inquiry into the Separation and Synthesis of Psychic Opposites in Alchemy* (Princeton NJ, Princeton University Press, 1963) xiv.

4

The Social Dimension of the EU

MANFRED WEISS

I. Introduction

The future of the European project to a great extent will depend on the fact whether it can provide social justice throughout the EU. The need for improving the 'European social dimension', to take up Jacques Delors' well-known formula, as a tool for the people to identify themselves with the European project has never been more urgent than it is today after the Brexit.

The Europeanisation of labour law was not on the agenda of the European Economic Community (EEC) in 1957. In its origins the European project was understood as being primarily an effort to construct a common market. Market freedoms and the guarantee of fair competition within the common market, therefore, were the pillars of the Treaty of Rome. Social policy almost exclusively was left to the Member States. The original Treaty did not contain legislative powers in this field.

In the meantime, the European integration of labour law has become an important part of the European project. The first steps in this direction were made in the 1970s. In spite of the lack of legislative powers of the EEC in the area of labour law, directives in this field were passed (in particular equal pay for men and women,[1] comprehensive equal treatment of men and women in employment,[2] protection of workers in case of collective redundancies,[3] in case of transfers of undertakings and in case of the insolvency of the employer).[4] They were based on articles in the original Treaty (100 and 205) which had nothing to do with labour law and which required unanimous voting in the Council. This shows that the Treaty is more or less irrelevant if there is a consensus between all Member States. In reference to labour law this was the case until 1979 when Thatcher came into power in the UK.

[1] Dir 75/117/EEC of 10 February 1976, L 45/19.
[2] Dir 76/207/EEC of 9 February 1976, OJ 1976, L 39/40.
[3] Dir 75/129/EEC of 22 February 1975, OJ 1975, L 48.
[4] Dir 77/187/EEC of 5 March 1977, OJ 1977, L 61.

Only when in 1987 the Treaty was amended by the Single European Act did the EEC become empowered to legislate in a very limited area of labour law (work environment) with qualified majority vote in the Council. By further amendments, by the social protocol to the Maastricht Treaty in 1992 and later on in 1998 by the Treaty of Amsterdam, the EEC not only was renamed the European Community (EC) but the legislative powers in the area of labour law were significantly extended. These amendments now simply were transferred into the Lisbon Treaty on the Functioning of the European Union (TFEU). Accordingly, the EU is empowered to establish minimum standards for practically all aspects of labour law except 'pay, the right of association, the right to strike and the right to impose lock-outs' (Article 153 paragraph 5 TFEU). Legislation is possible on most of the subject matters by qualified majority.

The indicated amendments have brought another innovation. If the Commission wants to initiate legislation it has twice to consult the social partners of the inter-professional social dialogue, the European Trade Union Confederation (ETUC) on the employees' side and the Confederation of European Enterprises (BUSINESS EUROPE), the European Association of Craft Small and Medium-Sized Enterprises (UEAPME) as well as the Centre of Employers and Enterprises providing Public Services (CEEP) on the employers' side. First, they are to be consulted on the question 'whether' a specific piece of legislation on subject matters listed up in Article 153 paragraph 1 TFEU should be initiated and second on the question 'how' such a piece of legislation should look. In the latter consultation the social partners are entitled to take away the project from the Commission and are invited to try within a certain period to reach an agreement by themselves. Such an agreement then by the social partners can be brought via the Commission to the Council which may transfer it into a directive. This happened only three times in the 1990s. Afterwards it did not work out again, except in reference to a minor amendment of the directive on parental leave. Therefore, this structural innovation should not be overestimated.

Finally, it should be remembered that after a long and very controversial discussion a Charter of Fundamental Rights of the EU was passed in 2000 as a legally non-binding declaration which expressed the consensus of all 15 Member States of that time.[5] The Charter now has become a legally binding part of the Lisbon Treaty. It contains a whole set of fundamental social rights, among them the right to protection against unjustified dismissal, the right to fair and just working conditions, the right to collective bargaining and collective action as well as rights for either workers or their representatives on information and consultation, to just give an impression.

These developments have to be kept in mind while in the following section the status quo of European labour law and industrial relations is briefly sketched.

[5] For the genesis and the content of the Charter see M Weiss, 'The Politics of the EU-Charter of Fundamental Rights' in B Hepple (ed), *Social and Labour Rights in a Global Context* (Cambridge, Cambridge University Press, 2002) 73.

This assessment is a necessary precondition to evaluate the impact of the Lisbon Treaty for further developments and to discuss the possibilities for further legislation on labour law.

II. The Status Quo of Social Minimum Standards

A. Labour Legislation

In individual labour law major progress has been made particularly in legislation on health and safety, on working time, on work and life balance, on atypical work, on protection of employees in case of transnational services and on discrimination. In addition, the directives on collective redundancy[6] and on transfer of undertakings[7] have been amended in a double sense: they now include cases where the decisions are taken by transnational headquarters and they are adapted to the case law as developed by the Court of Justice of the EU (CJEU).

The core instrument for protection of health and safety is the Framework Directive of 1989,[8] surrounded by a whole set of so-called daughter directives on specific risks for health and safety. The Framework Directive – at least in principle – covers all private or public areas of activity, contains the basic principles to fight risks of health and safety and lists up the duties of employers as well as of employees in this respect.

The Working Time Directive of 1983[9] not only serves health and safety considerations but to a great extent is devoted to the organisation of working time flexibility. Mainly three issues covered by the directive have become very controversial: the very notion of working time, the period within which an average maximum working time per week has to be reached and the possibilities of opting out. Many efforts to again amend the directive have not succeeded up to now.

In the area of work/life balance the already mentioned directive of 1996 on parental leave[10] is of importance, even if it is only a very small step in making work and family obligations more compatible. It is the first directive which is based on an agreement reached by the social partners. Parents thereby got a right to parental leave for a minimum period and the right to return – at least in principle – to the same job. However, due to the fact that pay is not part of the EU's legislative power the directive does not say anything to the financial conditions of parental leave, thereby neglecting a very relevant part. More important in the context of work/life

[6] Dir 98/59/EC of 20 July 1998, OJ 1998, L 225/16.
[7] Dir 01/23/EC of 12 March 2001, OJ 2001, L 82/16.
[8] Dir 89/391/EEC of 12 June 1989, OJ 1989, L 183/1.
[9] Dir 93/104/EC of 13 December 1993, OJ 1993, L 307/18, replaced by Dir 03/88/EC of 4 November 2003, OJ 2003, L 299/9.
[10] Dir 96/34/EC of 3 June 1996, OJ 1996, L 145/9.

balance is the directive of 1997 on part-time work,[11] the second directive based on an agreement by the social partners. Even if this directive can be understood as the lowest possible denominator, it contains two important elements: equal treatment pro rata in reference to working conditions and protection against dismissal if an employee refuses to transfer from full-time to part-time or vice versa. Thereby, part-time in quite a few Member States has been elevated to a much better status than before.

Of course, the directive on part-time work can also be put in the box 'atypical work' together with the directive of 1999 on fixed term contracts[12] and the directive of 2008 on temporary agency work which have to be put in context with the directive of 1991 on the health and safety of workers with a fixed-duration employment or a temporary employment relationship. The directive on fixed term contracts is the last one based on an agreement by the social partners. It contains two important elements: equal treatment with those in an undetermined employment relationship and prohibition of abuse of repeated fixed term contracts. However, the criteria for abuse are so wide that the repetitive use of fixed term contracts is almost unlimited. The directive on temporary agency work[13] is the result of a long and very controversial effort. In the very end a compromise was reached which is unsatisfactory. In principle equal treatment with the comparable employees in the user company is guaranteed. However, by way of collective agreement lower conditions for the temporary workers can be determined.

The EC's by far most important legislative input into individual labour law has been in the area of discrimination. In 1998 by the Amsterdam amendment in the EC-Treaty Article 13 was introduced which empowers the European legislator to take 'appropriate action to combat discrimination based on sex, racial or ethnic origin, religion or belief, disability, age or sexual orientation' (now Article 19 TFEU). This has become the basis for the two anti-discrimination-directives of 2000.[14] In addition, the concept of the already mentioned directive on sex equality has been brought fully in line with the spirit of these directives of 2000. The amendments now are integrated in a consolidated version of the directive.[15]

Even more important than the inputs into individual labour are the Community's legislative measures in the area of collective labour law: they shape the interaction and the power relationship between both sides of industry and, thereby, have an enormous impact on the structure of industrial relations. In particular three legislative steps in the area of workers' participation are of utmost interest, two referring to transnational undertakings and groups of undertakings and one referring to domestic structures within the Member States.

[11] Dir 97/81/EC of 15 December 1997, OJ 1998, L 14/9.

[12] Dir 99/70/EC of 28 June 1999, OJ 1999, L 175/43.

[13] Dir 08/104/EC of 19 November 2008, OJ 2008, L 327/9.

[14] Dir 2000/43/EC of 29 June 2000, OJ 2000, L 180/22 and Dir 2000/78/EC of 27 November 2000, OJ 2000, L 303/16.

[15] Dir 2006/54/EC of 5 July 2006, OJ 2006, L 204/23.

The first step in this context is the directive of 1994 on European Works Councils (EWC)[16] which has been amended in 2009.[17] It covers transnational undertakings and groups of undertakings with at least 1000 employees within the EU and with at least 150 employees of the undertaking or of different undertakings of the group in each of at least two different Member States. The amendment of 2009 mainly brought clarifications on the timing and content of information and consultation, has integrated the CJEU's judgments into the directive and has strengthened the link between EWC and national workers' representatives.

The second step in this context was the directive supplementing the statute for a European Company with regard to the involvement of employees.[18] This directive has to be read together with the Statute on the European Company[19] which contains the rules on company law. The main goal of establishing a European Company as an option is to save transaction costs, and to increase efficiency and transparency. It no longer should be necessary to create complicated structures of holding companies in order to overcome the problems arising from national company law.

A European Company only can be registered if the requirements of the directive are met. Thereby it is guaranteed that the provisions on employees' involvement cannot be ignored. The crucial and interesting topic of the directive refers to employees' participation in company boards.

Whereas these two directives refer to the transnational context, the directive on a framework for information and consultation of 2002[20] shapes the participation structure within the Member States. It covers public or private undertakings of at least 50 employees and establishments of at least 20 employees in Member States. It establishes a minimum level of workers' participation within the Member States leaving them a high amount of flexibility.

There are further directives on workers' participation. However, this very sketchy assessment should be sufficient to show that employees' involvement in management's decision making has become an important feature of European collective labour law.

B. Evaluation

Taking everything together, legislation on social minimum standards is unsystematic and fragmentary. Important areas as for example protection against unfair dismissals are still missing. This deficiency has become particularly evident when in the course of the management of the financial crisis in the context of

[16] Dir 94/45/EC of 22 September 1994, OJ L 254/64.
[17] Dir 09/38/EC of 6 May 2009, OJ L 122/28.
[18] Dir 01/86/EC of 8 October 2001, OJ L 294/22.
[19] Reg 01/2157/EC of 8 October 2001, OJ L 294/1.
[20] Dir 02/14/EC of 11 March 2002, OJ L 80/29.

the austerity strategy Member States in Southern Europe were forced to reduce their standards of dismissal protection and of minimum wage and also forced to dismantle their collective bargaining systems. The construction of social Europe needs a comprehensive floor of rights throughout the EU which cannot be undercut. This, of course, does not mean that diversity between the labour law systems of the Member States should be abolished. It only means that minimum standards are to be established which are in line with the worker's fundamental right to 'working conditions which respect his or her ... dignity' (Article 31 of the Charter). At least this minimal social coherence is to be achieved.

III. The Obstacles for Further Legislation

A. The Diversity of Interests

In spite of the fact that the EU has a comprehensive power to legislate in the area of labour law the obstacles for legislation in this field are significant. This is first of all due to the fact that – in particular since the enlargements of 2004, 2007 and 2013 when many formerly communist States of the EU were integrated in the EU – the interests of the Member States in the EU of 28 have become so heterogeneous that it is very unlikely to get even a qualified majority for a piece of legislation. It is understandable that low wage countries want to use lower labour standards as a competitive advantage in comparison to high wage countries.

IV. Alternative Strategies

Confronted with these difficulties the EU more and more has shifted the focus to alternative strategies. The main instrument in this context has become the Open Method of Coordination (OMC). It has first been developed in the context of the European Employment Policy (EEP) in the Amsterdam Treaty.[21] According to the OMC the genuine competence of the Member States remains uncontested. The EU merely is supposed to encourage co-operation between them, to support and, if necessary, complement their action. It is mainly based on the idea that best practices as discovered in one country may be imitated by other countries, thereby leading to social progress. Instead of regulation by way of legislation the EU only tries to put soft pressure on the Member States, leaving them the task to regulate. This method, however, runs into difficulties if the gap of the economic situation

[21] For the development of EEP see J Goetschy, 'European Employment Policy since the 1990s' in Reiner Hoffmann, Otto Jacobi Berndt Keller and Manfred Weiss (eds), *Transnational Industrial Relations in Europe* (Düsseldorf, Edition der Hans-Böckler-Stiftung, 2000) 137.

between Member States is too big to allow for similar remedies. Then the capacity of the OMC is quickly exhausted.

Since the beginning of the new century the EU has tried to combine OMC with specific goals to be reached. The first expression of this new approach was the Lisbon strategy launched in 2000 for the EU 'to become the most dynamic and competitive knowledge-based economy in the world by 2010 capable of sustainable economic growth with more and better jobs and greater social cohesion and respect for the environment'. A whole set of ambitious targets for 2010 were listed up, among them targets for employment rates and for full employment. The concepts for reaching these goals were put in vague notions as 'flexicurity' or 'employability'.

However, soon it turned out that the strategy was much too complex, that it was lacking a clear division of tasks between EU and member states and that there was no really functioning governance structure.[22] Therefore, the strategy was modified and re-launched in 2005. Of great importance were country specific recommendations. They were meant to help the Member States to better realise the objectives in their national reform programmes. The OMC as a mutual learning strategy was the underlying philosophy of the whole exercise.

The Lisbon strategy has, of course, not reached its goals but been replaced by the new agenda 'Europe 2020', a 'strategy for smart, sustainable and inclusive growth'[23] that focuses on five goals to be reached by so-called flagship initiatives. In essence it is nothing else but a slimmed Lisbon strategy in new clothes. There is still the reference to the flexicurity agenda, to new forms of work–life balance, to the problem-solving potential of social dialogue at all levels and to the European qualification framework. The new strategy remains to a great extent within the old paths.

These soft law strategies have to be seen in the context of the new institutional architecture for economic and social governance. At the heart of this new architecture is the 'European Semester' of policy coordination, through which the Commission, the Council and the European Council set priorities for the Union in the Annual Growth Survey, review National Reform Programmes and issue Country-Specific Recommendations to Member States, backed up in some cases by the possibility of financial sanctions. The European Semester brings together within a single annual policy coordination cycle a wide range of EU governance instruments with different legal bases and sanctioning authority. The problem with all these mechanisms is that social policy is conceived as a residual category under the imperative of economic considerations.

The focus of all these mechanisms is on economic efficiency and not on increase of labour regulation which in the neo-liberal perspective is understood

[22] For an assessment of the Lisbon Strategy see the report of the High Level Group chaired by W Kok, *Facing the Challenge: The Lisbon Strategy for Growth and Employment* (Luxemburg 2004).

[23] COM (2010) 2020 final.

to limit the effect of market forces. Therefore, social policy is supposed to end up in de-regulation, de-institutionalisation and de-collectivisation. Reduction of labour costs is the overarching goal of this economy-oriented paradigm. The measures taken in the course of the austerity politics for the Member States with high debts show very well this direction: reduction of wages and pensions, reduction of protection against dismissals and de-construction of the system of collective bargaining.

V. European Pillar of Social Rights

A new approach came up when in September 2015 President Juncker, addressing the European Parliament, announced a European Pillar of Social Rights for the EU. According to him this Pillar 'should complement what … already jointly (has been) achieved when it comes to the protection of workers in the EU'. It sounded like a rebirth of the idea to establish a framework of hard law. As a first step it was only meant to 'serve as a compass for the renewed convergence within the euro area', even if Juncker indicated that the single market as a whole should profit of it, thereby inviting the other Member States to join in.

The concretisation of Juncker's idea was left to the European Commission, which in March 2016 issued a Communication.[24] There it became clear that the Pillar of Social Rights is to be integrated in the overall economic agenda, as 'an essential feature of the process of economic policy coordination at EU level, now known as the European Semester. The rationale behind the Pillar of Social Rights follows this logic …'[25] The concept of flexicurity was reconfirmed, social benchmarking was stressed as well as mainstreaming social objectives in flagship initiatives. According to the Commission the 'Pillar should become a reference framework to screen the employment and social performance of participating Member States, to drive reforms at national level and, more specifically, to serve as a compass for renewed convergence within the euro area'.[26] This very vague and unspecific concept left open the most important question, namely whether the Pillar is meant to provide rights, meaning hard law, or whether it is merely an extension of the soft law approach. This uncertainty was not eliminated by the preliminary outline for the consultation process which was put at the end of the Communication.

The consultation with other EU institutions, national authorities and parliaments, trade unions and business associations, NGOs, social service providers, experts from academia as well as the public lasted until the end of 2016. In January 2017 the Commission held a European Conference in order to wrap up the results of the consultation and to define the future direction of the Pillar of Social Rights.

[24] 'Launching a consultation on a European Pillar of Social Rights', COM (2016), 127 final.
[25] ibid at 3.
[26] ibid at 7.

Now we have more clarity. On 26 April 2017, the Commission presented a Recommendation[27] and a Proposal for an Interinstitutional Proclamation[28] of the European Parliament, the Council and the Commission on the European Pillar of Social Rights. This pillar 'is primarily conceived for the euro area but is applicable to all Member States that wish to be part of it' and it 'shall not prevent Member States or their social partners from establishing more ambitious social standards'. It is divided into three chapters: (a) equal opportunities and access to the labour market, (b) fair working conditions and (c) social protection and inclusion. It lists goals and principles for 20 policy areas. Some of it is already part of the social acquis and some of it refers to rights contained in the Charter of Fundamental Rights. The powers of the EU as defined in the Treaties are not extended. Even if the set of principles and rights looks very impressive, most of the policy recommendations are meant as encouragement for the Member States to develop respective standards, among them the right to receive support for job search, training and requalification, the right to adequate minimum wages or the right to redress, including adequate compensation, in case of unjustified dismissal.

The pillar also provides a clarification of controversial notions in the Working Time Directive[29] and an initiative for a possible action addressing the challenges of access to social protection for people in all forms of employment.[30] It also contains, even if only to a very limited extent, a program for EU legislation on work–life balance for parents and carers[31] and on documentation of working conditions in labour contracts.[32] In this context the Directive on Parental Leave is to be repealed and the Directive on a Written Statement of Working Conditions is to be modernised. The question, however, where such legislative initiative can be realised in the very end, remains open. The indicated difficulties for legislation do not disappear by the proclamation of the pillar.

Undoubtedly the European Pillar of Social rights, providing a comprehensive social agenda, is a step in the right direction. However, it is too early for euphoria. There is, of course, pressure on them to implement the recommendations, but the pressure remains soft. Binding European law only can be expected to a marginal extent. Therefore, the need to reflect on possibilities for further hard law on the European level does not disappear.

[27] 26.4.2017 Com (2017) 2600 final.

[28] 26.4.2017 Com (2017) 251 final.

[29] Interpretative Communication on Directive 2003/88/EC of 4 November 2003 concerning certain aspects of the organization of working time, Brussels 26.4.2017, C (2017) 2601 final.

[30] First phase consultation of Social Partners under Article 154 on a possible action addressing the challenges of access to social protection for people in all forms of employment, Consultation document of 26.4.2017, C (2017) 2610 final.

[31] Proposal for a Directive of the European Parliament and the Council on work-life balance for parents and carers and repealing Council Directive 2010/18/EU, (SWD (2017) 202 and 203 final).

[32] Consultation Document of 26.4.2017 First phase consultation of Social Partners under Article 154 TFEU on a possible revision of the Written Statement Directive (Dir 91/533/EEC), (SWD (2017) 205).

VI. Possible Strategies to Overcome the Deficiencies of the Status Quo

A. Enhanced Cooperation

Therefore, we have to look for more promising strategies. One could be a Europe of different speeds as it has been suggested in the declaration at the celebration of the 60th anniversary of the Treaty of Rome. The mechanism for such a strategy is already contained in the Lisbon Treaty: it is called enhanced cooperation. In essence enhanced cooperation means that a group of at least nine member states 'within the framework of the Union's non-exclusive competences', as it is the case in labour law, may make use of the EU's institutions and exercise those competences. Any Member State can participate in this strategy. The final decision is made by the Council where only representatives of the Member States participating in enhanced cooperation have a voting right, even if all members are entitled to participate in the Council's deliberations. The acts adopted in the framework of enhanced cooperation only are binding the participating Member States. The competences, rights and obligations of the non-participating Member States are to be respected. Those Member States shall not impede the implementation by the participating Member States.

In a situation where – particularly in responding to the challenges implied by the refugee problem – it has become evident that solidarity between Member States is more than fragile, the temptation to take use of the possibility of enhanced cooperation is big. However, this option by necessity leads to an EU of different speeds. Whether in the long run these differences of speed can be equalised and whether the non-participating Member States eventually will join in, remains an open question. It is very ambiguous. The gap between core Europe and the periphery could become too big. And the incentive of those who are willing to build a social Europe for all citizens within the union might get lost. Whether the EU can survive under such perspectives, is at least uncertain. Therefore, I have my doubts whether this option should be chosen.

B. Extension of Competences

In my view for a really promising strategy to revitalise the social dimension the Treaty has to be significantly amended. First the legislative competences have to be extended. As indicated, the EU legislator still has no power to legislate on pay, the right of association, the right to strike and the right to impose lock-outs. This exclusion of competences is in sharp contrast to the fundamental social rights contained in the Charter of Fundamental Rights of the EU. But not only is this contrast puzzling, it is necessary to empower the EU to establish minimum standards also in these areas. Since only minimum standards are at stake, such legislative powers would not take away the Member States' power to legislate above this minimum level in favour of the employees. To just give two examples to show how important it would be to have minimum standards in this context: (a) a minimum wage for the EU could be established, of course not the same amount for each Member State but fixed as a percentage of the average wage in the respective country. This would guarantee a minimum wage for all employees and at the same time leave the national legislator and/or the parties to collective agreements to lift up this level according to the possibilities in each country; (b) it could be forbidden to undercut the level reached in collective agreements by agreements which are not concluded with trade unions but with other actors, a pattern which has been established in some Member States in the course of austerity politics. In short and to make the point: there is no need to leave these areas of legislation exclusively in the national context, an EU-wide floor of minimum standards should be made possible.

C. Reconstruction of the Legislative Procedure

Second the legislative machinery has to be changed. As already mentioned, under the present system of legislative procedure on the EU level it is almost impossible to expect further legislation on minimum social standards. Therefore, it is necessary to facilitate the production of European hard law by all means. First the right to initiate legislation should no longer be exclusively with the Commission as it has been up to now but should be extended to qualified minorities in the Parliament and in the Council. This to a much bigger extent would force the legislative bodies into discussions on the pros and cons of legislation, thereby increasing the transparency as well as the likelihood of legislative results. Second instead of requiring qualified majority or even unanimity in the Council, secondary law should be adopted by simple majority votes in both legislative bodies, the Parliament and the Council.[33] Third, the deliberations in the Council which so far are secret, should be made public in order to also increase transparency in this respect.

It, of course, is self-evident that in view of the unanimity requirement and the procedures for ratification in all the Member States amendments to the Treaty are an ambitious project. But perhaps the Brexit shock and the danger of populist right-wing movements all over might serve as a wake-up call to finally do something to improve the possibility for European citizens to identify with the social face of the European project.

[33] See in particular FW Scharpf, 'After the Crash: A Perspective on Multilevel European Democracy', *MPIfG Discussion Paper 14/21* (Cologne 2014) 17–22.

VII. Conclusion

The steps taken by the EU from an originally mere market approach to recognition of the social dimension are undoubtedly impressive. This, last not least, is symbolised by the fundamental social rights in the Charter of the Fundamental Rights of the EU which now has become legally binding.

This success story, however, cannot ignore that the obstacles for further development of minimum social standards for the EU have grown significantly in the meantime. New legislation in this controversial area has become very unlikely. To a great extent European involvement in shaping labour law and industrial relations now has become a soft law approach, an ongoing discourse on measures to be taken combined with mechanisms of soft pressure. This strategy which in addition is embedded in the manifold measures for economic governance is no real alternative to an EU-wide floor of minimum rights which cannot be undercut. The European Pillar of Social Rights only to a marginal extent is an innovation in this respect.

There is an urgent need to establish further social minimum standards in order to overcome the EU legitimacy crisis. Enhanced cooperation of Member States would be a possibility. But it is an ambiguous strategy, possibly increasing the gap within the EU too far. More promising might be an extension of legislative competences in the social field and facilitation of the legislative procedure. This, however, would require amendments to the Treaty. Whether such a perspective is too ambitious or whether the present legitimacy crisis and the Brexit shock turns it into a realistic project, remains an open question.

5

Geographical Scope and Diversity of EU Rules on Public Procurement

TRYGVE BEN HOLLAND

I. Introduction

Limitations of cross-border supply of services within the EU in the meaning of Article 56, I et seq Treaty on the Functioning of the EU (TFEU) are in principle abolished, if the provider is of Member States' nationality and established within the EU. Even though Article 56, II TFEU offers the possibility to extend this freedom to nationals of Third States, who provide services and who are established within the EU, the European Parliament and Council have not yet introduced such legislation, and legislation like this is not likely to be introduced in the near future. With respect to legal representation it is to be kept in mind that only a lawyer licensed in a Member State is entitled to represent, further, the EU institutions are not subject to any general obligation to inform the persons to whom their measures are addressed of the judicial remedies available or to any obligation to state the time-limits applicable to them.[1,2] However, the geographical scope is widely spread, usually with reference to the Government Procurement Act (GPA).

EU public procurement law is subject to various geographical scopes at different levels: first, the heartland territory of the 28 Member States, second, the outermost regions and especially the overseas countries and territories. Furthermore, a multiplicity of agreements between the EU and Third States are of relevance: the European Economic Area (EEA), Stabilisation and Association countries (SAAs), European Neighbourhood Policy (ENP) agreements (Partnership and Cooperation Agreements (PCAs) and Euro-Mediterranean Agreements (EMAs)), agreements of the EU with Canada, Chile, Israel, Japan, Korea, Mexico, Switzerland, Turkey, South Africa and USA as well as the Cotonou and the CARIFORUM agreements.

[1] cf ECJ, C-136/07, *Diy-Mar Insaat Sanayi ve Ticaret Ltd Sirketi a Musa Akar / European Commission*, ECR 2007, I-10125, para 41.

[2] cf ECJ, C-153/98, *Guérin automobiles / European Commission*, ECR 1999, I-1441, para 15.

II. Member States

Primarily, EU law is applicable within the territories of the Member States, as laid down in Article 52, I TFEU: founding members Belgium, France, Germany, Italy, Luxemburg and the Netherlands as well as the acceding countries Austria, Bulgaria, Croatia, Cyprus, Czech Republic, Denmark, Estonia, Finland, Greece, Hungary, Ireland, Latvia, Lithuania, Poland, Portugal, Romania, Slovakia, Slovenia, Spain, Sweden and the United Kingdom;[3] the rules on public procurement apply as from the date of that State's accession.[4]

Procurement laws are, for one reason or the other, not applicable to the Faroe Islands (Article 355, V lit a TFEU), Channel Islands and the Isle of Man (Article 355, V lit a TFEU), Gibraltar (Article 355, III TFEU), the United Kingdom Sovereign Base Areas, which addresses Akrotiri and Dhekelia (Article 355, V lit b TFEU),[5] Åland Island (to Finland, Article 355, IV TFEU) nor to Ceuta and Melilla (Spanish territory).

III. Outermost Regions and Overseas Countries and Territories

Article 355, I and II TFEU name as well the outermost regions as the overseas countries and territories, latter subject Article 199, IV TFEU, stipulating that for investments financed by the EU, participation in tenders and supplies shall be open on equal terms to all natural and legal persons who are nationals of a Member State or of one of the countries and territories.

The regions that are according to Article 349 subparagraph 1 TFEU are Guadeloupe, French Guiana, Martinique, Mayotte, Réunion, Saint-Martin, the Azores, Madeira and the Canary Islands. EU laws are applicable to these regions, but their structural social and economic situation is to be considered, which is compounded by their remoteness, insularity, small size, difficult topography and climate, economic dependence on a few products, the permanence and combination of which severely restrain their development.

Therefore, the Council, on a proposal from the European Commission and after consulting the European Parliament, shall adopt specific measures aimed, according to Article 349 subparagraph 1 TFEU, in particular, at laying down the conditions of application of EU law to those regions, including common policies; where these specific measures are adopted by the Council in accordance with a special legislative procedure, the same procedure applies.

[3] cf OJ L 157, 21.6.2005, p 11; OJ L 236, 23.9.2003, p 17 et seq.; OJ L 302 15.11.1985, p 0; OJ L 291 19.11.1979, p 0; OJ L 73 27.03.1972, p 0; OJ L 2 01.01.1973.

[4] cf ECJ, C-454/06, *Pressetext*, ECR 2008, I-4401, para 28; ECJ, C-76/97, *Tögel*, ECR 1998, I-5357, para 14.

[5] cf OJ L 236 23.09.2003, p 940 et seq.

The Overseas Countries and Territories (OCT) within the meaning of Article 355, II TFEU in conjunction with annex II TFEU are related to four Member States, since the foundation of the European Economic Community (EEC) they are considered associated territories, which distinguishes them from the outermost regions, them being an integral part of the EU territory. This specific status of the OCT is an impact of their historical relations to Denmark, France, the Netherlands and the United Kingdom; some former colonies have chosen the integration (outermost regions), others – essentially the African, Caribbean and Pacific (ACP) States – have chosen their sovereignty as Third States. The OCT are neither Members of the EU nor only Third States, therefore they have a specific status, governed by rules laid down in the TFEU.

The following regions are considered OCT: Anguilla (UK), Aruba (NL), Bermuda (UK), Bonaire (NL), British Antarctic Territory (UK), British Indian Ocean Territory (UK), British Virgin Islands (UK), Cayman Islands (UK), Curaçāo (NL), Falkland Islands (UK), French Polynesia (FR), French Southern and Antarctic Territories (FR), Greenland (DK), Montserrat (UK), New Caledonia and Dependencies (FR), Pitcairn (UK), Saba (NL), Saint Barthelemy (FR), Sint Eustatius (NL), Sint Maarten (NL), South Georgia and South Sandwich Islands (UK), Saint Helena, Ascension Island, Tristan da Cunha (UK), St. Pierre and Miquelon (FR), Turks and Caicos Islands (UK), and Wallis and Futuna Islands (FR). However, arrangements are not to be applied to Bermuda in accordance with the wishes of the Government of Bermuda.[6]

Generally, it is agreed:

> that the Council will seek to reach a solution which accords with the position of the Union. However, in the event that this proves impossible, the Conference agrees that the Member State concerned may act separately in the interests of the said overseas countries and territories, without this affecting the Community's interests. The Member State concerned will give notice to the Council and the Commission where such a divergence of interests is likely to occur and, when separate action proves unavoidable, make it clear that it is acting in the interests of an overseas territory mentioned above.[7]

Legal relations between the EU and the OCTs are, since 1 January 2014, governed by the Overseas Association Decision;[8] public procurement itself is not mentioned in the Decision, rather financial aid within the meaning of the EU's Financial Regulation.

[6] cf 2001/822/EC: Council Decision of 27 November 2001 on the association of the overseas countries and territories with the European Community ('Overseas Association Decision'), OJ 30.11.2001 No L 314, Recital 22, p 3; as last amended by 2007/249/EC: Council Decision of 19 March 2007 amending Decision 2001/822/EC on the association of the overseas countries and territories with the European Community, OJ L 109 26.04.2007, p 33 et seq.

[7] Treaty on European Union – Declaration on the representation of the interests of the overseas countries and territories referred to in Art 227(3) and (5)(A) and (B) of the Treaty establishing the European Community, OJ C 191 29.07.1992, p 103.

[8] Council Decision 2013/755/EU of 25 November 2013 on the association of the overseas countries and territories with the European Union ('Overseas Association Decision'), OJ L 344, 19.12.2013, pp 1–118.

The procedures governing the award of contracts shall be indicated in the respective financing agreements;[9] where assistance is granted by means of budgetary support, procedures for public procurement of the relevant OCT shall apply,[10] otherwise, the authorising officer responsible shall register in the European Development Fund (EDF) accounts, prior to signature for endorsement, the amount of each individual legal commitment which he has endorsed following a global commitment:[11,12] 'As regards budgetary support the Commission confirms that, in the procedures for granting budgetary support and before making transfers of funds, it ensures that the conditions of the Cotonou Agreement and of the financing agreements are met'.[13]

The Overseas Association Decision covers rules on non-discrimination concerning those economic operators formed in accordance with the law applicable in a given OCT and whose registered office, central administration or principal place of business is in that OCT; however, a company or enterprise having only its registered office in a country or territory must be engaged in an activity which has an actual and continuous link with the economy of that country or territory.[14]

With regard to these undertakings, the EU shall apply the conditions of the General Agreement on Trade in Services (GATS); Member States shall not discriminate between inhabitants, companies or enterprises of the OCTs. Accordingly, the OCT authorities shall afford nationals, companies or enterprises of the Member States treatment that is no less favourable than that which they extend to nationals, companies or enterprises of Third States and shall not discriminate between nationals, companies or enterprises of Member States.[15]

IV. European Economic Area

EU's public procurement rules apply 'not only throughout the European Community but, in accordance with the Agreement on the European Economic

[9] cf Art 10, I Council Regulation (EU) 2015/322 of 2 March 2015 on the implementation of the 11th European Development Fund, OJ L 58 of 3.3.2015, pp 1–16.

[10] cf ibid, Art 10, II.

[11] cf Art 78, II Reg (EC) No 215/2008 of 18 February 2008 on the Financial Regulation applicable to the 10th European Development Fund, OJ L 78 19.03.2008, p 1.

[12] cf Art 10, III Reg (EC) Council Regulation (EU) 2015/322 of 2 March 2015 on the implementation of the 11th European Development Fund, OJ L 58 of 3.3.2015, pp 1–16.

[13] Report from the Commission to the European Parliament on the follow-up to 2007 Discharge Decisions (Summary) – European Parliament Resolutions drafted pursuant to Art 276(3) of the EC Treaty and Art 180b of the Euratom Treaty, Art 147 of the Financial Regulation and Art 119(5) of the EDF Financial Regulation {SEC(2009)1427}.

[14] cf Art 50 lit b Council Decision 2013/755/EU of 25 November 2013 on the association of the overseas countries and territories with the European Union, OJ L 344 of 19.12.2013, pp 1–118.

[15] cf ibid, Art 51.

Area, also in Norway, Iceland and Liechtenstein'.[16] With regard to economic operators, established in accordance with the laws of the respective EEA State, the freedom to provide services is governed by Article 39 EEA,[17] especially Article 36, I EEA states:

> Within the framework of the provisions of this Agreement, there shall be no restrictions on freedom to provide services within the territory of the Contracting Parties in respect of nationals of EC Member States and EFTA States who are established in an EC Member State or an EFTA State other than that of the person for whom the services are intended.

According to Article 65, I EEA, 'annex XVI contains specific provisions and arrangements concerning procurement which, unless otherwise specified, shall apply to all products and to services as specified'.[18]

In Article 128 EEA, it is to be found, that any European State becoming a member of the EU shall apply to become a party to the EEA, and that the terms and conditions for such participation shall be the subject of an agreement between the Parties and the applicant State. The enlargement of the EEA to include the 10 countries that joined the EU on 1 May 2004 entered into force the same day; the latest enlargement of the EU took place in 2013 when Croatia joined the EU, the EEA Enlargement Agreement entered into force in 2014.[19] The enlargements of the EU in 2004, 2007 and 2013 added some EUR 60 billion in additional procurement opportunities, out of which some EUR 10 billion represent purchases in the utilities domain; the utilities procurement market within the EEA amounts to EUR 460 billion, of which about EUR 81 billion represent the above threshold procurement, governed by identical procurement rules.[20] By decision of the EEA Joint Committee, annex XVI and its appendices 1–14 EEA have been amended in 2019;[21] as an impact, EU's secondary legislation in the field of procurement is binding in Icelandic and Norwegian as well, the former legislation has been replaced by the currently applicable rules, and the terms of legislation were adjusted to the wording of the EEA. According to Articles 6, 105 and 106 EEA, the provisions of the EEA, in so far as they are identical in substance to corresponding rules of the

[16] Guide to the Community Rules on Public Works Contracts other than in the water, energy transport and telecommunication sectors, p 6.

[17] Agreement on the European Economic Area – Final Act – Joint Declarations – Declarations by the Governments of the Member States of the Community and the EFTA States – Arrangements – Agreed Minutes – Declarations by one or several of the Contracting Parties of the Agreement on the European Economic Area, OJ L 1 03.01.1994, p 3 et seq. (Agreement EEA).

[18] cf annex XVI Agreement EEA.

[19] Agreement on the participation of the Republic of Croatia in the European Economic Area, OJ L 170 of 11.06.2014, p 18 et seq.

[20] cf Report from the Commission concerning negotiations regarding access of Community undertakings to the markets of third countries in fields covered by the Directive 2004/17/EC, /* European Commission /2009/0592 final */.

[21] www.efta.int/media/documents/legal-texts/eea/the-eea-agreement/Annexes%20to%20the%20Agreement/annex16.pdf.

TFEU and to secondary legislation, shall, in their implementation and application, be interpreted in conformity with rulings of the ECJ.[22]

V. Stabilisation and Association Agreements

In talks with Western Balkan States who have expressed the wish to join the EU, the EU concludes Stabilisation and Association Agreements in exchange for commitments to political, economic, trade or human rights reforms in a country with the demanding aim to align respective Third States' existing and future legislation to that of the EU. These preparatory, pre-accession SAAs, typically running for ten years up from the date of entering into force, are part of the EU Stabilisation and Association Process, similar in principle to the Europe Agreements signed with the Central and Eastern European countries in the 1990s (and, to a certain extent, to the Ankara Association Agreement with Turkey of 1963, which, unlike the SAAs, does not provide for a deadline). The SAAs must be ratified by the associating state and all EU Member States, pending the ratification of a SAA, the European Commission concludes Interim Agreements to allow the trade and trade-related provisions of the SAA to enter into force as soon as possible. Since the aim of the SAAs is to help the countries concerned to build their capacity for the adoption and implementation of EU law, the reciprocal commitments are usually construed on an asymmetrical basis, which is also the case for the relevant procurement provisions. The economic operators of the signatory country, whether established or not in the EU, are granted access to contract award procedures in the EU pursuant to the EU public procurement rules as of the entry into force of the SAA, or of the Interim Agreement in cases where the latter makes such a provision; this rule applies also to contracts in the utilities sector once the signatory States have adopted the legislation introducing the EU rules in this area.

The SAA between the EU, the Member States and the Third States of the Western Balkans Albania,[23] Bosnia and Herzegovina,[24] former Yugoslav Republic of Macedonia (commonly referred to as FYROM),[25] Montenegro[26] and Serbia[27] show such asymmetric clauses on procurement. The opening-up of the award of public contracts on the basis of non-discrimination and reciprocity, in particular

[22] cf ECI, T-115/94, *Opel Austria*, ECR 1997, II-39, para 104 et seq.

[23] OJ L 107, 28.4.2009, p 166 et seq.; the SAA entered into force on 1 April 2009, market access is granted since 1 April 2013.

[24] OJ L 164, 30.6.2015, pp 2–547; market access is granted since 1 July 2013.

[25] OJ L 84 20.03.2004; the SAA entered into force on 1 April 2004, market access is granted since 1 April 2009.

[26] OJ L 345 28.12.2007, p 1; the Interim Agreement is applicable since 1 January 2008, market access is granted from that time on.

[27] OJ L 278, 18.10.2013, pp 14–471, market access is granted since end of 2018.

in the WTO context, has been agreed upon as a desirable objective.[28] Undertakings from the EU and those from the SAA States, whether established or not in the respective territory of the other Party, shall be granted access to contract award procedures according to the relevant applicable laws under treatment no less favourable than that accorded to their own companies as from the date of entry into force of the particular SAA.[29] Undertakings established according to laws within the EU, but not established in the respective SAA State, shall be granted access to contract award procedures in that State pursuant to the applicable national Law on Public Procurement under treatment no less favourable than that accorded to Albanian companies at the latest four years after the date of entry into force of this Agreement. It is stated explicitly, that the provisions on public procurement shall also apply to contracts in the utilities sector, once the respective SAA State has adopted the legislation introducing the EU rules in this area;[30] this articulates the asymmetric character of the SAAs.

VI. Partnership and Cooperation Agreements

The EU has concluded nine PCAs, one each with Armenia,[31] Azerbaijan,[32] Georgia,[33] Kazakhstan,[34] Kyrgyz Republic,[35] Moldova,[36] Russian Federation,[37] Ukraine[38] and Uzbekistan.[39] Currently, some of these PCAs are replaced with more comprehensive and enhanced Partnership Agreements:[40] the Association Agreement between the EU and the Republic of Moldova was signed in June 2014 and is in full effect since July 2016, the Association Agreement with Ukraine was signed in June 2014 as well and entered into force on 1 September 2017.

[28] cf Art 74, I SAA Albania; Art 76, I SAA Montenegro; Art 72, I SAA Macedonia; Art 74, I SAA Bosnia and Herzegovina; Art 76, I SAA Serbia.

[29] cf Art 74, II, III and IV subpara 2 SAA Albania; Art 76, II, III a. IV SAA Montenegro; Art 72, II subpara 1 a. subpara 3 SAA Macedonia; Art 74, II, III a. IV SAA Bosnia and Herzegovina; Art 76, II, III a. IV SAA Serbia.

[30] cf Art 74, II SAA Albania; Art 76, II subpara 2 SAA Montenegro; Art 72, II subpara 2 SAA Macedonia; Art 74, II subpara 2 SAA Bosnia and Herzegovina; Art 76, II subpara 2 SAA Serbia.

[31] OJ L 239, 09.09.1999, p 1 et seq.

[32] OJ L 246, 17.09.1999, p 1 et seq.

[33] OJ L 205, 04.08.1999, p 1 et seq.

[34] OJ L 196, 28.07.1999, p 3 et seq.

[35] OJ L 196 28.07.1999, p 48 et seq.

[36] OJ L 181, 24.06.1998, p 3 et seq.

[37] OJ L 327, 28.11.1997, p 3 et seq.

[38] OJ L 049, 19.02.1998, p 3 et seq.

[39] OJ L 229, 31.08.1999, p 1 et seq.

[40] Comprehensive and enhanced Partnership Agreement between the European Union and the European Atomic Energy Community and their Member States, of the one part, and the Republic of Armenia, of the other part (signed on 24 November 2017; ratification is pending); Enhanced Partnership and Cooperation Agreement between the European Union and its Member States, of the one part, and the Republic of Kazakhstan, of the other part (signed on 21 December 2015; ratification is pending).

All PCAs and new AAs have in common, that an important condition for strengthening the economic links between the respective Third State and the EU is the gradual approximation of the Third State's existing and future legislation to that of the EU;[41] this gradual approximation extends, among others, to public procurement.[42]

The intensity of aims differs, only the PCAs with Moldova and Ukraine cover co-operation concentrating on a more economic integration, including public procurement;[43] thus, the EU and Ukraine shall establish economic co-operation aimed at contributing to the process of economic reform and recovery and sustainable development of Ukraine. Such co-operation shall strengthen and develop economic links, to the benefit of both parties.[44] In relation to each of the eight PCA States, the clause applies, that the Parties shall cooperate to develop conditions for open and competitive award of contracts for goods and services in particular through calls for tenders.[45]

VII. Euro-Mediterranean Agreements

The nine association agreements between the EU and the Third States Algeria,[46] Egypt,[47] Israel,[48] Jordan,[49] Lebanon,[50] Morocco,[51] Palestine,[52] Tunisia,[53] Turkey,[54] cover rules on public procurement at different levels. The EMA with Syria has not yet entered into force, though its text was finalised in 2004. As a difference from the other EMAs, it entails detailed procedural procurement rules, and a comprehensive mutual market access, including utilities procurement; the EU continues the talks with Syria towards the signature of the EMA. The EMAs – except regarding Israel – aim, with almost the same wording, at the agreed objective of a progressive

[41] cf Art 43, I Agreement EC–Armenia; Art 43, I Agreement EC-Azerbaidjan; Art 43, I Agreement EC–Georgia; Art 43, I Agreement EC–Kazakhstan; cf Art 44, I Agreement EC–Kyrgyzstan; cf Art 50, I Agreement EC–Moldova; Art 50, I Agreement EC–Ukraine; Art 42, I Agreement EC–Uzbekistan.

[42] cf Art 43, II Agreement EC–Armenia; Art 43, II Agreement EC–Azerbaidjan; Art 43, II Agreement EC–Georgia; Art 43, II EC–Kazakhstan; Art 44, II Agreement EC–Kyrgyzstan; Art 50, II Agreement EC–Moldova; Art 50, II Agreement EC–Ukraine; Art 42, II Agreement EC–Uzbekistan.

[43] cf Art 51, III Agreement EC–Moldova; Art 52, III Agreement EC–Ukraine.

[44] cf Art 51, I Agreement EC–Moldova; Art 52, I Agreement EC–Ukraine.

[45] cf Art 48 EC–Armenia; Art 49 Agreement EC–Azerbaidjan; Art 50 EC–Georgia; Art 47 EC–Kazakhstan; Art 48 Agreement EC–Kyrgyzstan; Art 54 Agreement EC–Moldova; Art 55 Agreement EC–Ukraine; Art 47 Agreement EC–Uzbekistan.

[46] OJ L 265, 10.10.2005.

[47] OJ L 304, 30.9.2004.

[48] OJ L 147, 21.06.2000.

[49] OJ L 129, 15.05.2002.

[50] OJ L 143, 30.5.2006.

[51] OJ L 70, 18.3.2000.

[52] OJ L 187, 16.07.1997.

[53] OJ L 97, 30.03.1998.

[54] OJ L 35, 13.02.1996.

liberalisation of public procurement, while it is the Association Council's task to hold consultations on the implementation of this objective.[55]

Only the agreement with Israel covers detailed rules on the further progressive liberalisation of public procurement;[56] it is agreed to take measures with a view to a mutual opening of their government procurement markets and the procurement markets of undertakings operating in the utilities sectors for purchase of goods, works and services beyond the scope of what has been mutually and reciprocally covered under the GPA.[57] As laid down in the Joint Declaration, the Parties will open formal negotiations in a number of areas to open their procurement markets beyond what has been agreed under the GPA; These negotiations cover, inter alia, the procurement of goods, works and services by entities operating in the telecommunications and urban transport sector (not buses) as well as services purchased by GPA covered entities, in order to expand mutual commitments under Annex 4 of Appendix I of the GPA.[58] The Parties shall undertake to refrain from introducing additional discriminatory measures against economic operators of the other Party in the fields of heavy electrical and medical equipment beyond the provisions already agreed in the GPA and they shall seek to avoid introducing discriminatory measures which distort open procurement.[59]

The implementation of the agreement is periodically reviewed by the Parties with a view to further negotiations, aiming at an expansion of mutual coverage.[60] Additionally, the Parties will actively support the liberalisation of their respective telecommunications service markets and will participate in the GATS negotiating group on basic telecommunications.[61]

VIII. EU–Canada (CETA)

The Free Trade Agreement between the EU and Canada was signed on 30 October 2016 and awaits ratification still.[62] According to Article 19.4, each Party shall accord immediately and unconditionally to the goods and services of the other Party and to the suppliers of the other Party offering such goods or services, treatment no less favourable than the treatment the Party, including its procuring entities, accords to its own goods, services and suppliers. Such treatment includes within Canada, treatment no less favourable than that accorded by a province or

[55] cf Art 38 EMA EC–Egypt; Art 46 EMA EC–Algeria; Art 58 EMA EC–Jordan; Art 39 EMA EC–Lebanon; Art 41 EMA EC–Morocco; cf Art 41 EMA EC–Tunisia.

[56] cf Art 1, II EMA EC–Israel.

[57] cf ibid, Art 35.

[58] cf para 1 Joint Declaration on public procurement, EMA EC–Israel.

[59] cf ibid, para 2.

[60] cf ibid, para 3.

[61] cf ibid, para 4.

[62] Comprehensive Economic and Trade Agreement (CETA) between Canada, of the one part, and the European Union and its Member States, of the other part.

territory, including its procuring entities, to goods and services of, and to suppliers located in, that province or territory; within the EU, treatment no less favourable than that accorded by a Member State or a sub-central region of a Member State, including its procuring entities, to goods and services of, and suppliers located in, that Member State or sub-central region, as the case may be.

Set out in Article 19.7, procuring entities shall limit any conditions for participation in a procurement to those that are essential to ensure that a supplier has the legal and financial capacities and the commercial and technical abilities to undertake the relevant procurement.

With a view to rules on origin, Article 19.4 Nr. 5 sets out that no Party shall apply such rules to goods or services imported from or supplied from the other Party that are different from the rules of origin the Party applies at the same time in the normal course of trade to imports or supplies of the same goods or services from the same Party.

The territorial scope is defined in detail in Annex 19 CETA; Article 19.18 Nr. 6 sets out that in case of proposed rectifications to a Party's Annexes, the Party shall notify the other Party every two years, in line with the cycle of notifications provided for under the Agreement on Government Procurement, contained in Annex 4 of the WTO GPA, following the entry into force of this Agreement. However, there is no other reference to the GPA incorporated in the CETA.

IX. EU–Chile

The agreement between the EU and Chile,[63] in force since 1 May 2005, addresses, among others, public procurement; in general, cooperation in this field shall seek to provide technical assistance on issues connected with public procurement, paying special attention to the municipal level.[64] With regard to procurement, objectives of the agreement are: a) progressive and reciprocal liberalisation of trade in goods, respecting Article XXIV General Agreement on Tariffs and Trade (GATT); b) reciprocal liberalisation of trade in services, in conformity with Article V GATS; and c) effective and reciprocal opening of the government procurement markets of the Parties,[65] substantiated in Article 136 et seq of the agreement.[66]

Within the scope of the agreement, the rules apply to any law, regulation, procedure or practice regarding any procurement, by the entities of the Parties, of goods and services including works, subject to the conditions specified by each

[63] Agreement establishing an association between the European Community and its Member States, of the one part, and the Republic of Chile, of the other part – Final act, OJ L 352 30.12.2002, p 1 et seq (Agreement EC–Chile).

[64] cf Art 33 Agreement EC–Chile.

[65] cf Art 55 Agreement EC–Chile.

[66] cf Art 136 Agreement EC–Chile.

Party in the annexes XI, XII and XIII; neither Party may prepare, design or otherwise structure any procurement contract in order to avoid the obligations under the agreement. However, provided that such measures are not applied in a manner that would constitute a means of arbitrary or unjustifiable discrimination between the Parties or a disguised restriction on trade between them, exemptions are allowed.[67] Either Party may modify its coverage, provided that it notifies the other Party of the modification in advance and provides the other Party, within 30 days following the date of such notification, appropriate compensatory adjustments to its coverage in order to maintain a level of coverage comparable to that existing prior to the modification.[68]

Each Party shall ensure that its entities do not, in the qualification and selection of economic operators, goods or services, in the evaluation of bids or in the award of contracts, consider, seek or impose offsets, nor conditions regarding national preferences (eg margins allowing price preference).[69] While calculating the value of a contract, the procurement entity shall take into account all forms of remuneration (eg premiums, fees, commissions and interests, as well as the maximum permitted total amount, including option clauses) provided for by the contract; when, due to the nature of the contract, it is not possible to calculate in advance its precise value, entities shall estimate this value on the basis of objective criteria.[70] To ensure transparency, each Party shall promptly publish any law, regulation, judicial decision and administrative ruling of general application and procedure, including standard contract clauses, as well as any modifications regarding procurement in the appropriate publications referred, including officially designated electronic media;[71] this addresses, at Member State level, their official journals, at EU level the OJ as well as the European Commission's website (http://simap.eu.int), and in Chile the Chilean official journal and the relevant website (www.chilecompra.cl).[72] The Parties shall, to the extent possible, endeavour to use electronic means of communication to permit efficient dissemination of information on government procurement, particularly as regards tender opportunities offered by procurement entities, while respecting the principles of transparency and non-discrimination; with a view to improving access to government procurement markets and to encourage the use of electronic means for the transmission of offers, each Party shall endeavour to implement an electronic information system, which is compulsory for their respective entities.[73]

Procurement entities shall award their public contracts in principle by open or selective tendering procedures according to their national procedures only,

[67] cf Art 137 Agreement EC–Chile.
[68] cf Art 159, II Agreement EC–Chile.
[69] cf Art 140 Agreement EC–Chile.
[70] cf Art 141, III Agreement EC–Chile.
[71] cf Art 142, I Agreement EC–Chile.
[72] cf annex XIII, appendix 2 Agreement EC–Chile.
[73] cf Art 156 Agreement EC–Chile.

insofar as they are not discriminatory; open tendering procedures are those procedures whereby any interested economic operator may submit a tender, selective tendering procedures are those procedures whereby only economic operators satisfying qualification requirements established by the entities are invited to submit a tender.[74]

In selective tendering, entities may limit the number of qualified economic operators they will invite to tender, consistent with the efficient operation of the procurement process, provided that they select the maximum number of domestic economic operators of the other Party, and that they make the selection in a fair and non-discriminatory manner and on the basis of the criteria indicated in the notice of intended procurement or in tender documents; procurement entities maintaining permanent lists of qualified economic operators may select economic operators to be invited to tender from among those listed, and any selection shall allow for equitable opportunities for listed economic operators.[75]

However, in specific cases, procurement entities may use any other procedure than the open or selective tendering procedures, in which case the entities may choose not to publish a notice of intended procurement, and may consult the economic operators of their choice and negotiate the terms of contract with one or more of these.[76] Provided that the tendering procedure is not used to avoid maximum possible competition or to protect domestic economic operators, entities shall be allowed to award contracts by means other than an open or selective tendering procedure in the following circumstances; at least one of several defined conditions are required to justify the deviant procedure. Whenever it is necessary for procurement entities to resort to a procedure other than the open or selective tendering procedures based on the circumstances aforementioned, the entities shall maintain a record or prepare a written report providing specific justification for the contract awarded.[77]

As to the qualification of economic operators, any conditions for participation in procurement shall be limited to those that are essential to ensure that the potential economic operator has the capability to fulfil the requirements of the procurement and the ability to execute the contract in question. In the process of qualifying economic operators, entities shall not discriminate between domestic economic operators and economic operators of the other Party, a Party shall especially not impose the condition that, in order for an economic operator to participate in a procurement, the economic operator has previously been awarded one or more contracts by an entity of that Party or that the economic operator has prior work experience in the territory of that Party. Entities shall recognise as qualified economic operators all those who meet the conditions for participation

[74] cf Art 143 Agreement EC–Chile.
[75] cf Art 144 Agreement EC–Chile.
[76] cf Art 143, III Agreement EC–Chile.
[77] cf Art 145 Agreement EC–Chile.

in a particular intended procurement, base their qualification decisions solely on the conditions for participation that have been specified in advance in notices or tender documentation, and shall promptly communicate to economic operators that have applied for qualification their decision on whether or not they qualify. However, nothing shall preclude the exclusion of any economic operator on grounds such as bankruptcy or false declarations or convictions for serious crime such as participation in criminal organisations.[78]

Regarding the publication of notices, each Party shall ensure that its entities provide for effective dissemination of the tendering opportunities generated by the relevant government procurement processes, providing economic operators of the other Party with all the information required to take part in such procurement. Generally, for each contract entities shall publish in advance a notice inviting interested suppliers to submit tenders, or where appropriate, requests for participation for that contract.[79]

To be considered for award of contract, a tender must, at the time of opening, conform to the essential requirements of the notices or tender documentation and be submitted by an economic operator which complies with the conditions for participation; procurement entities shall make the award to the economic operator whose tender is either the lowest tender or the tender which, in terms of the specific objective evaluation criteria previously set forth in the notices or tender documentation, is determined to be the most advantageous.[80] In terms of bid challenges, procurement entities shall accord impartial and timely consideration to any complaints from economic operators regarding an alleged breach of this Title in the context of a procurement procedure; thus, each Party shall provide non-discriminatory, timely, transparent and effective procedures enabling operators to challenge alleged breaches arising in the context of procurements in which they have, or have had, an interest. Challenges shall be heard by an impartial and independent reviewing authority; a reviewing authority which is not a court shall either be subject to judicial review or shall have procedural guarantees similar to those of a court.[81]

X. EU–Israel

In addition to the EMA, two agreements between the EU and Israel are addressing public procurement: the agreement on public procurement[82] and the

[78] cf Art 146 Agreement EC–Chile.
[79] cf Art 147, II Agreement EC–Chile.
[80] cf Art 153 Agreement EC–Chile.
[81] cf Art 155 Agreement EC–Chile.
[82] Agreement between the European Community and the State of Israel on government procurement, OJ L 202 30.07.1997, p 85 et seq. (General Agreement EC–Israel).

sector-specific agreement on procurement by telecommunications operators.[83,84] While the first agreement expands the EU's and Israel's commitments to liberalise their respective public procurement markets through the GPA to improve mutual market access beyond the commitments laid down therein by broadening the scope of their respective Appendices I to GPA,[85] the sector-specific agreement on procurement by telecommunications operators considers granting reciprocal access to procurement by their respective telecommunications operators;[86] the personal scope of this agreements therefore covers any entities that pro-vide or operate public telecommunications networks or provide one or more public telecommunications services and which either are public authorities or undertakings or operate on the basis of special or exclusive rights granted by a state authority.[87] Thus, the agreement on telecommunication applies to any law, regulation or practice affecting procurement by those telecommunication service providers as defined in Annex I and to the award of all procurement contracts by them; with regard to services, including construction services, this Agreement applies to those listed in Annex II.[88] The agreement does not affect the rights and obligations of the Parties under the WTO or other multilateral instruments concluded under the auspices of the WTO.[89]

Any offsets prescribed in the qualification and selection of products, services, economic operators or service providers, or in the evaluation of tenders and award of contracts shall be prohibited; likewise, any law, procedure or practice, such as price preference, local content requirements, local investment or production requirements, terms of licence, authorisation, funding or bidding rights which discriminate, or require a Party's operator to discriminate, against the other Party's products, services, economic operators or service providers in the award of procurement contracts shall be prohibited.[90] The Parties shall apply the provisions of the WTO's TBT-Agreement[91] with regard to procurement by their respective operators;[92] moreover, it is of relevance that the Parties ensure that their operators (listed under A in Annex I) define the technical specifications set out in the tender documentation in terms of performance rather than design or descriptive

[83] Agreement between the European Community and the State of Israel on procurement by telecommunications operators – Art 1 (6) side letters – Agreed minutes, OJ L 202 30.07.1997, p 74. (Telecommunication Agreement EC–Israel).

[84] 97/474/EC: Council Decision of 24 February 1997 concerning the conclusion of two Agreements between the European Community and the State of Israel on, respectively, procurement by telecommunications operators and government procurement, OJ L 202 30.07.1997, p 72 et seq.

[85] cf Preamble General Agreement EC–Israel.

[86] cf Preamble Telecommunication Agreement EC–Israel.

[87] cf Art 1, II lit. a Telecommunication Agreement EC–Israel.

[88] cf Art 1, III and IV Telecommunication Agreement EC–Israel.

[89] cf Art 10, III Telecommunication Agreement EC–Israel.

[90] cf Art 2, II Telecommunication Agreement EC–Israel.

[91] Uruguay Round of Multilateral Trade Negotiations (1986– 1994) – Annex 1 – Annex 1A – Agreement on Technical Barriers to Trade (WTO–GATT 1994), OJ L 336 23.12.1994, p 86 et seq.

[92] cf Art 2, IV Telecommunication Agreement EC–Israel.

characteristics; such specifications shall be based on international standards, where such exist, otherwise on national technical regulations, recognised national standards or building codes. Any technical specifications adopted or applied with a view to, or with the effect of, creating obstacles to procurement by a Party's operators of products or services from the other Party and to related trade between the Parties shall be prohibited.[93] The Parties have to ensure that the procurement procedures and practices followed by their relevant operators comply with the principles of non-discrimination, transparency and fairness.[94]

The agreement provides for a challenge procedure as specified in Annex III; the Parties shall provide non-discriminatory, timely, transparent and effective procedures enabling economic operators or service providers to challenge alleged breaches of this Agreement arising in the context of procurements in which they have, or have had, an interest.[95] Thus, Parties shall ensure that decisions taken by bodies responsible for challenge procedures are enforced effectively,[96] relevant documentation is to be retained for at least three years.[97]

Additionally, the agreement provides for safeguard measures, if either Party considers that the other Party has failed to fulfil an obligation or if one Party fails to take measures specified in the decision by the arbitration panel or if a law, regulation or practice of either Party substantially reduces or threatens to reduce substantially the benefits accruing to the other Party, and the Parties are unable to agree promptly on appropriate compensation or other remedial action, the adversely affected Party may, without prejudice to its other rights and obligations under international law, suspend partly or completely, as appropriate, the application of this agreement and immediately notify the other Party thereof;[98] scope and duration of such measures shall be limited to what is necessary in order to remedy the situation and to secure, if necessary, a fair balance of rights and obligations.[99] Non-discrimination also covers interoperability on a reciprocal basis,[100] thus, the Parties shall cooperate with a view to ensuring that the type of procurement information, notably in tender notices and documentation, held on their respective databases is comparable in terms of quality and accessibility; likewise, they shall cooperate with a view to ensuring that the type of information exchanged through their respective electronic means between interested parties for the purposes of public procurement is comparable in terms of quality and accessibility.[101]

[93] cf Art 3, II Telecommunication Agreement EC–Israel.
[94] cf Art 3, I Telecommunication Agreement EC–Israel.
[95] cf Art 4, I and annex III Telecommunication Agreement EC–Israel.
[96] cf Art 4, III Telecommunication Agreement EC–Israel.
[97] cf Art 4, II Telecommunication Agreement EC–Israel.
[98] cf Art 7, I Telecommunication Agreement EC–Israel.
[99] cf Art 7, II Telecommunication Agreement EC–Israel.
[100] cf Art 9, II Telecommunication Agreement EC–Israel.
[101] cf Art 9, I Telecommunication Agreement EC–Israel.

XI. EU–Japan

The EU and Japan's Economic Partnership Agreement entered into force on 1 February 2019. Article 10.1 states that the GPA is incorporated into the agreement and made part of the provisions on public procurement. Consequently, the agreement does not provide for detailed arrangements deviating therefrom. Annex 10 of the agreement comprises some provisions for clarification purposes (listing procuring entities) and for the broadening of the GPA's scope (specification of certain categories of goods).

XII. EU–Korea

The Council of the EU adopted a Decision on the notification to Korea of the EU's withdrawal, on Korea's request, from its agreement with Korea on telecommunications procurement[102] because Korea considers that the agreement has become devoid of purpose because of the liberalisation of the Korean telecommunications market and the privatisation of Korea Telecom;[103] an FTA has been initiated. The FTA between the EU and Korea[104] aims at establishing a free trade area on goods, services, establishment and associated rules. To this end, the public procurement markets of the Parties shall, on a mutual basis, be liberalised.[105] With regard to establishment, nothing in this agreement shall be construed to impose any obligation with respect to government procurement,[106] thus, establishment is governed by the GATS and the GPA. The Parties reaffirm their rights and obligations under the GPA and their interest in further expanding bilateral trading opportunities in each Party's government procurement market. The personal and material scopes of the FTA are the same as in the GPA, with the exemption of BOT contracts and concessions. Within this limited scope of annex 9 of the FTA, each Party shall accord immediately and unconditionally to the goods, services and economic operators of the other Party treatment no less favourable than the treatment the Party accords to domestic ones. A Party shall not treat a locally established economic operator of the other Party less favourably than another locally established economic operator on the basis of degree of foreign affiliation or ownership. Each Party shall ensure that a procuring entity publishes a notice of intended

[102] Agreement on telecommunications procurement between the European Community and the Republic of Korea, OJ L 321 22.11.1997, p 32 et seq.

[103] cf Council of the European Union, Press release, 2600th Council Meeting, Justice and Home Affairs, Brussels, 19 July 2004.

[104] Free Trade Agreement between the European Union and its Member States, of the one part, and the Republic of South Korea, of the other part, OJ L 127 of 14.05.2011, p 6.

[105] ibid, Art 1.1.

[106] ibid, Art 7.1, II.

procurements in an appropriate official paper or electronic medium. These means of publication are for Korea the Internet homepage of each entity in Annexes 1 and 2 of Korea's GPA Appendix I and all local governments located in Seoul City, Busan City, Incheon City and Gyonggi-do and daily press; for the EU it is simap.europa.eu/index_en.html and the OJ. The notices shall be accessible to economic operators free of charge, if possible through a single point of access, so that they may submit tenders or requests for participation in that contract.[107]

Within a reasonable period of time after the award of each contract covered, each Party shall ensure that the award of that contract is made publicly available in an appropriate official paper or electronic medium, indicating the name and the address of the procuring entity and of the successful economic operator. Even though each Party shall ensure that there is an effective system of review of decisions by competent authorities covered, this obligation does not require the creation of a special system of administrative or judicial review. Subject to the requirement that such measures are not applied in a manner that would constitute a means of arbitrary or unjustifiable discrimination between the Parties where the same conditions prevail or a disguised restriction on international trade, nothing in Annex 9 shall be construed to prevent any Party from imposing or enforcing measures necessary to protect public morals, order or safety, to protect human, animal or plant life or health, to protect intellectual property, and/or relating to goods or services of persons with disabilities, philanthropic institutions or prison labour.[108]

XIII. EU–Mexico

The Economic Partnership and Cooperation Agreement between the EU and Mexico[109] addresses, among others, rules on public procurement, the Parties have agreed to the gradual and mutual opening of agreed government procurement markets on a reciprocal basis. To this end, the Joint Council decides on appropriate arrangements and timetable, particularly on coverage of the agreed liberalisation, non-discriminatory access to the agreed markets, threshold values, fair and transparent procedures, clear challenge procedures and the use of information technology;[110] the relevant decision was published in 2000[111] and provisions

[107] ibid, annex 9.

[108] ibid, Art 2, VIII.

[109] Economic Partnership, Political Coordination and Cooperation Agreement between the European Community and its Member States, of the one part, and the United Mexican States, of the other part, OJ L 276 28.10.2000, p 45 et seq. (Agreement EC–Mexico).

[110] cf Art 10 Agreement EC–Mexico.

[111] Decision 2/2000 of the EC–Mexico Joint Council of 23 March 2000, OJ L 157 30.06.2000, p 10 et seq (Decision 2/2000).

concerning public procurement entered into force on 28 February 2001;[112,113] Annexes VI-XIV are an integral and applicable part of the agreement.

Reciprocal liberalisation is expressed through the principles of national treatment and non-discrimination, thus each Party shall – with respect to all laws, regulations, procedures and practices regarding government procurement – provide immediately and unconditionally to the products, services and economic operators of the other Party treatment no less favourable than that accorded to domestic products, services and economic operators. Furthermore, with respect to all laws, regulations, procedures and practices regarding government procurement, each Party shall ensure that its entities do not treat a locally-established operator less favourably than another locally-established operator on the basis of the degree of foreign affiliation to, or ownership by, a person of the other Party, and that its entities do not discriminate against locally-established economic operators on the basis of the country of production of the good or service being supplied, provided that the country of production is the other Party.[114] As an impact of the principle of national treatment, no entity of a Party may make it a condition for the qualification of economic operators and for the awarding of a contract that the economic operator has previously been awarded one or more contracts by an entity of that Party or that the economic operator has prior work experience in the territory of that Party.[115]

Basically, national treatment and non-discrimination shall not apply to customs duties and charges of any kind imposed on, or in connection with, importation, the method of levying such duties and charges, other import regulations and formalities, and measures affecting trade in services other than laws, regulations, procedures and practices regarding government procurement.[116] Also, no Party may apply rules of origin to goods imported from the other Party for purposes of government procurement that are different from, or inconsistent with, the rules of origin which that Party applies in the normal course of trade. However, a Party may deny the benefits of this agreement to a service supplier of the other Party, subject to prior notification and consultation, where the Party establishes that the service is being provided by an enterprise that is owned or controlled by persons of a non-Party and that has no substantial business activities in the territory of either Party.[117] Institutional transparency is provided for: first, both Parties shall provide each other with illustrative information on their respective government enterprise markets in accordance with the format contained in Annex XIV subject to any applicable confidentiality provisions existing in their respective legal systems;[118]

[112] cf Art 38, III Decision 2/2000.

[113] cf Information concerning the entry into force of Title III 'Government procurement' of Decision No 2/2000 of the EC– Mexico Joint Council of 23 March 2000, OJ L 58 28.02.2001, p 23.

[114] cf Art 26 Decision 2/2000.

[115] cf Art 29, VI Decision 2/2000.

[116] cf Art 26, III Decision 2/2000.

[117] cf Art 27, II Decision 2/2000.

[118] cf Art 38, II Decision 2/2000.

second, the Parties have agreed on intensive exchange of information; third,[119] a Special Committee reports on the functioning of the agreement;[120] and fourth, comparable databases are to be introduced to ensure that the type of procurement information, notably in tender notices and documentation, are accessible.[121]

The geographic scope of the agreement covers Mexico and, generally, the EU. However, when a specific procurement may impair important national policy objectives, the Finnish or Swedish Governments, respectively, may consider it necessary in singular procurement cases to deviate from the principle of national treatment (a decision to this effect will be taken at Cabinet level); Finland also reserves its position to the Åland Islands; the provision of services, including construction services is subject to the conditions and qualifications for market access and national treatment as will be required by Austria in conformity with its commitments under the GATT.[122]

The material scope covers any law, regulation, procedure or practice regarding procurement by relevant entities (Annex VI), of goods (Annex VII), services (Annex VIII), construction services (Annex IX), where the value of the contract to be awarded is estimated to be equal to or greater than one of the relevant thresholds (Annex X). No Party may prepare, design or otherwise structure any procurement contract in order to avoid the obligations of the agreement.[123] Exemptions from the scope are provided for both contracting Parties, if such measures are not applied in a manner that would constitute a means of arbitrary or unjustifiable discrimination between the Parties or a disguised restriction on trade between the Parties.[124] If a Party wishes to modify its coverage, it shall only be possible in exceptional circumstances (also: the other Party has to be informed of the modification), and in connection with appropriate compensatory adjustments to its coverage in order to maintain a level of coverage comparable to that existing prior to the modification; exempted – ie no compensations need to be proposed – are, on the one hand, rectifications of a purely formal nature and minor amendments to Annexes VI–IX and XI, provided that it notifies such rectifications to the other Party and the other Party does not object to such proposed rectification within 30 days, a Party may, on the other hand, undertake reorganisations (not to avoid the agreement's obligations) of its entities, including programmes through which the procurement of such entities is decentralised or the corresponding government functions cease to be performed by any government entity, provided that it notifies such reorganisations to the other Party.[125] However, the Joint Council may adopt appropriate measures to enhance the conditions for effective access to

[119] cf Art 31 Decision 2/2000.
[120] cf Art 32 Decision 2/2000.
[121] cf Art 33 Decision 2/2000.
[122] cf annex XI Decision 2/2000.
[123] cf Art 25 Decision 2/2000.
[124] cf Art 34 Decision 2/2000.
[125] cf Art 35, IV Decision 2/2000.

a Party's covered procurement or adjust a Party's coverage so that such conditions for effective access are maintained on an equitable basis.[126] However, precedence is given to the North American Free Trade Agreement (NAFTA) in order to provide equivalence to the current value of the thresholds applied in the context of the NAFTA, thus Mexico shall apply the actual NAFTA thresholds instead of those mentioned above.[127]

Each Party shall ensure that its entities do not, in the qualification and selection of economic operators, goods or services, evaluation of bids or award of contracts, consider, seek or impose offsets (conditions imposed or considered by an entity prior to, or in course of, its procurement process that encourage local development or improve its Party's balance of payments accounts, by means of local content rules, licensing, investment, countertrade, etc).[128] With regard to procurement procedures, Mexico shall apply those specified in Part A of Annex XII and the EU shall apply the rules and procedures specified in Part B of Annex XII; both sets of rules and procedures are considered to provide equivalent treatment. In this context, NAFTA and GPA are of intense relevance: the rules and procedures specified in Annex XII may only be modified by the Party concerned in order to reflect amendments to the corresponding provisions of the NAFTA and the GPA, respectively. This clause is applicable only if these modifications continue to afford equivalent treatment, thus, a Party shall previously consult with the other Party and bear the burden of proving that the rules and procedures continue to afford equivalent treatment; the Party concerned shall notify the other Party of any modification no later than 30 days prior to their date of entry into force.[129]

The agreement covers a limited most-favoured nation (MFN) principle: in a case that the EU or Mexico offer a GPA or NAFTA Party additional advantages regarding access to their respective procurement markets beyond what has been covered in this agreement, they shall enter into mutual negotiations with a view to extending these advantages to the other Party on a reciprocal basis.[130] Where a Party considers that such modification affects access to the other Party's procurement market considerably, it can request consultations; if no satisfactory solution can be found the Party may have recourse to dispute settlement procedures (Title VI of the agreement), with a view to maintaining an equivalent level of access to the other Party's procurement market.[131] Bid challenges are arranged for in the event of a complaint by an economic operator that there has been a breach of this agreement. To this end, each Party shall provide its challenge procedures in writing and make them generally available, these procedures shall be non-discriminatory, timely, transparent and effective, enabling economic operators to

[126] cf Art 38, I Decision 2/2000.
[127] cf annex X part A No 3 Decision 2/2000.
[128] cf Art 28 Decision 2/2000.
[129] cf Art 29, IV Decision 2/2000.
[130] cf Art 37 Decision 2/2000.
[131] cf Art 29 Decision 2/2000.

challenge alleged breaches of the agreement arising in the context of procurements in which they have, or have had, an interest; all relevant documentation shall be retained for three years.[132]

XIV. EU–Switzerland

The agreement between the EU and Switzerland, as one out of seven,[133] encompassing 18 articles and Annexes I–X, addresses public procurement while taking into account the efforts and commitments so far to liberalise their respective public procurement markets, notably through the GPA and through the adoption of national rules providing for effective market opening in the field of government procurement through progressive liberalisation.[134] It improves and broadens the scope of their respective Annexes to Appendix I of the GPA, aiming to pursue liberalisation efforts among themselves by granting access to procurement of products, works and services by their respective telecommunications and railway operators, entities active in the field of energy other than electricity, and private utilities not covered by the GPA which operate on the basis of special or exclusive rights granted by a competent state authority and are active in the sectors of drinking water, electricity, urban transport, airports and maritime or inland ports.[135] The agreement includes 10 annexes: Annex I names the telecommunications operators covered, Annex II the railway operators, Annex III entities in the field of energy, Annex IV private utilities, Annex V the challenge procedure, Annex VI services, Annex VII works, Annex VIII exemptions applicable in Switzerland, Annex IX notified measures as to the integration process of the EU and the establishment and functioning of its internal market, as well as the development of the Swiss domestic market (until today, only Switzerland has notified such measure, concerning contracts below the thresholds), Annex X names a non-conclusive list of examples of areas where discrimination may be possible.

The territorial scope covers the EU, applied under the conditions laid down in the Lisbon Treaty, and the territory of Switzerland;[136] however, the agreement does not affect rights and obligations of the Parties under the GPA and other WTO agreements (see TBT).[137] The personal scope has been broadened in comparison to the GPA:

> In order to supplement and broaden the scope of its commitments vis-à-vis the Community under the GPA, Switzerland undertakes to amend its Annexes and General

[132] cf Art 30 Decision 2/2000.
[133] See the EU's database at ec.europa.eu/world/agreements.
[134] Preamble of Agreement between the European Community and the Swiss Confederation on certain aspects of government procurement, OJ L 114 30.04.2002, p 430 et seq. (Agreement EC–Switzerland).
[135] Preamble Agreement EC–Switzerland.
[136] cf Art 16 EC–Switzerland.
[137] cf Art 15 EC–Switzerland.

> Notes to Appendix I of the GPA as follows: Insert in Annex 2, under 'List of entities', the following new point after point 2: '3. Authorities and public bodies at district and municipality level'.[138]

This also has an impact on the agreement between the EU and USA. The material scope is "to secure reciprocal, transparent and non-discriminatory access of the relevant suppliers and service providers to purchases of products and services, including construction services, by telecommunications operators, railway operators, entities active in the field of energy other than electricity and private utilities of both Parties". The material scope of the agreement covers services and works within the meaning of Annexes VI and VII. Within these scopes, certain thresholds – estimated value, excluding VAT, of one or a series of contracts – are of relevance: the scope regarding thresholds is limited, for they shall not apply to those contracts, awarded by telecommunication operators, for purchases intended exclusively to enable them to provide one or more telecommunications services where other entities are free to offer the same services in the same geographical area and under substantially the same conditions; this provision shall apply under the same conditions also to contracts awarded by railway operators, entities active in the field of energy other than electricity and private utilities as soon as these sectors have been liberalised.[139] Moreover, urgent measures are addressed: if a Party considers that the other Party has failed to comply with its obligations under this agreement or that a law, regulation or practice of the other Party substantially reduces or threatens to reduce substantially the benefits accruing to it under this agreement, and the Parties are unable to agree promptly on appropriate compensation or other remedial action, the adversely affected Party may, without prejudice to its other rights and obligations under international law, suspend partly or completely, as appropriate, the application of this agreement; it shall immediately notify the other Party of any such suspension.[140]

XV. EU–South Africa

On the one hand, within the agreement between the EU and the Republic of South Africa,[141] the Parties agree to cooperate to ensure that access to the Parties' procurement contracts is governed by a system which is fair, equitable and transparent,[142] on the other hand, development cooperation between the EU and South Africa shall be conducted in a context of policy dialogue and partnership,

[138] cf Art 2 EC–Switzerland.
[139] cf Art 3, V EC–Switzerland.
[140] cf Art 9 EC–Switzerland.
[141] Agreement on Trade, Development and Cooperation between the European Community and its Member States, of the one part, and the Republic of South Africa, of the other part, OJ L 311 04.12.1999, p 3. (Agreement EC–South Africa).
[142] cf Art 45 Agreement EC–South Africa.

and shall support the policies and reforms carried out by the national authorities;[143] with respect to this, EU's financial regulation is applicable.

Both Parties have agreed to take appropriate steps to ensure that the EU character of development cooperation under this agreement is made known to the general public.[144] As an aim of the agreement in particular, development cooperation shall contribute to South Africa's harmonious and sustainable economic and social development and to its insertion into the world economy and to consolidate the foundations laid for a democratic society and a state governed by the rule of law in which human rights in their political, social and cultural aspects and fundamental freedoms are respected; within this context, priority shall be given to supporting operations which help the fight against poverty.[145] To this end, dialogue and partnership between public authorities and non-governmental development partners and actors will be promoted, programmes shall be focused on the basic needs of the previously disadvantaged communities and reflect the gender and environmental dimensions of development.[146] Cooperation partners eligible for financial and technical assistance shall be national, provincial and local authorities and public bodies, non-governmental organisations and EU-based organisations, regional and international organisations, institutions and public or private operators; any other body could be made eligible if so designated by both Parties.[147]

The means that may be deployed under the cooperation operations shall include in particular studies, technical assistance, training or other services, supplies and works, and also evaluation and monitoring audits and missions. Contribution from the partners shall in principle be required for each cooperation operation, the nature and amount of this contribution shall be adapted to the possibilities of the partner and nature of operations; however, opportunities may be sought for coherence and complementarity with other providers of funds (co-financing), particularly EU Member States.[148] This clause attempts to co-ordinate Member States' development programmes with EU's aims.

Multiannual indicative programming based on specific objectives and indicating modalities for the preparation, implementation and monitoring of the development cooperation and resulting operations during a reference period shall be carried out in the context of close contacts between the EU and South Africa with the contribution of the European Investment Bank (EIB); the outcome of these discussions shall be set out in a multiannual indicative programme signed by both Parties. Detailed operational procedures and provisions for implementation

[143] cf Art 65, I Agreement EC–South Africa.
[144] cf Art 68, V Agreement EC–South Africa.
[145] cf Art 65 Agreement EC–South Africa.
[146] cf Art 66 Agreement EC–South Africa.
[147] cf Art 67 Agreement EC–South Africa.
[148] cf Art 68 Agreement EC–South Africa.

and monitoring of the development cooperation shall be attached to the multiannual indicative programme.[149]

XVI. EU–USA

Between the EU and the USA, an agreement in form of an exchange of letters addresses public procurement.[150] The US and EU have agreed to cooperate and take all necessary steps to improve substantially the transparency of the notices of intended procurement in order to ensure that contracts covered under the GPA can be clearly identified as such;[151] moreover, it is agree to amend the respective Appendix I of the GPA,[152] the US shall grant to EU economic operators treatment no less favourable than for out-of-state economic operators for the Massachusetts Port Authority and for the states of West Virginia, North Dakota and as regards Illinois for procurement not covered by the GPA, and for out-of-city operators for the cities of Boston, Chicago, Dallas, Detroit, Indianapolis, Nashville and San Antonio.[153] Additionally, the US agreed to implement obligations with respect to Rural Electrification Administration (Annex 3, Appendix I) attached hereto as soon as possible after entry into force of this agreement, but no later than 1 January 1995 (entry into force of WTO agreement).[154,155] The agreement includes two Annexes (Annex 2 and 3), applicable to the USA, and the amended general notes and derogations from provisions of Article III of Appendix I GPA, with regard to the EU; the material scope remains unmodified: where a contract to be awarded by an entity is not covered by this agreement, it shall not be construed to cover any good or service component of that contract.[156]

Annex 2 covers the listed government entities at sub-central level. Relevant thresholds are Special Drawing Right (SDR) 355,000 for supplies and services and SDR 5 million for construction;[157] in case of construction services of the Republic of Korea and suppliers of such services, this agreement applies only to procurement of entities listed in Annexes 2 and 3 above a threshold of SDR 15 million.[158]

[149] cf Art 69 Agreement EC–South Africa.

[150] Agreement in the form of an exchange of letters between the European Community and the United States of America on government procurement, OJ L 134 20.06.1995, p 26. (Agreement EC–USA).

[151] cf No 3 Agreement EC–USA.

[152] cf No 1 Agreement EC–USA.

[153] cf No 2 Agreement EC–USA.

[154] cf Council Decision of 22 December 1994 concerning the conclusion on behalf of the European Community, as regards matters within its competence, of the agreements reached in the Uruguay Round multilateral negotiations (1986–1994), OJ L 336 23.12.1994; Uruguay Round of Multilateral Trade Negotiations (1986–1994) – Annex 4 – Agreement on Government Procurement (WTO), OJ L 336 23.12.1994, p 273 et seq.

[155] cf No 5 Agreement EC–USA.

[156] cf appendix 3 No 4 Agreement EC–USA.

[157] cf appendix 2 Agreement EC–USA.

[158] cf appendix 3 No 6 Agreement EC–USA.

However, a number of exemptions applies for both the USA and the EU.[159] All other aspects are governed by the GPA.

XVII. Agreement of Cotonou

The agreement between the EU, its Member States and the African, Pacific and Caribbean States[160] underlines 'the growing importance of services in international trade and their major contribution to economic and social development'; however, the EU and ACP States only agreed to reaffirm commitments under GATS – there is no reference to the GPA – and emphasise the need for special and differential treatment to ACP economic operators. Third State members of the agreement are: Angola, Antigua and Barbuda, Bahamas, Barba-dos, Belize, Benin, Botswana, Burkina Faso, Burundi, Cameroon, Cape Verde, Central African Republic, Chad, Comoros, Democratic Republic of Congo (Kinshasa), Congo (Brazzaville), Cook Islands, Cote d'Ivoire, Cuba, Djibouti, Dominica, Dominican Republic, East Timor, Equatorial Guinea, Eritrea, Ethiopia, Fiji, Gabon, Gambia, Ghana, Grenada, Guinea, Guinea-Bissau, Guyana, Haiti, Jamaica, Kenya, Kiribati, Lesotho, Liberia, Madagascar, Malawi, Mali, Marshall Islands, Mauritania, Mauritius, Micronesia, Mozambique, Namibia, Nauru, Niger, Nigeria, Niue, Palau, Papua New Guinea, Rwanda, St. Kitts and Nevis, St. Lucia, St. Vincent and the Grenadines, Samoa, Sao Tome and Principe, Senegal, Seychelles, Sierra Leone, Solomon Islands, Somalia, South Africa, Sudan, Suriname, Swaziland, Tanzania, Togo, Tonga, Trinidad and Tobago, Tuvalu, Uganda, Vanuatu, Zambia and Zimbabwe.

Significantly, the most-favoured nation principle is referred to: the Parties agree on the objective of extending, and after they have acquired some experience in applying MFN treatment under GATS, their partnership to encompass the liberalisation of services in accordance with the provisions of GATS and particularly those relating to the participation of developing countries in liberalisation agreements.[161]

Performance of works, supply and service contracts financed from EDF[162] shall be governed by general conditions applicable to contracts financed by the EDF,[163] or in case of co-financed projects and programmes, or where a

[159] cf ibid.

[160] Partnership agreement between the members of the African, Caribbean and Pacific Group of States of the one part, and the European Community and its Member States, of the other part, signed in Cotonou on 23 June 2000, OJ L 317 15.12. 2000, p 3, amended by 2005/599/EC: Agreement amending the Partnership Agreement between the members of the African, Caribbean and Pacific Group of States, of the one part, and the European Community and its Member States, of the other part, signed in Cotonou on 23 June 2000, OJ L 209 11.08.2005, p 27. (Cotonou Agreement).

[161] Art 41, IV Cotonou Agreement.

[162] 2006/608/EC: Decision No 1/2006 of the ACP–EC Council of Ministers of 2 June 2006 specifying the multiannual financial framework for the period 2008 to 2013 and modifying the revised ACP–EC Partnership Agreement, OJ L 247 9.9.2006, p 22 et seq.

[163] Art 29 lit a Cotonou Agreement.

derogation to third parties has been granted or in accelerated procedures or in other appropriate cases, such other conditions as may be agreed by the ACP State concerned and the EU (ie general conditions for contracts prescribed by the national legislation of the ACP State concerned or its established practices regarding international contracts, or any other international general conditions for contracts).[164] The procedure for award of contracts for public works and supplies forming part of the financial and technical cooperation provided for by the agreement involves a division of powers between the European Commission and the authorities of the ACP State concerned. Whilst it is incumbent on the European Commission to take financing decisions on behalf of the EU, the responsibility for preparing, negotiating and concluding the contracts falls to the authorities of the ACP State,[165] thus, the choice of the economically most advantageous tender is a matter for the administration of the ACP States,[166] for

> according to settled case-law contracts financed by the EDF remain national contracts which only the ACP States have the responsibility of preparing, negotiating and concluding. For their part, undertakings which submit tenders for or are awarded the contracts in question remain outside the exclusive dealings conducted on this matter between the European Commission and the ACP States.[167]

Contracts financed from EDF are regarded as national contracts, binding only the ACP State and the economic operator,[168]

> however, although there is no contractual relationship between the Commission and the applicant, it is clear from the case-law of the Court of Justice that the Commission may be liable [under Article 340, II TFEU] to make good damage suffered by third parties as a result of acts committed by the delegate in the performance of his duties.[169]

The European Commission appoints the Chief Administrative Officer (CAO) of the EDF, who shall be responsible for managing the resources of the EDF, commitment, clearance, authorisation and accounting of expenditure under the EDF:[170]

> Finally, the Commission has not only the right but also the duty to ensure, before any payments are made out of Community funds, that the conditions for such payments are in fact fulfilled. To that end, it is under a duty in particular to seek the necessary information in order to ensure the economical administration of the resources of the EDF.[171]

[164] Art 29 lit b No i Cotonou Agreement.

[165] cf ECJ, C-257/90, Italsolar SpA/European Commission, ECR 1993, I-9, head note.

[166] ibid para 24.

[167] ECI, T-175/94, *International Procurement Services SA/European Commission*, ECR 1996, II-729, para 43; ECJ, C-257/90, *Italsolar/European Commission*, ECR 1993, I-9, para 22; ECI, T-451/93, *San Marco/European Commission*, ECR 1994, II-1061, para 42.

[168] cf ECJ, 33/82, *Murri Frères*, ECR 1985, p 2759; ECI, T-451/93, *San Marco Impex*, ECR 1994, II-1061, para 42.

[169] ECI, T-451/93, *San Marco Impex*, ECR 1994, II-1061, para 43; ECJ, case 118/83, *CMC/European Commission*, ECR 1985, p 2325.

[170] cf Art 34, I Cotonou Agreement.

[171] ECI, T-175/94, *International Procurement Services SA/European Commission*, ECR 1996, II-729, para 45.

Thus, the European Commission has to ensure that the tender selected is economically the most advantageous, taking into account in particular the qualifications of and the guarantees offered by the economic operators, the nature and conditions of execution of the works and the price, utilisation costs and technical value of those works.[172]

Therefore, measures adopted by the European Commission's representatives during the procedure for conclusion or implementation of contracts concluded by States associated with the EU and financed by the EDF are solely intended to establish whether or not the conditions for EU financing are met; they are not intended to interfere with the principle that these contracts remain national contracts which the ACP States alone are responsible for.[173] It follows that European Commission's agents may not deal directly, in place of the ACP States, with undertakings which submit tenders for or are awarded contracts financed by the EDF, and those undertakings remain outside the exclusive dealings concluded on this matter between the European Commission and the ACP States; the measures adopted by the European Commission's representatives in the course of the procedure for the placing or implementation of those contracts cannot be regarded as being addressed to them. Such an undertaking has legal relations only with the ACP State responsible for the contract, and measures adopted by the representatives of the European Commission cannot substitute, in relation to the undertaking, an EU decision for an ACP State decision.[174]

The CAO commits, clears and authorises expenditure and keeps accounts, ensures that financing decisions are carried out, makes commitment decisions and financial arrangements in close cooperation with the NAO that prove necessary to ensure proper execution of approved operations from the economic and technical viewpoints, prepares the tender dossier before the invitations to tender are issued, approves the proposals for the placing of contracts subject to the powers exercised by the Head, ensures publication in reasonable time of international invitations to tender and, at the end of each year, makes available a detailed balance sheet of the EDF showing balances of contributions paid into the EDF by the Member States and global disbursements in respect of each financing heading. The Government of each ACP States shall appoint a NAO each to represent it in all operations financed from the resources of the EDF managed by the European Commission and the EIB.[175]

The European Commission shall be represented in each ACP State or in each regional grouping, which expressly so requests, by a delegation under the authority of a Head of Delegation, with the approval of the ACP State or States concerned. The crucial tasks of the Head of Delegation in the sphere of procurement procedures are, among others, to participate and give assistance, in close

[172] ECJ, C-370/89, *Société générale d'entreprises électro-mécaniques a. Roland Etroy/EIB*, ECR 1993, I-2583, para 30.
[173] cf ECJ, case 33/82, *Murri frères/European Commission*, ECR 1985, p 2759, para 33.
[174] ibid para 34.
[175] cf Art 35, I Cotonou Agreement.

cooperation with the NAO, in preparation of projects and programmes and in negotiating technical assistance contracts, if requested by the ACP State, participate in appraising projects and programmes, preparing tender dossiers and seeking ways to simplify project and programme appraisal and implementation procedures, prepare financing proposals, approve, before the NAO issues them, the local open invitation to tender and the emergency assistance contract dossiers within 30 days of their submission to him by the NAO, be present at the opening of tenders and receive copies of them and of the results of their examination, approve, within 30 days, the NAO's proposal for the placing of local open tenders, direct agreement contracts, emergency assistance contracts, service contracts and works contracts with a value less than EUR 5 million and supply contracts with a value less than EUR 1 million, for all other contracts, approve within 30 days the NAO's proposal for the placing of the contract wherever certain conditions are fulfilled (the tender selected is the lowest of those conforming to the requirements of the tender dossier, it meets all the selection criteria stated in the tender dossier, and it does not exceed the sum earmarked for the contract), ensure that projects and programmes financed from the EDF managed by the European Commission are properly executed from the financial and technical view-points, cooperate with authorities of the ACP State where he represents the European Commission in evaluating operations regularly, and to regularly inform national authorities of EU activities which may directly concern cooperation between the EU and the ACP States.[176] To simplify and streamline the general rules and regulations for competition and preferences for EDF financed operations, contracts shall be awarded through open and restricted procedures, framework contract, direct agreement contracts and direct labour.[177] Measures shall be taken to encourage the widest participation of natural and legal persons of ACP States in the performance of contracts financed by the EDF in order to permit the optimisation of the physical and human resources of those States. The ACP State may propose to prospective relevant economic operator's assistance of other ACP States' undertakings, national experts or consultants selected by mutual agreement; this may be either a joint venture, a subcontract or on-the-job training of trainees.[178]

XVIII. CARIFORUM

The EU signed an agreement[179] with Antigua and Barbuda, The Bahamas, Barbados, Belize, Dominica, Grenada, Guyana, Jamaica, Saint Lucia, Saint Vincent and the Grenadines, Saint Kitts and Nevis, Suriname, Trinidad and Tobago, and

[176] cf Art 36 Cotonou Agreement.
[177] cf Art 23, I lit a Cotonou Agreement.
[178] cf Art 26 lit e Cotonou Agreement.
[179] Economic Partnership Agreement between the CARIFORUM States, of the one part, and the European Community and its Member States, of the other part, OJ L 289 30.10.2008, p 3.

the Dominican Republic (Haiti signed in December 2009, but has not yet ratified the agreement); the agreement is provisionally applied as of 29 December 2008.

The agreement is not applicable to Haiti. The EU pledged to work with the Haitian government and Caribbean partners to ensure conditions for Haiti to join the CARIFORUM are in place.[180] The CARIFORUM Agreement commits its signatories to a very complete set of rules on transparency in government procurement but does not include any provisions on market access; thus, the EU and CARIFORUM have agreed to rules that would ensure that relevant information is freely disclosed in order to facilitate fair and acceptable processes in public tendering. However, in Article 165 to Article 182, the agreement rules on public procurement, Annex VI names the covered procurement entities and relevant thresholds.[181] The Parties recognise the importance of transparent competitive tendering for economic development with due regard being given to the special situation of the economies of the CARIFORUM States;[182] therefore the Parties and the CARIFORUM States shall ensure that procurements of their entities takes place in a transparent manner, treating any eligible economic operator of either the CARIFORUM States or the EU Party equally in accordance with the principle of open and effective competition.[183]

Enabling CARIFORUM States to comply with this agreement, they shall have an initial implementation period of two years from the entry into force of this agreement; where one or more CARIFORUM States need one more year for this, the period may be extended by one more year for the individual CARIFORUM States concerned. Derogating from this, Antigua and Barbuda, Belize, the Commonwealth of Dominica, Grenada, the Republic of Haiti, Saint Christopher and Nevis, Saint Lucia and Saint Vincent and the Grenadines shall benefit from an initial implementation period of five years.[184]

With respect to any measure regarding covered procurement, each CARIFORUM State, including its procuring entities, shall endeavour not to treat an economic operator established in any CARIFORUM State less favourably than another locally established economic operator; thus, the principle of non-discrimination is applied. Regarding measures of covered procurement, the Parties shall

- endeavour not to discriminate against an economic operator established in either Party on the basis that the goods or services offered by that economic operator for a particular procurement are goods or services of either Party,

[180] cf Report from the Commission concerning negotiations regarding access of Community undertakings to the markets of third countries in fields covered by the Directive 2004/17/EC, /* European Commission /2009/0592 final */.

[181] cf Art 167, I CARIFORUM.

[182] cf Art 165 CARIFORUM.

[183] cf Art 167, II CARIFORUM.

[184] cf Art 180 CARIFORUM.

- not treat a locally established economic operator less favourably than another locally established economic operator on the basis of degree of foreign affiliation to or ownership by operators or nationals of any signatory Party.

It follows that each Party shall with respect to any measure regarding covered procurement, accord to the goods, services and economic operators of the other Party treatment no less favourable than the treatment the Party, including its procuring entities, accords to domestic goods, services and economic operators. However, this treatment is conditioned: the Parties shall not be required to provide this treatment unless a decision by the Joint CARIFORUM–EU Council to this effect is taken, the decision may specify to which procurements by each Party the treatment would apply, and under which conditions; such a decision has not been taken yet. The agreement shall not be construed as preventing a CARIFORUM State or the EU Party from imposing or enforcing measures relating to goods or services of persons with disabilities, philanthropic institutions, or prison labour; additional exemptions apply.[185]

[185] cf Art 167 CARIFORUM.

6

Spatial Configurations of Welfare in the EU: The Case of Cross-border Healthcare

IRENE SOBRINO GUIJARRO

I. Introduction

Cross-border healthcare still constitutes a relatively modest area, both in terms of financial impact and numbers of people receiving healthcare in another Member State.[1] In this regard, it is estimated that, although patient mobility has progressively increased, its current volume is relatively low in terms of the overall public expenditure on healthcare.[2] However, the fact that patients are allowed to move between different health systems generates a complex reality that poses different questions in aspects such as the quality, security, health benefits, accessibility, financing, information, equity and legal responsibility of the Member States. These factors, together with the dense jurisprudential body that the Court of Justice of the European Union (hereinafter, CJEU) has developed on the rights related to cross-border healthcare provision, have made this question be moved to the top of the political agenda of Member States and the European Union over the last decade.[3]

On 9 March 2011, the Directive 2011/24/EU of the European Parliament and the Council on the application of patients' rights in cross-border healthcare in the

[1] W Palm and IA Glinos, 'Enabling Patient Mobility in the EU: Between Free Movement and Coordination' in E Mossialos and others (eds), *Health Systems Governance in Europe* (Cambridge, Cambridge University Press, 2010) 510–11.

[2] Specifically, it represents one per cent of overall public expenditure on healthcare, see European Parliament, *The Impact of the European Court of Justice Case Law on National Systems for Cross-Border Health Service Provision* (DG Internal Policies of the Union, Policy Department Economic and Scientific Policy, 2007) 2.

[3] The need to reach a shared European vision on the question led the European Commission to establish a 'High Level Process of Reflection on Patient mobility and health care developments in the European Union'" (26 June 2002), whose conclusions where further developed at the 'High Level Group on Health Services and Medical Care' (1 July 2004).

European Union, was finally enacted after a protracted process of political discussions. The adoption of the Directive not only responded to the need for providing a normative framework to codify the principles established by the CJEU jurisprudence on patient mobility, but also to the interest of Member States to take part in the delimitation of the terms of cross-border healthcare, in particular regarding the authorisation and reimbursement of the services, which until then had been shaped by the CJEU case law principles in application of the freedom to provide services.

The focus that structures the following analysis is linked to its most recent legal articulation through the Directive and its transposition into national law, as a concrete instance of the *sui generis* prevailing pattern of 'social construction' in the EU. The legal delimitation of this question unveils the existing tensions between, on the one hand, the application of the basic freedoms of the common market and, on the other hand, the Member States' protection of their welfare institutions, linked to national parameters of territorial solidarity and financial planning. In this context, the harmonising frame established by the Directive articulates important patients' rights on cross-border healthcare, taking as the main reference the case law established by the CJEU on free movement of services, as well as some common values and principles shared across the EU health systems. However, at the current stage of early implementation, there is a high degree of national variation as to the interpretation and transposition of key questions that may reduce the practicability of patients' rights.

II. Profiles of the EU 'Welfare' Structure

Although the EU has assumed shared powers on certain social areas, the core of its competences on welfare are reduced to a supporting or complementary role with the Member States. However, notwithstanding the relatively reduced responsibilities that it explicitly has on social issues, the EU law is having a significant impact on the laws and practices of the Member States in the area of welfare broadly conceived. De Búrca argues that two main aspects to the claim that the EU has an important impact in the area of social welfare can be distinguished: (1) the first refers to the impact that the EU economic law and policy (specifically, the CJEU jurisprudence on internal market and competition law) have on existing national laws and policies in this field, and (2) the second relates to the gradual emergence of elements of a distinct, albeit fragmented, EU welfare dimension alongside the conventional field of EU employment law.[4]

[4] For instance, the provisions and CJEU case law on EU citizenship; the EU Charter on Fundamental rights; the body of EU legislation regulating the coordination of social security benefits; the body of EU equality law; the emerging EU welfare law that aims at coordinating national social policies in areas such as employment, anti-poverty, pensions and health. See G De Búrca, 'Towards European Welfare?' in G De Búrca (ed), *EU Law and the Welfare State. In Search of Solidarity* (Oxford, Oxford University Press, 2005) 1–9.

From this perspective, the Union has definitely become a new territorial stratum involved in the social sphere regulation that interacts with the nationally based welfare state. It can be affirmed, therefore, that the 'spatial architecture of welfare'[5] is not confined anymore to that contained within the national boundaries, but it is being redrawn by the process of the European integration. However, notwithstanding the process of expansion experienced by the EU welfare dimension, there are certainly some structurally problematic aspects.

In this regard, it is widely emphasised that the 'fragmented'[6] or 'patchwork' form of EU social policy, is still far from a 'fully fledged' and coherent structure.[7] The cause of these characteristics is incardinated in the nature of the deeper structural logics underpinning the EU construction, related to the market-making core commitment of the European project that has had a determining influence on the nature and purpose of social policy shaping,[8] which has been consequently developed as a function of market integration.[9] The prevalence of this logic has resulted, according to F Scharpf, in an evident 'asymmetry' between policies promoting market efficiencies and policies promoting social protection and equality.[10]

With the aim to level out this 'asymmetry', there are increasing pressures from the political and doctrinal level to strengthen the social dimension of Europe. In broad terms, the main arguments underlying the claims for a more balanced equation between economic integration and the EU social dimension can be synthesised in three groups. The first emphasises the fact that as a result either of legal or economic competition constraints, European economic integration has generated pressures towards deregulation and has therefore challenged national social standards and welfare. This is seen as a spill-over effect of market integration rules into national economic and social regulations. The determinant assessment that would characterise this dynamic is what could be denominated the 'deficit on *compensation*', implying that the nascent 'gap' would not have been totally compensated for by social policies arising at the level of the European Union. The argument in favour of a European social policy would thus attempt to reintroduce political control over the economic sphere at the EU level.[11]

The secondary reason that has mobilised the claims of a more social Europe concerns the idea that the competence of the EU on social issues, albeit having

[5] M Ferrera, *The Boundaries of Welfare State. European integration and the New Spatial Politics of social protection* (OUP 2005) 51.

[6] de Búrca (n 4) at 1.

[7] C Barnard, 'EC Social Policy' in P Craig and G de Búrca (eds), *The Evolution of EU Law* (Oxford, Oxford University Press, 1999) 490.

[8] ibid, 491.

[9] M Poiares Maduro, 'Striking the Elusive Balance Between Economic Freedom and Social Rights in the EU' in P Alston (ed), *The EU and Human Rights* (Oxford, Oxford University Press, 1999) 462.

[10] FW Scharpf, 'The European Social Model: Coping with the Challenges of Diversity' (2002) 40(4) *Journal of Common Market Studies* 645–70.

[11] Poiares Maduro (n 9) at 464.

generally been limited, has been seen as a channel of opportunity to promote social policies against predominant deregulatory ideologies at the national level within the context of economic competition and efficiency criteria logics.[12] This point would be therefore placing the emphasis on the convenience of reinforcing a social regulatory framework at the European level to which national political initiatives could be to some extent effectively constrained.

Finally, it is also possible to identify an additional category of rationale underlying the European welfare construction, which would consist in the attempts to institutionalise certain shared conceptions of justice and equality as a way to deepen the democratic legitimation of the EU political power. From this viewpoint, this logic, although in practice bonded with the two previous ones, would be theoretically linked to considerations of the EU's endogenous constitutional and normative aspirations to progress in its legitimation as a political organisation, where the operationalisation of social or substantive equality would be a crucial factor. Discursively, claims on the needs to deepen on this dimension have been lengthily developed in academia and in the political sphere, and there is evidence of the growing and solid implementation of policies that articulate notions of real equality, be it territorially projected (eg cohesion policy as a manifestation of inter-territorial solidarity), at the individual rights level (eg transversality of certain social policy objectives in the EU's action required by the Treaty of Lisbon; reinforced legal character of social rights in the Charter of fundamental rights)[13] or through transnational solidarity commitments to provide certain essential services to citizens (eg cross-border healthcare).[14]

However, there are political and constitutional constraints in the process of articulating a social policy comprehensive vision in the EU. These tensions are not only due to the interest to the Members States to retain control of their domestic financial distributional schemes' equilibrium, but it is also the diversity of national welfare states, differing in levels of economic development, normative aspirations and institutional structures, that entails an added impediment for the embrace of a comprehensive European welfare dimension. This is derived from the basic premise that national welfare states' dynamics are essentially explained by traditional domestic policy and economic variables.[15]

[12] ibid, 464–66.

[13] See KA Armstrong, 'EU Social Policy and the Governance Architecture of Europe 2020' (2012) 18(3) *Transfer: European Review of Labour and Research* 285–300; J Ziller, 'L'Europe sociale dans la Constitution pour l'Europe' (2005) 2 *Droit Social* 197; M Poiares Maduro, 'The Double Constitutional Life of the Charter of Fundamental Rights of the European Union' in T Hervey and J Kenner (eds), *Economic and Social rights under the EU Charter of Fundamental rights: a legal perspective* (Oxford, Hart Publishing, 2003) 286.

[14] See F De Witte, *Justice in the European Union. The Emergence of Transnational Solidarity* (Oxford, Oxford University Press, 2015).

[15] MP Kleinman, *A European Welfare State?: European Union Social Policy in Context* (Basingstoke, Palgrave, 2001) 74.

III. The Case of Healthcare Law

The EU healthcare law represents an optimal case through which to explore the basic tensions and logics structurally linked to the 'welfare construction' in the EU. On health policy in the EU we can perceive a fundamental contradiction at its core. On the one hand, the Treaty on the Functioning of the European Union explicitly states that healthcare is the responsibility of the Member States, which preserve their own national health policy as part of their unique social policy. However, on the other hand, many national health systems are in fact subject to EU law and policy, given that health systems of Member States involve interactions with people (staff and patients), goods (pharmaceutical and devices) and services (the provision of healthcare itself), all of which are granted freedom of movement across borders by the same Treaty. Therefore, for instance, when national health systems seek to purchase medicines or medical equipment, or to recruit health professionals, we can see that their scope is largely determined by EU legislation.

Given that the EU has no formal legal powers to develop its own healthcare law, the EU's emergent healthcare policy is something of a patchwork. In this regard, EU healthcare law and policy is formed from a variety of provisions that belong to different policy domains, such as those of the internal market, employment law, public health and competition law. The influence of heterogeneous normative impulses from fields in which the EU does have legal competence has culminated in a fragmented EU healthcare law. From this viewpoint, it represents the concretion of analogous profiles that embodies the EU social law as a whole (ie fragmentation).

Both the case law and legislative development of cross-border healthcare accurately reflects the tension between the potential for patients to receive healthcare in other Member States based on the free movement of services, and the territorial solidarity and financial sustainability which national healthcare systems are built on. Such tensions are not just mere rhetoric. Conflicting political priorities and diverging positions translate into contentious relationships between the actors involved in the decision-making processes. Mirroring this, for instance, were the innumerable political hurdles and the protracted negotiation processes involved needed to enact the Directive on patients' rights in cross-border healthcare, mainly between Member States through the Council of the European Union and the European Commission's proposals.

IV. Cross-border Healthcare in the EU: The Directive 2011/24/EU

The progressive development of the cross-border healthcare policy embodies the aforementioned dynamic of the '*constitutional asymmetry*' that the lack of competence of the EU to regulate healthcare has resulted in, namely, the prevalence of negative integration (ie directly enforcing internal market Treaty provisions through litigation) over positive integration (ie adopting EU legislative measures). Such imbalance has raised significant uncertainties especially for the governments of the Member States and their healthcare institutions. Notably, for instance, by empowering the right to cross-border mobility of citizens, the case law has implicitly retracted the capacity of Member States to deny reimbursement when medical treatment has been provided outside the state of affiliation. This asymmetry has underlain the enactment of a regulatory framework for cross-border health mobility, which articulates the freedom of movement as the basis for a social right, involving financial commitments of two different countries (ie country of treatment and country of affiliation). The Directive is, ultimately, an optimal opportunity to analyse the mechanisms that frame the inevitable tensions that arise from attempts to harmonise rights, values and operating principles, and from the respect for the principle of subsidiarity, in the context of diverse national healthcare systems.

A. Legislative Background of the Directive 2011/24

Ever since the foundation of the European Community, the policy of awarding access to healthcare outside the State of social security affiliation has been essentially governed by some long-standing legislation, mostly by the coordination of social security schemes in order to facilitate the free movement of workers and their families (Regulation 883/2004). The material scope of the regulation covers sickness, invalidity and maternity benefits of those who fall within its personal scope.[16] Within this framework, it is important to differentiate two basic cases: (1) occasional medical need during the stay in another Member State (Article 19.1 Regulation 883/2004);[17] (2) travel to another Member State with the purpose of receiving healthcare during the stay. In this case, if the patients want the medical service be paid by their State of affiliation, they must always seek pre-authorisation from this (Article 20, Regulation 883/2004). The authorisation must be given, according to Article 20.2 Regulation 883/2004, if:

> the treatment in question is among the benefits provided for by the legislation in the Member State of affiliation and he cannot be given such treatment within a time-limit which is medically justifiable, taking into account his current state of health and the probable course of his illness.

Once the authorisation is granted, the medical treatment lies at the expense of the Member State of affiliation (ie the State where the person works and pays social security contributions).

[16] Reg 883/2004, Art 2 (1).
[17] ibid, Art 19.1.

The CJEU has developed a dense case law in the interpretation of this route, whose most problematic aspect has gravitated around the scope of the Member State's prior authorisation. The decisions have normally been framed within the context of preliminary rulings triggered by individual claims against refusals of pre-authorisations of their Member States.

In addition, since 1998, the CJEU has created an alternative procedure to that offered by the 'social security coordination' route, that also fosters patient mobility in the EU to seek scheduled care. In particular, this second route for cross-border healthcare is based on the fundamental principles of free movement of goods and services (Articles 56 and 57 TFEU, ex Articles 49 and 50 EC Treaty), and is the result of an interesting operation of translation of the fundamental principles of free movement into a right for patients to access healthcare services outside their home State.[18]

However, whereas the Court's case law generated over the years has allowed for a careful balance between free movement and the protection of public interest objectives, legal certainty could not be fully achieved, since, obviously, the particular circumstances of each case ultimately determine whether a refusal of authorisation by the State of origin for a person to be medically treated outside is considered necessary and reasonable under the rules on free movement. Hence, it is fundamentally the call for legal certainty for patients, Member States and health sector authorities, which underlie the policy response on cross-border healthcare on the 'alternative route' through Directive 2011/24.

B. Scope and Content of the Directive 2011/24

As a result of the briefly described processes, the planned patient mobility counts now on two different regulatory frameworks: Regulation 883/2004 (ie the social security coordination), and the one established by Directive 2011/24. In a nutshell, the Directive codifies and clarifies the main principles of the CJEU case law related to cross-border healthcare and it facilitates access to cross-border healthcare, under the premise that the health service in question is among the benefits to which the insured person is entitled in his/her home country (Article 7.1. *in fine*).

The Directive makes cross-border healthcare applicable both to nationals of Member States and to nationals of third countries that reside legally in a Member State. The legal base of the new regulatory framework lies on Article 114 TFEU (ex Article 95 TEC), that concerns the approximation of provisions laid down by law, regulation or administrative action in Member States which have as their object the establishment and functioning of the internal market.

[18] See, for instance, Case C-158/96 *Kohll* [1998] ECR I-1943; Case C-56/01 *Inizan* [2003] ECR I-12433; C-157/99 *Geraets-Smits and Peerbooms* [2001] ECR I-5528.

In terms of the delimitation of its scope, the Directive aims fundamentally at facilitating patients to receive healthcare services, or to buy medicines or medical devices in another Member State. It does not, however, encompass the regulation of aspects associated to the movement of the service provider (ie the healthcare professionals), or when the service itself moves (ie the medical treatment or healthcare). Furthermore, the Directive does not apply to services in the fields of long-term care, organs transplants or public vaccination programmes against infectious diseases which are exclusively aimed at protecting the health of the population on the territory of a Member State.[19]

An additional innovative question is the requirement to set-up 'National Contact Points' (hereinafter, NCPs), in charge of providing patients with information publicly available and easily accessible in relation to their rights on cross-border healthcare, as well as information regarding healthcare providers and the conditions that will apply to reimbursement and procedures for appeal if patients consider that their rights have not been respected.

The regulatory framework established by the Directive is explicitly articulated in accordance with the principle of subsidiarity and with respect for the exclusive responsibilities that Member States have on the organisation and delivery of healthcare, and on the definition of social security benefits.[20]

i. Need for Prior Authorisation

Article 8 of the Directive regulates the conditions in which prior authorisation by the Member State of affiliation may be required for the patient to be entitled to get a medical treatment in another Member State. The Directive basically codifies the criteria that the CJEU had developed regarding cross-border healthcare based on the free movement of services.[21] Consistently with the CJEU's case law, which conceptualised the system of prior authorisation as a barrier to the freedom to provide medical services, the request of authorisation is regulated as an option for Member States (Article 8.1: 'The Member State of affiliation may provide for a system of prior authorization …').

Therefore, in application of the CJEU's case law on this question, the existence of the authorisation needs to be justified and restricted to what is necessary and proportionate to the objective to be achieved (eg public objective interests that may act as legitimate justifications to exceptionally hinder the free movement of services, such as the financial balance of social security budget, needs for planning, etc), and may not constitute a means of arbitrary discrimination or unjustified obstacle to the free movement of patient (Article 8.1 Directive).

[19] Art 1.3 Directive.

[20] Explanatory memorandum of the Directive 2011/24, para 64.

[21] On the process of codification, see P Quinn and P De Hert, 'The European Patients' Rights Directive: A Clarification and Codification of Individual Rights Relating to Cross Border Healthcare and Novel Initiatives Aimed at Improving Pan-European Healthcare Co-operation' (2012) *Medical Law International* 11–12.

Whereas under the social coordination route, all healthcare must be authorised in advance, within the framework of the Directive, the *possibility* for Member States of affiliation to ask the patients for a prior authorisation is strictly limited to three cases (Article 8.2): (1) healthcare subject to planning requirements that either involves overnight hospital accommodation for at least one night or requires the use of highly specialised and cost-intensive medical infrastructure or medical equipment; (2) in case of treatments presenting a particular risk for the patient or the population; or (3) when the healthcare provider could give rise to serious concerns about the quality or safety of the care.

As regards the refusal of the authorisation, this is limited to four cases (Article 8.6): (1) when it implies a safety risk for the patient; (2) a safety risk for the population; (3) when there are concerns about the respect of standards on quality of care regarding the healthcare provider; (4) or when healthcare can be provided within the Member State of affiliation within a time which is medically justifiable.

In sharp contrast with precedent CJEU case law that had restricted authorisation to hospital treatments,[22] the Directive expanded the concept of 'hospital care' by including the use of highly specialised and cost-intensive infrastructure, even if not implying overnight accommodation, in the list of medical treatments that may justify their prior authorisation. In the Directive drafting process, the European Commission had proposed to set up a specific list at EU level of specialised healthcare subject to prior authorisation,[23] but this option was refused by the Council and the Parliament claiming that it would mean a breach of the subsidiarity principle. In the end, it was established that the Member States of affiliation will just have to make publicly available which healthcare is actually subject to prior authorisation (Article 8.7 Directive).[24] Additionally, the proposal of the Council to introduce a non-exhaustive list of criteria for refusing individual prior authorisation could, in the Commission's view, create risks of legal uncertainty for the patients. However, in order to allow the legislative process to move forward, the Commission did not stand against the position on these questions adopted by the Council.[25]

ii. Reimbursement

On this question, the Directive fully codifies the basic principles that the CJEU has established through its case law (eg the *Kohll-Decker* decision). The logic that applies is the following: if the healthcare in question is among the benefits to which the insured person is entitled in the Member State of affiliation, the costs of cross-border healthcare will be reimbursed by this State up to the level

[22] See, for instance, Case C-158/96 *Kohll* [1998] ECR I-1935, paras 42, 50–52, and Case C-120/95 *Decker* [1998], ERC I-1885, para 40.

[23] COM (2008) 414 final, 2.7.2008, Art 8.1 and 2.

[24] Council of the EU (11038/10) 6.

[25] COM (2010) 503 final, 20.9.2010.

of costs that would have been assumed by the Member State of affiliation, had this healthcare been provided in its territory without exceeding the actual costs of healthcare received (Article 7.4).

Hence, it is required an upfront payment of costs by the patients, who then have to cover these personally prior to being reimbursed. The main principle here is that the applicable reimbursement tariff is the one of the Member State of affiliation (in contrast to the logic of the social security coordination route, whose tariff of reference is that of Member State of treatment). These conditions could entail a situation of unequal access for patients, as clearly the requirement of upfront payment could favour wealthier patients disproportionately.

iii. Coordination of Both Routes

Importantly, the application of this route excludes the application of the social security coordination procedure.[26] In this regard, the Directive states that patients should not be deprived of the more beneficial rights guaranteed by the Union regulations on the coordination of social security systems when the conditions are met. Therefore, unless the patient explicitly requests to seek treatment under the terms of the Directive, any patient who requests an authorisation to receive treatment in another Member State should get it granted when the treatment in question is among the benefits provided for by the legislation in the Member State where the patient resides, and when the patient cannot be given such treatment within the time limit that is medically justifiable.[27]

iv. Patients' New Rights

In line with what has been called a 'patient-centred' or 'needs-based approach', which the CJEU, as well as the European Commission, have consistently supported,[28] the Directive establishes a new set of patients' rights that correlates to binding responsibilities of Member States, constituting one of the most innovative aspects in the Directive (Articles 4 and 5). The catalogue of rights has been inferred from the set of 'operating principles', common values and principles that are shared across the Union and are necessary to both ensure patients' trust in cross-border healthcare and to achieving patient mobility.[29]

[26] 'For patients, therefore, the two systems should be coherent; either this Directive applies or the Union regulations on the coordination of social security systems apply' (Explanatory memorandum, para 30). See also Art 8.3 of the Directive 2011/24.

[27] Point 31, Explanatory memorandum of the Directive 2011/24.

[28] See G Davies, 'The Community's Internal Market-based Competence to Regulate Healthcare: Scope, Strategies and Consequences' (2007) 14 *Maastricht Journal of European and Comparative Law* 229–30; W Sauter, 'The Proposed Patients' Rights Directive and the Reform of (Cross-border) Healthcare in the European Union' (2009) 36 *Legal Issues of Economic Integration* 111; Palm and Glinos (n 1) 513–14.

[29] Explanatory memorandum Directive 2011/24, paras 5, 21.

The core of the patients' rights concerns the obligation of the Member State of treatment to ensure that these receive information on healthcare providers, standards and guidelines on quality and safety, the accessibility of hospitals for persons with disabilities, legal and administrative options to settle disputes. The right to an informed choice involves particular information about availability, prices and outcomes of healthcare. Also, the Member State of treatment bears responsibility regarding the right of privacy while processing personal data, as well as the principle of non-discrimination on the basis of nationality. On the side of the Member States of affiliation, besides its duty to reimburse the costs of healthcare, its obligations focus on the need to ensure information to patients on their rights and procedures to receiving cross-border healthcare and, importantly, to make available a medical follow-up when it proves necessary.

V. Implementation of the Directive: Lack of Clarity and Fragmentation

The deadline for transposition of the Directive 2011/24 into Member States' legislation was 25 October 2013. Following Article 20 of the Directive, the Commission submitted a report in September 2015 to the European Parliament and to the Council on the operation of the Directive in the first years of its implementation.[30] Together with the report, other studies were issued monitoring the implementation and performance of the Directive.[31] Because of a generalised lack of compliance with the deadline of transposition, the Commission had to launch infringement proceedings against 26 Member States on the grounds of late or incomplete notifications of the transposition measures. In July 2015 four infringement procedures for incomplete transposition remained open. However, currently, all Member States seem to have complied with the obligation of transposition,[32] while the Commission is assessing whether this process has been conducted correctly.

The Commission report of 2015 shows a relatively low level of requests through this route across Member States, so it will be several years before we can have a real sense of how it is working on the ground. The relatively late transposition, together with the complexity of the procedure, may partially explain the low level of requests for this route.

[30] *Commission report on the operation of Directive 2011/24/EU on the application of patients' rights in cross-border healthcare*, 4 September 2015, COM (2015) 421 final. Subsequent reports on the functioning of the Directive will have to be released every three years.

[31] *Evaluative Study on the Cross-border Healthcare Directive* (2011/24/EU) (EC, 2015); *Member State data on cross-border healthcare following Directive 2011/24/EU* (EC, 2015); *Summary Report: Cross-border Healthcare: Main Conclusions and Recommendations Arising from the EPF Series of Regional Conferences-2014* (EPF, 2015).

[32] In this regard, it is important to emphasise that all NCPs have been set up across the Member States of the EU.

It is evident that Directive 2011/24 presented the quite difficult goal of making compatible the respect for the very different domestic financial balances of Member States' national healthcare systems (in particular, their territorial solidarity and financial sustainability), with principles of free movement and medical tourism between Member States. As regards some of the critical points of the Directive that generated a very high degree of friction in its drafting process (in particular, the scope of prior authorisation system or reimbursement), the Member States' interest in retaining substantive steering capacity certainly prevailed, to the detriment of a further expansion in the construction of a transnational medical space. At the same time, however, the new regulatory framework for cross-border healthcare mobility has arguably fostered the generation of more objective criteria, furthering the possibilities of harmonisation and 'positive integration' that the Directive aims at. In particular, as regards the codification of a set of patients' rights, the literature underlines the important potentiality of such rights as a step forward for patients seeking healthcare across the borders, but also for the patients receiving healthcare in their own Member State of affiliation.[33]

Additionally, it has to be taken into account that, while the adoption of the Directive ended the EU-level decision process, it represented the start of the implementation process, where 'regulation meets the national boundaries of welfare and stands as it ultimate test'.[34] In light of these questions, the following are some remarks regarding the new scenario triggered by the Directive's implementation, from the perspective of its potential and limitations to construct a cross-border social sharing on healthcare in the EU.

A. CJEU and the Directive

As the process of implementation develops in time, it will be interesting to assess the ways in which the existence of the Directive may shape, even indirectly, the CJEU's development of its own jurisprudence.[35] In this regard, Hatzopoulos and Hervey claim that from 2010, in the wake of the proposed Directive, the CJEU jurisprudence started to downgrade the 'revolutionary' scope of its previous rulings in favour of patients' rights, in order to align to the more restrictive Directive terms' on crucial questions.[36] The confirmation or alteration of the trend of progressive 'adjustment' of the CJEU jurisprudence to the Directive, will much depend on the subsequent approaches of the CJEU once the Directive's implementation gets to a more advanced stage.

[33] Sauter (n 28) at 121–22; Quinn and Hert (n 21) at 23–24, 41.

[34] See N Vasev and K Vrangæk, 'Transposition and National-Level Resources: Introducing the Cross-Border Healthcare Directive in Eastern Europe' (2014) 37(4) *West European Politics* 694.

[35] GI Cohen, *Patients with Passports: Medical Tourism, Law, and Ethics* (Oxford, Oxford University Press, 2015) 197.

[36] V Hatzopoulos and T Hervey, 'Coming into Line: the EU Court Softens on Cross-border' (2013) 8(1) *Health Economics, Policy and Law* 2–3.

Nevertheless, a relatively recent decision of the CJEU suggests that it may not have completely stepped down from its proactive stance, insofar as it applied an incisive understanding informed by a 'patient-centred' or 'needs-based' approach on a crucial concept for the articulation of healthcare provision in another Member State: the (im)possibility to provide a medical treatment in due time in the Member State of residence. In particular, this question was discussed in the *Petru* case in the framework of a preliminary ruling on the interpretation of the authorisation in the social security coordination on cross-border healthcare,[37] which involved a Romanian citizen who underwent a cardiovascular operation in Germany, while Romanian authorities refused to reimburse this treatment in the belief that this treatment could be provided in her own country within a reasonable period of time. The domestic court referred to the CJEU the question of whether the lack of medicines, basic medical supplies and infrastructure means could be equated with a situation in which the necessary medical treatment cannot be provided. The Court held that prior authorisation cannot be refused where the lack of medication, basic medical supplies and infrastructure, underlies the impossibility for hospital care to be provided in good time in the insured person's Member State of residence. Therefore, the CJEU linked for the first time the interpretation of the notion of 'timely available treatment condition' with absence of medicines and medical supply in the Member State, furthering this way the patient mobility concept in the EU.

B. Prior Authorisation

In coherence with the optional nature of the system of prior authorisation, a few Member States have not implemented (yet) such a system (ie the Czech Republic, Estonia, the Netherlands, Finland, Norway and Sweden). The rest of the Member States have done so, although following very different approaches. In particular, the majority of the Member States that require a prior authorisation, either just reproduce the terms of the Directive on this point (ie without further specification of the treatments that fall under the 'overnight stay' or the 'specialised care' criteria), or provide a non-exhaustive list of the specific medical categories.[38] An additional source of uncertainty derives from contexts where medical treatments imply an 'overnight hospital accommodation' in one Member State, but not in another. The Directive states that only in cases of treatments that require overnight stay in the home state, prior authorisation could be justified. But according to the Commission, some Member States wrongly relate that criterion to the way treatment is provided in the Member State of treatment.[39] At the same time, the fact

[37] See Case C-268/13 *Elena Petru v Romanian National Health Insurance Agency* [2014].

[38] 14 Member States in total, *Commission report on the operation of Directive* (n 27) at 4–5; W Palm, 'The Cross-border Care Directive: Implementation Status' (2016) 22(1) *Eurohealth* 22.

[39] *Commission report on the operation of Directive* (n 27) at 5.

that the Directive does not require that its information be provided in languages other than the official language(s) of the Member State of affiliation, may entail a further obstacle for the facilitation of cross-border mobility.

In view of this, and at the current early stage of implementation, the Commission's specific concerns on legal certainty on this question in the Directive drafting process, appear to have been justified. In the first place, the lack of specific information on the medical treatments subjected to authorisation seems to stand in direct breach with the obligation requested to Member States to make publicly available which healthcare is subject to prior authorisation. In the second place, in more substantive terms, despite the fact that the Directive restrained Member States' power to make the reimbursement of cross-border care subject to prior authorisation to certain cases (ie care that is subject to planning requirements and involves either overnight hospital stay or the use of highly specialised and cost-intensive medical infrastructure or equipment), the current state of the implementation demonstrates that many Member States are still maintaining comprehensive prior authorisation systems opened to general, wide and unspecified criteria.[40]

In relation with this last point, there is one question that further evidences the degree of uncertainty for patients in key questions of cross-border care mobility. Specifically, the Directive includes a fourth exemption to grant authorisation to those cases 'when healthcare can be provided within the Member State of affiliation within a time which is medically justifiable' (Article 8.6). As a consequence, wrongful denials of authorisation are linked here to a very undefined, and potentially small, category of cases where services are available at home but unduly delayed, which seems to excessively restrict the patients' rights.[41] This normative framework may entail not only a direct threat to transparency and legal certainty, but could also lead us to question the added value in terms of new rights on cross-border mobility established by the Directive, vis-à-vis the coordination route (EC) No 883/2004. In particular, in the social security coordination route, mobility on healthcare is granted as a right if two conditions are verified via authorisation (ie similar health service at home and undue delay), whereas in the framework of the Directive 2011/24, when the undue delay in the medical provision cannot be verified, the Member State of affiliation is allowed to decide to refuse prior authorisation. However, so far, this reason for refusal has been, by far, the most frequently one alleged by the Member States out of the several cases included in the Directive.[42] Furthermore, the Commission has confirmed that most of the Member States that count on a system of prior authorisation, albeit keeping formally distinct procedures of application, apply the same criteria for both EC

[40] Palm (n 38) at 21.
[41] Cohen (n 35) at 196; Quinn and De Hert (n 21) at 11–12.
[42] *Member State data on cross-border healthcare following Directive* (n 31) at 16.

coordination and the Directive.[43] This state of the question not only deepens the confusion and lack of clarity of rights for patients as regards the two different procedures, but also, more importantly, seems to dilute in practice the scope of prior authorisation and the limits of refusal thereof, as established in the Directive.

However, while it is true that the aggravated state of fragmentation on the national approaches in the implementation of the scope of prior authorisation may be due, to some extent, to a certain inaccuracy of an embryonic stage of development of such a complex matter, there are, however, structural concepts in the Directive that inevitably *institutionalise* a very high level of fragmentation and asymmetry across the systems. These are, for instance, the open category of specialised medical treatments subject to the prior authorisation and the wide set of reasons for refusal of the authorisation.[44] Such a scenario of national heterogeneity may impact negatively on the creation of conditions to foster a minimally uniform space where patients can exercise an equal core of entitlements on their right to cross-border healthcare.

There are, obviously, structural obstacles to further the cross-border space related to the *sui generis* nature and constitutional limits of the EU 'welfare' space. In this context, literature has shown how transposition strategies have largely been informed by resources and financial balance considerations, which have led some countries to incorporate more protectionist elements in the face of logical concerns over highly priced treatments.[45] It has been pointed out, for instance, wide concerns over the control and potential costs of access abroad to private health providers that do not have a contract with the respective national Department of Health.[46] Additionally, very importantly, the fact that reimbursement is only up to the level of coverage at the Member State of affiliation entails access inequality for patients of those Member States where prices for medical treatments are undervalued and not determined according to market principles.[47] Clearly, asymmetric financial conditions of Member States correlate to the varying degrees (and nature) of the challenges that the implementation of the Directive may entail for the sustainability of each health system.

In particular, in the context of austerity times which have impacted unequally on the financial conditions of Member States where welfare state robustness widely differ, together with the fragmentation that informs key questions of the Directive, it is difficult not to agree with the claim that this Directive may just reproduce or

[43] Y Jorens and J De Coninck, *Reply to an Ad Hoc Request for Comparative Analysis of National Legislations: Administrative Procedures for Cross-border Healthcare* (FreSsco, European Commission 2015) 6–9.

[44] *Evaluative Study on the Cross-border Healthcare Directive* (n 31) at 132.

[45] See Vasev and Vrangæk (n 34); H Ricardo 'Cross-border Healthcare Directive: Assessing Stakeholders' Perspectives in Poland and Portugal' (2016) 120 *Health Policy* 369–76.

[46] ibid, 371–74.

[47] Vasev and Vrangæk (n 34) at 703.

mirror the socio-economic unequal points of departure of each Member State, probably representing better conditions for certain Member States' patients, but narrow improvements for the majority of their counterparts.[48]

VI. Conclusion

The adoption of Directive 2011/24 and its implementation by Member States have given rise to interesting legal and policy-related questions. The Directive seems to reproduce a prevailing pattern in the *welfare* construction of the EU, according to which the 'positive integration' would be reactive to the asymmetry created by a first stage of intensive 'negative integration'. In the case of EU cross-border healthcare, the CJEU jurisprudence articulated the freedom of movement of services as the legal basis for the provision of a social right, involving financial commitments of two different countries (ie country of treatment and country of affiliation). The primary goal of the Directive was to facilitate access to cross-border healthcare by clarifying patients' rights through a normative framework that was structured in line with the principles established by the CJEU case law on patient mobility.

One of the most remarkable achievements of the Directive is the codification of a new set of patients' rights, which will benefit both patients seeking healthcare across the borders and also those receiving healthcare in their own Member State of affiliation. In particular, the national citizens and cross-border patients will be entitled to transparent and comparable information on healthcare providers, standards and guidelines on quality and safety and complaints procedures. However, the low level of request that so far has been experienced on the route established in the Directive evidences the complexity of the legal situation and the need to improve clarity in the differentiation of the two distinct regimes for cross-border healthcare (ie the Directive and the social security coordination route), in order to allow patients to be aware of their rights.

Concerns of the Member States over the financial balance and sustainability of their own health systems underlie the legal description of key concepts of the Directive on cross-border care (eg category of specialised medical treatments subject to the prior authorisation and the wide set of reasons for refusal of the authorisation) in an open, flexible and undefined fashion. The implementation status in the wake of this regulatory framework shows a very high level of fragmentation and asymmetry across the systems. However, the current state of national heterogeneity and variations in the specific transposition, transparency and interpretation of the articulation of cross-border healthcare mobility is so emphasised, at least at this early stage of implementation, that it threatens to dilute the effectiveness of the patients' rights mobility and weaken the general effect of the Directive.

[48] ibid, 707.

Undoubtedly, this scenario mirrors the basic tensions inherently linked to the 'welfare construction' in the EU. In this context, questions about the healthcare services to which citizens are entitled, the mechanisms used to finance and deliver that healthcare, such as the extent to which it is appropriate to rely on market mechanisms and competitive pressures to manage health systems, remained in the Directive in the decisional sphere of the national context. Nevertheless, in order to ensure the practicability of the patients' rights to access a safe and high-quality cross-border healthcare context as agreed in the Directive, further efforts would be required to enhance the convergence on both the key criteria of cross-border healthcare and the set of operating principles that are shared across health systems in the EU.

7

Godot is Finally Coming? The Great Convergence of Services Markets within the EU

PANAGIOTIS DELIMATSIS*

I. Introduction

The European Union is an ongoing, dynamic and multi-faceted experiment, which via deepening integration and widening its membership, has reached ever-increasing levels of integration within a diverse set of legal traditions and values.[1] The European recipe centered on market integration as a means of achieving broader economic, and ultimately political, goals.[2] What rose as the European Economic Community from a devastated Europe after WWII gradually evolved into an area where closer forms of integration were tested, with varying degrees of success.

Continuously feeding the level of interconnectedness of the European economies would create pressures for further integration from industries and interest groups.[3] Thus, integration within Europe, in accordance with Jean Monnet's vision,

* For useful insights and comments, I would like to thank the participants in the conference on 'the 60th anniversary of the Treaty of Rome – EU and Global Perspectives', 26–27 May 2017 in Hong Kong, China. Remaining errors are of the author's alone. Contact: p.delimatsis@uvt.nl.

[1] The European Union is the outcome of a series of subsequent treaties among several European countries. What started as a European Economic Community (EEC) among six European countries in 1957, evolved into a European Community with the Merger Treaty in 1967, and later into a European Union with the entry into force of the Treaty of Maastricht in 1993, which co-existed with the European Community in a so-called three-pillar structure. The Treaty of Lisbon, which entered into force in December 2009 and is the most recent amendment of the EU constitutive treaties, provides for the abolition of the three-pillar structure. Thus, the Community ceased to exist and is succeeded, for all practical purposes, by the European Union, which nowadays comprises 28 Member States.

[2] See the speech of the former Belgian Prime Minister, Paul-Henri Spaak at the *Chambre des Représentants*, 14 June 1961. See also the Lisbon judgment by the German Constitutional Court: BVerfG, 2 BvE 2/08 vom 30.6.2009, para 7.

[3] F Jacobs, 'The Evolution of the European Legal Order' (2004) 41 *Common Market Law Review* 303, at 304.

had to be conceived as technocratic, elite-led gradualism, along with corporatist-style engagement of affected interests, thereby creating pressures for 'more Europe' to increase prosperity internally[4] but also to become a compelling power at the international level.[5]

Market integration became a significant, overarching objective which was actively served by the European Court of Justice (ECJ; now Court of Justice of the European Union – CJEU), notably via the doctrine of *effet utile* or teleological interpretation of the provisions enshrined in the Treaties. These interpretations, often driven by an overarching vision of the EU as a single marketplace,[6] amounted to a progressive market manifesto.[7]

This narrative was built on the idea of an internal market[8] whereby products and factors of production could move freely in conditions of undistorted competition. This constitutional core of the European integration project was indeed exemplified in the promotion of the four internal market freedoms (goods, services, persons, capital). In subsequent years, the freedoms have been gradually upgraded and recognised as fundamental, a status virtually equivalent to fundamental rights,[9] against which fundamental freedoms should be weighed and balanced.[10] This was a very important judicial backing of the attempt made by the European Commission to promote the mobility of factors of production across the EU.

Against this background, this chapter focuses on regulatory convergence in the service sector within the EU and assesses the impact of the adoption and implementation of the Services Directive[11] towards market liberalisation in services.

[4] This theory has been framed as the neofunctionalist theory of European integration. See Paul Craig, 'The Nature of the Community: Integration, Democracy, and Legitimacy' in Paul Craig and Gráinne de Búrca (eds), *The Evolution of EU Law* (Oxford, Oxford University Press, 1999) 3–7.

[5] cf James Rogers, 'From "Civilian Power" to "Global Power": Explicating the European Union's "Grand Strategy" Through the Articulation of Discourse Theory' (2009) 47(4) *Journal of Common Market Studies* 831.

[6] cf Case 8/74, *Procureur du Roi v Dassonville*, ECLI:EU:C:1974:82; also Case 24/68, *Commission v Italy*, ECLI:EU:C:1969:29.

[7] G Davies, 'Trust and Mutual Recognition in the Services Directive' in I Lianos and O Odudu (eds), *Regulating Trade in Services in the EU and the WTO: Trust, Distrust and Economic Integration* (Cambridge, Cambridge University Press, 2011) 99, at 103.

[8] For the sake of simplicity, the terms 'single market', 'internal market' and 'common market' are used interchangeably here. For the nuances, see, generally, Catherine Barnard, *The Substantive Law of the EU – The Four Freedoms* 5th edn (Oxford, Oxford University Press, 2016) 9.

[9] The Court has invariably used terms such as 'fundamental freedom', 'one of the fundamental principles of the Treaty', a 'fundamental Community provision' or 'one of the foundations of the Community' to describe the significance of the four freedoms. See Peter Oliver and Wulf-Henning Roth, 'The Internal Market and the Four Freedoms' (2004) 41 *Common Market Law Review* 407.

[10] See also C-438/05, *The International Transport Workers' Federation and the Finnish Seamen's Union* ('*Viking Line*') ECLI:EU:C:2007:772.

[11] Directive 2006/123/EC of the European Parliament and of the Council of 12 December 2006 on Services in the Internal Market [2006] OJ L 376/36. For an early detailed account of the Directive, see Catherine Barnard, 'Unravelling the Services Directive' (2008) 45 *Common Market Law Review* 323; also M Klamert, *Services Liberalization in the EU and the WTO – Concepts, Standards and Regulatory Approaches* (Cambridge, Cambridge University Press, 2015) 174ff.

With all its imperfections, the EU single market for services has grown substantially even amidst the recent financial crisis. Such a finding applies to both intra- and extra-EU trade in services. However, in the case of the latter, we are yet to witness a concerted effort on the side of the EU as a whole to advance a global EU strategy in services trade.[12]

The present chapter advances three arguments: first, other than EU primary law, the Services Directive constitutes a powerful legal instrument in the CJEU's arsenal to pursue the objectives enshrined in the TFEU provisions relating to the freedom of establishment and that of services. Second, the implementation of the Services Directive has transparency-enhancing benefits which will have important trust-building effects. This will in turn allow for important compensatory measures of formal and informal nature that will likely facilitate mobility in the medium run. Third, the Services Directive, in its own right, cannot serve as an integration vector of the single market for services in the short run. Rather, its effectiveness will depend on the Member States' discretion and the capacity of public and private regulators to build trust among them amidst remaining regulatory divergence at the EU level.

II. The Economic Importance of Services for the EU

Within the EU, services trade appears to occur despite limited traction to further liberalisation in recent years. In the period 2004–14, the EU exports of services have doubled to exceed EUR 700 billion. The EU is the largest regional trade agreement, representing a share of 34 per cent of global trade in 2017. The block saw a double-digit increase of goods exports, totaling USD 5.9 trillion in 2017. An equally strong performance was recorded in the area of services exports, after a year of stagnation in 2016.

About 60 per cent of total trade in services takes place among EU Member States (ie intra-EU), which appears to be quite substantial but is significantly lower than intra-EU trade in goods (about 70 per cent), notably if one takes into account the importance of geographical proximity for certain services. Since 2010, extra-EU trade in services increased at a relatively rapid pace, with growth peaking at 11.3 per cent in 2015, to finally reach a moderate 2.4 per cent in 2016 (relative to 2015). In the period 2000–16, the EU-28 net surplus of services increased about 10-fold.

The EU-28 is currently the biggest trader of services in the world, accounting for over one fourth of global trade in services (excluding intra-EU trade).[13] In the period 2010–16, the EU has consistently recorded significant surpluses

[12] See also P Delimatsis, 'The Evolution of the EU External Trade Policy in Services – CETA, TTIP and TiSA after Brexit' (2017) 20(3) *Journal of International Economic Law* 583–625.

[13] See WTO, World Trade Statistical Review 2018, p. 128.

in services trade, exceeding EUR 100 billion every year. However, Eurostat statistics suggest that extra-EU trade in services is more concentrated among the EU's main trading nations than it is the case for intra-EU trade in services, suggesting that EU's globally present companies are concentrated in a handful of EU Member States, whereas certain EU Member States trade predominantly intra-EU.

Services account for two-thirds of total employment in the EU, while the growth-generating effects of services liberalisation are well-documented.[14] Services make nowadays about 40 per cent of the value of EU exported goods. Such intermingling also has important repercussions for intra-EU employment: companies supplying ancillary services like transport or logistics account for about one third of the jobs generated by exports in manufacturing.

If one considers the beneficial effects of services in enabling trade in manufacturing (coined as the 'servicification of manufacturing'), then more attention to services liberalisation can have widespread positive spillovers to the competitiveness of firms.[15] Such liberalisation would most likely also further boost the within-firm shift toward services in manufacturing services.[16] More generally, the growing interpenetration of services and goods in the supply and demand cycles means that any policy seeking the optimal allocation of productive resources must now take into consideration regulatory issues in both goods and services and their intermingling.[17]

However, much of 'services revolution' within the EU is not for the near future. Despite representing about 70 per cent of EU GDP, cross-border services account for some five per cent of EU GDP.

This disappointing result from an economic viewpoint lies in the extant sectoral diversity in services. Several service sectors such as health or education services are essentially regulated at the EU Member State level, while for several services such as tourism, distribution, construction, engineering and consultancy, certification and testing, no comprehensive internal market policy exists. Arguably, such fragmentation affects the productivity of the EU, which has declined significantly since the 1990s. This observation also applies at the firm level, whereby some frontier firms lead the race while the remaining firms lag behind, as the diffusion

[14] Inter alia, Aaditya Mattoo and others, 'Measuring Services Trade Liberalization and Its Impact on Economic Growth: An Illustration' (2006) 21(1) *Journal of Economic Integration* 64–98.

[15] For a literature review, see M Lodefalk, 'Servicification of Firms and Trade Policy Implications' (2017) 16(1) *World Trade Review* 59–83.

[16] See M Crozet and E Milet, 'The Servitization of French Manufacturing Firms' in L Fontagné and A Harrison (eds), *The Factory-Free Economy – Outsourcing, Servitization, and the Future of Industry* (Oxford, Oxford University Press, 2017) 111–35.

[17] P Delimatsis, *International Trade in Services and Domestic Regulations – Necessity, Transparency, and Regulatory Diversity* (Oxford, Oxford University Press, 2007) 62–63. For this intermingling, compare C-390/99, *Canal Satélite Digital* ECLI:EU:C:2002:34, paras 31–33. In the WTO context, see Appellate Body Report, China – Publications and Audiovisual Products. See also A Antimiani and L Cernat, 'Liberalizing Global Trade in Mode 5 Services: How Much is it Worth?', (2017), http://trade.ec.europa.eu/doclib/docs/2017/july/tradoc_155844.pdf, accessed 20 July 2019.

of knowledge and technology is not sufficient to cover for the difference.[18] In addition, administrative complexity and costs remain high and disproportionately hurt small and medium enterprises (SMEs), although many of these costs should be gradually phased out as the EU Services Directive is enforced.[19]

To be sure, the limited cross-border activity contradicts the ever-increasing role that services play for the smooth functioning of markets. Services are a crucial component of the information society networks on which relations between producers and consumers depend. Instantaneous interactive communication permits transactions in an increasing number of services to occur at the same time but in different places. This allows overcoming the previously indispensable requirement of proximity between consumer and service supplier and thus increases the tradability of services across borders and jurisdictions, calling for a more efficient reaction in regulatory-making terms from the side of the regulators at a cross-national level.

III. Implementing the Services Directive

A. The Need for a Legislative Instrument to Regulate Services Across Sectors

The Single Market Programme (SMP) set out by the European Commission in its 1985 White Paper 'Completing the Internal Market',[20] and the Single European Act (SEA) of 1986, formally completed in 1992, aimed at the removal of all barriers to trade and foreign direct investment (FDI) in the EU. While the SMP has improved competition, monetary integration, social protection and common policies relating to external action to address global challenges, several barriers to intra-EU trade in services remained virtually intact.

In its report on 'The State of the Internal Market for Services' in 2002,[21] the Commission identified the many challenges of completing the internal market for services and paved the way for the adoption of the EU Services Directive. The Directive was the legislative reaction to what has been considered as a self-defeating stalemate in regulating trade in services at the EU level.

[18] D Andrews, C Criscuolo and P Gal, 'The Best versus the Rest: The Global Productivity Slowdown, Divergence Across Firms And the Role of Public Policy', OECD Productivity Working Papers, No 5, OECD Publishing, 2016.

[19] Directive 2006/123/EC of the European Parliament and of the Council of 12 December 2006 on Services in the Internal Market [2006] OJ L 376/36.

[20] See European Commission, 'Completing the internal market', *White Paper*, COM(85)310 final, June 1985.

[21] European Commission, 'The State of the Internal Market for Services', COM(2002) 441 final, 30 July 2002.

However, the adoption of the Directive was only the beginning. Indeed, in his 2010 report commissioned by the European Commission, Mario Monti lamented that, in the case of services, the EU was still in a phase of 'market construction' that requires the abolition of barriers to cross-border activity, the dismantlement of national administrative and technical barriers and overcoming corporatist resistance.[22] Complex regulatory barriers have replaced physical and technical barriers, thereby diminishing the possibilities for a genuine, integrated internal market for services.[23] Furthermore, former monopolies in certain sectors such as postal services or energy utilities remained significant sources of market friction. In addition, Member States consistently fail to transpose promptly to national law EU legislation, notably in areas such as transport, finance and energy.

Both the Commission's work and the Monti Report confirmed the findings of previous studies on services trade: in the absence of tariffs charged at the border, services supply suffers from regulatory impediments that restrict their supply notably at the cross-border level. Services are vulnerable to this type of impediment: they are intangible, have limited storability, and are above all heterogeneous with limited possibilities of mass production. In addition, considerations of quality and consumer protection, the 'holy grail' of every law and regulatory measures governing services, are closely intertwined with the characteristics, education, qualifications or experience of individual service provider as well as the domestic preferences and traditions of each EU Member State.

These characteristics of services regulations increase transaction costs and can undermine any effort to achieve efficient outcomes when regulating this highly heterogeneous sector of the economy. Furthermore, numerous studies have identified the deadweight losses generated by existing barriers relating, for instance, to restrictive licensing conditions or to the lack of recognition of professional qualifications.[24] Additionally, self-regulated activities are routinely administered by the corresponding professional bodies which take decisions that can severely affect the supply of services in the 'shadow of the law'. Sometimes the rules that such bodies adopt can go against the spirit of state legislation or raise entry barriers aiming at the protection of incumbents whose income is maximised if access to a given activity is restricted.

While the results of integration efforts in previous years were mixed, it would be reductive to say that no progress towards more integration in the area of services was achieved. The liberalisation of various service sectors such as finance or infrastructure services produced tangible results, albeit at varying speed across

[22] Mario Monti, 'A New Strategy for the Single Market at the Service of Europe's Economy and Society', *Report to the President of the European Commission (Monti Report)* (2010), 37, http://ec.europa.eu/DocsRoom/documents/15501/attachments/1/translations, accessed 20 July2019.

[23] This is a phenomenon observed in other developed countries as well. See S Miroudot, J Sauvage and B Shepherd, 'Measuring the Cost of International Trade in Services' (2013) 12(4) *World Trade Review* 719–35.

[24] See Centre for Strategy and Evaluation Services, 'Barriers to Trade in Business Services – Final Report', commissioned by the European Commission (2001).

Member States. Again, harmonisation and mutual recognition efforts in the area of business services, and notably professional services, have met with limited overall success to date within the EU.[25]

Furthermore, despite the financial crisis, services are now central in the political and legislative agenda of the EU institutions, notably in the aftermath of the Monti Report in 2010 that recognised the important value-added role of further integration in services within the EU. In this regard, the promulgation and implementation of the two Single Market Acts and their accompanying measures,[26] which calls for achieving a single market notably in the areas of business and professional services, along with the full implementation of the Services Directive, shall significantly contribute to the pursuit of Europe's 2020 strategy objectives for smart, sustainable and inclusive growth.[27]

B. The Services Directive – A Pyrrhic Victory of Services Markets Integration

The core aim of launching the Services Directive has been to achieve more effective regulation and reap the economy-wide efficiency gains from more competitively supplied services within the Union. Earlier, the European Commission's Proposal for a Services Directive (hereinafter 'the Proposal')[28] recognised the importance of trust in the achievement and the smooth functioning of a genuine internal market for services. The lack of trust reveals the dominance of 'thinking national' mentality and is translated into protectionist interests that foreclose or impede foreign competition; negate the possibility of comparison; and thus dampen the incentives for domestic service suppliers to improve their services.[29] In turn, such lack of trust has a negative impact on prices and thus consumer welfare within the EU.

The tale of the EU Services Directive reveals how even within highly integrated areas such as the EU, services remain hostage to regulations impeding their supply. The timing of the Services Directive also was somewhat unfortunate, as it was associated with fears expressed in several Member States of uncontrolled flows of (especially lower-skilled) worker-migrants from the new Eastern European

[25] However, the consolidation of various directives relating to professional qualifications through the Directive 2005/36 did have a beneficial impact in the EU market for professional services and paved the way for further integration in recent times.

[26] See European Commission Communication, 'Single Market Act', COM(2011) 206 final, 13 April 2011, p 11, and EC Communication, 'Single Market Act II', COM(2012) 573 final, p 13.

[27] See European Commission Communication, 'Europe 2020 – A strategy for smart, sustainable and inclusive growth', COM(2010 2020 final, 3 march 2010, pp 20–21.

[28] European Commission, 'Proposal for a Directive of the European Parliament and of the Council on Services in the Internal Market', COM(2004) 2, 13 January 2004.

[29] For the positive effects of mutual trust more generally, see the seminal work by Francis Fukuyama, *Trust: The Social Virtues and the Creation of Prosperity* (New York, Free Press, 1995).

Member States to the old EU15 Member States. Shortly after it was presented by the Commission, the Directive became the 'legislative hot potato of the early twenty-first century'[30] and political resistance mounted rapidly.[31]

It is for this reason that one of the major tools to achieve full market integration in the area of services, ie the country of origin principle, did not ultimately see the light of the day. Economists took issue with this important text in the draft Directive. Static analyses had previously found that the removal of the country of origin principle alone could deprive the EU of an additional EUR 2–4 billion per annum. This represents up to 10 per cent of the expected welfare gains flowing from the adoption of the Directive.[32]

Even in the absence of the country of origin principle, several recitals of the Services Directive reveal its ambition to complete the internal market for services though a mix of various measures designed to ensure a high degree of legal integration by means of, inter alia, harmonisation regarding specific aspects of services-specific regulation.[33] The Services Directive takes a horizontal approach based on the understanding that, while ubiquitous and diverse, several service sectors call for regulatory intervention to pursue a set of legitimate public policy objectives which are common across sectors, such as consumer protection, the integrity of the profession or ensuring the quality of the service.

The Directive has a broad scope in that it aims to outlaw any requirement which may negatively affect access to or the exercise of a service activity.[34] The objective of the Directive is to enable both service suppliers and consumers *qua* service recipients to benefit from the fundamental freedoms guaranteed in Articles 49 and 56 TFEU, that is, the freedom of establishment and the freedom to provide services.[35] In this respect, the Directive consolidates previous CJEU case law on related issues.[36]

While several sectors such as gambling, audiovisual, telecommunication services or financial services are excluded from the scope of the Directive, it still

[30] For an early detailed account of the Directive, see Barnard (n 11) 323; also Klamert (n 11) 174ff.

[31] The lack of early involvement of critical stakeholders may have been one of the reasons for such resistance: see J Loder, 'The Lisbon Strategy and the Politicization of EU Policy-making: The Case of the Services Directive' (2011) 18 *Journal of European Public Policy* 566.

[32] See Copenhagen Economics, 'The Economic Importance of the Country of Origin Principle in the Proposed Services Directive' (2005) 9. In other studies, the negative effects of the non-incorporation of the country of origin principle appear to be even greater. See R de Bruyn and others, 'The Trade-induced Effects of the Services Directive and the Country of Origin Principle' (CPB document no. 108, February 2006) 42.

[33] Cf Joined Cases C-360/15 and C-31/16, *X*, ECLI:EU:C:2018:44, para 106. See also V Hatzopoulos, *Regulating Services in the European Union* (Oxford, Oxford University Press, 2012) 257ff.

[34] M Klamert, 'Way to Go? – More on the Services Directive and the Fundamental Freedoms' (2009) 64 *Zeitschrift für öffentliches Recht* 335.

[35] The Directive provides that suppliers already established in another Member State cannot be prevented from providing their services in a given Member State on the basis that they do not have an establishment in that Member State (Art 16:2(a)).

[36] See also P Delimatsis, 'From *Sacchi* to *Uber*: 60 Years of Services Liberalization, Ten Years of the Services Directive in the EU' (2019) 37 *Yearbook of European Law* 188.

applies to business services and covers, inter alia, most of the regulated professions as well as services of general economic interest (SGEI) within the EU, with the exclusion of non-economic services of general interest.[37] The latter category covers activities which, in themselves, are directly and specifically connected with the exercise of official authority, which requires a sufficient qualified exercise of prerogatives outside the general law, privileges of official power or powers of coercion.[38]

Furthermore, the Directive confirms the horizontal direct effect of EU law in this field, that is, that private action by professional associations when they self-regulate their activities or other restrictive measures taken by private parties are subject to the obligations laid down in the Directive. Crucially in this respect, the Directive adopts a sweeping definition of the term 'requirements' to cover obligations, prohibitions, conditions or limits imposed by law, administrative practice, judicial decisions or rules of professional bodies of self-regulatory nature.[39]

Other than codifying existing case law, the Directive validates the difficulty that Member States will have to justify any discriminatory measures and adduce evidence that proves that they comply with the principles of necessity and proportionality. In addition, the Directive confirms the view that in the case of services the home state is the primary regulator and thus, contrary to what happens under the freedom of establishment, the right to intervene in the case of the freedom to provide services is narrower.

In addition, the Directive calls for the creation of single contact points for service providers, the establishment or maintenance of electronic procedures, the promotion of the quality of the services supplied and the establishment of effective administrative cooperation among the Member States so that infrastructural heterogeneity is sufficiently tackled. The Directive also includes a convergence programme, which inter alia promotes the idea of creating pan-European codes of conduct in professional services.[40]

The Services Directive is widely acknowledged as a major step towards liberalisation and market integration but also the top-down creation of a culture of administrative cooperation. In the medium-term, this should be expected to lead to better regulation and the abolition of remaining barriers,[41] the modernisation

[37] See Joined Cases C-473/17 and C-546/17, *Repsol Butano*, ECLI:EU:C:2019:308, para 43.

[38] See C-397/17, *Kirschstein*, ECLI:EU:C:2019:563, para. 59 (where the Court found that the conferral of masters degrees by a private, for-profit entity under the supervision of and under conditions defined by the public authorities does involve the exercise of official authority).

[39] Art 4:7 of the Directive. See also European Commission (DG Internal Market and Services), 'Handbook on Implementation of the Services Directive' (2007) 16.

[40] See, in more detail, P Delimatsis, 'The EU Services Directive and the Mandate for the Creation of Professional Codes of Conduct' in I Lianos and O Odudu (eds), *Regulating Trade in Services in the EU and the WTO: Trust, Distrust and Economic Integration* (Cambridge, Cambridge University Press, 2011).

[41] Once again, such liberalisation happens in varying pace. For instance, a recent EU Commission's study showed that some of the most sweeping measures to reform domestic services markets were taken in EU Members States which have been subject to economic adjustment programmes after

of bureaucratic practices and the streamlining of administrative procedures that should also prove beneficial to service suppliers originating in EU Member States but also third-country service suppliers. Significant economic benefits across services sectors but also on EU's GDP generally are being reaped as the Directive is implemented voluntarily or through infringement proceedings initiated by the European Commission.[42]

The Directive has led to a regulatory deluge in the wake of its adoption but also after the end of the transposition period.[43] It incorporates obligations for Member States to conduct a screening and self-evaluate their regulations relating to services against EU law, whereas administrative simplification is encouraged or, under certain circumstances, required. EU Member States have, for the most part, introduced one horizontal law in their respective jurisdiction to comply with their obligation to transpose the Directive. Some Member States such as Germany or France have implemented several acts. According to the Directive, all EU Member States have to assess the impact of their legislation at all levels and reconsider domestic rules and measures that are out of proportion to their stated objectives and have negative effects on trade in services.

Shortly before the end of the transposition period, a mutual evaluation process and a performance check exercise took place. The former included a comprehensive evaluation of the regulatory framework that applied to services activities in EU Member States after the implementation of the Directive, in accordance with Article 39 of the Directive. This process was quite revealing as to the existence of remaining barriers to trade in services such as wide use of reserved service activities for certain operators; restrictions on legal form; shareholding requirements; or insurance obligations.[44] Performance checks, on the other hand, allowed for an assessment of the interaction among interrelated EU legislative instruments, including the Services Directive, the E-Commerce Directive and the Professional Qualifications Directive, in three key sectors (construction, business services and tourism).[45]

the financial crisis, that is, Grece, Portugal and Spain. For Greece in particular, the reforms in the period 2012-14 were estimated to increase the Greek GDP by 1.1 per cent in a period of 5–10 years. See European Commission, 'Assessment of the economic impact of the Services Directive: Update of the 2012 study', https://ec.europa.eu/docsroom/documents/13327/attachments/1/translations/en/renditions/pdf, accessed 20 July 2019.

[42] ibid. See also J Monteagudo and others, 'The Economic Impact of the Services Directive: A First Assessment Following Implementation' (2012) *Economic Papers 456*.

[43] See also M Klamert, 'Of Empty Glasses and Double Burdens: Approaches to Regulating the Services Market à propos the Implementation of the Services Directive' (2010) 37(2) *Legal Issues of Economic Integration* 111, at 114.

[44] For the key findings of the mutual evaluation process that took place in 2010, see European Commission Communication, 'Towards a better functioning Single Market for services – building on the results of the mutual evaluation process of the Services Directive', COM(2011) 20 final, 27 January 2011.

[45] See European Commission Staff Working Document on the result of the performance checks of the internal market for services (construction, business services and tourism), SWD/2012/147 final, 8 June 2012.

The Commission adopted a Services package in 2012 to report on the implementation of the Services Directive. While acknowledging the substantial progress made, the Commission identified barriers and restrictive measures that certain Member States maintained although they were prohibited by the Directive.[46] The Commission promised zero tolerance and indeed its strategy ever since has been to bring infringement proceedings against the Member States concerned. In the short run, the Commission identified that restrictions regarding legal form or shareholding did not cease to exist and thus conducted a peer review on this type of restrictions as well as a mutual evaluation of regulated professions as stipulated by the Professional Qualifications Directive.[47]

One of the lessons that the European Commission draws in all documents accompanying the implementation of the Directive was the failure of several Member States to properly assess the proportionality of national measures that affect trade in services but the Directive does not prohibit per se; rather it is for national authorities to assess the consistency with EU law of those (typically non-discriminatory) measures, including residency requirements, economic needs tests or legal form restrictions.

Member States' regulatory authorities have been confronted with significant difficulties in particular when called upon to review cross-border supply of services with a view to addressing double regulatory burdens. Avoiding such burdens would many times entail that the host regulatory authority has the regulatory tools and know-how to assess the equivalence of the home country laws with theirs in order to refrain from imposing similar requirements to service suppliers unnecessarily. Furthermore, this process of implementation review revealed the level of resources and effort needed when entertaining the peer-review and screening processes even in developed-country jurisdictions and the need to use infringement proceedings as a last resort to enforce the letter and spirit of the Directive.

C. The Recent 'Services Package'

In line with the Single Market Acts, the Juncker Commission has further prioritised services liberalisation by launching and implementing its Single Market Strategy in 2015.[48] The Commission emphasised the importance of introducing a 'services passport' for growth-generating sectors such as construction or business.

[46] See European Commission Communication, 'Implementation of the Services Directive – A partnership for new growth in services 2012–2015', COM(2012) 261 final, 8 June 2012; also see the Accompanying Staff Working Document encompassing detailed information on the implementation of the Services Directive, SWD/2012/148 final.

[47] See European Commission Staff Working Document on the outcome of the peer review on legal form, shareholding and tariff requirements under the Services Directive', SWD(2013) 402 final, and Commission Communication on Evaluating national regulations on access to professions, COM(2013) 676 final, both dated 2 October 2013.

[48] See European Commission Communication, 'Upgrading the Single Market: More opportunities for people and business', COM(2015)550 final, 28 October 2015.

In January 2017, the Commission presented three legislative proposals: one relating to a European services e-card (formerly known as 'services passport'), which would be an electronic document of voluntary nature issued by the home Member State of the service suppliers (in casu, construction and business service providers) to show compliance with applicable national rules when expanding their operations to other Member States;[49] a second on a comprehensive and transparent proportionality test to be undertaken prior to adopting or amending national rules on professional services;[50] and a third on improved notification of draft national laws on services allowing for the early filing of concerns regarding incompatibilities between national and EU law.[51] Finally, the Commission published a guidance document on reforming professional services at the domestic level, in particular engineering, legal, accounting, patent agent, real estate agent and tourist guide services.[52]

The implementation of the so-called 'Services package' is currently in full swing. Other than its substantive scope and breadth it also shows the dialectical relationship between the EU Services Directive and the EU legal framework relating to the recognition of professional qualifications with respect to the national regulation of professions. Naturally some requirements continue to fall under both the Professional Qualifications Directive[53] and the Services Directive

[49] European Commission, 'Proposal for a Regulation of the European Parliament and of the Council introducing a European services e-card and related administrative facilities', COM(2016)824 final, 10 January 2017; and 'Proposal for Directive of the European Parliament and of the Council on the legal and operational framework of the European services e-card introduced by [the proposed services e-card] Regulation', COM(2016)/ 823 final, 10 January 2017. The Internal Market Information System (IMI) would be used for the smooth functioning of the European services e-card, according to the Commission's proposal.

[50] European Commission, 'Proposal for a Directive of the European Parliament and of the Council on a proportionality test before adoption of new regulation of professions', COM(2016) 822 final, 10 January 2017.

[51] The proposed Directive would spell out the notification requirements under the Services Directive (see, for instance, Art 15:7 SD): European Commission, 'Proposal for a Directive of the European Parliament and of the Council on the enforcement of the Directive 2006/123/EC on services in the internal market, laying down a notification procedure for authorisation schemes and requirements related to services, and amending Directive 2006/123/EC and Regulation (EU) No 1024/2012 on administrative cooperation through the Internal Market Information System (IMI)', COM(2016)821 final, 10 January 2017.

[52] See European Commission Communication, 'Reform recommendations for regulation in professional services', COM(2016) 820 final, 10 January 2017.

[53] Directive 2005/36/EC on the recognition of professional qualifications [2005] OJ L 255/22 as amended by Directive 2013/55/EU [2013] OJ L 354/132. The latter Directive introduces the concept of EPC, an electronic certificate that proves that the conditions to provide services in a host Member State on a temporary and occasional basis or that professional qualifications for establishment in a host Member State are met. The Implementing Regulation 2015/983 clarifies the professions that can make use of the EPC but also technical matters such as format, documentation requirements, payment modalities, handling of applications or remedies. The EPC is now available for five professions (general care nurses, physiotherapists, pharmacists, real estate agents and mountain guides), thereby creating the first EU-wide fully online procedure for the recognition of qualifications in these professions. It bears mention that the EPC system is complementary and in no way affects the system of automatic or other recognition foreseen in the amended PQD other than diminishing considerably the transaction costs for certain professions. Discussions for extending the EPC to additional professions are ongoing.

(eg requirements relating to legal form or shareholding). Finally, the newly adopted Proportionality Directive[54] would be decisive for the notification to be made by the national authorities according to the Services Directive (which, in turn, would be determined by the new Directive on notification procedures included in the Services package).

D. The First 10 Years of Case Law under the Services Directive

In the early years after the transposition of the Services Directive, a period of judicial unease can be observed. Divergences between the Opinions of the Advocates-General and the Court (typically, in a Grand Chamber format) were not uncommon. More importantly, a clear line of case law faithful to the high level of ambition expressed in the introductory recitals of the Services Directive surfaced and solidified. In this respect, the Court has repeatedly stated that a broad interpretation of concepts enshrined in the Services Directive would be in line with its objective to remove restrictions to establishment and supply of services thereby contributing to the completion of a free and competitive internal market.[55]

Such consolidation occurs whereas at the same time the implementation of the Directive and ensuing actions are in full swing, ranging from benchmarking and mutual evaluation to peer reviews and targeted interventions by the European Commission – more recently, via the services package discussed earlier. In what follows, we take a critical stance vis-à-vis some of the most important clarifications brought forward by the recent jurisprudence and underline the emerging judicial patterns relating to various provisions of the Services Directive.

i. *Putting Advertising-related Restrictions to the Test*

The first case in which the CJEU was called upon to interpret the Services Directive related to a prohibition of canvassing by qualified accountants enshrined in the French Code of professional conduct and ethics of qualified accountants.[56] More specifically, under Article 12 of the Code, unsolicited contact by qualified accountants with third parties with a view to offering them their services was prohibited. The National Association of Qualified Accountants requested the annulment of the French Decree encompassing such a restriction. The Association based its request before the French Conseil d'Etat on the Services Directive and, in particular, its provisions relating to the removal of prohibitions relating to advertising.

[54] Directive 2018/958 on a proportionality test before adoption of new regulation of professions [2018] OJ L 173/25.

[55] See C-179/14, *Commission v Hungary*, para 63.

[56] See C-119/09, *Société fiduciaire nationale d'expertise comptable*, ECLI: EU:C:2011:208.

Generally, the Court is quite allergic to absolute prohibitions of any advertising in professional services even when it examines their compatibility with Article 56 TFEU or other secondary law instruments such as the E-Commerce Directive.[57] However, the task of the CJEU in the French case at issue was everything but easy. This is because Article 24 of the Directive appears to call for the removal of all *total* prohibitions on advertising by regulated professions but remains silent in the case of prohibitions of a given *form* of advertising (such as, in this case, canvassing).

The CJEU first found that, being a form of direct marketing, canvassing comes under the Directive's definition of commercial communication. The more important question, though, was whether the ban on canvassing could be regarded as a *total* prohibition of commercial communication pursuant to Article 24. After noting that the French law prohibits any canvassing, whatever its form, content or means employed, the CJEU ruled that the Directive should be interpreted as covering also those cases of a total prohibition of *a given form* of commercial communications. To substantiate its finding, the CJEU referred to Recital 100 of the Directive which makes clear that the intent of the Directive is to remove prohibitions on one or more forms of commercial communication such as a ban on all advertising in one or more given media.[58] The Court also underscored the importance of canvassing for professionals from other Member States who could use it to enter the French market.

Earlier, the CJEU had clarified that Article 24:2 of the Directive still preserves Members' right to lay down prohibitions relating to the content or methods of commercial communications, provided those rules are justified and proportionate for the purposes of ensuring, inter alia, the professional independence, dignity, integrity or secrecy. Nevertheless, being a total prohibition and not a prohibition relating to the content or methods of advertising, the restriction at issue fell under Article 24:1 and thus no leeway was available for the French government to defend the proportionality of the challenged measure.

In this regard, the Court disagreed with AG Mazak's view that canvassing is not a sufficiently separate form of commercial communication that can be distinguished from advertising but rather a mere method of advertising that should be subject to Article 24:2 of the Directive.[59] In condemning the French measure, the Court also took issue with the AG's ultimate conclusion that the measure not only falls under Article 24:2 but it is also proportionate to the public interest objectives it pursued.

Whereas it seems that both textual and contextual elements do not seem to support the Court's view in this case, the intention of the Court to show its intent to take a hard stance against remaining restrictions falling under the Directive becomes evident. It is submitted, however, that if it is so, then the Court should

[57] See C-339/15, *Vanderborght* (relating to a general and absolute prohibition of any advertising for dentists).

[58] ibid, para 29.

[59] AG Mazak's Opinion, Case C-119/09, ECLI:EU:C:2010:276, para 50.

have engaged in a more thorough discussion of the various relevant provisions, including the proportionality of the measure and the invoked justifications before reaching its final verdict.

ii. The Official Authority Exception and the Dichotomy between Establishment and Services Enshrined in the Services Directive

In the early years since the transposition of the Services Directive, the Court had the opportunity to clarify under which conditions certain restrictions to the freedom to provide services could be justified not based on the primary law exception of services in governmental authority (Article 51 TFEU) but based on the Services Directive.

The first such case arose from three disputes before the Italian *Consiglio di Stato* between Italian public authorities and an Italian company, Rina SpA, in connection with the State-imposed obligation for certification bodies to have their registered office in Italy.[60] The CJEU was requested to rule on, first, whether certification bodies (SOAs) fall outside the scope of the Directive because they exercise official authority pursuant to Article 2:2(i) of the Directive in conjunction with Article 51 TFEU; and, second, whether any of the liberalising provisions of the Directive, including Articles 14–16 would outlaw the requirement for a registered office imposed by Italian law.

The Court quickly dealt with the first question by noting that it answered the question in the negative indirectly in a previous case[61] where it affirmed that SOAs have no decision-making autonomy; they operate under strict State supervision and on conditions of competition, as companies seeking to participate in public works contracts can use the services of a SOA of their choice.[62]

The second question, however, was a rather novel, fundamental question of systemic importance for the interpretation of the Directive: how to classify a requirement to have a registered office in a Member State. The vagueness is partly due to the birth defects of the Services Directive after the abolition of the country of origin principle. It appears that such a requirement could be viewed as coming under Article 14(1), which deals with prohibited requirements, or Article 16 relating to the freedom to provide services.

While at first blush it may appear as inconsequential, the distinction has repercussions for the standard of review by the Court: if the requirement falls under Article 14 of the Directive, this means that it is per se prohibited and no possibility for justification is offered under the Directive. If, on the other hand,

[60] See C-593/13, *Rina Services and Others*, ECLI:EU:C:2015:399.

[61] See C-327/12, *SOA Nazionale Construttori*, ECLI:EU:C:2013:827, paras 28–35.

[62] More recently, the Court found that the activities of vehicle roadworthiness testing centres are not connected with the exercise of official authority, despite the fact that the operators of these centres have the power to take cars off the road in case of safety defects. See C-168/14, *Grupo Itevelesa SL*, ECLI:EU:C.2015:685, para 61.

Article 16 is applicable, then a Member State can justify such a restriction on public policy, public security, public health or environmental grounds provided that the principles of non-discrimination, necessity and proportionality are respected. Importantly, Article 14 is located within the Directive's provisions relating to establishment, whereas Article 16 is the introductory provision relating to services supply.

In *Rina Services*, the Court had to decide whether Article 14 or rather Article 16 should be the leading authority in legally classifying the measure at issue. AG Villalón took the latter view: whereas he admitted that the national measure at issue related to establishment, he also noted that, if properly viewed, the national measure also precluded any certification company established in another Member State from providing certification services in Italy. Thus, in the AG's view, both provisions could be relevant. However, the AG decided to examine the measure only under Article 16:2(a) of the Directive because the national measure constituted an absolute negation of the freedom to provide services.

The Court disagreed once again with the AG's interpretation of the Services Directive *tout court*, taking a stance in favour of the liberalising force of Article 14. Neglecting the AG's argument about the negation effect against the freedom to provide services, the Court noted that the requirement at issue relates to the location of the provider's registered office as laid down in Article 14(1) and in conjunction with Article 14(2), as the measure at stake indirectly prevents multiple establishments.

While this excessive textualism is unsatisfactory in view of the wording of Article 14 (indeed the requirement at stake was not technically based on the location of the registered office but actually *required* establishment), what seems to have played the most important role in the Court's decision was the dichotomy that the Services Directive aims to draw between restrictions relating to the establishment of service providers and those regarding the provision of services in a cross-border manner.[63] However, the Court could still contemplate on the potential challenges of a simultaneous application of both Articles 14 and 16 of the Directive, notably if one takes into account that the Court has previously accepted the simultaneous application of Articles 49 and 56 TFEU.

The Court has yet to clarify fully its intentions as to this issue. Recently, in *Commission v Hungary*,[64] the Court arguably took a different view in the dichotomy between establishment and services as laid down in Articles 14 and 16 of the Directive, respectively. Interestingly, the Court, again in a Grand Chamber format, rejected the Hungarian claim that a national measure requiring establishment cannot fall under both Articles 14 and 16. If this is true, then one wonders why in *Rina Services* the Court did not examine the measure at issue under both Articles 14 and 16.

[63] cf C-593/13, *Rina Services and Others*, para 31.
[64] See C-179/14, *Commission v Hungary*, ECLI:EU:C:2016:108, paras 108ff.

After *Commission v Hungary*, it appears that in cases where domestic measures require establishment, the Court would examine the measure under the obligations laid down in the Directive relating to both establishment and services. It appears that the latter would not be applicable only if the respondent can show that it would, in practice, be impossible for, and of no interest to, a service supplier established in another Member State to provide the relevant service in another Member State without any stable infrastructure there. Here the CJEU seems to require more tangible evidence regarding the violation of the freedom of establishment than mere speculation.

Going back to *Rina Services*, the CJEU has to decide on the possibility for invoking justifications if Article 14 of the Directive is found to be violated. The Court found that no justification can be submitted by the regulating Member State once a violation of Article 14 of the Services Directive is validated. According to the Court, any recourse to primary law (ie Article 52 TFEU) would undermine the ad hoc harmonisation intended by the Services Directive.

The Court underscored that the per se prohibition of Article 14 was intentionally chosen by the EU legislature to ensure the systematic and swift removal of certain restrictions on the freedom of establishment which were considered as negatively affecting the smooth functioning of the internal market.[65] In other words, the Directive intended to entail exhaustive harmonisation regarding those services that fall under its scope.[66] Thus, allowing recourse to primary law despite the lex specialis that the Directive created would amount to depriving the latter of its *effet utile*.[67]

A few years later, in *Hiebler*, the Court was given the opportunity to discuss again the concept of the governmental exception under the Directive. At stake was whether the trade of chimney sweep as exercised in the Land of Corinthia could be regarded as an activity in the exercise of official authority.[68] In its preliminary request, the Austrian Supreme Court appeared to suggest that this was the case because of certain tasks of public interest assigned to the chimney sweeps relating to fire safety regulation.

The CJEU took issue in that it found that the activity at stake was auxiliary to the exercise of official authority because the mayor delegates such tasks to chimney sweeps and is in charge of directly supervising their work. The chimney sweeps have no personal power of enforcement, constraint or coercion against their clients. The fact that they act in the public interest as part of their everyday activity is not sufficient for that activity to be regarded as directly and specifically connected to official authority. As the Court underlined previously in a series of cases relating to the inconsistency with EU law of a nationality requirement for notaries, it is not uncommon in various EU legal systems at the national level that

[65] ibid, para 46.
[66] Notably when it comes to Arts 9–14. See Joined Cases C-458/14 and C-67/15, *Promoimpresa srl*, ECLI:EU:C:2016:558, paras 59, 61.
[67] cf Joined Cases C-360/15 and C-31/16, *X*, para 93.
[68] See C-293/14, *Hiebler*, ECLI:EU:C:2015:843.

certain regulated professions have an obligation to act in pursuit of an objective in the public interest.[69] However, this alone is not sufficient for the activity to be deemed as part of the official authority exception.

iii. Spelling out the Basics of the Directive

In the first 10 years since the adoption of the Services Directive, the Court has clarified the meaning of various key concepts enshrined in the Directive. For instance, in *X*, the Court discussed the confines of the basic concept of 'service'.[70] In *X*, the question was whether the activity of retail sale of goods such as shoes and clothing comes under the above definition of 'service'.[71]

The question arose when Visser BV, a Dutch company owning commercial surfaces at the *Woonplein*, an outlet shopping area in Northern Netherlands, decided to rent shop premises to Bristol BV, a company wishing to open a discount retail outlet for shoes and clothing. However, this was against the zoning plan adopted by the local municipal council which reserved the area exclusively for retail trade in bulky goods.

At the outset, although one would not argue against retail being a self-employed activity provided for remuneration, the Court faced here the fundamental question whether the free movement of goods could be of relevance. However, the Directive could not be clearer in this regard: distributive trades fall under the scope of the Directive and the same goes for all requirements applicable to access to service activities or to the exercise thereof, to the exclusion of requirements applicable to goods as such. As the zoning plan at issue related to the conditions of access governing Woonplein where activities relating to the sale of specific goods can be established, the concept of 'service' must also include retail trade in goods such as clothing and shoes.[72]

Similarly, EU primary law on the freedom of establishment could not be applicable without depriving the establishment-related provisions for service providers of their *effet utile*. Following the AG's advice, the Court underscored the ever-changing nature of retail trade in goods, which nowadays extends to a considerable gamut of pre- and post-sale services.[73]

Another basic concept discussed in *X* was that of a 'requirement', which, according to the Directive, is a catch-all concept; it encompasses any obligation, prohibition, condition or limit provided for in national law, but also administrative

[69] See, among many, C-61/08, *Commission v Greece*, ECLI:EU:C:2011:340, para 88.

[70] Recall that Art 4(1) of the Directive provides that service is any self-employed economic activity, normally provided for remuneration, along the lines of Art 57 TFEU.

[71] See Joined Cases C-360/15 and C-31/16, *X*, paras 84ff.

[72] In a similar vein, the Court found previously that the marketing of non-alcoholic beverages and food in coffee shops is a catering activity characterised by an array of features and acts in which services (rather than the supply of the product itself) predominate: see C-137/09, *Josemans*, ECLI:EU:C:2010:774, para 49.

[73] Joined Cases C-360/15 and C-31/16, *X*, para 95. Also AG Szpunar's Opinion in *X*, ECLI:EU:C:2017:397, paras 102–03.

practice; rules of professional bodies and other associations that enjoy legal autonomy.[74] At issue was whether the zoning plan can fall under the concept of 'requirement' as set out in the Directive. After noting that the zoning plan at issue determines geographical zones where certain retail trade activities cannot be established but the addressees are not individuals in their private capacity, the Court confirmed that the measure at issue cannot fall under the exception of Recital 9 of the Directive relating to zoning restrictions but rather constitutes a restriction affecting the taking up and pursuit of a service activity.

As the measure at issue limits the establishment of retail traders outside the city centre, its compatibility with Articles 14 and 15 had to be examined. Whereas no clear violation of Article 14 was invoked, Article 15(2)(a), which obliges Member States to evaluate whether national measures impose territorial restrictions, and if so, to ensure that such measures are non-discriminatory, necessary and proportionate, was of relevance. By precluding access to a service activity in a given geographical area, the measure at issue came under Article 15(2)(a) and therefore had to comply with the principles of necessity, proportionality and non-discrimination.

While the Court found that it was for the domestic court to determine the compliance of the measure with these basic EU principles, it noted that protecting the urban environment[75] by maintaining the viability of the city centre of the municipality is in the interest of good town and county planning and could be an overriding reason relating to the public interest that may justify territorial restrictions of this type. AG Szpunar went a step further in this case to affirm the proportionality of the measure contending that no indication existed that the zoning plan at issue indirectly limited (or aimed at limiting) the overall number of retailers in the municipality.[76]

The contours of what type of requirements are covered by the Services Directive were further discussed in *Commission v Hungary*. At stake was the legality of a nationwide mobile payment system governed by a State-controlled company. The use of this system was mandatory, inter alia, for the mobile payment of public parking charges, tolls for use of the road network, public transport fares as well as fees connected with other services offered by the State.

Hungary argued that an SGEI was at stake which should result in the exclusion of the application of the Directive. While the Court admitted that the European Commission did not plausibly prove that the mobile payment service at stake is not an SGEI, it still held that the Directive applies to SGEI on condition that it does not obstruct the performance, in law and in fact, of the particular task assigned to such service providers.[77]

[74] Art 4(7) of the Directive. The provision excludes from its scope collective agreements negotiated by the social partners.

[75] cf C-17/00, *De Coster*, para 38.

[76] AG Szpunar's Opinion in *X*, paras 148–50.

[77] Art 15:4 of the Directive echoes Art 106:2 TFEU. According to established case law, it is for the Member State invoking the exception of Art 106:2 to prove that its requirements are met. See C-160/08, *Commission* v *Germany*, EU:C:2010:230, para 126.

Thus, the Court went on to examine the application of Article 15 of the Directive. Confirming the broad reach of the concept of 'requirement', the Court found that the national mobile payment system at stake is a requirement that falls under Article 15:2(d). This provision calls Member States to evaluate and ensure the compatibility with the principles of non-discrimination, necessity and proportionality of any condition that reserves access to a given service activity to particular providers by virtue of the specific nature of the activity concerned. Indeed, Article 15:2(d) appears to cover any newly established monopoly (of public or private nature) in a given service sector.

In examining the necessity of the system at stake, the Court found that Hungary itself accepted that a less restrictive measure was available, that is, a system of concessions based on a competitive process. In the Court's view, Hungary failed to prove that the system at stake was necessary to the performance, in a cost-effective manner, of the particular public service task at issue. For this reason, it found that it did not meet the necessity requirement of Article 15:3 nor had it proven the cost-effectiveness of the regulatory choice made pursuant to Article 15:4 of the Directive.

More recently, the Court was called upon to examine whether maximum tariffs for bottled liquefied petroleum gas (LPG) in certain gas containers and an obligation for home delivery imposed on the operators with the largest share in the market are consistent with Article 15:2 of the Directive.[78] Regarding the first requirement, Article 15:2(g) expressly classifies such maximum prices as a restriction on the freedom of establishment, whereas the second requirement constitutes another 'specific service' to be supplied jointly with the service of selling gas pursuant to Article 15:2(h). As noted earlier, such requirements are not ipso facto inconsistent with the Directive, but they have to satisfy the conditions of non-discrimination, necessity and proportionality, as provided for in Article 15:3.

In this case, the referring Court asked whether the principle of proportionality in this particular case should have a different meaning in light of the importance of the natural gas sector. The Court found that, indeed, in assessing a national requirement with the principle of proportionality, Courts' scrutiny may vary over time, depending on the relevant market and its evolution, keeping in mind that the requirements identified in Article 15:2 bear a certain negative weight that could perpetuate existing obstacles in EU services trade. For instance, measures of unlimited duration that prolong State interference with prices would most likely be outlawed, taking into account the general economic interest pursued.[79] Eventually, the Court found that several traits of the measure at issue supported its proportionate nature, including the periodic re-examination of the home delivery obligation and its focus on domestic consumers.

Article 15:2(g) of the Directive was again at the heart of a very recent dispute relating to the imposition of minimum and maximum tariffs for planning services

[78] Joined Cases C-473/17 and C-546/17, *Repsol Butano*, ECLI:EU:C:2019:308.
[79] cf C/265/08, *Federutility*, ECLI:EU:C:2010:205, paras 33, 35.

supplied by architects and engineers in Germany.[80] The Commission's complaint was partly based on *Cipolla*, where the Court found that setting minimum tariffs for lawyers is inconsistent with the freedom to provide services.[81] The Court started by underlying that Article 15 aims at reconciling the regulatory competence of Member States regarding all requirements listed in this provision and the genuine exercise of the freedom of establishment by EU nationals. This provision allows Member States to regulate as long as these requirements respect the principles of non-discrimination, necessity and proportionality.

In this case, the Court agreed with Germany that fixing the relevant tariffs is non-discriminatory and necessary to achieve the legitimate policy objectives that Germany has set for itself, notably, a high level of quality, consumer protection, building safety or ecological construction, but also transparency and prevention of excessive charges in the case of imposing maximum tariffs. In the Court's view, the peculiarities of the planning services market in Germany are such that, absent the fixing of tariffs, there is a risk that competition in this market may result in the offer of services at a discount or the elimination of suppliers offering quality services as a consequence of adverse selection due to asymmetric information.[82]

However, the Court went on to emphasize that the imposition of fixed tariffs can be regarded as proportionate only if it genuinely reflects a concern to pursue a legitimate objective in a consistent and systematic manner. Here, the Court agreed with the Commission that the German legislation at issue lacked consistency in relation to the objectives pursued because the supply of planning services subject to those tariffs was not circumscribed by minimal safeguards that ensure the quality of such services. Indeed, Germany conceded that service providers other than engineers and architects who were not subject to mandatory professional rules that can assess professional capability were still entitled to supply planning services.

Thus, the Court concluded by finding that Germany failed to show that minimum tariffs are suitable for securing the pursuit of the objectives of high quality and consumer protection set by Germany. Finally, with respect to the maximum tariffs, the Court found that Germany failed to show why increased information regarding prices for the various categories of services covered by the German legislation would not be a reasonably available measure that could be equally effective with a view to ensuring more transparency in the market. Interestingly, the Court did not refer at all to *Commission v Italy* where the Court found that the setting of maximum tariffs for lawyers was not a violation of the freedom of establishment and the freedom to provide services.[83] However, in the latter case, unlike in the

[80] See C-377/17, *Commission v Germany*, ECLI:EU:C:2019:562.

[81] See Joined Cases C-94/04 and C-202/04, *Cipolla and Others*, ECLI:EU:C:2006:758.

[82] The Court makes reference here to a situation akin to a market for lemons. See G Akerlof, 'The Market for "Lemons": Quality Uncertainty and the Market Mechanism' (1970) 84(3) *Quarterly Journal of Economics* 488.

[83] See C-565/08, *Commission v Italy*, ECLI:EU:C:2011:188.

present case of engineers, the measure at issue allowed for sufficient flexibility as to the maximum tariffs used.

Another important concept that the Court was called upon to decipher relates to authorisation requirements and procedures. The Directive provides that an authorisation scheme involves any procedure under which a service provider or recipient is in effect required to take steps with a view to obtaining from a competent authority a formal decision, or an implied decision regarding access to a given service activity or the exercise thereof.[84] Thus, the definition appears to be sufficiently broad to cover both explicit and implicit decisions as well as administrative procedures of public or private nature that have to be respected in order for a service supplier to commence her activity.

However, CJEU case law of late appears to suggest that a scheme of general application such as a zoning plan would not come under that concept because it does not require an administrative decision or act following a mandatory application by a service provider seeking to pursue an economic activity.[85] In *X*, AG Szpunar correctly identified three conditions for a particular situation to fall under an authorisation scheme: (a) the service provider has to request a decision from an authority; (b) the provider received a decision addressed to him specifically; and (c) that decision and the compliance therewith was a prerequisite for the service provider to start his activity.[86] We would add here that the decision could also be implicit. Such an extension seems plausible: if there is no reaction by the competent domestic authorities, the negative affected party should still be able to challenge an authorisation scheme or the manner it is applied.

Articles 9–13 of the Directive incorporate the conditions under which authorisation schemes can be compatible with EU law. In *Van Gennip*,[87] the Court was called upon to assess whether the requirement for a dual authorisation (a federal one relating to explosives and a regional environmental permit) in order to store pyrotechnic articles was consistent with Article 10 of the Directive which establishes certain criteria for authorisation schemes relating to non-discrimination, transparency, proportionality, objectivity and clarity.

Interestingly, the Court referred to the obligation for judicial deference when it comes to assessing the allocation of competences of the Member States' authorities granting authorisations; however, it still went on to examine the precise nature of the domestic dual authorisation scheme. While the Court found that it did not have sufficient information to examine the authorisation schemes at issue against all criteria, it noted, crucially, that the two schemes pursue different objectives, are subject to precise but different criteria and are transparent and accessible, as they are published in accordance with federal and regional legislation. Unfortunately, for our purposes, but wisely, for a supranational judicial instance, the Court

[84] Art 4(6) of the Directive.
[85] See Joined Cases C-360/15 and C-31/16, *X*, para 115.
[86] AG Szpunar's Opinion in *X*, para 126.
[87] C-137/17, *Van Gennip*, ECLI:EU:C:2018:771, paras 78ff.

decided to leave for the Belgian Court the assessment of proportionality of the measure of ceiling at 50kg the pyrotechnic composition at the federal level to protect public safety.

The Court delved into the adequate scope of Article 9 in *Kirschstein*.[88] At issue was a Belgian law imposing criminal penalties for persons who, without prior authorisation from the competent authority, conferred a master's degree. The Court underscored at the outset that provisions of criminal law do not escape the purview of the Directive. In order to examine the consistency of such provisions with the Directive, a review of the authorisation scheme at issue against the requirements of Articles 9 and 10 was warranted.

First the Court found that the scheme at issue does not discriminate among suppliers wishing to confer university degrees it covers. Then, the authorisation scheme would need to be justified by an overriding reason pursuing the public interest, which the Court found it did, as it was designed to ensure a high level of higher education and to protect the recipient of education services. In the Court's view, the requirement to hold an authorisation aimed at ensuring that sufficient safeguards are in place to guarantee the quality of the diplomas conferred. Finally, the scheme would need to comply with the principle of necessity pursuant to Article 9:1(c) of the Directive. Here, as well, the Court found that an inspection ex post would not be sufficiently effective. The Court finished its analysis confirming the relevance of the criteria of Article 10:2 of the Directive when evaluating the compatibility with the Directive of an authorisation scheme, as discussed in *Van Gennip*. However, the Court decided to exercise deference and leave this analysis for the referring Belgian Court.

The limits of authorisation procedures were discussed in *Hemming*,[89] where the compatibility with the Directive of a payment of a fee for the grant (or renewal) or a sex establishment licence in Westminster (London) was at issue. This fee consisted of two parts: one related to the administration of the application which is non-refundable in case of refusal of the application and the other (much higher) related to the management of and enforcement of the licensing regime, which was refundable in case of refusal. As the scheme resembled the fee structure of several professional associations, the case could have systemic repercussions for various categories of service providers.[90]

According to the plaintiff, this second part of the fee was inconsistent with Article 13(2) of the Directive. This provision requires that authorisation procedures and formalities not be dissuasive and unduly complicate nor delay the service supply. Crucially, it requires that charges incurred by the applicants are *reasonable* and *proportionate* to the cost of the authorisation procedures in question and not exceeding the cost of the procedures.

[88] C-393/17, *Kirschstein*, ECLI:EU:C:2018:918.

[89] C-316/15, *Hemming*, ECLI:EU:C:2016:879.

[90] Thus, it came as no surprise that the English professional associations of lawyers and architects were among the interveners in the proceedings.

Referring to previous case law suggesting that general supervisory activities cannot be financed in the case of granting individual licences in telecommunications services under the Directive 97/13, as it does not constitute administrative costs strictly generated by the work involved in implementing licences,[91] the Court found that Article 13(2) should be interpreted in a similar manner so that the fees charged by the city of Westminster exceed the cost of the authorisation procedure. The fact that such fees could be later reimbursed did not change the Court's conclusion.

Importantly, the Court noted that a different interpretation, which would essentially allow pre-financing the management costs, would contradict the aim of facilitating market access as incorporated in the Directive. In doing so, the Court followed a more liberalisation-friendly approach than AG Wathelet, who adopted a more fact-specific and evidence-based stance in that he considered the second part of the fee as unreasonable because the City Council could not give additional explanations and evidence as to the exact breakdown of that part of the fee.

Earlier, in *Trijber*,[92] the Court was requested to rule on the issue of duration of authorisations. Article 11(1) of the Directive provides that authorisations cannot be granted for a limited period except in cases where the number of available authorisations is limited; for instance, due to public interest grounds. In that case, the Court agreed that the protection of the environment and public safety are legitimate objectives that justify limiting in time and number the authorisations granted by the competent authorities.

In *Promoimpresa and Others*,[93] the Court also had to decide on the scope of Article 12 of the Directive, which relates to the specific case whereby the number of authorisations available for a given activity is limited due to scarcity of natural resources or technical capacity. In such cases, the Directive requires that Member States introduce a selection procedure and exclude automatic renewal. In this specific case, the issue at stake was whether the automatic extension of the period of validity of concessions of State-owned maritime and lakeside property contravened Article 12.

First, the Court found that the concessions at stake constitute formal decisions which a service provider must obtain from the national authorities to be able to commence his economic activity and thus they can be regarded as authorisations pursuant to the Directive. The Court went on to find that the State land at issue is located in place which can be deemed a natural resource but refrained from expressing a view as to whether such a resource was scarce.

Going back to the scope of Article 12, the Court contended that the automatic renewal foreseen by the domestic legislation disregarded the obligation for a selection procedure. Even if the Italian State's actions were based on public interest grounds, they could be taken into account in establishing the rules governing

[91] See Joined Cases C-392/04 and C-422/04, *i-21*, ECLI:EU:C:2006:586, paras 34–35.
[92] See Joined Cases 340/14 and C-341/14, *Trijber*, ECLI:EU:C:2015:641, paras 61ff.
[93] See Joined Cases C-458/14 and C-67/15, *Promoimpresa srl*, paras 49ff.

the selection procedure. However, Article 12 does not allow any justification of an automatic renewal on public interest grounds when no selection procedure is organised. Thus, the Italian measure was incompatible with the Directive.

In the case of the freedom to provide services under EU primary law, a key objective feature of a State measure in order for it to fall under the freedom to provide services is the presence of a cross-border element. Whereas the Court interpreted this requirement narrowly and in a manner that often looks into evidence of cross-border activity only marginally, the Services Directive appears to require no such activity in the case of the provisions relating to the freedom of establishment.

First, in *Rina Services*, the Court abstained from discussing the significance of the fact that the situation at issue was confined to one Member State only. Later, in *Trijber* the Court appeared to consider it necessary to identify cross-border elements before discussing the application of Chapter III of the Directive relating to establishment.[94] In doing so, it disregarded the advice of AG Szpunar to the Court to find that the provisions of the Directive relating to establishment of service providers also apply to purely internal situations.[95]

More recently, in *Hiebler*, the Court did not seem to mind that the territorial restrictions allowing chimney sweeps to offer their services only in the sweeping area where they are resident were confined to just one Austrian region (Corinthia) and applied the relevant provision of the Directive. The same approach can be observed in *Promoimpresa*, where the Court interpreted Chapter III provisions of the Directive that prohibited the automatic extension of concessions of State-owned maritime and lakeside property without considering that the purely internal nature of the facts had a bearing on the applicability of the Directive. The same stance was then reiterated in *Hemming*, whereby all facts of the case related to London.

Despite this case law, one could still argue – admittedly, in some cases more than others – that the dissuasive effect to service providers from other Member States potentially interested in establishing themselves in those Member States still was present and thus the Court was driven by considerations relating to potential trade opportunities.

This uncertainty was removed in *X*. The Court confirmed that the absence of a requirement for a cross-border element in the Directive as far as establishment is concerned shall have a meaning. In this regard, the Court drew a comparison with the provisions of the Directive relating to the services provision – Article 16 in particular – where the EU legislature clearly incorporated a cross-border element.

[94] See Joined Cases 340/14 and C-341/14, *Trijber*, para 41. On the other hand, when the Court discussed the second part of the case relating to a language requirement for window prostitution businesses as a condition for granting authorisations of that activity, it did not look for cross-border evidence: ibid, paras 67ff.

[95] See AG Szpunar's Opinion in *Trijber*, ECLI:EU:C:2015:505, paras 52–57 (referring to textual and contextual elements). The AG also found support in the Handbook on Implementation of the Services Directive (n 39) at 24.

In addition, the Court underscored that the conclusion could be no different if one takes into account the objective of the Directive to complete the internal market for services. This requires the elimination of obstacles encountered by those providers establishing in another Member State but also by those established in their own Member State, as such obstacles can adversely affect the supply of services throughout the Union.[96]

Finally, a concept that will most likely keep the Court and the Commission occupied in the short and medium run relates to commercial communications and the regulated professions. Recall that, in *Société fiduciaire nationale d'expertise comptable*, the Court confirmed that the concept of commercial communication includes any form of communication that promotes the product or service of an undertaking or a person engaged in an economic activity, including a regulated profession.[97] In this case, it found that canvassing is commercial communication as it constitutes a form of communication of information via personal contact between the service provider and potential clients with a view to acquiring new clients. Such communications are akin to direct marketing, according to the Court.

To be sure, whereas some coherence would be desirable, the fact that various professions are excluded from the scope of the Directive or are regulated by other legislative instruments clearly affects dealing with such national measures based on a single set of rules. In view of this fact, it should be expected that the Court will try to ensure some coherence informally between interpretations under Article 24 of the Services Directive and other secondary law instruments or, indeed, Article 49 and 56 TFEU.

This is all the more so because the Court has recognised over time the sensitivities of various professions when it comes to restrictions that ensure their integrity, professionalism or dignity.[98] The same case law, however, has revealed a certain difficulty on the side of the Court to clearly delineate ex ante under which conditions certain restrictions on advertising cannot be compatible with EU law.

In *Vanderborght*, for instance, the struggle on the side of the Court to explain in what sense the restrictions in that case were more burdensome than in *Konstantinides* (where the advertising restrictions were regarded as compatible with EU law) is quite telling. In a single sentence, the Court merely notes that in *Vanderborght*, the legislation at issue 'has a much broader scope' than in *Konstantinides*.[99]

Whether this statement indirectly introduces a new de minimis test is unclear. Be this as it may, more analytical guidance by the Court would be apposite and necessary in the future. A parallel development that may affect the interpretation of such restrictions would be the creation of codes of conduct for professions at

[96] See Joined Cases C-360/15 and C-31/16, *X*, para 105.
[97] See Art 4(12) of the Services Directive.
[98] C-339/15, *Vanderborght*, para 68.
[99] ibid, para 74.

the EU level as well as standardisation-related initiatives within the European standard-setting bodies.

iv. Delineating the Relationship between the Services Directive and Transport Services

Article 58:1 TFEU excludes from the scope of the freedom to provide services those activities provided in the field of transport.[100] By the same token, services in the field of transport, including port services, are excluded from the scope of the Directive pursuant to Article 2:2(d) of the Directive. In addition, recital 21 of the directive provides that not only port services but also urban transport, taxis and ambulances should equally be excluded.

More generally, this would appear to be in line with Article 100:1 TFEU, which provides that the transport-related provisions under the TFEU apply to transport by rail, road and inland waterway, but potentially also to sea and air transport. In view of the open wording adopted in the Directive ('including'), it appears that an a priori broad interpretation of this exclusion is apposite. This is all the more so not only because it would be too narrow an approach to restrict the exclusion to means of transport in themselves,[101] but also because the chapter on transport is an expression of the freedom to provide services which should lead to a common transport policy to be materialised by the EU legislature.[102]

In *Trijber*, the Court had the opportunity to demarcate the contours of this exception for the first time. At issue was whether a service of carrying passengers on a boat for a waterway tour of a city for event-related purposes against remuneration is a service in the field of transport. The Court started by noting that a review of the wording, purpose and general structure of the exception was necessary. After referring to the wording of primary law but also recital 21, the Court contended that no provision explicitly provides that any service consisting in waterway transport is ipso facto classified as 'transport' under the Directive. Rather, a review of the purpose of the service at issue was necessary.

In the Court's view, the Directive had to cater for a delicate balance between the elimination of obstacles to establishment and services supply and the need to safeguard the traits of certain sensitive activities, notably those relating to consumer protection. In this respect, the Court noted that services in the field of tourism, including tour guides, are consumer services falling within the ambit of the Directive.

The Court continued its analysis by noting that in the present case the consumers of the services were not interested in the point-to-point transport in Amsterdam but rather in the consumption of a service associated with tours and

[100] Crucially, however, the rules relating to the freedom of establishment apply in the case of transport: See C-338/09, *Yellow Cab Verkehrsbetrieb*, EU:C:2010:814, para 33.

[101] See C-168/14, *Grupo Itevelesa SL*, para 45.

[102] See also AG Szpunar's Opinion in *Tribjer*, ECLI: EU:C:2015:505, para 28.

rentals for festive occasions. Thus, the Court concluded, subject to verification by the referring court, the purpose of the service at issue was not a service in the field of transport pursuant to Article 2:2(d) of the Directive.

Almost about the same time period, the Court was confronted with another related *ratione materiae* question in *Grupo Itevelesa*:[103] are vehicle roadworthiness testing activities covered by the Directive? The Court had recourse to contextual and teleological techniques to answer the question. Overall, the Court appeared to follow a relative broad view of the transport exception included in Article 2:2(d) of the Directive.

First, it noted that the exclusion of this provision not only covers any point-to-point physical act of moving persons or goods by means of a vehicle, aircraft or waterborne vessel, but also any service inherently linked to such an act.[104] Viewed through this lens, tests relating to roadworthiness for motor vehicles are ancillary to and indispensable for the transport service. It seems that the existence of secondary law on the issue which used the relevant TFEU provisions on transport weighed significantly in favour of including the testing activities at issue as services in the field of transport.

The most recent cases discussing the scope of the provision excluding from the scope of the Directive services in the field of transport relate to Uber.[105] The cases before the CJEU could be regarded as quite narrow when compared to the breadth of litigation activity against Uber.[106] In *Elite Taxi*, at issue was whether the service that Uber offers is an information society service; a service coming under the Directive; or a service in the field of transport.

Crucially, the answer to this question was not free from important consequences; rather, it would determine the applicability and 'bite' of EU law: under EU secondary law, an information society services is a service provided for remuneration, at a distance, by electronic means at the request of the recipient.[107] The E-commerce Directive[108] requires that Member States not restrict the supply of such services but also that they notify the Commission of measures to be taken against providers of such services.

If, on the other hand, the Services Directive is deemed applicable, Article 9 on the conditions that authorisations schemes shall meet (in case of establishment)

[103] This decision was made public 15 days after *Trijber*.

[104] See also C-563/17, *Associação Peço a Palavra and Others*, ECLI:EU:C:2019:144, para 30.

[105] See C-434/15, *Asociación Profesional Elite Taxi*, EU:C:2017:981, para 35; and C-320/16, *Uber France SAS*, ECLI:EU:C:2018:221.

[106] For an overview, see V Hatzopoulos and S Roma, 'Caring for Sharing? The Collaborative Economy under EU Law' (2017) 54 *Common Market Law Review* 81–128, at 90.

[107] See Directive 98/34 laying down a procedure for the provision of information in the field of technical standards and regulations [1998] OJ L 204/37, as amended by Directive 98/48 [1998] OJ L 217/18, Art 1(2). The same definition is to be found in the Directive that replaced the Directive 98/34: See Directive 2015/1535 laying down a procedure for the provision of information in the field of technical regulations and of rules on information society services [2015] OJ L 241/1, Art 1:1(b).

[108] Directive 2000/31/EC on certain legal aspects of information society services, in particular electronic commerce, in the Internal Market [2000] OJ L 178/1.

and Article 16 (in the case of services) call for an assessment against the principle of non-discrimination, necessity and proportionality. Finally, if the service at issue is regarded as falling under the exception of Article 2:2(d) of the Directive relating to services in the field of transport, then the regulation of the activity is essentially a matter reserved to the EU Member States (with Article 49 TFEU nevertheless remaining directly relevant).

Depending on the solution chosen to this legal conundrum, negative effects on innovation could arise. While controversial from a competition or labour law perspective, online platforms have exerted a leadership role in disrupting various industries, ranging from hotels to tourism to transport.[109] Regulatory capture at the domestic level could lead to unduly protecting incumbents and prevent modernisation of performance and the launch of better or new forms of services. It may also prevent a proper and individualised assessment of the characteristics of the market at issue. More competition would rather increase the overall quality of the service in terms of choice, timing and performance.

AG Szpunar suggested that Uber is more than a mere intermediary between non-professional drivers willing to offer transport services occasionally and passengers looking for such services; in the AG's view, it is a genuine organiser and operator of urban transport services. Even if innovative and composite, as it combines an information society service with a transport service, the final service offered should be regarded as being offered in the field of urban transport.[110]

For all practical purposes, the Court agreed with AG Szpunar. At the outset, the Court appeared to see favourably the possibility of Uber being classified as an information society service due to the fact that it enables the transfer, by means of a smartphone application, of information regarding the booking of a transport service between the passenger and the non-professional driver who will carry out the transportation using his own vehicle. The Court, however, noted that the service offered by Uber also had a component relating to non-public urban transport services, which in fact was the predominant component of the service offered. In the Court's view, the intermediation service had to be regarded as being an integral part of an overall service which was transport-centered.

Such conclusion was corroborated by the fact that, first, Uber provided an application without which the non-professional drivers would not have decided to provide transport services, and the clients who wished to make an urban journey would not have used the services provided by those drivers; and, second, that Uber exercised decisive influence as to how those services were provided, notably by determining the maximum fare; by collecting that fare from the service recipients before paying part of it to the non-professional driver of the vehicle; and by exercising a certain control over the quality of the vehicles, the drivers

[109] See also European Commission Communication, 'Online Platforms and the Digital Single Market – Opportunities and Challenges for Europe', COM(2016) 288 final, 25 May 2016.
[110] See AG Szpunar's Opinion in *Asociación Profesional Elite Taxi*, ECLI:EU:C:2017:364, para 61.

and their conduct.[111] The Court concluded by noting that, in the current state of EU law, it is for the EU Member States to promulgate the conditions under which such services can be offered, keeping in mind the general TFEU rules.[112]

More recently, in *Uber France*, the Court build on the previous reasoning to shield from the scope of EU law a French law that foresees criminal penalties for the services that Uber offered without authorisation. In that case, Uber claimed that such penalties were imposed unlawfully because the relevant legislation was not notified to the European Commission as required by Directive 98/34. However, as the Court had previously found in *Elite Taxi* that the service offered by Uber was not an information society service pursuant to that Directive, no notification was required.[113]

This case law takes a conservative view which does not appear to encourage innovation in the emerging platform economy environment. On the contrary, it maintains a rather parochial view, which inhibits the opening of a thorough discussion on all issues surrounding disruptive models of service supply such as consumer protection or labour-related issues. More fundamentally, it appears to defy the purpose of primary law or the E-Commerce Directive.[114]

This line of case law is to be tested in the near future with respect to the regulatory fate of electronic platforms that redefine the shape and challenges of two-sided platforms. As is well-known by now, a two-sided platform offers different goods or services to two different groups who both intermediate between them through the platform. For instance, Uber brings together drivers and passengers, whereas Airbnb brings together in its marketplace hosts and guests; these parties need to be convinced of the value proposition for the platform to become a success.[115] As the two sides increasingly trust the platform and grow in numbers, the platforms benefit from important indirect network effects.[116]

In a pending case before the CJEU, the Court has been asked to determine whether the Airbnb service of connecting hosts (be it professionals or individuals) with accommodation available for rent with persons seeking accommodation is an information society service within the meaning of the E-Commerce Directive. Following the reasoning of the Court in the *Uber* case mutatis mutandis, the French government argued that Airbnb offers a service connected with real property and thus the rules relating to the exercise of the profession of real estate agents should be enforced against Airbnb, whereas Airbnb contended that all

[111] See C-434/15, *Asociación Profesional Elite Taxi*, paras 38–39.

[112] Similar considerations relating to online, collaborative platforms were identified by the Commission in a recent Communication: See European Commission Communication, 'A European agenda for the collaborative economy', COM(2016) 356 final, 2 June 2016, p 6.

[113] See C-320/16, *Uber France SAS*, para 26.

[114] For a critique along these lines, see D Adamski, 'Lost in the Digital Platform: Europe's Legal Travails With the Digital Single Market' (2018) 55 *Common Market Law Review* 719, at 738ff.

[115] See L Filistrucchi, D Geradin, E van Damme and P Affeldt, 'Market Definition in Two-Sided Markets: Theory and Practice' (2014) 10(2) *Journal of Competition Law and Economics* 293.

[116] Some of these traits were recently discussed by the US Supreme Court in the AMEX case: *Ohio et al v American Express Co et al*, 585 US__(2018).

the constituent elements of the definition of an information society service are met: Airbnb is a service provided for remuneration, at a distance by electronic means and at the individual request of the service recipient.[117] Based on this claim, Airbnb argued that the French government attempted to impose on Airbnb rules relating to the profession of real estate agent in contravention of the E-Commerce Directive.

AG Szpunar opined that Airbnb indeed meets all the above criteria and, unlike Uber, it does not exercise control over the essential procedures of the supply of the intermediate service it offers (that is, the connection of hosts and travellers).[118] It remains immaterial that the Airbnb also offers other services such as a photography service; a civil liability insurance; and a guarantee for damage to hosts, which have a material content as long as the service provided by electronic means remains independent of the services with a material content.

Furthermore, the AG recalled that the E-Commerce Directive is based on the country of origin principle with respect to supervision and otherwise foresees specific instances that could trigger the application of certain laws of the host Member State. However, it emphasised that the French government did not bring forward any of these possibilities that would allow for a derogation of the principle of free movement of information society services (eg, national measures necessary to protect public policy and security, or any attempt from the French government to notify the European Commission and ask Ireland, where Airbnb is based, to take measures with respect to information society services).

v. Health-related Services through the Lens of the Services Directive

The Services Directive excludes from its scope healthcare services, provided via healthcare facilities or not and regardless of the way organised and financed. Recital 22 equally excludes pharmaceutical services provided by health professionals to patients to assess, maintain or restore their state of health where such activities are reserved to a regulated health profession in the host Member State. From its wording already, the EU legislator appears to have intentionally broadened the scope of the healthcare exception.[119]

This means that, absent relevant, health services-specific secondary law, primary law remains the guiding legal basis for assessing compatibility with EU law when it comes to health-related professions. For instance, in *Ottica*, the Court found that the activities of opticians in Italy, where it is a regulated profession, ensure the protection of public health by, inter alia, conducting eye tests,

[117] See n 108.

[118] See Opinion of AG Szpunar in C-390/18, *Airbnb Ireland*, ECLI:EU:C:2019:336.

[119] However, the Handbook on the implementation of the Services Directive provided that the exception covers activities directly and strictly linked to the state of human health and therefore does not concern services which are designed to enhance well-being or provide relaxation such as sports or fitness clubs. See Handbook (n 39) at 12.

measuring visual acuity, detecting eye problems and using corrective optical devices and therefore are excluded from the scope of the Directive.[120]

Similarly, in *Femarbel*,[121] the Court confirmed the broad scope of the healthcare exception enshrined in the Directive and referred to the essential features of the activity: as long as the service is intended to assess, maintain or restore the state of health of patients and the activity is carried out by healthcare professionals recognised as such by the home Member State, the healthcare exception of the Directive should be triggered.

The Court, however, left it for the referring court to decide whether care activities in day-care centres and night-care centres shall be deemed as falling under the healthcare exception. Notably, the referring court has to assess whether the activity is genuinely intended to maintain or restore the state of health of elderly persons; is provided by a health professional; and constitutes a principal part of the services provided in these care centres.[122]

More recently, in *CMVRO*,[123] the Court confirmed that activities relating to the retail supply and use of organic products, special purpose anti-parasitic products and veterinary medicinal products do not constitute healthcare services for human beings and thus are subject to the requirements laid down in the Services Directive.[124] The Romanian law at stake limited to veterinary practitioners the retail and use of organic products, special purpose anti-parasitic products and veterinary medicinal products. It also required that the share capital of veterinary pharmacies and relevant outlets is owned only by registered veterinary practitioners.

Inspired by its case law relating to human health,[125] the Court found that the exclusive retail right, while falling under Article 15 of the Directive, was necessary and proportionate because of the importance of ensuring and protecting public health and the fact that the Romanian law did not appear to unduly use the discretion at its disposal. Regarding the shareholder requirement, the Court drew on previous case law[126] to find that good policy considerations may support the necessity of such a measure. However, the Court ultimately ruled that Member States' discretion in the field of animal health is not so important as to allow a total exclusion of non-veterinary professionals from establishments selling such products.[127]

[120] See C-539/11, *Ottica New Line di Accardi Vincenzo*, ECLI:EU:C:2013:591, paras 19–20.

[121] See C-57/12, *Fédération des maisons de repos privées de Belgique (Femarbel) ASBL*, ECLI:EU:C:2013:517.

[122] ibid, para 41.

[123] See C-297/16, *Colegiul Medicilor Veterinari din România (CMVRO)*, ECLI:EU:C:2018:141.

[124] See also Handbook (n 39) at 12, which provides that the healthcare exclusion concerns services relating to human health. Thus, services provided by veterinaries should be covered by the Directive.

[125] See, for instance, C-531/06, *Commission v Italy*, EU:C:2009:315.

[126] See Joined Cases C-171/07 and C-172/07, *Apothekerkammer des Saarlandes*, para 40.

[127] By ruling so, the Court denied the extension to animal health-related cases of its case law that accepted the compatibility of EU law with similar restrictions relating to shareholding acquisition in Italian pharmacies: case C-531/06, *Commission v Italy*.

IV. Conclusion

This chapter offered a succinct account of the great convergence that is taking place in the EU services markets as the implementation of the Services Directive occurs. Despite previous instances of political turmoil, a broader consensus seems to be emerging as to the economic benefits of integration in the field of services and the role that the Directive is expected to play in this process. Not only developments at the intra-EU trade level but also at the extra-EU level affect this process: the recent CJEU ruling in the *Singapore* Opinion[128] confirmed that the EU has exclusive competence in trade in services, including transport services. This will most likely have a significant impact on regulatory initiatives in this field both internally and externally in the short run.

The present chapter argued that the Services Directive constitutes an additional legal instrument to be used by the CJEU with a view to further pursuing the objectives of the fundamental freedoms of services and establishment. Early case law confirms that the Court will take a bold, expansive view in interpreting provisions of the Directive while maintaining a quite conservative view when it comes to exceptions such as those relating to social or healthcare services.

Having said this, the effects of the Directive on enhancing transparency, communication among regulatory authorities and the Commission and thus on further strengthening trust are already visible, notably at the informal level. Again, this does not mean that the Directive will complete the EU services internal market anytime soon. This has also to do with the weakened 'bite' of the services-related provisions of the Directive (as opposed to the establishment-related ones, notably Article 14 thereof). To be sure, the impact of the Directive will depend on the level of discretion that the CJEU will recognise to EU Member States and the dismantling of certain barriers in bottleneck industries and in the digital market that may lead to the expansion of services trade in a bottom-up manner.

[128] See Opinion 2/15, *Singapore-EU FTA*, ECLI:EU:C:2017:376.

8

Government, Culture and Movies

In Search of a Common Understanding from a European Perspective

SUSANA DE LA SIERRA

I. Introduction

> There is a growing feeling that the creation of a European culture must develop independently of the North American cultural model, perhaps even be prepared to defend itself against the latter, albeit this already has had a profound effect on the cultures of all the states of Europe. We must positively support the remarkable range of museums and art galleries and ancient buildings that we have, which in themselves perhaps indicate the way in which our future cultural development should go.[1]

Lord Slynn of Hadley, former judge of what is now the Court of Justice of the European Union (CJEU), puts forward in this wording a rarely heard statement, which is, however, implicit in many books, articles and conference proceedings and, most importantly, legal texts and case law. Culture could be considered, indeed, as many would argue, a European obsession.[2] European States, together with other countries, such as Canada, have fostered a protection system for culture in the international relations and, especially, in international trade.[3] This is not

[1] Lord Slynn of Hadley, 'Law and Culture – a European Setting', The Tanner Lectures on Human Values, delivered at Brasenose College, Oxford, 19 and 28 October 1993. See https://tannerlectures.utah.edu/_documents/a-to-z/s/Slynn95.pdf, all links accessed 16 May 2019. Some authors have warned against the use of the notion 'American culture' in singular, since the United States is – as it happens with other countries – 'a land of many cultures'. See Rachael Craufurd Smith, 'Article 151 EC and European Identity' in Rachael Craufurd Smith (ed), *Culture and EU Law* (Oxford, Oxford University Press, 2004) 277.

[2] This is most notably perceived in the audiovisual field, where some have even spoken of a 'challenge to [the European] civilisation', due to the fact that American products are, allegedly, 'colonising' the European market. See, for instance, Jean-Claude Batz, *L'Audiovisuel Européen: Un Enjeu de Civilisation [The European Audiovisual: A Civilisation Challenge]* (Paris, Atlantica, 2005) 53.

[3] Some have argued that Canada's cultural policy in international trade responds to the need to defend itself from the erosion of its national culture by US dominance of the cultural market. See Joseph Devlin, 'Canada and International Trade in Culture: Beyond National Interests' (2004) 14 *Minnesota Journal of Global Trade* 177.

only a long standing tradition in the countries which are now members of the European Union (EU) but it has also been inherited by the European Union itself. The underlying reasons will be explored in this chapter, bearing in mind that culture has been a goal of the European Communities since the very beginning of the European project in the 1950s, although it has acquired legal recognition only at a later stage.[4]

The main purpose of this chapter is to analyse the different legal approaches in Europe and the United States regarding culture and cultural policies. As I will develop further later, culture is understood here both in its broader and in its narrower meaning. The broader meaning links culture to concepts such as civilisation, traditions and customs, whereas the narrower meaning relates it to something more specific: the arts. Focus is put mainly on the European experience, since the research is carried out through the lens of a European lawyer. Yet the purpose is to try and identify certain parameters that enable the comparison of both approaches, the European and the American, and deduce elements for a common understanding in a framework of an ever closer legal globalisation. Culture is, by definition, something that should be excluded from the socio-economic phenomenon of globalisation, and therefore the law regulating culture should be the last, if at all, to be globalised. Anyway, there are already some international reference points, such as the negotiations on the cultural exception at the World Trade Organization, or the implementation of international treaties such as the UNESCO Convention on the Protection and Promotion of the Diversity of Cultural Expressions.[5] Therefore, it is now a task for scholars to study this issue and propose ways of understanding, accordingly.

II. The United States and the European Union in a Conundrum: What is Culture and What is a Film?

The differences in the approach to cultural policies in the United States and the European Union correspond to the existence of opposed or, at least, diverging, answers to the following questions: what is the relationship between the government and culture/the arts? Are there any constitutional constraints or obligations to establish a cultural agenda? Who is in charge of the political agenda in the government? Who defines the paths to follow? Who administers the money? Who decides where to allocate the funds? Are the agencies independent in this area?

[4] As Paul Craig and Gráinne de Búrca have maintained, 'the connection between Community law and culture goes back considerably further, to the origins of the EEC Treaty'. See preface to the pioneering book Rachael Craufurd Smith (ed), *Culture and European Union Law* (Oxford, Oxford University Press, 2004) 277. This book can be considered a milestone for this literature, before which we relied on academic contributions on this issue, written mostly by the contributors to this book.

[5] Full text available at the following address: https://en.unesco.org/creativity/convention.

Is it possible to confer the implementation of this policy to private parties? What other types of constitutional problems arise in this field? What are the criteria that should guide the funding of the arts? What are the implications for fundamental rights, such as freedom of expression?[6] The debate on censorship is of course crucial here.[7]

The general framework on culture that has been exposed will be exemplified with one of the key policies that has given rise to controversy between the two sides of the Atlantic: the film industry and film policies, if we are indeed allowed to speak of policies in such an area. According to some recent developments, it seems that, in this respect, the European and the American perspectives are slowly converging. There is an increasing common trend to approach films from a manifold perspective, admitting that it does not belong to the world of culture/the arts exclusively or to the world of economics only. And this is an important step towards a mutual (legal) understanding.

In Europe,[8] although the emphasis is always put on the cultural meaning of movies, public policies are now treating the film industry precisely as an industry. This has implications for the internal organisation of public bodies, and also for the relationship between those public bodies and others. Independence and autonomy from political choices are the key elements here. The rationale behind these new organisational models is the will to help this industry and use it as a means to promote economic growth and development, something which will be allegedly better achieved through independent bodies rather than through more traditional and hierarchical units. This perspective actually belongs to the United States and, as will be explored later, new agencies are being created in the Member States of the European Union to promote film production in accordance with this perspective.

In the United States, movies are approached from a very different perspective than Europe. Movies are conceived of as part of the general entertainment

[6] In the United States, the debate on cultural public policies has been addressed from the perspective of the protection of fundamental rights, and mainly freedom of expression. See on this, among others, Symposium, 'Art, Distribution & The State: Perspectives on the National Endowment for the Arts' [Amy Schwartzman (Moderator); John Tuskey; Robert W. Peters; Hope O'Keeffe; Roberto Bedoya; David Cole; Marci Hamilton] (1999) 17 *Cardozo Arts & Entertainment Law Journal* 705.

[7] The following statement is highly illustrative in this regard: 'The requirement that the NEA, in making funding decisions take respect and decency into consideration, does not have anything to do with prohibiting art. Rather, it has to do with funding art. Simply because art is not funded does not necessarily mean that it is prohibited. Even if Karen Finley does not receive government money for smearing chocolate on herself, she is still perfectly free to do so. There is no censorship at all.' See Symposium, 'Art, Distribution and the State: Perspectives on the National Endowment for the Arts' (1999) 17 *Cardozo Arts & Entertainment Law Journal* 708 (John Tuskey). For a perspective of how private actors can interfere with freedom of expression (which, of course, puts forward a different set of problems than a case involving interference by a public body), see also Lawrence Lessig, *Free Culture. How Big Media Uses Technology and the Law to Lock Down Culture and Control Creativity* (New York, The Penguin Press, 2004).

[8] Meaning not only the EU, but also the States which are not *yet* Members of this international organisation.

business and are therefore subject, in general, to ordinary market rules. Nevertheless, some changes have occurred lately and new perspectives can be identified in film public policies.[9] More and more public funding is increasingly being devoted to the film industry. On the one hand, direct public funding is being given to film production, usually to support creativity or access to films for certain communities. Thus, it is linked to policies of access to culture and education.[10] On the other hand, there is a system of tax credits, conferred indistinctly of the artistic value of the movie. Therefore, its aim is not strictly speaking a cultural aim, but an economic one, since it pursues a positive impact in the development of certain areas and regions.

From a more general perspective, it is interesting to examine whether these cultural/film policies can be seen through the lens of constitutional welfarist theories.[11] Can new (substantive) rights and freedoms be deduced from the Constitution? Or, even, can these rights and freedoms be 'found' in documents such as the Declaration of Independence, the Ninth Amendment, and the 'citizenship' and 'privileges and immunities' clauses of Section 1 of the Fourteenth Amendment?[12] This theory, which is not widespread in the United States, is well understood by Europeans, since it is linked to the system of fundamental rights in countries such as Germany, Italy and Spain. Others, such as the United Kingdom,[13] are reluctant, just as the United States are, insofar as a theory of duties addressed to public powers and based on fundamental rights is not as common as in the aforementioned European countries.[14]

Yet the idea that underlies the whole debate could be, whether culture/the arts are public goods that justify an obligation for public powers to act. For precisely

> as societies become more complex and differentiated, there may be disagreement about what constitutes social and political 'health' and how it may best be ensured. … With increasing sophistication, people can eventually come to believe that the best way to ensure the vitality of society is by ensuring the well-being of the constituent members

[9] This will be further developed in the second part of this chapter.

[10] It is important to note here that aids to film production refer to the whole 'life' of the film, ie pre-production, production, post-production, distribution, exhibition and promotion. This implies that the budget for this is fairly relevant.

[11] See, for instance, Sotirios A Barber, *Welfare & The constitution* (Princeton NJ, Princeton University Press, 2003). This topic, which is not as popular in the United States as it is in Europe, has been developed in the former at State level rather than at the federal level. See Helen Hershkoff, 'Welfare Devolution and State Constitutions' (1999) 67 *Fordham Law Review* 1403.

[12] See Charles L Black, Jr, *A New Birth of Freedom* (New Haven CT, Yale University Press, 1997) *xix*.

[13] Although, as some observers have noted, the United Kingdom is becoming more and more 'European', and this evolution is of special interest in the legal arena. See JE Levitsky, 'The Europeanisation of the British Legal Style' (1994) 42 *The American Journal of Comparative Law* 347.

[14] In the British bibliography, see Andrew J Harding, *Public Duties and Public Law* (Oxford, Clarendon Press, 1989). See also, related to this issue, Ross Cranston, *The Legal Foundations of the Welfare State* (London, W & N, 1985); Harry Street, *Justice in the Welfare State* 2nd edn (London, Stevens, 1975).

> in the *widest* possible sense, and that may mean leaving it up to them to determine themselves in what their human flourishing consists.[15]

In this chapter some legal norms and public policies will be tackled, where culture and the arts are indeed considered public goods and therefore it is possible to identify public duties which should pursue this goal.

The questions that have been posed in the preceding lines will be given an answer, at least a tentative one. One of the main features of the new scenario of cultural and film policies is that both perspectives, the American and the European, are converging. In both cases, the constitutional and economic implications of film production should be analysed through an array of different legal instruments, ie films are not homogeneous from a legal perspective. Their nature is rather multifold and therefore various film legal policies and not just one should be developed. Thus, to begin with, the relationship between government and culture in the European Union and the United States will be discussed, in order to canvass at a later stage the relationship of the government and films.

III. Culture and the Arts in Today's Global Law

Global law is increasingly becoming a reality, even though its features are still far from clear. Both the supporters and opponents of this phenomenon alike are aware of the fact that globalisation is a process which cannot be stopped. Differences lie rather in the way both groups approach this process: some would like to reduce its scope as much as possible, whereas others consider that people should benefit from its positive aspects. Among such positive aspects, in the first instance, it is the economic development in those areas of the world which require so. And, in later instances, the respect for human rights, including social and cultural rights, are found on the agenda.

Culture is, by definition, opposed to the idea of globalisation. Culture is what characterises a specific society and is therefore peculiar to that society. No global society strictly speaking exists so far and, indeed, globalisation has provoked nationalist and regionalist movements which foster their own identity and fear the homogenisation effect that could be purported by it.[16] Notwithstanding this, there is a *global trend* to try and establish a common protection system for culture, or, better expressed, for *cultures*. Diversity – *cultural* diversity – is here the key concept, and it derives from an understanding of culture which will be now explored.

[15] Raymond Geuss, *Public Goods, Private Goods* (Princeton NJ, Princeton University Press, 2001) 37–38.

[16] This is clear in Europe, where Member States are not only afraid of losing their identity as single entities in the globalisation process, but also and specially in the framework of the European Union, due to the ever deeper integration.

There are many theories on the concept of culture. Yet a major tentative division is the one which distinguishes between a broad and a narrow concept of culture. The broad concept understands culture as civilisation, ie as the group of customs, beliefs and institutions that form a society. Anthropologists following Edward B Tylor's theories would argue that culture is an accumulative process, and therefore there are different degrees in the evolution towards the ideal of culture or civilisation.[17] On the other hand, theories following Franz Boas' approach would focus on the fact that there are not different degrees towards a common idea of culture, but there are different cultures, all of them equally valuable.[18] This second approach is the one underlying modern international legal scholarship interested in the concept of cultural diversity.

On 18 March 2007, a new international treaty entered into force: The Convention on the Protection and Promotion of the Diversity of Cultural Expressions,[19] a Convention that was framed by the UNESCO, the agency of the United Nations for Science, Education and Culture. Only two States voted against it: the United States and Israel, and there were four abstentions: Australia, Honduras, Liberia and Nicaragua. There is a general trend whereby culture is regarded, in general, as a minor political issue. Yet the (hard) negotiations proved that the topic was indeed highly political. There was fear that the Treaty might lead to an increase in the so-called 'cultural exception' in areas where the World Trade Organization (hereinafter, WTO) did not really want it to happen. In the framework of the WTO it is well known that the principle of free trade might be subject to some exceptions, one of them being the abovementioned 'cultural exception'.[20]

[17] Edward B Tylor, *Primitive Culture* 7th edn (New York, Brentano's, 1924) 1871. Tylor was the father of cultural evolutionism and gave this most famous definition of culture: 'That complex whole which includes knowledge, belief, art, morals, law, custom, and any other capabilities and habits acquired by man as a member of society'.

[18] Franz Boas wrote also against theories generally accepted in that time, according to which some races are superior to others. See, mainly, Franz Boas, *The Mind of Primitive Man* (Whitefish MT, Kessinger, 2007) 1911.

[19] https://en.unesco.org/creativity/convention.

[20] See Serge Regourd, *L'Exception Culturelle [The Cultural Exception]* 2nd edn (Paris, Presses Universitaires de France, 2004); Bruno de Witte, 'Trade in Culture: International legal regimes and EU constitutional values' in Gráinne de Búrca and Joanne Scott (eds), *The EU and the WTO* (Oxford, Hart Publishing, 2001) 238; Anna Herold, 'European Public Film Support within the WTO Framework', *IRISplus, Legal Observations of the European Audiovisual Observatory* (2003-6) 2ff; Anna Herold, *European film policies in the context of EU and international law: a misalliance of culture and free market* (PhD thesis written at the European University Institute, Florence and published in Europa Law Publishing, 2009). It is also interesting to reproduce here the words of S Nikoltchev, Head of Department of Legal Information at the European Audiovisual Observatory, in the editorial to that very issue 2003-6: 'The promotion of cultural diversity and a competitive European film and programming industry continues to be the subject of much debate this year. … However, Europeans are also currently faced with a contradictory suggestion: various states have called for audiovisual services to be made subject to WTO regulations, partly in order that potentially anti-competitive effects of the various support programmes might be recognized and reduced. The European Union has already taken a stance through statements made by the Commission and Parliament in relation to preparations for the fifth Ministerial

Movies are the classical example of this cultural exception, an exception which goes back to the post-Second World War period, when France used it to stop the increasing presence of American movies in its theatres. However, this was not a unilateral decision, since it responded to agreements signed between France and the United States.[21] The US accepted it. The UNESCO Convention on the Protection and Promotion of the Diversity of Cultural Expressions is, indeed, intended to be left aside from any negotiation on trade regulation products or goods with some kind of cultural or artistic value.[22] Even if it is not its main intention, it is at least one of its major consequences. Thus its political and economic importance is apparent.

Cultural diversity is also a key legal concept in European Union law. The European Community Treaty (hereinafter, the EC Treaty) grants powers to the European Community to preserve its cultural diversity. European culture in the broad sense, as mentioned before, is thus a complex phenomenon, since it purports a somewhat delicate equilibrium between the cultures of the Member States and an ideal of European culture in the strict sense, which is still developing.

So far, I have referred to the broad concept of culture. As for the narrow concept, it implies that culture is only related to the fine arts, or simply the arts, admitting here that some entertainment activities – such are movies – can also be considered to be culture in this sense.

The question of culture is indeed relevant in the international sphere. This is so not only due to the existence of international treaties on the protection of culture, but also due to 'cultural clauses' or 'exceptions' in other types of treaties. In the international arena, such as in the framework of the negotiations of the WTO, one can perceive a major fracture between the United States and the European States. And the fracture is fostered even more since the European States take common positions under the umbrella of the European Union and develop therefore a common cultural policy. The relevance of this issue was put forward by some scholars back in the 1990's and, as Schlesinger framed it at that time, 'culture is going to be one of the main political battle camps in the future'.[23] It should be assessed whether this has actually proved to be so.

Conference in the World Trade Organisation (WTO), being held in Cancún, Mexico in September. It appears determined not to enter into any commitments in the audiovisual sector'. Indeed, as we know now, the European Union has still not entered into any commitment in the audiovisual sector. The negotiations at the WTO being halted for the moment, and the problems within this organisation being more far-reaching, it might be the case that this question will remain undisputed in the near future.

[21] On the Blum-Byrnes Agreements see Association française de recherche sur l'histoire du cinéma, Blum-Byrnes. L'arrangement 1945-1948 (1895, 1993, nº 13).

[22] See Art 20 of the UNESCO Convention on the Protection and Promotion of the Diversity of Cultural Expressions.

[23] See Philip Schlesinger, 'Europeanness: A New Cultural Battlefield' in John Hutchinson and Anthony Smith (eds), *Nationalism* (Oxford, Oxford University Press, 1994).

'Culture' is understood here as equivalent to 'the arts'.[24] However, its broader meaning will also be considered, since public policies on the arts, and more specifically film policies, usually lay on a preconception of what a certain culture is or should be and how it can be preserved.[25]

IV. The European Perspective: Changing Patterns in EU Law

A. Cultural Policies in the Member States of the European Union

For many years, some Member States of what is now the European Union, developed strong cultural policies, where films played a very important if not decisive role. France, of course, is the leading example of this, since it expeditiously created a specific public body to deal with these policies: the Department of Culture (*Ministère de la Culture*).[26] But also other countries, such as Germany, Italy,[27] and Spain, among others,[28] have traditionally devoted an important part of their public budget to subsidise culture/films in various forms: grants to fund the artistic creation, protection of cultural/artistic heritage, funds to support the film industry in all its phases – pre-production, production, post-production, distribution, exhibition, promotion, etc. However, other European countries, such as the United Kingdom, have a different tradition in this regard. Although they are in favour of aiding and supporting artistic activities, yet it is for very different motives. For instance, aids are granted in the United Kingdom to promote culture as an educational goal and not *usually* just for the art's sake.[29] This echoes the widespread notion of culture, one that links culture with education, and has given rise to the birth of a constitutional theory on the so-called 'Culture State' in Europe.[30]

[24] See here, in the British literature, P Kearns, *The Legal Concept of Art* (Oxford, Hart Publishing, 1999).

[25] On this see Batz (n 2). This reference is particularly interesting, because it focuses the analysis on audiovisual policies in Europe.

[26] For a classical critique on the French interventionism in the field of culture, see Marc Fumaroli, *l'état culturel. Essai sur une religion moderne [The Culture State. Essay on a Modern Religion]* (Paris, Fallois, 1991).

[27] See Lucia Bellucci, *Cinema e Aiuti di Stato Nell'Integrazione Europea. Un Dirittto Promozionale in Italia e in Francia [Film and State Aid in European Integration. A Supporting Law in Italy and France]* (Milan, Giuffrè, 2006).

[28] See an early publication on this in Council for Cultural Co-operation of the Council of Europe, *Art of the cinema in ten European countries* (1967).

[29] It should be mentioned here that the UNESCO Convention on the Protection and Promotion of the Diversity of Cultural Expressions defines cultural activities, goods and services 'irrespective of the commercial value they may have. Cultural activities may be and end in themselves, or they may contribute to the production of cultural goods and services' (art 4.4).

[30] This theory will be further developed later, but it should be noted already that it was first treated thoroughly in Enrico Spagna Musso, *Lo Stato di Cultura nella Costituzione italiana [The Culture State in the Italian Constitution]* (Naples, Morano, 1961).

Present-day public powers *in Europe* have 'discovered' the economic potential of culture and of cultural industries.[31] And here lies a new basis for public intervention which has developed recently and with a certain amount of success.[32] Governments, and more importantly, local authorities foster culture and film production, in order to increase the economic growth of the areas subject to their jurisdiction. This is generating a delocalisation of film production from the United States to Europe, since American producers can benefit – under certain circumstances – from European public funds, and they can also benefit from the indirect support to the film industry which is provided by facilitating access to locations, technical personnel, etc.[33]

The tradition in the EU Member States of placing culture in the political agenda and giving it support has been inherited by the European Union itself. The three founding Treaties of the European Communities, drafted back in the 1950s, are said to be just of economic nature and their purpose being to reach a European economic integration.[34] Yet some early political documents indicate that the goals of the European project were already ambitious at that time.[35] This is the case, for instance, in the Schuman Declaration, presented by the French foreign minister, Robert Schuman, on 9 May 1950, where it was stated that '[the] proposal will lead to the realization of the first concrete foundation of a European federation indispensable to the preservation of peace'. In fact, it is not even necessary to remember here that the idea of placing the coal and steel industry under

[31] Speaking of cultural 'industries' might sound oxymoronic to some, especially in Europe, but the truth is that such industries exist and some laws have been passed to establish their legal framework, and their importance for the general economy is continuously growing. See Rostam Neuwirth, *The Cultural Industries and the Legacy of Article IV GATT* (Conference on Cultural Traffic: Policy, Culture and the New Technologies in the European Union and Canada of 22–23 November 2002, Carleton University).

[32] On this see *The economy of culture in Europe*, EU Publications www.keanet.eu/ecoculture/executive_summary_en.pdf. See also *Eurobarometer qualitative study on the Europeans, culture and cultural values* at http://ec.europa.eu/culture/eac/sources_info/studies/eurobarometer_en.html. In Spain, a recent study (2007) has just been published by the Department of Culture: *El valor económico de la cultura (2000–2004)* [*The economic value of culture (2000–2004)*]. See www.cultura.mecd.es/estadisticas/MC/VecE/Presentacion.html. The areas considered therein are common heritage, archives and libraries, books and press, fine arts, visual arts, audiovisual and multimedia (films, video, music, television and radio). On the issue of economic value of culture for the United States, see Devlin (n 3). In the first paragraph of this article it is argued: 'The United States and Canada trade with each other more than any two other countries on earth. Part of this trade involves cultural products, an important export industry for the United States. Unlike the United States, Canada is primarily an importer of cultural products. Seventy-five percent of Canadian cultural products are imported, and the vast majority comes from the United States'.

[33] See, among others, Toby Miller and others, *Global Hollywood* (London, British Film Institute, 2005) 2: and in particular ch 2: 'The New International Division of Cultural Labour'.

[34] On the different theories about European integration, its various causes and its evolution, see Paul Craig and Gráinne de Búrca, *EU Law* 3rd edn (Oxford, Oxford University Press, 2003: 4th edn 2008) 3–52. For the Euro-American dialogue it is interesting to refer here to the explanation the authors provide as to the organisational needs the USA encountered in order to administer the Marshall Plan. The administration of the funds was first structured in the Organization for the European Economic Co-operation (OEEC: 1948) and led to co-operation mechanisms which would later prove useful for other organisations to come.

[35] ibid, 8, for instance.

one and the same authority (which was the aim of the European Coal and Steal Community in 1951), co-ordinated by two countries which had been enemies for centuries – France and Germany – was to help to maintain peace in the old continent.[36]

A specific legal basis for cultural policies was not included in the European Community Treaty until the Treaty of Maastricht modified the former in 1992 and introduced Article 128 EC Treaty (now Article 167 of the Treaty on the Functioning of the European Union/TFEU).[37] Culture was initially not a goal of the European Communities. However, it was present in some policies or regulations. For instance, culture could be invoked to limit the four fundamental freedoms of the internal market: free movement of goods, persons, services and capitals. This can be illustrated with the landmark ruling of the European Court of Justice (ECJ) in *Cinéthèque SA v Fédération Nationale des Cinémas Français* (1985).[38] Here, the French government established a minimum period of time that had to elapse between the time when a movie was first shown in theatres and the time when the same movie could be sold or rented through other means, such as video tapes. The Tribunal de Grande Instance of Paris[39] asked for a preliminary ruling to the ECJ, in order for it to determine whether this regulation was at all compatible with the European fundamental freedoms and, if it was not compatible, whether it could be considered as an exception to the general regime. The ECJ argued that such a system was common to many Member States of the European Union, and that its goal was to promote film production. It was indeed a restriction of the freedom of movement of goods (video tapes), but it was justified in order to pursue a legitimate goal in Community law. Culture was thus considered a legitimate objective in Community law which could affect its core, ie the fundamental freedoms.

Culture, therefore, was present in Community law before the Treaty of Maastricht, first, due to the fact that it could constitute an exception to fundamental freedoms. Second, it should also be borne in mind that policies which might very well be regarded from a cultural point of view can also be tackled from other perspectives. Film policies, for instance, have been adopted by the European Community even before the Treaty of Maastricht incorporated a legal basis for it. The so-called MEDIA programmes, which have been in motion since 1991, were carried out then under the legal basis of Article 130 EC Treaty, now Article 173 TFEU, which gives competence to the European Community to act in the field of industry. After a specific legal basis for culture was included in the Treaty, the

[36] See Martin Holland, *European Integration from Community to Union* (London, Pinter, 1993).

[37] This might well be regarded as a symptom of the new drift the European Community received at that time, a question which was tackled in Joseph Weiler, 'The Transformation of Europe' (1991) 100 *Yale Law Journal* 2403.

[38] Cases 60 & 61/84 [1985] ECR 2605.

[39] The Tribunal de Grande Instance of Paris is defined by Ass'n and others (eds), *The Bluebook: A Uniform System of Citation* 18th edn (New York, Columbia Law Review, 2005, 5th prtg 2007) 265 as the 'ordinary court of original jurisdiction'.

MEDIA programmes have *still* been linked to industry, but it is important to note that the cultural dimension has always been put forward.[40] So culture was implicit even when it wasn't formally present.

Third, culture was also present before 1992, not only to justify restrictions to the fundamental freedoms, but also to admit exceptions to another core principle of European Community law, being the prohibition of State aids.[41] There are several exceptions to this principle, which are included in various provisions. Agriculture is one of the well-known examples, and culture is another of these examples. Article 107 TFEU, paragraph 3 indicates which aids may be considered compatible with the common market. The Commission should indicate case by case (here including case categories) which aids affect trade in a manner that they are not compatible with the common market.[42] Amongst these types of aids, the Treaty specifically defines aids related to culture in the following terms: '[A]id[s] [devoted] to promote culture and heritage conservation where such aid[s] [do] not affect trading conditions and competition in the Community to an extent that is contrary to the common interest'. The aforesaid Article also mentions other categories of aids that can constitute an exception and that are related to economic development: this is important to note, since some measures adopted in Member States to promote film production could easily be included here. As already stated, public policies on the film industry are increasingly focusing now on using film production as a means to promote economic development in certain areas.

B. The European Identity. Towards a Legal Basis for Cultural Policies

The legal basis for European institutions to pursue cultural policies was introduced in 1992. Notwithstanding the foregoing, there is a long history of political attempts to take consideration of culture in the European integration process. This will be briefly summarised in the following lines, with a view to show the path

[40] See Herold (n 20) (both references).

[41] TFEU art 107 establishes that '[s]ave as otherwise provided in this Treaty, any aid granted by a Member State or through State resources in any form whatsoever which distorts or threatens to distort competition by favouring certain undertakings or the production of certain goods shall, in so far as it affects trade between Member States, be incompatible with the common market'.

[42] This decision is subject to judicial review. Although the Commission enjoys a high level of discretion in this type of decision, it does not imply that it is not susceptible of any type of control. A case where the Court of First Instance of the European Communities annulled the decision of the Commission denying the right of the party to have access to Community funds for film distribution (MEDIA II – Development and distribution, 1996–2000) is case T-233/00, *Scanbox Entertainment A/S v Commission of the European Communities*, 2002 ECR II-2749. I find particularly illustrative the distinction proposed by Peter Strauss between 'discretion' and 'DISCRETION!', which would help to categorise the cases in which judicial review can play a role in controlling the activity of the administration. This distinction can be found, for instance, in Peter Strauss, *Administrative Justice in the United States* 2nd edn (Durham NC, Carolina Academic Press, 2002) 91–94.

the EC and the EU have followed until now. It might seem difficult to find just one purpose behind this new policy and the political documents that preceded its incorporation to the EC Treaty. Various goals lie behind national cultural policies and therefore various goals also lie behind cultural policies in the framework of the EC. Education can be one of them. Indeed, from an organisational point of view, it is interesting to note that education and culture have been policies undertaken in one and the same General Direction at the European Commission, and today the programmes developed under both policies are conferred to one executive agency, which was recently created: the Executive Agency for Education, Audiovisual and Culture.[43] Economic development can also be a goal of cultural policies, as already indicated. However, to end with, one of the most important goals of cultural policies is to defend, to protect, to construct or to foster a specific identity. This can be traced in the opening statement to this article, put forward by Lord Slynn, and it is also one of the concepts that have guided the attempts to make the EC act in the cultural field.[44]

The Schuman Declaration showed the aim of the framers of the European project to reach an ever-growing union which at the end would not only be economic. Later documents show this ambition even better. As early as 1961, the so-called Fouchet Plan,[45] fostered by General de Gaulle, mentioned the need to foster cultural cooperation, with the view to protect the common heritage and also the values precious to the European civilisation. This document intended to promote a Union between European people, a Union based upon an intergovernmental model rather than upon an integrative one.[46] Yet the basic principle of its organisation was the one that has inspired the whole project since the very beginning: unity and common *spiritual* heritage, on the one side, and diversity and respect of the various cultures, on the other side.

Later, in 1969, at the Summit of The Hague, in The Netherlands, the – then – six Member States drafted a final Communiqué which contained the details of a real *momentum* in the history of the European Union.[47] Here, it was decided that the European Economic Community should be transformed into an economic and monetary union, that it should be enlarged and that goals other than economic should be pursued. Therefore, they stated that '[they had] a common conviction that a Europe composed of States … is indispensable for preserving an

[43] See http://eacea.ec.europa.eu/index.htm.

[44] This attempt, however, might bring negative consequences with it, such as the increase of 'the sense of alienation felt by certain sectors of Europe's population'. See Craufurd Smith (n 1) 277, 294.

[45] It should be remembered that neither the United Kingdom nor Ireland were members of the European Communities at that time. This is the reason why English was not an official language, so usually references to the *Plan Fouchet* are made in French, even when addressed to English speakers. The text can be found, in French, at www.leforum.de/artman/publish/printer_520.shtml.

[46] It was promoted by General De Gaulle, but some representatives of other Member States were firmly against it. The Fouchet Plan was reviewed on several occasions but finally did not lead to the project it was supposed to foster.

[47] This document can be found at http://aei.pitt.edu/1451/01/hague_1969.pdf.

exceptional seat of development, of progress and culture, for world equilibrium and for peace'.[48]

The Paris Summit in 1972 introduced a 'qualitative development'[49] in the European Economic Community. The Member States decided to go further with new objectives and policies. Economic expansion, again, was considered not to be an end in itself, but a means towards something more ambitious. This was the year in which new Accession Treaties for Denmark, Ireland and the United Kingdom were signed, thus meaning that the Communities would be nine Member States Communities from 1973 onwards. It can be inferred from the Statement of the Paris Summit an express awareness of the destiny and role of Europe:

> [N]ow that the tasks of the Community are growing, and fresh responsibilities are being laid upon it, the time has come for Europe to recognize clearly the unity of its interests, the extent of its capacities and the magnitude of its duties; Europe must be able to make its voice heard in world affairs, and to make an original contribution commensurate with its human, intellectual and material resources. It must affirm its own views in international relations, as befits its mission to be open to the world and for progress, peace and co-operation.[50]

A special mention to the 'genius of Europe' is to be found in the text, as well as the need to take into consideration European 'intangible values'. This is (clearly?) linked to a concept of identity that the European Communities might be willing to build or identify.[51] The idea of a common identity is found further in the section related to external relations, where a distinct approach, common to all Member States, but recognisable as pertaining to a different subject, is to be fostered.[52] The idea of an identity based on diversity might seem apparent.

The European identity will be a key concept at a later stage, the European Summit in Copenhagen, in 1973. The Europe of Nine drafted a new document, precisely about identity, which starts with the following statement:

> The Nine Member Countries of the European Communities have decided that the time has come to draw up a document on the European Identity. This will enable them to achieve a better definition of their relations with other countries and of their

[48] In point 11 of the Communiqué the States even mention the desire to create a European University. This is a reality now, after the creation in 1972 of the European University Institute in Florence, Italy.

[49] So it has been qualified in Marcos Vaquer, *Estado y Cultura* (Madrid, CEURA, 1998) 153.

[50] It is highly interesting, and must therefore be highlighted, that the word 'Europe' is mentioned here instead of the 'European Communities'. This far-reaching ambition, to unite (or re-unite) the whole continent under one and the same project, can be perceived in later documents and has been confirmed in the Berlin Declaration on 25 March 2007, where the new Member States, Bulgaria and Rumania, are warmly welcomed. I will refer to the Berlin Declaration later in this same text.

[51] This will be a recurrent argument: every time an enlargement takes place, the question of identity is tackled.

[52] 'The construction of Europe will allow it, in conformity with its ultimate political objectives, to affirm its personality while remaining faithful to its traditional friendships and to the alliances of the Member States, and to establish its position in world affairs as a distinct entity'. See in the document 'To this end', number 7.

> responsibilities and the place which they occupy in world affairs. They have decided to define the European Identity with the dynamic nature of the Community in mind. They have the intention of carrying the work further in the future in the light of the progress made in the construction of a United Europe.

Identity is constructed upon an idea of opposition to others, as it was already visible in the Statement at the Paris Summit, and responsibilities are thus to be defined. One of the key words in the document is 'dynamism', and it indicates the need to redefine the identity as new Member States are included in the European project. The European identity is considered in this document from a twofold perspective, which has been a constant *leit motiv* since the early beginning of the European Communities and explains European cultural policies now. On the one hand, there is a need to concentrate on the common values. On the other hand, cultural diversity (and diversity in general) is to be respected.[53] This formula is now in Article 167 TFEU, ie in the legal basis for cultural policies.

The European identity, according to the Declaration adopted in 1973 at the Summit in Copenhagen, is based on four main elements: representative democracy, rule of law, social justice (which is, according to the document, the ultimate goal of economic progress) and respect of human rights. And the premises for those elements to exist at the supranational level are the common European civilisation, the attachment to common values and principles, the increasing convergence of attitudes to life, the awareness of having specific interests in common and the determination to take part in the construction of a United Europe. It is clear that these ambitious goals go way beyond the economic nature of the European Economic Community, but it is also clear that they are not easy to achieve, not the least because Member States might not be really willing to reach that end.

The Copenhagen Declaration can be considered a milestone on the path towards a political union, at least *on paper*, and some years later it leads, implicitly or explicitly, to the idea of a people's Europe. This starts to take shape at the European Council in Fontainebleau, in 1984, and the Conclusions to this Council revisit the notion of identity and common image. Identity and people's Europe might well be considered as two elements of one and the same reality. Yet this chapter does not endeavour the (fascinating) task of building a theory on identity in Europe,[54] but to simply try and explain why cultural policies developed in the European Communities at a certain point in time.

[53] 'The Nine wish to ensure that the cherished values of their legal, political and moral order are respected and to preserve the rich variety of their national cultures'.

[54] Joseph Weiler is critical of the institutional attempts to foster a European identity. See Joseph Weiler, *The Constitution for Europe, 'Do the New Clothes have an Emperor'* (Cambridge, Cambridge University Press, 1999) 344. On the new momentum in the EU see, among others, R Comella, *New Governance Fatigue? Administration and Democracy in the European Union* (Jean Monnet Working Paper No 06, 2006), https://jeanmonnetprogram.org/paper/new-governance-fatigue-administration-and-democracy-in-the-european-union/.

Finally, mention should be made of a recent political document which was drafted precisely, in order to set the new conceptual framework in the EU. The last enlargement of the EU and the need to define the European project for the future brought European political leaders, under the German Presidency, to sign the Berlin Declaration on 25 March 2007.[55] The type of Declaration under discussion here, and where the document signed in Berlin can be integrated, very much reminds us of Constitution Preambles. Of course, I do not mean here that the Berlin Declaration should be considered a Constitution Preamble (since this would imply many assumptions that are not the object of this chapter), but the constitutional moment and the political process in which the EU is now embedded magnify the importance of this document.

It is perhaps not surprising that no reference to a European identity is to be found in this text. Experiences that are still perceived as very recent, such as the negative results in the French and Dutch referenda about the European Constitution, may lie beneath this choice. From a political point of view it might not have been an appropriate moment to foster the idea of a European identity when the popularity of the European project may not be as high as it used to be.[56] Thus, the Berlin Declaration does not refer to the European identity, contrary to previous documents of the same kind, but it does include references to unity and to the citizens of the Union in a way very reminiscent of earlier utterances to the European identity:

> For centuries Europe has been an idea, holding out hope of peace and understanding. That hope has been fulfilled. European unification has made peace and prosperity possible. It has brought about a sense of community and overcome differences. Each Member State has helped to unite Europe and to strengthen democracy and the rule of law. Thanks to the yearning for freedom of the peoples of Central and Eastern Europe the unnatural division of Europe is now consigned to the past. European integration

[55] The text can be found at http://europa.eu/50/docs/berlin_declaration_en.pdf.

[56] After the negative results of the referenda in France and The Netherlands, the European Commission launched a campaign focused on culture in order to involve the citizens in the European project. Thus, the Commission stated the following: 'Opinion polls confirm that Europeans are generally concerned about the speed of economic and technological change, as well as the phenomenon of globalization. They feel a loss of identity and often have a sense of disconnection from the European Union. Against this backdrop, there is a growing recognition that the EU must bring itself closer to the citizen and that art and culture can make an important contribution. Indeed, art and culture offer an inspiring way of looking at reality. They can provide a more human dimension to the integration project, a so-called "Soul for Europe". In this context, the perception and role of culture in the EU is gradually changing. Whereas, in the past, the question was what Europe could do for culture, there is a growing recognition that culture lies at the heart of the European project and has a unique and indispensable role to play. It is therefore increasingly necessary to also ask what culture can do for Europe. The Directorate General for Education and Culture (DG EAC) is preparing a Communication on culture which seeks to address these issues. Please visit our website … Participate in the consultation.' E-mail from Edith Guetta (27 September 2006) (on file with author). See *Eurobarometer qualitative study on the Europeans, culture and cultural values* (n 32). Maybe in order to fight the euro-sceptisicism, the Berlin Declaration concludes, '[F]or we know, Europe is our common future'.

> shows that we have learnt the painful lessons of a history marked by bloody conflict. Today we live together as was never possible before.
>
> We, the citizens of the European Union, have united for the better.
>
> …
>
> We have a unique way of living and working together in the European Union.
>
> …
>
> We preserve in the European Union the identities and diverse traditions of its Member States. We are enriched by open borders and a lively variety of languages, cultures and regions. There are many goals which we cannot achieve on our own, but only in concert.

The many references in various parts of this document to *aspects* or *perspectives* of the notion of identity are apparent; as is also apparent the emphasis put on the existence of *various* identities under one common umbrella which is the European Union. The consolidation of a 'European society' and of a 'European model' – which are mentioned by the Declaration – should/could be achieved, precisely, through cultural policies, that preserve the identities, the traditions, and the variety of languages, cultures and regions. Again, unity in the diversity.

To conclude with, it should be noted that documents other than the ones signed at the highest political level of the European Communities and the European Union were also drafted in order to promote specific actions in the area of culture. The first one of this sort was the Commission's Communication *Community Action in the Cultural Sector*, issued in 1977, on the basis of former resolutions of the European Parliament.[57] Here, the Commission recalls that at the Copenhagen Summit, culture was recognised at the highest political level as one of the fundamental elements of European identity. It is one of the elements that contribute to the feelings of being part of a whole and to solidarity. The Commission provides a definition for the cultural sector, which is considered as 'the socio-economic whole formed by persons and undertakings dedicated to the production and distribution of cultural goods and services'. It is interesting to note that this definition includes both an economic and a social view of culture. Community action in this area should focus in two main types of activities: solution of specific problems (taxes, preservation of common heritage) and support of culture, which might be considered the very European approach. This actually allows the existence of different European cultural policies, and not just one cultural policy. Finally, there is an insistence upon cooperation, with other international organisations, such as UNESCO and the Council of Europe,[58] and also cooperation with Member States. Later documents only emphasise on this specific line, such as the Communication of Commission and Parliament on *Stronger Action in the Cultural Sector* (1982) and *Cultural Action in the European Community. New Orientations Envisaged*, Commission Staff Working Paper (1991).

[57] 13 May 1974 and 8 March 1976.

[58] This organisation deals and works with basic concepts such as cultural democracy, socio-cultural leadership and integrated preservation.

C. The Legal Basis for Culture: 'Culture Constitution' and 'Culture State'

All the aforementioned political precedents should not overshadow the main legal achievement of the Treaty of Maastricht in 1992: the inclusion of a legal basis for the European Community to pursue cultural policies. What is now Article 167 TFEU reads as follows:

> 1. The Union shall contribute to the flowering of the cultures of the Member States, while respecting their national and regional diversity and at the same time bringing the common cultural heritage to the fore.
>
> 2. Action by the Union shall be aimed at encouraging cooperation between Member States and, if necessary, supporting and supplementing their action in the following areas:
>
> - improvement of the knowledge and dissemination of the culture and history of the European peoples,
> - conservation and safeguarding of cultural heritage of European significance,
> - non-commercial cultural exchanges,
> - artistic and literary creation, including in the audiovisual sector.
>
> 3. The Union and the Member States shall foster cooperation with third countries and the competent international organisations in the sphere of culture, in particular the Council of Europe.
>
> 4. The Union shall take cultural aspects into account in its action under other provisions of the Treaties, in particular in order to respect and to promote the diversity of its cultures.
>
> 5. In order to contribute to the achievement of the objectives referred to in this Article:
>
> - the European Parliament and the Council acting in accordance with the ordinary legislative procedure and after consulting the Committee of the Regions, shall adopt incentive measures, excluding any harmonisation of the laws and regulations of the Member States,
> - the Council, on a proposal from the Commission, shall adopt recommendations.

A modification to the initial version of 1992 was introduced in 1998, and what is now paragraph 4, was inserted to incorporate a transversal provision, implying that all measures adopted under any other provision of the Treaty (such as trade or industry, for instance) should take consideration of the 'cultural aspect' of the measure. These types of transversal provisions, which also exist in other areas, such as environmental law, imply here that all policies can be indirectly addressed to support culture, something which is especially applicable to film policies, because they can pursue different goals. It should also be noted that the regulation of Article 167 TFEU is coherent with the classical twofold perspective which appeared in previous political documents: although a common culture is to be fostered, support of diversity is at the core of Community cultural policies.

In Article 167 TFEU, some authors see an embryo of the so-called 'Culture Constitution'. The theory of the 'Culture Constitution' (*Kulturverfassung, Costituzione culturale, Constitución cultural*) has been developed by scholars in some European States, departing from the fact that some European Constitutions include specific provisions on culture and the arts.[59] These *constitutional* provisions are designed, among other aims, to preserve cultural heritage, to provide access to culture for citizens, to protect artistic freedom or to include cultural transversal clauses such as the one now existing at the European Community law level. Culture, both in the broad as in the narrow sense is considered here, and therefore public duties towards culture are, in principle, wide in scope (of course, as in other cases of public duties, there are always difficulties in enforcing them). It should be noted that the notion of 'Culture Constitution' does not refer to a type of Constitution based on customs or traditions. It has a very precise meaning, which is the set of constitutional provisions dealing with public action in the field of culture and the arts, the whole of principles and choices of the supreme norm in relation to culture. The theory should not be confused with other anthropological notions which might share some common elements with it, but which do not have the legal dimension that is being referred to here.

The theory of the 'Culture Constitution' argues that, along history, different norms have regulated various aspects of culture (museums, theatre, education …) but only recently – mostly after Second World War – have Constitutions incorporated these types of provisions.[60] This could be applied to the EU. As to the European Union, some authors maintain that some articles of the TFEU build what is usually considered as the Culture Constitution. Article 167 TFEU is one clear example, but mention should also be made of Article 3.3 of the EU Treaty, insofar as it includes culture as one of the competencies, goals and policies of the EU. The fact that these Articles exist implies specific obligations for public powers, like the one included in paragraph 4 of Article 167 TFEU, the transversal provision that was referred to previously: Thus, '[t]he Community shall take cultural aspects into account in its action under other provisions of this Treaty, in particular in order to respect and to promote the diversity of its cultures'. So, an action related to trade, to industry, to economy in general, to environmental protection … any action should take into consideration possible cultural implications and take them into account in the final decision.

From a wider perspective, the existence of a 'Culture Constitution' is linked to a specific State type or model, which has been characterised by some authors as

[59] Apart from the references that are provided in other notes, see also Peter Häberle, *Kulturstaatlichkeit und Kulturverfassungsrecht* (Darmstadt, Wissenschaftliche Buchgesellschaft, 1982); Jesús Prieto de Pedro, *Cultura, Culturas y Constitución* (Madrid, Centro de Estudios Políticos y Constitucionales, 1992).

[60] This is a similar phenomenon to the one that occurred between World War I and World War II with the concept of 'Economic Constitution'.

the 'Culture State'.[61] The 'Culture State' is, of course, linked to the Welfare State, but the emphasis is put on one specific public policy, which is considered to be the key element to build up the public space and to allow citizens to take part fully in that public space. Supporters of this theory thus argue – in coherence with the theory of the 'Culture Constitution' – that there are constitutional provisions that compel public powers to adopt cultural measures, usually intended to facilitate access to culture for all citizens, to fight against social exclusion, and to support artistic creativity and free expression through the arts. Film policies are clearly included here. There might be some problems, on applying a broad concept of culture here as there won't be a clear priority in terms of cultural goals, and the judges will be unable to decide on clear constitutional patterns in case of conflict. But a wide concept of culture is also useful, as it allows consideration of wide-ranging policies and can confer, if needed, higher protection.[62]

The original concept of the 'Culture State' links culture to education, which should be understood in the most far-reaching way, ie as a means to educate future citizens who will fully participate in the democratic process. Only thus would theoretical democracy be transformed into real democracy. I do not pretend here to deal, even tentatively, with theories of democracy. The research question is much more specific, but the overall picture should not be forgotten. Culture and democracy go hand-in-hand according to this theory, and it could be asked whether cultural policies at the EU level might be directed explicitly or implicitly towards the building up of a concept of democracy at the supranational level.

V. The US Perspective: Changing Patterns in US Law

It is frequently argued that culture has not played a political, legal or public role in the United States as it has in Europe. This might be true if the figures of public budgets are compared,[63] but American public policies in the cultural field should not be underestimated. In the following section, the various stages in the history of cultural policies of the United States will be briefly summarised. Interestingly, the attempt to create a public body somehow comparable to a Department or a Ministry for Culture (the National Endowment for the Arts, hereinafter NEA) was pursued approximately at the same time as some European countries, such

[61] See the early works of Otmar Jung, *Zum Kulturstaatsbegriff* (Meisenheim, Anton Hain, 1976) and Spagna Musso (n 30).

[62] The potential breadth of the concept of culture and the dangers surrounding it might have been one of the reasons why some European countries have been historically against granting the EC competences in the cultural field. Since culture is, in principle, a concept with positive connotations, its use might lead to abuse by public powers, which could adopt putative cultural policies with the real intention to intervene in areas where the countries had not actually conferred competences.

[63] Figures for the NEA, 2017, can be found in the following link: www.arts.gov/sites/default/files/2017%20Annual%20Report.pdf. As for the European Union, see references in note 32.

as France, decided to establish similar types of bodies. The creation of the NEA led ultimately to important controversies in Congress, but also throughout the country, as public funding was given to certain artistic projects that some found 'indecent'.[64] This debate is clearly applicable to the funding of the film industry and is therefore the context in which the latter should be considered. Indeed, attention will be devoted, first, to the general question of presence of public policies and public bodies in the cultural field, bearing in mind the previous considerations in the European experience, which should serve to draw conclusions from a comparative law perspective. Second, film policies will be specifically discussed and some final remarks, again from a comparative law perspective, will be made.

A. A Brief Introduction to the History of Cultural Policies in the United States

The history of the relationship between government and culture in the United States is clearly different from the one in Europe and is determined by the very origins of the country. According to historical studies, colonial America was unsupportive of the arts and people were prosecuted for producing or rehearsing plays.[65] This might have been a reaction against European countries, mainly England, since plays reflected precisely a specific culture which might have been perceived as alien and hostile. Apart from this, another fact that should be taken into consideration is that theatre was also controversial at that time in Europe, and that theatre censorship and prohibitions were developed during that period, due to various reasons, such as political or those related to alleged decency issues.[66]

Cultural policies in the United States go back to the period of the Depression, when two projects were created: the Federal Arts Project and the Federal Theatre Project. Yet these projects did not pursue strict cultural or artistic aims,

[64] See, eg, Symposium, 'Art, Distribution & the State: Perspectives on the National Endowment for the Arts' (1999) 17 *Cardozo Arts & Entertainment Law Journal* 705. See further GE Devlin, 'NEA v Finley: Explicating the Rocky Relationship between the Government and the Arts' (2000) 27 *Pepperdine Law Review* 345; M Mustokoff, 'National Endowment for the Arts v Finley: Striking the Balance between Art and the State or Sealing the Fate of Viewpoint Neutrality?' (1998) 9 *Temple Political & Civil Rights Law Review* 135; Th Scelza and KT Murray, 'The Big Chill: Is the Exotic Cow, Tutto Nudo, an NEA Endorsement?' ("002) 164 *Education Law Reporter* 2; Cara Putman, 'National Endowment for the Arts v. Finley: The Supreme court Missed an Opportunity to Clarify the Role of the NEA in Funding the Arts: Are the Grants a Property Right or an Award?' (1999) 9 *George Mason University Civil Rights Law Journal* 237, 248; Lackland Bloom, Jr, 'NEA v. Finley: A Decision in Search of a Rationale' (1999) 77 *Washington University Law Quarterly* 1, 25–26.

[65] See, among others, Enrique R Carrasco, 'The National Endowment for the Arts: A Search for an Equitable Grant Making Process' (1986) 74 *Georgetown Law Journal* 1521, 1534. See further George B Bryan, *American Theatrical Regulation* (Metuchen NJ, The Scarecrow Press, Inc, 1993) 1607–900.

[66] See, in Spanish, Ingenio fecundo y juicio profundo. *Estudios de Historia del Teatro en la Edad Moderna* (Carmen Sanz Ayan, ed, Universidad Complutense de Madrid 1999), and also edited by Carmen Sanz Ayan (a Member of the Spanish Royal Academy of History) see Teatro y Fiesta *del Siglo de Oro en Tierras Europeas de los Austrias* (Madrid, SEACEX 2003).

but were rather conceived to foster employment.[67] Although there are, of course, some precedents, it was not until the 1950s that the American Federal Government clearly developed the idea of creating an agency for the arts and the education, which would lead some years later, in 1965, to the establishment of the NEA.[68] Since then, some have seen a (constant) increase in the role of the government through various bodies and techniques.[69]

In his thorough and well-documented study,[70] Martel submits that there is indeed public intervention in the field of culture and the arts, but this is 'invisible'. There is usually, contrary to what happens in Europe, no public funding for individuals, as is usually the case in Europe. Yet tax deductions to foundations or private institutions are fairly common in the system.[71] This is an important example of the presence of private funding,[72] which leads the author to describe this 'decentralised system' in its singular details. All together it might be qualified as a mess or a disorder, which nonetheless builds a system.[73] This is, definitely, the case for films, since film production depends on private business, public policies and private initiative based on cultural, artistic or other non-profit interests.[74]

So there is in fact a history of cultural policies in the United States. But does it have the same implications for the question of identity as it might have in Europe/the EU? The arts and culture do play an important role in the United States law, and in reality it could be considered that they contribute to the concept of cultural identity or identification, as much as they do in Europe. Indeed, as some authors have argued:

> [w]e depend upon our arts community for cultural identification. Moreover, tolerance and understanding are often drawn from the arts. … Indeed, it is said that philosophers

[67] See Carrasco (n 65).

[68] For a thorough description and analysis of the development of cultural policies in the US see Frédéric Martel, *De la Culture en Amérique* (Paris, Gallimard, 2006). The author of this 'tocquevillian' approach to cultural policies in the US worked at the department of cultural affairs at the French Embassy in Washington for some years.

[69] This is one of the major arguments of Frédéric Martel (n 68). I am translating here the French word 'État' for 'Government'. Yet it should be noted that the way Martel uses the word 'État' might be more far-reaching, as it is related to any public intervention by any type of public body.

[70] ibid.

[71] I would like to refer again here to the discussion on indirect public aids. See on this Vanessa Hernández Guerrero, 'Defining the Balance between Free Competition and Tax Sovereignty in EC and WTO Law: the "Due Respect" to the General Tax System' (2004) 5 *German Law Journal* 1.

[72] This is one of the *leit motivs* of the book (cited in n 68). *Ad ex* see p 289: 'De sorte que si le ministère de la Culture n'est nulle part, la vie culturelle est partout' [Thus if the Department for Culture is nowhere, cultural life is everywhere].

[73] See also on this general idea E Abrahamson and D Freedman, *A Perfect Mess: The Hidden Benefits of Disorder* (2007).

[74] Something more specific – and leaving the film industry for later comment – is the public policy on museums. As Congress declared at the time of the framing of the Museums Act, 'an advanced civilization must not limit its efforts to science and technology alone, but must give full value and support to the other great branches of scholarly and cultural activity in order to achieve a better understanding of the past, a better analysis of the present, and a better view to the future', reported in Marilyn E Phelan, *Museum Law* 2nd edn (Evanston, Kalos Kapp Press, 2001). The author argues that museums in the US should 'foster and support a form of education, and access to the arts and the humanities'

> are half a generation ahead of cultural trends and that artists are half a generation ahead of philosophers.[75]

Others have scrutinised the impact of the film industry on American cultural identity, since film exportation implies the exportation of a cultural image to the world.[76] This is not the place to propose a tentative definition of what cultural identity is, or what identity in general is. But it is interesting to note how it is possible to locate an approach here rather similar to the one existing in Europe, an approach which might have legal implications.

Films are not *necessarily* regarded as culture in the United States, but some novelties – which will be developed later – are worth mentioning. First, subsidies for film production are increasing, be it through direct aids or through tax benefits. Second, state and local bodies are developing film policies in order to foster economic development. And, third, there are some concerns in the film industry regarding audiences in Europe. This is due to the fact that many American films are more successful in Europe than in America, something that implies that a part of the market is oriented towards Europe and not towards America.

It could be concluded from the previous lines that in the US there is indeed a public system of regulating and funding the arts, a system completely different from the European system, but which pursues similar aims. From a legal perspective, it is interesting to see how the system works, what kind of public bodies pursue these policies, what kind of limits and conditions constrain their activity and how it can be controlled. Some of these questions will be considered in the following section, which will link the general question with the more specific one of film policies.

B. Culture and Agencies: The NEA

The NEA is an independent agency of the federal government which was established in 1965[77] with the following goals: to support the excellence in the arts, to bring the arts to Americans and to provide leadership in arts education.[78]

that will 'provide models of excellence to the American people' [at 1]. See also Stephen E Weil, *Beauty and the Beasts. On Museums, Art, the Law and the Market* (Washington DC, Smithsonian Institution Press, 1983).

[75] See Kristine M Cunnane, 'Maintaining Viewpoint Neutrality for the NEA: National Endowment for the Arts v Finley' (1999) 31 *Connecticut Law Review* 1445, 1482.

[76] See Paul C Weiler, *Entertainment, Media and the Law, Entertainment, Media and the Law 997* (St Paul MN, West Group, 1997).

[77] The agency was created under the presidency of Lyndon Johnson, following the path of President John F Kennedy. Its greatest development arrived only later, under President Nixon, paradoxically enough, since Republicans had been contrary to the creation (and preservation) of such an agency.

[78] The National Foundation on the Arts and Humanities Act of 1965. The NEA is not a regulatory agency, but an adjudicatory one. On rulemaking, from an American-European comparative perspective, particularly interesting for this article, see Peter L Strauss, 'Rulemaking in the Ages of Globalization and Information: What America Can Learn from Europe, and Vice Versa' (2006) 12 *Columbia Journal of European Law* 645.

The key words here are creativity, access to culture and education, ie just the same ones that guide cultural public policies in Europe.[79]

Attention should be paid to the fact that this agency does not simply support culture or the arts for themselves, in the belief that they might be considered public goods worth protecting and promoting.[80] The NEA does so, but it also does something else. It links the arts to other public policies, such as education and the fight against social exclusion (through access to culture).[81] This is something common to other countries and, more specifically, to the European Union, as has already been mentioned. Thus, another element for a common understanding can be found here.

One of the major problems with public bodies dealing with cultural and artistic issues in the US is the fact that it is not easy to convince tax-payers that their money is devoted to cultural enterprises,[82] especially when those cultural enterprises are capable of offending some of them. In this regard, significant controversies have arisen in the judicial arena, as some funds allocated by the NEA to cultural projects were considered indecent by some.[83] Thereafter, many voices asked Congress to cut or even eliminate funds to the NEA, and this turned into one of the ongoing discussions between Democrats and Republicans. The latter proposed the NEA had to disappear, whereas the former put forward its value and its need for the development of a society of free people. Finally, there was an agreement that the NEA was indeed necessary, but there was still discrepancy in the way it should work. Republicans would rather fund the preservation of cultural heritage, where

[79] Some have identified less pious aims in the creation of this (type of) agency, which would have been proposed by some intellectuals, at the time of the Cold War, in order to show the excellence of American culture to the world. On American cultural policy at the time of the Cold War, see eg Martel (n 68) 27–28.

[80] On culture as a public good in the US see Weiler (n 76): 'The further question, though, is whether the cultural environment (like the physical environment) has the qualities of a public good that are not sufficiently served by individual choices in the consumer market, such that there is a need for collective citizen action through the political process'.

[81] This might be clear when referring to action in small communities. See J Weatherup, 'Agencies and the Arts: The Dilemma of Subsidizing Expression' (2004)24 *Journal of the National Association of Administrative Law Judges* 271, 307: 'While private parties may provide support for the arts in a major metropolis, programs bringing art and culture to local communities would be unlikely to survive without the aide of the NEA'. The NEA programmes to bring the arts to Americans including specific actions on reaching every community.

[82] ibid: 'Rather than being conclusive, Finley leaves many questions unanswered, and its broad grant of discretion to the NEA obscures the extent to which the agency may have duties to protect the First Amendment rights of grantees while maintaining taxpayers' confidence in the institution', at 307. See also Neil P Patten, 'The Politics of Art and the Irony of Politics: How the Supreme Court, Congress, the NEA, and Karen Finley Misunderstand Art and Law in National Endowment for the Arts v Finley' (2000) 37 *Houston Law Review* 559.

[83] Among the most relevant cases, see: *Nat'l Endowment for the Arts v Finley*, 524 US 569, 602 (1998) (Souter, J dissenting); *Advocates for the Arts v Thomson*, 532 F. 2d 792 (1st Cir. 1976) cert. denied, 429 US 894 (1976); *Southeastern Promotions, Ltd v Conrad*, 420 US 546 (1975); *Brooklyn Inst Of Arts & Scis v New York*, 64 F. Supp. 2d 184 (EDNY); *People for the Ethical Treatment of Animals v Giuliani*, 105 F. Supp. 2d 294 (SDNY); *Rosenberger v Rector & Visitors of Univ of Va*, 515 US 819 (1995); *Bella Lewitzky Dance Foundation v Frohanmayer*, 754 F. Supp. 774, 776 (CD Cal 1991); *Miller v California*, 413 US 15 (1973).

Democrats would see the value in supporting artists even if their projects may in some cases raise doubts as to the respect of the limits of the First Amendment.

The NEA takes decisions on what is art and what is not art when giving funds to the various projects, and is setting the framework of artistic freedom as a manifestation of freedom of expression.[84] But this should be and is controlled by judges. The Supreme Court did not find that the 'aggressive' projects that were funded by the NEA and which gave rise to various cases had gone beyond the First Amendment limits. It actually advised political parties to reach some balanced agreement amongst them. New trends at the NEA show a move towards educational policies, something which might imply that this balanced (de minimis) agreement has been reached. From a practical point of view, this has had positive consequences, such as a funding increase in the last few years.[85]

From the preceding lines it can be deduced that although culture has allegedly not played a major role in public policies in the United States, there is an interesting bibliography on the NEA and on the limits and justification for this kind of public policy. Also, other public and private initiatives illustrate this statement. Americans for the Arts was created in 1996 as a result of the merger between the National Assembly of Local Arts Agencies (NALAA) and the American Council for the Arts (ACA). Even though it is a non-profit organisation, its links with public organisations are strong. They present themselves in the following way:

> Americans for the Arts is the nation's leading non-profit organization for advancing the arts in America. With 45 years of service, we are dedicated to representing and serving local communities and creating opportunities for every American to participate in and appreciate all forms of the arts.[86]

This far-reaching objective seems fairly similar to European proposals, and its main purpose is carried out through local arts agencies, something which is again coherent with similar initiatives in Europe. The development of cultural public policies through local agencies is especially relevant in the area of film law, as has already been indicated and as will be developed later.

According to one of the organisations devoted to cultural policies, the Center for the Arts and Culture,[87] three major issues are:

> pre-eminent legal concerns for the next decade [writing in 2005], as regards the laws affecting culture and creativity:
>
> copyright and intellectual property
>
> free expression and content control
>
> consolidation and consumer choice
>
> Legal challenges, court decisions, and a changing regulatory framework will make a tremendous impact upon our cultural life.[88]

[84] See, eg, J. Weatherup (n 81) 309–10.
[85] See Weatherup (n 81) 309.
[86] Americans for the Arts: www.americansforthearts.org/.
[87] It existed until 2005. See www.culturalpolicy.org.
[88] See www.culturalpolicy.org/issuepages/issuetemplate.cfm?issue=Law.

This type of prediction reminds of the statement made by Schlesinger some years ago.[89] Culture and the arts are and will be, for various different reasons, a major political issue. The challenge is to identify exactly the public good we are talking about, to discuss if it is a public good at all, and to decide what type of legal framework we are going to provide for it. Indeed, the Center for the Arts and Culture developed an Art, Cultural & the National Agenda Project, intended to promote the regulation of the arts. In the framework of this project, it identified seven areas where policy and culture intersect: law, globalisation, access, preservation, community, investment and education. It should be noted that the major topics that are addressed in this chapter can be subsumed within these seven major areas.

C. Constitutional Framework for Cultural Policies

In 1989, the Congress reacted to the controversies in the cultural and arts field regarding public funding of works with an 'indecent' content, and amended the NEA's statute, so as to avoid NEA funding being allocated to works that the agency considered obscene. The District Court in the *Bella Lewitzky* case held the amendment to be unconstitutional and the Congress reformed its grants procedures.[90] For this, the Congress was helped by a commission of constitutional law scholars. In the commission's report it can be read that

> *there is no constitutional obligation to provide arts funding*, but also recommended that the NEA rescind the certification requirement and cautioned against legislation setting forth any content restrictions. Instead, the Commission suggested procedural changes to enhance the role of advisory panels and a statutory reaffirmation of the high place the nation accords to the fostering of mutual respect for the disparate beliefs and values among us. (emphasis added)

Although minor, there exists a line of thought among constitutional lawyers in the United States that considers constitutional rights to have always been narrowly interpreted. Charles L Black, Jr suggested that more efforts to develop substantive rights in American law are required, something that would help a real citizenship to be built up.[91] The starting point of Black's argument is the Preamble of the Constitution, which states that a purpose of the Constitution is to 'promote the general Welfare', and from there on he disseminates the concept of 'general welfare', as the key concept which could justify the existence of affirmative constitutional duties.[92] In a similar way as Black's, Barber asks himself what constitutes well-being and concludes that '[f]aring well in this society might best be viewed

[89] See Schlesinger (n 23). Schlesinger foresaw the impact of culture and the arts in the legal and political sphere. Here, emphasis is put on the other side of the story: the law will have an impact on cultural life.
[90] The *Bella Lewitzky* case (n 83).
[91] See Black, Jr (n 12).
[92] ibid, at 133.

not as actually possessing good things … but as developing or possessing the capacity to get them by one's lawful efforts to the extent that one reasonably wants'.[93] So welfare is not getting things, but developing the capacity to get them. Access to culture could play here an important role.

According to this theoretical framework, it could be considered that educational policies (to which, as it has been already indicated, cultural policies are linked) are at the core of this welfarist interpretation. Indeed, as Black later argues, '[b]ecause government must maintain the conditions for developing and exercising the capacities in whose possession well-being consists, well-being in America would also include the education, economic independence, and self-respect sufficient for the electoral choices that the Constitution envisions'.[94]

This line of thought could well be linked to the European efforts to give content to the concept of 'Culture State'. But there are also other constitutional implications regarding culture.[95] An apparent example of this would be the First Amendment, which as has been already mentioned, gave rise to a series of court decisions dealing with controversial arts funding.[96]

D. Subsidising Films. Executive Agencies and Films: A New Model of Public Administration

It is frequently heard that the film industry in the United States is not subsidised. However, there has always been some kind of public funding, a tendency that has been increasing in the last few years.[97] Federal, State and local agencies give

[93] See, in a similar way, Barber (n 11) 107. Barber bases his theories on Martin Diamond, 'Ethics and Politics: The American Way' in Robert H Horwitz (ed), *The Moral Foundations of the American Republic* (Charlottesville VA, University Press of Virginia, 1986).

[94] See Black, Jr (n 12) at 113–14.

[95] On the implications of welfarist theories for Administrative Law, which is the legal academic background of the author, see Matthew Diller, 'The Revolution in Welfare Administration: Rules, Discretion and Entrepreneurial Government' (2000) 75 *New York University Law Review* 1121.

[96] On this issue, see the Supreme Court's decision in *Finley* (n 83), where the Court indicates that 'the First Amendment certainly has application in the subsidy context' [at 587]. See further Frederick Schauer, 'Principles, Institutions, and the First Amendment' (1998) 112 *Harvard Law Review* 84, 98–99. More specific are the following studies: Celia A Cohen, 'An Endangered Species? Artistic Grants as a Vehicle for the Evolution of Entitlements Law' (1999) 49 *Syracuse Law Review* 1277, 1284; Craig J Flores, 'Indecent Exposure: An Analysis of the NEA's "Decency and Respect" Provision' (1998) 5 *UCLA Entertainment Law Review* 251, 257; Robert Vosburgh, 'Government Subsidies of Controversial Art: Dung, the Virgin Mary, and Rudy Giuliani' (2001) 11 *Temple Political & Civil Rights Law Review* 221, 234.

[97] On film law in the United States see, eg Donald Biederman and others, *Law and Business of the Entertainment Industries* 4th edn (Westport CT, Greenwood, 2001); Sherri Burr, *Entertainment Law in a Nutshell* (Eagan MN, Thomson/West, 2004); Robert Fremlin and Michel *Landau, Entertainment Law* (Eagan MN, Thomson/West, 2006); Schuyler M Moore, 'The Film Industry' in Howard Siegel (ed) *Entertainment Law* 3rd edn (New York, New York State Bar Association, 2004); Philip Miller, *Media Law for Producers* 3rd edn (Waltham MA, Focal Press, 1998) (with some interesting insights for public lawyers); Peter Muller, *Show Business Law* (Westport CT, Quorum Books, 1991); Thomas Selz and

aids to film production for different reasons. Also, an amendment to the Internal Revenue Code incorporated tax credits for film production, after the Department of Commerce 'estimated that run-away production drains as much as $ 10 billion per year from the US economy'.[98]

At the Federal Level, the National Endowment for the Arts gives grants to the media arts (film, radio and television) with the intention to encourage

> the artists and organizations that participate in advancing and preserving the media arts, and to supporting the production of media art works that celebrate the arts – visual arts, music, dance, literature, design, theater, musical theater, opera, folk & traditional arts, etc. – in an engaging and creative manner.[99]

So, creativity is the key word for this funding programme, and the projects funded for 2007 range from financial aid to certain film festivals, to foster curated film production in specific regions of American independent films at film festivals, to support the distribution to communities and libraries, to promote film production by young producers, to support a retrospective of Spanish director Pedro Almodóvar in Seattle, among others.[100] In many cases, only organisations can qualify for these grants and the amounts range from USD 7,500 to USD 70,000. Of course, this is not going to help Hollywood-like productions, but this is precisely the aim of these types of policies.

It could be considered that another kind of public funding, although strictly speaking it is not 'funding', are tax credits. The so-called 181 Section in the Internal Revenue Code, as amended in 2004, permits the deduction of qualifying film's production costs. But, in order to qualify for the deduction, the film must meet certain conditions. One of them is that the production costs not more than USD 15 million, or USD 20 million (depending on specific criteria), and the costs must have 'significantly incurred' in a low-income community or distressed area. It should be indicated that it is fairly difficult for an average film to stick to USD 15 million, as various different costs should be included (development cost, administrative costs, certain financing costs, costs of acquiring rights or a production, pre and post-production). In addition to that, in many cases it is not possible to know the final cost until the film has been in circulation for several months or years.

Agencies other than federal also help the film industry financially. In the State of New York, for instance, different bodies share competences on

others, *Entertainment Law: Legal Concepts and Business Practices* 3rd edn (Eagan MN, Thomson/West, 2006).

[98] See Senate Committee Report (S REP N° 108-192). On the position of American movies in international trade, see W Wayne Fu, 'Concentration and Homogenization of International Movie Sources: Examining Foreign Film Import Profiles' (2006) 56 *Journal of Communication* 813.

[99] See www.arts.gov/grants/apply-for-a-grant.

[100] All these projects and the amount given to all of them can be found at www.arts.gov/grants/recent-grants.

the same areas: the New York State Council on the Arts,[101] the New York State Governor's Office for Motion Picture and Television Development[102] and the New York City Film Office.[103]

At the State level, the New York State Council on the Arts and the New York State Governor's Office operate from different perspectives. The Office for Motion Picture, or New York Film Commission, is one of the many bodies existing in the United States to promote film production in their territories. They do this by means of tax credits, which vary from State to State, and also by other means. These include, for instance, help provided for obtaining licences and permits, help to find locations, contacts to local personnel who provide stages and equipment, etc.

The so-called 'Film Commissions' (although the actual name may vary from case to case) are reunited in the Association of Film Commissioners International.[104] The history of this Association, which is based in the United States (in Helena, Montana) goes back to 1975 and it defines itself as a non-profit *educational* organisation.[105] Yet, its origins are more remote. As early as in the decade of the 1940s, these commissions were timidly created, at the time when film producers decided to shoot outside studios as practical needs for film production started to increase. Permits requirements, police supervision, even coordination with fire departments, as well as the fact that film production usually has a positive economic impact on the area where films are produced, led these commissions to provide the services desired by film producers and, at the same time, they would promote the economic development of their own areas. This is still their main focus.

Film Commissions have a public nature, in the sense that they must be created by a public body and are usually operated and funded by government agencies. As stated by the Association of Film Commissioners International,

> [t]heir primary responsibility is to attract film and video production to their area in order to accrue locally-realized benefits from hiring local crews and talent, renting local equipment, using hotel rooms, rental cars, catering services, or any number of goods and services supplied on location. While attracting business to their area, they also attract visitors. Film scenes at a particular location are in themselves 'soft-sell' vehicles that also promote that location as a desirable site for future tourism and industry.

From a general more theoretical perspective, this is very interesting, because this shows a type of public body very different from classical public bodies which would limit themselves to funding. Here, it is actually possible to

[101] See www.nysca.org/public/home.cfm.
[102] See www.nylovesfilm.com/index.asp.
[103] See www.nyc.gov/html/film/html/index/index.shtml.
[104] See https://afci.org/.
[105] See https://afci.org/about-afci/#afci-history.

distinguish one good example of what some scholars have called 'entrepreneurial government'.[106]

So the New York State Governor's Office for Motion Picture and Television Development is one of these bodies and is therefore more focused in the economic aspect of films that in the cultural one. Its main aim is to promote economic development in the State of New York through film production. And the same nature shares the New York City Film Office, which acts at the local level.

On the other hand, the New York State Council is, as the National Endowment for the Arts at the Federal level, more focused on the artistic aspect of film production. And on this basis, it gives grants with 'the goal to bring high-quality artistic programs to the citizens of the state through supporting the activities of nonprofit arts and cultural organizations'.[107] This is another typical aim of cultural policies in the strict sense, ie to provide access to culture to all citizens, thus contributing to full participation of citizens in society. The grants conferred by the Agency in the Electronic Media and Film Program for 2006–07 summed up to USD 2,185,300, of which the minimum grant was USD 2,500 and the maximum was USD 136,500.[108]

VI. Conclusions

The US and the EU have, logically, different histories regarding cultural policies, where 'cultural policies' mean the intervention of public bodies in the cultural and artistic field. The tradition of (some) European States to treat culture as a public good, pursuing therefore cultural policies, has been inherited in the European Union. The political documents that led to the introduction of a legal basis for cultural policies in the EC Treaty, the aims of these policies and the problems they pose have been discussed in this article. And, as it has been developed here, culture and cultural policies are narrowly linked to the concept of identity. From a legal perspective, it is interesting to focus on the theories of 'Culture Constitution' and of 'Culture State', which were proposed in some Member States of the EU and have now been inherited in some scholarship dealing with the European Union itself. According to this theory, culture is related to the very concept of democracy, as it implies public duties addressed to public powers in order to facilitate access to

[106] See Diller (n 95), particularly at 1172ff. See also, as the major piece proposing a reconception of public administrations, Michael C Dorf and Charles F Sabel, 'A Constitution of Democratic Experimentalism' (1998) 98 *Columbia Law Review* 267, where the authors argue in favour of a decentralisation of government power and the distribution to citizens. See also Michael Barzelay, *Breaking Through Bureaucracy: A New Vision for Managing in Government* (Berkeley CA, University of California Press, 1992); David Osborne and Ted Gaebler, *Reinventing Government: How the Entrepreneurial Spirit is Transforming the Public Sector* (New York, Perseus, 1992).

[107] See www.nysca.org/public/home.cfm.

[108] See www.nysca.org/public/home.cfm.

culture and education for citizens. Cultural policies in Europe are manifold, but one of the key areas of them all, including EU cultural policies, is films. Films are particularly linked to the idea of identity, since they reflect and idiosyncrasy and they help to understand other customs, traditions, and ways of living. In Europe there is a long tradition of subsidising films, as they are conceived as cultural products. Yet new trends in film law show that public bodies, especially at the local level, are developing different policies. Considering films from an economic or industrial perspective, new mechanisms are being established, so as to take advantage of the positive effects on the economy.

In the US, the principle of freedom that justified the new political system after independence and the 'rebellion' against certain traditions and customs of the European States might be the reason why from the very beginning the decision of not subsidising the arts was consciously taken. Yet in the twentieth century, this changed slightly and the new situation gave rise in the 1960s to the creation of the National Endowment for the Arts, which is not equivalent to a Department or Ministry for Culture *à la européen*, but which developed some cultural policies and provoked some case law and bibliography on the relationship between the government and the arts. In some circles and in some legal writing, culture has been considered a public good, though the concrete consequences of this statement are still to be developed. There is no theory of a 'Culture Constitution' in the US or of a 'Culture State' as it exists in Europe, but some scholarly efforts to provide a more 'generous' interpretation of the American Constitution are interesting for comparison. Cultural policies in the US are being conducted at the State and the local level, rather than at the federal level. Here it is to be noted that films are, as it happens in Europe, at the core of those policies. Local and State authorities have for a long time favoured the production of films in their territories through various means. Also, different systems of tax benefits have been implemented in the last years, not least due to the fact that film production, as any other activity, is increasingly being delocalised.

In Europe, public bodies are approaching films and film production from an economic perspective as they usually did not do in the past. In the US more attention is being paid now to the film industry, from a public law perspective in comparison to the situation in the past. The reasons for the same have been discussed in this article, and the future of these converging perspectives is still to be awaited. One final conclusion could be that films are complex in their nature. They might not be regarded just as cultural products or as economic products. They can be both and they can be objects of different public policies which pursue different objectives. This complexity should be borne in mind in the relationship between the US and the EU, be it bilateral, be it multilateral, such as in the frameworks such as the WTO or the UNESCO, even if the latter is now being questioned by the US. Complex situations require complex solutions. Many problems are still to be solved, but this is the story so far. To be continued.

PART II

The European Union as a Global Actor: Issues and Partners

9

The European Union and Global Economic Governance

A Leader Without a Roadmap?

JAN WOUTERS AND AKHIL RAINA

I. Introduction

The European Union ('Union' or 'EU') has been called 'the world's most successful case of *multilateralism*'.[1] This is probably because of its repeated, unwavering declarations of multilateral commitment, in particular in Article 21(1), second paragraph, of the Treaty on European Union (TEU), in which the Union undertakes to 'promote multilateral solutions to common problems, in particular in the framework of the United Nations'. However, herein lies a puzzle: while the EU and its Member States are among the architects of today's multilateral order, at the same time, the Union has rigorously pursued *regional* endeavours. Two recent developments illustrate this dichotomy: on 20 March 2018, the European Council (Council) gave the European Commission (Commission) the mandate to negotiate a 'Multilateral Investment Court';[2] exactly one month later, the Commission announced an 'in principle' trade agreement with Mexico.[3] How can these two approaches, i.e multilateralism versus regionalism, be reconciled? How does the EU 'square the circle' – i.e how does its regional engagement (various and varied as it is)[4] fit with its stated dedication to multilateralism? Does the future of global

[1] KV Laatikainen and KE Smith (eds), *The European Union at the United Nations: Intersecting Multilateralisms* (Basingstoke, Palgrave Macmillan, 2006) 2 (emphasis added).

[2] European Council, 'Multilateral investment court: Council gives mandate to the Commission to open negotiations' (20 March 2018) 144/18.

[3] Officially called a 'global agreement', it is more or less, a regular 'deep and comprehensive' trade agreement. See: European Commission, 'EU and Mexico reach new agreement on trade' (21 April 2018), http://trade.ec.europa.eu/doclib/press/index.cfm?id=1830, accessed 13 May 2018.

[4] See Commission, 'Overview of FTA and other Trade Negotiations' (March 2018), http://trade.ec.europa.eu/doclib/docs/2006/december/tradoc_118238.pdf, accessed 13 May 2018.

economic governance have only one playbook, that of multilateralism or of regionalism, or do they, and can they, co-exist? Finally, and most critically, how successful a multilateral player is the EU? We take on these questions, and more, in this chapter.

We begin with a reality check on multilateralism, since this gives perspective as to what the Union is trying to achieve with its somewhat dual strategy. So, staunch multilateralists like Bhagwati, who famously called regional (preferential) trade agreements 'termites in the trading system', are being increasingly challenged.[5] But while it has become *bon ton* to say that multilateralism is in crisis,[6] 'global governance' is still largely effectuated on the multilateral table. Both sides flag factual evidence. With the World Trade Organization (WTO), one side points to the death of the Doha Development Agenda after nearly two decades of trials and tribulations, while the other side urges managed expectations: it claims that the Uruguay Round (UR) dynamic(s) no longer exist, and that in any case, the 2013 conclusion of the Trade Facilitation Agreement (TFA) is a sign of progress. One side cites 'Brexit' and withdrawals (or threats thereof) from international institutions,[7] while the other hails the birth of the Paris Climate Accord (Paris Accord). This debate is taken up for proper examination in Part II of our chapter. Part III uses a recent study by García-Durán Huet and Eliasson[8] to question the validity of the following Commission justification: regional endeavours are not dangerous for multilateralism because once 'critical mass'[9] is reached, regional deals will be multilateralised. García-Durán Huet and Eliasson find – and we agree – that the Commission's reasoning leaves out one very important analytical element: the state of multilateral negotiations. Part IV analyses the EU's status in, and strategy for, formal and informal international economic institutions. As we will see, though the EU may claim to be a bastion of multilateralism, it lacks a coordinated strategy to bring its declarations to life. This leads to our concluding remarks.

[5] Some have challenged what they see as 'multilateralism for multilateralism's sake'. This is understandable, since, as Alvarez puts it: '[m]ultilateralism is our [international lawyers'] shared secular religion'. José E Alvarez, 'Multilateralism and Its Discontents' (2000) 11(2) *European Journal of International Law* 393, at 394.

[6] Axel Marx, Bregt Natens, Dylan Geraets and Jan Wouters, 'Global Governance *Through* Trade: An Introduction' in Jan Wouters and others (eds), *Global Governance through Trade: EU Policies and Approaches* (Cheltenham, Edward Elgar, 2015) at 1–4.

[7] Bolivia, Ecuador and Venezuela from the International Centre for Settlement of Investment Disputes (ICSID); and Burundi from the Rome Statute (Philippines has also signalled an intention to leave; and though South Africa, the Gambia, Zambia, Kenya and Uganda requested withdrawal, they later changed their mind). The United States of America's (US) withdrawal from the Paris Accord is also significant.

[8] Patricia García-Durán Huet and Leif Johan Eliasson, 'Squaring the Circle: Assessing whether the European Union's Pursuit of Bilateral Trade Agreements is Compatible with Promoting Multilateralism' (2018) 6(1) *Journal of Self-Governance and Management Economics* 7.

[9] For an explanation, see Gary Winslett, 'Critical Mass Agreements: The Proven Template for Trade Liberalization in the WTO' (2017) 1 *World Trade Review* 2–4.

II. Multilateralism Revisited

The critique of multilateralism is as old as the system. Over time, however, some factors have contributed to the rise in protest decibels. We lay out some major ones here.

Arguably the biggest arsenal against multilateralism is the snail-slow pace of negotiation.[10] This mostly boils down to decision-making, particularly in bodies like the WTO, where consensus is held up with almost religious fervour.[11] This is interesting because while a large part of the philosophy behind multilateralism is the cession of (some) sovereignty, a strong attachment to consensus, which effectively gives everybody a veto, is an overt manifestation of the sovereignty principle. In fact, one could even argue that it is *post*-sovereign, in that a single country could block agreement between the remaining 163 Members. Theorising aside, multilateral negotiations take time to produce results, leading many to greener (quicker) pastures. This is often coupled with the belief that multilateral rules are (or have been) unfair to developing countries. For instance, some have argued that countries like India were forced to take up onerous Intellectual Property Rights (IPR) obligations during the UR; 'single package' was the name of the game, and if India wanted more market access, it had to swallow the bitter IPR pill.[12]

Cohen has recently argued that multilateralism's ills stem, ironically, from its success.[13] He claims that 'multi-polarity' (as opposed to the Cold War era of 'bi-polarity') was a 'fulfillment of the mission of post-World War II multilateralism, which promised … [the] growing and spreading of wealth'.[14] No country is totally dependent on another anymore, and, for example, a new power dynamic now exists at the WTO: the old 'quad' (Canada, EU, Japan and the United States (US)) that dominated and dictated trade UR negotiations has turned into an odd 'quad-plus-one' of the US, EU, India, China and (maybe) Brazil/Russia. While in itself this can be seen as the result of organic power shifts, negotiations have (so far) been hampered because there is little convergence of policy preferences between the new powers. Add to this the sheer *number* of developing (and least developed)

[10] To understand why WTO negotiations ran out of steam, post-UR, see inter alia Richard Baldwin, 'The World Trade Organization and the Future of Multilateralism' (2016) 30(1) *Journal of Economic Perspectives* 95 (in particular, see his explanation of internal and external sources of WTO's 'woes' at 106–09).

[11] On the other hand, this also adds legitimacy to the international organisation at hand: see Gregory Shaffer and others, 'The Extensive (but Fragile) Authority of the WTO Appellate Body' (2016) 79 (1) *Law and Contemporary Problems* 237 at 258.

[12] In general, see Jayashree Watal, 'Patents – An Indian Perspective' in Jayashree Watal and Antony Taubman (eds), *The Making of the TRIPS Agreement: Personal Insights from the Uruguay Round Negotiations* (Geneva, WTO, 2015) 295.

[13] Harlan Grant Cohen, 'Editorial Comment: Multilateralism's Life Cycle' (2018) 118 *American Journal of International Law* 47 at 59–61.

[14] ibid at 54. He also cites other reasons for multilateralism's decline, for example, the reduced importance of trade-linkages (see 55–59).

countries that have joined, and it is not hard to see why negotiations are going nowhere fast.[15] Cohen believes that multilateralism, as a concept, is undergoing a natural decay, and that soon a new system will emerge, containing the DNA of the old.[16]

Further, most international organisations – stars in the multilateral universe[17] – are relatively old, and many of their working arrangements have not kept up with the times.[18] Representation, for example, is a big source of discontent.[19] The United Nations Security Council (UNSC) – arguably *the* most important international body in terms of direct action – is still in the palms of the 'P5' (US, United Kingdom (UK), China, Russia, France).[20] Voting/power dynamics are also problematic in institutions like the International Monetary Fund (IMF) where the US still holds a uniquely large voting 'quota'.[21] Some organisations, like the UN, have come under fire for becoming extremely bureaucratic; moreover, there are those who claim that selections to high offices are not done on merit, and that the system has been 'politicised'.[22] This is not exclusive to personnel: recently Sudan was elected as Vice-Chair of the UN Committee on Non-Governmental Organizations (NGOs),[23] and Saudi Arabia, hardly known as a champion of women's rights, was invited to be a part of the UN Commission on the Status of Women.[24] All this adds fodder to criticism's fire, and has resulted in a proliferation of regional (preferential) trade agreements;[25] and in a feed-in fashion this has amplified the voice(s) against multilateralism.[26]

[15] This is particularly true in today's time, when major player(s), like the US, have opted for what can be most optimistically described as 'lukewarm' international engagement.

[16] Cohen (n 13) at 52.

[17] In general, see: Michael N Barnett and Martha Finnemore, 'The Politics, Power, and Pathologies of International Organizations' (1999) 53 *International Organization* 699.

[18] A general call for updating international organizations can be found in Niels M Blokker and Ramses A Wessel, 'Editorial: Updating International Organizations' (2005) 2 *International Organizations Law Review* 1. See also Giulio M Gallarotti, 'The Limits of International Organization: Systematic Failure in the Management of International Relations' (1991) 45 (2) *International Organization* 183.

[19] For detailed reading, see Jacob Katz Cogan, 'Representation and Power in International Organization: The Operational Constitution and Its Critics' (2009) 103 *American Journal of International Law* 209.

[20] United Nations, Charter of the United Nations (1 UNTS XVI) (24 October 1945), art 27(3), which requires the 'concurring votes of permanent members' for all non-procedural matters.

[21] International Monetary Fund, 'IMF Members' Quotas and Voting Power, and IMF Board of Governors', www.imf.org/external/np/sec/memdir/members.aspx, accessed 13 May 2018.

[22] See eg Frederik Trettin, 'Spoilers from Within: Bureaucratic Spoiling in United Nations Peace Operations' (2014) 1(5) *Journal of International Organizations Studies* 13.

[23] 'UN elects genocidal Sudan Vice-Chair of Committee on NGOs' *UN Watch* (Geneva, 2017), www.unwatch.org/u-n-elects-genocidal-sudan-vice-chair-committee-ngos/, accessed 13 May 2018.

[24] Amanda Erickson, 'Believe it or not, Saudi Arabia was elected to the UN women's rights commission' *The Washington Post* (2017), www.washingtonpost.com/news/worldviews/wp/2017/05/03/saudi-arabia-where-women-arent-allowed-to-drive-was-just-elected-to-the-u-n-womens-rights-commission/?utm_term=.23896df5ea3a, accessed 13 May 2018.

[25] For a succinct description of the reasons for this proliferation, see: Alessandro Antimiani and Luca Salvatici, 'Regionalism versus Multilateralism: The Case of European Union Trade Policy' (2015) 49(2) *Journal of World Trade* 253 at 254.

[26] Also note that, in general, civil society has become more and more vocal about its dissatisfaction with trade – be it regional or multilateral. There are groups advocating the 'end' of the WTO

Here the defenders step in. They point to Bhagwati's 'small think' danger – that trade diversion (caused by regionalism) would reduce global welfare, and his 'big think' danger – that regionalism would impede progress towards global free trade.[27] As noted above, the WTO's TFA and the Paris Accord are cited as success stories.[28] Again, the WTO's consensus rule is a strong guarantor of fairness and equality. Further, this side points out, the spectre of withdrawals is grossly overstated. That the US pulled out of the Paris Accord (or, more recently, from the Iran Deal) can be squarely chalked up to the current administration's populist preferences. All of the recent International Criminal Court (ICC) withdrawals (except Burundi) were taken back.

As it stands, the current global governance landscape exhibits 'regime complexity':[29] both multilateralism and regionalism exist, and cross-intersect with one another. While regional pacts have no doubt exploded in number, not a single international organisation has shut down for lack of interest or relevance. As Baldwin explains:

> [t]he rise of preferential tariffs within bilateral and regional agreements has not blocked the path to overall global tariff-cutting. Virtually all of the developing-nation WTO members who engaged in bilateral, discriminatory liberalization have simultaneously been engaged in unilateral, non-discrimination liberalization.[30]

Two important questions emerge from this: first, what can/do we learn from history and the status quo? And second, what does the future of trade governance look like? As to the first, what is important to understand is that there is probably no 'right' way. Regionalism and multilateralism have long existed side-by-side and have often fed into one another.[31] Even empirical economics is unable to give a straight, black-and-white answer.[32] As for the future, there are some predictions. Baldwin foresees a 'two-pillar' system, where 'the WTO continues to govern traditional trade … [alongside] the second pillar, [is] a system where disciplines on trade in intermediate foods and service, investment and intellectual property protection, capital flows, and the movement of key personnel are multilateralized in mega-regionals'.[33] In a somewhat similar vein, Cohen argues for 'thinner' multilateral agreements, leaving the meatier bits for regional deals (that could later be multilateralised).[34] Keohane and Morse, on the other hand, have argued for the

(Third World Network (www.twn.my) and Public Citizen (www.citizen.org), and there was a strong anti-TTIP campaign in Europe (particularly targeting its investment dispute settlement chapter).

[27] Baldwin (n 10) at 112.

[28] The fact that China has agreed to ratify the Paris Agreement is also a small success. Cohen (n 13) at 47.

[29] Karen J Alter and Kal Raustiala, 'The Rise of International Regime Complexity' (2018) *Annual Review of Law and Social Science*. Note that this 'patchwork of bilateral agreements' can have negative effects on developing states and the environment. Huet and Eliasson (n 8) at 3.

[30] Baldwin (n 10) 113.

[31] For examples see García-Durán Huet and Eliasson (n 8) 11–12.

[32] Antimiani and Salvatici (n 25).

[33] Baldwin (n 10) 114.

[34] Cohen (n 13) at 65–66. The rational being that 'justice' is probably more effectively delivered bottom-up, ie from a local level. Note: this concerns *implementation*, not rule-making.

possible alternative of 'counter-multilateralism', which occurs when 'the objective of the members is not to substitute multilateralism with bilateralism but rather to create an alternative to *established* multilateralism … to create a new form of multilateralism through competitive regime creation'.[35] What the future will really look like, can of course only be answered when the future arrives. Till then, the debate carries on.

III. Can the EU 'Square the Circle'?:[36] Yes, but No

We have now approached the test-subject: the EU. As noted before, the Commission has claimed allegiance to multilateralism while pursuing a thorough regional agenda. In fact, 1999 onwards, there was an informal 'moratorium' on regional deals (in favour of Doha negotiations)[37] that ended in 2006 with the Commission's 'Global Europe' strategy. In it the Commission announced a need for 'new priorities and new approaches',[38] possibly as a prelude to the 'new generation' Free Trade Agreements (FTAs), whose creation it was about to embark on. Despite this, the overall message was still the same: there would be 'no European retreat from multilateralism', and it (the EU) was prepared to 'pay … to keep the system thriving'.[39] The Commission assured the world that new FTAs would be 'stepping stones, not a stumbling block for multilateral liberalisation'.[40] From then, till now, all Commission strategy papers have endorsed this understanding.[41] Also the EU's 2016 Global Strategy 'reiterates and reinforces the EU's defence of a liberal rules-based order'.[42] This is in line with Articles 21(1) and 21(2)(h) TEU that requires the Union to 'promote multilateral solutions … and an international system based on strong[er] multilateral cooperation and good global governance'.[43]

[35] García-Durán Huet and Eliasson (n 8) at 12, 13 (emphasis added). The authors point out that though the Transatlantic Trade and Investment Partnership (TTIP) can be such an alternative, not all bilateral agreements have the potential to be counter-multilateral yet.

[36] An exceedingly common phrase in trade and investment literature, the inspiration for this particular title is García-Durán Huet and Eliasson (n 8).

[37] See: Pascal Lamy, 'Stepping Stones or Stumbling Blocks? The EU's Approach Towards the Problem of Multilateralism vs Regionalism in Trade Policy' (2002) 25 (10) *The World Economy* 1399.

[38] Commission, 'Global Europe: Competing in the World – A Contribution to the EU's Growth and Jobs Strategy' COM (2006) 567 final, 10.

[39] COM (2006) 567 final, 15 and 11–13.

[40] ibid.

[41] García-Durán Huet and Eliasson (n 8) at 2.

[42] High Representative of the EU for Foreign Affairs and Security Policy, 'Shared Vision, Common Action: A Stronger Europe. A Global Strategy for the EU's Foreign and Security Policy' (2016). See Joris Larik, 'The EU's Global Strategy in the Age of Brexit and 'America First' *Leuven Centre for Global Governance Studies Working Papers* (2017) 193.

[43] Consolidated Version of the Treaty on European Union [2016] OJ C202, arts 21(1) and 21(2) (h).

So how does this dedication to multilateralism fit with the EU's pursuit of FTAs? The idea, based loosely on 'open regionalism',[44] is this: regional agreements will formulate new rules (for example: WTO+ and WTO-X),[45] and once 'critical mass' is reached, the agreements will be multilateralised. This is based on three premises: first, that bilateral and multilateral approaches to trade governance need not be mutually exclusive; second, that preferential agreements have the ability to either bolster or hamper multilateral progress, depending on how they are designed; and third, that the potential technical feasibility of multilateralising bilateral/regional agreements is ensured by the WTO+ and WTO-X nature of the agreements.[46]

Regarding the first premise, García-Durán Huet and Eliasson note that 'both instruments [ie approaches] may be needed to deal with the complexities of an interdependent world', especially since all WTO Members have at least one Preferential Trade Agreement (PTA) with another Member.[47] In fact, the WTO – the very embodiment of the multilateral trading system – contemplates derogation from the fundamental principle of most favoured nation treatment (MFN) in favour of regional engagement, given the fulfilment of certain circumstances.[48] Consider this line from ex-WTO Director General Pascal Lamy:

> Half the world's economists seem determined to prove that policy-makers should choose between being a multilateralist and a regionalist, and tell us that we can't be both at the same time. The problem is that life is messier and more complicated than economic theory.[49]

García-Durán Huet and Eliasson point out that the Commission's second premise is based largely on the seminal work of Viner, who argued that regionalism has the capacity to both create *and* divert trade.[50] However, academics diverge here: Baldwin claims that the two systems can feed into one another,[51] while Bhagwati, forwarding his famous 'spaghetti bowl', focuses on regionalism's eroding effects (due to trade diversion).[52] On this point, García-Durán Huet and Eliasson conclude that

> since both the 'stepping stone' and the 'stumbling block' positions are based on empirical evidence, it is logical to assume that the *content* of a particular PTA determines its compatibility with the multilateral system: the more an agreement favors trade

[44] C Fred Bergsten, *Open Regionalism*, Working Paper Series WP97 -3, Peterson Institute for International Economics (1997).

[45] For elaboration, see: García-Durán Huet and Eliasson (n 8) at 6.

[46] ibid at 4.

[47] ibid at 5.

[48] Art XXIV, General Agreement on Tariffs and Trade (GATT) 1994, Apr 15, 1994, Marrakesh Agreement Establishing the World Trade Organization, Annex 1A, 1867 UNTS 187, 33 ILM 1153 (1994).

[49] Lamy (n 39).

[50] Jacob Viner, *The Customs Union Issue* (Washington DC, Carnegie Endowment for International Peace, 1950).

[51] The WTO's creation is a prime example: plurilateral (non-multilateral) 'codes'' on dumping, technical barriers etc was eventually multilateralised, after critical mass, through the concept of a single undertaking.

[52] For references see: García-Durán Huet and Eliasson (n 8).

creation over trade diversion, the more likely it is to support the multilateral system and vice-versa.[53]

Finally, García-Durán Huet and Eliasson find that the third premise is also supported by legal and economic literature.[54] However, the authors identify one very important element that is missing from the Commission's analysis: the state of multilateral negotiations.

The authors posit that there is 'no guarantee' that the bilateral approach will feed into the multilateral one, and that the technical possibility/feasibility of multilateralisation is a necessary but not sufficient condition. Using the studies of Baldwin and Evenett, and of Jeffery Schott, the authors argue that multilateralism must be 'alive' for multilateralisation to occur, ie negotiations must not be stalled.[55] Though it may sound intuitive, the fact that the Commission is forwarding a rather contradictory approach necessitates this clarification.

As García-Durán Huet and Eliasson submit, the purpose and rationale of EU regional agreements has changed over time. Until 2006 (before Doha began stalling), they principally served non-economic purposes, like neighbourhood and development objectives. Since then, the EU has chosen to protect its economic interests through PTAs – from 2006 to 2009 with important trade players like India and South Korea, and after that with old 'quad' partners, ie Japan, US and Canada. Thus, in their assessment, the Commission's stated justification is only valid until 2008. Since then the EU's bilateral agreements or negotiations should be seen as substitutes for a multilateral strategy (or in the case of TTIP, *counter-multilateralist*).[56]

Now, a pedantic question: what does a 'responsibility' to engage multilaterally entail? Does it only mean participation in multilateral negotiations, and to claim it to be the best form of governance? If so, the Union has probably discharged its duty and respected its mandate. If, however, it is more – if it means playing the role of a mediator or a conciliator when negotiations are stuck, or to repeatedly and persistently push for more engagement from other members, then there is a lot more that the EU could do. To justify its current (less than ideal) contribution(s), the 2016 Global Strategy provides that the Union will pursue 'targeted engagement', with 'co-responsibility' being a guiding principle.[57]

True, EU negotiations are constrained by their own complicated nature. With the exception of trade policy, competences are typically shared between the EU

[53] ibid at 5 (emphasis added); see also Antimiani and Salvatici (n 25).

[54] García-Durán Huet and Eliasson (n 8) at 6–9.

[55] ibid at 11; see also: Richard Baldwin and Simon Evenett (eds), *Why World Leaders Must Resist the False Promise of another Doha Delay* (London, VoxEU.org eBook, 2011); and Jeffery Schott, 'Regionalism and Multilateralism' (Washington DC, IMF, 1997). Though Garcia-Duran Huet and Eliasson (n 8) accept that it is difficult to precisely determine when a multilateral negotiation is stalled, especially since most of them progress very slowly.

[56] García-Durán Huet and Eliasson (n 8) at 19.

[57] Global Strategy (n 42) 17–18. Also significant: the EU will '*partner selectively* with players whose cooperation is necessary …' (emphasis added) (ibid, at 18).

and its Member States. Sometimes, as we will see, the Union and its Member States are members to an IO, or a club, and more than once there is no coordination between them. As mentioned before, new powers, particularly the BRICS countries, contest the EU's position as a leader. And on the home front, the EU has troubles of its own. The refugee crisis takes up a lot of discussion time, and Brexit has hardly made things easier. But how far are these merely excuses?

Yes, the Union is going through a tough time, but so are several other international players who are not as economically fortunate as the EU and who are still seriously pushing the multilateral agenda. The Treaty on European Union (TEU) stipulates that the Union '*shall promote* multilateralism' (emphasis added), not just participate in it. Thus, the Union is under a (self-imposed) legal obligation to play a leading role in ensuring multilateralism's robust sustenance.[58] And so it must do more. A solid, coordinated strategy in international economic bodies would be a good starting point. With that in mind we turn to our chapter's core.

IV. The EU's Status and Strategy in International Economic Bodies: Between Words and Action

Let us for a minute assume, for the sake of argument, that there is no contradiction between the EU's stated dedication to multilateralism and its regional pursuits, and that the Commission's justifications over the years contain no logical (or analytical) loopholes. Does the EU have a strategy in place to effectuate this multilateral progress, which it claims to deeply desire? Is the Union in-tune with its Member States' priorities and interests, or do the Member States and the EU present uncoordinated positions that lead to a loss in the 'European voice'? We take on these questions now.

A. Informal 'Clubs'

i. Group of 7 (G7)

The G7 was born in 1973 as the G5, comprising of the US, UK, West Germany, France and Japan. It was 'progressively consolidated in the immediate aftermath of the 1973 oil crises and the abrupt end of the Bretton Woods system',[59] with

[58] See Jan Wouters, Anna-Luise Chané and Thomas Ramopoulos, 'Improving the European Union's Status in the United Nations and the UN System: An Objective without a Strategy?' in Christine Kaddous (ed), *The European Union in International Organizations and Global Governance: Recent Developments* (Oxford, Hart Publishing, 2015) 45.

[59] Chiara Oldani and others, 'The G7, Anti-Globalism and the Governance of Globalization: Setting the Scene' in Chiara Oldani and Jan Wouters (eds), *The G7 and Global Governance in Times of Anti-Globalization* (Abingdon, Routledge, 2018).

an aim to promote global neoliberalism and move towards 'shared hegemony'.[60] Italy joined in 1975, and a year after that Canada was brought in. The G7 then became 'G7+1' with Russia's addition in 1998. In 2014 Russia was expelled over its annexation of Crimea. Together, the G7 members cover 33 per cent of global GDP (adjusted to purchasing power).[61] And though the 2005 Gleneagles Summit led to the creation of the G8+5 meeting (comprising additionally of Brazil, India, China, Mexico and South Africa – the 'outreach countries'), the G7 is probably best described as a 'minilateral' body.[62] Dobson suggests we understand the G7 as operating at the 'highest levels of global governance, overarching global intuitions, in a setting conducive to testing new ideas, re-igniting cooperation and putting items on the agenda of formal multilateral fora'.[63] For example, the 1996 communiqué encouraged the UN to enhance its efficiency and coordination, particularly regarding its various funds and programmes.[64] The next year the communiqué urged the IMF and the WTO to 'finalize governance policies consisting of principles and guidelines of best governance' (in the wake of the 1997 financial crisis), and the year after that the communiqué directly addressed the IMF Executive Board, calling for '[s]trengthening the architecture of the international monetary system'.[65]

The G7 has no formal charter or statute, and therefore no fixed procedure or agenda. Instead, it is founded upon what has been described as an '*esprit de corps*', which leads only to morally binding decisions.[66] The subject-areas covered in the 2017 meetings give a snapshot of the club's priorities; these include: culture, energy, foreign affairs, finance, environment, transport, labour, agriculture, home affairs, health and gender equality.[67] Thus the G7's initial remit (macroeconomic policy coordination, international trade, the monetary system, North-South relations) has greatly broadened.[68] Most recently, gender and terrorism have gained attention, while environmental discussions and coordination is at an 'all-time low'.[69] And though informality is the body's greatest strength (in terms of ease of negotiations, evidenced by a high number of meetings), it is also, circularly, its greatest weakness, in so far as legitimacy and accountability are concerned.[70]

[60] ibid.
[61] ibid.
[62] ibid.
[63] ibid. See Hugo Dobson, *The Group of 7/8* (Abingdon, Routledge, 2006).
[64] Oldani and others (n 59). See also: Peter I Hajnal, *The G8 System and the G20: Evolution, Role and Documentation* (Abingdon, Routledge, 2016).
[65] Oldani and others (n 59); see Hajnal, ibid.
[66] Oldani and other (n 59) at 3.
[67] ibid.
[68] ibid at 6.
[69] Oldani and others (n 59).
[70] ibid.

Since 1977 (initially on invitation from the UK), the EU has been an 'active participant' in the G7. Initially its participation was limited to items that fell under EU competence (such as trade), but now it extends to cover all G7 agenda items.[71] Thus, the Union is directly represented (through the Presidents of the European Council and the Commission), and indirectly through its four largest Member States, ie France, Germany, Italy and the UK. There is no clear coordination between the EU and its Member States.[72] The Commission believes that a legal mandate for the G7 may be unnecessary since no formal decision-making takes place and discussions remain mostly of a political nature.[73]

A pertinent question to ask is: are EU Member States in the G7 obliged to pursue EU's interests, especially over their own? The answer is in the affirmative, considering the principle of sincere cooperation laid down in EU law.[74] The lack of coordination will get worse once Brexit becomes real, because the UK will look after its own interests.[75] It may take up power-sources earlier held by (or in line with) the EU, and may even challenge it on some matters. Signs of this have already started to appear, with the UK proposing for additional sanctions on Russia during the Lucca Summit in April 2017 (resisted by Italy and Germany) and the lack of condemnation by the UK for the US's withdrawal from the Paris Accord (which the EU and its other Member States criticised).[76] For the EU, this concern exists in other clubs as well where the UK is an independent member. At the same time, some foresee a thin silver lining:

> [d]ue to the UK leaving the EU, the interests of the EU G7 Member States and the Union are more aligned. In combination with the Russian suspension, the EU might be able to become a more pivotal player within the G7, which could increase its voice and importance in this summitry.[77]

ii. Group of Twenty (G20)

The G20 was created (at the level of ministers of finance and central bank governors) in the light of the financial crisis in South East Asia in 1999. In 2008, when a financial crisis struck the West, it was elevated to the level of heads of State

[71] Jan Wouters and Sven Van Kerckhoven, 'The Role of the EU in the G7 in Times of Populism, Nationalism and Anti-Globalism' in C Oldani and J Wouters (eds), *The G7 and Global Governance in Times of Anti-Globalization* (Abingdon, Routledge, 2018).

[72] Though the 2016 Global Strategy does mention the EU's desire to 'acquire greater … cohesion … across multilateral fora': Global Strategy (n 42) at 40.

[73] Judith Huigens and Arne Niemann, 'The EU within the G8: A Case of Ambiguous and Contested Actorness', *College of Europe EU Diplomacy Papers* (2009) 5.

[74] TEU, art 4(3).

[75] Wouters and Van Kerckhoven (n 71), citing Skander Nasra and others, 'The EU in the G8 system: Assessing EU Member State's Involvement' *EUI Working Papers* (2009) 45.

[76] In general, see: Wouters and Van Kerckhoven (n 71).

[77] ibid at 17.

and government. In 2009 the G20's leaders heralded it as the 'premier forum for [our] international economic cooperation'.[78] It aims to

> promote informal dialogue on a wide range of economic and financial issues among systemically important countries within the framework of the Bretton Woods institutions … and to enhance the cooperation between its members in order to achieve stable and sustainable world economic growth that benefits all.[79]

It comprises 19 individual countries (including the four largest EU Member States, as in the G7) and the EU, which is represented by the President of the European Council and the President of the Commission for summits, and by the Commission and the European Central Bank for meetings of ministers of finance and central bank governors.[80] The Union is the only non-state member and has full rights except the right to host summits.[81] Together, the G20 membership represents more than 85 per cent of global GDP, 80 per cent of world trade (including intra-EU trade), and two-thirds of the world population.[82] Critics however, point to the under-representation of the developing world and of Africa in particular: there is only one African G20 member, South Africa.[83] Brookings argues that the lack of developing country representation results in under-prioritisation of the developmental agenda.[84] Further, the G20 has not been able to dissociate itself from its past: some view the G20 agenda as 'G7-driven',[85] and Kirton points to the risk that the G20 may be acting to 'legitimize G7 agendas and outcomes'.[86]

Both the EU and the G20 'mark, in their own very different ways, a changing world order in which states are cooperating ever more closely in order to tackle

[78] G20, 'G20 Leaders Statement: The Pittsburgh Summit' (2009), www.g20.utoronto.ca/2009/2009communique0925.html, accessed 9 April 2018, pt 19. See also: Jan Wouters and others, 'The International Financial Crisis, Global Financial Governance and the European Union' in A Antonis Antoniadis and others (eds), *The European Union and Global Emergencies: Law and Policy Analysis* (Oxford, Hart Publishing, 2011) 141, at 147.

[79] Jan Wouters and Sven Van Kerckhoven, 'A European Perspective on the G20 and the BRICS' (2018) 13 *International Organisations Research Journal* 60. See also John Kirton, *G20 Governance for a Globalized World* (Farnham, Ashgate, 2013); G20, 'Declaration on the Summit of Financial Markets and the World Economy' (2008).

[80] For a detailed study on EU's role in the G20, see: European Research Centre for Economic and Financial Governance (EURO-CEFG), 'The European Union's Role in International Economic Fora Paper 1: The G20' (2015) IP/A/ECON/2014-15.

[81] Jan Wouters and others, 'The EU at the G20 and the G20's Impact on the EU' in Bart Van Vooren and others (eds), *The EU's Role in Global Governance: The Legal Dimension* (Oxford, Oxford University Press, 2013) 259.

[82] Wouters and others (n 78) at 145.

[83] ibid, 146. See also John Kirton, 'The G20: Representativeness, Effectiveness, and Leadership in Global Governance' in Kirton and others (eds), *Guiding Global Order: G8 Governance in the 21st Century* (Aldershot, Ashgate, 2001).

[84] Wouters and others (n 78) 146; see also Homi Kharas, 'Passing the Development Football from the G8 to the G-20' *Recovery or Relapse: The Role of the G-20 in the Global Economy, Global Economy and Development at Brookings* (2010) 10, at 11–12.

[85] Wouters and others (n 78) at 146.

[86] ibid; see also Kirton (n 83).

transnational challenges'.[87] There are many interactions between the two entities and they can push each other's agendas forward.[88] The Union views the G20 as a venue to push its own (internal) agenda on other countries[89] and to 'promote global cooperation'.[90] Recently, it has urged the G20 to consider issues like refugees and terrorist threats, and to explore the possibility of a global financial tax.[91] Conversely, the EU needs the G20 in order to align its policies with the global order, as this makes EU's responses more effective.[92]

The EU's seven per cent world population translates into 25 per cent membership in the G20, and although Spain and the Netherlands – large economies in their own right – are not G20 members, they are regularly invited to meetings. Importantly, the fact that only the largest (and most powerful) EU Member States are the European G20 members could have the following 'perverse side-effect': if and when these powerful countries cannot get their preferred policies though the EU, they could try and push for them independently at the G20 platform.[93] Interestingly, the 'large number of Europeans' at the G20 table is seen by some as a disadvantage. 'If [the] Europeans find common ground, the repetition of the same message might irritate other G20 members … and [if] EU and the [MS] fail to find common ground, the European voice is lost'.[94]

While there is no specific strategy in place to coordinate between the Union and its Member States, some discussion does take place, before G20 meetings, at the Council level.[95] In advance of the first G20 summit in November 2008, in Washington DC, the Council agreed on principles of reform for the international financial system and the approach that the EU would take towards it at the G20.[96] The next summit, in April 2009 in London, was even more thoroughly prepared, and the Union and its Member States agreed upon stricter supervision by the IMF, more thorough regulation of financial markets, and the unification of international rating-agencies procedures.[97] This resulted in 'agreed language' of the EU and its Member States; significantly, the Council and the Commission were called upon to ensure appropriate follow-up to the summit.[98] The end result was a success, since

[87] Wouters and others (n 81) at 259.

[88] Wouters and Van Kerckhoven (n 79).

[89] Jan Wouters and Sven Van Kerckhoven, 'The EU's Internal and External Regulatory Actions after the Outbreak of the 2008 Financial Crisis' (2011) 8(5) *European Company Law* 201.

[90] Wouters and Van Kerckhoven (n 89); see also: European Commission, 'Economic Crisis in Europe: Causes, Consequences and Responses' (2009) 7 European Economy.

[91] Wouters and Van Kerckhoven (n 89), see particularly footnotes 9–12.

[92] Communication from the Commission, 'From financial crisis to recovery: A European framework for action' (OJ 2010 C76/28).

[93] Wouters and others (n 81) at 261.

[94] Peter Debaere, 'The Output and Input Dimension of the European Representation in the G20' (2010) 63(2) *Studia Diplomatica* 141, at 141.

[95] Wouters and others (n 81) at 260–66.

[96] ibid at 261; see also: European Commission (n 92).

[97] Wouters and others (n 81) at 262; see also Meeting of the European members of the G20 in Berlin, 23 February 2009, http://europa-eu-un.org/articles/en/article_8511_en.htm.

[98] Wouters and others (n 81) at 262; see also European Council Presidency, *Conclusions 19/20 March 2009* (7880/1/09) Brussels, 29 April, para 22.

the EU agenda was almost perfectly reflected in the G20 declaration.[99] The 2010 Toronto summit is also, largely, considered by the Europeans as a success.[100]

This is not, however, always the case. Some point out that, although the Union is successful in setting up the G20 agenda (and implementing its decisions), it has failed on specific issues.[101] An example of this was the 2009 Pittsburgh summit, where despite EU 'agreed language', the G20 adopted 'broad and vague statements on most issues' and failed to take up the EU's proposals on 'Everything but Arms', Basel II and climate change.[102] A similar story unfolded at the 2010 Seoul summit.[103] Again, an important reason for this is the lack of attention paid to building a proper G20 strategy. The 2016 Global Strategy mentions the G20 only once, and that too in passing, with no substantive statements regarding a strategy, particularly when it comes to economic decision-making.[104] This is especially problematic because without a policy or legal basis for unified external representation, EU Member States can still deviate from 'agreed language'. However, elsewhere it has been argued that this lack of strategy is less worrying (compared to BRICS, for instance) because the Member States have, until now, mostly worked with the 'agreed language', thus allowing the EU to steer in its preferred direction.[105]

The impact of G20 commitments on EU law and policy is fairly heavy. This can be seen by the repeated references to G20 commitments in EU legislation and policy documents.[106] A significant example of the Union taking G20 commitments seriously is the creation of the European Systemic Risk Board (ESRB), which was brought to life on the recommendation of the *de Larosiere Report*, which urged the EU to work more closely with its partners in, inter alia, the G20.[107] In some fields, such as banking regulation, the EU has been a frontrunner; but in others, such as OTC derivatives regulation, it has lagged behind.[108]

B. Formal Bodies

i. WTO

The WTO is the largest multilateral economic governance institution in existence today. It boasts of 164 Members, and deals with everything from tariffs and technical barriers to agriculture, services and intellectual property rights. The EU's status and its relationship with its Member States (who are all WTO Members

[99] Wouters and others (n 81) at 262.
[100] ibid at 264.
[101] Wouters and others (n 81) at 270.
[102] ibid at 263.
[103] ibid at 264–65.
[104] Global Strategy (n 42) at 43. See Wouters and Van Kerckhoven (n 79).
[105] Wouters and others (n 78) at 147, see particularly fn 25.
[106] Wouters and others (n 81) at 267.
[107] ibid.
[108] Wouters and Van Kerckhoven (n 79).

themselves) is clearer at the WTO than in the aforementioned informal clubs. The Union is a full Member, independent of the fact that its Member States have the same status. It is represented by the Commission, and it is *the* forum where the EU speaks with one voice. The following aspects of the WTO system help us understand EU Member State dynamics better: voting, committee discussions, budget and dispute settlement.

WTO decision-making processes are special because of their penchant for consensus. Everybody must agree, or any progress made until then falls apart. It is also special for 'equality' since each Member has one vote. The Marrakesh Agreement, which set up the WTO, stipulates that '[w]here the European Communities exercise their right to vote, they shall have a number of votes equal to the number of their member States which are Members of the WTO'[109] and that 'the number of votes of the European Communities and their member States shall in no case exceed the number of the member States of the European Communities'.[110] Van den Bossche and Zdouc explain that '[i]t is [thus] clear that either the European Union or the EU Member States (each individually) will participate in a vote. Who participates in a vote is not a matter of WTO law but of EU constitutional law'.[111]

Discussions in the WTO are segregated by committee(s). Different ones discuss different aspects of trade in meetings. The Union speaks for itself and its Member States, even if the committee deals with matters not within the exclusive competence of the EU.[112] While Member States attend these meetings, they do not speak (or vote), unless (procedural) matters like budget, finance and administration are being discussed.[113] Member States get to make 'short [formal] statements' at (the now almost fruitless)[114] Ministerial Conferences. All this is significant in displaying the parental role of the EU in the WTO, even though – and this is significant – the budget for the WTO comes from EU Member States, not the EU.[115]

Dispute settlement is an important function of the WTO. To date, no EU Member State has ever filed a complaint against another WTO Member at the WTO: it is the EU which requests for consultations (first stage in WTO dispute settlement), and if a case is filed against an EU Member State, the defence is carried out by the EU.[116]

There is little coordination mismatch here, if any. The EU, and not its Member States, is the real participant at the WTO.

[109] Marrakesh Agreement Establishing the World Trade Organization, Apr 15, 1994, 1867 UNTS 154, 33 ILM 1144 (1994), art IX:1.

[110] ibid. Fn 2 to art IX: 1.

[111] Peter Van den Bossche and Werner Zdouc, *The Law and Policy of the World Trade Organization: Text, Cases and Materials* 4th edn, (Cambridge, Cambridge University Press, 2017) 147.

[112] ibid, 148.

[113] ibid, 148.

[114] The latest one was disappointingly result-less, even by WTO standards.

[115] Van den Bossche and Zdouc (n 111) at 158.

[116] See: Gracia Marin-Duran, 'The EU and its Member States in WTO Dispute Settlement: A "Competence Model", or A Case Apart, for Managing International Responsibility?' in Marise Cremona and

In terms of engagement, the Union seems to have opted for a change of track. As noted above, the EU was initially fully invested in the multilateral track. Indeed, it was one of the principal architects of the WTO system. However, after the Doha Round did not grant an(y) outcome, year after year, the Union gradually became convinced that the future lay in bilateral and/or regional trade. It has since embarked on negotiations of a 'new generation' of 'deep and comprehensive FTAs', which means that they address more than 'pure trade' (tariffs, customs) matters. The first such agreement to be provisionally applied was the EU–Korea FTA, in 2011. The EU–Colombia–Peru–Ecuador FTA has been provisionally applied since 2013, whereas the EU–Vietnam FTA has been finalised and was signed in June 2019.[117] A number of FTAs – with important players in Asia, like India and Thailand – are locked in (often stalled) negotiations. TTIP negotiations ran out of steam already at the end of the Obama administration's mandate; latest news reports suggest that the US may be looking to re-start talks.[118]

Significantly, these FTAs are signed by both the EU *and* its Member States. The recent Court of Justice of the European Union (CJEU) opinion on the EU–Singapore FTA (finalised in 2014) declared that other than matters of non-direct foreign investment, and the dispute settlement system provided for under such FTAs, the Union has exclusive competence for negotiation(s).[119] This has important consequences for any future EU–UK FTA as well.

Thus, while the EU may have been a truly active participant in WTO governance in the old days, it seems to have shifted its priorities to non-multilateral forms of negotiations.[120] If the Union wishes to stay true to its word, then it needs to return, in good spirit, to the multilateral table, especially now that today the US seems to disengage from the WTO system.

ii. Organisation for Economic Co-operation and Development

The Organisation for Economic Co-operation and Development (OECD) is a cross-regional intergovernmental organisation comprising of 35 countries, most of which are high-income economies. In its own words, the OECD, 'uses

others (eds), *The European Union and International Dispute Settlement* (Oxford, Hart Publishing, 2017).

[117] See: Commission, 'Vietnam', http://ec.europa.eu/trade/policy/countries-and-regions/countries/vietnam/, accessed 14 May 2018.

[118] Richard Bravo and Julia Chatterley, 'Trump Is Willing to Reopen TTIP Amid EU-US Trade Dispute, Ross Says' *Bloomberg Politics* (2018) www.bloomberg.com/news/articles/2018-03-29/trump-willing-to-reopen-ttip-amid-eu-u-s-trade-spat-ross-says, accessed 14 May 2018; the EU, it would seem, is also on board. See Global Strategy (n 42) at 37.

[119] Court of Justice of the European Union, 'The free trade agreement with Singapore cannot, in its current form, be concluded by the EU alone' Press Release No 52/17 (2017), https://curia.europa.eu/jcms/upload/docs/application/pdf/2017-05/cp170052en.pdf, accessed 14 May 2018.

[120] Again, the EU concurrently also claims that it wants the WTO to be the 'centre of global negotiations'. Global Strategy (n 42) at 41.

its wealth of information on a broad range of topics to help governments foster prosperity and fight poverty through economic growth and financial stability … [they] help ensure the environmental implications of economic and social development are taken into account'.[121] The Organisation's work spans the economy, social and environmental policies, tax, education, trade and investment, science and innovation and more.[122]

EU Member States – 22 out of 35 – are in a 'dominant' position.[123] In 1960, through Supplementary Protocol No. 1 to the OECD Convention, the European Commission was given the right to 'take part' in the work of the Organisation. This gives life to Article 220 of the Treaty on the Functioning of the European Union (TFEU), which requires the Union to establish 'all appropriate forms of cooperation' with, inter alia, the OECD. Carroll and Kellow remind us that the EU–OECD relationship has 'changed significantly' over time: 'they began on a limited and somewhat competitive basis, slowly becoming more cooperative … as the various member countries, the European Commission and the OECD Secretariat became familiar with each other's role and capacities'.[124] However, Carroll and Kellow also point out that the relations are 'still subject to occasional stress'.[125] An example of this came in 2004, when the EU was keen for the OECD to take up membership of six of its 10 new members. To the EU's surprise, its proposal was met with considerable resistance – the new members were seen as being 'too small … to warrant membership',[126] and then there was Turkey's opposition to Cyprus' accession. In the end, only two new members (Estonia and Slovenia) were invited to join.[127]

The Union is a 'quasi-member' in the OECD.[128] It is represented in the governing body (the OECD Council), and participates in discussions and can make proposals and amendments. It is also a full member of the Development Assistance Committee. In fact, along with its Member States, the EU is the largest donor to the Official Development Assistance (ODA) programme.[129] However, the Union has no right to vote on legal acts, and does not contribute to the OECD budget (except voluntary contributions).[130]

[121] See: www.oecd.org/about/whatwedoandhow/.
[122] ibid.
[123] Wouters and others (n 78) at 159.
[124] Peter Carroll and Aynsley Kellow, 'The OECD' in Knud Erik Jørgensen and Katie Verlin Laatikainen (eds), *Routledge Handbook on the European Union and International Institutions: Performance, Policy, Power* (Abingdon, Routledge, 2013) 247 at 247–48.
[125] ibid at 250.
[126] ibid; see particularly Andrew Beatty, 'EU gives ground in OECD membership battle' The Economist Intelligence Unit Ltd. As reported in *EIU ViewsWire, New York*: April 5 2007.
[127] Carroll and Kellow (n 124) at 250.
[128] Wouters and others (n 78) at 159.
[129] See figures at: www.oecd.org/about/budget/member-countries-budget-contributions.htm.
[130] For the origin and development of EU–OECD relations, see Carroll and Kellow (n 124) at 247–50.

iii. United Nations

The United Nations (UN) and the UN family of organisations is the largest global multilateral system in existence today. Its institutional structure is diverse and complex, and naturally, EU participation in the system is equally uneven.[131] The UN itself is a Westphalian organisation *par excellence* since it comprises of only nation states,[132] and thus, as such, the EU is barred from becoming a full member. This does not, however, 'prevent the various UN bodies and fora from including provisions in their governing instruments that allow for membership'.[133] This has happened, for instance in the UN Food and Agriculture Organization (FAO), where the Union is, since 1991, the first and only member-organisation.[134] However, in most UN bodies the EU currently only has an observer status.[135] Significant amongst them are: the UN General Assembly (UNGA), the Economic and Social Council (ECOSOC), the International Labour Organization (ILO), the World Health Organization (WHO), and the UN Educational, Scientific and Cultural Organization (UNESCO). Over time the EU has tried to improve its observer status by enhancing its participation rights. The UNGA is a successful example of this (though the enhanced status proposal was initially resisted, even by traditional allies like Australia, Canada and New Zealand). The EU's enhanced participation rights in the UNGA since 2011 include the right to: be on the list of speakers among representatives of major groups and to make interventions; participate in the general debate at the UNGA; have its communication circulated directly; present proposals and amendments orally; and exercise the right of reply.[136] At the same time the Union does not have the right to vote, to co-sponsor draft resolutions or decisions, or to submit candidates.[137]

On the other side of the spectrum is the UN Security Council (UNSC), where the EU has no formal status and has to rely on its Member States that have a permanent seat (ie France, since the UK will soon lead its own path), or a temporary seat (on average two, sometimes even three, Member States).[138] Proposals for a single UNSC EU seat have not found support, and some claim that the reason

[131] For a detailed analysis see: Anna-Luise Chané and Jan Wouters, 'The European Union in the United Nations Economic Governance Fora' in M Bungenber and others (eds), *European Yearbook of International Economic Law* (New York, Springer International Publishing, 2017) 541.

[132] UN Charter, Art 4(1).

[133] Jan Wouters and Anna-Louise Chané, 'Brussels Meets Westphalia: The European Union and the United Nations' in Piet Eeckhout and Manuel Lopez-Escudero (eds), *The European Union's External Action in Times of Crisis* (Oxford, Hart Publishing, 2016) 299 at 305.

[134] ibid at 306 (originally as EEC).

[135] ibid.

[136] See UNGA Res 65/276, 'Participation of the European Union in the Work of the United Nations', 3 May 2011, UN Doc A/RES/65/276. Wouters and Chané (n 133) at 307.

[137] ibid 308.

[138] ibid; in particular see: Sieglinde Gstöhl, '"Patchwork Power" Europe: The EU's Representation in International Institutions' (2009) 14(3) *European Foreign Affairs Review* 385 at 400.

behind this is the desire of France and the UK to maintain their strong position.[139] Be that as that may, since the entry into force of the Treaty of Lisbon the High Representative of the EU for Foreign Affairs and Security Policy can represent the Union in the UNSC to present the EU position on an subject which is on the UNSC's agenda.[140]

The EU takes the UN seriously. There are multiple references to the UN and its Charter in the TEU and the Treaty on Functioning of the EU (TFEU),[141] particularly Articles 3(5) and 21 of the TEU. Other provisions oblige EU institutions to comply with commitments taken in the UN system when implementing EU policies, and to cooperate with UN bodies. It is also heartening to note that there is some clear strategy for UN engagement.[142] The 2003 European Security Strategy (ESS) recognised the UN Charter as the 'fundamental framework for international relations', and states that 'the strengthening of the UN, equipping it to fulfil its responsibilities and to act effectively, is a European priority'.[143] It further states that 'the [then] Community should be given the possibility to participate fully in the work of the UN bodies where matters of the [then] Community are concerned, and MS should contribute effectively towards this'.[144] In the same year the Commission published 'The European Union and the United Nations: The choice of multilateralism', which sets out a general strategy for EU–UN cooperation.[145] Wouters and Chané note that voting cohesion at the UN is quite high, indicating the success of the internal coordination mechanisms.[146] Split votes have been rare and reserved for sensitive issues like Israel/Palestine and usage of drones.[147] This is notwithstanding the fear of a 'silent competence creep', vis-a-vis the UK.[148]

Though on the ground and in terms of funding the EU–UN relationship is generally seen as favourable, not everything is rosy, since their *institutional* relationship is still rather fraught. Wouters and Chané point out that as a regional entity in a state-centric institution, the Union faces challenges of multilateral diplomacy.[149] The acquisition of participatory rights required considerable investment of diplomatic and political capital, and the implementation of rights often

[139] Wouters and Chané (n 133) at 309; Commission, 'Proposal for a Council Decision laying down measures in view of progressively establishing unified representation of the euro area in the International Monetary Fund' COM (2015) 603. This point also finds utterance in Global Strategy (n 42) at 40.

[140] Art 34(2), third paragraph, TEU. See Wouters and Chané (n 133) at 308.

[141] Wouters and Chané (n 133) fn 11.

[142] In general see Chané and Wouters (n 131).

[143] Wouters and Chané (n 133) at 300; see also: European Council, 'European Security Strategy: A Secure Europe in a Better World' (Brussels, 2003).

[144] Wouters and Chané (n 133) at 305.

[145] ibid; see also European Council (n 143). See also (for the legal framework), Wouters and Chané (n 133) at 302–04.

[146] Wouters and Chané (n 133) at 319.

[147] ibid at 320.

[148] ibid at 321, 322.

[149] ibid at 301.

and others. Ultimately, the European countries had to give up two Executive Director positions in favour of emerging countries, and another six per cent of voting shares were transferred to them. It was the smaller Member States, in particular Belgium and the Netherlands, which paid the price for this. This further fosters the fear of the IMF becoming dominated by the largest European countries, almost completely negating the initial objection to their position.

In this context, the proposal for a single Eurozone seat becomes relevant again. Is this a solution? The idea of a single Eurozone seat predates the Euro.[165] Logically, it would solve, both, European overrepresentation (since the voting shares could be dramatically lowered), and under-effectiveness (since the EU would speak with 'one voice'). Some also claim that a single seat would sit better with the image of a single entity in international relations.[166] On the other hand, the Euro's creation (or existence) is, in itself, not a convincing enough argument, since, as has been pointed out, 'the main focus of IMF activities has shifted from exchange rate surveillance to the stability and integrity of the international financial system'.[167] Further, there is disagreement about the practical aspects of such a shared seat. Regardless of *how* such a seat would come into existence, there are two issues to deal with – one legal and one political. First, the IMF only grants membership to countries and the EU's accession would require an amendment of the IMF's Articles of Agreement. Politically, many EU Member States fear that a consolidated representation would undermine their ability to forward national interests; this fear is most strongly held by the smaller Member States, who are well represented in the status quo.

v. World Bank

The World Bank (WB) is an international financial institutional group that comprises the International Bank for Reconstruction and Development (IBRD) and the International Development Association (IDA). It provides loans to countries for capital projects. Though the World Bank initially focused on post-war reconstruction of Western Europe, over the years, and as a result of persistent criticism, its agenda has evolved to include: development issues in post-colonial and post-Soviet transition countries, and the handling of the debt crisis of the 1980s and the financial crises of the 1990s.[168]

[165] See, for example, P Maystadt, 'Implications of EMU for IMF' in Mason and others (eds), *EMU and the International Monetary System* (Washington DC, IMF, 1997).

[166] Kathleen R McNamara and Sophie Meunier, 'Between National Sovereignty and International Power: What External Voice for the Euro?' (2002) 78 (4) *International Affairs* 173.

[167] Lorenzo Bini Smaghi, 'A Single EU Seat in the IMF?' (2004) 42 (2) *Journal of Common Market Studies* 229 at 247.

[168] Eugenia Baroncelli, 'The World Bank' in Knud Erik Jørgensen and Katie Verlin Laatikainen (eds), *Routledge Handbook on the European Union and International Institutions: Performance, Policy, Power* (Abingdon, Routledge, 2013) 205 at 208.

Only EU Member States are members, and only three (France, Germany and the UK) can appoint their own Executive Director at the World Bank Board. The EU does not even have an observer status.[169] As is the case with the IMF, some see the Union as the 'accidental player': 'a weighty Union that seeks to become more influential but, apparently, does not succeed to punch at its weight'.[170] And, like in the IMF, there have been calls for a single EU seat at the World Bank (on grounds of enhanced legitimacy and improved effectiveness), but to date, EU Member States have not seriously taken up this proposal. Such a single seat is also made difficult by the 'persistence of the US veto' at the IMF.[171]

In sum, the EU has potentially substantial voting shares (ie in the hands of its Member States), but there have been repeated calls for a more influential role of the Union. Closer coordination between EU and its Member States has been reported since 2003,[172] and both parties are to be given credit for this. However, on a policy level, coordination still takes place on an ad hoc basis.[173]

V. Conclusion

This chapter gives a bird's eye view of the EU's engagement in global economic governance. As we found out, the Union has pursued regional deals while strongly reiterating its attachment to multilateralism. We first questioned whether the Union's words and actions can be reconciled; subsequently, in order to see if it is possible for the EU to fulfil its multilateral agenda, we assessed its status and strategy in various formal and informal economic governance bodies.

We agree with García-Durán Huet and Eliasson that the Commission's justification for regional pursuits has (so far) omitted one important (and almost obvious) element: the state of multilateral negotiations. Without multilateral progress, the Union's regional deals can never be multilateralised, as it would supposedly like. In any case, there is a lot more that the Union can do if it is serious about its declarations of multilateral devotion. A starting point would be the formulation of a clear and coordinated (vis-à-vis its Member States) strategy in economic bodies. This, we find, is mostly missing as of now.

At the G7 the Commission has questioned whether a strategy is even required. The answer is: it is, especially since the UK will soon compete for power and position. At the G20, the Member States have largely stuck with the EU's 'agreed language' on issues. The WTO is probably the place where the EU's actorness

[169] ibid at 205.

[170] ibid at 209, citing Bini Smaghi, 'Going Forward: Regulation and Supervision after the Financial Turmoil', *Paolo Baffi Centre Research Paper* (2009) 47.

[171] Baroncelli (n 168) at 211.

[172] ibid at 216.

[173] ibid at 211.

is most obvious: the EU is the real player, and there is very little (if any) policy confusion. At the OECD, European countries are in a dominant position, but the EU, as such, is at best, a 'quasi member'; no strategy for coordination seems to be in place. The UN's case is complex because of institutional reasons: the Union has 'enhanced participation rights' at the General Assembly but no formal position at the Security Council, and only an observer status in most other bodies. There are some slivers of strategy in place, but they are either outdated (eg the Commission's 2003 paper) or do not address the UN family comprehensively (eg the EU's 2016 Global Strategy). Finally, in the Bretton Woods institutions (IMF and World Bank) the EU is manifestly punching below its weight: we are light years removed from a single Euro seat and policy coordination remains ad hoc.

The concluding thought, in light of all the foregoing, is that, if the Union is serious about multilateralism, the first step should be the formulation of a comprehensive strategy for coordinating with its Member States in order to display a united front before global economic governance bodies.

10

Lessons from European Constitutionalism for Reforming Multilevel Governance of Transnational Public Goods in Asia?

ERNST-ULRICH PETERSMANN

I. 'Constitutionalism' as Universally Adopted 'European Political Invention'

During most of the recorded history of the *homo sapiens*, law and governance were justified by 'mandates of heaven' invoked by feudal rulers. When the 'first humanism' since about 500 BC enabled the emergence of *autonomous* rather than *heteronomous* political and legal orders, *democratic constitutionalism* (eg in ancient Athens) and *republican constitutionalism* (notably in ancient Rome) were designed and justified (eg by political philosophers like Plato, Aristotle and Cicero) as more inclusive, more legitimate and more effective 'political strategies' for protecting public goods (PGs) for the benefit of citizens; they empowered ancient Athens and Rome to protect internal and external peace and trade in large parts of the Mediterranean. Democratic constitutionalism focused on improving the *input legitimacy* of law and governance through citizenship rights, democratic elections, participatory democracy (eg in popular assemblies and armies), deliberative democracy and institutional 'checks and balances' (eg among legislative, executive and judicial institutions). Republican constitutionalism focused on additional constitutional mandates and restraints aimed at improving the *output legitimacy* of law and governance (eg in terms of protecting non-domination, judicial remedies of Roman citizens and other PGs like the Roman legal system that became accepted by many other jurisdictions throughout Europe).[1] Even after

[1] Notwithstanding disagreements on whether 'freedom as non-domination', civic virtues, active citizenry, political equality, self-government, rule of law, the community, the common good or the struggle against domination are the core values of 'republicanism', modern liberal and republican

the ancient city republics around the Mediterranean ceased to exist (eg due to the West and East Roman empires), new city republics emerged (eg in Florence, Venice and the Northern European city republics participating in the 'Hanseatic League' protecting peace and trade throughout the Baltic sea). They developed new law and governance institutions (eg maritime law, transnational financial law, arbitration protecting multinational banks and investments abroad) that continue to influence modern legal systems.

Law (eg as self-commitment to rules of a higher rank) is part of individual and social self-constitution in order to realise 'personality' (eg one's 'moral powers' of choosing a 'good life' and 'social justice') and order society. Constitutionalism differs from feudalism and related value traditions (eg including Confucianism) by the ideas that (1) all legal public power must be justified vis-à-vis citizens through (2) limited delegation of governance powers for protecting PGs and (3) remain accountable subject to (4) agreed 'higher law' as acts of individual and social self-constitution.[2] As a 'social contract' theory on the relationship between the source of the authority of political power (*potestas*, government by the people), the control of its limited delegation and exercise (*auctoritas*, government of the people), and of the duty of governments to protect PGs for the benefit of citizens (*res publica*, government for the people), constitutionalism evolved differently in different societies, for instance depending on the ideas prevailing in particular societies regarding the relationship of their own legal, ideal and real social orders with social conceptions of divine or cosmic order (eg justification of legal rules and ultimate sources of public authority by religious beliefs), natural law and justice (as 'higher law' limiting legislation), and of human nature and the 'human condition' (eg contractual justifications and constructions of social and legal order).[3] Societies and their ideas of constitutionalism distinguished between the *legal constitution* (eg as reflected in the positive law of a society), the underlying *constitutional ideals* (eg the constitutional mandates for realising a better future), and

theories overlap (eg in their separation of powers and of public and private spheres). In national and international law, republicanism is more ancient than liberalism and majoritarian democratic decision-making.

[2] The distinction between 'sovereignty' and 'government' appointed by the sovereign people was increasingly discussed since the sixteenth century in view of the impossibility of applying the Athenian model of permanent self-governance through democratic assemblies in city-republics to nation states with vast territories and people. Hobbes's suggestion (in *De Cive*, 1642) that the sovereign – after appointing a government – may be considered as 'sleeping', contributed to the invention of representative 'parliamentary sovereignty' (eg in England) and of 'constitutional democracy' (eg in the USA and France) constituting, limiting, regulating and justifying limited government powers through democratically agreed, constitutional rules of a higher legal rank and constitutional rights of citizens aimed at 'constitutionalising' the overall structures of society; cf R Tuck, *The Sleeping Sovereign: The Invention of Modern Democracy* (Cambridge, Cambridge University Press, 2016).

[3] cf P Allot, *The Health of Nations. Society and Law beyond the State* (Cambridge, Cambridge University Press, 2002) ch 12.

the *real constitution* (eg abuses of power and other 'constitutional failures' in social realities). Today:

All 193 UN Member States have adopted national (big C) Constitutions (written or unwritten) constituting, limiting, regulating and justifying the basic legal order of their respective peoples based on agreed 'principles of justice', which are progressively clarified and developed through national and international legal instruments (like UN treaty commitments to respect human rights, rule of law, democratic self-governance and protection of other, transnational PGs for the benefit of citizens).

This *positive constitutional law* also includes mandates for the progressive realisation (eg through additional constitutional, legislative, administrative, judicial and international rules and institutions) of the *ideal constitution* (eg as reflected in the objectives of national Constitutions and specified, inter alia, in the 2000 'millennium goals' and 2015 'sustainable development commitments' of UN Member States).

The social and '*constitutional realities*', however, often differ from the constitutional law and ideals set out in the multilevel constitutional commitments adopted by peoples and governments in the name of their citizens. For instance, inside many UN Member States, governments do not effectively protect human and constitutional rights of citizens and corresponding PGs as prescribed in national Constitutions, UN law or regional human rights law.

Since the 'glorious revolution' in England during the seventeenth century and the human rights revolutions in the USA and France during the eighteenth century, constitutionalism has been progressively transformed:

'*Constitutionalism 1.0*' (like the democratic American and French Constitutions during the eighteenth century, the German and Swiss Constitutions during the nineteenth century) had focused on emancipation of peoples in nation states, the constitution of government powers, and the creation of common markets.

A second wave of '*human rights constitutionalism 2.0*' after World War II was based on national, regional and worldwide commitments (eg in UN law) to protection of civil, political, economic, social and cultural human rights and popular self-determination. The customary law requirement of interpreting treaties 'in conformity with the principles of justice', including also 'human rights and fundamental freedoms for all' (as recalled in the Preamble and Article 31 of the 1969 Vienna Convention on the Law of Treaties (VCLT)), induced national and international courts of justice to increasingly interpret international law in conformity with the human rights obligations of UN Member States.

Post-war European economic integration prompted adjustments of many national Constitutions and the emergence of functionally limited, multilevel constitutional law among the 28 Member States of the European Union (EU) as well as among third states participating in the European Economic Area (EEA), as illustrated by the interpretation of EU and EEA law by national courts, the European Court of Justice (CJEU) and the European Free Trade Area (EFTA) Court as multilevel constitutional legal systems protecting constitutional and human rights of citizens. This multilevel European '*cosmopolitan constitutionalism 3.0*'[4] aims at protecting and emancipating citizens vis-à-vis abuses of national foreign policy powers through multi-level treaty law and institutions constituting, limiting, regulating and justifying multi-level governance of transnational PGs (like common markets, transnational rule of law, protection of monetary stability and of the environment, multi-level legal and judicial protection of cosmopolitan rights). The repercussions of this multilevel constitutionalism on international economic law (IEL) are illustrated by European constitutional and common market law, EU membership in worldwide organisations like the World Trade Organization (WTO) and Food and Agriculture Organization (FAO), and by the ever larger number of international courts protecting rights not only of governments, but also of individuals and non-governmental organisations.

Designing and controlling multilevel governance powers remains the biggest 'constitutional challenge' of modern legal systems.

II. 'Constitutional Failures' in Multilevel Governance of PGs

Many countries have made the historical experience that their 'revolutionary Constitutions' (like the French Constitution of 1791, the German Weimar Constitution of 1919, China's Constitutions of 1912 and of 1982) failed to effectively protect equal rights of citizens and to re-establish legitimate, political authority lost by previous political regimes.[5] Also some international 'treaty constitutions' mandated to protect transnational 'aggregate PGs'[6] – like international rule of law, peaceful settlement of disputes, an international monetary and trading system, public health, international labour and human rights – have failed to fully realise their constitutional objectives (like protection of human rights, international peace and legal security by UN institutions). Some of the founding treaties – eg for

[4] cf EU Petersmann, *Multilevel Constitutionalism for Multilevel Governance of Public Goods – Methodology Problems in International Law* (London, Bloomsbury, 2016); A Somek, *The Cosmopolitan Constitution* (Oxford, Oxford University Press, 2014).

[5] cf S Gardbaum, 'Revolutionary Constitutionalism' (2017) 15 *International Journal of Constitutional Law* 173–200.

[6] On the defining characteristics and different kinds of 'pure PGs' (whose use is 'non-rival' and 'non-excludable' like human rights) and 'impure PGs' (like 'club goods' excluding free-riders, common pool resources with rival uses), the related 'collective action problems', and their limitation through 'multilevel constitutionalism' see Petersmann (n 4) ch 2.

the International Labor Organization (ILO), World Health Organization (WHO), FAO, and UN Educational, Scientific and Cultural Organization (UNESCO) – are explicitly called 'constitutions' and link their legislative and executive mandates to specific human rights (like labour rights, health rights, rights to food and education) and corresponding PGs (like public health and education systems, food security, collective bargaining between employers and employees). Yet, due to the intergovernmental domination of UN/WTO governance and their 'disconnect' from democratic and judicial protection of rights of citizens, UN/WTO governance often remains dominated by special interest groups (eg special producer interests rather than general consumer interests, governmental self-interests in limiting legal, democratic and judicial accountability vis-à-vis citizens). For instance, toxic tobacco products have killed more than 100 million smokers during the twentieth century before the WHO finally adopted the Framework Convention on Tobacco Control in 2003, which has now been ratified by 181 countries. From the point of view of citizens as 'constituent powers' and 'democratic principals' of governments, the power-oriented 'disconnect' of the 'inter-governmental domination' of the decision-making processes of many international organisations and their inadequate democratic control reveal 'constitutional failures' ushering in unnecessary poverty and inadequate protection of human rights of billions of adversely affected citizens in UN Member States.

There are numerous reasons why the self-constitution of individuals and societies in the twenty-first century requires an extension of constitutionalism beyond state borders to the ever more intense, transnational cooperation and 'republican emancipation' of citizens and (non)governmental institutions in their collective supply of private and PGs. For example:

The more 'globalisation' transforms national into *transnational PGs* which no state can protect unilaterally without international law and multilevel governance institutions, the more necessary become constitutional restraints and democratic control of discretionary foreign policy powers to tax and restrict citizens and redistribute domestic income through foreign policy measures (like import tariffs, export subsidies, discriminatory trade, investment and internet restrictions).

The 'disconnect' between intergovernmental UN/WTO governance and domestic rights of citizens – such as intergovernmental treaty provisions and practices preventing citizens from invoking 'PGs treaties' in domestic jurisdictions – risks undermining constitutional rights of citizens (eg as 'democratic principals' of multilevel governance agents with limited, delegated powers) and democratic control of international 'PGs treaties', whose primary and secondary law often eludes effective parliamentary and judicial review and remedies of citizens.

Citizen-driven 'network governance' (eg protecting reasonable, common self-interests of citizens though labour rights, human rights, competition, commercial and common market law and adjudication, global supply chains, climate change governance) has proven to be more effective than intergovernmental UN and

WTO 'chessboard governance' treating citizens as mere objects. As legal subjects and 'democratic principals', citizens must assume republican responsibilities and use their knowledge and energy for promoting transnational PGs.

The widespread disregard for human rights in many UN Member States creates 'negative externalities' (eg more than 60 million refugees fleeing civil wars and unnecessary poverty) that call for 'constitutional restraints' on abuses of power and collective assistance limiting 'governance failures' and 'constitutional failures' (like impunity of rulers violating human rights and committing crimes against humanity).

As human rights recognise individual and democratic self-development as ultimate values, autonomous individual and social 'self-constitution' based on 'recognition of the inherent dignity and of the equal and inalienable rights of all members of the human family (a)s the foundation of freedom, justice and peace in the world' (Preamble of the Universal Declaration of Human Rights (UDHR)) must be extended to the ever more intensive, transnational cooperation among citizens, as recognized in everyone's rights 'to a social and international order in which the rights and freedoms set forth in this Declaration can be fully realized' (Article 28 UDHR). The universally recognised principle – that '(i)n the exercise of his rights and freedoms, everyone shall be subject only to such limitations as are determined by law solely for the purpose of securing due recognition and respect for the rights and freedoms of others and of meeting the just requirements of morality, public order and the general welfare in a democratic society' (Article 29:2 UDHR) – requires constitutional protection of all human beings against abuses of multilevel governance powers.

Democratic, republican and cosmopolitan constitutionalism do not aim at the utopia of a 'global super-constitution' overruling domestic law in multilevel governance of global PGs. They rather argue for functional 'bottom-up constitutionalisation' of multilevel governance of transnational PGs through stronger cosmopolitan rights and remedies (eg in constitutional laws, labour laws, human rights law, competition, common market and environmental legislation) inducing citizens to participate in, and support multilevel governance of transnational PGs (eg by protecting economic and social rights in the global division of labour, rights to participation, privacy and remedies in global communication systems). The fragmented 'constitutionalisation of multilevel governance' is facilitated by the simultaneous 'internationalisation of national constitutional law principles' as reflected in the jurisprudence of international courts and the emergence of 'global administrative law' (GAL).[7] They promote a convergence of national

[7] cf S Cassese (ed), *Research Handbook on Global Administrative Law* (Cheltenham, Edward Elgar, 2016); A Peters, 'The Globalisation of State Constitutions' in J Nijman and A Nollkaemper (eds), *New Perspectives on the Divide between National and International Law* (Oxford, Oxford University Press, 2007) 251–308.

constitutional law principles by linking the 'constitutional functions', principles and 'constitutional methodologies' in multilevel regulation and governance of transnational PGs (eg judicial use of 'proportionality balancing' of competing rights and constitutional principles').[8] The increasing use by national and regional courts in Europe of 'constitutional methodologies' for interpreting the 'rules of recognition, change and adjudication' of multilevel legal systems (like EU, EEA law and European human rights law) as 'principal-agent relationships' among citizens and multilevel governance agents remains context-specific and differs, eg, from multilevel judicial cooperation in Asian countries.[9]

III. Dialectic Evolution of European Constitutionalism

Since the 1950s, the treaties establishing the European Convention on Human Rights (ECHR), the European Communities, the EFTA, EEA and other European organisations continue to transform the state-centred 'international law among European states' (as it evolved notably since the Westphalian peace treaties of 1648) into a citizen-centred European integration law recognising constitutional rights of citizens, transnational rule of law, multilevel democratic rights and multilevel parliamentary, governmental and judicial institutions as common foundations of an emerging European constitutional law.[10] In contrast to power-oriented conceptions of 'international law among states' that risk 're-feudalising' international relations by prioritising rights of governments over rights of citizens (eg in many areas of UN and GATT/WTO law),[11] the dynamically evolving European constitutional law reconnects with the ancient idea of European public law including both domestic, transnational and international public law for multilevel governance of PGs inside and beyond the EU, the EEA and the 47 Member States of the Council of Europe. The more the different domestic and transnational public laws interact both vertically and horizontally, the more the doctrinal separation of the national, transnational, international and supranational levels of legal regulation

[8] cf EU Petersmann, *Constitutional Functions and Constitutional Problems of International Economic Law. International and Domestic Foreign Trade Law and Policy in the United States, the European Community and Switzerland* (Fribourg, Fribourg University Press/Oxford, Boulder Press, 1991); M Hilf and EU Petersmann (eds), *National Constitutions and International Economic Law* (Deventer, Kluwer, 1993).

[9] cf PJ Yap, *Constitutional Dialogue in Common Law Asia* (Oxford, Oxford University Press, 2015), who emphasises the advantages of 'dialogic judicial review' over alternatives of legislative or judicial supremacy.

[10] cf A von Bogdandy and J Bast (eds), *Principles of European Constitutional Law* 2nd edn (Oxford, Hart Publishing, 2010).

[11] cf Allot (n 3) 289 ff ('It was a sad day in the history of humanity when the subtle and complex concept of law was crudely split into two – national law and the law between nations').

neglects the transformative and 'compensatory functions' of multilevel legislative, administrative and judicial governance for protecting rights of citizens and transnational PGs in the common European space.[12] 'European constitutionalism' has, at least, the following five defining characteristics:

The multilevel constitution, limitation, regulation and justification of governance powers (eg in the EU, EEA, EFTA, ECHR and the European Energy Charter Treaty) are based on respect for constitutional rights, multilevel protection of rule of law and democratic governance, rules-based 'economic constitutionalism' (eg of competition and common market regulations), and protection of 'constitutional pluralism' and diverse 'constitutional identities' of peoples (cf Article 4 TEU).

The multilevel regulatory structures (eg of EU, EEA and EFTA law) have more successfully protected transnational PGs (like transnational common markets, rule of law, non-discriminatory conditions of competition, fundamental rights and social welfare of citizens) than in any previous period of European history – notwithstanding 'populist contestations' (eg prompting the British government – in 2017 – to invoke medieval 'royal prerogatives' and 'Henry VIII powers' for implementing its 'Brexit' withdrawal from the EU pursuant to Article 50 TEU ushering in the unilateral termination of the fundamental rights of British citizens under EU law).

Even if European integration law could often not progress in 'linear ways' (eg due to popular opposition against 'political' and 'defence communities' proposed in the 1950s), the economic 'integration dynamic' promoted 'functional spill-overs' (eg from the customs union to the progressive creation of a common market and 'competitive social market economy', monetary union, 'area of freedom, security and justice' and multilevel legal and judicial protection of ever more fundamental rights as codified in the EU Charter of Fundamental Rights (EUCFR)).

The history of European law confirms that intergovernmental power politics can be 'constitutionalised' in diverse ways through multilevel constitutional, parliamentary, participatory and deliberative 'democratic principles' (cf Articles 9–12 TEU) and multilevel, judicial protection of transnational rule of law accommodating very diverse constitutional traditions (eg of common law and civil law countries) inside EU Member States and third states insisting on participation in the common market without supra-national constitutional restraints (eg EEA member countries like Norway, EFTA member countries like Switzerland, authoritarian Muslim countries like Turkey).

[12] cf A von Bogdandy, 'The Idea of European Public Law Today. Introducing the Max Planck Handbooks on Public Law in Europe', *MPIL Research Paper Series* (2017).

The 'economic logic' (eg of creating an EU monetary union without common economic policies) and 'public reason' driving European integration (eg its 'social market economy' prescribed in Article 3 TEU) remain contested, as illustrated by the 'financial crises' since 2008/2010, the debt crises in so far 10 EU member states,[13] the refugee crises and related 'rule of law crises' (as illustrated by widespread disregard for the 'Schengen rules' on free movements of persons and of the EU budget and debt disciplines in Article 126 TFEU). Yet, the 'governance failures' have often been pragmatically used as 'opportunities' for far-reaching reforms (eg by creating a 'banking union' in response to private and public debt crises inside EU Member States). The EU's 'cosmopolitan foreign policy constitution' prescribing (eg in Articles 3 and 21 TEU and the EUCFR) 'protection of human rights', 'strict observance of international law' and mutual coherence of internal and external market regulations illustrates political limits of 'EU constitutionalism', for instance if decisions in EU external relations are not 'taken as openly as possible and as closely as possible to the citizen' (contrary to Article 1 TEU), or if EU free trade agreements (FTAs) preclude citizens from invoking and enforcing FTA obligations in domestic jurisdictions (contrary to the guarantees of fundamental rights and judicial remedies in the EUCFR).[14] Yet, this pragmatic and 'dialectic evolution' of European integration law remains constantly exposed to 'constitutional challenges' (eg from national constitutional courts and European courts contesting EU regulations, 'illiberal' EU Member State governments – like currently in Hungary and Poland – defying compliance with EU law) that may enable future constitutional reforms (eg of the European monetary union, the re-allocation of refugees from Mediterranean 'arrival countries' to other EU Member States). Notwithstanding 'populist dissatisfaction' with certain 'governance failures' inside the EU (like monetary crises, financial austerity measures, uncontrolled immigration in 2015, social inequalities, youth unemployment), citizen support for constitutional, parliamentary, participatory and deliberative democracy remains very high in Europe.

[13] The global financial crisis of 2008 ushered in increasing disregard by EU Member States for the budget and debt disciplines of Art 126 TFEU. The 'bail out'- and related 'credit facility'-prohibitions in Arts 123–125 TFEU, which reflected Germany's insistence on constitutional commitments to fiscal and monetary stability, did not prevent the EU and its Member States to respond positively to requests for – so far – 10 'sovereign debt programmes' disbursing around 500 billion euros since 2008 in favour of euro area states (Greece, Ireland, Portugal, Cyprus) as well as balance of payments loan assistance under Art 143 TFEU for other EU Member States (Hungary, Latvia, Romania). Also Greece formally ended its 'sovereign debt programme' and resumed borrowing in private, international capital markets in 2019. This illustrates not only the success of most of these programmes; it also seems to confirm the 'constitutional problem' that – in weak political systems where politicians fail to defend the rule of law (eg the budget and debt disciplines of Art 126 TFEU) – the public debt is high because the government is willing to pay for the losses of small, well-organised groups rather than to defend the collective interests of taxpayers.

[14] cf EU Petersmann, 'The EU's Cosmopolitan Foreign Policy Constitution and its Disregard in Transatlantic Free Trade Agreements' (2016) *European Foreign Affairs Review* 449–69.

IV. Lessons from European Constitutionalism for Multilevel Governance of Public Goods in Asia?

The human desire for individual and social self-realisation and for its legal protection ('self-constitution') against abuses of 'bounded rationality' can be seen all over the world (eg in 'struggles for justice' liberating peoples from feudalism, colonization and other suppression of human rights). Since Plato's book on *The Republic* (circa 375 BC), the metaphor of the 'state ship' is used in Western republicanism for describing the governance challenges of protecting society from the dangers surrounding it. During discussions on how to reform multilevel trade governance in the WTO, China's WTO Ambassador referred to the Chinese proverb (attributed to the Confucian philosopher Xunzi 298–220 BC) using this metaphor of the 'state ship': 'The heavens create the people and appoint the ruler. The ruler is like a boat, the people are like the water. The water may support the boat, and it may also capsize it.' The Ambassador used this proverb as an illustration of the communitarian, Chinese traditions of 'benevolent governance' aimed at promoting social welfare.[15] My response to the Ambassador emphasised the different use of the 'state ship metaphor' in Western political thought: in Plato's example, society and its rulers are on the boat together; the captain acts as an *agent* of the people, who are recognised as *democratic principal* and '*constituent power*'. The Chinese metaphor describes the people as keeping the state afloat without being on board the ship and without being capable of reforming or steering it. Such different 'pre-conceptions' of law, the state and of citizens are bound to influence law, legal interpretations and governance. For instance, in his comparison of 'rights' in traditional China and 'Western countries', Lubman concluded that the two philosophical schools of Confucianism and Legalism in China 'shared a vision of society in which individual lives were led within hierarchies and social distinctions and proper behaviour derived from an individual's status in those hierarchies' … 'Western thought makes the individual the bearer of rights and bases rights on the fundamental dignity and equality of every human being. There were no such concepts in Chinese thought'; in the Confucian view, 'identity constantly changes, varying with the context; duties and, correspondingly, rights/rites are also constantly being redefined as other actors change'.[16]

As Asian countries continue to adopt ever more legislation and international agreements protecting trading rights, investment rights, intellectual property

[15] The mandate of heaven required benevolent virtues of the ruler, promotion of economic welfare, and consent or acquiescence by the people; economic subsistence rights were considered to be more important than civil and democratic rights against state power as defined by American and European constitutionalism; cf EJ Perry, 'Chinese Conceptions of "Rights": From Mencius to Mao – and Now', (2008) 6 *Perspectives on Politics* 37–50.

[16] SB Lubman, *Bird in a Cage: Legal Reform in China after Mao* (Stanford CA, Stanford University Press, 1999) 15–16, 19.

rights and other economic, social and constitutional rights, historical generalisations about 'rights in the East' and in 'the West' may no longer be justifiable.[17] China seems to comply with most WTO rules and WTO dispute settlement rulings; it has used WTO law for justifying domestic 'rule of law' and judicial reforms inside China. Yet, China's totalitarian interventions into the economy (eg by means of non-notified subsidies, tax- and regulatory-privileges for state-owned companies, 'forced technology transfer' by foreign investors, restrictions of internet freedoms) run counter to the 'liberal understanding' underlying the General Agreement on Tariffs and Trade (GATT 1947), as it was made explicit in the UDHR of 1948 and, less so, in the stillborn Havana Charter for an International Trade Organisation of 1948. China's maritime expansion disregarding its legal and judicial obligations under the UN Convention on the Law of the Sea (UNCLOS)[18] has contributed to the increasing disintegration of the WTO legal and dispute settlement system by hegemonic US power politics using the geopolitical rivalry between China and the US as justification for discriminatory 'trade wars' as protectionist tools for containing Chinese economic and military power. China's political use of history for justifying its territorial and maritime claims over large swaths of the South China Sea reflects long-standing, imperial strategies following the logic of the ancient Chinese board game *wei qui* (also known in the West by its Japanese name *go*), eg building artificial islands and extending military positions surrounding oil, gas and other natural resources aimed at occupying territories and excluding other countries without regard to the UNCLOS provisions on exclusive economic zones and archipels. Similarly, many non-democratic rulers (eg in African and Asian countries) resist constitutional and judicial safeguards of 'rule of law' in order to protect their power, privileges and selfish interests. How should reasonable citizens respond to such power politics? Can the EU Treaty requirements (eg in Articles 2, 9–12 TEU) of promoting constitutional, representative, participatory and deliberative democracy – inside and beyond the EU -as constitutional restraints of multilevel governance of PGs[19] serve as a model for 'constitutionalising' multilevel governance in societies outside Europe with communitarian rather than individualist constitutional traditions? Or is this deliberate self-constitution

[17] Also the proposal by J Chan, *Confucian Perfectionism. A Political Philosophy for Modern Times* (Princeton NJ, Princeton University Press, 2014) – eg that China should adopt liberal democratic institutions which are shaped by the Confucian conception of the good rather than the liberal conception of equal rights – seems to neglect the human reality of reasonable conflicts of interests among free and equal citizens, whose peaceful reconciliation requires mutually agreed human and constitutional rights and remedies.

[18] See China's rejection of the arbitration award of 12 July 2016 under UNCLOS Annex VII concerning the Chinese claims to control more than 80 per cent of the South China Sea without regard to UNCLOS obligations: Permanent Court of Arbitration Case No 2013-19 in the matter of the South China Sea Arbitration (*The Republic of the Philippines v The Peoples Republic of China*). The award is published on the PCA website at www.pcacases.com/web/view/7.

[19] cf EU Petersmann, 'EU Citizenship as a Constitutional Restraint on the EU's Multilevel Governance of Public Goods' (2018) 43 *European Law Review* 89–105.

of the EU as a 'civilised soft power' – in a world of increasing rivalry between hegemonic US 'hard power', revanchist Russian power and totalitarian Chinese power – dangerous and naïve?

A. Constitutionalism as a Means for Reconciling Competing Conceptions of International Economic law

Asian legal traditions often focus on the communitarian dimensions of legal systems (eg on governmental 'duties to protect' PGs rather than corresponding individual rights, communitarianism as a necessary response to the reality of social interdependence and the mutually beneficial effects of social cooperation). European and North-American democracies, by contrast, tend to prioritise equal freedoms as 'first principle of justice' and cosmopolitan, human rights as individualist foundations of democratic and republican constitutionalism, thereby recognising the individual human being and her dignity as ultimate moral concerns that need protection against the frequent abuses of power in communities, nations and states.[20] Hence, in contrast to the regional human rights conventions and regional economic integration agreements with multi-level judicial protection of cosmopolitan rights in Europe, Africa and in the Americas, similar regional agreements and courts do not exist in Asia. Due to the 'globalisation' and 'great convergence' of the modern division of labour – based on information technologies enabling transnational corporations to move labour-intensive work and know-how (eg for production, management and marketing) abroad to developing countries propelling their rapid industrialisation through 'global production' and trade of goods, services and technologies[21] – the shifting of industries from the 'North' to the 'South' (notably to BRICS countries like Brazil, India, China and South Africa) continues to change also conceptions of IEL.

For example, (1) traditional conceptions of IEL as public international law among states (eg the 1944 Bretton Woods Agreements, GATT 1947)[22] and as (2) private international commercial law and 'conflicts law'[23] are criticised by (3) legal conceptualisation of IEL – and notably the law of the hundreds of

[20] For an analysis of IEL from the cosmopolitan perspective of individuals and their human rights see: EU Petersmann, *International Economic Law in the 21st Century. Constitutional Pluralism and Multilevel Governance of Transnational Public Goods* (Oxford, Hart Publishing, 2012). More generally on the status of individuals in modern international law see: A Peters, *Beyond Human Rights: The Legal Status of the Individual in Public International Law* (Oxford, Oxford University Press, 2016).

[21] cf R Baldwin, *The Great Convergence. Information Technology and the New Globalization* (Cambridge MA, Harvard University Press, 2016).

[22] For this view see, eg, G Schwarzenberger, 'The Principles and Standards of International Economic Law' (1966) 117 *Recueil des Cours* 1–98; I Seidl-Hohenveldern, 'International Economic Law' (1986) 198 *Receuil des Cours* 3–264.

[23] An example is: B Schöbener, J Herbst and M Perkams, *Internationales Wirtschaftsrecht* (Hamburg, Müller, 2010). Also the *Internationales Wirtschaftsrecht* edited by C Tietje (Berlin, De Gruyter, 2009)

worldwide and regional organisations for the collective supply of transnational PGs – as global administrative law ('GAL').[24] In view of European human rights law and the legal primacy and 'direct effects' of European common market law vis-à-vis domestic legal systems, EU law and – in less supra-national ways – also EEA law are also (4) construed by European and national courts as multilevel constitutional law. The more the regulation of international monetary, financial, trade and investment organisations became influenced by economic theories (eg on the 'separation of policy instruments' and their 'optimal, efficient ranking' in GATT/WTO law), the more legal doctrines further recognised (5) the need for understanding IEL, and protecting its coherence, in terms of multilevel economic regulation (eg of tariffs and non-tariff border barriers, domestic regulations 'behind borders' like competition rules, subsidies and taxes).[25] Even though most advocates of these five competing conceptions of IEL admit the need for 'methodological pluralism' (eg in interpreting IEL), national, regional and worldwide economic courts increasingly recognise 'constitutional limits' of multilevel economic regulation and governance of transnational PGs, for instance by invoking multilevel human rights guarantees and the customary law requirement of interpreting treaties 'in conformity with the principles of justice', including also 'human rights and fundamental freedoms for all' (as codified in the Preamble and Article 31 VCLT), as constitutional restraints of regulatory economic discretion.[26] Yet, the 'judicialisation' of the WTO legal and dispute settlement system through more than 380 WTO panel, appellate and arbitration reports settling disputes over the interpretation of WTO rules through third-party adjudication has prompted the US, since 2016, to block the filling of Appellate Body vacancies and disregard WTO law through discriminatory trade restrictions that risk undermining the whole WTO legal and dispute settlement system.[27]

B. Five Lessons from European Constitutionalism for Asian Economic Law

Most countries in Asia have embraced 'constitutionalism' only in the twentieth century after having overcome feudal and colonial regimes. The need for limiting

and M Herdegen's *Principles of International Economic Law* (Oxford, Oxford University Press, 2013) include chapters on 'international business law' and transnational private law.

[24] See note 7 above and, eg, R Stewart and RM Ratton Sanchez Badin, 'The WTO and Global Administrative Law' in C Joerges and EU Petersmann (eds), *Constitutionalism, Multilevel Trade Governance and International Economic Law* (Oxford, Hart Publishing, 2011) ch 16.

[25] For detailed explanations of these five competing conceptions of IEL see Petersmann (n 20) ch 1.

[26] cf EU Petersmann, 'Legal Methodology Problems in International Economic Law and Adjudication' (2016) 7 *Jindal Global Law Review* 279–332.

[27] cf EU Petersmann, 'The 2018 Trade Wars as a Threat to the World Trading System and to Constitutional Democracies' (2018) X *Trade, Law and Development* 179–225; EU Petersmann, 'How Should WTO Members React to their WTO Governance Crises?' (2019) 18 *World Trade Review* 503–525.

abuses of public and private, national and intergovernmental power politics in Asia is no less urgent than in Europe and other parts of the world, notably by reviewing how human rights, rule of law and democracy commitments of Asian countries can be protected more effectively in multilevel governance of transnational economic, political and legal PGs. As human rights also protect individual and democratic diversity (eg different democratic preferences and cultural traditions), 'Asian constitutionalism' (eg in common law countries like India, Malaysia, Singapore and Hong Kong (China)) is likely to remain different from European constitutional traditions and experiments.[28] From the perspective of constitutionalism as (1) a normative conception for the input-legitimacy of public law; a (2) constitutional mandate for its output legitimacy; and (3) a legal methodology for interpreting and developing PGs systems, European constitutional and economic law offer important lessons for extending democratic, republican and 'cosmopolitan constitutionalism' beyond national borders also in relations among Europe and Asian countries – with due respect for diverse constitutional traditions at national levels of governance (eg 'Commonwealth constitutionalism' permitting national legislatures to ignore or reverse national judicial decisions inconsistent with parliamentary majority views).[29]

First lesson: constitutionalism as welfare-enhancing, legal methodology. The constitutional core principles (like human rights, rule of law, democracy, republicanism) and their mutual 'proportionality balancing' have empirically proven to be the most effective 'legal method' for protecting PGs also beyond states, like

mutually beneficial common markets and 'social market economies' (cf Article 3 TEU) promoting general consumer welfare;

citizen-driven health rights and public health protection, environmental rights and protection of the environment, equal rights of access to justice and protection of privacy rights in global communication systems; and

multilevel judicial protection of fundamental rights and transnational rule of law beyond national borders.[30]

Constitutional agreement on shared reasons for just rules helps not only to maintain a 'stable equilibrium', social legitimacy and rule of law in the decentralised

[28] cf EU Petersmann, 'International Economic Law without Human and Constitutional Rights? Legal Methodology Questions for my Chinese Critics' (2018) 21 *JIEL* 213–31.

[29] More generally on the reasons of why the historical evolution from 'emancipatory constitutionalism 1.0' and post-World War II 'human rights constitutionalism 2.0' to multilevel 'European constitutionalism 3.0' suggests that – also beyond Europe – some kind of functionally limited 'multilevel constitutionalism 4.0' is both a necessary and politically realistic methodology see Petersmann (n 4).

[30] For empirical case-studies confirming the greater effectiveness of citizen-driven 'cosmopolitan international law' empowering citizens through individual rights and remedies see: R Pierik and W Werner (eds), *Cosmopolitanism in Context. Perspectives from International Law and Political Theory* (Cambridge, Cambridge University Press, 2010); Petersmann (n 20) 59 ff, 321 ff.

application and enforcement of rules by individual agents.[31] It also recognises that economic markets and 'political markets' are legal constructs (rather than 'gifts of nature'), which can protect general consumer and citizen welfare only if 'market failures', 'governance failures' and 'constitutional failures' (eg of protecting civil, political, economic and social rights and remedies of citizens) are legally and institutionally limited. 'Constitutional' and inclusive 'cosmopolitan interpretations' of PGs treaties recognising citizens as legal subjects (as, arguably, required by Article 31:3 VCLT in view of the worldwide recognition of human rights) can promote 'democratic law' empowering citizens and enhancing the democratic capacities of peoples to protect PGs and individual and democratic 'self-constitution' more effectively. Historical evidence confirms that – also in Asia – countries protecting civil, political, economic freedoms, social rights, open markets and transnational rule of law (eg through WTO and FTA Agreements) were capable of producing more social welfare than, eg, communist countries suppressing economic freedoms and human rights.

Second lesson: globalisation requires multilevel constitutionalism. In Asia no less than in Europe, globalisation has transformed national Constitutions into incomplete, 'partial constitutions' that can no longer protect most PGs without international law and multilevel governance institutions. In view of the 'intergovernmental disconnect' of UN/WTO governance from citizens and their constitutional rights, citizens and their democratic and judicial institutions have to struggle for holding intergovernmental power politics legally, democratically and judicially more accountable for protecting PGs more effectively. Citizen-driven 'cosmopolitan network governance' beyond national frontiers – based on individual rights and remedies (eg in the context of competition, trade and investment law remedies, the WHO Framework Convention on Tobacco Control, global supply chains, the Internet, climate change prevention) – has empirically proven to protect PGs more effectively than power-oriented, state-centred 'chess-board governance' disconnected from citizens and civil society.[32] By 'localising PGs' through decentralised 'ownership by citizens' and their empowerment to use 'republican virtues' and constitutional rights for civil society support of transnational PGs, multilevel governance of PGs can be legitimised and strengthened bottom-up.[33]

[31] The constant interaction between 'law as a legal order' and 'law as legal practices' is emphasised by 'critical legal positivism', according to which law and its legal changes should be examined on (1) the surface level of positive law, (2) the legal culture, and (3) the deeper structures of law and underlying principles; cf K Tuori, *Critical Legal Positivism* (Farnham, Ashgate, 2002).

[32] cf note 30 and AM Slaughter, *The Chess-Board and the Web. Strategies of Connection in a Networked World* (New Haven CT, Yale University Press, 2017) (elaborating strategies for designing, improving and managing social networks for resolving collective action problems at local, national and transnational levels of governance). On the 'disruption' of multilateral PGs treaties by populist power politics of the US Trump administration see Petersmann (n 27).

[33] cf EU Petersmann, 'Cosmopolitan Constitutionalism: Linking Local Engagement with International Economic Law and Human Rights' in L Biukovic and P Pitman (eds), *Local Engagement with International Economic Law and Human Rights* (Cheltenham, Edward Elgar, 2017) 26–54.

Third lesson: human rights require democratic constitutionalism. The instrumental function of law for the 'self-constitution' of individuals and peoples – and for social regulation more generally – depends on 'inclusive rule-making' and 'socialisation' of law through 'citizen struggles for justice' (like decolonisation, liberation from feudal suppression of human rights, democratic self-government). European law respects the diversity of national democracies (like parliamentary sovereignty in Britain, rights-based constitutional democracy in Germany, 'illiberal democracies' as currently practised by populist rulers in Hungary, Poland and Turkey). But the EU requirements of constitutional, representative, participatory and deliberative 'democratic principles' (eg in Articles 2, 9–12 TEU) prescribe different levels of democratic legitimation of multilevel EU governance; they reflect the constitutional insight that the lack of a single *demos* and of effective *parliamentary and democratic control* beyond nation states requires stronger protection of constitutional rights of citizens and of non-governmental actors in multilevel governance of PGs. The 'secondary rules of recognition, change and adjudication' in UN/WTO law (eg Article 38 ICJ Statute on the sources of international law) justify citizen-oriented 'constitutional interpretations' and mutually 'consistent interpretations' (eg of the international law rules on state sovereignty, popular sovereignty and 'individual sovereignty' as protected by 'inalienable' and 'indivisible human rights') protecting 'constitutional justice' (eg in constitutional law-making, courts of justice) and judicial remedies of citizens (eg as universally recognised in UN and regional human rights law). Even if international courts adopt 'conservative interpretations' (eg the ICJ judgment of 2012 in *Germany v Italy* denying conflicts between 'old rules' on state immunity and 'new' *jus cogens* prohibitions of genocide and crimes against humanity), national constitutional courts (eg the 'Solange jurisprudence' of the German Constitutional Court regarding the constitutional limits of EU law, the Italian Constitutional Court judgment of 2014 denying the domestic implementation of the 2012 ICJ judgment on grounds of Italian constitutional law) increasingly invoke constitutional arguments protecting the 'constitutional identity' of national democracies and justifying or limiting 'judicial comity' between national and international jurisdictions on grounds of human rights and other constitutional law principles.[34]

Fourth lesson: protection of PGs requires republican constitutionalism. The 'human condition' (like unequal distribution of human capacities, economic resources and power; 'bounded rationality', individual utility-maximisation, diversity and reasonable disagreements) excludes utopias of 'global justice' and 'global democracy'. Multilevel constitutionalism has enabled 'piecemeal reforms' aimed at limiting the ubiquity of public and private abuses of power by enhancing the input- and output-legitimacy and effectiveness of multilevel governance of PGs. The history of democratic, republican, cosmopolitan and 'economic

[34] cf F Francioni, 'From Deference to Disobedience: The Uncertain Fate of Constitutional Court Decision No 238/2014' (2014) XXIV *The Italian Yearbook of International Law* 1 ff.

constitutionalism' (eg promoting 'economic efficiency' and the use of 'optimal policy instruments' in trade and competition law) offers a rich 'tool-box' for limiting abuses of intergovernmental 'top-down chessboard governance' by citizen-driven 'bottom-up network governance' focusing on common interests and PGs rather than on political and economic interest group politics. There is no 'one size fits all' strategy for promoting individual, social and global 'self-constitution' of citizens, peoples and the emerging 'international community of states' (Article 53 VCLT) and individuals, as illustrated by the comparatively lesser development of regional human rights conventions, economic integration agreements and regional courts in Asia than in Africa, the Americas and Europe. Legal and policy priorities must respond to diverse, democratic preferences and local conditions of peoples, which differ among and inside countries (eg due to colonial determination of state borders and distribution of economic resources). Even if the dissatisfaction by citizens and voters with traditional political parties and with their 'governance failures' has prompted 'protest votes' in favour of 'populist politicians' so as to increase democratic pressure for resolving social, economic and environmental crises, the constitutional constraints continue to limit abuses of power and to promote citizen-driven crisis-solutions.

Fifth lesson: transnational rule-of-law requires cosmopolitan constitutionalism. Empirical evidence suggests that 'cosmopolitan legal systems' enabling citizen-driven 'network governance' have protected PGs more effectively than intergovernmental conceptions of 'international law among sovereign states'.[35] Hence, UN Member States have good reasons for limiting the context-specific 'collective action problems' in multilevel governance of PGs by limiting abuses of public and private power through stronger rights, participation and remedies of citizens. For instance, incentives for private and public protection of PGs and limitation of related collective action problems can be set by

promoting transparency and accountability through 'republican countervailing rights' and judicial remedies of citizens (eg regarding toxic tobacco products);

limiting 'free-riding' through transformation of 'pure PGs' (like an open, rules-based world trading system) into 'club goods' (like the WTO and FTAs admitting membership only on conditions of reciprocal trade liberalisation and regulation); and

reducing the non-rival nature of certain PGs (eg in case of pollution of the atmosphere, fishing and pollution in the High Seas, over-use of forests) through creation of 'private-public partnerships' in the joint administration of 'common pool resources'.[36]

[35] Examples include national and international contract, commercial, trade and investment law, labour law, human rights, competition, common market and intellectual property law; cf nn 30, 32 and 33.

[36] cf the research of economic Nobel Prize winner E Ostrom on more efficient 'private-public governance' of common pool resources allowing resource appropriators and local institutions to participate

V. Beyond Rational Choice: Multilevel Constitutionalism as Constraint on Harmful Power Politics

European integration law goes far beyond 'rational choice assumptions' that citizens and governments rationally choose 'optimal policy instruments' for realising private and public goals. As explained by public choice theory, democratic, republican, cosmopolitan and multilevel constitutionalism limits selfish utility-maximisation (eg through rent-seeking and political 'two-level games') by inducing 'boundedly rational actors' to use their 'moral powers' (eg to pursue their individual conceptions of a good life and of social justice) for their individual and democratic 'self-constitution' in ways that respect the equal civil, political, economic, social and cultural rights of EU citizens and other human beings. Constitutional constructivism can institutionalise corresponding 'public reason' and PGs (like multilevel constitutional democracies, rule of law, public health, food and environmental security systems) without unduly limiting national sovereignty (as illustrated by Britain's protectionist 'Brexit' decision to leave the EU). National courts, the CJEU, the EFTA Court and the European Court of Human Rights (ECtHR) have not only recognised the ECHR and EU treaties as 'constitutional instruments' supplementing the national constitutional systems of European states.[37] European courts have also held EU institutions and Member States legally accountable for respecting human rights in the implementation of UN Security Council sanctions and in other fields of the EU's external relations.[38] The micro-economic common market constitution and macro-economic monetary constitution of the EU respond to European governance failures (like nationalism and imperialism provoking World Wars I and II, post-war monetary instability, East–West divide) that remain different from the governance challenges in Asia. Yet, wars, dictatorships and other abuses of government powers have existed outside Europe no less than in Europe. 'Constitutionalisation' of PGs regimes outside Europe often differs, as illustrated by 'non-democratic constitutionalism' (eg in China) and by broader parliamentary powers, more limited judicial powers, less comprehensive 'common law freedoms' and 'human rights charters' in countries practising 'Commonwealth constitutionalism'.[39] The more

in the governance (like the atmosphere as a global commons): E Ostrom, *Governing the Commons: The Evolution of Institutions for Collective Action* (Cambridge, Cambridge University Press, 1990); E Ostrom, *Understanding Institutional Diversity* (Princeton NJ, Princeton University Press, 2005).

[37] cf A Rosas, *EU Constitutional Law* (Oxford, Hart Publishing, 2012); K Tuori, *European Constitutionalism* (Cambridge, Cambridge University Press, 2015).

[38] For surveys of 'sectoral constitutional fragments' and 'societal constitutionalism' in the jurisprudence of UN, WTO, European and private law jurisdictions see: A Peters, 'Constitutionalisation', in *Max Planck Institute for Comparative Public Law and International Law MPIL Research Paper Series* 2017-08; EU Petersmann, '"Constitutional Constructivism" for a Common Law of Humanity? Multilevel Constitutionalism as a "Gentle Civiliser of Nations"', in *MPIL Research Paper Series* 2017–24.

[39] cf J Komarek and M Avbelji (eds), *Constitutional Pluralism in Europe and Beyond* (Oxford, Hart Publishing, 2011).

multilevel regulation is based on vertically coherent principles (like subsidiarity, rule of law, human rights), the easier it may be for multilevel governance institutions to protect the overall legal coherence between fragmented PGs regimes (like trade law, investment and environmental law, human rights law). The unnecessary poverty of billions of peoples without effective access to protection of human rights confirms that citizens must struggle for further limitations of state-centred conceptions of 'international law among sovereign states' that risk 're-feudalising' transnational cooperation by limiting human and democratic rights and remedies of citizens as the ultimate 'agents of justice' and guardians of individual and democratic 'self-constitution'. The limitation of intergovernmental protectionism under 'GATT 1947' by the WTO legal, trading and compulsory dispute settlement systems has contributed to reducing absolute poverty to now less than 10% of the world population, notably by assisting China, India and developing countries to benefit from rules-based, global division of labour promoting consumer welfare.

This contribution has suggested that also UN 'treaty constitutions' (eg for the ILO, WHO, FAO and UNESCO) can fulfil their respective mandates of protecting human rights and corresponding PGs (like labour rights and collective bargaining aimed at protecting 'social justice', health rights protecting public health, human rights of access to food promoting food security, rights to education promoting public reason) more effectively by overcoming the authoritarian 'disconnect' between the 'law in the books' (eg explicit treaty commitments to protection of human rights) and the 'law in action' (eg prioritising rights of governments over legal, democratic and judicial rights of citizens, domestic non-implementation of UN human rights law). The European history of democratic, republican, cosmopolitan and multilevel constitutionalism suggests that also beyond Europe – eg in regional cooperation among Asian countries – multilevel PGs regimes cannot be enforced top-down through intergovernmental power politics without support from citizens using their constitutional and republican rights – as 'democratic owners' of PGs – to hold multilevel governance institutions legally, democratically and judicially more accountable. As law exists only in the minds and practices of human beings, their individual and democratic conceptions of law remain inevitably contextual depending on their diverse 'constitutional imaginations' and 'ordinary virtues'.[40] The constitutional task of limiting collective action problems by 'institutionalising public reason' at national and transnational levels of governance and regulation must aim at building an 'overlapping consensus' among national, regional and functionally limited, global regulatory systems with due respect for the inevitable diversity of constitutional conceptions.

[40] cf M Ignatieff, *The Ordinary Virtues: Moral Order in a Divided World* (Cambridge MA, Harvard University Press, 2017) (explaining why the moral language resonating with most people – notably in authoritarian countries in Asia – remains that of local everyday virtues and community-based solidarity rather than the human rights discourse of liberal elites in constitutional democracies).

Individual, social and democratic 'self-constitution' of peoples in Asia remains shaped by different cultures, democratic preferences and legal traditions. The EU example of regional market integration based on GATT/WTO rules continues to be successfully used by many countries outside Europe, for instance by China (eg using WTO rules for peaceful recreation of a common market among the four Chinese WTO members) and by Eurasian countries (eg participating in the Eurasian customs and economic union) for promoting economic welfare and peaceful cooperation. The WTO and FTA rules confirm the 'constitutional insight' that market-driven, economic and legal systems offer decentralised incentives for resolving 'constitutional problems', knowledge problems, coordination and reputation problems of social cooperation among millions of self-interested producers, investors, traders, consumers and other citizens more efficiently and more legitimately than discretionary power politics.[41] The signing of the Trans-Pacific Partnership Agreement (TPP) by 12 diverse developed and less-developed countries (Australia, Brunei, Canada, Chile, Japan, Malaysia, Mexico, New Zealand, Peru, Singapore, USA and Vietnam) in 2016 – and, following the US withdrawal from the TPP in 2017, its transformation into a Comprehensive and Progressive TPP among the remaining 11 trading countries – illustrate how an 'overlapping consensus' among members of mega-regional FTAs may progressively reduce regulatory 'gaps' among worldwide and regional agreements (eg in fields like trade, labour, investment, competition regulation and environmental protection).

The universal recognition of human rights may not have changed the 'everyday virtues' of many people (eg in communist countries like China and Vietnam). But it entails government duties to protect PGs that – as illustrated by European law – require some kind of multilevel constitutionalism constituting, limiting, regulating and justifying multilevel governance powers for the benefit of citizens as 'constituent powers', 'democratic principals' and legal subjects of 'transnational communities', which must protect 'voice' and remedies of citizens in international rule-making protecting transnational PGs. The regulatory self-constitution of peoples in Asia can learn from both the 'constitutional failures' in Europe (like communist and socialist dictatorships) and from Europe's experimental struggles for 'constitutionalising' public power and multilevel governance of PGs. Asian countries have reasonable self-interests to support the EU's constitutional obligations (under Articles 3 and 21 of the 2009 Lisbon Treaty) to protect 'strict observance of international law' in foreign policies so as to contain hegemonic power politics undermining multilateral treaties protecting global PGs like the WTO, the rule-based maritime order based on UNCLOS, and climate change prevention based on the 2016 Paris Agreement. By starting hegemonic 'trade wars' and undermining multilateral 'PGs treaties' (like the WTO and Paris Climate

[41] cf EU Petersmann, 'Constitutional Functions and Constitutional Problems of International Economic Law in the 21st Century' (2011) 3 *Collected Courses of the Xiamen Academy of International Law* 149–236.

Agreements), the US Trump administration undermines also the regulatory task of designing new multilateral WTO rules limiting 'totalitarian Chinese market distortions' (eg by means of state-owned enterprises, non-transparent subsidies, 'forced technology transfers', arbitrary restrictions of the internet and human rights). Replacing China's communist 'sham constitution' of 1982 (as amended) by democratic constitutionalism limiting the totalitarian powers of China's 'communist party state' would offer the most effective contribution to avoiding a 'new cold war' and 'great power rivalry' among China and the USA, which risk destroying the WTO trading system and harming the welfare of citizens all over the world.

11

The EU's Civil Justice Policy Field: Perspectives for Asia?

HELEN E HARTNELL

I. Introduction

In the late 1990s, the EU Member States agreed[1] to add 'building an Area of Freedom, Security and Justice' (AFSJ) as a goal of European integration. The 'justice' component of the large AFSJ policy field includes the goal of creating a 'European Judicial Area' (EJA), which, in turn, includes a subfield that the European Commission calls *civil justice*. Formally based on a narrow notion of measures aimed at enhancing *judicial cooperation in civil matters*, the EJA's civil justice dimension has evolved to incorporate a wide array of issues relating to civil procedure, conflict of laws (private international law), and the administration of justice.

This chapter begins by asking why European developments might be of interest in Asia (section II). Next, it explores the scope of the EU's civil justice policy field (section III) and the overarching policy objectives that animate this field of EU policy-making (section IV). The chapter concludes with reflections on the significance of developments in the civil justice policy field for the larger process of European integration, along with their potential relevance for Asia (section V).

II. Civil Justice beyond the Nation-State

Historically, European nations have engaged in sustained efforts towards transnational harmonisation or unification in regard to civil justice issues over a period of

[1] The Treaty of Amsterdam, which amended the Treaty on European Union (TEU) and the Treaty Establishing the European Community (EC Treaty), was signed in 1997 and entered into force in May 1999. The EC Treaty was renamed the Treaty on the Functioning of the European Union (TFEU) as of 2009.

more than a century. The most important multilateral efforts in Europe have been carried out by the Hague Conference on Private International Law (HCCH)[2] – the 'World Organisation for Cross-border Co-operation in Civil and Commercial Matters'[3] – which works toward 'progressive unification of the rules of private international law'[4] as a way to resolve difficulties that stem from the diversity of legal systems and affect 'personal and family or commercial situations … connected with more than one country'.[5] The overarching aims of this enterprise are to provide legal security for transborder actors, and to promote the 'orderly and efficient settlement of disputes, good governance and the rule of law, while respecting the diversity of legal traditions'.[6] The principal tool used by the Hague Conference is the traditional public international law convention, that is, a set of rules negotiated among member countries operating under the norm of consensus, signed at the conclusion of negotiations, and subsequently available for ratification by individual countries or regional actors (such as the EU, which became a member of the Hague Conference in 2007). HCCH conventions aspire to create 'hard' legal norms that are designed to solve concrete problems on a wide range of topics affecting international judicial and administrative co-operation in the area of private law, especially as it affects children and the family, civil procedure, trusts and estates, and commercial law.

Another traditional multilateral forum is the International Institute for the Unification of Private Law (UNIDROIT), which was established in 1926 to 'study needs and methods for modernising, harmonising and co-ordinating private and in particular commercial law as between States and groups of States'.[7] Like the Hague Conference, UNIDROIT was at work long before World War II, and is independent of the EU. Yet unlike the Hague Conference, UNIDROIT has focused the bulk of its efforts on *substantive* harmonisation of civil and commercial law, rather than on civil justice issues.[8] In recent years, however, UNIDROIT has become active in regard to one subset of civil justice issues, namely its work on developing Transnational Principles of Civil Procedure, first in conjunction with the American

[2] First convened in 1883, the Hague Conference was founded as an international organisation in 1893.

[3] Homepage, Hague Conference Website, www.hcch.net/, accessed 2 February 2018.

[4] Statute of the Hague Conference on Private International Law, art 1, adopted on 31 October 1951 (in force on 15 July 1955); as amended on 30 June 2005 (in force on 1 January 2007).

[5] Overview, Hague Conference Website, www.hcch.net/index_en.php?act=text.display&tid=26, accessed 20 December 2017.

[6] Vision and Mission, Hague Conference Website, www.hcch.net/en/about/vision-and-mission, accessed 20 December 2017.

[7] Purpose, UNIDROIT Website, www.unidroit.org/about-unidroit/overview, accessed 20 December 2017.

[8] Another significant difference is that UNIDROIT has been more innovative, methodologically speaking, and has supplemented the use of traditional 'hard' conventions with a variety of 'soft' instruments, notably model laws, legal guides and general principles addressed directly to judges, arbitrators and contracting parties.

Law Institute for global transactions, and more recently, with the more recently created European Law Institute,[9] to adapt those rules for regional usage.[10]

Asian countries are no strangers to the work of either the Hague Conference or UNIDROIT. While founded by European countries – among them the nineteenth-century incarnations of the six countries that founded the European Communities[11] in the 1950s – the Hague Conference currently has 83 members from across the globe, including all current EU members, as well as a growing number of countries in Asia.[12] For its part, UNIDROIT currently has 63 members, including all EU Member States, as well as a handful of members from Asia.[13] Particularly noteworthy is the activity of the Hague Conference, which opened a new Regional Office for Asia and the Pacific (ROAP) in Hong Kong in 2012, with the aim of increasing awareness of the value of membership in the HCCH and encouraging states in the region to adopt its conventions.[14]

Questions about the need for reform or even transnational regulation of civil justice issues have been raised by a growing number of Asian scholars. Some authors have published studies about private international law in various countries,[15] while others look beyond national developments and call attention to

[9] The European Law Institute was founded in 2011 as an 'entirely independent organization … to improve the quality of European law' and to 'study and stimulate European legal development in a global context'. About the ELI, www.europeanlawinstitute.eu/about-the-eli, accessed 21 May 2019.

[10] ELI – UNIDROIT Transnational Principles of Civil Procedure, www.unidroit.org/work-in-progress/transnational-civil-procedure, accessed 29 December 2017.

[11] Before there was a European Union, there were three communities: the European Coal and Steel Community (ECSC), the European Atomic Energy Community (Euratom) and the European Economic Community (EEC). The ECSC expired in 2002, while Euratom and the EEC (later renamed the European Community or EC) have been fully superseded by and absorbed into the EU, by virtue of the Lisbon Treaty (effective December 2009).

[12] The countries, in chronological order, including their dates of membership and the number of conventions they have ratified, are: Japan (1957, seven); China (1987, three, not including those applicable to Hong Kong and Macao), Republic of Korea (1997, four); Russian Federation (2001, six); Malaysia (2002, zero); Philippines (2010, three); Singapore (2014, three); and Viet Nam (2013, two).

[13] The countries, in chronological order, including their dates of membership, are: Japan (1954); Republic of Korea (1981); China (1986); Russian Federation (1990); and Indonesia (2009).

[14] The opening ceremony was attended by more than 100 distinguished guests, including Consuls General and representatives from over 30 countries and international organisations. Hague Conference on Private International Law, 'Official opening of the Hague Conference on Private International Law Asia Pacific Regional Office in Hong Kong' (2012) www.hcch.net/en/news-archive/details/?varevent=294, accessed 20 December 2017.

[15] The following articles published in English suggest the breadth of interest: Hyun Suk Kwang, 'The New Conflict of Laws Act of the Republic of Korea' in Petar Sarcevic and Paul Volken (eds), *Yearbook of Private International Law* (Alphen aan den Rijn, Kluwer, 2003) 99; Koji Takahashi, 'A Major Reform of Japanese Private International Law' (2006) 2 *Journal of Private International Law* 311; Masato Dogauchi 'New Private International Law of Japan: An Overview' (2007) *The Japanese Annual of International Law* 3; Zhengxin Huo, 'An Imperfect Improvement: The New Conflict of Laws Act of the People's Republic of China' (2011) *International and Comparative Law Quarterly* 1065; Kwang Hyun Suk, 'Some Observations on the Chinese Private International Law Act: Korean Law Perspective' (2011) *Zeitschrift fuer Chinesisches Recht (ZChinR)* 105; Jin Huong and Zhengxin Huo (eds), 'A Commentary on Private International Law in East Asia – From the Perspective of Chinese Law' in Wen-Yeu Wang (ed), *Codification in East Asia* (New York, Springer, 2014); Qingkun Xu, 'The Codification of Conflicts Law in China: A Long Way to Go' (2017) 65 *The American Journal of Comparative Law* 919.

the need to address private international law issues – such as jurisdiction, choice of law, and the recognition and enforcement of judgments – in order to enhance regional integration and create an internal market.[16] For example, Jie (Jeanne) Huang has proposed adoption of an interregional judgment recognition and enforcement (JRE) system for Mainland China, Hong Kong and Macao in order to alleviate current difficulties,[17] while Xinyi Gong advocates a similarly interregional approach to insolvency cases.[18] For its part, the Special Commission on Inter-Regional Conflict of Laws of the Chinese Society of Private International Law has carefully considered EU experience in developing its own approach to the taking of evidence.[19] Another major initiative is the project undertaken by private international law scholars in ten East and Southeast Asian jurisdictions to harmonise the region's private international law rules – the Asian Principles of Private International Law (APPIL) – which were finalised in 2017.[20] The APPIL contain non-binding principles on a wide range of civil justice issues, notably choice of law, international jurisdiction, recognition and enforcement of foreign judgments, and judicial support for international commercial arbitration.[21] These soft law principles are intended as a model law, which can be used by national and regional legislators when applying or adopting national instruments, or even applied by national courts and arbitral tribunals in appropriate cases. Another new actor in the field is the Singapore-based Asian Business Law Institute (ABLI), whose ambitious 'Project on Convergence in International Civil Procedure' is working towards harmonising rules on the recognition and enforcement of foreign judgments in ASEAN, Australia, China, India, Japan and South Korea.[22] As this

[16] Weidong Zhu, 'A Plea for Unifying or Harmonizing Private International Law in East Asia: Experiences from Europe, America and Africa' (2011) 117 *Studies on Private International Law* http://ssrn.com/abstract=2194347, accessed 20 December 2017.

[17] Jie (Jeanne) Huang, *Interregional Recognition and Enforcement of Civil and Commercial Judgments: Lessons for China from US and EU Law* (London, Bloomsbury Publishing, 2014).

[18] Xinyi Gong, *China's Insolvency Law and Interregional Cooperation: Comparative Perspectives from China and the EU* (Abingdon, Routledge, 2017).

[19] Mainland China concluded a Taking of Evidence Arrangement with Macau in 2001 and with Hong Kong in 2017. Guangjian Tu, 'The Special Commission on Inter-Regional Conflict of Laws of the Chinese Society of Private International Law Organized Its Third Annual Symposium on Inter-Regional Taking of Evidence Within China' http://conflictoflaws.net/2017/the-special-commission-on-inter-regional-conflict-of-laws-of-the-chinese-society-of-private-international-law-organized-its-third-annual-symposium-on-inter-regional-taking-of-evidence-within-china/, accessed 22 May 2019.

[20] Weizuo Chen and Gerald Goldstein, 'The Asian Principles of Private International Law: Objectives, Contents, Structure and Selected Topics on Choice of Law' (2017) 13 *Journal of Private International Law* 411.

[21] In this respect, the scope of the APPIL is broader than the EU's civil justice field, which does not cover international commercial arbitration at this time.

[22] Adeline Chong (ed), *Recognition and Enforcement of Foreign Judgments in Asia (Compendium)* (Asian Business Law Institute (ABLI) Legal Convergence Series 2017) http://abli.asia/PROJECTS/Foreign-Judgments-Project, accessed 21 May 2019. The first phase of this project, which was concluded in December 2017, maps the rules for recognition and enforcement of foreign judgments in ASEAN, Australia, China, India, Japan and South Korea, while the second (ongoing) phase aims to 'determine common principles which will be published as a set of *Asian Principles for the Recognition and Enforcement of Foreign Judgments*'. ibid. See also Sai Ramani Garimella and Stellina Jolly (eds), *Private International Law: South Asian States' Practice* (New York, Springer, 2017).

brief survey of recent Asian scholarship (available in English) shows, the topic of regional harmonisation and unification in the field of civil justice has arrived, and is being embraced by a range of public and private (including academic) actors throughout Asia.[23]

These developments aside, the challenge of devising appropriate solutions for Asia is just beginning. It would be unwise to assume that solutions devised in the context of a federal state such as the United States, or in a quasi-federal entity such as the EU, can be adapted in Asia. While regional integration efforts show many similarities worldwide, particularly in the general approach to economic integration, it is risky to compare the very advanced – even if currently troubled – state of integration in the EU with efforts underway elsewhere, however ambitious the latter may be.[24] This is particularly true in Asia, with its great number and wide variety of countries, its enormous population and linguistic diversity, its diverse political and legal systems, and its strong cultural traditions. While APEC's work focuses on economic integration, ASEAN's mandate extends beyond the economic realm and includes dimensions of political, security and socio-cultural cooperation. Still, neither regional initiative currently envisions a level of legal harmonisation or administrative cooperation as pervasive as that which the EU is pursuing in the civil justice field. Given the close nexus between the EU's civil justice measures and its far-reaching political goals – notably free movement of persons and the concept of European citizenship – it is possible that legal harmonisation and unification will remain a low priority for these regional organisations, despite urgent calls by Asian scholars for progress in this field. Moreover, absent legislative capacities with at least some of the features found in the EU, among them largely autonomous institutions and qualified majority voting rules, it is difficult to imagine that regional organisations in Asia (or elsewhere in the world) could achieve the level of dynamism seen in the EU over the past two decades since 'judicial cooperation in civil matters' was communitarised by the Treaty of Amsterdam.

[23] ABLI (ibid) reports that 63 per cent of its contributors are academics and 38 per cent are practitioners.

[24] For example, the activities of the Asia-Pacific Economic Cooperation (APEC) on the Comprehensive and Progressive Trans-Pacific Partnership (CPTPP) – the name of which was altered from Trans-Pacific Partnership (TPP) after President Trump withdrew the United States in 2017 – and of the Association of Southeast Asian Nations (ASEAN) on the Regional Comprehensive Economic Partnership (RCEP), both exemplify ambitious efforts towards regional integration in the Asia-Pacific area. In regard to the former, the CPTPP entered into force on 30 December 2018 for Australia, Canada, Japan, Mexico, New Zealand and Singapore, and in January 2019 for Vietnam. Government of Canada, CPTPP, https://international.gc.ca/trade-commerce/trade-agreements-accords-commerciaux/agr-acc/cptpp-ptpgp/index.aspx?lang=eng, accessed 21 May 2019. In regard to the latter, negotiations continue among ASEAN Member States and ASEAN's free trade agreement (FTA) partners (ie, Australia, China, India, Japan, South Korea and New Zealand). 'Joint Leaders' Statement on the Regional Comprehensive Economic Partnership (RCEP) Negotiations' (14 November 2018) https://asean.org/joint-leaders-statement-regional-comprehensive-economic-partnership-rcep-negotiations/, accessed 21 May 2019.

III. Scope of the EU's Civil Justice Policy Field

This section provides a conceptual map of the EU's civil justice policy field. Given the wide (and sometimes conflicting) variance in the literature on how particular labels are used and concepts bundled, some introductory remarks are needed. Scholars use various terms to discuss these developments, such as 'European Private Law', 'European (Civil) Procedure' and 'European Private International Law'. These choices often reflect the author's own disciplinary 'home' field or institutional base. Terminological diversity does not mean, however, that there is no consensus. In fact, few still invoke the official label found in the Treaty – 'judicial cooperation in civil matters' – which is too narrow to capture the sweep of the EU's policy field. I use the term 'civil justice' for three reasons. First, it does not correspond to any recognised academic specialisation, thus neither reproduces peculiar national (or systemic) subdivisions, nor tries to force one legal subfield into unnatural subordination to another. Second, this is the term that the EU itself uses, as seen most prominently on the website of, and in documents prepared by, the Commission's Directorate-General (DG) Justice. And third, this term resonates with the overarching concern for justice that animates the broader AFSJ project.

The scope of the EU's civil justice field is defined by multiple parameters. First, scope depends on the EU's *formal competence*, which is delineated by the Treaty on the Functioning of the European Union (TFEU). Article 81(1) TFEU calls upon the EU to

> develop judicial cooperation in civil matters having cross-border implications, based on the principle of mutual recognition of judgments and of decisions in extrajudicial cases. Such cooperation may include the adoption of measures for the approximation of the laws and regulations of the Member States.

In particular, as per Article 81(2) TFEU:

> the European Parliament and the Council, acting in accordance with the ordinary legislative procedure,[25] shall adopt measures, particularly when necessary for the proper functioning of the internal market, aimed at ensuring: (a) the mutual recognition and enforcement between Member States of judgments and of decisions in extrajudicial cases; (b) the cross-border service of judicial and extrajudicial documents; (c) the compatibility of the rules applicable in the Member States concerning conflict of laws and of jurisdiction; (d) cooperation in the taking of evidence; (e) effective access to justice; (f) the elimination of obstacles to the proper functioning of civil proceedings, if necessary by promoting the compatibility of the rules on civil procedure applicable in the Member States; g) the development of alternative methods of dispute settlement; [and] (h) support for the training of the judiciary and judicial staff.

[25] Footnote added by author. The ordinary legislative procedure entails qualified majority voting and full participation by the EP. In regard to family law matters, however, the EU uses a special legislative procedure, which requires unanimity and limits the EP's role in the legislative process (TFEU Art 81(3)).

This treaty basis is, however, just the starting point.

The scope and content of the field are also established by goals and parameters laid out in EU *policy statements and programmes* (section IV below). In addition, they are manifested by the actual *exercise* of the EU's competence. Finally, the Court of Justice of the European Union (CJEU) plays a growing role in demarking the civil justice field.

At the incipient stage of its development,[26] 'judicial cooperation in civil matters' comprised *private international law*, which encompassed choice of law as well as international/transnational civil procedure. It also included a broad general reference to *civil procedure*, along with one dimension of the *administration of justice*, namely access to justice. *Substantive law*, on the other hand – the private law of contract, tort, family law, etc – was not formally part of the civil justice field at all. The term 'civil justice' used here includes all types of measure listed in Article 81 TFEU, as well as some that are not explicitly mentioned in the Treaty, but are nevertheless formally part of, or at least informally linked to the growth of the AFSJ. I organise these measures according to the following schema:

- [European] Procedural Law[27]

  Jurisdiction and Mutual Recognition and Enforcement of Judgments and Decisions in Extrajudicial Cases (Articles 81(2) (a) & (c) TFEU)[28]

  International Judicial Assistance:

  Cross-border Service of Judicial and Extrajudicial Documents (Article 81(2)(b) TFEU)

  Cooperation in the Taking of Evidence (Article 81(2)(d) TFEU)

  Elimination of Obstacles to the Proper Functioning of Civil Proceedings (if necessary by promoting the compatibility of the rules on civil procedure applicable in the Member States) (Article 81(2)(f) TFEU)

- Institutional Measures: The Administration of Justice

  Judicial Network & E-Justice

  Support for Training of the Judiciary and Judicial Staff (Article 81(2)(h) TFEU)

  Effective Access to Justice (Article 81(2)(e) TFEU)

  Alternative Methods of Dispute Settlement (Article 81(2)(g) TFEU)

- Conflict of Laws

  Choice of Law Rules (Article 81(2)(c) TFEU)

[26] The precursor to Art 81 TFEU was Art 65 of the EC Treaty, which was added by the 1997 Treaty of Amsterdam (effective May 1999).

[27] My conceptual framework simplifies discussion by abandoning the traditional legal category of *private international law*, and by merging 'international/transnational civil procedure' into '[European] civil procedure'.

[28] I bundle these two sets of issues, even though the TFEU does not, because this reflects how the issues are treated in legislative measures, such as the Brussels I and Brussels II Regulations.

IV. Policy Objectives in the Civil Justice Arena

While ineluctably pragmatic, the EU's efforts in the civil justice field are also oriented towards overarching policy goals. Moreover, it is arguable that the EU would not have succeeded in gaining its current broad authority to regulate civil justice issues, had it not been for the ambitious political goals that animate the field, or the historical junctures that led to creation of the AFSJ.[29] This section looks behind labels in order to illuminate the vision that drives the policy field. In particular, it examines the evolution of the conceptual schema from inception until the present, by tracing discursive shifts in policy statements and financial programmes relating to civil justice. The analysis is divided into two periods – Preparation and Implementation – with most attention devoted to the latter period.[30]

A. Preparation (June 1977–October 1999)

Serious efforts to develop the EU's new civil justice policy field began between the signing of the Treaty of Amsterdam and its entry into force in May 1999, despite the EU's lack of legislative competence during that period. The AFSJ rapidly took on a life of its own, thanks to the Commission, the Council, the European Parliament (EP) and the European Council, who together articulated justifications for the AFSJ and elaborated visions for the civil justice subfield of the AFSJ.

Six policy statements on the EU's emerging 'genuine European area of justice' were issued during the preparation phase:

- Commission Communication on Judgments (January 1998)[31]
- European Council: Cardiff Presidency Conclusions (June 1998)[32]
- Commission AFSJ Communication (July 1998)[33]
- European Council and Commission: Vienna Action Plan (December 1998)[34]

[29] Helen E Hartnell, *Europeanizing Civil Justice in Amsterdam (1997) and Tampere (1999): Legal Elites and the Politics of Private International Law, Civil Procedure, and the Administration of Justice in the European Union* (PhD Dissertation, University of California, Berkeley, 2018).

[30] For a detailed examination of the early phase, see Helen E Hartnell, 'EUstitia: Institutionalizing Justice in the European Union' (2002) 23 *Northwestern Journal of International Law and Business* 65; Eva Storskrubb, *Civil Procedure and EU Law – A Policy Area Uncovered* (Oxford, Oxford University Press, 2008). For a comprehensive recent analysis of EU developments, see Hartnell (n 29).

[31] Commission Communication to the Council and the European Parliament, 'Towards Greater Efficiency in Obtaining and Enforcing Judgments in the European Union' [1998] OJ C 33/3 (Commission Communication on Judgments).

[32] Presidency Conclusions, Cardiff European Council [1998] *Bulletin EU* 6-1998, paras I.1–I.35 (Cardiff Presidency Conclusions).

[33] Communication from the Commission, 'Towards an Area of Freedom, Security and Justice' [1998] COM(1998) 459 final (Commission AFSJ Communication).

[34] Council and Commission Action Plan of 3 December 1998 on how best to implement the provisions of the Treaty of Amsterdam on the creation of an Area of Freedom, Security and Justice [1999] OJ C 19/1 (Vienna Action Plan).

- European Parliament (EP) Resolution on the Draft Action Plan (April 1999)[35]
- European Council: Tampere Milestones (October 1999)[36]

Together, these foundational documents reveal not only the preliminary schematics for developing Europeanised civil justice (EUstitia), but also the driving vision behind the profusion of new measures that have followed in the wake of communitarisation by the Treaty of Amsterdam.

These early policy statements articulate both the 'negative' and 'positive' integration goals to be pursued in the civil justice arena. Negative integration refers to measures that eliminate national barriers or 'restraints on trade and distortions of competition',[37] while positive integration pertains to 'common European policies to shape the conditions under which markets operate'.[38] These notions, which are anchored in trade of goods, required rethinking in connection with civil justice, which is linked to free movement of persons – the 'cornerstone of … freedom and democracy' in the EU[39] – rather than to free movement of goods. Civil justice is thus oriented both towards the 'negative' goal of removing barriers to free movement of persons, and towards the grander 'positive' goal of establishing the AFSJ, conceived as a European legal order that has a crucial role to play in establishing European political order. The Vienna Action Plan, for example, emphasises that 'freedom' includes the 'freedom to live in a law-abiding environment … complemented by the full range of fundamental human rights, including protection from any form of discrimination'.[40]

The Commission was quick to take up the challenge of developing the 'positive' integration face of civil justice. It showed early concern, for example, with the principle of *efficiency*,[41] and later added *certainty* to the roster.[42] These systemic goals, while closely linked to the logic of negative integration, have increasingly been characterised as ends in themselves, rather than as instrumental means to

[35] European Parliament Resolution A4-0133/99 on the Draft Action Plan of the Council and Commission on How Best to Implement the Provisions of the Treaty of Amsterdam on an Area of Freedom, Security and Justice [1999] OJ C 219/61 (EP Resolution on the Draft Action Plan).

[36] Presidency Conclusions, Tampere European Council [1999] *Bulletin EU* 10-1999, paras I.1–I.16 (Tampere Milestones).

[37] For example, the Commission Communication on Judgments [1998] characterises national legal institutions as *impediments* to the internal market, noting that 'widely-divergent procedural systems … render procedures less transparent than they might be', and that such 'barriers impede the free movement of judgments between Member States' [1998] para 6. Such deficiencies are problematic in 'an integrated area', where 'all ought to have easy access to the rules of the game, and ought to know, before deciding to embark on proceedings, what their rights and duties are, what formalities are to be complied with, what the effect of the resultant documents will be, what effect the judgment will have and what redress procedures are available, not to mention the rules governing enforcement of judgments' (ibid).

[38] Fritz Scharpf, 'Negative and Positive Integration in the Political Economy of European Welfare States' in Gary Marks and others (eds), *Governance in the European Union* (London, Sage, 1996) 15.

[39] European Parliament Resolution A4-0034/99 on Strengthening the Union's Institutions with a View to Establishing an Area of Democracy and Liberty [1999] OJ C 150/359, para 4.

[40] Vienna Action Plan [1998] para I.6.

[41] The Commission Communication on Judgments emphasises the 'extreme importance' of measures "to eliminate obstacles to the smooth working of civil rulings … for European integration and for the efficiency of the internal market in particular' [1998] para 13.

[42] Vienna Action Plan [1998] para I.16.

an end. Even more fundamental than those principles are the overarching goals of promoting *equality* and *non-discrimination*. The Commission thus deplored that the 'heterogeneity of national procedural systems' places litigants in the EU on an unequal footing, and deprives them of 'access to instruments of equal performance levels', since '*equality* of citizens and business partners in an integrated area *presupposes equal access to the weapons of the law*'.[43] In this context, 'equality' refers both to the fundamental principle of EU law that prohibits discrimination on the basis of nationality, as well as to the notion of 'equality of armaments',[44] which is considered a precondition to access to justice, and later assumes an iconic role in the EU's civil justice arena.

Meeting in Cardiff in June 1998, the European Council emphasised that the 'genuine European area of justice' is part of a 'sustained effort … to bring the Union closer to people' by achieving 'progress in policy areas which better meet the real concerns of people, notably through greater openness, and progress on … justice and home affairs'.[45] The idea embraced by the European Council in Cardiff was initially elaborated by the Commission:

> The ambition is to give citizens a common sense of justice throughout the Union. Justice must be seen as facilitating the day-to-day life of people and bringing to justice those who threaten the freedom and security of individuals and society. This includes both access to justice and full judicial cooperation among Member States. What Amsterdam provides is a conceptual and institutional framework to make sure that those values are defended throughout the Union.[46]

Moreover, 'law-abiding citizens have a right to look to the Union to simplify and facilitate the judicial environment in which they live in the European Union context'.[47]

Ultimately, EUstitia is more than just a set of policy tools aimed at making the wheels of civil justice turn more smoothly. It is, in addition, the lynchpin of a rights-based strategy aimed at generating legitimacy for EU governance through concrete measures designed to enhance the rule of law and rights *in action*. The goal of ensuring to 'each European citizen security for themselves and their property and the respect of individual freedoms and fundamental rights' is a crucial component of the evolving notion of European citizenship.[48] The EP forcefully articulated the view

> that the establishment of [the AFSJ] is urgently demanded by European public opinion … that its consolidation is intimately linked to the development of real – and

[43] Commission Communication on Judgments [1998] para 30 (emphasis added).
[44] ibid para 12.
[45] Cardiff Presidency Conclusions [1998] para I.1.37.
[46] Vienna Action Plan [1998] paras I.2 and I.15.
[47] ibid para I.16.
[48] French Ministry of Justice, Declaration of Avignon (16–17 October 1998), 'The European Judicial Area: A New Challenge for Tomorrow's Europe' [1998] www.justice.gouv.fr/anglais/adefieuro.htm, accessed 15 November 2002.

> not merely theoretical – European citizenship, and that it constitutes the only possible outcome of the internal market.[49]

The preliminary policy documents surveyed above suggest a general approach and philosophy for the AFSJ. However, the decisive event that set the stage for the explosive development of the civil justice field was the October 1999 meeting of the Tampere European Council during the first Finnish Presidency. At that special summit, the European Council refined and expanded the earlier proposals, and agreed on a detailed five-year plan for making the newborn AFSJ a reality. That plan was embodied in the Tampere Presidency Conclusions – the 'Tampere Milestones' – in which the European Council elaborated the 'policy orientations and priorities' needed to build the AFSJ, placed the goal of making the AFSJ 'a reality' as quickly as possible 'at the very top of the political agenda', and promised to make 'full use of the possibilities offered by the Amsterdam Treaty'.[50] Moreover, the Tampere Milestones operationalised these goals with great specificity, and established supporting institutional mechanisms that contributed to the unusual dynamism of the policy field after the Treaty of Amsterdam entered into force in 1999.

In terms of general policy orientations, the Tampere Milestones took the new civil justice rhetoric to a higher level, in two ways. First, they cemented the fusion of the negative and positive integration logics, as seen in the claim that 'individuals and businesses *should not be prevented or discouraged from exercising their rights* by the incompatibility or complexity of the legal and administrative systems in the Member States'.[51] And second, Tampere imagined the end-point (*telos*) of the dawning era – a 'genuine European area of justice' – in which people

> can approach courts and authorities in any Member State as easily as in their own … Judgements and decisions should be respected and enforced throughout the Union, while safeguarding the basic legal certainty of people and economic operators. Better compatibility and more convergence between the legal systems of Member States must be achieved.[52]

Crucially, however, the Tampere European Council did not stop at rhetoric, but also mapped out a detailed programme for the ensuing five years. The Tampere Milestones divided the civil justice field into three components:

- Better access to justice
- Mutual recognition of judicial decisions, and
- Greater convergence in civil law.

[49] European Parliament Resolution A4-0133/99 on the Draft Action Plan of the Council and Commission on How Best to Implement the Provisions of the Treaty of Amsterdam on an Area of Freedom, Security and Justice [1999] OJ C 219/61, preamble, para K.

[50] Tampere Milestones [1999] introduction, para 2.

[51] ibid para 28 (emphasis added).

[52] ibid para 5.

Of these three, the only one that was explicitly added by the Treaty of Amsterdam is the recognition of judicial decisions. Thus, Tampere was the EU's first – but by no means its last – expansive policy reach beyond the parameters established in the foundational treaty text. First, the Tampere Milestones added two entirely new parameters: access to justice and convergence in civil law. The former is conceptualised in very pragmatic terms, rather than in the abstract language of fundamental human rights, while the latter refers explicitly to substantive law as well as procedural law.[53] Second, the Tampere Milestones stretched the notion of 'recognition' of judicial decisions to mean 'mutual recognition' which, in the context of EU law, unmistakably invokes the radically deregulatory logic developed in the jurisprudence of the Court of Justice (CJEU). The far-reaching character of these components exposes 'judicial cooperation in civil matters' as a modest treaty basis upon which to erect an ambitious agenda to transform the rule of law in action throughout the EU.

The combination of Tampere's detailed agenda and timetable for the first five years after the entry into force of the Treaty of Amsterdam (1999–2004), and the changing institutional dynamics that have been introduced since 1999, resulted in a period of legislative frenzy akin to a perpetual-motion machine. Despite some delays along the road mapped out in Tampere, the pace of change was, at times, breakneck.

B. Implementation (since October 1999)

Post-Tampere, the EU continued to articulate overarching visions and justifications for building the 'genuine European area of justice' in the form of five-year policy blueprints and multiannual funding frameworks, although much policy initiative was channelled into work on particular legislative proposals. The following discussion examines the shifting discursive terrain based on selective reading of five policy statements (along with pertinent related reports) issued during the implementation phase:

- Hague Programme (2005–09)
- Multiannual Funding Framework (2007–13)
- Stockholm Programme (2010–14)
- Multiannual Funding Framework (2014–20)
- Post-Stockholm 'Strategic Guidelines' (2015–20).

These documents demonstrate how the logic of integration plays out in terms of concrete shifts in policy goals and methods of implementation.

[53] ibid paras 38–39.

i. *The Hague Programme (2005–09)*

The 1999 Tampere Summit established a five-year cycle for major policy statements about the future direction of the AFSJ (including civil justice). The European Council is responsible for defining the 'strategic guidelines for legislative and operational planning within the [AFSJ]' (Article 68, TFEU), but it does so with considerable help from the European Commission, which conducts mid-term reviews, conducts public debates on the future of the AFSJ, communicates its views to the other EU institutions and makes proposals. The Commission's June 2004 Tampere Assessment[54] notes that – despite 'undeniable and tangible' progress – Tampere's 'original ambition was limited by institutional constraints, and sometimes also by a lack of sufficient political consensus' (3–4). The Commission proposed inter alia to:

- Establish a European judicial area respecting the legal traditions and systems of the Member States, and closely associating those working in relevant areas (paragraph 2.6), and
- Establish a judicial area in civil and commercial matters to facilitate cooperation and access to justice (paragraph 2.7).

According to the Commission, paragraph 2.6 is oriented towards the twin goals of implementing the principle of mutual recognition while simultaneously preserving the legal and judicial traditions of the Member States, which are in tension with each other. Mutual recognition presupposes 'a common basis of shared principles and minimum standards' as a means to 'strengthen mutual confidence', yet the 'effectiveness of [EU] policy on judicial matters' can only be achieved if there is a 'high degree of involvement of those working in this field'. It is hardly conceivable that enrolling members of the Member States' national judiciary and legal professions in the project of establishing shared principles and standards would not alter their national legal and judicial traditions. For its part, paragraph 2.7 emphasises the perceived needs of European citizens, and expands on Tampere's goal of making tangible improvements in the daily life of individuals and businesses by enabling them to assert their rights at Union level. In this regard, the Commission's Tampere Assessment broadens its gaze from the narrow issue of *judgments* to include recognition of *documents* and of the *civil status of persons*.[55]

[54] Communication from the Commission, 'Area of Freedom, Security and Justice: Assessment of the Tampere Programme and Future Orientations' [2004] COM(2004) 401 final (Tampere Assessment).

[55] First, the Commission asserts the need to 'concentrate on fields where there are as yet no Community rules on mutual recognition', such as the property-law aspects of death and of relationship breakdown (marriage or co-habitation). Second, it recognises that Tampere's emphasis on the 'traditional problem of the recognition of judgments' fails to address the needs of ordinary people, who are more likely to encounter problems arising out of the non-recognition of *documents* – such as those arising in family or succession or property law contexts – than problems relating to enforcement of *judgments* resulting from litigation. Similarly, the Commission considers it 'useful to facilitate mutual recognition in new fields such as the civil status of individuals, family or civil relations between individuals (partnerships) or paternity'. Tampere Assessment [2004], para 2.7.

Finally, the Commission cautioned against creating a more complex legal environment, in which 'two separate legal regimes' exist in each Member State, 'one relating to the disputes with a cross-border implication and the other to purely internal disputes'.

The European Council adopted the second AFSJ five-year plan – the Hague Programme – in November 2004, with the aim of improving 'the common capability of the Union and its Member States to guarantee fundamental rights, minimum procedural safeguards and access to justice'.[56] The Hague Programme nicely illustrates the 'widening' and 'deepening' dynamics of European integration. First, the EU *widens* the number of measures that are included under the already familiar headings, such as by endorsing the move into civil law areas – property, family and inheritance law – over which the EU had no legislative jurisdiction in regard to substantive law, and by adding 'certificates' that affect a person's status to the mutual recognition mandate, which heralds the extension of this paradigm into the realm of personal documents. And second, the EU *deepens* its work in the civil justice field by proposing measures designed to make existing rules pertaining to mutual recognition more effective.[57] On the institutional side, the Hague Programme asserts the need for 'progressive development of a European judicial culture based on diversity of the legal systems of the Member States and unity through European law',[58] in order to build confidence and trust in the European legal area. The aim of improving 'mutual understanding among judicial authorities and different legal systems' is to be furthered by EU support for networks of judicial institutions and organisations, as well as judicial training.[59]

Finally, the Commission prepared a plan to translate the Hague Programme into action,[60] which adds the goal of 'guaranteeing an *effective* European area of justice for all'.[61] The claim that the European area of justice is 'more than an area where judgements obtained in one Member State are recognised and enforced

[56] Presidency Conclusions, Hague European Council [2004] *Bulletin EU* 11-2004, para II.15 and Annex I (Hague Programme) 12.

[57] The Hague Programme (para III.3.4.2) calls for increasing the effectiveness of existing mutual recognition instruments by 'standardising procedures and documents and developing minimum standards for aspects of procedural law, such as the service of judicial and extra-judicial documents, the commencement of proceedings, enforcement of judgments and transparency of costs'.

[58] The Hague Programme, para III.3.2.

[59] According to the Hague Programme, 'an EU component should be systematically included in the training of judicial authorities. The Commission is invited to prepare as soon as possible a proposal aimed at creating, from the existing structures, an effective European training network for judicial authorities for both civil and criminal matters…' [2004] para III.3.2. In addition, the Hague Programme aims to enhance cooperation by requiring Member States to 'designate liaison judges or other competent authorities based in their own country', and invites the Commission to 'organise EU workshops on the application of EU law and promote cooperation between members of the legal professions (such as bailiffs and notaries public) with a view to establishing best practice' (ibid at para III.3.4.3).

[60] Communication from the Commission, 'The Hague Programme: Ten priorities for the next five years – The Partnership for European renewal in the field of Freedom, Security and Justice' [2005] COM(2005) 184 final (Hague Programme Priorities).

[61] Para 2.3(9) (emphasis added).

in other Member States, but rather an area where *effective access to justice* is guaranteed in order to obtain and enforce judicial decisions'[62] opens the way towards an important change in how the EU approaches the implementation of policy goals in the justice arena. This additional step not only compels the EU to strive towards 'progressive creation of a "European judicial culture"', but also compels greater attention to the quality of justice in the Member States.[63] The Commission's growing emphasis on ensuring the high quality of national justice systems is hardly surprising, in light of concerns about the integrity of the rule of law in a few of the post-Communist countries that have joined the EU since 2004. While the quoted language is explicitly linked to developments in the *criminal* justice field, the logic that dictates trust-building measures applies equally in the civil justice field, and later was extended by the second Multi-annual Funding Framework (2007–13) to include civil in addition to criminal justice. However, it took some time for the shift towards quality of justice to gain traction in practice.

ii. Multiannual Funding Framework (2007–13)[64]

The Multiannual Funding Framework (2007–13) was the second funding framework for the AFSJ, after an earlier one in 2002. It expanded the civil justice objectives as follows:[65]

(a) to foster judicial cooperation in civil matters aiming at:

- (i) *ensuring legal certainty* and improving access to justice;
- (ii) promoting mutual recognition of decisions in civil and commercial cases;
- (iii) eliminating obstacles to cross-border litigation created by disparities in civil law and civil procedures and promoting the necessary compatibility of legislation for that purpose;
- (iv) *guaranteeing a proper administration of justice* by avoiding conflicts of jurisdiction;

(b) *to improve mutual knowledge of Member States' legal and judicial systems in civil matters and to promote and strengthen networking, mutual cooperation, exchange and dissemination of information, experience and best practices*;

[62] ibid (emphasis added).

[63] The Commission's Hague Programme Priorities call for 'measures which build confidence and mutual trust among Member States, creating minimum procedural standards and *ensuring high standards of quality of justice systems*, in particular as regards fairness and respect for the rights of defense' [2005] para 2.3(9) (emphasis added).

[64] European Parliament and Council Decision 1149/2007/EC establishing for the period 2007–2013 the Specific Programme 'Civil Justice' as part of the General Programme 'Fundamental Rights and Justice' [2007] OJ L 257/16 (the Funding Framework).

[65] Changes vis-à-vis the 2002 funding framework are noted in italics.

(c) to ensure the sound implementation, the correct and concrete application and the evaluation of Community instruments in the area of judicial cooperation in civil and commercial matters;
(d) to improve information on the legal systems in the Member States and access to justice;
(e) to *promote the training of legal practitioners* in Union and Community law;
(f) to *evaluate the general conditions necessary to reinforce mutual confidence, while fully respecting the independence of the judiciary*;
(g) to facilitate the operation of the European Judicial Network in civil and commercial matters.

The Funding Framework for 2007–13 both *elaborates* goals that had already been articulated in earlier documents, but also *supplements* them in subtle but important ways. Notably, it spells out mechanisms for building trust and mutual understanding, and engages in more systematic reflection on this fundamental challenge. Even more important, conceptually, is that it frames the policy challenge holistically, as 'guaranteeing proper administration of justice'.[66] Finally, it explicitly adds legal practitioners to the EU's training remit.[67]

iii. Stockholm Programme (2010–14)[68]

By the time the third five-year plan was needed, an air of crisis surrounded the AFSJ. Within a decade after coming into being, the AFSJ had grown to massive proportions, and was attracting ever more institutional and public attention. The Commission had struggled since 1999 to stay abreast of developments in the entire field, using semi- and later annual scoreboards to track the moving targets. The topical matrices used to organise the ever-growing welter of legal instruments had grown in length and complexity, and the conceptual headings and subheadings shifted with each programmatic iteration. This reflected in part the artificiality of the 'big tent' nature of the AFSJ, which houses an ever-growing array of topics, and the ceaseless efforts to render it coherent by imposing some semblance of order. In preparation for the Stockholm Programme, the Commission and EP prepared voluminous reports.

The Stockholm Programme that emerged from this in-depth review process rejigged the conceptual architecture of the AFSJ field, in a major step towards increasing the internal coherence of the policy arena. Overall, justice was 'elevated' to a position above security concerns, rather than being left to bring up the rear, as in prior five-year plans. At the same time, however, justice appears to have been 'demoted' in terms of its political import, insofar as it is described as having more

[66] The Funding Framework, para 3(a)(iv).
[67] ibid, para 3(e).
[68] 'Stockholm Programme – An open and secure Europe serving and protecting citizens' *approved by* Stockholm European Council [2010] OJ C 115/1-38.

to do with convenience – ie, making citizens' lives easier – than with justice as such. This first impression vanishes, however, upon close reading of the text, where access to justice is clearly presented as the flip-side of the 'rights' coin.

The Stockholm Programme in paragraph 1.1 articulated a vision of a 'Europe of law and justice':

> The achievement of a European area of justice must be consolidated so as to move beyond the current fragmentation. Priority should be given to mechanisms that facilitate access to justice, so that people can enforce their rights throughout the Union. Training of and cooperation between public professionals should also be improved, and resources … mobilised to eliminate barriers to the recognition of legal decisions.

New here is the emphasis on the need to overcome the bewildering fragmentation of the justice field. *Not* new, but still noteworthy, is the elevation of efforts focused on 'public professionals' from a pragmatic project to a fundamental political priority. The Stockholm Programme also emphasised the importance of legal consciousness – of 'raising overall awareness of rights'[69] – as a key element in the EU's strategy for the justice arena.

Also noteworthy is that the Stockholm Programme *did not* endorse the Commission's earlier (and oft repeated) proposal to emphasise 'quality of justice systems'.[70] It did, however, elaborate an approach towards the goal of 'strengthening mutual trust'[71] among Member State legal systems that is quite solicitous of Member State sensitivities in regard to their national legal sovereignty: 'The Union should support Member States' efforts to improve the efficiency of their judicial systems by encouraging exchanges of best practice and the development of innovative projects relating to the modernisation of justice'. Strengthening mutual trust also requires deeper efforts directed towards professional training and networking. However, the Stockholm Programme *did not* endorse the EP's call for 'root-and-branch revamping of university curricula' as a way to build 'European judicial culture'.[72]

As in prior five-year plans, the Stockholm Programme expanded the scope of EU policy activity, including a call for a wider range of measures in core civil law areas, and a strong push to supplement the mutual recognition approach by adopting 'common minimum [procedural] standards or standard rules of civil procedure'.[73] It also took an important conceptual step by exploring further 'benefits for citizens of the European judicial area',[74] and pushed beyond concerns

[69] ibid, para 3.
[70] Hague Programme Priorities 2005, para 2.3(9).
[71] ibid, para 3.2.
[72] European Parliament Resolution P7_TA(2009)0090 on the … area of freedom, security and justice serving the citizen – Stockholm Programme [2009], para O.
[73] Hague Programme, para 3.2.2.
[74] ibid, 3.4.

about access to justice for ordinary citizens to include a strong statement about the role of civil justice in 'supporting economic activity',[75] thereby linking the civil justice agenda to political concerns arising from financial crisis.[76]

The Stockholm Programme was a moment of reckoning with the volume of new measures that had been adopted since 1999. The European Council urged Member States to implement the EU measures that had been put in place, and stressed the need for 'consolidation of the instruments adopted so far'.[77] Yet despite the fact that Member States were struggling to come to grips with the mushrooming policy field,[78] the Commission and the EP were preparing increasingly ambitious proposals for ever more far-reaching EU action.[79]

iv. Multiannual Funding Framework (2014–20)[80]

After much delay, agreement on the EU's budget for 2014–20 – the Multiannual Financial Framework (MFF) – was finally reached in 2013. Given the economic and financial crisis, the MFF reflects an overarching paradigm shift that was already visible in the Stockholm Programme, but has come to permeate every area of EU policy,[81] including civil justice. The European Council's 2013 MFF Conclusions in paragraph 1 state:

> the [EU] and its Member States have taken important steps in response to the challenges raised by the economic and financial crisis. Looking to the future, the next Multiannual Financial Framework (MFF) must ensure that the [EU's] budget is geared to lifting Europe out of the crisis … [and] must be a catalyst for growth and jobs

[75] ibid, para 3.4.2.

[76] Notably, the Stockholm Programme contains proposals aimed at adopting civil justice measures on debt collection in the context of bankruptcy or litigation, contract and company law, and other commercial matters.

[77] Hague Programme, para 3.2.1.

[78] As in prior AFSJ policy cycles, the Commission prepared a plan to put the Stockholm Programme into action. Communication from the Commission, 'Delivering an area of freedom, security and justice for Europe's citizens: Action Plan Implementing the Stockholm Programme' [2010] COM(2010) 171 final. This time, however, the European Council refused to endorse the Commission's plan, because it went too far. Rolf Wagner 'Das neue Programm zur justiziellen Zusammenarbeit in Zivilsachen – Ein Wendepunkt?' (2014) *6 IPRax (Praxis des internationalen Privat- und Verfahrensrechts)* 469, 470.

[79] In 2010, the EP adopted two far-reaching resolutions that make the Commission's vision look modest in comparison: European Parliament Resolution P7_TA(2010)0242 on judicial training – Stockholm Programme; and European Parliament Resolution P7_TA(2010)0426 on civil, commercial, family and private international law aspects of the action plan implementing the Stockholm Programme. In 2011, the Commission issued another path-breaking civil justice document: Communication from the Commission 'Building Trust in EU-Wide Justice: A New Dimension to European Judicial Training' [2011] COM(2011) 551 final.

[80] Conclusions, Brussels European Council 'Multiannual Financial Framework' [2013] EUCO 37/13 (MFF Conclusions).

[81] For example, Communication from the Commission, 'Annual Growth Survey 2013' [2012] COM(2012) 750 final, at 2 (emphasising the need to 'lay the foundations for future growth and competitiveness that will be smart, sustainable and inclusive').

> across Europe, notably by leveraging productive and human capital investments … [S]pending should be mobilised to support growth, employment, competitiveness and convergence …

In this context, the Commission emphasised the goal of ensuring that '*economic, cultural and social growth* may develop in a stable, lawful and secure environment'.[82]

In terms of funding, justice and rights-related issues fall under the general heading 'Security and Citizenship', and constitute the smallest – around two per cent – among the five major appropriations categories.[83] Civil justice policies themselves are divided between two subheadings, 'Rights' and 'Citizenship and Justice', with funds to be allocated according to priorities articulated in the Rights, Equality and Citizenship Programme for 2014–20[84] and in the Justice Programme for 2014–20,[85] respectively.

The Rights, Equality and Citizenship Programme, which builds on the Stockholm Programme's goal of making 'the achievement of a Europe of rights'[86] a political priority, formulates this ambition in very broad terms:

> The [EU] is founded on the values of respect for human dignity, freedom, democracy, equality, the rule of law and respect for human rights and fundamental freedoms. Those values are common to the Member States in a society in which pluralism, non-discrimination, tolerance, justice, solidarity and equality between women and men prevail. Persons are entitled to enjoy in the Union the rights conferred on them by the [TFEU] and the [TEU]. Furthermore, the [Charter of Fundamental Rights] … reflects the fundamental rights and freedoms to which persons are entitled in the Union. Those rights should be promoted and respected. The full enjoyment of those rights, as well as of the rights deriving from international conventions to which the Union has acceded, … should be guaranteed and any obstacles should be dismantled.[87]

From the Commission's pragmatic perspective, the goal is to 'make people's rights and freedoms effective in practice by making them better known and more consistently applied across the EU'.[88] This goal is to be achieved by a host

[82] European Commission 'One trillion euro to invest in Europe's future – the EU's budget framework 2014–2020' [2013] IP/13/1096 (emphasis added). The Commission's conception of "economic, cultural and social growth" is – consistent with past practice – broader than the European Council's formulation, which aims to 'support growth, employment, competitiveness and convergence' (MFF Conclusions [2013] para 1).

[83] MFF Conclusions [2013] 47. The heading 'Security and Citizenship' includes a wide range of issues, including asylum, migration, both external and internal security, in addition to measures in the field of justice.

[84] Council and European Parliament Regulation (EU) 1381/2013 establishing a Rights, Equality and Citizenship Programme for the period 2014 to 2020 [2013] OJ L 354/62 (Rights, Equality and Citizenship Programme).

[85] Council and European Parliament Regulation (EU) 1382/2013 establishing a Justice Programme for the period 2014 to 2020 [2013] OJ L 354/73 (Justice Programme).

[86] Rights, Equality and Citizenship Programme, preamble, art 2.

[87] ibid, preamble, art 1.

[88] European Commission, 'Commission strengthens the justice and fundamental rights dimension of future EU budgets' [2011] IP/11/1349 (Future Budget Press Release).

of measures having 'European added value', including 'national and small-scale projects'.[89]

The Justice Programme aims to 'to contribute to the further development of a European area of justice based on mutual recognition and mutual trust, in particular by promoting judicial cooperation in civil and criminal matters'.[90] It is largely consistent with the features outlined for the Rights, Equality and Citizenship Programme, but differs in its specific aims – which are not limited to measures designed to 'facilitate and support judicial cooperation'[91] – as well as in some of the means outlined for achieving them.[92] Two details regarding civil justice are noteworthy. First, the Justice Programme places great emphasis on the role of training the judiciary and judicial staff, which is seen as 'central to building mutual trust and [improving] cooperation between judicial authorities and practitioners' throughout the EU, and is recognised as an 'essential element in promoting a genuine European judicial culture'.[93] Moreover, the term 'judiciary and judicial staff' is expansively defined to include 'judges, prosecutors and court officers, as well as other legal practitioners associated with the judiciary, such as lawyers, notaries, bailiffs, probation officers, mediators and court interpreters'.[94] And second, the Justice Programme aims to 'facilitate access to justice for all',[95] which is defined broadly to 'include … access to courts, to alternative methods of dispute settlement, and to public office-holders obliged by the law to provide parties with independent and impartial legal advice'.[96]

[89] Rights, Equality and Citizenship Programme, preamble, art 22. Of particular interest, from the civil justice perspective, is that the Rights, Equality and Citizenship Programme, art 3(2), foresees measures aimed at: '(a) enhancing awareness and knowledge of Union law and policies as well as of the rights, values and principles underpinning the Union; (b) supporting the effective, comprehensive and consistent implementation and application of Union law instruments and policies in the Member States and the monitoring and evaluation thereof; (c) promoting cross-border cooperation, improving mutual knowledge and enhancing mutual trust among all stakeholders; and (d) improving knowledge and understanding of potential obstacles to the exercise of rights and principles guaranteed by the TEU, the TFEU, the Charter, international conventions to which the Union has acceded, and secondary Union legislation'.

[90] Justice Programme, art 3.

[91] ibid, art 4(1)(a).

[92] The Justice Programme, art 4(2), foresees the following: '(a) enhancing public awareness and knowledge of Union law and policies; (b) … ensuring efficient judicial cooperation in civil and criminal matters, improving knowledge of Union law, including substantive and procedural law, of judicial cooperation instruments and of the relevant case-law of the [CJEU], and of comparative law; (c) supporting the effective, comprehensive and consistent implementation and application of Union instruments in the Member States and the monitoring and evaluation thereof; (d) promoting cross-border cooperation, improving mutual knowledge and understanding of the civil and criminal law and the legal and judicial systems of the Member States and enhancing mutual trust; (e) improving knowledge and understanding of potential obstacles to the smooth functioning of a European area of justice; (f) improving the efficiency of judicial systems and their cooperation by means of information and communication technology, including the cross-border interoperability of systems and applications'.

[93] ibid, preamble, para 5.

[94] ibid, preamble, para 4.

[95] ibid, art 4(1)(c).

[96] ibid, preamble, art 8.

v. Post-Stockholm 'Strategic AFSJ Guidelines' (2015–20)[97]

Review of the Stockholm Programme lagged behind schedule, but agreement on a new multiannual plan was finally reached in June 2014, following a lengthy debate over whether any new AFSJ five-year plan should be drawn up at all.[98] Opponents insisted that there was 'little need' for a new programme that would add to the 'significant number of rules' that had already been adopted, since the AFSJ field is 'today and will remain for the next couple of years in "implementation mode"'.[99] Proponents of new strategic guidelines, conversely, drew attention to 'unfilled gaps … which call for further action', and pointed to 'new challenges' that 'modify the landscape in which action is taking place'.[100] Institutional factors – including institutional squabbling during the second Barroso Commission[101] – also impeded the budget process. Moreover, 2014 was a 'turnover' year for the EU, in the wake of EP elections in May 2014. EU institutions tend to be weak during such transitions, in part owing to doubts about the legitimacy of allowing outgoing stakeholders to commit incoming ones.

Despite these delaying factors, AFSJ policy planning wheels continued to turn. The Commission announced as early as 2013 that it saw no need for another detailed five-year policy programme, appealed to Member States to resist the temptation to put forward detailed wish lists, and expressed its preference for a set of strategic guidelines instead.[102] Notwithstanding calls for restraint, the Commission itself as well as the EP presented detailed visions of the future trajectory of the AFSJ prior to the June 2014 European Council meeting: the Commission's Justice Agenda 2020[103] and the EP Stockholm Programme Resolution.[104]

[97] Conclusions, Brussels European Council 'Strategic Guidelines for Legislative and Operational Planning for the coming years within the EU's Area of Freedom, Security and Justice' [2014] EUCO 79/14 (Strategic AFSJ Guidelines).

[98] Jörg Semmler, 'Das Instrument der Mehrjahresprogramme in der europäischen Justiz- und Innenpolitik' (2009) 1 *integration* 63; Sergio Carrera and Elspeth Guild, 'Does the Stockholm Programme Matter? The Struggles over Ownership of AFSJ Multiannual Programming' *Centre for European Policy Studies (CEPS) Papers in Liberty and Security in Europe*, No 51 (2012).

[99] European Policy Centre, 'The Stockholm programme: what's next?' (2013) www.epc.eu/pub_details.php?pub_id=3671, accessed 3 February 2018.

[100] ibid.

[101] The division of Commission Directorate-General Justice, Freedom and Security (DG JAI) in 2010 into DG Justice and DG Home did not resolve *inter*-institutional squabbling, but rather led to border skirmishes between the two separate DGs for the AFSJ policy field. Moreover, the fact that these two policy subfields are large and amorphous also resulted in *intra*-DG squabbling.

[102] Wagner (n 78) 469, 470 (observing that both the Hague and Stockholm Programmes involved lengthy, difficult and strength-sapping negotiations, and arguing that an extremely strong political will would have been required to find consensus on AFSJ matters, in view of the different priorities and interests of the Member States, and the fact that none of the Member States occupying the presidency during the relevant periods were keen to take on this challenge). The Commission's posture, which ultimately prevailed, is consistent with its sole right of legislative initiative in the civil justice field, in contrast to the European Council's more limited policy role under Art 68 TEU.

[103] Communication from the Commission, 'The EU Justice Agenda for 2020 – Strengthening Trust, Mobility and Growth within the Union' [2014] COM(2014) 144 final (Justice Agenda 2020).

[104] European Parliament Resolution P7_TA(2014)0276 – Mid-term review of the Stockholm Programme [2014] (EP Stockholm Programme Resolution).

The Commission's Directorate-General for Justice (DG Justice) was especially proactive under the leadership of Commission Vice-President and Justice Commissioner Viviene Reding (2010–14). In 2013, two far-reaching DG Justice measures laid the foundation for the Commission's ambitious Justice Agenda 2020. First, DG Justice organised a civil society forum in Brussels (21–22 November 2013) – the *Assises de la Justice* on the theme of 'Shaping Justice Policies in Europe for the Years to Come' – which drew more than 700 people to discuss civil justice, criminal justice, administrative justice, the rule of law, and fundamental rights. According to Commissioner Reding, who hosted the event,

> In the space of just a few years, justice policy has come into the limelight of European Union activity – comparable to the boost given to the single market in the 1990s. We have come a long way, but there is still a lot more than we can do to develop a true European area of Justice.[105]

On that occasion, the Commission publicised results of a Eurobarometer poll on 'Justice in the European Union' – which it creatively interpreted as showing that 'two thirds of [respondents] think that the functioning of national judicial systems is a matter of Common European concern' – in order to advance its ambitious agenda for knitting the EU legal order more tightly.[106]

The Commission's second major innovation was the new *Justice Scoreboard* programme, which presents annual data on the 'quality, independence and efficiency of *national* justice systems', with the aim of 'ensuring the effectiveness of EU law'.[107] It explained on page 2 that, in the reform process that followed in the wake of the EU's economic and financial crisis,

> the national justice systems play a key role in restoring confidence and the return to growth. An efficient and independent justice system contributes to trust and stability. Predictable, timely and enforceable justice decisions are important structural components of an attractive business environment.

[105] European Commission, 'Building Trust in Justice Systems in Europe: *Assises de la Justice* forum to shape the future of EU Justice Policy' [2013] IP/13/1117.

[106] ibid.

[107] Communication from the Commission, 'The EU Justice Scoreboard: A Tool to Promote Effective Justice and Growth' [2013] COM(2013) 160 final, 4 (emphasis added). Recall that the Commission had tried to add *quality of justice* to the Hague Programme a decade earlier, but the European Council was unwilling to embrace this objective at that time. On this later occasion, however, DG Justice not only asked the European Council once again to endorse this goal, but also – to be on the safe side – enshrined it formally in a document that identified five priority areas designed to guide Member States through the financial crisis and back to growth. The goal of *modernising public administration* elaborated there includes 'improving the quality, independence and efficiency of judicial systems as well as ensuring that claims can be settled in a reasonable time frame and promoting the use of alternative dispute mechanisms', so as to 'reduce costs for businesses and increase the attractiveness of the country to foreign investors'. Communication from the Commission, 'Annual Growth Survey 2013' [2012] COM(2012) 750 final, para 5 (2013 Justice Scoreboard).

The Commission's move into the 'quality of justice' arena upset some Member States, which felt that they were being unfairly targeted,[108] as well as some in Strasbourg, who felt that DG Justice had appropriated the role, methodology, and findings of the Council of Europe's Commission on the Efficiency of Justice (CEPEJ). The EP reacted quickly to endorse the Commission's foray into benchmarking, but also to smooth ruffled feathers in those Member States that were unfavourably reviewed in the 2013 Scoreboard,[109] as well as in Strasbourg.[110]

The Commission's Justice Agenda 2020, which builds on the *Assises de la Justice* and the 2013 Justice Scoreboard, is every bit as ambitious as its title suggests. It 'sets out the political priorities that should be pursued in order to make further progress towards a fully functioning common European area of justice oriented towards trust, mobility and growth by 2020',[111] asserting that 'EU justice policy … has a major role to play in enforcing the common values upon which the Union is founded, in strengthening economic growth and in contributing to the effectiveness of other EU policies'.[112] It emphasises the need to build 'bridges between the different justice systems',[113] and to fortify the 'bedrock' of mutual trust, which presupposes 'the independence, quality and efficiency of the judicial systems and the respect of the rule of law'.[114]

To achieve these goals, the Commission proposed a tripartite approach that aims to *consolidate* what has already been achieved,[115] *codify* EU law 'when

[108] As a result of the 2013 Justice Scoreboard, the Council of the EU made recommendations to 10 Member States – Bulgaria, Hungary, Italy, Latvia, Malta, Poland, Romania, Slovenia, Slovakia and Spain – to improve the independence, quality and/or efficiency of their justice system or to further strengthen the judiciary. Council Recommendations [2013] OJ C 217 passim.

[109] European Parliament Resolution P7_TA(2014)0064 – EU Justice Scoreboard – Civil and Administrative Justice in the Member States [2014] (EP Resolution on 2013 Justice Scoreboard). Reflecting the sensitivities of some Member States, this EP Resolution states that 'any comparison of national justice systems, especially in relation to their previous situation, must be based on objective criteria and on evidence which is objectively compiled, compared and analysed; points out the importance of assessing the functioning of justice systems as a whole, without separating them from the social, historical and economic situation of the Member States or from the constitutional traditions that they stem from; [and] stresses the importance of treating Member States impartially, thus ensuring equality of treatment between all Member States when assessing their justice systems' (para 4). In order to avoid blind-siding Member States in the future, the EP 'calls on the Commission to discuss the proposed method at an early date, in a transparent procedure involving the Member States' (para 5), and 'points out that benchmarks must be set before information on national justice systems is gathered in order to develop a common understanding of methodology and indicators' (para 6).

[110] The EP Resolution on 2013 Justice Scoreboard (ibid) 'takes note of the EU Justice Scoreboard with great interest; calls on the Commission to take this exercise forward in accordance with the Treaties and in consultation with the Member States, while bearing in mind the need to avoid unnecessary duplication of work with other bodies' (para 1); and 'underlines the role of the CEPEJ in gathering and presenting the relevant data at both national and regional level; considers that the EU institutions should seek to cooperate with the CEPEJ, as it provides an excellent basis for the exchange of best practices, and duplication needs to be avoided' (para 19).

[111] Justice Agenda 2020, 2.

[112] ibid, 10.

[113] ibid, 3.

[114] ibid, 4.

[115] ibid, para 4.1.

necessary and appropriate',[116] and *complement* the existing framework with new initiatives.[117] In the Commission's view, '*every national legal practitioner* – from lawyers and bailiffs on the one hand, to judges and prosecutors on the other – should also be knowledgeable in EU law and capable of interpreting and effectively enforcing EU law, alongside his or her own domestic law'.[118] This theme is reiterated in the Commission's 2014 Justice Scoreboard, which insists that 'effective justice requires *quality throughout the whole justice chain*'.[119] This language aims to broaden the (already quite broad) 'judicial training' mandate.

On the theme of *codification*, the vision expressed in the Commission's Justice Agenda 2020 is equally breath-taking:

> Codification of existing laws and practices can facilitate the knowledge, understanding and the use of legislation, the enhancement of mutual trust as well as consistency and legal certainty while contributing to simplification and the cutting of red tape. In a number of cases, the codification of certain parts of the existing EU legislation relating to justice or to relevant case-law of the Court of Justice of the Union in the area of justice can be beneficial in terms of providing consistency of legislation and clarity for the citizens and users of the law in general.[120]

The Commission's codification proposal extends inter alia to civil, commercial and consumer law, and also suggests that a code of private international law rules 'could be useful'.[121] Even more startling than the list of projects contemplated here is the wholesale embrace of codification as an appropriate paradigm for the EU legal order.

When compared to the sweeping vision contained in the Commission's Justice Agenda 2020 and its 2014 Rule of Law Framework, the 2014 EP Stockholm Programme Resolution takes a more sober view. The Parliament's report drew attention to the fact that only a few of the civil justice measures proposed in the prior Stockholm Programme had been achieved, and urged continuing efforts along those lines.[122] However, the EP also noted that 'legislative initiatives in the field of civil law have so far been focused largely on substantive law', and called for 'a greater focus on procedural law in the future'.[123] Finally, the EP repeated its call

[116] ibid, para 4.2.

[117] ibid, para 4.3.

[118] ibid, para 4.1(iii) (emphasis added).

[119] Communication from the Commission, 'The 2014 EU Justice Scoreboard' [2014] COM(2014) 155 final, 16 (2014 Justice Scoreboard) (emphasis added).

[120] Justice Agenda 2020, para 4.2.

[121] ibid.

[122] European Parliament resolution P7_TA(2014)0276 of 2 April 2014 on the mid-term review of the Stockholm Programme (2013/2024(INI)), paras 36–37.

[123] ibid, para 39. Along these lines, the EP commenced work in 2015 on common minimum standards of civil procedure in the EU. See European Parliament Resolution P8_TA(2017)0282 resolution of 4 July 2017 with recommendations to the Commission on common minimum standards of civil procedure in the European Union [2017]. See also Burkhard Hess and Xandra E Kramer (eds), *From Common Rules to Best Practices in European Civil Procedure* (Baden-Baden, Nomos Verlagsgesellschaft, 2017).

for a 'truly European legal culture', along with 'common standards and an understanding of other legal systems', observing that 'mutual recognition and trust can lead to gradual changes in national civil law traditions through an exchange of best practices between Member States', which does not necessarily 'detract from the value of national legal traditions'.[124] Here appears in incipient form, an acknowledgement – indeed an endorsement – of the idea that training and other measures aiming at fostering European legal culture may over time lead to spontaneous harmonisation of national legal orders.

In June 2014, the European Council agreed on Strategic AFSJ Guidelines for 2015–20. These Guidelines are less visionary than previous five-year programmes, as well as less detailed. They embody the Commission's preferred approach, which limits the European Council to general strategic guidelines and allows the Commission itself greater flexibility. Scholars have criticised them as a regressive throw-back to the 'Third Pillar' mentality, at least in some AFSJ policy subfields.[125] In terms of concrete policy statements, the new Guidelines state unambiguously that the 'priority now is to consistently transpose, effectively implement and consolidate the legal instruments and policy measures in place'.[126] However, they also express ongoing commitment to the goal of ensuring 'the protection and promotion of fundamental rights',[127] and identify a few desirable new measures for each AFSJ policy subfield.

In regard to civil justice, the European Council once again refrained from embracing 'quality of national justice' as an overarching political priority for the EU, despite the Commission's repeated urging. Rather, the Strategic AFSJ Guidelines note that the goal in the civil justice field is to ensure the 'smooth functioning of a true European area of justice' that simultaneously respects the 'different legal systems and traditions of the Member States' and enhances 'mutual trust in one another's justice systems', as a way to 'contribute to economic growth'.[128] This reference to the different legal systems and traditions of the Member States, which would have been considered inappropriate during the early years after

[124] European Parliament resolution P7_TA(2014)0276, para 38.

[125] Carrera and Guild argue that the Strategic AFSJ Guidelines aim to 'limit and prevent the emergence of plural and competing policy agendas and strategic programmes by the next European Commission and European Parliament', and to 'sideline the EU Charter of Fundamental Rights and rule of law in the wider EU AFSJ policy landscape'. (It must be noted, however, that their criticisms are aimed at more controversial AFSJ subfields, such as migration and criminal law, rather than at civil justice.) Sergio Carrera and Elspeth Guild, 'The European Council's Guidelines for the Area of Freedom, Security and Justice (2020): Subverting the "Lisbonisation" of Justice and Home Affairs?' [2014] *Centre for European Policy Studies (CEPS) Papers in Liberty and Security in Europe*, No 51, 2.

[126] Strategic AFSJ Guidelines, para I.3. For Wagner, the consolidation mandate appears to be the most important one: 'The period of actionism, during which one legal instrument after another was rapidly pulled out of thin air, is over'. ('Die Zeit des Aktionismus, in der mit hoher Geschwindigkeit ein Rechtsinstrument nach dem anderen aus dem Boden "gestampft" worden ist, soll vorbei sein'.). Wagner (n 78) 469, 471.

[127] Strategic AFSJ Guidelines, para I.4.

[128] ibid, para I.11.

communitarisation,[129] was added to the TFEU by the Lisbon Treaty.[130] This restrained vision of civil justice is supplemented, however, by a few new objectives found in the Strategic AFSJ Guidelines, notably: promoting the 'consistency and clarity of legislation'; simplifying access to justice by promoting 'effective remedies and use of technological innovations including the use of e-justice'; reinforcing the 'rights of persons, notably children, in proceedings to facilitate enforcement of judgements'; and enhancing 'training for practitioners'. Yet even with these new additions, this falls far short of the sweeping vision of civil justice in the EU that former Commissioner Reding espoused.

Indeed, when one considers the Strategic AFSJ Guidelines for 2015–20 in conjunction with Commission President Juncker's reorganisation of the Commission, it is difficult to escape the conclusion that DG Justice's wings have been clipped.[131] The trajectory of civil justice (and other AFSJ policy subfields) under the Juncker Commission has depended in large part on the actions of Juncker's right-hand man – Frans Timmermans, the Commission's First Vice-President in charge of Better Regulation, Inter-Institutional Relations, the Rule of Law and the Charter of Fundamental Rights – whose mandate includes supervising and coordinating the activities of DG Justice and DG Migration & Home,[132] and trying to keep the subordinate Commissioners[133] on a short leash. Since assuming this position, Timmermans has become increasingly preoccupied with rule of law backsliding in some of the post-Communist Member States that joined the EU in 2004 and 2007, notably Hungary, Poland, Romania and, most recently, Bulgaria.[134]

[129] Wagner (n 78) 472 ('nicht salonfähig').

[130] Art 67(1) TFEU (as amended by the Lisbon Treaty in) states: 'The Union shall constitute an area of freedom, security and justice with respect for fundamental rights and the different legal systems and traditions of the Member States'.

[131] The Juncker Commission, which took office on 1 November 2014, made substantial changes to the Commission structure, including some that disaggregate (and even downgrade) DG Justice, in the wake of Commissioner Reding's ambitious leadership as Commissioner for Justice, Fundamental Rights and Equality. Commissioner Reding's portfolios were broken apart and redistributed, while some new mandates were added to DG Justice. First, overarching questions relating to *fundamental rights* and *rule of law* have been 'traded up' to Commission First Vice-President Timmermans, one of whose express responsibilities is to guide the work of the Commissioner for Justice, Consumers and Gender Equality. Second, the overarching topic of *citizenship* has also been transferred out of DG Justice. The initial proposal was to bundle it with Education, Culture, and Youth, but this engendered controversy when the portfolio was assigned to the Hungarian Commissioner. In the end, citizenship was transferred to Dimitris Avramopoulos, Commissioner for Migration, Home Affairs and Citizenship. Third, DG Justice's *equality* portfolio has been disaggregated, with the rights of persons with disabilities and equal treatment at work moved to DG Employment, Social Affairs and Inclusion. Gender equality, on the other hand, remains in DG Justice. Fourth, DJ Justice gained a number of new portfolios, notably consumer and marketing law, data protection, and the monitoring of 'effective justice'.

[132] Carrera and Guild (n 125) 11.

[133] During the Juncker Commission, DG Justice is under the stewardship of Věra Jourová (Commissioner for Justice, Consumers and Gender Equality).

[134] See Verfassungsblog – On Matters Constitutional, 'Debate on Protecting the Rule of Law in the EU' (March 2018) https://verfassungsblog.de/category/debates/protecting-the-rule-of-law-in-the-eu/, visited 22 May 2019. Commission First Vice-President Timmermans has proposed to bolster the tools at the EU's disposal for dealing with Member States that infringe the rule of law. Eszter Zalan,

While some uncertainty remains as of July 2019, in the wake of the May 2019 EP elections, concerns about rule of law are likely to remain on the EU's agenda.[135] Ursula von der Leyen has been confirmed as the next Commission President, and Timmermans is widely expected to remain a prominent member of the College of Commissioners. In this regard, he has stated publicly that he 'has no doubt whatsoever' that the von der Leyen Commission will be 'as forceful, as concrete, as clear, as determined as the [Juncker] commission' on threats to the rule of law in some EU Member States.[136]

In conclusion, the Strategic AFSJ Guidelines for 2015–20 signalled a turning point away from hectic growth towards greater attention to quality and coherence of the EU's civil justice policy field.[137] Institutionally speaking, the Commission emerged from the post-Stockholm policy process as the winner, insofar as it gained relatively free rein to pursue the goals articulated in its Justice Agenda 2020, bearing in mind the priorities articulated by the European Council in the Strategic AFSJ Guidelines. This was a Pyrrhic victory for the Commission, in view of the institutional retrenchment introduced by the Juncker Commission,[138] which curbed the widening spyre of developments in the civil justice field, and prioritised improving civil justice legislation over adopting new measures.[139] The pace of new legislation has accordingly slowed since 2014 in the 'area of Justice and Fundamental Rights based on mutual trust',[140] but efforts continue – particularly within the Commission and the European Parliament,

'EU Commission plans bolstering the rule of law toolbox' *EUobserver* (3 April 2019). For comprehensive analysis, see Daniel Hegedüs, 'What Role for EU Institutions in Confronting Europe's Democracy and Rule of Law Crisis?' *The German Marshall Fund of the United States*, No 4 (March 2019). On Bulgaria, see Radosveta Vassileva, 'Is Bulgaria's Rule of Law about to Die under the European Commission's Nose? The Country's Highest-Ranking Judge Fears So' (23 April 2019) https://verfassungsblog.de/is-bulgarias-rule-of-law-about-to-die-under-the-european-commissions-nose-the-countrys-highest-ranking-judge-fears-so/, visited 22 May 2019.

[135] In his 2017 State of the Union speech, Commission President Juncker urged relying on European values – 'three fundamentals, three unshakeable principles: freedom, equality and the rule of law' – as the compass to navigate the EU's uncertain future. 'President Jean-Claude Juncker's State of the Union Address 2017' http://europa.eu/rapid/press-release_SPEECH-17-3165, visited 23 May 2019.

[136] Irene Kostaki, 'Timmerman says EU Commission under von der Leyen will be tough on rule of law' *New Europe* (19 July 2019) www.neweurope.eu/article/timmermans-says-eu-commission-under-von-der-leyen-will-be-tough-on-rule-of-law/, visited 23 July 2019.

[137] Wagner (n 78) 473.

[138] The incoming Juncker Commission set out to 'restructure the internal set-up of the College [of Commissioners] to enable the so-called "last chance" Commission to turn the corner'. Steven Blokmans (ed), 'What Comes After the Last Chance Commission? Policy Priorities for 2019–2024' [2019] *Centre for European Policy Studies (CEPS)*, 1. One of the 10 priorities identified at that time was to enhance cooperation between different EU justice systems and preserve the rule of law (ibid at 1–2). Juncker's intentions aside, 'political circumstances deteriorated', resulting in a 'poly-crisis' that 'blew the Commission off course' (ibid at 1). See Commission White Paper on the Future of Europe: Reflections and scenarios for the EU 27 by 2025, [2017] COM(2017) 2025.

[139] Communication from the Commission, 'Commission Work Programme 2018 – An agenda for a more united, stronger and more democratic Europe' [2017] COM(2017) 650 final (Commission Work Programme 2018).

[140] ibid, 7.

but also among academic and other civil society actors – to advance the civil justice agenda.[141]

V. Conclusions: Civil Justice Perspectives for Asia?

This chapter has documented key EU policy statements about the civil justice field, and sketched basic features of the EU's institutional landscape. Viewed as a whole, the rhetoric of 'judicial cooperation in civil matters' reveals that civil justice (EUstitia) is expected to play a key role in transcending the EU's humble origins as a mere market and constructing an 'ever closer union' (TFEU, preamble). The lofty rhetoric and ambitious proposals surveyed above suggest that EUstitia is more than the sum of its parts. Indeed, it is linked to overarching political as well as pragmatic goals. From its inception, the civil justice subfield of the AFSJ has been linked to debates about governance, judicialisation and legitimacy in the EU. In particular, the EU has framed civil justice as a vital dimension of European citizenship.

Many of the steps that have been taken to create a 'genuine area of justice'[142] in the field of civil law are highly technical, and address themselves to concrete procedural problems arising from the diversity of the Member State legal systems that are bound together into the Union. However, EU action in the field is also directed towards institutional aspects of the administration of justice itself, which may yet have far-reaching consequences. Technocratic tinkering in procedural fields not only affects outcomes in particular cases, but can also alter the sheer availability of justice within the EU, and spur the development of substantive EU law, given that litigation is a complex form of governance,[143] and one which is historically linked to the advancement of European integration.[144] Like the Commission's influential 2001 Governance White Paper,[145] which was a tool-kit designed to narrow the EU's legitimacy gap, the EU's civil justice project is not limited to the perennial concern with ensuring adequate enforcement of EU law, but also yoked to the enormous tasks of enhancing the legitimacy of EU governance and putting meat on the bones of EU citizenship.

The EU's civil justice project conceptualises Member State courts as arenas where actors may drive the process of integration while resolving particular cases, and would strengthen the courts' capacity to participate in European

[141] For an up-to-date and authoritative overview, see Rolf Wagner, 'Zwanzig Jahre justizielle Zusammenarbeit in Zivilsachen' (2019) 3 *IPRax (Praxis des internationalen Privat- und Verfahrensrechts)* 185.

[142] Tampere Milestones.

[143] Martin Shapiro and Alec Stone Sweet, 'Judges and Company' in Martin Shapiro and Alex Stone Sweet, *On Law, Politics, and Judicialization* (Oxford, Oxford University Press, 2002) 292, 294.

[144] Alec Stone Sweet, *Governing with Judges* (Oxford, Oxford University Press, 2000); Alec Stone Sweet, *The Judicial Construction of Europe* (Oxford, Oxford University Press, 2004).

[145] European Commission, 'European Governance: A White Paper' [2001] COM(2001) 428 final.

governance through the process of judicialisation,[146] in which the judiciary is seen 'not … standing in an aloof place in the political order, … opposed to society, but rather as part of a continuum on which other governance arrangements are also placed'.[147] As such, national courts are 'glocal' fora where transnational governance can be generated from the interaction of social, economic and political forces in the pursuit of private justice. The judicialisation dynamic links the micro-level strategic behaviour of individual actors to the development of the macro-level normative structure,[148] via 'an increasingly common chain of precedent'.[149]

The EU's 'genuine area of justice', according to an early formulation, aims to ensure to 'each European citizen security for themselves and their property and the respect of individual freedoms and fundamental rights'.[150] The invocation of positive integration goals such as these, together with the explicit incorporation of private citizens into the governance narrative surrounding the emerging civil justice field, reveal that the civil justice subfield of the AFSJ is envisioned as part of a strategy for alleviating the EU's problematic legitimacy. The 2001 Governance White Paper aimed to overcome 'disenchantment' by rendering policy-making 'more inclusive and accountable' and by 'connecting the EU more closely to its citizens'.[151] It envisioned an increasing role for civil society in which 'everyone, or at least potentially everyone, is … seen as a participant' in the governance process.[152] The White Paper itself paid little heed to the role of courts, beyond their traditional role as implementers and interpreters of Community law. In contrast, the AFSJ's 'genuine area of justice' connects concerns about citizenship and legitimacy to the judicial context. Consonant with the aims of the 2001 Governance White Paper, EUstitia is dedicated to the goals of connecting Europe with its citizens, and getting 'more people and organizations involved in shaping and delivering EU policy'.[153] By increasing access to justice and enhancing the capacity of Member State courts to participate in the development of European norms, the EU's civil justice project clears one avenue by which social and economic actors can participate in European governance. Civil litigation in Member State courts provides a forum close to home where citizens can invoke their rights, interact with the European legal order, and play an active (albeit indirect) role in developing EU law and policy.

[146] Stone Sweet (2000) (n 144).

[147] Oliver Gerstenberg, 'Expanding the Constitution Beyond the Court: The Case of Euro-Constitutionalism' (2002) 8 *European Law Review* 172, 184.

[148] Stone Sweet (2000) (n 144) 196.

[149] Gerstenberg (n 147) 191.

[150] Avignon Declaration (1998). The Avignon Declaration, which was issued at the conclusion of a seminar on the criminal judiciary held in Avignon during a French Presidency, is not an official EU document, but is frequently quoted by EU institutions, including the EP and the Justice and Home Affairs Council.

[151] European Commission (n 145) 8.

[152] Martin Shapiro, 'Administrative Law Unbounded' (2001) 8 *Indiana Journal of Global Legal Studies* 369, 369.

[153] European Commission (n 145) 3.

Participation – whether in litigation, or in regulatory or political processes – can generate a sense of belonging and authorship, and thus has an 'identity-forging constructivist dimension'.[154] Litigation – even if adversary – is a social process that has the potential to shape the identity of European citizens and firms, and feeds into the political process by pushing normative development.[155] In contrast to Haas's neo-functionalist view of European integration, which linked integration to a transfer of actors' 'loyalties, expectations and political activities' from nation-states to EU institutions,[156] EUstitia imagines the possibility of boot-strapping loyalty to the EU political order from interactions in national courts. The scope of civil justice is broad enough to touch everyone, at least potentially. As such, EUstitia's impact is not limited to the traditional beneficiaries of EU law, namely economic actors and persons who exercise their free movement rights to live, work, or study in another Member State.

The EU's civil justice project is conceptualised as a key strategy for legitimating European governance through enhanced emphasis on European citizenship, rights and justice. Drawing litigants into the process of articulating norms in Member State courts goes hand-in-hand with giving citizens a greater personal rights-based stake in Europe. In this sense, EUstitia offers a set of predominately procedural means towards profoundly substantive ends. If the 'people's Europe' is being constructed through law,[157] then EUstitia aims at nothing less than transforming the judicial arenas where European citizens' claims are resolved, and thereby rendering EU citizenship relevant by making the benefits of European integration 'more tangible to the populations of the member states'.[158]

Asian countries need not embrace the full vision of civil justice in order to benefit pragmatically from the pioneering technocratic work carried out by the EU to craft a transnational (or interregional) legal order for civil justice issues. However, given the extraordinary difficulties that attend efforts to unify laws of such a complex and technical nature, it is an open question whether sufficient consensus can be achieved without an ambitious political agenda that renders civil justice more salient by conceptualising it as a fundamental element of a larger politico-legal construction. The demonstrated commitment of Asian actors to pursuit of solutions for concrete civil justice problems suggests that earnest work towards these goals will continue in the short term and bear fruit in the long term.

[154] Gerstenberg (n 147) 183.

[155] Neil Fligstein, 'The Process of Europeanization' (2000) 1 *Politique Européenne* 25, 37–40.

[156] Ernst Haas, *The Uniting of Europe: Political, Social, and Economic Forces 1950-1957* (Stanford CA, Stanford University Press, 1958) 16.

[157] Harm Schepel and Erhard Blankenburg, 'Mobilizing the European Court of Justice' in Gráinne de Búrca and Joseph Weiler (eds), *The European Court of Justice* (Oxford, Oxford University Press, 2001) 9, 9.

[158] Richard Bellamy and Alex Warleigh, 'Introduction: The Puzzle of EU Citizenship' in Richard Bellamy and Alex Warleigh (eds), *Citizenship and Governance in the European Union* (New York, Continuum, 2001) 1, 3.

12

Bilateralism in an Interregional World?

From EU Negotiations with MERCOSUR to a Bilateral Strategic Partnership with Brazil

KATHARINA L MEISSNER

I. Introduction[1]

The European Union (EU) has a dense network of diverse trade relations across the globe. It has engaged in the Doha Round negotiations of the World Trade Organization (WTO); it has negotiated free trade agreements (FTA), Association Agreements and Economic Partnership Agreements (EPA). The EU has also recently established a diverse set of Strategic Partnerships (SP) with important economic powers. The design of these relations have varied in scope from multi-, and plurilateral, interregional, to bilateral.[2] The EU has neither developed a coherent strategy nor has it treated its partners consistently. On the contrary, in the South African case the EU has shifted from a bilateral to an interregional framework;[3] in the Southeast Asian case it has switched to reverse order;[4] in other cases it has maintained interregional relations.[5] In the South American case,

[1] This chapter appeared previously as an RSCAS Working Paper 2015/37 entitled 'The Time has Come to Look at Brazil: The EU's Shift from Interregional Negotiations with MERCOSUR to a Bilateral Strategic Partnership with Brazil'. Elements of the work presented in this chapter have been published in the article 'Resorting to Bilateralism: the EU, MERCOSUR, and the Strategic Partnership with Brazil' (2017) 40 *Journal of European Integration* 51–66.

[2] Bilateral relations mean the EU's relationship with one selected member of a region; interregionalism defines the EU's relations with the exact number of members of a region; plurilateralism defines the EU's relations with at least two members of a region; and multilateral relations characterise the EU's interaction with more countries than the members of a region.

[3] The EU has a trade, development and co-operation agreement with South Africa, and later negotiated an EPA with the Southern African Development Community.

[4] The EU switched from interregional negotiations with the Association of the Southeast Asian Nations to bilateral negotiations with Singapore and other Member Ztates.

[5] As of 1991 the EU conducted interregional negotiations with the Gulf Cooperation Council.

the EU has engaged in three overlapping venues of trade relations: the South American countries and the EU were part of the Doha Round negotiations (multilateralism); the EU negotiated an Association Agreement with the Mercado Común del Sur (MERCOSUR) (interregionalism); and it launched an SP with MERCOSUR's most important member Brazil in 2007 (bilateralism).

Why has the EU maintained such diverse trade strategies, and why has the design of its negotiations varied over time, across regions, and even towards one particular region? To unravel this puzzle, the analysis will compare the interregional negotiations between the EU and MERCOSUR (1999–2004) and the EU–Brazil SP (since 2007). The focus on the EU's relations with Brazil serves as a least likely case study to test a recent theoretical framework which I developed in more detail elsewhere.[6] It is a least likely case because, first, the EU has already negotiated trade issues with Brazil in the multilateral Doha Round and the Association Agreement talks.[7] Second, before the launch of the SP, the EU committed itself to interregional relations by signing the Interregional Framework Cooperation Agreement. Further to this commitment, the mandate for the Association Agreement negotiations forbade any bilateral move towards South America. Third, the MERCOSUR customs union has forced its members to region-by-region talks on rules of market access and services. Yet, the EU approached Brazil bilaterally in 2007 by launching an SP.

The literature on EU–South America relations has highlighted the EU's endogenous motivation for its continuous engagement in the region. So far, scholars have focused on interregionalism, and they have stressed the EU's affection towards regional integration. Tanja Börzel and Thomas Risse, for instance, have argued that the

> promotion of regional integration has become part of the governance package the EU seeks to export … And Inter-regionalism as a way to promote socio-economic development, democracy and good governance … has developed into one of the foundations of its foreign policy.[8]

The EU's increasing use of bilateralism since 2006, in contrast, was conceived of as an endogenous change of the EU's preferences based on the Global Europe strategy paper.[9] In fact, the Global Europe paper, which the EU released in 2006, makes the pragmatic nature of trade policy explicit, but does not contain much information about the EU's preferred design of negotiations. As opposed to emphasising

[6] KL Meissner, *Commercial Realism and EU Trade Policy: Competing for Economic Power in Asia and the Americas* (Abingdon, Routledge, 2018).

[7] The EU first negotiated an Association Agreement with MERCOSUR from 1999 to 2004. The talks stagnated in 2004, but were resumed in 2010, and were just recently concluded in July 2019.

[8] T Börzel and T Risse, 'Diffusing (Inter-)Regionalism: the EU as a Model of Regional Integration', *KFG Working Paper* (2009) 7, 10.

[9] European Commission, 'Global Europe: Competing in the World. A Contribution to the EU's Growth and Jobs Strategy', *European Commission* (2006); D Furby, *Global Trade: The fall of Doha and the rise of bilateral agreements* (London, Business for New Europe, 2012).

bilateralism, the Global Europe paper highlights *MERCOSUR* and other *regions* as a priority.[10] An alleged endogenous shift of preferences cannot explain why the EU varied the design of trade strategies before 2006, and why it returned to interregional relations with some partners after 2006.

In order to investigate this gap in the literature of why the EU switched from interregionalism to bilateralism and why the EU has varied the FTA's design over time, and across and within regions, this chapter's theoretical part will develop an alternative explanation. This theoretical model emphasises extra-regional factors as opposed to endogenous preferences, and material interests as opposed to an affection for certain norms – that is the EU's affection towards regional integration. The EU feared losing South America's most influential country, Brazil, to its competitors, the US and China. In its endeavour to counterbalance US and Chinese initiatives, the EU singled Brazil out when interregionalism began to seem fruitless. The EU's commitment to support regional integration has begun to waver in the face of MERCOSUR's increasing fragmentation and competition over privileged relations with Brazil. Material interests have, thus, pre-empted the EU's affection for regional integration in South America.

By explaining the theoretical argument and by demonstrating its empirical validity, the sections will introduce the reader to the outcome to be explained, first, to the explanatory factor, second, and to the causal mechanism between the two, third. The chapter will begin with the theoretical framework, proceed with the EU–MERCOSUR negotiations, and continue with the EU–Brazil SP. The conclusion will summarise the results. The analysis relies on self-generated data from 29 interviews and 165 newspaper articles of Mercopress.

II. Theorising the Impact of Regional Cohesion on EU Trade Strategies

Two strands of research inform the theoretical model presented in this chapter: the literature on interregionalism, and the literature on foreign trade policy-making. The theory links these two strands of research by conceiving of interregionalism and bilateralism as one variation in the design of foreign trade policy-making.[11] Interregionalism and bilateralism as possible venues of EU trade strategies are the outcomes which the theoretical model seeks to explain. The research design is therefore outcome-, or Y-centered,[12] so that the structure will begin by explaining

[10] European Commission (n 9) 11.

[11] V Aggarwal and E Fogarty, 'Explaining Trends in EU Interregionalism' in V Aggarwal and E Fogarty (eds), *European Union Trade Strategies: Between Globalism and Regionalism* (London, Palgrave Macmillan, 2004); M Elsig, 'The EU's Choice of Regulatory Venues for Trade Negotiations: A Tale of Agency Power?' (2007) 45 *Journal of Common Market Studies* 927.

[12] T Gschwend and F Schimmelfennig, *Forschungsdesign in der Politikwissenschaft: Ein Dialog zwischen Theorie und Daten* (Frankfurt am Main, Campus, 2007) 21.

the dependent variable, and then move on to the independent variable, and the causal mechanism between the two.

A. Bilateralism and Interregionalism in the Design of Trade Policy

Interregionalism and bilateralism are foreign policy tools which states or state-like entities choose over other instruments.[13] Among other features, the selection of these tools characterise a trade policy's regime design. Interregionalism and bilateralism are two possible designs[14] in addition to multilateralism or plurilateralism. If we treat the EU as a unitary actor on the international stage, the definition of these designs rests on the counterpart region. Interregionalism describes relations between the EU and all members of a regional organisation. Bilateralism describes relations between the EU and one single member state of a regional organisation. Multilateralism describes relations between the EU and the members of a regional organisation plus at least one third country, and plurilateralism describes relations between the EU and at least two member states of a regional organisation.

By offering this definition of interregionalism, the theoretical model considers the micro level and actors' interests, which alternative descriptions of this concept lack. Ralf Roloff, for instance, has defined interregionalism as a 'process of widening and deepening political, economic, and societal interactions between international regions'.[15] Similarly, Frederik Söderbaum et al have understood interregionalism as a process or an outcome.[16] Although these definitions are not wrong, they tell us little about the actors' interests, and they offer little help in contrasting the concept of interregionalism to other trade policy regime designs such as bilateralism. The theoretical framework presented here, however, requires a definition of interregionalism which leaves room for its alternatives – such as bilateralism – and which leaves room to consider states' preferences for an interregional versus a bilateral design.

B. Regional Cohesion as an Explanatory Factor

The relevant literature on interregionalism and on foreign trade policy-making has so far neglected possible explanatory factors related to the counterpart region.

[13] V Aggarwal and E Fogarty, 'The Limits of Interregionalism: The EU and North America' (2005) 27 *Journal of European Integration* 327.

[14] A Thompson and D Verdier, 'Multilateralism, Bilateralism and Regime Design' (2014) 58 *International Studies Quarterly* 15.

[15] R Roloff, 'Interregionalism in Theoretical Perspective: State of the Art' in H Hänggi, R Roloff and J Rüland (eds), *Interregionalism and International Relations* (New York, Routledge, 2006) 18.

[16] F Söderbaum, P StÅlgren and L van Langenhove, 'The EU as a Global Actor and the Dynamics of Interregionalism: a Comparative Analysis' (2005) 27 *Journal of European Integration* 365.

However, they may explain the EU's variation between bilateral and interregional regime designs. Although, interestingly, the literature has not considered features of the counterpart region, its cohesion seems to be intuitively important to EU trade policy. Cohesion is *the process or fact of sticking together and remaining united in satisfying members' interests.*[17] The Member States are united when they agree on the goal of representing the entire group to the international environment. The more divergent their interests are, the more difficult it is to represent the group to the external environment; consequently, the less cohesion there is. Cohesion presents a low degree of diverging interests, whereas a divergence of interests is, concisely, non-cohesion.[18] The concept comes close to *team spirit*, which Eugénia da Conceição-Heldt and Sophie Meunier describe as follows:

> The concept … captures the intuition … [to] be more effective on the international scene by being united internally. It is a measure of the resistance of the members to leave the group, their willingness to co-ordinate their efforts, and their overall level of 'team spirit'. When it comes to displaying cohesiveness to the rest of the world, it is the degree to which the group comes up with a single message and manages to present that message with a single voice, without members of the group breaking away and undermining the collective message.[19]

Cohesion is a fuzzy concept and it may cover a range of aspects such as disputes, institutions and material interests. Given its fuzzy character, the concept describes a continuum rather than a dichotomy. We shall therefore distinguish cohesion into five dimensions: process and procedure, institutionalisation, policy outputs, preference homogeneity and economic convergence. Each dimension is ascribed a set of indicators,[20] leading to an index of cohesion with 15 indicators. The higher the number of indicators in which the region is cohesive, the higher the overall degree of cohesion is.

C. Developing a Causal Mechanism Towards Varying Trade Strategies

Because the EU fears losing important regions or regional actors to its competitors such as the US or China, it counterbalances their initiatives towards these

[17] KL Meissner, 'Resorting to Bilateralism: The EU, MERCOSUR, and the Strategic Partnership with Brazil' (2018) 40 *Journal of European Integration* 51; KL Meissner, 'Cherry Picking in the Design of Trade Policy: Why Regional Organizations Shift between Inter-regional and Bilateral Negotiations' *Review of International Political Economy* (forthcoming).

[18] E da Conceição-Heldt and S Meunier, 'Speaking with a Single Voice: Internal Cohesiveness and External Effectiveness of the EU in Global Governance' (2014) 21 *Journal of European Public Policy* 961.

[19] ibid 964.

[20] These indicators are: number of trade disputes; intensity of trade disputes; settlement of trade disputes; supranational institutions; deepening of institutions; enlargement of institutions; unity in international institutions; unity in non-regulated areas; unity in presidential summits; priority of negotiation partner; priority of negotiation issue; convergence of trade; investment by partner; type of trade; and type of investment.

regions. The EU's underlying aim is to secure its position as a powerful actor on the international stage. One facet of power is economic, and one way to achieve economic competitiveness is to arrange trade relations with foreign markets.[21] Such trade arrangements, which offer the advantage of being exclusive by targeting a specific partner and of being comprehensive by encompassing several issues, are FTAs or SPs. The EU tries to set up these types of trade relations in such a way that they establish, maintain, or strengthen the EU's economic power.[22] If the EU's competitors engage in such activities with a certain region, the EU will launch counter-initiatives.[23]

Where there are competing activities between the EU and its competitors, this may turn out to the partner region's advantage. Simultaneous trade relations or trade negotiations increase the region's or state's bargaining power because it can play competing actors off against each other. By playing them off or by prolonging simultaneous negotiations, the regions or the states can insist on more favourable outcomes and on concessions. The more actors, thus, negotiate simultaneously with a state or a group of states, the higher the bargaining power of the respective state or group is.

Given this presence of competing actors for one region or a state, developing countries can improve their bargaining power by three means. First, when countries coordinate their trade preferences and enter negotiations as a block, they build a coalition. Coalition building gives developing countries more leverage because they can thereby balance the asymmetric, economic power of industrialised states. Second, developing countries can commit themselves to a regional format by building a customs union and setting up a common external tariff.[24] If states belong to a customs union they would have to exit the entire organisation if they wanted to negotiate on a bilateral basis. Third, if there is a regional power among the developing countries, it is able to provide leadership and to push collaboration.[25] The existence of a regional power may sometimes be crucial to keep a group of countries together.

[21] H Zimmermann, 'Realist Power Europe? The EU in the Negotiations about China's and Russia's WTO Accession' (2007) 45 *Journal of Common Market Studies* 813, 816–18.

[22] JM Grieco, *Cooperation among Nations: Europe, America, and non-Tariff Trade Barriers to Trade* (Ithaca, Cornell University Press, 1990); R Gilpin, *The Political Economy of International Relations* (New Jersey, Princeton University Press, 1987); R Gilpin, *Global Political Economy: Understanding the International Economic Order* (New Jersey, Princeton University Press, 2001); AO Hirschmann, *National Power and the Structure of Foreign Trade* (Los Angeles, University of California Press, 1969); Zimmermann (n 22).

[23] Having said this, other factors may equally trigger and explain design changes in EU trade policy. Such variables may be interest groups or institutional struggles between the European Commission and EU Member States. A systematic test of these factors vis-à-vis extra-regional factors can be found in Meissner (n 6).

[24] R Fernández, 'Returns to Regionalism: An Evaluation of Nontraditional Gains from Regional Trade Agreements' *NBER Working Paper* (1998) 5970, 22; RJ Langhammer and U Hiemenz, 'Regional Integration among Developing Countries' (1990) 232 *Kieler Studien* 9.

[25] W Mattli, *The Logic of Regional Integration: Europe and Beyond* (New York, Columbia University Press, 1999); D Nolte, 'How to Compare Regional Powers: Analytical and Research Topics' (2010)

Decisive for whether a region appears as a group of states or as individual states and for whether they make use of the three above-mentioned means is their degree of regional cohesion. The higher the degree of regional cohesion, the more likely it is that the region will appear as a group on the international stage. In contrast, if a region is diverse, it will be difficult for it to appear as a group. The region's *team spirit* decides whether states try to increase their bargaining power by collective appearance.

Where there are competing actors, the region's cohesion will influence the European trade regime design as to whether it is interregional or bilateral. In cases where there are competing actors and the region is cohesive, the EU will feel pressured into counter-initiatives. In such situations, the EU adjusts its trade strategies to features of the counterpart region, so that it will choose an interregional design to increase the likelihood of an FTA. Where there are competing actors and the region is non-cohesive, the EU will choose a bilateral design in such a way that it increases the likelihood of an agreement. Hence, the higher the degree of cohesion within the counterpart region, the more likely the EU is to use an interregional design. Whereas in reverse, the lower the degree of cohesion within the partner region, the more likely the EU is to switch to a bilateral design.[26]

The next two sections test this expectation in a least likely case study, which comprises the EU's interregional negotiations with MERCOSUR and the EU's SP with Brazil. The analysis seeks to explain the outcome – interregional versus bilateral design – and the research design is therefore *backward-looking*.[27] This is why the sections start by describing the policy outcome; second, explain the degree of cohesion; and, third, explain the causal mechanism between South America's cohesion and the policy outcome.

III. EU–MERCOSUR Negotiations (1999–2004)

In 1994, Brazil, Argentina, Uruguay and Paraguay formalised the (imperfect) MERCOSUR customs union. The customs union was a Brazilian project and its top foreign policy priority.[28] It helped to prevent bilateral negotiations by Brazil's

36 *Review of International Studies* 881; S Schirm, 'Leaders in Need of Followers: Emerging Powers in Global Governance' (2010) 16 *European Journal of International Relations* 197; MG Schoeller, *Leadership in the Eurozone: The Role of Germany and EU Institutions* (London, Palgrave Macmillan, 2019).

[26] For a more detail elaborating see Meissner (n 17) (both references); Meissner (n 6).

[27] FW Scharpf, *Games Real Actors Play: Actor-Centered Institutionalism in Policy Research* (Boulder, Westview Press, 1997) 24–26.

[28] LAM Bandeira, 'Brazil as a Regional Power and its Relations with the United States' (2006) 33 *Latin American Perspectives* 12, 25; MRS De Lima and M Hirst, 'Brazil as an Intermediate State and Regional Power: Action, Choice and Responsibilities' (2006) 82 *International Affairs* 21, 29; A Malamud, 'Presidential Diplomacy and the Institutional Underpinnings of Mercosur: An Empirical Examination' (2005) 40 *Latin American Research Review* 139, 425.

smaller neighbours with the US or the EU,[29] and was played out by Brazil as a means for increasing leverage in international negotiations.[30] In 2000, the EU and MERCOSUR were ready to start negotiating an Association Agreement, which covered political issues, cooperation and an FTA. The EU's mandate laid out the content of the Association Agreement, which went far beyond a traditional FTA by including also services, investments and non-tariff trade barriers. The negotiation directive forbade any bilateral talks between the EU and MERCOSUR, but was interregional in substance.[31]

A. A Phase of High Cohesion[32]

MERCOSUR's degree of cohesion was high between 1997 and 2003. The index of cohesion reached 12 out of 15 indicators (Figure 1). In the 1990s, MERCOSUR as a regional organisation became very successful. MERCOSUR's success can be seen in the settlement of disputes, in establishing institutions, and in the group's economic and external dimension.

Figure 1 Degree of cohesion, 1997–2003

Index Cohesion	
Indicator	**Fulfilled demands**
Trade disputes	XXX
Supranational institutions	XXX
Unity	XXX
Trade and commerce	XXX
Sum	12

Reference: Own illustration

MERCOSUR's success and high degree of cohesion is reflected in trade disputes and their settlement. MERCOSUR started out with a relatively high number of trade disputes (127) in 1995, but this number gradually decreased, reaching the modest amount of 33 in 1998.[33] These low-scale conflicts could be resolved within the structure of MERCOSUR. Its Member States brought only one dispute

[29] F Duina and J Buxbaum, 'Regional Trade Agreements and the Pursuit of State Interests: Institutional Perspectives from NAFTA and Mercosur' (2008) 37 *Economy and Society* 193.

[30] M Carranza, 'Can MERCOSUR survive? Domestic and International Constraints on MERCOSUR' (2004) 45 *Latin American Politics and Society* 67.

[31] Interview, *Expert at UDELAR*, Montevideo, Uruguay, 8 August 2014, Katharina L Meissner.

[32] This section is based on Meissner (2018) (n 17).

[33] IDATD, 'Integrated Database of Trade Disputes for Latin America and the Caribbean' (2011) idatd.eclac.cl/controversias/index_en.jsp.

to a third dispute settlement mechanism outside of MERCOSUR. One year after bringing the conflict to an international body, MERCOSUR's members settled it voluntarily based on a mutual agreement. In the same spirit, most of MERCOSUR's trade disputes were low-scale. Only two conflicts occurred that were more serious: the automobile sector crisis (1995), and the footwear industry dispute (1999). Both disputes were, however, settled rapidly and easily by using the regional dispute settlement mechanism.

MERCOSUR's cooperation was high, too, in establishing new institutions. The permanent dispute settlement mechanism was MERCOSUR's first *supranational* institution, established by the Protocol of Olivos in 2002.[34] One year later, the Member States announced the second *supranational* institution, which was the MERCOSUR parliament Parlasur. Besides setting up new institutions, MERCOSUR's members deepened its institutions by signing nine protocols or agreements. The Member States agreed on the Protocol of the Harmonization of Intellectual Property Norms (1995), the Protocol for the Defense of Competition (1996), the Legal Framework on the Regulations Regarding Dumping on Imports from non-MERCOSUR Countries (1997), and the Protocol of Montevideo on Trade in Services (1997). Two International Commercial Arbitration Agreements (1998), and the Agreement for the Regulation of the Protocol of Competition Policy, the Protocol of Olivos for the Solution of Controversies, and the Agreement for International Freight Contracts Jurisdiction between MERCOSUR countries (2002) followed. Further to setting up new institutions and deepening existing institutions, MERCOSUR paved the way for enlargement. Venezuela's and the Andean countries' accession was prepared when Chavez participated at a presidential summit (2001),[35] and when MERCOSUR's members agreed on Peru's anticipated accession (2003).[36]

On the international level, too, MERCOSUR appeared united and reached important achievements. Brazil was particularly successful when it initiated the Initiative for the Integration of Regional Infrastructure in South America (IIRSA) (2000). IIRSA attempted to integrate South America in commerce, energy and infrastructure.[37] In international institutions, too, Brazil appeared as a leader when it led the group of developing countries in the WTO's Doha Round negotiations. Therein, Brazil mobilised the G20 to pressure the US and the EU into significant reforms in agriculture.[38] Within MERCOSUR, Brazil was also very

[34] C Arnold and B Rittberger, 'The Legalization of Dispute Resolution in Mercosur' (2013) 5 *Journal of Politics in Latin America* 97.

[35] Mercopress, 'Venezuela next Mercosur member' (2001) en.mercopress.com/2001/04/06/venezuela-next-mercosur-member.

[36] Mercopress, 'Regional parliament and expansion' (2003) en.mercopress.com/2003/06/12/regional-parliaments-and-expansion.

[37] D Small, 'South American Summit: Infrastructure Integration is the New Name of Peace' (2005) 32 *Executive Intelligence Review* 29.

[38] K Hopewell, 'New Protagonists in Global Economic Governance: Brazilian Agribusiness at the WTO' (2013) 18 *New Political Economy* 603.

active, when it pushed the *regional* format of South America's negotiations. To ensure this regional format, Brazil assisted its fellow members materially and institutionally. In this endeavour, Brazil provided safeguard measures and special rules for financing transactions to Argentina, which had entered a recession.[39] Brazil also voluntarily restricted exports,[40] and agreed to macroeconomic coordination. These were significant steps, which injected energy into MERCOSUR's integration based on the organisation's *inter-presidential* character.[41]

The two most important states – Brazil and Argentina – had converging positions on MERCOSUR's foreign trade agenda, too. They agreed to strengthen MERCOSUR's negotiation capacity, and they emphasised the content of negotiations with the US and the EU over their timetable.[42] Brazil and Argentina preferred an agreement with the EU over an agreement with the US, which demonstrates that MERCOSUR's members had similar preferences over the negotiation partner. Over negotiation issues, too, MERCOSUR's member had similar preferences by wanting a single undertaking – namely an agreement, which includes all negotiation issues at once. Trade data resemble MERCOSUR's cohesion in its external trade agenda. Trade with European countries increased for all MERCOSUR's Member States.[43] Although there does not appear to be any systematic data on investment numbers, the above-mentioned indicators allow for MERCOSUR to be ascribed a high degree of cohesion between 1997 and 2003. MERCOSUR's cohesion proved to influence the EU's trade policy towards South America as the next section will explain.

B. Regional Cohesion and the EU–MERCOSUR Negotiations

In 1999, when the EU and MERCOSUR started the Association Agreement negotiations, the EU launched a counter-initiative to the US's Free Trade Area of the Americas (FTAA). The FTAA targeted the entire Latin American continent, attempting to integrate the continent peacefully into the US sphere of influence.[44] Scholars have widely interpreted the EU's initiative as a reaction to the US approach and perceived the EU and the US as rivals for influence over the continent of South America.[45] Interviewees from the EU and MERCOSUR, too, confirmed that there was always a sense of competition between the EU's and

[39] GM Genna and T Hiroi, 'Brazilian Regional Power in the Development of Mercosul' (2007) 34 *Latin American Perspectives* 43.

[40] W Bear, T Cavalcanti and S Peri, 'Economic Integration without Policy Coordination: The Case of Mercosur' (2002) 3 *Emerging Markets Review* 269.

[41] Malamud (n 28).

[42] Mercopress, 'Argentina Brazil joint position' (2000) en.mercopress.com/2001/02/14/argentina-brazil-joint-position.

[43] DataIntal, 'Inter-American Development Bank Trade Statistics System' (2012) iadb.org/dataintal/default/aspx.

[44] Carranza (n 30) 320.

[45] J Faust, 'The EU's Trade Policy towards MERCOSUR' *PEIF Working Paper* (2002) 7.

US's approaches towards Latin America.[46] The European Association Agreement and the American FTAA talks became so interlinked that failure on one side was replicated on the other,[47] because the EU wanted 'at all costs avoid an upsurge of US influence in the continent'.[48]

MERCOSUR's members, using the competition between the EU and the US over South America to their advantage, promoted a regional format of negotiations. Brazil and Argentina admitted that they negotiate on multiple fronts to pressure their partners into concessions and to reach the best result.[49] Brazil was also open about the fact that it would discuss in a *regional* format only.[50] Brazil's former president declared that the country needs MERCOSUR 'to tackle the complex challenges of the Americas Free Trade Association discussions, relations with the European Union and other world blocks'.[51] Prior to the negotiations with the EU and the US, Brazil successfully insisted on an interregional format and a single undertaking of the negotiations, so that 'negotiating as a group has been retained'[52] for the EU–MERCOSUR discussions.

In the EU–MERCOSUR talks, the EU was, from the beginning, mainly interested in concluding an agreement with Brazil, whether it was with or without MERCOSUR.[53] The EU understood, however, that Brazil would have never opted for a bilateral track because MERCOSUR means a geopolitical vision for Brazil.[54] The country openly favoured negotiations with a 'strong Mercosur block'[55] and not on a region-to-country basis, because a regional format gives the group bargaining power.[56] In fact, when Argentina and Uruguay voiced the idea of bilateral talks with external actors, Brazil insisted on the regional format, and made it clear that bilateralism is not compatible with membership in the customs union.[57]

If the EU wanted to conclude a deal with Brazil, it thus needed to go the interregional way. Although the Commission has a somewhat natural inclination towards

[46] Interviews, *Embassy*, Brussels, Belgium, 4 April 2014, Katharina L Meissner; Interview, *European Commission*, Brussels, Belgium, 8 April 2014, Katharina L Meissner; Interview, *Former Diplomat*, Montevideo, Uruguay, 8 August 2014, Katharina L Meissner.

[47] M Doctor, 'Why Bother with Inter-Regionalism? Negotiations for a European Union-Mercosur Agreement' (2007) 45 *Journal of Common Market Studies* 281.

[48] Inter-American Development Bank, *MERCOSUR Report No 5* (1998–1999) (Buenos Aires, IDB-INTAL, 1999) 34.

[49] V Bulmer-Thomas, 'The European Union and MERCOSUR: Prospects for a Free Trade Agreement' (2000) 42 *Journal of Interamerican Studies and World Affairs* 1.

[50] Mercopress, 'Lula in Buenos Aires and Chile' (2002) en.mercopress.com/2002/12/01/lula-in-buenos-aires-and-chile.

[51] Mercopress, 'Mercosur Lula's Priority' (2002) en.mercopress.com/2002/09/30/Mercosur-lula-s-priority.

[52] Inter-American Development Bank (n 48) 33–35.

[53] Interview, *European Commission*, Brussels, Belgium, 18 March 2014, Katharina L Meissner; Interviews (n 46).

[54] FS Christensen, 'Brazil's Foreign Policy Priorities' (2013) 34 *Third World Quarterly* 271, 274.

[55] Mercopress, 'Mercosur expanding regional trade' (2000) en.mercopress.com/2001/02/21/expanding-regional-trade.

[56] Mercopress, 'Caracas Summit' (2001) en.mercopress.com/2001/04/09/caracas-summit.

[57] Interviews (n 46).

region-to-region talks, the format of negotiations is a case-by-case decision rather than a general preference. Following Brazil's insistence on MERCOSUR's customs union, there was little leeway for the EU in deciding about the negotiation format.[58] The same happened in 2010, when the Commission re-launched the Association Agreement negotiations. Given MERCOSUR's customs union, the EU chose an interregional format. If, however, MERCOSUR had reconfigured and if Brazil had been open for bilateral negotiations, the Commission would have tried to reshape its negotiation mandate in favour of bilateralism.[59] In fact, when the Commission re-launched the Association Agreement negotiations, the bilateral option was discussed internally, but it was not aired because Brazil wanted to retain the customs union at any cost.[60]

Given Brazil's geopolitical vision for MERCOSUR, the EU had little flexibility in deciding about the venue for negotiations whether it should be bilateral or interregional.[61] MERCOSUR and *interregional* relations are Brazil's foreign policy tools, and therefore Brazil insisted on the regional format. In the same vein, Brazil prevented its neighbours from negotiating bilaterally with third actors,[62] and it preferred MERCOSUR's enlargement over its deepening.[63] Brazil 'hijacked MERCOSUR as its child',[64] and it created MERCOSUR as a political brand. Brazil's insistence on MERCOSUR as a political block coupled with the EU's fear of losing political and economic presence in South America[65] explains why the Association Agreement negotiations were so important to the EU. The fact that relations with South America do not only have an economic but also a political dimension to the EU also explains why the EU chose an Association Agreement instead of a pure FTA. Pascal Lamy declared in 2006 that 'indeed the EU's profound motivation in this agreement has always been geopolitical; it is not just a trade agreement'.[66]

IV. A Bilateral Strategic Partnership

In 2004, however, the Association Agreement negotiations between the EU and MERCOSUR stagnated, and the EU showed no further interest in the talks. This stagnation was triggered by the breakdown of the FTAA negotiations by the US, so that the EU needed to search for alternatives. In fact, in 2005 the EU discussed internally the possibility of bilateral relations with Brazil, which led to the SP

[58] Interview, *European Commission*, Brussels, Belgium, 18 March 2014, Katharina L Meissner.

[59] Interview, *European External Action Service*, Brussels, Belgium, 20 March 2014, Katharina L Meissner.

[60] Interview, *European Commission*, Brussels, Belgium, 8 April 2014, Katharina L Meissner.

[61] Interview (n 31).

[62] Interview (n 46).

[63] Christensen (n 54).

[64] Interviews, *Foreign Ministry*, Montevideo, Uruguay, 6 August 2014, Katharina L Meissner.

[65] Interview (n 46).

[66] Inter-American Development Bank, *Mercosur Report No 10* (2004–2005) (Buenos Aires, IBD-INTAL, 2006) 86.

in 2007.[67] The SP was a result of the EU's new perspective on South America after it had realised that the region was not as homogeneous as the EU had perceived.[68]

The SP served the EU as a means to deepen economic ties with Brazil and to eventually move towards an agreement. Although the possibility of an EU–Brazil FTA has never officially been on the table, the European Commission would not hesitate to follow this path if Brazil were ready or willing to consider it.[69] Because a bilateral FTA outside of MERCOSUR's customs union has been unacceptable to Brazil, the EU had to focus on issues other than market access rules. The SP covers political dialogues, economic matters, environment and sustainable development, bi-regional cooperation, science and technology, cultural matters and transnational relations.[70] Furthermore, the SP serves to discuss investment and non-tariff trade barrier issues to eventually smooth an either regional or a bilateral FTA.[71]

A. A Phase of Low Cohesion[72]

What had changed during the interregional negotiations between 2000 and 2004 was the degree of cohesion within MERCOSUR. Brazil's smaller neighbours started to feel disappointed about the customs union and the progress of the FTA negotiations. The rising tensions and increasing divergence manifested in the external agenda, but also in the resolution of trade disputes, or the institutional dimension. On the index of cohesion, MERCOSUR reached only three indicators out of 15 in the time between 2003 and 2007, which means a low degree of team spirit (Figure 2).

Figure 2 Degree of cohesion 2003–2007

Index Cohesion	
Indicator	**Fulfilled demands**
Trade disputes	X
Supranational institutions	-
Unity	-
Trade and commerce	XX
Sum	3

Reference: Own illustration

[67] A Carlos Lessa, 'Brazil's Strategic Partnerships: An Assessment of the Lula Era (2003–2010)' (2010) 53 *Revista Brasileira de Política Internacional* 115, 128.

[68] ibid.

[69] Interview, *European External Action Service*, Brussels, Belgium, 20 March 2014, Katharina L Meissner; Interview, *European Commission*, Brussels, Belgium, 8 April 2014, Katharina L Meissner.

[70] European Union, *Factsheet: EU-Brazil Summit: EU-Strategic Partnership with Brazil* (Brussels, European Commission, 2011).

[71] Interview, *European Commission*, Brussels, Belgium, 18 March 2014, Katharina L Meissner.

[72] This section is based on Meissner (2018) (n 17).

Before the EU and Brazil launched the SP, between 2004 and 2006, the number of trade disputes in MERCOSUR increased from 11 to 15. Only two of them were solved through MERCOSUR's dispute settlement mechanism, whereas the members brought two other conflicts to international bodies. Brazil brought one dispute on anti-dumping duties to the WTO. The other conflict concerned a pulp mill, which Argentina brought to the International Court of Justice (ICJ) although Uruguay took it to the MERCOSUR dispute settlement mechanism. Argentina even rejected the competence of MERCOSUR on this issue.[73] Although the pulp mill dispute was considered one of the most serious conflicts in South America, Brazil decided not to intervene, but perceived the dispute as a purely bilateral issue.[74] Meanwhile, Brazil had its own ongoing disputes with its neighbours. One of them was a conflict in 2006 with Paraguay over the Itaipu dam.[75] As a consequence of this conflict, Paraguay leaned closer to the US in commercial and military issues.

Institutionally, MERCOSUR's integration has stagnated since 2003. Between 2003 and 2007, the members did not set up further supranational institutions. Although the MERCOSUR parliament started working in 2007, it was only three years later that those citizens could vote its members directly, despite this having been scheduled for the same year.[76] Neither did MERCOSUR deepen integration between 2003 and 2007. It signed only two agreements, one on rules of origin, and the other on the accession of Venezuela to MERCOSUR. The members took no steps to further enlarge the regional organisation.

The low degree of cohesion becomes most obvious in MERCOSUR's external agenda. The members had divergent positions in international institutions. First, in 2005, Brazil bid for a permanent seat in the United Nations Security Council, receiving no support from its MERCOSUR partners; Argentina even opposed Brazil's bid.[77] Second, in 2005, Brazil submitted its candidature for director-general of the WTO, but was rejected after the first round. The second of four applications came from Uruguay, whose representative made it to the last round.[78] Third, in 2005, Brazil and Colombia both applied for a leadership position in the Inter-American Development Bank. MERCOSUR's members supported the Colombian candidate but not the Brazilian one.[79] Fourth, in 2008, Argentina's president bid

[73] LA Di Martino, 'Institutional Deficit for Cross-Border Conflict Resolution: The Conflict over the Construction of a Pulp Mill near the Uruguay River' (2010) e.okayama-u.ac.jp/jafee/paper/a21.pdf; R Luchi and A Llorente, 'Rules of Entanglement: The River Uruguay's Pulp Mills International Dispute: A Case Study' (2011) iae.edu.ar/pi/Documentos%20Investigacin/Research%20Seminars/PulpMills Dispute.pdf.

[74] A Malamud, 'A Leader without Followers? The Growing Divergence Between the Regional and Global Performance of Brazilian Foreign Policy' (2011) 53 *Latin American Politics and Society* 1.

[75] Mercopress, 'Kirchner Lula address Mercosur fragility' (2006) en.mercopress.com/2006/04/26/kirchner-lula-address-mercosur-fragility.

[76] S Caballero Santos, 'Brasil y la region: una potencia emergente y la integración regional sudamericana' (2011) 54 *Revista Brasileira de Política Internacional* 158.

[77] Malamud (n 74); Christensen (n 54).

[78] Malamud (n 74).

[79] ibid.

for the chair of UNASUR. Although he was the only promising candidate he failed because Uruguay decided not to support him.[80]

The members of MERCOSUR also started to have divergent preferences on the substance of the external trade agenda. In the Doha Round, for instance, Brazil and Argentina allocated themselves to opposing working groups because Argentina could not accept Brazil's pro-liberalisation agenda on manufactured goods.[81] At several presidential summits, the members aimed at reforming the double tariff system, but they were not able to find a compromise.[82] This led observers to conclude that MERCOSUR had nothing to show other than an unfinished agenda.[83] Anecdotally, the former Brazilian finance minister and the former Brazilian president judged that MERCOSUR was in a devastating state by being extremely divided and by lacking a true regional leader.[84]

Brazil's neighbours started to feel disillusioned about MERCOSUR and its external agenda. In 2003, Argentina and Uruguay aired the possibility of degrading the customs union to a free trade area. This would allow the members to negotiate FTAs on a bilateral basis. Although this did not materialise, Uruguay and the US agreed bilaterally on an investment treaty[85] and a free trade understanding.[86] In terms of substance, the countries no longer had a common preference over the negotiation partner. While in the beginning, the members agreed that an FTA with the EU would be favourable, Argentina, Uruguay and Paraguay became dissatisfied with the lack of progress in negotiations. Argentina, Uruguay and Paraguay wanted to move forward with the EU and the US, whereas Brazil favoured a wait and see approach. Moreover, the members perceived each other increasingly as competitors in agriculture, and they had diverging positions on manufactured goods. In brief, the members had increasingly 'diverging interests within the trade area'.[87]

However, in numbers, trade with European countries had actually risen for every MERCOSUR member between 2003 and 2007. The same is true for trade between MERCOSUR's members and the US and China. The only country that had not seen constantly rising trade numbers was Paraguay. Trade in agriculture and trade in manufactured goods had increased, too, between 2003 and 2007.

[80] Mercopress, 'Argentina furious with Uruguay's veto to Mr Kirchner' (2008) en.mercopress.com/2008/10/24/argentina-furious-with-uruguay-s-veto-to-mr-kirchner.

[81] Christensen (n 54).

[82] Mercopress, 'Mercosur summit challenge: how not to deepen differences' (2007) en.mercopress.com/2007/12/03/mercosur-summit-challenge-how-not-to-deepen-differences.

[83] ibid.

[84] Mercopress, 'Mercosur has become irrelevant and too complicated' (2007) en.mercopress.com/2007/12/02/mercosur-has-become-irrelevant-and-too-complicated; Mercopress, 'Mercosur an illusion of integration: Brazil no longer leads' (2007) en.mercopress.com/2007/05/30/Mercosur-an-illusion-of-integration-brazil-no-longer-leads.

[85] Mercopress, 'Mercosur rebel member seen from Buenos Aires' (2006) en.mercopress.com/2006/01/19/mercosur-rebel-member-seen-from-buenos-aires.

[86] Mercopress, 'US Uruguay free trade accord not on the agenda' (2006) en.mercopress.com/2006/02/04/us-uruguay-free-trade-accord-not-on-the-agenda.

[87] Christensen (n 54) 275.

Brazil, Argentina and Uruguay could boost their trade by commodities, and only Paraguay witnessed some minor ups and downs in numbers of trade. Systematic reliable investment data were unfortunately not available.

B. Lacking Regional Cohesion and the EU–Brazil Strategic Partnership

After the FTAA negotiations started to stagnate, the US made it clear that it was no longer interested in MERCOSUR, but that it wanted to focus on Brazil. The US trade representative Peter Allgeier revealed that the regional format 'is something which does not interest the US'.[88] The US concentrated its efforts on facilitating trade with Brazil, but no longer discussed market access rules. Thus, in 2006, the US and Brazil signed a letter of intent in order to boost trade, investments, and business exchanges. Further, the agreement included ethanol, which was important to the US aviation industry.[89] In 2007, the US and Brazil signed a strategic bio-fuels promotion agreement, which was followed by further memorandums of understanding on different issues.[90]

When the FTAA talks stagnated, the EU lost interest in its own FTA negotiations.[91] Instead, it searched for alternatives, and started discussing the possibility of an SP as early as 2005.[92] The SP served the EU as a possibility to keep economic and political ties with Brazil outside the framework of the customs union.[93] For the EU, Brazil is a 'strong ally'[94] in the sense that they have common cultural heritage and common goals, so that it did not want to lose Brazil to the US. Every initiative on the US side was followed by a counter-initiative on the EU's side.[95] The SP, in brief, was a clear political message to Brazil,[96] with which it demonstrated how important Brazil is to the EU.

Why did, first the US and then the EU switch to a bilateral approach after having invested five years of negotiating with MERCOSUR? As of 2003, it became clear that MERCOSUR was facing problems and internal tensions. Uruguay and Argentina were dissatisfied with the customs union and voiced the idea of degrading it to a free trade area. While initially Brazil had tried to keep the group together, this had changed over time. In a situation of growing tensions and

[88] Mercopress, 'US reject 4-1 agreement with Mercosur' (2005) en.mercopress.com/2005/02/09/us-reject-4-1-agreement-with-mercosur.

[89] Mercosur, 'Brazil US closer to a formal trade agreement' (2006) en.mercopress.com(2006/06/08/brazil-us-closer-to-a-formal-trade-agreement.

[90] BrazilCouncil, 'US-Brazil Bilateral Agreements' (2014) brazilcouncil.org/bilateralagreements.

[91] Interviews (n 46).

[92] Carlos Lessa (n 67).

[93] Interview (n 46).

[94] Interview (n 69).

[95] Interview (n 31).

[96] Interviews (n 46).

severe problems with regional integration, Brazil was basically absent.[97] In 2007, the former Brazilian president Cardoso summed up the situation as follows: 'Latinamerica has never been so divided, Mercosur is but an illusion of integration and Brazil has lost its leadership and convergence capacity'.[98] Brazil was no longer willing to lead, and in 2007 the former Brazilian Foreign Finance minister admitted that 'Mercosur has become irrelevant and too complicated'.[99]

The decision to launch the SP with Brazil was a result of the EU's earlier perspective on MERCOSUR as a united block, which had not matched reality.[100] Thus, one interviewee reflected that if the negotiations on an Association Agreement had been finished there would have been no need for an SP between the EU and Brazil.[101] The EU singled out Brazil as a strategic partner because of its political and economic weight in the region.[102] In other words, the difficulties within MERCOSUR led the EU to consider alternatives to strengthen ties with Brazil bilaterally.

The suggestion of launching an SP with Brazil came therefore from the EU side, and although it does not include market access issues, the SP manifests the worry that the EU and Brazil could move forward with an FTA bilaterally.[103] So far, however, this option has never been on the table. An anecdotal fact, which demonstrates how divided MERCOSUR was in 2007, is that Brazil's partners heard about the SP from the press. Brazil did nothing to inform its neighbours about the SP, and they asked for information from EU diplomats (and not Brazilian diplomats) when they learned about it.[104]

V. Concluding Discussion

The chapter explained why the EU launched an SP with Brazil although it has conducted interregional relations and negotiations with MERCOSUR since 1995. In 1999, the EU started negotiations on an Association Agreement with MERCOSUR, the mandate for which talks explicitly foresaw no bilateral moves between the regions. Brazil insisted on region-to-region talks also because it had earlier established the MERCOSUR customs union. Simultaneously, the EU engaged in the multilateral Doha Round negotiations, which included the MERCOSUR members, too. Yet, in 2007, the EU launched an SP with Brazil.

[97] Mercopress, 'Mercosur is on flames and Brazil absent' (2006) en.mercopress.com/2006/12/09/mercosur-is-on-flames-and-brazil-absent.

[98] Mercopress (n 84).

[99] ibid.

[100] Carlos Lessa (n 67) 209.

[101] Interview, *European External Action Service*, Brussels, Belgium, 20 March 2014, Katharina L Meissner.

[102] ibid.

[103] Interview (n 31).

[104] Mercopress, 'Brazil to become a strategic partner of the European Union' (2007) en.mercopress.com/2007/07/04/brazil-to-become-a-strategic-partner-of-the-european-union.

In studying this question, the chapter suggested a theoretical framework and tested it against the EU's shift from interregional to bilateral talks with Brazil as a least likely case. The theoretical model speaks to three strands of literature. First, it took into account extra-regional factors of EU foreign trade policy-making, which the literature had not done before. Second, the chapter spoke to the literature on interregionalism, which conceived of the EU's interregional negotiations as a normative support for regional integration. While the EU seeks to support regional integration through its external relations, interregionalism is equally a foreign policy tool to foster European commercial and political interests. Third, the model highlights exogenous factors as opposed to an endogenous change of preferences for explaining the EU's shift to bilateralism.

The results of the analysis show that the EU shifted from interregionalism with MERCOSUR to bilateralism with Brazil due to external pressures. Because the EU wanted to secure its economic and regulatory power in South America and because it did not want to lose Brazil to its main competitor the US, the Commission adjusted its design of trade policy to Brazil. When the interregional strategy clashed with rising tensions and increasing divergence within MERCOSUR, the EU shifted to a bilateral approach. This was informed by a perceived urgency to find an agreement with Brazil given the US activities on the subcontinent. These results demonstrate that the EU to a certain extent departed from its normative commitment to support regional integration in other parts of the world, once this approach was at odds with its own material interests.

13

Reclaiming the Comprehensive Strategic Partnership through the EU–China Partnership and Cooperation Agreement

Taking Stock and Moving Forward

CHIEN-HUEI WU*

I. Introduction

In 2003, the European Commission updated its 1998 Communication *Building a Comprehensive Partnership with China*[1] by adopting the communication *A Maturing Partnership – Shared Interests and Challenges in EU-China Relations.*[2] The European Commission maintained that various sectorial agreements and cooperative efforts had brought about a maturation of the partnership.[3] In response, China in 2003 adopted its first country/region policy paper, *China's Policy Paper on EU*[4] in which China committed to develop 'a long-term, stable and full partnership with the EU. Subsequently, in the *European Security Strategy* (ESS) adopted in 2003, the EU explicitly voiced its intent to pursue strategic partnership with China.[5] Thus was a strategic partnership between the EU and China launched.

* The author wishes to express his gratitude for the grant of the Ministry of Science and Technology (108-2410-H-001-060-) which makes this research possible.

[1] COM (1998) 181.

[2] COM (2003) 533 final.

[3] 'A Maturing Partnership – Shared Interests and Challenges in EU-China Relations', 6.

[4] www.chinamission.be/eng/zywj/zywd/t1227623.htm accessed 01 May 2019.

[5] European Security Strategy: A Secure Europe in a Better World (ESS), adopted 12 December 2003, 14.

The maturation of EU–China relations into a comprehensive strategic partnership was again recognised by the leaders of the EU and China at the 9th EU–China Summit in 2006.[6] The leaders declared that

> [i]n order to reflect the full breadth and depth of today's comprehensive strategic partnership between the EU and China, the two sides agreed to launch negotiations on a new Partnership and Co-operation Agreement which will encompass the full scope of their bilateral relationship, including enhanced cooperation in political matters.[7]

The Partnership and Co-operation Agreement (PCA) is thus seen as an instrument to reflect and solidify this comprehensive strategic partnership.

The PCA negotiations were regularly mentioned in subsequent joint statements of EU–China Summits, but there has been no further reference since 2009. In fact, since the launching of the negotiations with a view to upgrading the 1985 Trade and Economic Cooperation Agreement in 2007, little progress has been reported and the negotiations have been stalled since 2011 due to divergences between the mandates and expectations of the parties.[8]

Such a result is not surprising. In setting forth the objective of launching PCA negotiations, the leaders in the 9th EU-China Summit mentioned several critical issues that anchor the EU–China relations in general, and EU–China PCA negotiations in particular. These issues include, from the China side, the 'One China' policy, the arms embargo and Market Economy Status (MES), and from the EU side, human rights and China's ratification of International Covenant on Civil and Political Rights (ICCPR), China's accession to the Rome Statute and the International Criminal Court, Climate Change, complete and faithful implementation of China's WTO commitments and the establishment of a transparent, open and predictable regulatory environment.

Indeed, most of these issues continue to plague both the EU and China and prevent PCA negotiations from breaking through the deadlock. This chapter traces the evolution of the EU–China strategic partnership, explores the role of a PCA in this partnership, and investigates major challenges facing the two parties for its successful conclusion. This chapter will focus on two dimensions of the proposed partnership: political and security; trade and economy. In the context of the political and security dimension, this chapter addresses the troubling relationship between sovereignty and human rights and the EU's call for China's collaboration in building a rules-based international order and advancing effective multilateralism. In the trade and economic dimension, this chapter examines China's pursuit of MES and the EU's demand for a transparent, open and predicable regulatory environment in China. This chapter then points to the difficulties in

[6] 9th EU–China Summit Joint Statement, Helsinki 9 September 2006, para 2.
[7] ibid, para 4.
[8] Overview of FTA and other Trade Negotiations, update in July 2019, http://trade.ec.europa.eu/doclib/docs/2006/december/tradoc_118238.pdf, accessed 1 July 2019. See also Julien Chaisse, China-European Union Investment Relationships-- Towards a New Leadership in Global Investment Governance? (London: Edward Elgar, 2018) 328 p.

issue linkages or human rights prioritisation in the PCA negotiations, and probes whether a comprehensive investment agreement (CAI) constitutes a satisfactory alternative to the PCA.

II. What does EU–China Strategic Partnership Signify?

'Strategic partnership' is not clearly defined in EU treaties or policy instruments, but the European Parliament suggests that use of the term 'strategic partnership' 'represents the EU's response to an increasingly interdependent world, since cooperation with key powers is necessary to ensure that the EU's values and interests are preserved at the global level'.[9] Therefore, a strategic partnership between the EU and third countries entails two dimensions: inter se relations between the EU and its strategic partners and their cooperative efforts in managing international affairs and shaping global governance. The institutionalisation of the EU strategic partnership can be traced back to the 2003 ESS where the EU identified a list of strategic partner countries, and the list has gradually expanded.

For China, strategic partnership was originally an instrument to regulate its relations with great powers, but gradually expand to cover a wide range of countries with various weight in international relations.[10] There is no clear-cut definition of strategic partnership and the criteria for the partner countries remain vague in view of the diversity of the partner countries. Addressing the EU–China comprehensive strategic partnership, during a visit to Brussels in 2004, the former Premier Wen Jiabao stated:

> By 'comprehensive', it means that the cooperation should be all-dimensional, wide-ranging and multi-layered. It covers economic, scientific, technological, political and cultural fields, contains both bilateral and multilateral levels, and is conducted by both governments and non-governmental groups. By 'strategic', it means that the cooperation should be long-term and stable, bearing on the larger picture of China–EU relations. It transcends the differences in ideology and social system and is not subjected to the impacts of individual events that occur from time to time. By 'partnership', it means that the cooperation should be equal-footed, mutually beneficial and win-win. The two sides should base themselves on mutual respect and mutual trust, endeavour to expand converging interests and seek common ground on the major issues while shelving differences on the minor ones.[11]

[9] Library of European Parliament, 'EU Strategic Partnerships with Third Countries' *Library Briefing,120354REV1* (2012) 1.

[10] Zhongping Feng and Jing Huang, 'China's Strategic Partnership Diplomacy' (27 June 2014). ESPO Working Paper No 8. Available at SSRN: https://ssrn.com/abstract=2459948, 10–11.

[11] Vigorously Promoting Comprehensive Strategic Partnership Between China and the European Union, Speech by HE Wen Jiabao at the China-EU Investment and Trade Forum, Brussels, 6 May 2004, www.chinamission.be/eng/zt/t101949.htm, accessed 1 May 2019.

Therefore, in China's view, a strategic partnership between the EU and China refers to pan-dimensional, wide-ranging and multi-layered, long-term cooperation based on equal footing.

Since the establishment of EU–China strategic partnership in 2003, EU–China relations have made significant progress and the cooperation has extended to various areas. Nonetheless, doubts and suspicions about such a partnership persist. In 2004, David Shambaugh, a US expert on China, wrote that, unlike Sino – American relations, the EU and China have no military competition in the Asia Pacific and the EU strictly adheres to 'One China' policy and is under no obligation to safeguard Taiwan. The EU–China relations constitute an emergent axis in the multipolar world, by virtue of which they can constrain American power and hegemony in particular under the Bush Administration in the post-September 11 era. Shambaugh believed that EU–China strategic partnership would continue to grow steadily.[12] However, other scholars seem not so confident regarding the future of the EU–China strategic partnership.

In 2014, Jing Men, the EU–China Chair in College of Europe, Bruges, rhetorically posed the question: is there a strategic partnership between the EU and China? Whereas she answered in the affirmative with some reservation in her conclusion, she noted the different nature of the two powers: the EU being liberal power and China realist power. She concluded by saying that 'without a common political vision and normative understanding, it is premature to define the partnership as "strategic"'.[13] Similarly, Richard Maher noted in 2016 the clashes on political values, geopolitical interests and priorities, and vision of world order between the EU and China have prevented the forge of meaningful strategic partnership and will continue to complicate the bilateral relationship. Maher further cautioned China's fever for the EU has gradually faded away as China sees the EU weak and politically divided.[14]

Ayse Kaya, a US political scientist, argued in 2014 that the EU has a China problem, which may undermine its normative or civilian image. According to Kaya, the EU is a new type of sovereignty project, in which sovereignty is pooled. Under this new arrangement, states are expected to protect human rights within and across borders. By contrast, China endorses a traditional model sovereignty that draws the boundary between foreign and domestic issues, which include human rights. The pivotal difference between the new and traditional sovereignty lies in their views on the contemporary contestations between the 'responsibilities' and 'governance without interference'. New sovereignty links the two concepts

[12] David Shambaugh, 'China and Europe: the Emergent Axis' (2004) 103 *Current History* 243, 243–47.

[13] Jing Men, 'Is There a Strategic Partnership between the EU and China' (2014) 19 *European Foreign Affairs Review* 5, 17.

[14] Richard Maher, 'The Elusive EU-China Strategic Partnership' (2016) 93 *International Affairs* 959, 975.

and maintains that governance without inference is contingent upon the respect of human rights; by contrast, traditional sovereignty prefers the de-linkage.[15] In the same vein, Jing Men wrote in 2011 about the divergent views on sovereignty and human rights between the EU and China. According to Men, the EU holds that human rights are a universal value whereas China gives greater weight to sovereignty and collective rights.[16]

The value-based depiction of the EU–China strategic partnership is not shared by all academics. Jonathan Holslag, a Brussels-based political scientist, argued in 2014 that the EU could benefit from a strategic partnership with China but it failed to seize the opportunity. Holslag argued that with an aim to sustaining the strategic partnership, and in view of the shared strategic interests of the EU and China, an approach with more realism is needed. 'Realism will also make relations less prone to setbacks over symbolical issues, permit Europe to reap larger gains from other powers and to form a worthy alternative for the EU's defective soft power'.[17]

The challenges facing the EU and China in forging a strategic partnership are not limited to their divergent perceptions on sovereignty, political values and human rights, but extend to concrete policy practices impacting EU–China relations. As Men noted, the visit of the Dalai Lama, China's ratification of the ICCPR, the arms embargo and Taiwan issues have continuously plagued the EU–China political relations.[18] Even in the low-politics of trade and economic, the chronic trade deficit, growing economic disputes, and most importantly the EU's continuous resistance to recognising China as a market economy also trouble the EU–China strategic partnership.[19]

In addition to inter se relations clouding the EU–China strategic partnership, divergent visions of world order also lead to different approaches in managing international affairs and shaping global governance, which subsequently impact the two strategic partners' cooperative efforts in international relations. Whereas it is subject to debate whether China is a revisionist or status quo power, it is settled that China demands a greater voice and redistribution of power in international relations and global governance regimes. The EU, as a non-conventional actor in international relations, also aims to demonstrate its actorness and secure an appropriate role. From appearances, their common desire to have a greater voice and role in international relations helps to solidity the strategic partnership.

[15] Ayse Kaya, 'The EU's China Problem: A Battle over Norms' (2014) 51 *International Politics* 214, 218–19.

[16] Jing Men, 'Between Human Rights and Sovereignty – An Examination of EU-China Political Relations' (2011) 17 *European Law Journal* 534, 537–48.

[17] Jonathan Holslag, 'The Elusive Axis: Assessing the EU-China Strategic Partnership' (2016) 49 *Journal of Common Market Studies* 293, 294.

[18] Men (n 16) 537–48.

[19] Mingjiang Li, 'China-EU Relations: Strategic Partnership at a Crossroads' (2009) 7 *China: an International Journal* 227, 241–46.

A closer look nonetheless proves otherwise, as can be best illustrated by the terminology the EU and China use in articulating their views in international relations. The EU has endorsed multilateralism while China prefers multipolarity. China's vision of world order is still dominated by power politics and its advocacy of a multipolar world reflects that vision. In this multipolar world, the poles are the US, China and the EU. China views multipolarity as a way to constrain US hegemony, and recognising that the EU constitutes a pole reflects China's hedging strategy. By contrast, the EU prefers multilateralism, and terminology supportive of that vision is found in the legal texts of its founding treaties. Multilateralism signifies a rule-based international order which binds the EU and other powers, including China and the US. Under multilateralism, norms take precedence over power.[20] These parties' differing preferences with respect to multipolarity and multilateralism correspond to Men's depiction of China as a realist power and the EU as a liberal power.

Below, I will demonstrate how divergences between the EU and China over political values, trade and economic interests and vision of world order emerge as thorny issues in EU–China PCA negotiations. I will also clarify what a Partnership and Cooperation Agreement is meant to accomplish, and which type of PCA the EU and China are pursuing.

III. What is a Partnership and Cooperation Agreement and What is it for?

The EU treaties and official documents do not provide a clear-cut definition of 'partnership and cooperation agreement'.[21] As observed by EU Monitor,

> A partnership and cooperation agreements (PCA) is a legally binding agreement between the EU and third countries. It is one of three special types of international agreements. By means of a partnership and cooperation agreement the EU works to support the democratic and economic development of a country.[22]

PCAs were first widely used as an instrument to regulate the Union's relations with Russia and newly Independent states of Eastern Europe, the Southern Caucasus and Central Asia following the dissolution of the Soviet Union. 'The general principles [of PCAs] concern respect for democracy, the principles of

[20] David A Scott, 'Multipolarity, Multilateralism and Beyond … ? EU-China Understandings of the International System' (2013) 27 *International Politics* 30, 33–38.

[21] In contrast, 'association agreement' is a specific genre of EU external agreement explicitly provided in the EU founding treaties.

[22] www.eumonitor.eu/9353000/1/j9vvik7m1c3gyxp/vh7gkuhng0wh accessed 1 May 2019. According to EU Monitor, these three types of international agreements are: partnership and cooperation agreements, association agreements and trade agreements.

international law and human rights. The market economy is also an objective set out in all the PCAs'.[23] The practice of concluding PCAs with a view to regulating bilateral relations has been extended to Asian countries, including Indonesia, the Philippines and China. Sometimes, the term 'strategic partnership agreement' may be used when concluding a political agreement with strategic partners, such as Canada and Japan. As observed, one of the characteristics of EU trade diplomacy is the formal and legalist manner in which politics and economics are linked. The EU aims to use its huge market as leverage to shape or transform the political behaviours of third countries. PCAs represent the political arm, and trade agreements the economics arm, of that lever though PCAs usually also include trade and economic dimensions. Typically, the conclusion of a political agreement constitutes the prerequisite for free trade talks; nonetheless, given long process of its negotiation and ratification process, in recent practice the negotiation of political and trade agreements maybe held in parallel.[24]

The linkage between politics and economics, or even the prioritisation of human rights, may not always work in the EU's favour, especially when facing a strong counterpart, as in the case of China. Economically, it may be argued that the EU depends more on China than China does on the EU. Moreover, whereas China has indicated its interest in negotiating an FTA with the EU, the EU has responded coldly. Since launching the Global Europe strategy, the EU has adopted a position of negotiating a stand-alone bilateral investment treaty, rather than an FTA, with China, given the opportunities and challenges presented by China.[25] If the EU–China PCA has not substantial trade and economic elements, it is doubtful that China would be willing to swallow the EU's preaching on political values and human rights. Therefore, it is essential to explore which type of PCAs the EU–China PCA will resemble and whether it will cover deep trade liberalisation obligations or commitments.

The time span for the EU's PCA negotiations, starting from the late 1990s, covers almost three decades and the context and coverage of PCAs display some similarities and diversities. Some examples are archetypical of EU PCA practices: EU–Russia PCA signed in 1994, EU–Indonesia PCA in 2009, and EU–Canada Strategic Partnership Agreement in 2017. Will the EU–China PCA resemble the EU–Russia PCA, which has 102 articles, 10 annexes and two protocols with strong economic and trade dimensions? Or is the EU–China PCA to be modelled on the EU–Indonesia PCA, which contains 50 articles setting out a general and broad framework for cooperation and dialogues? Or alternatively, in view of China's and Canada's similar status of strategic partners to the EU, will the EU–China PCA be

[23] European Union, Summaries of EU Legislation, 'Partnership and Cooperation Agreements (PCAs): Russia, Eastern Europe, the Southern Caucasus and Central Asia', https://eur-lex.europa.eu/legal-content/EN/TXT/?uri=LEGISSUM%3Ar17002, retrieved 1 May 2019.

[24] Maiike Okano-Heijmans, 'Trade Diplomacy in EU-Asia Relations: Time for a Rethink' (2014) *Clingendael Report* 14.

[25] Global Europe – Competing in the World, COM (2006) 567 final, 9–10.

more like the EU–Canada SPA, which has 34 articles addressing mainly political and diplomatic issues and was concluded together with the EU–Canada Comprehensive Economic and Trade Agreement (CETA)?

In addressing this question, three factors have to be taken into consideration: the status of the EU's strategic partner, its WTO membership and parallel FTA talks. In view of the fact that China, just as Russia and Canada, is a strategic partner of the EU, one is tempted to assume that the EU–China PCA will resemble more the EU–Russia PCA or EU–Canada SPA. Both the EU and China may prefer the title of 'strategic partnership agreement', however that intuitive thought may not be warranted. It is to be remembered that the EU–Russia PCA was concluded before Russia's accession to the GATT/WTO, and therefore the EU–Russia PCA sets out for the legal framework regulating the trade between EU and Russia. In view of the fact that China acceded to the WTO in 2001, the EU–China PCA need not reproduce the work of the WTO to regulate trade and economic relations between the two sides. Therefore, the EU–China PCA might not take a form similar to the EU–Russia PCA. On the other hand, the EU–Canada SPA was concluded together with the CETA, with the SPA dealing with political and diplomatic issues and CETA trade and economic issues. In view of the fact that China's wish to enter into FTA talks has been received coldly by the EU, it seems that the pattern of parallel negotiations of two agreements (one political, one trade) will not be followed in EU–China negotiations. Thus, it is reasonable to assume that an EU–China PCA will more closely resemble the EU–Indonesia PCA than the EU–Russia PCA or EU–Canada SPA in view of the EU's position that the EU–Indonesia PCA constitutes a prerequisite stepping-stone to an EU–Indonesia FTA. This position seems to be embraced as well by the EU in the context of the EU–China PCA and potential EU–China FTA.

Nevertheless, as noted above, China has repeatedly expressed its wish to pursue FTA talks with the EU, which has consistently declined. As the EU makes it clear,

> [t]he EU is developing a new generation of modern, high standard trade agreements, and could consider broader ambitions such as a deep and comprehensive FTA with China, when the conditions – including implementation of the necessary economic reforms in China – are right.[26]

The key message here is the implementation of the necessary reforms in China and the implementation of the WTO commitments are necessary parts of those reforms. During its WTO accession negotiations, China committed to a high degree of market access. The critical issue here is China's willingness and capability to implement its WTO commitments. Therefore, the gravity of the trade and economy dimension of the EU–China PCA is to convince, and ensure, that China faithfully and effectively implements its WTO obligations. However, one may wonder what the EU may offer in exchange. Supposing that detailed commitments

[26] Joint Communication to the European Parliament and the Council, Elements for a new EU strategy on China, Brussels, 22.6.2016 JOIN(2016) 30 final, at 8.

on market accession and trade liberalisation are left to FTA negotiations in later stage, it seems that the EU has little to offer. The mismatch of mandate and expectation explains the stalemate in the PCA negotiations.

IV. The Mismatch of Mandate and Expectation in EU–China PCA Negotiations

The lack of progress in EU–China PCA negotiations is reflective of the mismatch between mandate and expectation between the two sides, which is rooted in differences in the nature of power, their visions of world order and growing conflicts in economic interests.

A. Political and Security Dimension

i. Sovereignty and Human Rights

In translating Kaya's depiction of the EU and China as units of new and traditional sovereignty into the context of PCA negotiations, one would not be surprised to find that the political and security dimension of the PCA negotiation is replete with controversies and challenges. Sovereignty and territorial integrity are sensitive issues for China and are, from time to time, claimed as core interests of China. As it jealously guards its sovereignty, China frequently accuses the EU of interfering in its domestic affairs when issues relating to Taiwan are at stake. Although the EU and its Member States have adopted and maintain a 'One China' policy, what this 'One China' policy entails is subject to dispute. While China is eager to enshrine its 'One China' policy in the legal text of the PCA, for the EU, the political wisdom of bowing to this demand is questionable.

Taiwan-related issues may take different forms in the context of EU–China PCA negotiations. On the one hand, the 'One China' policy would impact Taiwan's participation in the international conventions and organisations – the underlying structure on which the EU's pursuit of multilateralism is founded. On the other hand, Taiwan issues may constitute a hurdle to the EU's trade diplomacy, as happened in the export embargo case.

In the EU's latest policy paper on China, *Elements for a new EU strategy on China*, the EU claims that it should 'promote practical solutions regarding Taiwan's participation in international frameworks, wherever this is consistent with the EU's "One China" policy and the EU's policy objectives'.[27] Nonetheless, it is difficult to translate lip service into concrete deeds. Taiwan's current pursuit of observer status in the World Health Assembly (WHA) is a case in point.

[27] ibid, at 4.

While Article 21 of the TEU instructs the Union, in its actions on the international scene, to promote multilateral solutions to common problems and to consolidate and support human rights, in actuality the EU, with the exception of one Member State, Germany, remains reluctant to extend support for Taiwan's bid for the WHA observer status – a position which may run counter to the idea of effective multilateralism in conducting infectious diseases and the objective of upholding the right to health. In view of this, to write a controversial 'One China' policy into the legal text of the EU–China PCA may constrain the EU's policy space and undermine its normative image as it suggests that the EU yields to China's sovereignty claims out of power politics calculation in the sacrifice of multilateralism spirit.

Taiwan issues played different roles in the context of China's push to have the arms embargo lifted, which was imposed by the EU in response to the Tiananmen Square massacre in 1989. China has expressed its wish for the embargo to be lifted on various occasions and has devoted tremendous diplomatic resources to this matter. The rationale for lifting the arms embargo is that, in the context of a comprehensive strategic partnership, the EU should not lump China in with Zimbabwe and Burma/Myanmar which are also under arms embargoes. China has claimed that the imposition of an arms embargo constitutes a form of 'political discrimination'. The debates on the arms embargo against China were significantly intensified during 2004–05 and some Member States, such as France and Germany, were in favour of ending this embargo; eventually, the US intervened to exert great pressure to prevent the EU from lifting the arms embargo.[28] The EU was thus put into a difficult position in balancing its transatlantic partnership and economic interests. Ironically, the EU–China strategic partnership was originally spurred on by US unilateralism, in particular the second war against Iraq, that divided the EU. Debate on lifting the arms embargo nonetheless came to an end in 2005 with China's adoption of the Anti-Secession Act, which obliges China to force unification with Taiwan under three scenarios.[29]

In view of the sensitive issues mentioned above, Shambaugh's observation that the EU–China strategic partnership would continue smoothly to grow and strengthen owing to the fact that the EU, unlike the US, is under no obligation to sell defensive arms to Taiwan, nor to maintain peace across the Taiwan Strait, and has no conflicting security interests with China in the Asia Pacific, might not be sustainable. Taiwan issues may constitute thorny issues, particularly when

[28] See Kristin Archick and Richard F Grimmett, 'European Union's Arms Embargo on China: Implications and Options for US Policy' CRS Report for Congress, Order Code RL32870, Updated 27 May 2005; Jerker Heiiström, 'The EU Arms Embargo on China: a Swedish Perspective', Swedish Defence Research Agency (2010).

[29] Anti-Secession Act, Art 8 ('In the event that the 'Taiwan independence' secessionist forces should act under any name or by any means to cause the fact of Taiwan's secession from China, or that major incidents entailing Taiwan's secession from China should occur, or that possibilities for a peaceful reunification should be completely exhausted, the state shall employ non-peaceful means and other necessary measures to protect China's sovereignty and territorial integrity.')

sovereignty concerns are in the spotlight. Moreover, while adhering to the 'One China' policy, the EU stresses that the future of Taiwan should be resolved through peaceful means, which explains why China's adoption of the Anti-Secession Act terminated debates on lifting the arms embargo.

Also sovereignty and territorial integrity issues are not limited to Taiwan but extend to Tibetan and Chinese minority rights. The climate of the EU–China strategic partnership is, from time-to-time, clouded by visits by the Dalai Lama to European countries. For example, when the former French President Nicolas Sarkozy met with the Dalai Lama in 2008, the EU–China Summit was cancelled in retaliation.[30] Minority rights again touch upon the sensitive issues of sovereignty and human rights. According to Kaya, the EU's conception of sovereign power is contingent upon the protection of human rights. Men also wrote that the EU holds human rights as universal and unbound by territorial boundaries. The same cannot be said of China. Sovereignty and territorial integrity are core interests of China, and according to the government cannot be subject to foreign interference. This speaks to the EU's painful efforts to insert human rights and rule of law clauses into the EU–China PCA.[31]

From the perspective of the EU, first and foremost the priority in the EU–China PCA is to overcome difficulties associated with the inclusion of human rights and rule of law clauses.[32] As noted above, in the context of the external actions in international scene, Article 21 of the TEU directs the EU to consolidate and support the rule of law and human rights,[33] and a human rights clause constitutes a distinctive and important feature of EU external agreements.[34] The EU has long encouraged China to ratify the ICCPR, which it signed in 1998, and which it repeatedly states it will soon ratify. However, no substantial efforts have been devoted to this objective, and no substantial progress is anticipated in the near future. In the *Elements for a new EU strategy on China*, the EU reiterates that human rights will continue to be a core part of the EU's engagement with China and expresses its deep concerns with recent China's crackdown on defence lawyers, labour rights advocates, publishers and journalists; the EU is particular concerned about the new and worrying extraterritorial dimension of Chinese suppression.[35] In view of the consistent

[30] On the effect of meeting with the Dalai Lama on trade with China, see Andreas Fuchs and Nils-Hendrik Khann, 'Paying a Visit: The Dalai Lama Effect on International Trade' (2013) 91 *Journal of International Economics* 164.

[31] See eg, Lingliang Zen, 'A Preliminary Perspective of Negotiations of EU–China PCA: A New Bottle Carrying Old Wine or New Wine or Both?' (2009) 15 *European Law Journal* 121; Antoine Sautenet, 'The Current Status and Prospects of the "Strategic Partnership" between the EU and China: Towards the Conclusion of a Partnership and Cooperation Agreement' (2007) 13 *European Law Journal* 699.

[32] In fact, this clause also contains the objective to consolidate and promote democracy. Nonetheless, this objective is too idealistic to be included in the PCA. This chapter thus chooses not to discuss democracy clause.

[33] TEU, 21(2)(b).

[34] See Lorand Bartels, *Human Rights Conditionality in the EU's International Agreements* (Oxford, Oxford University Press, 2005).

[35] Elements for a new EU strategy on China (n 26) 4.

divergences between the EU and China on human rights and rule of law, the early conclusion of a PCA that includes human rights or rule of law clauses is unlikely.

ii. Effective Multilateralism and Rules-based International Order

The EU has been a key proponent for effective multilateralism with the United Nations at its core[36] and a rules-based international order. The EU sees China as a beneficiary from this rules-based international order and expects China to assume its responsibilities.[37] Multilateralism does not necessarily correspond to multipolarity. Whereas China wants to have a greater voice in global governance and international relations, China has not always endorsed the idea of rules-based international order. Indeed, China may prefer a power-oriented international order in view of its political, economic and military might. That said, it is clear that in the international world today, it is difficult, if not impossible, to address global issues without China on board. Therefore, the EU–China PCA will address their cooperation in international relations, which duly reflects that cooperative efforts in managing international affairs and shaping global governance constitutes a key element of the strategic partnership. Two issues are of critical importance to the EU and have already been raised in previous EU–China Summit statements: the International Criminal Court and United Nations Framework Convention on Climate Change (UNFCCC).

The adoption of the Rome Statute and the establishment of the International Criminal Court correspond to the constitutional objectives of the EU's external actions in consolidating and promoting principles of international law and fostering a rules-based international order.[38] As international criminal justice carries strong normative implications, the EU's support for the International Criminal Court reinforces its self-image as a normative power. Therefore, the EU has been a key proponent of the adoption of Rome Statute and the success of the International Criminal Court.[39] In line with this policy, accession to the Rome Statute or cooperation with International Criminal Court has been included in a number of

[36] See generally, Edith Drieskens and Louise G van Schaik (eds), *The EU and Effective Multilateralism: Internal and External Reform Practice* (Abingdon, Routledge, 2014); Katie Verlin Laatikainen and Karen E Smith (eds), *The European Union at the United Nations: Intersecting Multilateralisms* (Basingstoke, Palgrave Macmillan, 2006).

[37] Elements for a new EU strategy on China (n 26) 4.

[38] See Joris Larik, *Foreign Policy Objectives in European Constitutional Law* (Oxford, Oxford University Press, 2016).

[39] Martijn Groenleer and David Rijks, 'The European Union and the International Criminal Court-The politics of international Criminal Justice' in Knud Erik Jørgensen (ed), *The European Union and International Organizations* (Abingdon, Routledge, 2009) 167–87; Jan Wouters and Sudeshna Basu, 'The Creation of Global Criminal Justice System: The European Union and the International Criminal Court' in Cedric Ryngaert (ed), *The Effectiveness of International Criminal Justice* (Cambridge, Intersentia, 2009) 117–42; Antonis Antoniadis and Olympia Bekou, 'The European Union and the International Criminal Court: An Awkward Symbiosis in Interesting Times' (2007) 7 *International Criminal Law Review* 621, 621–56.

EU external agreements, such as the Cotonou Agreement[40] and the PCA between EU and Southeast Asian countries, including the Philippines,[41] Vietnam[42] and Indonesia.[43] In the Stabilization and Association Agreement between the EU and Balkan countries, including Montenegro[44] and Serbia,[45] and the Interim Agreement on Trade and Trade-related Matters between the European Community, of the one part, and Bosnia and Herzegovina,[46] cooperation between these third countries and International Criminal Tribunal for the former Yugoslavia constitute an essential element of the agreements, the violation of which would result in suspension of the application of the agreements.

Regarding the International Criminal Court, China has reservations on the universal jurisdiction of the Court, the inclusion of 'armed conflict not of an international character', the definition of wars of aggression as those occurring without the intervention of the UN Security Council, and the power of the ICC's prosecutor to initiate an investigation at its own initiative. Given that the PCAs between the EU and Southeast Asian countries only encourage the third countries to accede to the Rome Statute, it is expected that the EU–China PCA will provide a similar arrangement. The obstacle presented by the Rome Statute on the EU–China PCA negotiations appears rather modest.

The fight against climate change has been explicitly referred to in the Lisbon Treaty, and the EU has been a key participant in the UNFCCC and Kyoto Protocol[47] and played a significant role in the adoption of Paris Agreement. China signed the Paris Agreement and ratified it on 3 September 2016. Therefore, unlike human rights issues, climate change presents an area for the EU and China to forge a constructive partnership. Since 2005, the EU has established a climate change partnership with China.[48] On the sidelines of the G20 energy ministerial meeting in Beijing 2016, the EU and China also agreed to the EU–China Energy Roadmap to addressing climate change and energy security.[49] Since China is plagued with environment degradation and aims to upgrade its economy and transit into a low-carbon economy, and as, in fact, China has already benefited from a number

[40] Cotonou Agreement, Art 11(6).

[41] EU–Philippines PCA, Art 7.

[42] EU–Vietnam PCA, Art 11(4).

[43] EU–Indonesia PCA, Art 4(3).

[44] EU–Montenegro SAA, Art 2.

[45] EU–Serbia SAA, Art 2.

[46] Interim Agreement on Trade and Trade-related Matters between the European Community, of the one part, and Bosnia and Herzegovina, on the other part, Art 1.

[47] See eg, John Vogler and Charlotte Bretherton, 'The European Union as a Protagonist to the United States on Climate Change' (2006) 7 *International Studies Perspectives* 1; Sebastian Oberthür and Claire Roche Kelly, 'EU Leadership in International Climate Policy: Achievements and Challenges' (2008) 43 *The International Spectator: Italian Journal of International Affairs* 35.

[48] EU and China Partnership on Climate Change, MEMO/05/298, Brussels (2005), https://ec.europa.eu/clima/sites/clima/files/international/cooperation/china/docs/joint_declaration_ch_eu_en.pdf, accessed 1 May 2009.

[49] EU–China Roadmap on energy cooperation (2016–2020), https://ec.europa.eu/energy/sites/ener/files/documents/FINAL_EU_CHINA_ENERGY_ROADMAP_EN.pdf, accessed 1 May 2019.

of cooperation projects under the Clean Development Mechanism, the EU and China have an opportunity to develop positive synergy in the context of climate change.

With the retreat of Trump Administration from efforts to combat climate change and the US withdrawal from the Paris Agreement, the EU looks to China for climate change leadership. In the 2017 June EU–China Summit, climate change emerged as the main theme. As the President of the European Council Donald Tusk remarked in the joint press conference:

> Today, we are stepping up our cooperation on climate change with China. Which means that today, China and Europe have demonstrated solidarity with future generations and responsibility for the whole planet. We are convinced that yesterday's decision by the United States to leave the Paris Agreement is a big mistake, bigger than not ratifying the Kyoto Protocol, because Paris is fairer. But the fight against climate change, and all the research, innovation and technological progress it will bring, will continue, with or without the US.[50]

This statement signifies the EU's frustration about the US withdrawal from the Paris Agreement and the EU's expectation that China can play a bigger role in climate change action. A stronger partnership on climate change action between the EU and China may spill-over to other fields. In fact, the Trump Administration's preference for unilateral action and bilateralism has pushed the EU toward striking partnerships with third countries to safeguard multilateralism. This is not limited to climate change action but extends to the liberal international economic order underpinned by the multilateral trading system and the fight against protectionism, to which now I will turn.

B. Trade and Investment Dimension

i. Protectionism and Multilateral Trading System

The economic dimension of the EU–China strategic partnership is characterised by their economic interdependence and huge trade volumes. The political economy of this strategic partnership is rather ambivalent. On the one hand, with the preference of the Trump Administration for bilateralism and sometimes protectionism, and its increasing attacks on the WTO and its Appellate Body,[51] China

[50] Remarks by President Donald Tusk after the EU-China Summit in Brussels, 2 June 2017, www.consilium.europa.eu/en/press/press-releases/2017/06/02/tusk-remarks-eu-china-summit-june/, accessed 1 May 2019.

[51] See, eg the USTR Robert Lighthizer's statement in Centre of Strategic and International Studies on 19 September 2017. According to Lighthizer, 'the United States sees numerous examples where the dispute-settlement process over the years has really diminished what we bargained for or imposed obligations that we do not believe we agreed to. There have been a lot of cases in the dumping and countervailing-duty, the trade-remedies laws, where, in my opinion, the decisions are really indefensible, and even a lot of people who have much more free-trade orientation who read these question(s).'

has become an important ally for the EU as it seeks to ensure the principles and spirit of free trade and to safeguard the multilateralism. On the other hand, China's state capitalism and continuous intervention in markets through subsidies and state-owned enterprises (SOEs) and other regulatory measures have led the EU, in conjunction with the US and Japan, to issue a statement implicitly criticising China at the WTO ministerial conference in Buenos Aires in 2017.[52] The difficulty is that neither the US under the Trump administration, nor China, has really endorsed free trade and sought to abide by WTO rules. The EU is, in fact, trapped in a dilemma between the souring traditional transatlantic partnership with the US and the uneasy new strategic partnership with China. The question of whether or not to grant China MES provides a case in point.

ii. Market Economic Status

With regards to MES, China has made tremendous efforts through diplomatic channels to persuade the EU to grant China MES. To date, those efforts have been fruitless. In 2016, the European Parliament adopted a resolution, calling for the use of non-standard methodologies in anti-dumping and anti-subsidy investigations in accordance with, and giving full effects to, Paragraph 15 of China's Accession Protocol until China meets all five EU criteria for qualifying as a market economy.[53] Out of frustration and anger, China, on the second day after the expiry of the 15 years period for the regulation of price comparison in anti-dumping investigations as provided in Paragraph 15 of China's Accession Protocol, brought a complaint against the EU, and the US, in the WTO.

The relevant part of Paragraph 15 of China's Accession Protocol reads as follows:

> (ii) The importing WTO Member may use a methodology that is not based on a strict comparison with domestic prices or costs in China if the producers under investigation cannot clearly show that market economy conditions prevail in the industry producing the like product with regard to manufacture, production and sale of that product.

Further, according to subparagraph (d) of Paragraph 15, 'the provisions of subparagraph (a)(ii) shall expire 15 years after the date of accession'. A different interpretation of Paragraph 15 (a)(ii) read in conjunction with Paragraph 15(d) leads to different positions on whether China should be automatically granted MES upon the expiry of the 15 year transition period. Apparently, China maintains so, but the EU and the US find otherwise. Regarding the MES issue, the EU is

www.csis.org/analysis/us-trade-policy-priorities-robert-lighthizer-united-states-trade-representative, accessed 1 May 2019.

[52] Taos Turner, 'EU and Japan Join US in Criticizing China at WTO Summit', *Financial Times* (2017), www.wsj.com/articles/eu-and-japan-join-u-s-in-criticizing-china-at-wto-summit-1513122372, accessed 1 May 2019.

[53] European Parliament resolution of 12 May 2016 on China's market economy status (2016/2667(RSP)), para 6.

faced with internal and external challenges. Internally, Member States are divided. Nordic countries and the UK are in favour of granting China MES in exchange of preferential market access to China or strategic/diplomatic purchase from China. Mediterranean countries, in particular Italy, are against the idea to grant China MES due to the overlapping of industrial structure. Central and Eastern European countries are ambiguous due to their complicated political and diplomatic ties with China and weak capacity to accommodate if retaliation is imposed by China. Externally, if the EU chooses to unilaterally recognise China as an MES, it may be rewarded by China in economic terms, but risk undermining the transatlantic partnership with the US in diplomatic and strategic terms. The issue is even thornier under the Trump Administration, which seems not to hold dear the transatlantic partnership.

The EU finally decided to side with the US on the issue of MES. In fact, the EU turned out to be the main target in China's pursuit of MES through litigation. Whereas China sent its request for consultation under the Understanding on Rules and Procedures Governing the Settlement of Disputes (DSU) with the US and the EU on the same day, the speed of these two proceedings differ. *US–Measures Related to Price Comparison Methodologies*[54] is still at the consultation phase as China on 3 November 2017 requested additional consultation with the US,[55] which the EU and other countries requested to join. In contrast, *EU–Measures Related to Price Comparison Methodologies*[56] has entered the panel phase, with the US and other countries intervening as third parties.[57] The US sided with the EU and argued against China automatically obtaining MES. It is interesting to note that the EU, which aims to forge a stronger strategic partnership, came under direct fire while the US, whose hegemony is challenged by China's rise, only backed the EU's position. This litigation thus illustrates the difficulty for the EU to navigate between EU–China strategic partnership and EU–US transatlantic partnership.

iii. Transparent, Open and Predictable Regulatory Environment

Good governance/good administration in economic and trade aspects has been a key objective since China's accession to the WTO. The aim to establish a transparent, open and predictable regulatory environment is not a single legal obligation, but an attempt to transform the Chinese economy into one that is more in line with the western economic and development path, including liberalisation, rule of law, property rights. To this end, China's accession protocol is specially designed to deviate from standardised form and to contain a number

[54] WT/DS515.

[55] www.wto.org/english/tratop_e/dispu_e/cases_e/ds515_e.htm, accessed 1 May 2019.

[56] WT/DS516.

[57] Third Party Submission of the United States of America, *EU–Measures Related to Price Comparison Methodologies* (DS516), https://ustr.gov/sites/default/files/enforcement/DS/US.3d.Pty.Su.pdf, accessed 1 May 2019.

of substantial obligations, covering transparency, uniform administration of laws and regulations, and impartial and independent judicial review. These obligations are intended to contribute to the establishment of transparent, open and predictable regulatory environment.

While there has been substantial progress in China's trade regulatory regime, other trade nations still find it unsatisfactory. As the European Commission notes, '[l]egal reform and strengthening the rule of law in China are preconditions for the overall success of China's reforms. A transparent and impartial legal system is an essential part of the institutional bedrock for a market-based economy'.[58] Regulatory cooperation through technical assistance or capacity building can play an important role in contributing to the establishment of transparent, open and predictable regulatory environment in China. An EU–China PCA could facilitate and enhance regulatory cooperation or technical assistance processes. The major part of the trade and economic arm of the EU–China PCA will thus be regulatory cooperation in trade and economic matters, which have been, to varying degree, covered by sectoral agreements. As the current position of the EU is to leave these sectoral agreements intact, the added value of an EU–China PCA seems limited. Moreover, the WTO accession was originally seen as an instrument to contribute to good economic governance in China, and has already proven to fail to meet the expectations of existent WTO members; what difference will regulatory cooperation under the EU–China PCA framework make for the establishment of transparent, open and predictable regulatory environment if China does not see it as feasible and beneficial? The critical issue here is that the western model of good governance and market economy has become less and less attractive, and China is determined to, and has demonstrated its capacity to, shape a different model of development path.

C. Issue Linkage and Human Rights Prioritisation

The EU–China PCA is a manifestation of the uneasy EU–China strategic partnership. The EU emphasises the political and diplomatic dimension of the PCA while China wants to inject more trade and economic elements. As the EU–China PCA, unlike the EU–Russia PCA, has not sufficient elements of trade and economic issues, and unlike the EU–Japan or EU–Canada SPAs, its negotiations are not held in parallel to a trade agreement, without the possibility of issue linkage, the EU has little leverage to exchange China's acceptance of political issues, such as a human rights clause. Moreover, the hands of the European Commission are tied. As the European Parliament made clear in its resolution, the EU cannot grant China MES unless the five criteria are met. China has long adopted a position that the prerequisite to enter into FTA or economic partnership agreements talks with

[58] Elements for a new EU strategy on China (n 26) 7–8.

China is to recognise China's MES. It is thus highly unlikely that the two sides will conclude a PCA without the EU's recognition of China as an MES. Moreover, the PCA negotiations differ significantly from WTO accession negotiations in that in the latter negotiations, the existent WTO Members have de facto veto power and China has no choice but to swallow the bitter terms existent Members demanded. As much as the EU may want to insert a human rights clause into the legal text of the EU–China PCA to reinforce its image of normative power, it simply does not have an upper hand vis-à-vis China in the negotiation processes. By virtue of its economic growth in the past decades and its increasing influence in international relations, the EU is more dependent on China than China is on the EU, in economic, political and strategic terms. The discrepancy between expectation and mandate, and shift in global power explain the deadlock in the EU–China PCA negotiations.

V. Is a Comprehensive Agreement on Investment an Alternative?

Due to the stagnation of EU–China PCA negotiations and the EU's hesitation to enter into FTA talks with China, the two sides launched negotiations on Comprehensive Agreement on Investment (CAI) as an alternative to advance and deepen their trade and economic ties at the 15th EU–China Summit in February 2012. The EU's pursuit of a CAI with China is in line with its Global Europe strategy. In 2013, the European Commission requested, and was granted, a negotiating mandate for CAI negotiations. The launch of the CAI negotiations was announced at the 16th EU–China Summit and the first round of talks was held in January 2014.

It is not entirely clear whether the turn of a CAI as an alternative for the PCA is a good strategy as the nature and scope of these two agreements differ. To begin with, a PCA aims to lay down a solid legal foundation for the EU–China strategic partnership and in so doing upgrade the partnership. Therefore, the PCA has great political, diplomatic and strategic implications. By contrast, if the CAI focuses narrowly on investment liberalisation and investment protection with a view to its earlier conclusion, it is doubtful whether the CAI has the sufficient capacity underpinning the strategic partnership. Alternatively, if the CAI has a greater ambition to move beyond traditional investment treaty and become a comprehensive agreement as its name suggests, similar obstacles troubling the PCA negotiation will inevitably impact the CAI negotiations. In fact, in its recommendation for a Council Decision authorising the CAI negotiations, the European Commission complained about 'the lack of an open, predictable and secure environment' in China.[59] The European Parliament in 2013 adopted

[59] COM (2013) 297, final, at 3.

a resolution on EU–China CAI emphasising the importance of sustainable and inclusive development.[60] The European Parliament further stressed that 'investment agreements concluded by the EU must not be in contradiction with the fundamental values that the EU wishes to promote through its external policies'.[61] In view of the critical importance of SOEs in Chinese economy, the European Commission also presented a draft chapter on SOEs.[62]

In view of the above, it is doubtful whether the two sides can completely avoid a human rights clause or sustainable environment clause in the CAI, if the European Parliament stands firmly on its position and threatens to veto the deal. In the context of the EU–China PCA negotiations, one of the key objectives is to establish a transparent, open and predicable regulatory regime through good governance/good administration, similar regulatory demand is present in the context of CAI negotiations. As can be seen in the statement of the European Commission's proposal for Council Decision, one of the priorities of the CAI negotiations is to ensure a transparent, open and predicable investment regulatory regime in China. In addition, the MES saga may be lingering in the CAI negotiations, taking the form of the SOE issue though the scope of SOE issue may be more limited and its nature less politicised. Therefore, whereas the CAI deals with narrow scope and specific issues, on the one hand, it cannot serve as the legal foundation to sustain the EU–China strategic partnership; on the other hand, it cannot sidestep all the challenges facing the PCA without addressing them. An EU–China CAI is thus not a sufficient and satisfactory alternative for the EU–China PCA.

VI. Conclusion

This chapter traced the evolution of the EU–China strategic partnership since its inception in 2007, examined the efforts to solidify this strategic partnership through a new PCA, identified the obstacles preventing the successful conclusion of this PCA and reflected whether an alternative CAI negotiation may sidestep the difficulties and help to underpin the strategic partnership. This chapter argued that the EU–China strategic partnership represents the two powers' efforts to engage with other major powers in the international relations and shape the course of global affairs. The divergences of the EU and China on their self perception, the hierarchy between sovereignty and human rights and on their visions on world

[60] European Parliament Resolution, 2013/2674(RSP), para 22.

[61] European Parliament Resolution, 2013/2674(RSP), para 23.

[62] European Commission, EU–China Investment Agreement: Report of the 15th Round of negotiations Beijing – 9 to 12 October 2017, http://trade.ec.europa.eu/doclib/docs/2017/october/tradoc_156353.pdf, accessed 1 May 2019. See also Julien Chaisse 'Demystifying Public Security Exception and Limitations on Capital Movement-- Hard Law, Soft Law and Sovereign Investments in the EU Internal Market' (2015) 37(2) *University of Pennsylvania Journal of International Law* 583–646.

order, have introduced various challenges to this strategic partnership. The stalemate of the EU–China PCA negotiations is reflective of the contradictory nature of this strategic partnership, which is manifested in the concrete subject-matters on the negotiation table.

The challenges troubling the EU and China relate to inter se EU–China relations, such as China's MES, economic reform and the establishment of transparent, open and predicable regulatory environment therein, the EU's arm embargo and 'One China' policy. The challenge also relate to how the EU and China should cooperate to shape the form and substance of global governance, such as China's ratification of the ICCPR and accession to the Rome Statute and how to combat climate change in UNFCCC. As far as the PCA is concerned, the EU emphasises the political and strategic dimension whereas China expects more substantial trade and economic elements. Due to the mismatch of mandate and expectation, the EU and China decided to pursue for CAI as an alternative for the PCA. The same challenges facing the PCA negotiations will plague the CAI negotiators as well if the human rights and sustainable development clauses as demanded by the European Parliament are written into the legal text of the CAI. Moreover, the CAI cannot achieve the objective for upgrading the EU–China relations and sustain the EU–China strategic partnership.

14

Legalisation of International Economic Relations: Is Asia Unique?

SHINTARO HAMANAKA

I. Introduction

It is not easy to conduct a theoretically informed comparative study of de jure economic integration, namely, economic integration in terms institutional development. Therefore, we tend to have a simplistic argument that economic relations in Europe are more institutionalised or legalised than those in Asia, which has adopted an 'informal' approach, without further elaboration. As a result, Asian scholars and policy makers are often preoccupied to learn lessons from Europe and to contemplate what Asia should do to achieve a comparable level of institutionalisation or legalisation as Europe. Alternatively, Asian elites simply argue that Asia is very different from Europe and it should pursue its own way of regionalism without having careful reference to integration efforts in other regions. In essence, there is a lack of real comparative study of de jure economic integration across regions.

One of the reasons for the lack of serious attempts at comparative study are the limited scholarly interactions between international economic lawyers and international relations experts.[1] International economic lawyers tend to focus on the interpretation of rules on a case by case basis, without too much generalisation, such as a European or Asian way of setting international rules. International relations theorists, in contrast, are preoccupied in identifying the causes of institutionalisation (conditions under which international relations are institutionalised), without paying great attention to differences in institutional and/or legal design. In addition, area study experts (eg European studies experts in Asia) who are interested in comparative regionalism studies seem to keep some distance from disciplinary studies such as laws and international relations, which has resulted in another knowledge gap, the one between area studies and disciplinary studies.

[1] Anne-Marie Slaughter Burley, 'International Law and International Relations Theory: A Dual Agenda' (1993) 87(2) *American Journal of International Law* 205–39.

However, several important theoretical works that look into the legal aspects of institutions have been conducted by international relations theorists since 2000. One area of research that achieved remarkable theoretical development is 'legalisation of institutions'. While earlier studies do not clearly distinguish the difference between the two terms (institutionalisation and legalisation), and often use them interchangeably, Abbott and others define legalisation as a particular form of institutionalisation characterised by three components: obligation, precision and delegation.[2] International relations experts are now studying specific questions regarding legalisation of institutions, such as the impact of flexible languages and the form of delegation of power.[3]

This chapter asks a very simple but important question: is Asia unique in terms of legalisation of economic relations? I try to answer this question by reviewing the legalisation of Association of Southeast Asian Nations (ASEAN) trade liberalisation. The chapter mainly discusses the liberalisation of goods trade and dispute settlement mechanisms, but it also touches upon services trade liberalisation in ASEAN.[4] While past influential studies argue that international relations in Asia are less legalised, implying that rules are imprecise and non-binding and Asian countries are reluctant to delegate power, such an observation needs careful re-examination, given the number of economic agreements signed in Asia since the early 2000s.[5] We should also not rule out the possibility that Asia has a distinct approach to legalisation, different from Europe or elsewhere. Moreover, it is important to ask which aspects of legalisation (precision, bindingness and

[2] Kenneth Abbott and others, 'The Concept of Legalization' (2000) 54 (3) *International Organization* 401–19.

[3] Linos and Pegram argue that the impact of flexible languages in a treaty often have unexpected impacts on state behaviours. When an agreement specifies some tasks firmly and provisions on other expected tasks include flexible languages, governments may respond strategically redirecting efforts towards firmly specified tasks. Katerina Linos and Tom Pegram. 'The Language of Compromise in International Agreements' (2016) 70(3) *International Organization* 587–621; Duina argues that delegation of power takes a different form between FTAs among civil law countries and those among common law countries. The former prefer a permanent court to solve dispute, while the latter prefer an ad hoc dispute settlement mechanism. Francesco Duina, 'Making Sense of the Legal and Judicial Architectures of Regional Trade Agreements Worldwide' (2016) 10(4) *Regulation & Governance* 368–83.

[4] Investment is another important area where international economic relations are legalised. However, we will not discuss investment in this chapter because legalisation of investment relations deeply involve private entities, such as investor-state dispute, which makes the nature of delegation of power very different from the case of trade. For the legalisation of international investment relations, see Jeswald W Salacuse, 'The Treatification of International Investment Law' (2007) 13 *Law and Business Review of the Americas* 155–66.

[5] Interestingly, Kahler argues that economic cooperation is one of the areas that achieves a relatively high level of legalisation in Asia, unlike security. Note, however, that many international economic lawyers are of the view that economic cooperation in Asia is poorly legalised, despite the number of FTAs. See Paul J Davidson, 'The Asean Way and the Role of Law in Asean Economic Cooperation' (2004) 8 *Singapore Year Book of International Law* 165–76 and Michael Ewing-Chow, 'Culture Club or Chameleon: Should ASEAN Adopt Legalization for Economic Integration' (2008) 12 *Singapore Year Book of International Law* 225–38. Miles Kahler, 'Legalization as Strategy: The Asia-Pacific Case' (2000) 54(3) *International Organization* 549–71.

delegation) have been most developed in Asia, because there is a possibility that Asian institutions are legalised in terms of one or two aspects of legalisation, but not all.

The next section reviews the development of international relations theories on institutions and explains the studies on legalisation of institutions in detail. Section III discusses ASEAN countries' attitudes towards precision and bindingness in developing international rules or commitments. Section IV discusses the third aspect of legalisation, namely, the delegation of power. In addition to the arrangement of delegating power, it discusses the actual exercise of delegated power. The final section concludes, and attempts to answer the question whether Asia is unique.

II. Review of Theories: From Regime to Legalised Institution

There was a rise of regionalism in the 1960s, which was triggered by the launch of the European Commission in 1957.[6] Naturally, scholars started to analyse the interesting development of regionalism and some comparative analysis was conducted. The focus then was *organisation*, which is an interstate association with some physical body such as permanent secretariat. In fact, Nye states that 'regionalism in the descriptive sense is the formation of interstate associations or groupings on the basis of regions; and in the doctrinal sense, the advocacy of such formations'.[7] Interestingly, one of the leading journals of international relations has the title of *International Organization*, which was launched in 1947.

International relations scholars started to think that the focus of analysis was too narrow if they stuck to the concept of organisations. Krasner started to use the term regime, which means 'sets of implicit or explicit principles, norms, rules, and decision-making procedures around which actors' expectations converge in a given area of international relations'.[8] The scope was widened, to capture various mechanisms that affect state behaviours, going beyond written rules and formal organisations. Moreover, an emphasis was placed on regimes, which are the accumulation of or networks of various mechanisms, such as the security regime and human rights regime.[9] However, conducting sound empirical analysis using the concept of regime was often very difficult because of its broad scope.[10]

[6] Edward D Mansfield and Helen V Milner. 'The New Wave of Regionalism' (1999) 53(3) *International Organization* 589–627.

[7] Joseph S Nye, *International Regionalism* (Boston MA, Little, Brown and Co, 1968).

[8] Stephen D Krasner, 'Structural Causes and Regime Consequences: Regimes as Intervening Variables' (1982) 36(2) *International Organization* 185–205.

[9] Robert Jervis, 'Security Regimes' (1982) 36(2) *International Organization* 357–78; Jack Donnelly, 'International Human Rights: A Regime Analysis' (1986) 40(3) *International Organization* 599–642.

[10] Stephan Haggard and Beth A Simmons, 'Theories of International Regimes' (1987) 41(3) *International Organization* 491–517.

After this, the literature developed in two ways. A first group of scholars conducted analysis on international norms. While norms are included in the concept of regime because they affect state behaviours, their treatment was marginal in empirical studies because positive analysis of norms is difficult – norms are often unwritten. Finnemore and Toope, who belong to this group of scholars, heavily criticise legalisation literature (the second half of this section) that intends to contribute to 'positive' empirical studies, on the grounds that the concept of legalisation is vast and summarising it into a limited number of 'variables' misses the point.[11]

What is interesting is that literature on regional institutions that emphasises the role of norms has developed in the context of Asian regionalism. This is particularly evident in the study of ASEAN, whose institutionalisation started more than half a century ago. For example, Acharya called the institutionalisation of cooperation in Southeast Asia as the 'ASEAN' way.[12] It is very interesting to note that several key words to describe the ASEAN way use somewhat contradictory terms. 'Flexible consensus' means that decision making is based on consensus, which does not necessarily require the consent of all parties. Proponents of the ASEAN way distinguish consensus and unanimity. Consultations to reach flexible consensus are held at 'informal official' meetings. Such a meeting is not an unofficial meeting. What is agreed as a result of such consultations becomes a 'non-binding commitment'. Countries need to implement commitments, but non-fulfilment does not lead to punishment. Above all, the overarching attitude of ASEAN negotiations can be said to be 'agree to disagree'.[13]

Other scholars return to the analysis of organisations. The paper by Abbott and Snidal that tackles the question 'why states act through *formal* international organizations' (emphasis added) is one of the illustrative examples.[14] It is important to note that theorists start to make a conscious effort to develop concepts that are useful for empirical studies. So-called rational institutional design projects made a very important contribution in this regard.[15] They argue that institutions have five key features (membership rules, scope of issues covered, centralisation

[11] Martha Finnemore and Stephen J Toope, 'Alternatives to "Legalization": Richer Views of Law and Politics' (2001) 55(3) *International Organization* 743–58.

[12] Amitav Acharya, 'Ideas, Identity, and Institution-building: From the "ASEAN way" to the "Asia-Pacific way"?' (1997) 10(3) *The Pacific Review* 319–46. See also Debashis Chakraborty, Julien Chaisse and Xu Qian, Is It Finally Time for India's Free Trade Agreements? The ASEAN "Present" and the RCEP "Future" (2019) 9(2) *Asian Journal of International Law* 359–391.

[13] Gonzalo Villalta Puig and Lee Tsun Tat, 'Problems with the ASEAN Free Trade Area Dispute Settlement Mechanism and Solutions for the ASEAN Economic Community' (2015) 49(2) *Journal of World Trade* 277–308.

[14] Kenneth Abbott and Duncan Snidal, 'Hard and Soft Law in International Governance' (2000) 54(3) *International Organization* 421–56. See also Julien Chaisse and Xueliang Ji '"Soft Law" in International Law-Making: How Soft International Taxation Law is Reshaping International Economic Governance' (2018) 13(2) *Asian Journal of WTO Law and Health Policy* 463–509.

[15] Barbara Koremenos and others, 'The Rational Design of International Institutions' (2001) 55(4) *International Organization* 761–99.

of tasks, rules for controlling the institution and flexibility of arrangements), from which angle sound empirical studies, including comparative studies, of international institutions can be conducted.

It was in this context that the concept of legalisation of institutions was developed by Abbott and others.[16] Legalisation is a particular set of characteristics that institutions may possess: obligations, precision and delegation. Obligation means that states or other actors are legally bound by a rule or commitment in the sense that their behaviour thereunder is subject to scrutiny under the general rules, procedures and discourse of international laws. Precision means that rules unambiguously define the conduct they require, authorise or proscribe. Delegation means that third parties have been granted authority to implement, interpret and apply the rules; to resolve disputes. While there has been a criticism that legalisation is only one aspect of institutionalisation, ignoring other important institutional features, there seems to be a wide consensus that the concept is useful for empirical studies.[17]

Whether rules or commitments are hard or soft has been one of the principal concerns among scholars studying international relations. When they satisfy the three conditions of legalisation (obligation, precision and delegation), such is hard law or highly legalised institutions. When one or more aspects of legalisation are insubstantial, such can be called soft law. There would be an extreme argument by neo-realists that even precise and binding rules do have little impact on states' behaviour. However, for many, when obligations are binding and precise, they are likely to have a large influence on state behaviours. In other words, there is an assumption that 'the harder, the better', regarding international rules. Many arguments that support the value of soft law actually take it for granted that hard law is the very best solution, with soft law being the second best. Because agreeing upon hard legalisation is difficult due to sovereignty cost, states compromise and accept soft legalisation, with some actors holding an expectation that institutions would be more legalised in future. Probably, the only factor that would make soft legalisations superior to hard ones is 'uncertainty'.[18] Because what will happen in the future is uncertain, the soft approach that has an ambiguous and broad scope is better at governing state behaviours. Institutions or rules that are too hard tend to be broken down or outdated easily when something unexpected happens.

Kahler examines Asian institutions such as ASEAN and Asia-Pacific Economic Cooperation (APEC), using the concept of legalisation developed by Abbott and others.[19] He convincingly concludes that Asian institutions are less legalised from

[16] Abbott and others (n 2).

[17] Finnemore and Toope (n 11); Judith Goldstein and others, 'Response to Finnemore and Toope' (2001) 55(3) *International Organization* 759–60.

[18] Some international economic lawyers are critical to soft laws; proliferation of soft laws might destabilise the international system (P Weil, 'Towards Relative Normativity in International Law' (1983) 77(3) *The American Journal of International Law* 413–42). Abbott and others (n 2).

[19] Abbott and others (n 2).

the angle of all three aspects, and asks why this is the case. He carefully examined two possibilities: legal culture in Asia and authoritarian governments. He argued that Asia's uniform rejection of legalisation should have been persistent, if those are the reasons. In reality, however, he found that Asia's attitude towards legalisation is mixed, which implies that those constant factors do not explain why Asia often, but not always, prefers a low level of legalisation. In addition, regarding legal culture, he rejects such a possibility on the grounds that Asian states adopt a legalisation approach in developing *domestic* legal institutions. Then, he argued that legalised institutions are a means to other ends and Asian countries adopt legalisation only when that serves their goal, though an important question of when Asia accepts legalisation goes unanswered.

The following sections discuss whether there is an Asian way of legalisations of international economic relations and whether Asia has a distinctive approach to legalisation of institutions. First, we will analyse precision and bindingness of rules. There may be a trade-off between the two aspects of legalisation. Then, we will analyse the delegation of power. We will also discuss the exercise of delegated power, which is different from the delegation of power per se.

III. Priority on Precision over Bindingness: 'Asian' Rules?

Asian countries including ASEAN Members prefer adopting declarations or political statements. By looking at the website of ASEAN, one can find that it is full of declarations and political statements. Declarations and political statements are usually non-binding and imprecise – they are hardly hard law. Another interesting phenomenon is that ASEAN likes to sign framework agreements, which may or may not be followed by the signing of detailed agreements. ASEAN's project on trade liberalisation starts with the signing of the Framework Agreement for Enhancing ASEAN Economic Cooperation signed on 28 January 1992. Service liberalisation projects are also conducted under the ASEAN Framework Agreement on Services (AFAS), signed in 1995. The Framework Agreement can be said to be a first step into the legalisation of international relations, because the signing of framework agreements is a manifestation of Members' interests in developing legalised institutions.

When economic liberalisation commitments are legalised, ideally, rules or commitments should be both precise and binding. But when precise 'and' binding rules are too much, one of them should be prioritised. What is the case of ASEAN? It seems that Asia and ASEAN start to have very precise rules with regard to economic liberalisation commitments. Trade liberalisation of the ASEAN Free Trade Area (AFTA) is precise enough; it is very clear that by when and to what degree tariff should be reduced for each specific tariff line. ASEAN's liberalisation of services trade is also precise enough. The schedules of service liberalisation commitments show the minimum level of liberalisation that Members shall maintain in future. It is clear which sector and which mode of service supply are subject to which regulations.

Hence, it seems that ASEAN prioritises precise commitments over binding commitments. In other words, ASEAN members' commitments tend to be precise but non-binding. The 'Temporary Exclusion List' used in the AFTA Common Effective Preferential Tariff (CEPT) Scheme is an illustrative example of this. Article 1 of Protocol Regarding the Implementation of the CEPT Scheme Temporary Exclusion List signed in 2000 states:

> Article 1 Objective and Scope
>
> The objective of this Protocol is to allow a Member State to temporarily delay the transfer of a product from its [Temporary Exclusion List] TEL into the Inclusion List (hereinafter referred to as "IL"), or to temporarily suspend its concession on a product already transferred into the IL, if such a transfer or concession would cause or have caused real problems, by reasons which are not covered by Article 6 (Emergency Measures) of the Agreement.

Haggard notes that the High Level Task Force on ASEAN Economic Integration argued for flexibility in meeting commitments, but at the same time proposed that commitments be more precise and transparent. In his observation, all commitments undertaken by ASEAN Members are precise, but there is differentiation in terms of the timing of implementation across countries, including a possibility of temporary opt-out.[20] There is even a possibility of perpetual opt-out based on the 'ASEAN minus X' formula. This is in line with ASEAN's original idea of a Temporary Exclusion List introduced in the CEPT scheme. The idea is to make the commitments non-binding for a temporary period, not to make them imprecise.

The negotiation position of ASEAN at the multilateral services trade negotiations also suggests ASEAN's preference to precision over bindingness. At the World Trade Organization (WTO) Doha Round services trade negotiations, ASEAN Members insisted that they can submit ambitious services liberalisation commitments, which are precise in nature, provided that new rules on Emergency Safeguard Measures (ESM) are agreed. With the system of ESM, WTO Members can be exempted from the liberalisation commitments when something unexpected happens. ASEAN countries have the Asian financial crisis in 1997/98 in mind. Hence, for example, ASEAN's commitment of financial services liberalisation can be suspended, if another financial crisis hits the region and ESM is in place. It should be noted that WTO services trade liberalisation follows the so-called positive list approach wherein liberalisation is required only in the sectors that each member agrees to liberalise. While ASEAN Members have an option to take advantage of this rule by offering poor-quality commitments rather than requesting the ESM, they decided to insist upon the new rules on ESM, which enables

[20] Stephan Haggard, 'The Organizational Architecture of the Asia-Pacific: Insights from the New Institutionalism (No. 71)', *ADB Working Paper Series on Regional Economic Integration* (2011).

them to submit ambitious offers. In short, ASEAN wants to relax the bindingness of WTO services trade liberalisation commitments, while keeping them precise (and ambitious).

Then, the question is why precision is prioritised over bindingness. There are two possible explanations. First, because the methodology of the commitment is globally standardised, Asia should follow it. Asian countries do not have room to make imprecise commitments because of the globally harmonised way of liberalisation. This is especially true for Asian countries' commitment under the WTO, but this is also true for commitments under Asian free trade agreements (FTAs) that often follow global standards. The second possibility is that the level of bindingness can be adjusted relatively easily, even after the enforcement of rules. In contrast, reducing the precision of text involves additional negotiations to agree upon a new set of ambiguous languages and commitments, which is time consuming.

IV. Delegation of Power and the Exercise of Delegated Power

As one can imagine, international relations tend to focus on 'which country has more power'. The early days of international relations scholarship tried to clarify what power means. Power can be military power, which is essentially based on material capability. But, as Nye says, there is soft power as well. Nonetheless, the question of soft power is which country has the larger influence, which is essentially on the same paradigm as hard power.[21] The legalisation literature made a very important contribution in this regard. Power is delegated to a third party, not other states. With the concept of delegation of power, we can go beyond a question regarding which country has more power. Institutionalism literature (neoliberal institutionalism) argues that institution to prevent prisoners' dilemma situation is beneficial to all members. Institutionalists emphasise the importance of the mechanism that guarantees cooperation such as monitoring, side payment and punishment (in the case of incompliance), while the legalisation literature makes it very clear that power delegated to such a compliance mechanism is the key to understanding the nature of institutions.

The first protocol on Dispute Settlement Mechanism (DSM) of ASEAN was signed in 1996 (1996 Protocol), but this was never invoked due to its excessively bureaucratic nature.[22] Based on Abbott and others, Davidson reviewed the legalisation of economic cooperation among ASEAN achieved by the early 2000s.[23]

[21] Joseph S Nye, 'Soft Power' (1990) 80 *Foreign Policy* 153–71.
[22] Villalta Puig and Tsun Tat (n 13) 282.
[23] Abbott and others (n 2); Davidson (n 5).

While he acknowledges the growing momentum of delegation of power, he concludes that the delegation is the most difficult aspect of legalisation in ASEAN economic relations because of the norm of the ASEAN way.

The institutional design of ASEAN services trade liberalisations also implies that delegation is the lowest priority in ASEAN. As discussed, at the WTO services trade negotiations, ASEAN Members are the proponents of ESM, which reduces the bindingness of commitments. However, ASEAN's regional services trade liberalisation called AFAS does not have ESM. This is perhaps partly because ASEAN Members are unlikely to exercise delegated power even if power is delegated (for further discussion on the exercise of delegated power, see the next section). As long as the initiation of a dispute settlement mechanism is unlikely, ASEAN Members accept not only precise but also binding commitments. Because this assumption does not hold for the case of WTO services trade liberalisation, ASEAN needs to insist upon the ESM. Hence, we can say that the delegation of power is the lowest priority of legalisation in ASEAN services trade liberalisation.

However, by the mid-2000s, an attempt was made to legalise the delegation of power in the dispute settlement mechanism of ASEAN. In 2004, ASEAN adopted the Protocol on Enhanced Dispute Settlement Mechanism (2004 Protocol), which establishes a near rule-based dispute settlement mechanism for AFTA.[24] Does this mean that ASEAN's economic relations are fully legalised in terms of all of three aspects, namely, precision, bindingness and the delegation of power? In order to tackle this question, it seems helpful to distinguish the two questions below:

(i) whether states delegate power to dispute settlement mechanisms
(ii) whether power delegated to dispute settlement mechanisms are actually exercised.

Voeten argues that, in general, countries are not keen to use dispute settlement mechanisms and attempt to solve problems diplomatically through consultation and consensus. And such an attitude is not unique in Asia as many non-Asian countries also solve problems without using dispute settlement mechanisms.[25] However, it should be noted that what Voeten found was that there is no evidence that Asian countries are less likely than other states to refer trade, investment or territorial disputes to dispute settlement mechanism at the *global* level, such as WTO Dispute Settlement.

Then, the real question is why ASEAN countries refrain from using the ASEAN dispute settlement mechanism against fellow ASEAN states, despite the fact that they initiate the WTO dispute settlement proceedings as frequently as other states.

[24] Villalta Puig and Tsun Tat (n 13).

[25] Erik Voeten, 'Regional Judicial Institutions and Economic Cooperation: Lessons for Asia?' *ADB Working paper Series on Regional economic Integration No 65* (2010).

Articles 26 and 27 of ASEAN Charter that came into force on 15 December 2008 give us some idea on this problem.

> Article 26 Unresolved Disputes
>
> When a dispute remains unresolved, after the application of the preceding provisions of this Chapter, this dispute shall be referred to the ASEAN Summit, for its decision.
>
> Article 27 Compliance
>
> Any Member State affected by non-compliance with the findings, recommendations or decisions resulting from an ASEAN dispute settlement mechanism, may refer the matter to the ASEAN Summit for a decision.

While ASEAN trade dispute settlement mechanism developed to a certain degree, ASEAN is essentially an institution that solves problems through consultation and consensus. The ASEAN Charter anticipates that if disputes remain unresolved, the dispute shall be referred to the ASEAN Summit, which is very likely to follow consultation and consensus rather than majority voting.[26]

In this regard, the difference between Asian countries and others is substantial. As Kahler argues, non-Asian countries also solve problems outside legalised institutions. Nevertheless, the difference between the two should be emphasised.[27] Asian countries are more explicit in accepting the fact that legal solutions have limitations and it is diplomatic efforts that ultimately solve legal problems. In contrast, Westerners try to make the loopholes of legalised institution as small as possible and try to make legalised institutions as perfect as possible. While Asian countries *formally* accept *informal* way of solving problems, it seems Westerners only *informally* accept the fact that an *informal* way is necessary to solve disputes.

In this context, we should remember that ASEAN started as an institution that mainly focuses on security issues. Even after ASEAN developed new rules and procedures to handle new issues such as trade and environment, the underlying norms developed during the early era, such as non-interference and consultation and consensus, are still present. Because the enforcement of new specific rules is constrained by the meta-regime that is based on old norms and values, they do not function as they were expected to.[28] The ASEAN way was effective in solving security problems or effective in putting sensitive security problems on the shelf. One could argue that security and trade issues are totally different in terms of dispute settlement because the latter deals with more time-sensitive problems that have huge commercial implications, and the ASEAN way is not effective in solving those immediate disputes at hand.[29] At the same time, one could also argue that

[26] Ewing-Chow (n 5).

[27] Kahler (n 5).

[28] Vinod Aggarwal and Jonathan T Chow, 'The Perils of Consensus: How ASEAN's Meta-regime Undermines Economic and Environmental Cooperation' (2010) 17(2) *Review of International Political Economy* 262–90.

[29] Because the fact that ASEAN Dispute Settlement has been never used to solve trade dispute shows the clear limitation of ASEAN way, Puig and Tat suggest the arbitration model for trade dispute settlement in ASEAN. Villalta Puig and Tsun Tat (n 13).

everything is related to security and this is especially true for ASEAN where the concept of 'non-traditional' security issues is widely accepted.[30]

V. Conclusion

Legalisation is a particular form of institutionalisation characterised by three aspects: obligation, precision and delegation. During the recent two decades, international economic relations among ASEAN Members have experienced the substantial process of legalisation. While earlier studies tend to conclude that legalisation of economic liberalisation in ASEAN was insubstantial in terms of all of the three aspects of legalisations, it is timely to re-examine, because of the progress of economic integration in ASEAN and Asia.

It seems that liberalisation commitments of ASEAN trade liberalisation are as precise as liberalisation elsewhere. Because the 'template' of liberalisation has been globally standardised, ASEAN needs to follow it. The bindingness of rules is also acceptable to ASEAN. Only when the exercise of delegated power is likely, ASEAN tries to keep rules non-binding. ESM under the WTO services trade negotiation is one illustrative example of this. Other than this scenario, ASEAN usually accepts precise and binding rules. The most difficult part of legalisation in ASEAN is the delegation of power. Even if ASEAN Members agree to delegate power, there is an implicit understanding that trade disputes should be ultimately solved diplomatically outside the legalised system. In fact, the ASEAN dispute settlement mechanism has never been used, despite the fact that ASEAN's use of the WTO dispute settlement mechanism is as frequent as other states. So, the situation is ironic; only when ASEAN Members agree not to use the legal mechanism, they can agree upon the establishment of such legal mechanism. This does not, of course, mean legalisation in ASEAN is of no value. As long as disputes are not too critical to national interests, they are likely to be solved legally.

The difference between Asia or ASEAN and the Western world in terms of legalisation is substantial. While Asians formally accept an informal way of solving problems, it seems Westerners only informally accept the fact that the informal way is necessary to solve problems. One plausible explanation why ASEAN makes it explicit that non-legal method should always be on the table is that ASEAN is essentially a security institution that tries to solve problems in an amicable way and the implication of trade disputes to security is not negligible. ASEAN does not deny the value of legalisation, but explicitly keeping the option of a non-legal solution is the prerequisite to legalisation. In order not to over-write the solution suggested by legalised institutions by last-minute diplomatic negotiations, legal and diplomatic methods always go hand-in-hand in ASEAN economic cooperation.

[30] Andrew Tian Huat Tan and Ken Boutin (eds), 'Non-traditional Security Issues in Southeast Asia', *Institute of Defence and Strategic Studies* (Singapore 2001).

PART III

European Union's Trade Policy: Global and Regional Trade Challenges

15

Trade for All? Transparency in the EU's Common Commercial Policy

FERNANDO DIAS SIMÕES

I. Crafting a Common Commercial Policy in Times of Anti-trade Backlash

The last years have witnessed intense public debate over international trade policies, with a growing anti-trade rhetoric in political discourses sweeping across Europe and elsewhere. While the mounting backlash against the globalisation process is caused by different reasons, trade policies are certainly among them.[1] The election of Donald Trump in the United States and Brexit in the United Kingdom both seem to be related to angered citizens who feel ostracised by globalisation.[2] This resentment has been used by populist candidates for electoral gain.[3] Populists reject the 'liberal internationalism' that they associate with 'globalisation', namely the support for supra-national integration and regulation, trade and investment treaties.[4] The electoral ascendance of political groups who take advantage of citizens' feeling of economic insecurity has been described as the largest threat to free trade since the Second World War.[5] The rising wave of nationalism is especially dangerous for the post-sovereign, post-nationalist European project.[6]

[1] C Fred Bergsten, Edwin M Truman and Jeromin Zettelmeyer, 'G-7 Economic Cooperation in the Trump Era' *Peterson Institute for International Economics Policy Brief No. 17-15* (2017) 4, https://piie.com/publications/policy-briefs/g-7-economic-cooperation-trump-era, accessed 23 January 2018.

[2] Michele Veeman, 'North American Trade Policy for Agriculture and Forestry: Can Economics Trump Politics?' (2017) 65(1) *Canadian Journal of Agricultural Economics* 43, 52.

[3] ibid.

[4] Grahame F Thompson, 'Populisms and Liberal Democracy – Business as Usual?' (2017) 46(1) *Economy and Society* 43, 52.

[5] 'Playing with fear', *The Economist* (12 December 2015) www.economist.com/news/leaders/21679792-america-and-europe-right-wing-populist-politicians-are-march-threat, accessed 23 January 2018.

[6] Karen E Smith, 'The European Union in an Illiberal World' (2017) 116(788) *Current History* 83.

The European Union (EU) has exclusive competence in the area of common commercial policy.[7] Under this institutional architecture, the European Commission conducts negotiations in consultation with a special committee appointed by the Council and within the framework of such directives as the Council may issue to it.[8] This chapter reviews the experience of the European Commission in its role as leading negotiator and discusses the strongest criticism it currently faces – an alleged lack of transparency.[9] This critique is part of a grander, older debate about the apparent lack of transparency in EU decision-making processes.[10]

Transparency is essential for the operation of any international organisation and forms part of the broader notion of good governance.[11] The concept is one of the most important principles of globalisation,[12] with an author asserting that it has 'attained quasi-religious significance in debate over governance and institutional design'.[13] Pursuant to the Treaty on the Functioning of the European Union, in order to promote good governance and ensure the participation of civil society, the EU's institutions, bodies, offices and agencies shall conduct their work as openly as possible.[14]

Over the last years transparency became one of the most pressing topics in international law. However, like many fundamental concepts, transparency eludes a precise definition. In the realm of trade and investment negotiations, transparency refers basically to the access of the general public to negotiating documents, position papers and consolidated draft texts.[15] Official papers created during negotiations can be separated into three categories. First, public documents to which everyone has access. Second, limited documents to which only people working on specific issues have access. Third, restricted documents, which can only be accessed by a selected number of individuals.[16]

[7] Consolidated version of the Treaty on the Functioning of the European Union [2012], OJ C326/47, art 3(1) e).

[8] ibid art 207(3).

[9] See, eg, Miguelángel V Garrido, 'Business as Usual: On Untransparency, Lack of Participation, and Unnacountability in Free Trade Negotiations' in Daniel Cardoso and others (eds), *The Transatlantic Colossus: Global Contribution to Broaden the Debate on the EU/US Free Trade Agreement* (Berlin Forum on Global Politics, Internet & Society Collaboratory and FutureChallenges.org, 2013) 38, 39; Magda Stoczkiewicz and Erich Pica, 'EU and US both Threatened by Secret Trade Talks' *EU Observer* (16 December 2013) https://euobserver.com/opinion/122467, accessed 23 January 2018.

[10] See Deirdre Curtin and Maarten Hillebrandt, 'Transparency in the EU: Constitutional Overtones, Institutional Dynamics, and the Escape Hatch of Secrecy' in Adam Lazowski and Steven Blockmans (eds), *Research Handbook on EU Institutional Law* (Cheltenham, Edward Elgar, 2016) 190.

[11] See Allen Buchanan and Robert O Keohane, 'The Legitimacy of Global Governance Institutions' (2006) 20(4) *Ethics and International Affairs* 405.

[12] John Braithwaite and Peter Drahos, *Global Business Regulation* (Cambridge, Cambridge University Press, 2000) 508.

[13] Cristopher Hood, 'Transparency in Historical Perspective' in Cristopher Hood and David Heald (eds), *Transparency: The Key to Better Governance?* (Oxford, Oxford University Press, 2006) 3, 4.

[14] Treaty on the Functioning of the European Union (n 7) art 15(1).

[15] Panagiotis Delimatsis, 'TTIP, CETA, and TiSA Behind Closed Doors: Transparency in the EU Trade Policy' in Stefan Griller and others (eds), *Mega-Regional Trade Agreements: CETA, TTIP, and TiSA: New Orientations for EU External Economic Relations* (Oxford, Oxford University Press, 2017) 2.

[16] Adrienne Héritier and others, 'The European Parliament as a Driving Force of Constitutionalisation' European Parliament, Directorate General for Internal Policies (2015) 93, www.europarl.europa.eu/RegData/etudes/STUD/2015/536467/IPOL_STU(2015)536467_EN.pdf, accessed 23 January 2018.

The fact that official envoys are discussing a wide range of regulatory issues with potential impact on citizens' lives understandably elicits public interest. Civil society groups and the community at large wish to have access to the decision-making process and gauge the impact of prospective agreements on their futures. A proper level of transparency in international negotiations may help to diminish public hesitancy, evade mistrust and boost the legitimacy of the process.

The reality, however, is that transparency in diplomatic negotiations is a paradox.[17] There is no rule of public international law prohibiting confidential negotiations between governments.[18] In fact, the privacy of trade and investment negotiations, be it at the bilateral, regional or multilateral level, is a time-honoured practice.[19] The EU has also been following this praxis for a long time.[20] The EU is represented in the negotiation process by officials from the European Commission Directorate-General for Trade who meet with officers from partner countries in private. According to some commentators, the negotiation behind closed doors of an international agreement with tremendous economic and social impact undercuts democratic values.[21] The secrecy of the negotiations is perceived by others as a symbol of a hidden agenda against the interests of European citizens, directed at increasing the profit of multinational corporations.[22] The opacity or downright secrecy of trade and investment negotiations contributes to the citizen's loss of trust in European policymaking. This is particularly relevant when there are low levels of trust in politics and institutions.[23] The discussion therefore turns on the democratic legitimacy of the EU's trade policy.[24]

Seeking to address public furore, in October 2015 the European Commission unveiled its new trade and investment policy, titled 'Trade for all: Towards a More Responsible Trade and Investment Policy'.[25] The new strategy is centred on

[17] Delimatsis (n 15) at 3.

[18] Cristoph Herrmann, 'Transleakancy' in Christoph Herrmann and others (eds), *Trade Policy between Law, Diplomacy and Scholarship* (Berlin, Springer, 2015) 39, 41.

[19] ibid.

[20] Vigjilenca Abazi, 'European Parliamentary Oversight Behind Closed Doors' (2016) 5 *Cambridge Journal of International and Comparative Law* 31, 34.

[21] George Monbiot, 'This Transatlantic Trade Deal is a Full-frontal Assault on Democracy', *The Guardian* (London, 4 November 2013) www.theguardian.com/commentisfree/2013/nov/04/us-trade-deal-full-frontal-assault-on-democracy, accessed 23 January 2018.

[22] Hans Pitlik, 'Lack of Trust, Campaigning and Opposition against the TTIP' in Ernest Gnan and Ralf Kronberger (eds), *Transatlantische Handels- und Investitionspartnerschaft zwischen der EU und den USA (TTIP)* (Vienna, Facultas, 2016) 221.

[23] Sebastian Dullien and others, 'A Fresh Start for TTIP' European Council on Foreign Relations (2015) 6 www.ecfr.eu/page/-/ECFR124_-_TTIP.pdf, accessed 23 January 2018.

[24] Elisabeth Winter, 'Trade for All or Unity at Stake? Reclaiming a Legitimate and Single Voice for EU Trade Policy' *Transatlantic Policy Symposium 2016 at Georgetown University* (2016) 4, http://tapsgeorgetown.com/wp-content/uploads/2016/02/Elisabeth-Winters-Trade-for-All-or-Unity-at-Stake.pdf, accessed 23 January 2018.

[25] European Commission, 'Trade for All: Towards a More Responsible Trade and Investment Policy' (2015) http://trade.ec.europa.eu/doclib/docs/2015/october/tradoc_153846.pdf, accessed 23 January 2018.

three basic principles: effectiveness, transparency and values. This seems a promising response to the most debated traits of European trade policymaking.[26] This chapter examines the present-day level of transparency in European trade and investment negotiations. It argues that the level of transparency adopted by the European Commission, while open to improvement, is already quite satisfactory. The current practice strikes a sensible balance between the principles of transparency and democratic scrutiny and the need to ensure orderly, fruitful international negotiations. Still, a greater measure of transparency and public participation in the negotiation process could help to restore the image of the EU as a credible institution that negotiates on behalf of all Europeans.

II. A Start on the Wrong Foot

International trade and investment agreements have been attracting unprecedented levels of attention and criticism. The negotiations for the Transatlantic Trade and Investment Partnership (TTIP), the proposed mega-trade agreement between the EU and the United States, were a turning point in this regard. A number of civil society organisations have been vigorously working to increase mobilisation against the agreement.[27] Political opposition to the TTIP is also substantial in several European countries.[28] The confidentiality of the negotiating mandate is presented by critics as a token of how the TTIP negotiation process has been concealed from civil society.[29] When the Council of the European Union issued the negotiating directives, the public was promptly informed.[30] However, the full text of the mandate was not liberated. As the negotiations started drawing public attention, calls for derestricting the negotiating mandate augmented, including inside the Commission[31] and the Parliament.[32] In February 2014 several

[26] Winter (n 24) at 6.

[27] See, eg, Corporate Europe Observatory, 'International Trade' https://corporateeurope.org/international-trade; STOP TTIP, 'European Initiative Against TTIP and CETA' https://stop-ttip.org; The Greens and European Free Alliance in the European Parliament, 'TTIP: Beware What Lies Beneath' http://ttip2016.eu/home-en.html; Global Justice Now, 'What is TTIP?' www.globaljustice.org.uk/what-ttip-0; War on Want, 'What is TTIP?'www.waronwant.org/what-ttip, all accessed 23 January 2018.

[28] Pitlik (n 22).

[29] Dalila Ghailani and Aída Ponce del Castillo, 'The Transatlantic Trade and Investment Partnership (TTIP): Converging Interests and Diverging Opinions' in David Natali and Bart Vanhercke (eds), *Social Policy in the European Union: State of Play 2015* (European Trade Union Institute and European Social Observatory, 2015) 215, 221.

[30] Council of the European Union, 'Council Approves Launch of Trade and Investment Negotiations with the United States' (2013) http://europa.eu/rapid/press-release_PRES-13-255_en.htm, accessed 23 January 2018.

[31] European Parliament, 'Statement by Commissioner Karel De Gucht on TTIP' (2014) http://europa.eu/rapid/press-release_SPEECH-14-549_en.htm, accessed 23 January 2018.

[32] Bernd Lange, 'TTIP Debate Suffering from Lack of Transparency' *The Parliament Magazine* (31 October 2014) www.theparliamentmagazine.eu/articles/opinion/ttip-debate-suffering-lack-transparency, accessed 23 January 2018.

civil society organisations submitted a request for access to several documents, including the negotiating mandate. The petition was submitted under Regulation (EC) no 1049/2001, of 30 May 2001, which regulates the right of European citizens or legal persons to access documents of European institutions.[33] The request was rejected by the Commission,[34] arguing that the release of the documents could 'weaken the negotiating position of the EU in the negotiations with the United States and therefore compromise the protection of the EU international relations'.[35] The then-Director-General for Trade, Jean-Luc Demarty, stated:

> [w]hile the EU holds dear the principles of transparency, a certain level of discretion and special care in handling negotiating documents is … necessary in order to allow mutual trust between negotiators. The success of the negotiations depends to a large extent on the protection of objectives, tactics and fallback positions of the parties involved. In addition, as the negotiations are ongoing, the publication of these documents would also be likely to prejudice the decision-making process of the EU …[36]

Demarty declined to take a position on the disclosure of the negotiating mandate since it was a Council document. The Commission also provided the internet links to some documents that were already public at the time.[37]

After several complaints from civil society organisations, the European Ombudsman, Emily O'Reilly, decided to open an investigation.[38] O'Reilly called on the Council to publish the negotiating directives, arguing that 'a proactive approach to transparency could enhance the prospects of success by enhancing the legitimacy of the negotiating process in the eyes of citizens'.[39] The Ombudsman also addressed a letter to the Commission suggesting a range of measures to facilitate timely public access to TTIP documents.[40] In response to mounting pressure, the Council made the negotiating mandate public on 9 October 2014[41] – more than one year after the decision was made.

[33] Regulation (EC) 1049/2001, OJ 2001 L 145/43.

[34] European Commission, 'Letter to Mr Paul de Clerck, of 6 May 2014' (2014) www.foeeurope.org/sites/default/files/reply-1-dg_trade-gestdem_2014_0884.pdf, accessed 23 January 2018.

[35] ibid.

[36] ibid.

[37] ibid.

[38] European Ombudsman, 'Ombudsman asks Council and Commission to publish more TTIP documents' (2014) www.ombudsman.europa.eu/en/press/release.faces/en/54636/html.bookmark, accessed 23 January 2018.

[39] ibid; European Ombudsman, 'Letter to the Council of the EU requesting an opinion in the European Ombudsman's own-initiative inquiry OI/11/2014/MMN concerning transparency and public participation in relation to the Transatlantic Trade and Investment Partnership (TTIP) negotiations, of 29 July 2014' (2014) www.ombudsman.europa.eu/en/cases/correspondence.faces/en/54634/html.bookmark, accessed 23 January 2018.

[40] European Ombudsman (n 38); European Ombudsman, 'Letter to the European Commission requesting an opinion in the European Ombudsman's own-initiative inquiry OI/10/2014/MMN concerning transparency and public participation in relation to the Transatlantic Trade and Investment Partnership (TTIP) negotiations, of 29 July 2014' (2014) www.ombudsman.europa.eu/en/cases/correspondence.faces/en/54633/html.bookmark, accessed 23 January 2018.

[41] Council of the European Union, 'TTIP Negotiating Mandate Made Public' (2014) www.consilium.europa.eu/uedocs/cms_data/docs/pressdata/en/foraff/145014.pdf, accessed 23 January 2018.

It is evident that the negotiations started on the wrong foot. In an opinion piece published in October 2014,[42] Bernd Lange, then chair of the European Parliament's International Trade Committee, stated:

> [s]ince the start of discussions, opposition has been growing among the civilian population and certain political parties, despite the fact that the final content of the project cannot be discussed in detail, even one year on. This leaves a lot of room for interpretation and speculation. Therefore, many critics are spreading horror stories and predicting that an agreement will result in a loss of democratic values. This criticism should have been addressed with maximum transparency from the outset.

The tardy publication of the negotiating directives only contributed to amplify public concerns. The disclosure of the mandate was a noteworthy decision, since it was the first time the EU has circulated such a document since it began negotiating trade agreements.[43] Nevertheless, as acknowledged by Lange:

> this step has come several months too late. In order to hold a debate based on facts rather than myths and allegations, basic information is required. The negotiating mandate, which the member states use to instruct the commission to negotiate an agreement and its content, does, without a doubt, constitute such a basic document.[44]

While it was a reactive decision, prompted by public clamour, the release of the negotiating directives reveals the recognition by the European institutions that the old-style secrecy of negotiation processes will be tolerated no more. Civil society is increasingly calling for a higher degree of transparency in the negotiations, and making use of the available information to monitor their evolution.

III. A Fresh Start

One month after the divulgation of the negotiating mandate, the European Commission unveiled its 'Transparency Initiative'.[45] The Commission accepted that the negotiations on TTIP had

> become the object of increased public scrutiny and a certain amount of concern in public opinion. It is important to ensure that the general public has accurate and full information of the EU's intentions in the negotiations, to address the concerns and to evacuate misperceptions.[46]

Different actions were advanced as part of a 'fresh start' on the TTIP in order to 'win public trust and support'.[47] These measures were expected to 'help to ensure

[42] Lange (n 32).
[43] Ghailani and Ponce del Castillo (n 29) at 222.
[44] Lange (n 32).
[45] European Commission, 'Communication to the Commission Concerning Transparency in TTIP Negotiations', C(2014) 9052 final.
[46] ibid 2.
[47] ibid.

greater access to trade documents by the general public and the European Parliament, and legitimacy EU trade policy at large'.[48] The list of actions included the provision of more extensive access to documents, notably by making public all the negotiating texts that the Commission already shared with Member States and the European Parliament; the review of the classification of information related to TTIP; and the decision to keep such information classified only up to the point when it is shared with the other party.

The 'transparency initiative' goes beyond anything seen before in the EU.[49] The Commission started to make available the EU's negotiating texts and position papers.[50] This is the first time that these kind of documents have been made public at an early period of the negotiations and constitutes a significant landmark in the Commission's efforts to promote the transparency of the negotiating process.[51] The initiative was designed to give TTIP a 'fresh start'. This is an implicit acknowledgement that there was something wrong with the original approach. The negotiations started from a point of near absolute secrecy,[52] causing significant damage that had to be repaired.[53] The Commission's new professed philosophy is that '[g]etting TTIP right means … being as open as possible about what we're negotiating'.[54] On a dedicated webpage, the Commission makes available the EU's negotiating texts and position papers, chapter by chapter.[55]

A second impulse towards greater transparency took place on 14 October 2015, when the European Commission presented its new trade and investment policy, titled 'Trade for all: Towards a More Responsible Trade and Investment Policy'.[56] The document starts with a sort of *mea culpa* by the EU Trade Chief, Cecilia Malmström:

> In recent years we have seen an intense debate about trade across the European Union which has some important lessons for EU trade policy. It is clear Europeans want … to know more about trade negotiations carried out in their name. In this new strategy … the Commission is adapting its approach to trade policy to take all of these lessons on board. As a result, trade policy will become more responsible, meaning it will be more effective, more transparent and will not only project our interests, but also our values. To make trade negotiations more transparent, the strategy commits to publishing

[48] ibid.

[49] Erin Hannah, *NGOs and Global Trade: Non-state Voices in EU Trade Policymaking* (Abingdon, Routledge, 2016) 119.

[50] European Commission, 'The EU's Position in the Negotiations' http://ec.europa.eu/trade/policy/in-focus/ttip/documents-and-events/index_en.htm#eu-position, accessed 23 January 2018.

[51] Delimatsis (n 15) at 18.

[52] Monique Goyens and Léa Auffret, 'TTIP: What Is in It for Consumers?' (2015) 50(6) *Intereconomics* 333.

[53] Tereza Novotná, 'European View: Four Reasons Why TTIP May Fail and Why It Will be Europe's Fault' *LSE Ideas Special Report* (2016) 34, 37 www.academia.edu/26313108/Four_Reasons_Why_TTIP_May_Fail_and_Why_It_Will_be_Europe_s_Fault, accessed 23 January 2018.

[54] European Commission, 'How We'll Make TTIP Happen' http://ec.europa.eu/trade/policy/in-focus/ttip/about-ttip/process/#_transparency, accessed 23 January 2018.

[55] ibid.

[56] European Commission (n 25).

key negotiating texts from all negotiations, as happens in the Transatlantic Trade and Investment Partnership (TTIP).[57]

The document acknowledges that '[t]rade policy is more debated today than at any time in recent years, with many asking whether it is designed to support broad European interests and principles or the narrow objectives of large firms'.[58] The Commission claims to take 'these concerns seriously. Policymaking needs to be transparent and the debate needs to be based on facts'.[59] The new trade and investment policy adds:

> [l]ack of transparency undermines the legitimacy of EU trade policy and public trust. There is demand for more transparency in trade negotiations, particularly when they deal with domestic policy issues like regulation. The Commission has taken unprecedented steps in response to this demand, in particular in publishing EU negotiating proposals.[60]

According to the document, '[t]ransparency should apply at all stages of the negotiating cycle from the setting of objectives to the negotiations themselves and during the post-negotiation phase'.[61] The Commission pledges to 'actively engage with civil society and the public at large in the context of the civil society dialogues and citizens' dialogues …'[62] In addition, the Commission will

> at launch, invite the Council to disclose all FTA negotiating directives immediately after their adoption; during negotiations, extend TTIP practices of publishing EU texts online for all trade and investment negotiations and make it clear to all new partners that negotiations will have to follow a transparent approach; and after finalising negotiations, publish the text of the agreement immediately, as it stands, without waiting for the legal revision to be completed.[63]

It appears that the European Commission is committed to a higher level of transparency in trade negotiations than ever before.[64] This is particularly true if we think about the negotiations for the EU–Canada Comprehensive Economic and Trade Agreement (CETA), which were marked by a notorious lack of transparency.[65]

IV. Dimensions of Transparency

Is the current practice of the European Commission, the leading negotiator, enough to allay public fears and curb allegations of secrecy? The answer to this

[57] ibid 5.
[58] ibid 18.
[59] ibid 5.
[60] ibid 19.
[61] ibid.
[62] ibid 18.
[63] ibid 19.
[64] Delimatsis (n 15) at 20.
[65] ibid 12.

question requires an analysis of different angles from which transparency in trade and investment negotiations can be considered.

A. In General

The first dimension of transparency refers to the access of the general public to the negotiation process.

From an optimistic perspective, the new approach of the Commission to the negotiation process makes TTIP's transparency record quite unique.[66] Naturally, the public clamour for greater access to negotiating documents and the ensuing involvement of the European Ombudsman played a decisive role in this change of attitude.[67] Furthermore, the European Parliament has also increased its involvement in the negotiations, thanks to the TTIP's political prominence.[68] The level of transparency of the TTIP negotiations seems exceptional when compared to the secrecy that traditionally marks intergovernmental negotiations.[69] From this viewpoint, the TTIP represents a turning point towards a standard of transparency that is completely innovative in the panorama of intergovernmental negotiations.[70]

Some commentators, however, are not so enthusiastic. The initial release of a few negotiating texts was labelled by some as a sham since many of those documents had already been leaked online. The perception that the new posture of the Commission was nothing more than window dressing only contributed to fuel criticism.[71] While acknowledging that the Commission's efforts to publish its proposals are positive and even laudable, some authors believe that they are insufficient.[72] It has been argued that released documents on negotiating positions only contain general statements of intent that do not offer any meaningful information.[73] A higher level of transparency should be pursued, namely through the publication of consolidated negotiating texts as soon as possible.[74] However, since the United States refuse to disclose their proposals and consolidated negotiating texts, it seems impossible for the European Commission to elevate its transparency standard.[75] This is problematic. As the general public only has access to the

[66] ibid 22.
[67] ibid.
[68] Héritier and others (n 16) at 94.
[69] Stefano Rossi, 'The TTIP: a New Generation Treaty' (2015) 28(2) *The Federalist Debate* 18, 19.
[70] ibid 21.
[71] Winter (n 24) at 4.
[72] Goyens and Auffret (n 52) at 334.
[73] Glyn Moody, 'European Commission Announces Major Transparency Initiative for TAFTA/TTIP' (2015) www.techdirt.com/articles/20150107/07102529619/european-commission-announces-major-transparency-initiative-taftattip.shtml, accessed 23 January 2018.
[74] See, eg, Trans Atlantic Consumer Dialogue, 'Letter to Ambassador Michael Froman and Commissioner Cecilia Malmström, of 30 January 2015' (2015) http://tacd.org/wp-content/uploads/2015/01/TACD-letter-to-Froman-and-Malmstr%C3%B6m.pdf, accessed 23 January 2018.
[75] Goyens and Auffret (n 52) at 334.

initial position of one of the parties – the EU – there is the risk that, once texts are consolidated, the public is unaware of fundamental alterations.

B. The Sustainability Impact Assessment Mechanism

A different – and more technical – dimension of transparency results from the conduction of impact assessment studies. Sustainability Impact Assessment (SIA) studies, which have been carried out on all trade agreements negotiated since 1999, are described by the European Commission as follows:[76]

> The Sustainability Impact Assessment (SIA) is a DG Trade-specific tool for supporting major trade negotiations. SIAs provide the Commission with an in-depth analysis of the potential economic, social, human rights, and environmental impacts of ongoing trade negotiations. These assessments are an opportunity for stakeholders in both the EU and in the partner countries to share their views with negotiators.
>
> SIAs have several purposes, including:
>
> - feeding information into and helping steer the negotiations
> - assessing the changes that are likely to be caused by a trade agreement
> - helping to identify possible trade-offs
> - ensuring that the related policy choices are optimised
>
> SIAs contribute to sound, evidence-based and transparent trade negotiations.

Trade SIAs are a well-established instrument to inform trade negotiators and policymakers and steer their decision-making processes.[77] Quantitative and qualitative data on the relationship between proposed trade policies and their potential effects is collected in a scientific fashion.[78] The goal is to calculate the probable positive or negative consequences of a selection of alternative measures.[79] This information may contribute to adjust existing policies, generate new ones, or change the way problems are identified and policies are formulated.[80]

[76] European Commission, 'Sustainability Impact Assessments' http://ec.europa.eu/trade/policy/policy-making/analysis/policy-evaluation/sustainability-impact-assessments/index_en.htm, accessed 23 January 2018.

[77] Stephen White and Jakub Koniecki, 'How Informed Should Decisions be?' in Anneke von Raggamby and Frieder Rubik (eds), *Sustainable Development, Evaluation and Policy-Making: Theory, Practise and Quality Assurance* (Cheltenham, Edward Elgar, 2012) 129.

[78] Colin Kirkpatrick and Clive George, 'Assessing the Sustainability of Trade Policies and Agreements' in Organisation for Economic Co-Operation and Development (ed), *Conducting Sustainability Assessments* (OECD, 2008) 119, 120.

[79] Tom Bauler, 'The Commission's Impact Assessment Process: Handling the External Dimensions of Sustainability' in Marc Pallemaerts and Albena Azmanova (eds), *The European Union and Sustainable Development: Internal and External Dimensions* (Brussels, Brussels University Press, 2006) 277, 278.

[80] See Ivan Scrase and William Sheate, 'Integration and Integrated Approaches to Assessment: What do they Mean for the Environment?' (2002) 4 *Journal of Environmental Policy and Planning* 275.

These studies also inform the general public about the potential effects of projected policies by including mechanisms for public participation and consultation.[81] Consultation with stakeholders and experts can shed light on relevant issues that are frequently overlooked during negotiations.[82] This open, participatory debate about the consequences of international agreements might help policymakers to integrate societal concerns such as sustainable development more fully into trade policies.[83] In the words of the Commission:

> SIAs consist of two equally important and complementary components:
>
> (i) a robust analysis of the potential economic, social, human rights and environmental impacts that the trade agreement under negotiation could have, in the EU, in the partner country(ies) and in other relevant countries;
>
> (ii) a continuous and wide-ranging consultation process which ensures a high degree of transparency and the engagement of all relevant stakeholders in the conduct of the SIA inside and outside the EU.[84]

In 2016 the Commission published the second edition of its Handbook for Trade Sustainability Impact Assessment, which also emphasises the importance of transparency:

> Transparency is a central element of SIAs. By relying on a genuine, wide-ranging and continuous consultation of stakeholders, SIAs contribute to fulfilling the Commission's commitment to ensure transparent trade negotiations. They are a prime opportunity for stakeholders to inform EU negotiators of their views on the potential economic, social, human rights and environmental consequences of ongoing trade negotiations.[85]

The handbook underlines the importance of 'close dialogue with all relevant stakeholders, including the more vulnerable ones …' in order to 'capture the wider implications of our policy choices and to prevent unintended side-effects. With this prevention-driven approach, we can ensure that our trade policy genuinely works for all'.[86]

The positive influence of trade impact assessment studies on the outcome of the policymaking process is not unanimous among experts.

[81] Gerald Berger, 'Sustainability Impact Assessment: European Approaches' in Organisation for Economic Co-Operation and Development (ed), *Conducting Sustainability Assessments* (OECD, 2008) 15, 19.

[82] Markus Gehring and Marie-Claire Cordonier Segger, 'Overcoming Obstacles with Opportunities: Trade and Investment Agreements for Sustainable Development' in Stephan Schill and others (eds), *International Investment Law and Development: Bridging the Gap* (Cheltenham, Edward Elgar, 2015) 93, 103.

[83] See Hussein Abaza and Robert Hamwey, 'Integrated Assessment as a Tool for Achieving Sustainable Trade Policies' (2001) 21 *Environmental Impact Assessment Review* 481.

[84] European Commission, 'Handbook for Trade Sustainability Impact Assessment, 2nd ed' (2016) 5–6, http://trade.ec.europa.eu/doclib/docs/2016/april/tradoc_154464.PDF, accessed 23 January 2018.

[85] ibid 4.

[86] ibid 3.

Some authors recall that the adoption by the Commission of trade SIAs was a strategic political decision aimed at reducing civil society opposition to trade liberalisation policies.[87] From this perspective, it can be argued that SIAs have a positive impact since they engage civil society in a process of consultation and dialogue, thereby contributing to a greater consideration by the Commission of the impact of trade policies.[88] The Commission comments on the findings of these studies through 'position papers' defining points of agreement, responding to disagreements and considering further actions to be implemented.[89] Civil society groups and parliamentarians in both the EU and its partner countries also make use of the findings of SIAs in their submissions to governments, thus seeking to influence the negotiation process.[90] These studies are also receiving increasing attention from the European Parliament.[91] By offering opportunities for greater transparency and public dialogue, these studies help to build capacity and increase cooperation, thus enhancing the credibility and legitimacy of trade and investment agreements.[92]

Other commentators express doubts about any meaningful impact of SIAs on the trade negotiating process. The Commission is not bound by the results of impact assessment studies.[93] Even if these studies recommend measures to mitigate the negative impact of proposed policies, there is no guarantee that they will be implemented.[94] Impact assessment studies in general have been criticised for focusing on justifying the Commission's proposals.[95] Instead of being used by trade negotiators to develop and implement sustainable policies, trade SIA studies may simply provide an appearance of legitimacy that justifies pre-existing trade

[87] Clive George and Colin Kirkpatrick, 'Political Challenges in Policy-Level Evaluation for Sustainable Development: The Case of Trade Policy' in Anneke von Raggamby and Frieder Rubik (eds), *Sustainable Development, Evaluation and Policy-Making: Theory, Practise and Quality Assurance* (Cheltenham, Edward Elgar, 2012) 73, 84–85.

[88] ibid 85.

[89] Clive George and others, 'EU Trade Strategy and Regionalism: Assessing the Impact on Europe's Developing Country Partners' in Philippe De Lombaerde and Michael Schulz (eds), *The EU and World Regionalism: The Makability of Regions in the 21st Century* (Abingdon, Routledge, 2016) 63, 74–75.

[90] ibid 84.

[91] ibid 75.

[92] Rok Zvelc, 'Environmental Integration in EU Trade Policy: the Generalised System of Preferences, Trade Sustainability Impact Assessments and Free Trade Agreements' in Elisa Morgera (ed), *The External Environmental Policy of the European Union: EU and International Law Perspectives* (Cambridge, Cambridge University Press, 2012) 174, 191–92.

[93] Fabiane Baxewanos and Werner Raza, 'Human Rights Impact Assessments as a New Tool for Development Policy?' *Austrian Foundation for Development Research* (2013) 11, www.econstor.eu/handle/10419/98807, accessed 23 January 2018.

[94] ibid 12.

[95] The Evaluation Partnership, 'Evaluation of the Commission's Impact Assessment System. Final Report (2007) 5–6, http://ec.europa.eu/smart-regulation/impact/key_docs/docs/tep_eias_final_report.pdf, accessed 23 January 2018.

negotiations.[96] These studies are not intended to influence policymaking directly, but rather indirectly through the promotion of public dialogue.[97]

From this viewpoint, the SIA process fails to allow for sufficient consultation from non-corporate stakeholders and civil society organisations.[98] The choice of relevant stakeholders has been deemed selective, with those consulted frequently not having the necessary information to make their participation in an effective way.[99] Some non-governmental organisations have revealed difficulties in devoting sufficient resources to commenting on the complex and lengthy process of SIAs, leading to a decrease in interest, attention and resources devoted to this mechanism.[100]

Improvements in terms of public participation are needed.[101] The creation of a proper legal framework on trade SIAs should include specific procedures for public participation.[102] New mechanisms to increase transparency and consultation should be implemented. The European Economic and Social Committee, for instance, has suggested the creation of a civil society monitoring mechanism including actors from business, trade unions, NGOs, academia and others.[103]

V. Concluding Remarks

The European Commission seems committed to a higher level of transparency in the negotiation of international trade agreements. This is a positive development that contributes to the democratisation of a process that can have significant

[96] Baxewanos and Raza (n 93) at 12.

[97] Clive George and Colin Kirkpatrick, 'Sustainability Impact Assessment of Trade Agreements: From Public Dialogue to International Governance' (2008) 10 *Journal of Environmental Assessment Policy and Management* 67, 69.

[98] See Marc Maes, 'Civil Society Perspectives on EU-Asia Free Trade Agreements' (2009) 7 *Asia Europe Journal* 97.

[99] Baxewanos and Raza (n 93) at 12.

[100] Lisa Alf and others, 'Towards a Transatlantic Dialog on Trade and the Environment: A Comparison of Approaches to Environmental Impact Assessments of Trade Agreements in the US and EU' (2008) 20, http://ecologic.eu/sites/files/event/2013/transatlantic-lunch-jan-08-final_report.pdf, accessed 23 January 2018.

[101] See Ingmar von Homeyer and others, 'Improving Public Participation in Sustainability Impact Assessment of Trade Agreements' in Paul Ekins and Tancrède Voituriez (eds), *Trade, Globalization and Sustainability Impact Assessment: A Critical Look at Methods and Outcomes* (London, Earthscan, 2009) 189.

[102] Markus Gehring and others, 'Sustainability Impact Assessments as Inputs and as Interpretative Aids in International Investment Law' (2017) 18 *Journal of World Investment and Trade* 163, 188.

[103] European Economic and Social Committee, 'Opinion of the European Economic and Social Committee on the Role of Civil Society in the Free Trade Agreement Between the EU and India' (2011) REX/316CESE 1612/2011 9–10, www.eesc.europa.eu/?i=portal.en.rex-opinions.20331, accessed 23 January 2018.

impact on the lives of European citizens.[104] This heightened standard of transparency is totally innovative in the panorama of intergovernmental negotiations, especially when compared with the current situation on the other side of the Atlantic.[105]

Still, the European Commission also seems to be aware of the need to strike a balance between a high standard of transparency and the secrecy or *privacy* necessary to ensure a fruitful negotiation. Access to information regarding the negotiating process is generally limited to prevent the ultimate failure of negotiations.[106] An excessive measure of transparency may cause delays, hamper the efficiency of the process, or even conduct to a breakdown in negotiations.[107] Furthermore, restrictions to public access to documents might be necessary to safeguard a legitimate interest in the protection of strategic elements of the negotiations.[108] Even if certain documents have already been transmitted to the other party that does not mean that they should be made public, as disclosure can put the EU's interests regarding international relations at a risk.[109]

The benefits of transparency need to be balanced against its potential drawbacks, adopting a balanced approach to the secrecy–transparency dichotomy. Whereas a certain level of privacy ensures that negotiating parties have sufficient room for bargaining, negotiation results should be disclosed after every negotiation round to allow for public discussion and input.[110] This methodology combines public and private stages of negotiation, depending on their timing and sensitiveness, and achieves a high level of transparency without compromising the need to create mutual trust between all the involved parties.[111]

As for the SIA mechanism, while the direct influence of these studies on the decision-making process seems low, it can be said that they nevertheless contribute to raising public awareness about the broader consequences of trade policies.[112] Impact assessment studies force policymakers to collate and evaluate evidence as they make decisions and to produce a statement to explain their options. SIAs allow for a discussion between a broad range of stakeholders about a diversity of issues

[104] Rossi (n 69) at 19.

[105] ibid 21.

[106] Laura Puccio, 'TTIP: Access to Consolidated Texts and Confidential Documents' *European Parliamentary Research Service* (2016) 2, www.europarl.europa.eu/thinktank/en/document.html?reference=EPRS_BRI(2016)580909> accessed 23 January 2018.

[107] Delimatsis (n 15) at 25.

[108] ibid 10.

[109] ibid.

[110] Holger Janusch, 'Public Protests and FTA Negotiations with the United States: Lessons for the TAFTA/TTIP' in Daniel Cardoso and others (eds), *The Transatlantic Colossus: Global Contribution to Broaden the Debate on the EU/US Free Trade Agreement* (Berlin Forum on Global Politics, Internet & Society Collaboratory and FutureChallenges.org 2013) 24, 27.

[111] Thomas Cottier and Michelangelo Temmerman, 'Transparency and Intellectual Property Protection in International Law' in Andrea Bianchi and Anne Peters (eds), *Transparency in International Law* (Cambridge, Cambridge University Press, 2013) 197, 207.

[112] Clive George and Colin Kirkpatrick, 'Creation of Processes: Sustainability Impact Assessments' in Diana Tussie (ed), *The Politics of Trade: The Role of Research in Trade Policy and Negotiation* (Leiden, Republic of Letters, Brill, International Development Research Centre, 2009) 55, 69.

that would not be included in a traditional trade agenda.[113] One should also take into account the power of public pressure. If concerns are raised by civil society groups that are refuted without proper justification, they may trigger significant public opposition.[114] The existence of impact assessment studies requires policymakers to engage in a discussion with the general public.[115] This is a significant, incremental step when compared with the secretive way trade negotiations were traditionally conducted.

Finally, one should bear in mind that besides the two dimensions of transparency discussed above there is a third, internal facet to the concept, referring to the exchange of information between the European Commission and the European Parliament. Under the institutional architecture of the EU, the Commission has the obligation to report regularly to the Parliament on the progress of negotiations.[116] Where agreements between the EU and third countries or international organisations need to be negotiated and concluded, the Parliament shall be immediately and fully informed at all stages of the procedure.[117] Furthermore, consent by the Parliament is required before the conclusion of the agreement by the Council.[118] Being the chamber of European citizens, the European Parliament plays a decisive role in monitoring the negotiations and ensuring that they comply with high standards of transparency and democratic participation.

In its new trade and investment policy the European Commission states:

> As co-legislator alongside the Council, the European Parliament also has a central role in ensuring full democratic scrutiny and accountability of trade policy. The Parliament and the Commission have intensified their interaction, ensuring the close involvement of the Parliament at every step of the negotiations. The Commission will also step up its efforts to promote an informed debate in Member States and a deeper dialogue with civil society at large. This is an opportunity to raise people's awareness about ongoing and planned trade and investment negotiations, and to get feedback on issues from stakeholders concerned.[119]

European negotiators are well aware that consent by the European Parliament will be directly influenced by public opinion.[120] If accusations of secrecy and opacity of the negotiating process become unbearable, members of the Parliament may succumb to the pressure and reject the trade agreement. The European Parliament's rejection of ACTA in 2012 is a vivid example that lack of transparency leads to a reduction in public trust that may result in the failure of the agreement.[121]

[113] James Harrison, 'Human Rights Impact Assessments of Trade Agreements: Reflections on Practice and Principles for Future Assessments' (2010) 16, www.humanrights.ch/upload/pdf/100719_Background_paper.pdf, accessed 23 January 2018.

[114] Alf and others (n 100) at 48.

[115] ibid.

[116] Treaty on the Functioning of the European Union (n 7) art 207(3).

[117] ibid, art 218(10).

[118] ibid, art 218(6) a).

[119] European Commission (n 25) at 18.

[120] Goyens and Auffret (n 52) at 337.

[121] Cottier and Temmerman (n 111) at 220.

Avoiding the repetition of this precedent requires paying greater attention to the issue of transparency in the conduct of the negotiations.[122]

Transparency should be a basic component of trade and investment negotiations. Taking into account the overall decline in trust, both in national governments and parliaments as well as in the EU, policymakers cannot conduct negotiations as they traditionally did.[123] The Commission's emphasis on transparency over the last few years is an auspicious step in the right direction.[124] The availability of relevant information pertaining to trade and investment agreements may diminish public criticism and help to restore the image of the EU as a credible institution that negotiates on behalf of all Europeans.[125] While the current practice can always be improved and fine-tuned, it already strikes a reasonable, sensible balance between the principles of transparency and democratic scrutiny; and the need to ensure orderly, fruitful international negotiations.

[122] Elvire Fabry and others, 'The TTIP Negotiations: a Pirandello Play' *European Policy Center and Jacques Delores Institute* (2014) 6, www.notre-europe.eu/media/ttipnegotiationsfabrygarbassopardone-jdijan14.pdf?pdf=ok, accessed 23 January 2018.
[123] Dullien, Garcia and Janning (n 23) at 9.
[124] Winter (n 24) at 6–7.
[125] ibid 7.

16

Investor to State Dispute Settlement Mechanisms

A Comparison of Evolving Legal Approaches in Brazilian and Latin American Relations with the European Union

DANIELE BIANCHI AND KIRSTYN INGLIS*

I. Introduction

The reform of investor to state dispute settlement (ISDS) and potential alternatives to it, is a priority for the EU today. Foreign direct investment (FDI) by the European Union in Brazil and Latin America is considerable, and vice versa.[1] Various forms of settling disputes between investors and states are incorporated into agreements carrying FDI.

Classical Investor to State Dispute Settlement (ISDS) mechanisms have become increasingly contentious in recent years, and with the growth in the number of ISDS agreements, public fears that investors may gain control of

* All views expressed here are the authors' alone. The support of the European Commission for the project support and production of this publication is not in accordance with its content, which is the responsibility of the authors. The Commission is not responsible for any use that may be made of the information contained in this publication.

[1] See the Europa website, 'Foreign Direct Investment Statistics' (2017), http://ec.europa.eu/eurostat/statistics-explained/index.php/Foreign_direct_investment_statistics. As at end 2015, EU outward FDI stocks in Latin America were EUR 490.2bn (7.1 per cent of global EU outward FDI). In terms of inwards FDI into the EU, Brazil was in fourth place among states investing in the EU in 2015, and Mexico in eighth place, the former accounting for EUR 127.6bn and the latter, EUR 36.5bn: see Table 2, to be found at http://ec.europa.eu/eurostat/statistics-explained/index.php/File:Top_10_countries_as_extra_EU-28_partners_for_FDI_stocks,_EU-28,_end_2012%E2%80%932015_(billion_EUR)_YB17.png.

sensitive areas of public policy have grown also (see section II below). Compared to State-to-State Dispute Settlement (SSDS) mechanisms, investor to state dispute settlement mechanisms are criticised for enabling companies and multinationals the potential to undermine a country's public policy objectives with the threat to national sovereignty that this implies. Justifications for ISDS boil down to states' provision for protection of investors in order to progress with their development goals. However, the core drivers of globalisation are changing rapidly and the rise of countries capable of exponential growth, accentuates the negatives to ISDS, including the lack of democratic accountability of and scrutiny over third country investors, the use of private arbitrators, the secrecy of proceedings and rulings and no participatory rights for third parties holding a direct interest in the process.

To date, investment protection has been confined to case-specific international agreements, rather than through overarching bilateral agreements. Legally speaking, these agreements span the public international law basis of the treaties and the public law nature of the relationship between the investor and sovereign state concerned, and asymmetry between states in international agreements further complicates multilateral approaches to reforming ISDS. At EU level, Foreign Direct Investment was included in the European Union's powers under the Common Commercial Policy under the Treaty of Lisbon (ToL) in 2009, but such initiatives when involving ISDS reform remain complex and must respect the EU Member States' competences.[2] Thus, the entry into force of the Comprehensive Economic and Trade Agreement (CETA) between the EU and Canada in September 2017 is preliminary: all the EU Member States must ratify it, raising again the spectre of political resistance to its ISDS clause as experienced in 2016, particularly in the Belgium State of Wallonia. The ISDS mechanisms in CETA must respect the delineation between EU and Member State competences established by the Court of Justice of the European Union (CJEU) in May 2017, and Belgium raised important questions for the CJEU in September 2017 on the compatibility of CETA with EU law, even before the preliminary entry into force of CETA[3] to which the CJEU recently gave an answer (see section III.A below).

Following EU Commission President Jean Claude Juncker's State of the Union Address in September 2017, the EU is committed to making ISDS fit for purpose both within the EU 28 Member States but also in the EU's external relations with

[2] See Consolidated version of the Treaty on the Functioning of the European Union [2008] OJ C 115/47, Art 207(1): 'The common commercial policy shall be based on uniform principles, particularly with regard to changes in tariff rates, the conclusion of tariff and trade agreements relating to trade in goods and services, and the commercial aspects of intellectual property, foreign direct investment, the achievement of uniformity in measures of liberalisation, export policy and measures to protect trade such as those to be taken in the event of dumping or subsidies. The common commercial policy shall be conducted in the context of the principles and objectives of the Union's external action.'

[3] See Belgian Ministry for Foreign Affairs, Foreign Trade and Development Co-operation, 'Minister Reynders Submits Request for an Opinion on CETA' (2017) https://diplomatie.belgium.be/en/newsroom/news/2017/minister_reynders_submits_request_opinion_ceta. For the form and content of the request, see 'CETA: Belgian Request for an Opinion from the European Court of Justice', https://diplomatie.belgium.be/sites/default/files/downloads/ceta_summary.pdf.

third countries.[4] The EU is abiding by its commitment to unprecedented transparency in all its trade and investment actions[5] following the pathway set down by President Juncker. Improved democratic controls over ISDS to improve public trust at home and abroad, will also be an important yardstick. Already the United Nations Commission on International Trade Law (UNCITRAL) working group began work in November 2017 on the topic of ISDS reform and the EU has been advocating the Multilateral Investment Court (MIC) to this end.

This contribution focuses on ISDS in EU external relations. Section III explores EU policy reform of ISDS – notably proposing a new permanent, judge-based MIC for investor-state disputes – to set a level playing field at global level for the protection of FDI while also guaranteeing states and society their democratic rights to shape public policy. Section IV then examines the experience of Brazil and Latin America, revealing a long-established refusal of any transfer of sovereignty through bilateral agreements regarding ISDS, resorting more to experimental forms of mediation based on the willingness of the state concerned.

Given that investor protection clauses have not been incorporated within the EU–MERCOSUR draft trade agreement, and the consistent refusal of Brazil's parliament to ratify agreements containing ISDS, would a multi-lateral investment court render ISDS more palatable to Brazil and other ISDS averse countries? Or is there indeed a sufficient critical mass of problem cases to justify the EU's bazooka approach in the form of the MIC. Is this solution proportionate as well as acceptable democratically and legally speaking, even if the questions as to the compatibility of the MIC with EU law are apparently now solved?[6] While the European Commission can negotiate and ratify agreements containing provisions for the protection of direct foreign investments of third country nationals in the EU (and vice versa),[7] the EU Member States must be involved in the negotiation of clauses on dispute settlement between investors and states, as well as in relation to non-direct foreign investment ('portfolio' investments made without any intention to influence the management and control of an undertaking). The Member States' national constitutional procedures must be respected in the ratification of

[4] See European Commission, *President Jean Claude Juncker's State of the Union Address 2017* (Brussels 13 September 2017) http://europa.eu/rapid/press-release_SPEECH-17-3165_en.htm.

[5] The initial time table foresaw agreement by end 2017. For the European Union's Europa Portal dedicated to this 13th round of EU–MERCOSUR negotiations, go to http://trade.ec.europa.eu/doclib/press/index.cfm?id=1761. See also European Commission factsheet introducing the deal so far, to be found at http://trade.ec.europa.eu/doclib/docs/2017/december/tradoc_156465.pdf. In the policy *Factsheet* explaining the agreement, the European Commission makes clear that the EU–MERCOSUR Agreement will include provisions for civil society's input regarding the implementation, including any environmental concerns. However, there is no provision for ISDS: transparency reporting on the negotiations mentions dispute settlement although ISDS will not be dealt with in the body of the EU–MERCOSUR Agreement itself.

[6] See Opinion 1/17, 30 April 2019, press release no 52/19, https://curia.europa.eu/jcms/upload/docs/application/pdf/2019-04/cp190052en.pdf.

[7] See Opinion 2/15 of the CJEU, Press Release 52/17 of 16 May 2017, to be found at https://curia.europa.eu/jcms/upload/docs/application/pdf/2017-05/cp170052en.pdf.

such clauses in multilateral or bilateral agreements between the European Union and third countries.

All this said, the conclusions consider whether Latin American approaches present a viable alternative that the EU might emulate – even in part – in the modernisation of its ISDS system, or whether these approaches present more of a blank cartridge in addressing sovereignty and democracy concerns (see section V below). Is there any intermediate solution in-between the European legal bazooka and the Latin American blank cartridge?

II. ISDS: Advantages, Disadvantages and Alternatives to ISDS

As of the late 1990s, ISDS claims by investors exploded, notably in the framework of the NAFTA,[8] and put the spotlight on the potential for investors to make use of it to shape sensitive public policy in a host state. The most recent data relating to investment cases globally from 1986 to 2018,[9] show a surge over the last 20 years both in terms of the number of new cases opened every year and in the number of arbitral decisions issued every year: combined over time, the number of cases launched rose from under 50 in the mid-1990s to nearly 800 in 2015, and the combined number of decisions issued rose from under 50 in the mid-1990s to over 700 in 2015.

A few milestone examples of investor-state disputes have contributed to this snowballing in societal resistance to ISDS mechanisms. In the late 2000s, the *Vattenfall* claims against Germany awakened the public protests in Europe.[10] In Australia, the fire was started by the Philip Morris claim under UNCITRAL rules challenging Australian tobacco Advertising Restrictions,[11] pushing the Australian government to announce in 2011 that it would discontinue the practice of seeking inclusion of investor state dispute settlement provisions in trade agreements with developing countries.[12] Other countries are moving in the same direction.[13]

[8] See eg Julien Chaisse 'The Issue of Treaty Shopping in International Law of Foreign Investment – Structuring (and Restructuring) of Investments to Gain Access to Investment Agreements' (2015) 11(2) *Hastings Business Law Review* 225–306.

[9] See Julien Chaisse and Rahul Donde 'The State of Investor-State Arbitration – A Reality Check of the Issues, Trends, and Directions in Asia-Pacific' (2018) 51(1) *The International Lawyer* 47–67.

[10] In 2012 Vattenfall filed suit at the Washington-based International Center for Settlement of Investment Disputes (ICSID), demanding $6 billion in compensation in reaction to the 'nuclear exit' programme to close down all German nuclear plants by 2021.

[11] See www.ag.gov.au/internationalrelations/internationallaw/pages/tobacco-plainpackaging.aspx.

[12] Australian Government, Department of Foreign Affairs & Trade, Gillard Government Trade Policy Statement, *Trading Our Way to More Jobs and Prosperity* (2011). See Jürgen Kurtz, 'The Australian Trade Policy Statement on Investor-State Dispute Settlement' (2011) 15 American Society of International law.

[13] South Africa has stated it will withdraw from treaties with ISDS clauses, and India is also considering such a position. Indonesia plans to let treaties with ISDS clauses lapse when they need renewal. Brazil has refused any treaty with ISDS clauses.

The usual system of dispute settlement became increasingly contentious in the face of negative public attention and criticism, snowballing into concerted societal resistance to the system in operation, but also to proposed modernising approaches to ISDS. Currently, ISDS relies on a court of arbitrators that decides behind closed doors and does not publish its decisions. The lack of transparency in the dispute resolution goes to the heart of public suspicions,[14] giving rise to fears that ever more powerful multinationals operating globally, are thus enabled – without democratic accountability – to side-step public policies and the democratic processes that have formulated them. Large scale infrastructure investment decisions today under one government, are capable of locking a country into time frames lasting well beyond the term of office of the government undertaking the commitment, in some cases even lasting generations. The exponential growth potential of emerging economies has compounded these concerns in a globalising world.

In October 2014 *The Economist* printed an opinion piece[15] summing up the situation in a sweeping generalisation:

> If you wanted to convince the public that international trade agreements are a way to let multinational companies get rich at the expense of ordinary people, this is what you would do: give foreign firms a special right to apply to a secretive tribunal of highly paid corporate lawyers for compensation whenever a government passes a law to, say, discourage smoking, protect the environment or prevent a nuclear catastrophe. Yet that is precisely what thousands of trade and investment treaties over the past half century have done, through a process known as 'investor-state dispute settlement', or ISDS.

The Economist is a mainstream media outlet following high journalistic standards and received as a source of quality, but in this case serves rather to conflate the negative dimension of ISDS mechanisms, oversimplifying the technical legal and political challenges facing governments and policy makers seeking common ground in international negotiations to respect democratic values in line with public policies while importantly also, providing the legal certainty for investors enabling development in other countries. There are indeed negative facets to ISDS mechanisms, and yet the ultimate purpose provides a legitimate justification for ISDS: investors underwriting the development of other countries need legal certainty when investing in foreign jurisdictions where domestic rule of law and governance cannot be trusted.

For some, the central rationale justifying ISDS is obvious, while for others it is less so. The main justifications for ISDS essentially rely on the procedural legitimacy of an investor to initiate claims concerning the application of an investment

[14] See European Ombudsman, 'Ombudsman: "Further steps to increase TTIP transparency necessary"' (2015); S Preschal and ME De Leeuw, 'Transparency: A General Principle of EU Law?' in U Bernitz and others (eds), *General Principles of EC Law in a Process of Development* (London, Kluwer Law International, 2008) 204–29; Pierpaolo Settembri, 'Transparency and the EU Legislator: "Let he Who is Without Sin Cast the First Stone"' (2005) 43 *Journal of Common Market Studies* 637–54.

[15] See 'The Arbitration Game' (n 14).

treaty – based on the mistrust of the judicial system of the host country – as well as political dependence in the state SSDS system.

On procedural legitimacy, it allows a foreign investor to avoid the host state's national courts where their independence, efficiency or competence is questionable. In some countries an ISDS system may be faster than domestic court procedures, for instance by removing state-immunity obstacles that might otherwise complicate domestic legal claims. Recourse to independent and experienced arbitrators under ISDS – in theory – ensures adjudication of claims by a qualified and neutral third party. Finally, it also allows for the recognition and enforcement of arbitral awards in many jurisdictions, especially if the ISDS mechanism employed is governed by the Convention on the Settlement of Investment Disputes between States and Nationals of Other States (the ICSID Convention)[16] or the New York Convention.

In terms of the potential for political interference, the ISDS approach gives the investor a directly-actionable right to avoid recourse to diplomatic protection which would be the case under SSDS. The investor here is not reliant on its home state's willingness to bring claims or exercise diplomatic protection.

Also, whereas the dispute settlement mechanism (DSM) is undergoing an apparent 'depoliticisation', the ISDS confers an autonomous and actionable right to start or continue litigation that is less dependent on politics or the willingness of the investor's home country.[17] Nevertheless, certain cases of a particularly sensitive nature might prevent a state from initiating a procedure against another state, in which case a state would simply be hiding behind its investor. Another procedural argument in favour of ISDS is that in many countries, investment agreements are not directly enforceable in domestic courts. Therefore, an investor suffering discrimination, or whose investment is expropriated even, may not seek redress by invoking investment protection rules before these domestic courts. Investor to state dispute settlement here would allow the investor to rely directly on the rules specifically designed to protect their investment.

In its 2010 Communication *Towards a Comprehensive European International Investment Policy*,[18] the European Commission also sees the advantage that 'an investment involves the establishment of a long-term relationship with the host state which cannot be easily diverted to another market in the event of a problem with the investment', and that the absence of an ISDS 'would in fact discourage investors and make a host economy less attractive than others'. However, when examining the Transatlantic Trade and Investment Partnership (TTIP),

[16] André de Carvalho Ramos, 'O diálogo das cortes: o Supremo Tribunal Federal e a Corte Interamericana de Direitos Humanos' in Amaral Junior and others (orgs), *O STF e o Direito Internacional dos Direitos Humanos* (São Paulo, Quartier Latin, 2009).

[17] See JAF Costa and VDR Gabriel, 'A Proteção dos investidores nos acordos de cooperação e favorecimento de investimentos: perspectivas e limites' (2016) 49 *Revista de Arbitragem e Mediação* 127–55.

[18] See European Commission Communication, 'Towards a Comprehensive European International Investment Policy', *COM* (2010) 343.

the European Parliament took the opposite view. It saw the inclusion of ISDS in the EU-negotiated agreements not as a necessity but rather as 'a conscious and informed policy choice that requires political and economic justification' and that 'the question whether to include ISDS should be decided for each International Investment Agreement in the light of the particular circumstances'.[19]

Turning to the disadvantages of ISDS systems, it seems that the positive aspects can be neutralised by the political context in which the ISDS operates. Most obviously, by its very nature ISDS grants foreign investors greater rights than those enjoyed by domestic investors, creating unequal competitive conditions, even more so in the case of forum shopping. Multinational companies are effectively enabled to opt for 'nationality planning' when resolving a dispute, choosing the most favourable location giving access to ISDS. In democratic terms, this would enable investment protection rules to be abused because it would bring into question the legitimate policy choices of countries. This is no minor fault or any simple imperfection in the current system.[20]

Strong public concerns have arisen in some of the most recent cases brought by investors against states, as demonstrated in the above *Vattenfall v Germany* and in *Philip Morris v Australia* cases. Both implied negative impacts on national choices in sensitive public policy areas (health and energy), and both have been treated in absolute secrecy. Neither Germany nor Australia have made any changes to their public policies as a result of these investors' lawsuits, nor can either be forced to do so by the ISDS tribunals concerned. But this in no way diminishes the concerns as to the legitimacy of ISDS as a means of 'rendering justice'. Additionally, host states are exposed to legal and financial risks as a result of actual or threatened ISDS suits. The legitimacy of ISDS is questionable first and foremost because it is modelled on private commercial arbitration where confidentiality reigns. Indeed, most existing Bilateral Investment Treaties (BITs) provide for disputes to be settled behind closed doors unless both Parties agree otherwise.[21] The lack of transparency raises concerns as to the independence and impartiality of both the arbitrators and process.

[19] See Amendment 2, Justification in the *European Parliament Report on the Proposal for a Regulation Establishing a Framework for Managing Financial Responsibility Linked to Investor-State Dispute Settlement Tribunals Established by International Agreements to Which the European Union Is Party*, COM(2012)0335–C70155/2012–2012/0163(COD) of 26 March 2013.

[20] See Commission, *Fact sheet, Investment Protection and ISDS in EU agreements* (2013) 5.

[21] The World Bank's International Centre for the Settlement of Investment Disputes (ICSID) is required by ICSID Administrative and Financial Regulation 22 to make public, information on the registration of all requests for arbitration and to indicate in due course the date and method of the termination of each proceeding. It also publishes the vast majority of awards with the consent of the parties. If the parties do not consent, ICSID publishes excerpts showing the tribunal's reasoning. The ICSID website has published awards for most completed arbitrations, and decisions in investor-state arbitrations outside of ICSID are also publicly available online. See 'International Centre for the Settlement of Investment Disputes, ICSID Cases', Icsid.worldbank.org; 'International Centre for the Settlement of Investment Disputes, View Decisions and Awards'. For the website, go to https://icsid.worldbank.org/en/>.

There are instances of companies initiating disputes as a tactic to pressurise the host state to influence or refrain from certain policy measures. While such cases are usually unsuccessful in the end, they do take up time, money and resources for the host state, implying a threat to the latter's right to regulate. Also, ISDS does not allow for the correction of an erroneous decision, as normally arbitrators' decisions are not subject to appeal. Moreover, it fails to ensure consistency between decisions adopted by different tribunals on identical or similar issues because there is no formal system for precedent setting in relation to the arbitrators' decisions, and even though they will recall the reasoning in previous cases in their rulings, they are under no obligation to do so. Ultimately also, ISDS is typically a very expensive system on both sides, and in any case in terms of outcome, because normal jurisdictions are subject to quantitative limits as regards, for instance, reimbursements that do not apply to arbitrators.

Alternative dispute resolution (ADR) mechanisms should be mentioned here: frequently combining SSDS or ISDS, they help appease the critics of the system and offer practical advantages. Typically, ADR precedes the commencement of international investment arbitration and is subject to the willingness of both parties to accept mediation instead of arbitration. While it cannot make up for all the disadvantages of ISDS, it does reduce the number of disputes taken to full-scale arbitration. The large number of cases resolved by ADR models is not in itself a guarantee of the system's success, but it does prove that parties are much more inclined to opt for clarification over litigation where there is a focal point through which to address concerns. ADR can help resolve disputes at an early stage, preventing them from severely and permanently damaging the relationship between the investor and host country. The more informal and flexible nature of ADR could similarly benefit investor to state arbitration, helping also to save time and money. Should the parties nevertheless go on to arbitration, they would have prepared the field and perhaps even solved some minor questions. Being familiar with the role of an Ombudsman at both European and national levels, the EU no doubt considered this when, for instance, creating an Investment Ombudsman at EU level.

As we know, the origin of BITs goes back to the post-colonisation era[22] and the need to ensure protection of foreign investment in countries under political transition or where governance is weak or lacking. ISDS is difficult to justify in well-governed domestic legal systems, such as Canada or the USA, countries characterised by sound legal systems, general good governance and relevant expertise

[22] The first one recollected in the German Pakistan BIT of 1959. We are fully in the post colonialism era. Previously States had other means to protect their investments. First of all, essentially, they consisted in public investments or investment made by state owned companies or, in the simplest case, investments made by the occupants in the colony. There was no need of special protection beside the one already given by the military presence in the country and by the jurisdiction exercised by the judicial order set up by the occupant. Or, as last resort, the 'gunboat diplomacy' applied. See Kenneth J Vandevelde, 'A Brief History of International Investment Agreements' (2005) 12 *UC Davis Journal of International Law & Policy* 157.

in local courts. Nevertheless, as concerns the potential for any agreement between the EU and the US, the asymmetry between the partners remains a source of concern in Europe that undermines any truly balanced agreement, particularly in terms of the degree of completion of their respective domestic markets and the unresolved extraterritorial issues of US law.[23] However, to impose a model on a case by case basis, according to a judgement on the performance of the judicial system of a sovereign country is certainly not the best way to start diplomatic relations. This was one of the reasons (perhaps the only reason) for the inclusion of an ISDS clause in the EU agreements with Canada and the USA, both of which are undoubtedly fully developed judicial systems that certainly compare to the EU Member States for the purposes of equivalence. To impose an ISDS system on Canada and the USA, might be received as implying its imposition on all other trade partners, in a kind of blanket, non-discriminatory approach.

Of course, other ways could also be explored, such as negotiating only with trade partners that provide equivalent judicial systems in vital respects. In its above 2010 Communication, the European Commission recommended only negotiating with countries that respect the rule of law. In the influential Namur Declaration (see section III below), it was suggested that: 'the ratification of the key instruments for the defense of human rights, the core ILO conventions, the recommendations of the BEPS project (base erosion and profit shifting) and the Paris Climate agreement shall be obligatory for the parties'.[24] This is certainly reflected in the approach of the EU today: to ensure that so-called 'new generation' economic and trade treaties do not weaken the laws protecting the socio-economic, sanitary and environmental values pursued by the EU and its Member States in any ways, and further, they contribute to sustainable development, the reduction of poverty and inequalities and the fight against climate change. To this can now be added 'minimum corporate tax rates and verifiable targets for the reduction of greenhouse gas emissions'.

Following EU Commission President Jean Claude Juncker's State of the Union Address in September 2017, the EU is committed to making ISDS fit for purpose both within the EU 28 Member States but also in its external relations with third countries.[25] Looking at inwards investment, the EU published its paper on *Welcoming Foreign Direct Investment while Protecting Essential Interests*.[26] It promises a departure from previous EU approaches to resolving disputes arising between states over foreign investments through ISDS mechanisms. As concerns ISDS

[23] See *Declaration of Namur* of 5 December 2016, available at http://declarationdenamur.eu/en/index.php/namur-declaration/.

[24] See *The Declaration of Namur* (2015), adopted by the 6th conference of Ministers Responsible for cultural Heritage, Council of Europe, Namur, Belgium, 24 April 2015.

[25] See European Commission, *President Jean Claude Juncker's State of the Union Address 2017*, Brussels 13 September 2017, to be found at http://europa.eu/rapid/press-release_SPEECH-17-3165_en.htm.

[26] See COM(2017) 494 of 13 September 2017, available at https://ec.europa.eu/transparency/regdoc/rep/1/2017/EN/COM-2017-494-F1-EN-MAIN-PART-1.PDF.

and EU external relations, which is the primary focus of this paper, the pursuit of a multi-lateral investment court (MIC) is the culmination of the EU's policy research and consultations since December 2016. Any analysis and anticipation of the form and structure of the multi-lateral investment court will be affected by President Juncker's State of the Union Address, insisting on the values underpinning EU trade relations today, which significantly, includes unprecedented transparency for all the EU's trade dealings with other countries. According to the European Commission's *Reflection Paper on Harnessing Globalisation*, this means an end to ISDS as such, to be replaced by the multi-lateral investment court based on the principles of fairness and transparency in particular.[27] Ongoing negotiations at UN level have begun in November 2017 within the UNCITRAL Working Group set up for this purpose and are also demonstrating the influence of trends towards transparency.[28]

In the meantime, with signature in Chile on 8 March 2018 of the Trans-Pacific Partnership Agreement (TPP) by 11 Pacific Rim countries – excepting the USA – and the inclusion of ISDS provisions,[29] ISDS mechanisms are developing in parallel. The approach there is one of using a system of arbitrators, combined with transparency provisions making the hearings open to the public but also for experts and the public to make submissions, as well as for the decisions of the tribunals to be made public. Japan is signatory to the TPP while at the same time, has only just concluded the Economic Partnership Agreement with the EU, the latter containing no investor protection clauses. The EU has put its reformed Investment Court System on the table[30] and is reaching out to all partner countries, including Japan, to work towards the setting up of a Multilateral Investment Court. The revival of the TPP by continuing ISDS forms, further muddies the waters for ISDS reform and the shift towards a multilateral investment court in particular, although the scope and use of ISDS clauses has been considerably narrowed within the TPP.[31] As mentioned above, no provision for investor protection is made in the EU–MERCOSUR trade agreement either.

[27] See European Commission *Reflection Paper on Harnessing Globalisation*, COM(2017) 240 of 10 May 2017, at 15, to be found at https://ec.europa.eu/commission/sites/beta-political/files/reflection-paper-globalisation_en.pdf.

[28] See the UNCITRAL Working Group III website, to be found at www.uncitral.org/uncitral/en/commission/working_groups/3Investor_State.html. It includes submissions from two international intergovernmental organisations, International Centre for Settlement of Investment Disputes (ICSID) and the Permanent Court of Arbitration (PCA). The submissions of the ICSID and the PCA can be found at https://documents-dds-ny.un.org/doc/UNDOC/LTD/V17/073/14/PDF/V1707314.pdf?OpenElement.

[29] See the website of the Australian Department of Foreign Affairs and Trade, for reporting on developments, http://dfat.gov.au/trade/agreements/tpp/Pages/trans-pacific-partnership-agreement-tpp.aspx.

[30] See European Commission Memo: Key elements of the EU–Japan Economic Partnership Agreement, to be found at http://trade.ec.europa.eu/doclib/press/index.cfm?id=1687.

[31] See for examples, an interview with Minister David Parker, of the New Zealand Ministry for Foreign Affairs on 12 November 2017, in *The Standard*, to be found at https://thestandard.org.nz/the-tpp11-negotiations-isds-provisions-are-gone-almost/.

III. The Evolution of ISDS: From Bilateral Investment Treaties to a Multilateral Investment Court

To understand the policy evolution at EU level that has led to today's proposal for a Multilateral Investment Court, two European Commission Communications provide valuable insight into the evolution of the strategic negotiating course for the design of dispute settlement mechanisms involving investors and state, at EU and Member State levels.

The first is the 2010 Communication *Towards a Comprehensive European International Investment Policy*,[32] where the European Commission explained why a one-size-fits-all model for investment agreements with third countries was neither feasible nor desirable. Each specific negotiating context demands that the Commission elaborate specific further comment on certain common recommendations, broad principles and parameters for future investment agreements. The first of five recommendations listed deals with basic criteria for the selection of partner countries. According to this Communication, the EU's interest in pursuing investment negotiations depends, in the first place, on:

> the political, institutional and economic climate of our partner countries. The 'robustness' of investor protection through either host country or international arbitration would be important determinants in defining priority countries for EU investment negotiations. In particular, the capacity and the practice of our partners in upholding the rule of law, in a manner that provides a certain and sound environment to investors, are key determinants for assessing the value of investment protection negotiations.

The second recommendation relates to the very rationale of foreign investments:

> it is important that a common international investment policy not only enables the execution of a direct investment itself – the acquisition of a foreign enterprise or the establishment of one – but also that it enables and protects all the operations that accompany that investment and make it possible in practice: payments, the protection of intangible assets such as Intellectual Property Rights.

Third, the search for: 'balance between the different interests at stake, such as the protection of investors against unlawful expropriation or the right of each Party to regulate in the public interest, needs to be ensured'.

By extension, the fourth recommendation concerns the enforcement of investment commitments, importantly without yet mentioning the notion of a permanent court as such. Equally importantly however, it stresses the key EU-motivation of ensuring the effective enforceability of investment provisions through binding dispute settlement. In its recently concluded Free Trade Agreements (FTAs), the European Union has incorporated a SSDS system. To ensure effective enforcement, investment agreements also feature ISDS, which permits an

[32] See European Commission Communication *Towards a Comprehensive European International Investment Policy*, COM (2010) 343 final of 7 July 2010.

investor to make a claim against a government directly to binding international arbitration. Most obviously among these is the Energy Charter Treaty to which the EU is a party, and which contains investor-state dispute settlement mechanism, as do all the Member States' BITs.

Finally, the fifth recommendation addresses international responsibility: the exclusive external competence of the European Union rests in the European Commission for the negotiation of trade agreements, and which has argued that the European Union is the sole defendant regarding any measure taken by EU institutions as well as by a Member State 'which affects investments by third country nationals or companies falling within the scope of the agreement concerned'. In developing its new international investment policy, 'the Commission will address this issue, and in particular that of financial compensation, relying on available instruments, including, possibly, new legislation'. As the next section of this chapter makes clear, the so called 'Singapore' ruling of the Court of Justice of the European Union of May 2017 has since clarified somewhat the tensions between Member States and the EU, but further legal questions remain outstanding and Belgium has requested clarifications from the CJEU.

Significantly also, in that same 2010 Communication, the Commission indicated that future EU agreements including investment protection should include investor-state dispute settlement, but that to do so would be complicated by the fact that 'the Union has not historically been a significant actor in this field. Current structures are to some extent ill-adapted to the advent of the Union'.[33] Therefore, in approaching investor-state dispute settlement mechanisms, the Union should build on Member State practices to arrive 'at state-of-the art investor state dispute settlement mechanisms'.

In the framework of the negotiations of CETA and TTIP,[34] the EU opted to retain an ISDS system but with significant improvements to transparency and institutional structure. In line with the EU's approach before the WTO, a new EU system for ISDS should ensure transparency in requests for arbitration,

[33] For example, the ICSID Convention is open to signature and ratification by states members of the World Bank or party to the Statute of the International Court of Justice. The European Union qualifies under neither. In its communication, the Commission indicates that it will explore with interested parties the possibility that the European Union seek to accede to the ICSID Convention (noting that this would require amendment of the ICSID Convention).

[34] The TTIP mandate on ISDS (doc 11103/13 MP/sy 8 DG C 1 RESTREINT UE/EU RESTRICTED) refers to: 'Enforcement: the Agreement should aim to provide for an effective and state-of-the-art investor-to-state dispute settlement mechanism, providing for transparency, independence of arbitrators and predictability of the Agreement, including through the possibility of binding interpretation of the Agreement by the Parties. State-to-state dispute settlement should be included, but should not interfere with the right of investors to have recourse to the investor-to-state dispute settlement mechanisms. It should provide for investors as wide a range of arbitration fora as is currently available under the Member States' bilateral investment agreements. The investor-to-state dispute settlement mechanism should contain safeguards against manifestly unjustified or frivolous claims. Consideration should be given to the possibility of creating an appellate mechanism applicable to investor-to-state dispute settlement under the Agreement, and to the appropriate relationship between ISDS and domestic remedies.'

submissions, open hearings, *amicus curiae* briefs and publication of awards, and so forth.[35] Other improvements would involve granting public access to arbitration documents, including settlement agreements, and arbitral hearings, and allowing the participation of interested non-disputing parties such as civil society organisations in the process.[36]

Under public pressure, in 2014 the EU published its negotiating mandate, and as the negotiations progress, different papers are made partially available.[37] The Commission considers that improvement of ISDS is not conceivable without transparency.[38] NAFTA already gave an example of progress in transparency.[39]

Whether the accusations of lack of transparency and democratic legitimacy are well-founded or not, the only answer is that of more transparency and more participation to weaken the arguments of protesters. As regards the trade agreements themselves, there can be no sense in undertaking years of negotiations only to see them thrown out in the end, with all the waste of resources and energy that implies, not to mention the loss of face with commercial partners, who would likely hesitate to embark on further negotiations where a successful outcome would be so precarious.

The need for improvement in European consultation was clear. Wide public debates surrounding the signing of CETA revealed how the EU's way of negotiating international trade agreements and their content, is being challenged by ever broader sections of public opinion. The debates on the approval process of the CETA agreement raised concerns. An attempt to find a solution led to the *Declaration of Namur* of 5 December 2016,[40] which was the idea of the Belgian politician

[35] See also *UNCITRAL Rules on Transparency in Treaty-based Investor-State Arbitration* (New York: UN 2014). The Rules are found at www.uncitral.org/uncitral/en/uncitral_texts/arbitration/2014 Transparency.html.

[36] See 'ICSID, Arbitration Rules'. Icsid.worldbank.org: 'Under Art 29 of the US Model-BIT of 2004, all documents pertaining to ISDS have to be made public and amicus curiae briefs are allowed. However, no investment treaty allows other parties who have an interest in the dispute, other than the claimant investor and respondent government, to obtain standing in the adjudicative process'. #Under the Trans-Pacific Strategic Economic Partnership, the tribunals shall, subject to the consent of the disputing parties, conduct hearings open to the public. The tribunal will make available to the public documents relating to the dispute such as the notice of intent, the notice of arbitration, pleadings, memorials, minutes or transcripts of the hearings of the tribunal, where available; orders, awards and decisions of the tribunal. In addition, third parties can and increasingly do participate in investor-state arbitration by submitting amicus curiae petitions'.

[37] Communication to the Commission concerning transparency in TTIP negotiations, 25 Nov 2014, C(2014) 9052 final. See Marise Cremona, 'Guest Editorial: Negotiating the Transatlantic Trade and Investment Partnership (TTIP): Context and Scope of TTIP' (2015) 52 *Common Market Law Review* 351–62.

[38] On transparency, see F Ortino, 'Transparency of Investment Awards: External and Internal Dimensions' in J Nakagawa (ed), *Transparency in International Trade and Investment Dispute Settlement* (London and New York, Routledge, 2013) 119–58; C Titi, 'International Investment Law and Good Governance' in M Bungenberg and others (eds), *International Investment Law: A Handbook* (Baden Baden, Nomos, 2015) 1768; S Menétrey, 'La transparence dans l'arbitrage d'investissement' (2012) 1 *Revue de l'Arbitrage*; A Newcombe and L Paradell, *Law and Practice of Investment Treaties* (Alphen aan den Rijn, Kluwer Law International, 2009).

[39] See Titi, ibid 1768.

[40] See *Declaration of Namur* (n 24).

Paul Magnette, Minister-President representing the Walloon State of Belgium, who together with more than 40 lead academics from the EU, the US, and Canada, forged the *Declaration of Namur*. Insisting on EU values of solidarity, democracy and progress that constitute the European Union, it was certainly intended as a shot across the bows for any business as usual approach by the EU in negotiating trade agreements. It has proved highly influential on the evolution of the EU external relations today, specifically as concerns trade and investment. The approach advocated goes further than the current transparency rules and procedures envisaged at the multilateral level by UNCITRAL in December 2014,[41] calling for further advances in transparency and informed debate:

> Public analyses and contestation of the potential effects of a new economic and commercial treaty should be conducted before establishing a negotiating mandate, in order to guarantee that it will contribute to sustainable development, the reduction of poverty and inequality, and the fight against climate change;
>
> The negotiating mandates regarding mixed agreements should be the object of a prior parliamentary debate in the national and European Assemblies (as well as the regional Assemblies with equivalent powers), involving as much as possible representatives of civil society;
>
> The interim results of the negotiations should be made public and accessible in due course, so that civil society is ensured full knowledge and a parliamentary debate can take place before closing the negotiations;
>
> The 'provisional application' of agreements should not be favored, so that parliaments keep their full powers in the assent procedure of mixed agreements.[42]

There is no doubt that the CETA marked the application of a welcome new approach to transparency in trade negotiations which should help prevent the further spread of anxiety and campaigns based on rumour. Such relatively simple rules provide full respect of democratic checks and balances in the process and are inclusive of both civil society and democratic parliamentary control

[41] See the UNCITRAL Rules on Transparency in Treaty-based Investor-State Arbitration of 10 December 2014 to be found at www.uncitral.org. The Transparency Registry is also a key feature of the United Nations Convention on Transparency in Treaty-based Investor-State Arbitration (the 'Mauritius Convention on Transparency') adopted in December 2014, which extends the application of the Rules to investment treaties concluded before 1 April 2014. The Rules, the Convention and the Transparency Registry constitute the UNCITRAL standards on transparency. Original proposals to make all UNCITRAL arbitration under investment treaties public were not adopted after opposition by some states and by representatives of the arbitration industry who participated in the UNCITRAL working group negotiations as state representatives. See also the United Nations Convention on Transparency in Treaty-based Investor-State Arbitration ('Mauritius Convention') which will render the UNCITRAL Rules on Transparency in Treaty-based Investor State Arbitration also applicable to disputes arising out of investment treaties that were concluded prior to 1 April 2014 if both parties to the investment treaty are also party to the Mauritius Convention, to be found at www.uncitral.org/pdf/english/texts/arbitration/transparency-convention/Transparency-Convention-e.pdf. For the state of ratification, go to www.uncitral.org/uncitral/en/uncitral_texts/arbitration/2014Transparency_Convention_status.html. Latin American countries do not employ ISDS and are not signatories to the Mauritius Convention.

[42] See *Declaration of Namur* (n 24).

procedures – not forgetting the improved role for the European Parliament, which must now give its assent to trade agreements and has the right to be kept informed throughout the negotiations.

As for structural institutional aspects, this should also address ongoing concerns about the appointment of all arbitrators and potential conflicts of interest, by opting for the use of quasi-permanent arbitrators and/or appellate mechanisms. All those persons adjudicating disputes should possess the requisite skills, be fully independent, impartial, free from conflicts of interest, be 'affordable' to the parties, and subject to rules on qualifications, conduct and remuneration, through a code of conduct for example.

The second relevant European Commission Communication, issued in September 2015, formally proposed a new Investment Court System to replace ISDS clauses.[43] This Investment Court System was intended to replace the existing ISDS mechanisms in all ongoing and future EU investment negotiations, including the now failed EU–US negotiations on a Transatlantic Trade and Investment Partnership (TTIP). The ISDS chapter of the initial draft of the TTIP did not foresee such an idea. It was limited to a review of the way in which the ISDS arbitration tribunals work, on how to appoint the arbitrators, on creating a system of appeal, and on how to strengthen EU governments' rights to regulate in the public interest by clarifying and limiting the rights that investors are granted.[44]

The European Parliament's influence in shaping the proposal was substantial,[45] as was that of the Member States, national parliaments and stakeholders through the public consultation.[46] On the occasion of the proposal's launch, First Vice-President of the European Commission Frans Timmermans said:

> With our proposals for a new Investment Court System, we are breaking new ground. The new Investment Court System will be composed of fully qualified judges, proceedings will be transparent, and cases will be decided on the basis of clear rules. In addition, the Court will be subject to review by a new Appeal Tribunal. With this new system, we protect the governments' right to regulate, and ensure that investment disputes will be adjudicated in full accordance with the rule of law.

The then EU trade Commissioner, Cecilia Malmström, declared this 'a new, modernized system of investment courts, subject to democratic principles and public scrutiny'.

[43] See http://europa.eu/rapid/press-release_IP-15-5651_en.htm.

[44] On SSDS the proposal wanted to use the same method in place at WTO and to ensure that it is fully transparent.

[45] See EP Resolution(2015) 0252 of 8 July 2015 requiring 'a new system for resolving disputes between investors and states which is subject to democratic principles and scrutiny, where potential cases are treated in a transparent manner by publicly appointed, independent professional judges in public hearings and which includes an appellate mechanism, where consistency of judicial decisions is ensured, the jurisdiction of courts of the EU and of the Member States is respected, and where private interests cannot undermine public policy objectives' (XV).

[46] See http://trade.ec.europa.eu/consultations/index.cfm?consul_id=179.

The reform is driven by the intent to establish trust in the system. It aimed to replace the old, traditional form of dispute resolution suffering from a fundamental lack of trust, with 'a new system built around the elements that make citizens trust domestic or international courts'. The Commission intended that the new system would not be allowed to override the European ban on chicken carcasses washed with chlorine, nor could companies use legal technicalities to build frivolous cases against governments. With the opening up of investment tribunals to public scrutiny, documents would be public and interested parties, including NGOs, able to make submissions. Also, the EU system would eliminate any conflicts of interest by making sure that the arbitrators deciding on EU cases be above suspicion.

The formal report on the results of the consultation, released on 13 January 2015, identified four areas of particular concern, where further improvements to the EU approach should be explored:

i. the protection of the right to regulate;
ii. the establishment and functioning of arbitral tribunals;
iii. the review of ISDS decisions through an appellate mechanism;
iv. the relationship between domestic judicial systems and ISDS.

All this progress was made before the emergence of political and societal resistance to CETA's progress or the new Trump administration in the US made short shrift of TTIP. The idea of a permanent court had been accepted by Canada once CETA had been finalised, but it is still under discussion and probably will never be accepted by the Americans within the TTIP.[47]

This explains the European Commission's unexpected suggestion, on Christmas Eve 2016, to make a joint proposal with Canada exploring the introduction of a Multilateral Investment Court and to launch an impact assessment and a public consultation thereon.[48] The examples set with the CETA and TTIP – their arduous negotiation and ratification and ultimate defeat bringing to mind the metaphor of 'Caudine Forks' – provide a considerable hurdle for the survival of further such mechanisms. Attempts at including such a court in future agreements face a dicey passage through the democratic processes required of an agreement's ratification.

The impact of all this on balancing values on the current policy path set for EU trade and investment is clear today, particularly in terms of transparency and inclusion of civil society and interested parties beyond the direct parties to investor protection mechanisms. These values must be seen as including the EU's respect for its international commitments, notably including the Global Compact and the Paris Agreement. Rooted in the two new 2017 Communications on

[47] See US–EU Joint Report on TTIP Progress to Date, 17 January 2017, available at http://trade.ec.europa.eu/doclib/docs/2017/january/tradoc_155242.pdf.

[48] See http://europa.eu/rapid/press-release_MEMO-16-4350_en.htm.

A Progressive Trade Policy to Harness Globalisation[49] and on *Welcoming Foreign Direct Investment while Protecting Essential Interests*[50] – and not forgetting work already done under the previous 2015 *Communication on Trade for All: Towards a More Responsible Trade and Investment Policy*[51] – initiatives on trade and investment are to be balanced with global governance in human rights and working conditions, food safety, public health, environmental protection and animal welfare. Very significant also is the new Advisory Group on EU trade agreements specifically designed to include civil society in trade policy formulation.[52]

A. From a Permanent Investment Court to a Multilateral Investment Court

In theory three models offer alternatives to ISDS. The first two rely on existing models: by replacing ISDS by SSDS,[53] by replacing ISDS with domestic dispute resolution[54] or a combination of both.[55] With the lessons learned from the beleaguered CETA and TTIP negotiations, and CETA's ratification at EU level, the European Union has been recoiling from proposing such a system in its trade negotiations.

The third option was the creation of a permanent international investment court. Opting for this approach, in its new generation of bilateral FTAs, the EU proposed a permanent bilateral investment court: this proposed new model would apply to conflicts arising between investors and states under the implementation of bilateral investment treaties, and would be governed by a permanent court composed of judges subject to a code of conduct and working in a more transparent manner.

[49] See COM(2017) 492 of 13 September 2017, to be found at https://ec.europa.eu/transparency/regdoc/rep/1/2017/EN/COM-2017-492-F1-EN-MAIN-PART-1.PDF. See the European Commission Communication, *Towards a Comprehensive European International Investment Policy*, COM (2010) 343 final of 7 July 2010.

[50] See COM(2017) 494 of 13 September 2017, to be found at https://ec.europa.eu/transparency/regdoc/rep/1/2017/EN/COM-2017-494-F1-EN-MAIN-PART-1.PDF.

[51] On the rational and concrete next steps for trade and investment, see COM(2015) 497 of 14 October 2015 http://trade.ec.europa.eu/doclib/docs/2015/october/tradoc_153846.pdf.

[52] The EU civil society dialogue on trade can be followed at http://trade.ec.europa.eu/civilsoc/index.cfm, and the procedure for establishing the list of trade experts was published 13 September 2017, COM(2017)6113, to be found at http://trade.ec.europa.eu/civilsoc/index.cfm.

[53] This is the WTO system under its dispute settlement mechanism (DSM).

[54] This option has merits mainly in countries where reliance on ISDS is less important because of their sound legal systems, good governance and local courts' expertise. Different will be the interest in countries with weak governance.

[55] For instance this is the option chosen by Australia in its recent agreements with Japan, Malaysia, New Zealand and USA, or by Brazil in its CFIAs. These treaties leave investment disputes subject to domestic courts but complement this process with the possibility of state-state proceedings under the treaty.

Initially welcomed as a novelty, there was hardly enough time for commentators to reflect upon this permanent bilateral investment court[56] before upgrading it to the even more ambitious idea of an MIC.[57]

It is true that the idea of a MIC was already proffered during the 2014 public consultation on investment protection, where various stakeholders suggested that investment dispute resolution would best be undertaken multilaterally rather than through bilateral reforms.[58] At that time, the European Commission took a first step with the introduction of a bilateral Investment Court System (ICS), which was incorporated into the EU trade agreements with Canada and Vietnam. After the public consultation in the summer of 2014, the European Commission modified its proposal for the TTIP by proposing a permanent court instead of the traditional – even if improved – ISDS system. The new system would bring improvements on two fronts: clarify and improve investment protection rules on the one hand, and improve the operation of the dispute settlement system on the other.

On the first front, the improvements were intended to appease concerns as to the negative impact of ISDS on state's right to regulate, by actually specifying that the states' right to regulate is preserved[59] so that companies could not successfully bring claims against a state's right to regulate where these claims are based on public policy reasons.

[56] Among others, see Catharine Titi, 'The European Union's Proposal for an International Investment Court: Significance, Innovations and Challenges Ahead' (2016) 1(3) *Transnational Dispute Management* 122–45; Ingo Venzcke, 'Investor-State Dispute Settlement in TTIP from the Perspective of a Public Law Theory of International Adjudication' (2017) 17 *Journal of World Investment & Trade* 374–400.

[57] Interesting to mention that this idea was already suggested by Professor Van Harten in 2008, see 'A Case for International Investment Court', for the *Inaugural Conference of the Society for International Economic Law*, 16 July 2008, available at http://papers.ssrn.com/sol3/papers.cfm?abstract_id=1153424.

[58] See S Hindelang and C-P Sassenrath, 'The Investment Chapters of the EU's International Trade and Investment Agreements in a Comparative Perspective', for the European Parliament (2015) 105, available at http://bookshop.europa.eu/uri?target=EUB:NOTICE:QA0115679:EN:HTML; S Hindelang, 'Study on Investor-State Dispute Settlement ("ISDS") and Alternatives of Dispute Resolution in International Investment Law', *Study for the European Parliament* (2014) 63, http://ssrn.com/abstract=2525063.

[59] Some arbitrators already judged on this issue: see *Saluka Investments BV v The Czech Republic* (2006): 'It is now established in international law that States are not liable to pay compensation to a foreign investor when, in the normal exercise of their regulatory powers, they adopt in a non-discriminatory manner bona fide regulations that are aimed at the general welfare'. *Methanex v United States* (2005): 'As a matter of general international law, a non-discriminatory regulation for a public purpose, which is enacted in accordance with due process and, which affects, inter alia, a foreign investor or investment is not deemed expropriatory and compensable unless specific commitments had been given by the regulating government to the then putative foreign investor contemplating investment that the government would refrain from such regulation'. The EU–South Korea FTA appears to be the first EU document to explicitly refer to the right to regulate (EU–South Korea FTA, OJ 2011 L 127/6, Art 7.1(4); see also the preamble and Arts 13.3, 13.4.3, 13.5.2 and 13.7). In the current FTAs under ratification or being negotiated a provision will refer to the right of Governments to take measures to achieve legitimate public policy objectives, on the basis of the level of protection that they deem appropriate. Is it enough? All depends, as in any legal order, from the way an ISDS tribunal, even if it was a properly constituted court, would interpret any legal text intended to protect public policy objectives.

Operationally, the new court system envisages a public system composed of a First Instance Tribunal and an Appeals Tribunal. Judgments would be issued by publicly appointed judges with high qualifications, comparable to those required for the members of permanent international courts, such as the International Court of Justice and the WTO Appellate Body. The system would be transparent, with open hearings and comments available on-line, and a right for interested parties to intervene. Rules on forum-shopping and frivolous claims would improve the current system by avoiding multiple and parallel proceedings.

The progression towards a multilateral system of investment dispute settlement was to appease the adverse national and public reactions to the CETA with Canada, and also the recent anti-EU movements that arose within the European Union itself in 2016, ranging from Brexit to the referendum on the EU Agreement with Ukraine, for example. Other countries faced the same kinds of criticism in respect of ISDS systems. On Christmas Eve 2016, the Commission launched the public consultation[60] on a multilateral reform of investment dispute resolution, including the possible establishment of a permanent Multilateral Investment Court.

There are obvious advantages to a multilateral international investment court, not least that a standing international investment court would guard against the non-transparent and non-democratic nature of ISDS. By replacing the system of multiple ad hoc arbitral tribunals with one single institutional structure, a standing international investment court would safeguard national sovereignty and supranational governance, as it would be composed of adjudicators (or judges)[61] appointed by States on a permanent basis and could also comprise an appeals chamber. It would be like any other typical international judicial body,[62] but would also operate as a public institution serving the interests of investors and states alike. And more broadly speaking, it would not only strengthen the legitimacy of the investor-state regime. It would contribute to enhancing consistency and

[60] The consultation was open until 15 March 2017. See http://trade.ec.europa.eu/consultations/index.cfm?consul_id=233.

[61] For being different from current arbitrate procedures and guarantee independence and impartiality of adjudicators, it should be composed by judges with security of tenure and exclusivity of function, ie judges, unlike arbitrators in the present regime, would not be permitted to continue serving as counsel or expert witnesses.

[62] According to Christian Tomuschat, an international judicial body, to be classified as such, must meet five basic criteria: (i) it must be permanent; (ii) it must have been established by an international legal instrument; (iii) it must resort to international law in order to decide the cases submitted to it; (iv) it must decide the cases on the basis of preexisting rules of procedure; and (v) its decisions must be legally binding. Christian Tomuschat, 'International Courts and Tribunals with Regionally Restricted and/or Specialized Jurisdiction', *Judicial settlement of international disputes: international Court of Justice, other courts and tribunals, arbitration and conciliation: an international symposium* (Max-Planck Institute, 1987) 285–416. Cesare Romano adds two other criteria: (i) the judicial body must be composed (at least in its majority) of judges who have not been appointed ad hoc by the parties, but rather who have been chosen before a case is submitted through an impartial mechanism; (ii) among the parties to the dispute, at least one must be a sovereign state or an international organisation. Cesare PR Romano, 'The Proliferation of International Judicial Bodies: the Pieces of the Puzzle' (1999) 21 *International Law and Politics* 713–15.

predictability in the interpretation of international treaties, especially in today's tangled and fragmented spider's web of some 3000 BITs.

The shared interest on this project was also evident in the exploratory talks held at the technical level by the EU with third countries on 13 and 14 December 2016 in Geneva.[63] On that occasion the European Commission and Canadian Government[64] co-hosted discussions on a multilateral investment court. Reporting on this event, the European Commission found that the:

> very positive attendance (almost 170 delegates from more than 60 countries and eight international organizations representing all major trade and investment world actors) is evidence that there is an appetite for reforming the current system of investor-state dispute settlement and significant interest in the idea of establishing a permanent multilateral investment dispute settlement mechanism.

Discussions continued among trade ministers on the margins of the World Economic Forum in Davos in January 2017. Meanwhile at European Commission level, an impact assessment process on the option of establishing a multilateral investment court was ongoing. A 12-week online public consultation process was launched in December 2016 and a stakeholder meeting held in Brussels in February 2017. In July 2017, UNCITRAL agreed to work on the possible reform of ISDS[65] and actual work at UNCITRAL level on the proposal began on 27 November 2017.[66] In line with the European Commission's commitment to transparency, all activities and related documentation are published on the Europa website,[67] including videos of public consultations, of which the last was held on 20 November 2017.

Certainly, the current proposal for a permanent bilateral court – even though not yet operational – provides food for thought on what a multilateral investment court might look like. The first instance and the appeal level will be retained, but for multilateral negotiations various issues arise for which the bilateral context

[63] See www.trade.ec.europa.eu/doclib/press/index.cfm?id=1606.

[64] In the EU–Canada Joint Interpretative Instrument it is stated: 'Therefore, CETA represents an important and radical change in investment rules and dispute resolution. It lays the basis for a multilateral effort to develop further this new approach to investment dispute resolution into a Multilateral Investment Court. The EU and Canada will work expeditiously towards the creation of the Multilateral Investment Court. It should be set up once a minimum critical mass of participants is established, and immediately replace bilateral systems such as the one in CETA, and be fully open to accession by any country that subscribes to the principles underlying the Court.'

[65] See press release at www.unis.unvienna.org/unis/en/pressrels/2017/unisl250.html.

[66] See Note by the UNCITRAL Secretariat, 'Possible reform of investor-State dispute settlement (ISDS)' A/CN.9/WG.III/WP.142 of 18 September 2017, to be found at <www.uncitral.org/pdf/english/workinggroups/wg_3/142-e.pdf. For the EU response to the UNCITRAL, see *The identification and consideration of concerns as regards investor to state dispute settlement* (2017), to be found at http://trade.ec.europa.eu/doclib/docs/2017/november/tradoc_156402.pdf. See also United Nations Commission on International Trade Law Working Group III (Investor-State Dispute Settlement Reform) Thirty-fourth session Vienna, 27 November–1 December 2017 to be found at www.uncitral.org/uncitral/en/commission/working_groups/3Investor_State.html.

[67] To be found at http://trade.ec.europa.eu/doclib/press/index.cfm?id=1608, for comprehensive links to EU and UN documents, including explanatory information and videos.

cannot provide answers, such as the scope of the tribunal, its membership, the appointment of its adjudicators, geographical balance, whether it will be permanent, provision for enforcement, cost allocation.[68] At the same time, whether a permanent multilateral investment court can become be part of an already existing international organisation is a matter that has been kept open.

Among crucial questions to be addressed was the compatibility of such courts with the EU legal order.[69] The question on the nature of such agreements has been solved,[70] and it is clear now that the Member States retain control over investor to state dispute settlement mechanisms. A public consultation and an impact assessment are also relevant but the opinion of the Court of Justice, especially after its opinion on the accession to ECHR,[71] on such a controversial and crucial issue was all the more necessary.[72]

[68] Projected costs would be comparable to those of other international tribunals, such as the International Law of the Sea Tribunal, which costs around USD 10 million per year to run or the WTO Appellate Body which costs around USD 7 million to operate per year.

[69] See Laurens Ankersmit, 'The Compatibility of Investment Arbitration in EU Trade Agreements with the EU Judicial System' (2016) 13 *Journal for European Environmental & Planning Law* 46–63; Inge Govaere, 'TTIP and Dispute Settlement: Potential Consequences for the Autonomous EU Legal Order' *College of Europe Legal Studies* (2016); J Kokott and C Sobotta, 'Investment Arbitration and EU Law' (2016) *Cambridge Yearbook of European Legal Studies* 3–19; Cremona (n 39). See recently Gisèle Uwera, 'Investor-State Dispute Settlement (ISDS) in Future EU Investment-Related Agreements: Is the Autonomy of the EU Legal Order an Obstacle?' (2016) 15 *The Law & Practice of International Courts and Tribunals* 102–51; Ana Lopéz Rodríguez, 'Robbing Peter to Pay Paul? ISDS and ICS from an EU law perspective' (2017) 86 *Nordic Journal of International Law* 470–98; D Bianchi, 'Bazooka ou cartouches à blanc? Une comparaison des approches juridiques en évolution au Brésil et dans l'Union européenne en matière de mécanismes de règlement des différends entre investisseurs et États', at Tour's conference on 'Le nouveau système européen des règlements des différends relatif aux investissements', November 2018, available at www.canal-u.tv/producteurs/irji/le_nouveau_systeme_europeen_de_reglement_des, *Revue du Droit de l'Union européenne* (forthcoming).

[70] See case A-2/15 on the Singapore Free Trade Agreement. The Opinion of Advocate General Sharpston in Opinion 2/15, was delivered on 21 December, the same day of the launching of the public consultation on the MIC. AG Sharpston concludes on the mixed nature of the agreement. The ECJ, in its opinion delivered on 16 May 2017, largely confirmed it. In the opinion on the nature of the Singapore agreement, see Opinion of the ECJ of 16 May 2017, Case A-2/15, the Court made clear that the opinion relates only to the issue of whether the EU has exclusive competence and not to whether the content of the agreement is compatible with EU law. See also CJEU, Opinion 2/13, paragraphs. 145–46: 'It must be borne in mind in that regard that, under Article 218(11) TFEU, the Parliament, the Council, the Commission or a Member State may obtain the Opinion of the Court of Justice as to whether an envisaged agreement is compatible with the provisions of the Treaties. That provision has the aim of forestalling complications which would result from legal disputes concerning the compatibility with the Treaties of international agreements binding upon the EU (see Opinions 2/94, EU: C: 1996:140, paragraph 3; 1/08, EU: C: 2009:739, paragraph 107; and 1/09, EU: C: 2011:123, paragraph 47)'. See Opinions 3/94, EU:C:1995:436, paragraph 17, and 1/09, EU:C:2011:123, paragraph 48: 'A possible decision of the Court of Justice, after the conclusion of an international agreement binding upon the EU, to the effect that such an agreement is, by reason either of its content or of the procedure adopted for its conclusion, incompatible with the provisions of the Treaties could not fail to provoke, not only in the internal EU context, but also in that of international relations, serious difficulties and might give rise to adverse consequences for all interested parties, including third countries'.

[71] See CJEU opinion 2/13 on the draft agreement on the accession of the European Union to the European Convention for the Protection of Human Rights and Fundamental Freedoms of 13 December 2014.

[72] Among others, the European Association of Judges (representing 44 national associations of judges), the German Association of Judges (representing 160000 German judges and public prosecutors),

The investment court system provisions under CETA did not take effect as part of the provisional entry into force of the CETA, and further measures have to be taken to give effect to CETA investment court system provisions. The Council of the European Union, comprising all the EU Member States of course, remains competent to decide these rules, upon proposals from the European Commission. Moreover, national constitutional provisions must be respected for the ratification and entry into force of these dispute settlement provisions.

With all this in mind, the preliminary opinion of the CJEU requested by Belgium on 6 September 2017 promises answers on the matter of compatibility with European Union law. Specific reference to the investment court system provided for in the CETA (which will be as a precursor to a multilateral court), Belgium has put four questions on its compatibility with:

> The exclusive competence of the CJEU to provide the definitive interpretation of European Union law;
> The general principle of equality and the 'practical effect' requirement of European Union law;
> The right of access to the courts;
> The right to an independent and impartial judiciary.[73]

The CJEU's opinion is likely to cause much ink to flow. In a nutshell, the Court recalled the principles governing the autonomy of the EU legal order and concluded on the compatibility of the ISDS a proposed in the CETA. While recognising the legitimacy of these tribunals, the Court reaffirms that the CETA contains provisions that deprive those tribunals of any power to call into question the choices that have been democratically made within a Party to that agreement in relation to, inter alia, the level of protection of public order or public safety, the protection of public morals, the protection of health and life of humans and animals or the preservation of food safety, protection of plants and the environment, welfare at work, product safety, consumer protection or, equally, fundamental rights. Consequently, that agreement does not adversely affect the autonomy of the EU legal order. In order terms the principle of autonomy is diluted with the democratic considerations typical of the principle of sovereignty. Following the opinion of AG Bot, the Court further distinguishes CETA from intra-EU BITs by highlighting

101 law professors in an open letter, have objected to ICS inter alia on the ground that the system might not be compatible with EU law.

[73] See the Belgian Request for an Opinion from the CJEU (n 4) 2. On the matter of the right to an independent and impartial judiciary, further sub-questions address: the conditions regarding the remuneration of the members of the Tribunal and the Appeals Body; the appointment of members of the Tribunal and the Appeals Body; the release of members of the Tribunal and the Appeals Body; the guidelines of the International Bar Association regarding conflicts of interest in international arbitration and the introduction of a code of conduct for the members of the Tribunal and the Appeals Body; the external professional activities related to investment disputes of members of the Tribunal and the Appeals Body.

that the principle of mutual trust, which was at the core of its decision in Achmea,[74] is not applicable to the relations between the EU and third countries, but it's more a question of reciprocity.[75] The opinion confirms that the issue is rather mainly a political one: a question of negotiation with the third country but as well as a question of acceptance by the European civil society opposing investor-state arbitration. An adverse opinion would have had serious political consequences, as it would have required the amendment of CETA.

Nevertheless, even if the legal dispute is solved, still the political question remains: is this belts and braces approach really necessary? Would the creation of a multilateral International Investment Court be tantamount to using a bazooka to kill a mosquito? Does the current 10 per cent of problem cases[76] provide the critical mass to justify such an independent international jurisdiction? How many states would have to participate for it to be workable? Would only new BITs refer to it explicitly or should it be subject to consensus of the parties and be competent to adjudicate over other investment treaties? Would the eventual court be competent to adjudicate on investment disputes under a BIT involving both investor-state and state-state proceedings? Why create such a new body where others already exist?

In the international arena in particular, how would the multilateral investment coexist with well-established supranational courts? An outright negative answer would make the MIC redundant before it could take concrete form.

And last but not least, the fact that a proposed system is now recognised as legal would definitively prevent discussion of other systems that might otherwise be more democratically acceptable to European public opinion.

Nevertheless, recent practice bears out how the Juncker Commission is fundamentally reforming the existing system for settling investment-related disputes. In a fact sheet published on 1 July 2017,[77] the European Commission clearly stated that 'for the EU ISDS is dead'. Moreover, the same fact sheet mentions that, 'Investment is part of the Commission's negotiating mandate: EU governments want the Commission to improve the access of EU investors to the Japanese market and negotiate rules to promote and protect EU investors'. It states that this is 'the EU's agreed approach that it is pursuing from now on in its trade agreements. This is also the case with Japan'. Anything less ambitious, including a return to the old investor to state dispute settlement, is no longer acceptable.

[74] See CJEU 6 March 2018, C-284/16, *Slovak Republic c/Achmea BV*. See Denys Simon, 'L'arbitrage en matière d'investissement remis en cause par la Cour de justice? À propos de l'arrêt du 6 mars. 2018' (2018) 5 *Achmea, Europe* 1.

[75] See para 105 of Advocate General Bot's Conclusions.

[76] According to the United Nations Conference on Trade and Development (UNCTAD), there are 2953 Bilateral Investment Treaties of which 2322 in force, and to which should be added 362 Treaties with Investment Provisions (TIPs) of which 294 in force. Around 1400 concern EU Member States. Of the ones in force, 90 per cent operated without a single investor claim of a treaty breach. According to the figures of UNCTAD, there are 608 known treaty-based ISDS cases (decided and pending).

[77] European Commission, 'A new EU trade agreement with Japan', *fact sheet* (2017).

This is the approach reflected in the new EU–Japan Economic Partnership Agreement. The partners only announced the agreement at the conclusion of the 2017 EU–Japan Summit on 6 July 2017,[78] and on the eve of the G20 summit. It was concluded on 8 December 2017 and has been hailed as the most important bilateral trade agreement ever concluded by the EU. The Commission continues with legal verification and translation of the agreement into all EU official languages[79] and then submitting it for the approval of EU Member States and the European Parliament.

It would be difficult not to interpret the official press releases quoting Commissioner Malmström as saying 'we believe in building bridges, not walls', as anything other than a direct answer to President Trump's unhappy declarations. Similarly, the inclusion of an express reference to the Paris Agreement on Climate Change in the draft text demonstrates the determination of both parties to go ahead with such multilateral initiatives in spite of President Trump's recent declaration of the US withdrawal from the Paris Agreement. However, in spite of the innovative provisions concerning sustainable development, environmental protection and corporate governance, there is one blatant omission that may signal a longer-term problem for the EU's trade negotiators: investment protection remains outside the scope of the agreement. The EU has put its reformed Investment Court System on the table[80] and is reaching out to all partner countries, including Japan, to work towards the setting up of a Multilateral Investment Court.

With the absence of any substantive investment protection or ISDS mechanism in the EU–Japan Agreement, nor any explicit reference to the MIC as a potential future option, it remains to be seen whether the EU and Japan might eventually be able to reach agreement on investment protection and an alternative dispute resolution process for investor-state disputes.[81] We are left in the dark as to the future of investor protection and investor state dispute settlement. An overcautious interpretation of the ECJ's opinion on Singapore agreement[82] could plead in favour of a separate agreement (or protocol) on investments perhaps even including a reference to the multilateral court as a system for resolution of disputes.

[78] Japan–EU Economic Partnership Agreement ('JEEPA'), to be found at http://ec.europa.eu/trade/policy/in-focus/eu-japan-economic-partnership-agreement/.

[79] The preliminary text is already available in respect of the transparency commitments of the EU. See the web address ibid. The dispute settlement provisions do not include investor protection disputes.

[80] See European Commission, 'Memo: Key elements of the EU-Japan Economic Partnership Agreement' (2017), to be found at http://trade.ec.europa.eu/doclib/press/index.cfm?id=1687.

[81] However, the vast majority of Japan's international investment agreements contain traditional ISDS mechanisms and it recently supported the inclusion of such a mechanism in the context of the Trans-Pacific Partnership ('TPP'). In the Australia–Japan economic partnership agreement in 2015, the ISDS was substituted by a reference to the domestic courts, pending future agreement on an appropriate dispute resolution mechanism.

[82] See Opinion of the ECJ of 16 May 2017, Case A-2/15, the Court focused its criticisms on the inclusion of portfolio investment, which it considered to be outside the scope of the EU's exclusive competence. However, there is no reason why the EU should be hesitant to include pure foreign direct investment within the scope of the agreement.

IV. The Latin American Experience

Without attempting to study in detail all the mechanisms dealing with solving investment disputes worldwide, it is possible to focus on Latin America in order to evaluate implementation of these mechanisms in bilateral or multilateral trade agreements. The American continent is the EU's main trading partner, while MERCOSUR alone is the fourth largest regional economy in the world after NAFTA, the European Union and Japan. Brazil has traditionally been a leader in the inter-American community and plays an important role in economic cooperation, is a founding member of the Organization of American States (OAS) and the Inter-American Treaty of Reciprocal Assistance (Rio Treaty), and Brazil gives high priority to expanding relations with its South American neighbours and strengthening regional bodies such as the Latin American Integration Association (ALADI), the Union of South American Nations (UNASUR) and MERCOSUR.

EU–MERCOSUR negotiations were relaunched in 2010 and aim at concluding an overall trade agreement. In 2011, Brazil signed a trade agreement with the US which included regulatory issues affecting trade and investment. In recent years,[83] traditional Latin American resistance to the participation in an international system of investment protection has undergone some rethinking relating to investment standards and the elaboration of new models. This is evident in Brazil's cooperation and facilitation investment agreements (CFIAs), the negotiations on the creation of a regional dispute settlement centre under the aegis of the Union of South American Nations (UNASUR),[84] and in some political positions and amendments to national arbitration laws for disputes involving the State in other Latin American countries.

Only in 2014 and 2015[85] at least 13 international investment agreements were negotiated and signed by countries in the region. Half of these agreements are intra-Latin American. Four among them were BITs. Brazil was the most active negotiator, with six CFIAs being signed, all in 2015. Colombia and Mexico came next with four each. Moreover, the recently revived TPP[86] (not now including the US) involves several southern America countries (Chile, Mexico and Peru),

[83] See Katia Fach Gómez and Catharine Titi (eds), 'The Latin American Challenge to the Current System of Investor-State Dispute Settlement' (17)4 *Journal of World Investment & Trade: Special Issue.*

[84] See María José Luque Macías, 'Reliance on Alternative Methods for Investment Protection through National Laws, Investment Contracts, and Regional Institutions in Latin America' in Steffen Hindelang and Markus Krajewski (eds), *Shifting Paradigms in International Investment Law. More Balanced, Less Isolated, Increasingly Diversified* (Oxford, Oxford University Press, 2016) 291; Verónica Villaruel, 'Estados del Sur ponen en marcha Observatorio sobre Inversiones Transnacionales' (2014) 10 *Revista Diplomacia ciudadana* 18. To be found at https://issuu.com/cancilleriaec/docs/revista_diplomacia_ciudadana_d__cim.

[85] See María José Luque Macías, 'Current Approaches to the International Investment Regime in South America' in Christoph Herrmann and others (eds), *European Yearbook of International Economic Law* (Heidelberg, Springer-Verlag Berlin, 2013) 285.

[86] See most recent version of the full text is dated 26 January 2018 and can be found at http://tpp.mfat.govt.nz/text. See Ch 9, *Investment*, to be found at https://ustr.gov/about-us/policy-offices/press-office/fact-sheets/2015/march/investor-state-dispute-settlement-isds.

and incorporates dispute settlement guidelines between governments and foreign investors.[87]

Common to these agreements is the dual provision made for arbitration together with alternative dispute resolution or investor-state mechanisms that are less adversarial than their predecessors. Some Latin American countries have even developed preventive mechanisms aimed at reducing the number of conflicts in relation to international investment.[88]

However, it would be a misconception to consider Latin America as one 'continent' insofar as ISDS is concerned. The picture is much more complex and fragmented in terms of regional approaches to the investor-state dispute settlement mechanism[89] because:

> the (minority of) countries that, in the last decade, took significant actions against investment arbitration, and countries working on shaping transversal and long-term models for ISDS;
> the revival of inter-state mechanisms in the settlement of disputes in recent regional agreements and national laws (with the imposition of local litigation requirements and the promotion of less adversarial investor-state mechanisms), and;
> the flourishing of regional or regionally-designed mechanisms for the Settlement of Investment Disputes (the UNASUR Centre[90] or the intra-MERCOSUR investment agreement).

This testifies as to the progressive transformation of some Latin American countries' approaches to ISDS, which will undoubtedly have important consequences for the region – provided, that is, 'its liberation from the tutelage exercised by the industrialized world'[91] is not to be compromised by the economic crisis, and

[87] For the version of the TPP prior to the US' Trump Presidency, see https://ustr.gov/about-us/policy-offices/press-office/fact-sheets/2015/march/investor-state-dispute-settlement-isds: 'Despite having 50 ISDS agreements in place, the United States has never lost a case and nothing in our agreements has inhibited our response to the 2008 financial crisis, diluted the financial reforms we put in place, or has challenged signature reforms like the Affordable Care Act or any of the other new regulations that have been put in place over the last 30 years'. President Trump signed a merely symbolic (as the agreement was never ratified by the US Congress) Presidential memorandum to withdraw the US from the TPP on 23 January 2017, leaving open the ratification among the remaining in the absence of the US.

[88] See the Colombian National Agency for the Legal Defence of the State (Agencia nacional de defensa jurídica del Estado (ANDJE)) www.defensajuridica.gov.co/Paginas/Default.aspx and the Peruvian Coordination and Response System for International Investment Disputes (Sistema de Coordinación y Respuesta del Estado en Controversias Internacionales de Inversión–SICRECI, to be found at www.mef.gob.pe/index.php?option=com_content&view=article&id=3970&Itemid=100906&lang=es.

[89] See generally Catharine Titi, 'Investment Arbitration in Latin America: The Uncertain Veracity of Preconceived Ideas' (2014) 30 *Arbitration International* 357.

[90] An English unofficial translation of the texts can be found in María Gabriela Sarmiento, 'The 2012 Draft Constitutive Agreement of the Centre for the Settlement of Investment Disputes of the UNASUR' http://papers.ssrn.com/sol3/papers.cfm?abstract_id=2698574, and in María Gabriela Sarmiento, 'The 2014 Draft Constitutive Agreement of the Centre for the Settlement of Investment Disputes of the UNASUR', http://ssrn.com/abstract=2703651.

[91] See Fach Gómez and Titi (n 87).

which for Brazil extends to the political turmoil linked to its Presidency. This supports the conclusion that 'numerous signs predict that Latin America may play a decisive role in the worldwide design of the future investment dispute settlement system', especially in the event that the new models should eventually be implemented and – successfully – tested.

A. The Brazilian Case

Brazil is one of the most popular destinations for foreign direct investment, despite being entrenched in desisting from the international system of investment protection.[92] Brazil's reluctance is not the fruit of some left-wing ideology but rather, a consistent position defended by governments of both left and right, from the beginning of the twentieth century when at The Hague Conference of 1907, Brazil already expressed its reluctance to giving up any kind of sovereignty.[93] Based on the Calvo Doctrine – named after its author, the Argentinian diplomat, Carlos Calvo – those who live in a foreign country must introduce their demands or complaints to the jurisdiction of the local courts there, avoiding recourse to diplomatic pressure or armed intervention of its own State or Government.[94] It has since been adopted in several Latin American countries.

Based on this doctrine, Brazil has neither been party to any BITs, nor has it ever ratified the ICSID Convention.[95] The Brazilian delegate in the negotiations of the ICSID Washington Convention, argued that the text of the Convention not only raised constitutional questions but also conferred upon investors a privileged position in relation to the host state, for only the investor enjoyed the prerogative of commencing arbitral proceedings, which would disadvantage Brazil.[96]

Nonetheless, Brazil went on to sign the Convention that established the Multilateral Investment Guaranty Agency (MIGA) in 1985.[97] In the 1990s Brazil signed several BITs[98] that were never ratified by the Brazilian Parliament, in spite of the

[92] See in general Daniel de Andrade Levy and others (eds), *Investment Protection in Brazil* (Alphen aan den Rijn, Kluwer Law International, 2014).

[93] Carlos Henrique Cardim, *A raiz das coisas: Rui Barbosa: o Brasil no mundo* (Rio de Janeiro, Civilização Brasileira, 2007) 153.

[94] *Derecho internacional teórico y practico de Europa y América* (1868).

[95] Ramos (n 17).

[96] History of the ICSID Convention, vol II-1, 306, and Jean Kalicki and Suzana Medeiros, 'Investment Arbitration in Brazil: Revisiting Brazil's Traditional Reluctance towards ICSID, BITs and Investor-State Arbitration' 14 *Revista de Arbitragem e Mediação* 57, 68.

[97] Decree No 698 of 8 December 1992, www.planalto.gov.br/ccivil_03/decreto/1990-1994/D0698.htm. The text of the Convention is available at www.miga.org/quickref/index_sv.cfm?stid=1583.

[98] Brazilian BITs with the Belgian–Luxembourg Economic Union (6 January 1999), Chile (22 March 1994), Cuba (26 June 1997), Denmark (4 May 1995), Finland (28 March 1995), France (21 March 1995), Germany (21 September 1995), Italy (3 April 1995), Korea (1 September 1995), Netherlands (25 November 1998), Portugal (9 February 1994), Switzerland (11 November 1994), United Kingdom (19 July 1994) and Venezuela (4 July 1995). Information available at www.unctad.org/sections/dite_pcbb/docs/bits_brazil.pdf.

fact that Brazil had signed the two protocols of the MERCOSUR Agreement on foreign investments (the Protocols of Colonia and of Buenos Aires),[99] both of which provide for investor-state arbitration. None of these, unsurprisingly, were ratified by the Brazilian Parliament.

The arguments invoked in the Brazilian parliamentary debates are similar to those invoked in world-wide debates on CETA and TTIP: disagreements over submitting to an international arbitration tribunal; questions of a constitutional nature that should normally be reserved to a national judge; and the possibility of creating a system that might privilege foreign investors' nationals;[100] as well as restrictions on the right to regulate and the ability of the host states to adopt public policies. Other arguments relate to the high economic and political cost of the arbitration procedure, the imposition of onerous reparations, and the lack of transparency of arbitration awards. But importantly, this has not prevented Brazil from developing alternative negotiating models both at the multilateral level (MERCOSUR) or at the bilateral level (CFIAs).[101] However, even though the Brazilian government negotiates such agreements, typically they are shot down by the Parliament at ratification, in objection to the ISDS provisions.

Nevertheless, it is relevant to now consider whether Brazil might become a land of the future[102] in the field of investment protection?

i. Brazilian Cooperation and Facilitation Investment Agreements: An Innovative Model for Dispute Prevention

Given its traditional opposition to ISDS, the Ministry of Trade of Brazil developed some guidelines and an innovative model[103] that are followed in the negotiations of BITs. Even the name of the agreements is different, as they are called *Acordo de Cooperação e Facilitação de Investimentos* (ACFI), which translates into English

[99] Protocol of Colonia for the Promotion and Reciprocal Protection of Investments within MERCOSUR, which applies to investment within the MERCOSUR zone (Common Market Council's Decision No 11/93 of 17 January 1994, available at www.sice.oas.org/trade/mrcsr/colonia/pcolonia_p.asp. Buenos Aires Protocol for the Promotion and Protection of Investment made by Countries that are not Parties to MERCOSUR (Common Market Council's Decision No 11/94 of 5 August 1994, available at www.sice.oas.org/Trade/MRCSRS/Decisions/dec1194p.pdf.

[100] Carmen Tibúrcio, 'A Arbitragem de Investimento no Brasil' in Marilda Rosado de Sá Ribeiro (org.), *Direito Internacional dos Investimentos* (Rio de Janeiro, Renovar, 2014) 237.

[101] See Matatias Lucas Lopes Parente, *O modelo brasileiro de acordo de cooperação e facilitação de investimentos 2015: considerações a respeito do impacto dos acordos internacionais de investimentos estrangeiros sobre o ordenamento jurídico interno*, available at www.conpedi.org.br/publicacoes/c178h0tg/p2qwwuu8/7018K6Lq63OTKYbP.

[102] Reference is here made to Stefan Zweig, *Brazil, Land of the Future* (NewYork, Viking Press, 1941) 282.

[103] To be found at www.mdic.gov.br/comercio-exterior/negociacoes-internacionais/218-negociacoes-internacionais-de-investimentos/1949-nii-acfi.

as 'Cooperation and Investment Facilitation Agreements'.[104] The word 'protection' does not appear, which is certainly intended. This is a complete departure from traditional BITs because CFIAs are characterised by the absence of any ISDS mechanism and in general also, by a recognition of a reduced set of guarantees, advantages or benefits for the investor compared to bilateral treaties.[105] The investor is clearly subordinate to the willingness of its state of origin – not having any autonomous, legitimate procedural *locus standi* – as well as to the laws and institutions of the host state benefiting from the investment.

Brazil's new model is intended to remove the internal legal barriers that had prevented the ratification of earlier BITs, which had been deemed incompatible with the Brazilian Constitution due to their provisions on expropriation and ISDS. The CFIA is based on three pillars:

a) risk mitigation;
b) institutional governance;
c) thematic agendas for cooperation and facilitation of investments.[106]

It provides a set of measures aimed at reducing investor exposure to risks, avoiding the creation of situations that could lead to controversy before the host state. Thus, inter alia, the instrument expressly establishes guarantees of non-discrimination, including the principles of national treatment and most-favoured-nation treatment, together with transparency provisions and specific conditions to deal with direct expropriation, compensation in case of conflicts and currency transfer.

The philosophy underlying the new model clearly differs from the traditional model of BITs. It no longer focuses on investment protection and dispute settlement. ISDS is not possible on the basis of the CFIAs. The focus has shifted to investment promotion and dispute prevention, objectives which are expressly

[104] V Gabriel, 'The New Brazilian Cooperation and Facilitation Investment Agreement: An Analysis of the Conflict Resolution Mechanism in Light of the Theory of the Shadow of the Law' (2016) 34 *Conflict Resolution Quarterly* 1; VDR Gabriel and JAF Costa, 'O Mercosul e as Controvérsias sobre Investimentos' (2015) 3 *Revista da Secretaria do Tribunal Permanente de Revisão* 267–84. JAF Costa and VDR Gabriel, 'O Brasil, ACFIs e a arbitragem de investimentos' in Associação Portuguesa de Arbitragem (ed), *Revista Internacional de Arbitragem e Conciliação – Ano VIII – 2015* (Lisbon, Almedina, 2015) 63–82. VDR Gabriel, 'O Brasil e a Regulamentação Jurídica Internacional dos Investimentos Estrangeiros: Uma Análise Comparada com a Proteção Jurídica Americana e Argentina' in Vladmir Oliveira da Silva, Karine de Souza Silva, Rosângela Angelin (eds), *Direito internacional. I. Encontro Nacional do CONPEDI/UFSC* (Florianópolis, CONPEDI, 2014) v I, 374–97. Renato Souza, 'Cooperation and Facilitation Investment Agreement – CFI', Presentation, *UNCTAD Expert Meeting on The Transformation of the International Investment Agreement Regime* (2015), to be found at http://unctad-worldinvestmentforum.org/wp-content/uploads/2015/03/Brazil_side-event-Wednesday_model-agreements.pdf.

[105] See Costa and Gabriel (n 18).

[106] On the three pillars of Brazilian CFIAs, see generally Catharine Titi, 'International Investment Law and the Protection of Foreign Investment in Brazil', *Transnational Dispute Management*, advance publication on 13 July 2015, forthcoming in *Transnational Dispute Management Special Issue on Latin America* (eds Ignacio Torterola and Quinn Smith), 9 *et seq.*

cited in the recent agreements. Dispute prevention in particular, involves 'extensive planning in order to reduce the number of conflicts that escalate or crystallize into formal disputes'.[107]

In this respect, the innovative element of CFIAs in terms of governance and dispute settlement mechanisms, is the establishment of focal points or Ombudsmen (Article 5), in each of the states parties, in addition to the creation of a Joint Committee. These instances can be considered the institutional core of the agreement because they contribute to the achievement of the commitments and the strengthening of the dialogue between the parties on the investments. The focal point of each party serves as a facilitator in the technical relationship between investors.

It should function as an additional channel of dialogue and governmental support in order to improve the environment for the attraction and maintenance of investment. In Brazil, the CAMEX[108] – an inter-ministerial body linked to the Presidency of the Republic – will act as the Ombudsman for the agreement, with the purpose of prevention and amicable settlement of disputes involving bilateral investments.

There is no provision for ISDS in line with the Calvo Doctrine. Investors need to go through their investors' state of origin in order to introduce any complaints and start the dialogue foreseen with the other Party.

The Brazilian approach emphasises the prevention of disputes based on dialogue and bilateral consultation prior to initiating an arbitration procedure, thus encouraging a more dynamic interaction between the parties (Article 15). Such instruments include the direct and permanent activities of the aforementioned focal points, in addition to extensive discussions within the Joint Committee (Article 4), which is composed of representatives of both governments and is responsible for the preliminary examination of specific issues demanded by the signatories.

As a starting point, the investor directly addresses the Ombudsman to seek an amicable solution for both. The focal points serve as communication channels between foreign investors and the host state, inter alia to propose improvements to the business environment, prevent disputes and facilitate their resolution. However, should this be unsuccessful, it will then be up to the investor's state of origin to assess the situation and then to forward the demand for a Joint Committee analysis, in which representatives of both governments discuss and review the implementation of the CFIAs. The Joint Committee is responsible for sharing opportunities for the expansion of mutual investment, monitoring the implementation of the Agreement, preventing disputes and solving possible disagreements in an amicable manner.

[107] See UNCTAD, *Investor–State Disputes: Prevention and Alternatives to Arbitration* (2010) 129.
[108] To be found at www.camex.gov.br/.

This system seeks to prevent disputes through 'dialogue and bilateral consultation, prior to the initiation of State-State arbitration procedures'. It is only in the event that this procedure does not culminate in a solution, that arbitration between states is reverted to *ultima ratio*, as this is the only option available as a juridical mechanism in CFIAs.

The Brazilian Focal Point is inspired by the Office of the Foreign Investment Ombudsman (OFIO)[109] that was created as a grievance-settlement body within the South Korea Trade-Investment Promotion Agency (KOTRA) to help improve the investment environment thereby providing assistance in resolving difficulties that foreign companies might face when investing in South Korea, whether in business activities and day-to-day management.[110] Operating on the basis of a 'Home Doctor' system – under which specialists from various fields such as labour, taxation, finance, law, etc provide services to foreign-invested companies – according to their data from 1999 to 2015, the OFIO has resolved 4976 grievance cases (with an annual average of 311 cases) while a total of 360 cases were handled as a result of the OFIO's contribution to system improvements.[111]

However, the Brazilian model differs from the South Korean one on certain substantial points that could serve to undermine its success. The South Korean OFIO is an independent office created by law and directed by a high-level civil servant appointed by the President of the Republic, and seconded experts in the different areas related to investments. The OFIO is accessible to all trade partners and free of charge. As in the Brazilian model, should this stage prove unsuccessful, the investor may then begin the arbitration procedure.

In the South Korean case, the ICSID procedure applies. Protection by means of arbitration between states is reserved for extremely serious situations, such as those caused by nationalisation, or those affecting companies or individuals holding powerful influence over the government. Enshrining it in treaty form prevents access to the system by foreign investors not covered by the agreements as is envisaged in the Brazilian model. Moreover, the OFIO is more than simply a facilitator for dispute settlement as it cooperates with the South Korean trade agency and has the power to make recommendations.[112] Another substantial difference is the traditional independence of the office of an ombudsman. The Brazilian focal point – the CAMEX, *Câmara de Comércio Exterior* – is an inter-ministerial body linked to the Presidency of the Republic.

[109] See *South Korea Foreign Investment Ombudsman Annual Report 2014* (2015), http://125.131.31.47/Solars7DMME/004/15Foreign_Investment_Ombudsman_Annual_Report2014.pdf and http://english.kotra.or.kr/foreign/biz/KHENKO140M.html?TOP_MENU_CD=INVEST.

[110] See Hi-Taek Shin (ed), *Commentaries on Selected Model Investment Treaties* (Oxford, Oxford University Press, 2013) 1018.

[111] South Korea. Foreign Investment Promotion Act (Republic of Korea). Art 15-2(1), http://legal.un.org/avl/pdf/ls/Shin_RelDocs.pdf.

[112] F Nicolas, S Thomsen and M Bang, 'Lessons from Investment Policy Reform in Korea', in *OECD Working Papers on International Investment* (OECD Publishing, 2013), http://dx.doi.org/10.1787/5k4376zqcpf1-en.

In summary, the Brazilian alternative model compared to traditional investment agreements, recognises the essential role of governments[113] in fostering an enabling environment for investment that meets both the concerns of the private sector and the development needs of the countries that are signatories to the agreement. Currently, the following CFIAs have been signed: in 2015, the first ACFIs with Mozambique followed by Angola, Malawi, Mexico, Colombia and Chile, and in 2016, with Peru, in 2018 with Ethiopia and Suriname.[114]

The aim pursued – a balanced outcome combining the promotion of an attractive environment for investors while preserving space for public policies – is certainly achievable in the case of those partners involved. On one hand they are certainly more dependent on Brazilian investments than vice versa, and, on the other hand, they have a less developed economical structure, either because they have no big potential investors, or the investors potentially involved have no power to put pressure on local governments.

The new model has allowed the Brazilian Parliament to overcome the traditional objections. The agreement with Angola is the first to enter into force on 11 October 2017, and others will follow as the process of ratification seems not to haven any further ideological obstacle.[115]

By preferring the governmental role and SSDS, it is clear that Brazil takes control over any eventual disputes arising. But the system is completed by a dialogue mechanism, which is something of novelty. The efficiency and success of this model will depend on the room for manoeuvre that the focal points will have to seek a fair solution. The fact that it is directly dependent on the government will probably reduce its appeal[116] because it has no juridical authority or any possibility to adjudicate the case, even *ex aequo e bono*. Its role will simply be to help clarify the situation, analyse the questions of the investor, and forward them to the relevant authorities responsible for addressing specific doubts or difficulties facing the investor.

Then again, is this Brazilian resistance to investor-state arbitration a critical issue? It appears simply to be another way of solving the issue of the regulatory

[113] For some considerations on inter-state arbitration on the basis of Brazil's CFIAs, see María José Luque Macías, 'Inter-State Investment Dispute Settlement in Latin America: Is There Space for Transparency?' in Katia Fach Gómez and Catharine Titi (eds), 'The Latin American Challenge to the Current System of Investor-State Dispute Settlement' (2016) 17 *Journal of World Investment & Trade*; N Bernasconi-Osterwalder and MD Brauch, 'Comparative Commentary to Brazil's Cooperation and Investment Facilitation Agreements (CIFAs) with Mozambique, Angola, Mexico, and Malawi' (2015), www.iisd.org/library/comparative-commentary-brazil-cooperation-and-investment-facilitation-agreements-cifas; F Morosini and MR Sanchez Badin, 'The Brazilian Agreement on Cooperation and Facilitation of Investments (ACFI): A New Formula for International Investment Agreements?' (2015) 6 *Investment Treaty News* 3–5, www.iisd.org/itn/2015/08/04/the-brazilian-agreement-on-cooperation-and-facilitation-of-investments-acfi-a-new-formula-for-international-investment-agreements.

[114] For the full text of each agreements see www.mdic.gov.br/comercio-exterior/negociacoes-internacionais/218-negociacoes-internacionais-de-investimentos/1949-nii-acfi.

[115] See para 2.40 of *WTO Report on Brazil*, doc n WT/TPR/S/358, 12 June 2017, www.wto.org/french/tratop_f/tpr_f/s358_f.pdf.

[116] See Costa and Gabriel (n 18).

freedom and alternative institutional mechanisms created by ISDS mechanisms, which is, apparently, so problematic in the CETA or TTIP.

ii. Brazil Proposal within Intra-MERCOSUR Negotiations

Brazil has traditionally always been against any transfer of competence on investment protection to foreign organisations or arbitral systems. Interestingly, in the framework of MERCOSUR, it proposed[117] the negotiation of an intra-MERCOSUR investment agreement including a system for settling disputes between states instead of the traditional scheme under which private investors may sue states before international courts.

It is worthwhile mentioning that MERCOSUR has its own dispute settlement mechanism[118] and Brazil proposes to apply that system with some differences. The aim is to negotiate an 'Intra-MERCOSUR Cooperation and Investment Facilitation Protocol', which is currently being discussed by Working Subgroup No 12 (Investments). In the past, in 1993, the MERCOSUR signed an agreement for the promotion and mutual protection of intra-bloc investments, and another for the treatment of investment flows with the rest of the world in 1994 (the Colonia and Buenos Aires Protocols, respectively): neither have ever entered into force.[119]

The proposal put forward by Brazil is modelled on the CFIAs that it has signed with Mexico, Colombia, Mozambique, Malawi and Angola in recent years. The agreement will cover direct investments and will establish commitments regarding non-discrimination, conditions of expropriation and compensation for losses, transparency, exchange of information between states, cooperation between investment promotion agencies, a regional agenda for further cooperation and investment facilitation, the free transfer of investment-related resources in local or convertible foreign currencies, with the possibility of temporarily restricting these flows in the event of a balance of payments crises, provided certain conditions are met.

[117] On 22 and 23 September 2015 at the 99th Regular Meeting of the Common Market Group (GMC) which took place in Asunción, Paraguay.

[118] See Gabriella Giovanna Lucarelli de Salvio and Jeanine Gama Sá Cabral, 'Considerations on the Mercosur dispute settlement mechanism and the impact of its decision in the WTO dispute resolution system', (2006) 4 CEBRI Papers. See also Francisco Domíngues and Marcos Guedes de Oliveira (eds), *Mercosur: Between Integration and Democracy* (Bern, Peter Lang AG, 2004); Luiz Olavo Baptista, 'Mercosur, its institutions and juridical structure. Foreign Trade Information System', http://ctrc.sice.oas.org/geograph/south/mstit2_e.pdf; Nadia Araújo, 'O Tribunal Permanente de Revisão do MERCOSUL e as Opiniões Consultivas: análise dos laudos arbitrais, sua ligação com o common law e algumas idéias para o future' in Lauro da Gama e Souza Junior (ed), *Revista de Direito da Associação dos Procuradores do Novo Estado do Rio de Janeiro Vol XV – Direito Internacional. Lumen Juris* (Rio de Janeiro, 2005) 111; Wilfrido Fernándesz, 'El Nuevo Tribunal Arbitral del Mercosur' in *Anuario de Derecho Constitucional Latinoamericano* (2006), www.juridicas.unam.mx/publica/librev/rev/dconstla/cont/20061/pr/pr27.pdf.

[119] See *Decisão do Conselho do Mercado Comum* no 11/93 of 17 January 1994, www.sice.oas.org/trade/mrcsr/colonia/pcolonia_p.asp.

However, the most relevant difference in comparison with previous protocols and the bilateral investment agreements already signed by the MERCOSUR countries, is the provision for a dispute settlement system. While all the MERCOSUR countries have signed agreements of this kind, they have never entered into force in Brazil as they have not been ratified by the Parliament precisely because of the inclusion of ISDS.

Brazil's proposal provides for dispute settlement between states within the framework of the provisions set out in the Olivos Protocol – instead of the traditional system in which private investors may sue states before national and international courts. Nevertheless, before applying the dispute settlement system of the Olivos Protocol, a solution must be found under the auspices of a system of prevention of disputes based on the appointment of an ombudsman, one for each counterpart who will act as national focal point. The principal function of these ombudsmen will be to provide support to investors of the counterparts on its territory. Clearly modelled on the CFIAs however, the system will suffer the same disadvantages already commented upon above. The central element will of course be the preventative mood inspiring such proposals. Ultimately however, two important questions remain. Would it be enough for and acceptable to all trading partners within MERCOSUR? And is it really an exportable model? Does this model effectively amount to a blank cartridge in the ISDS debate?

V. Conclusions: Bazookas and Blank Cartridges

With the inclusion of Foreign Direct Investment in the European Union's powers under the Common Commercial Policy under the Treaty of Lisbon in 2009, the EU is leading the push to revolutionise the antiquated, secretive and politicised arbitrator system that has characterised foreign investment protection globally for centuries.[120] The EU's reform will institutionalise the procedure and fill out its substantive juridical scope and content. Procedurally this means establishing a permanent court and formally providing an appellate mechanism. In terms of substantive content, this means guaranteeing a state's right to regulate, as well as defining principles and/or indirect expropriation, transparency, ethics, appointments of judges, costs, rules on procedure, forum shopping, frivolous claims, as well as specific provisions for SMEs. This addresses the threats to states' governance as well as negative political and public opinion on international trade and investment agreements.

However, it remains valid to question whether this reform is sufficient, adequate and necessary to address the negative dimensions of ISDS as such: *cui prodest*? Given the strength of current political and societal opposition to investment

[120] This explains the strong opposition of all of the associations of arbitrators against the new model, seemingly more motivated by the fear of losing their monopoly and huge fees than by sound argument.

treaties, doubts remain as to the true usefulness of such agreements. Who do they truly serve? Is their global economic impact in terms of GDP and employment growth meaningful? While ISDS mechanisms are not questioned per se in the EU – and considered part of the framework for the various reasons examined – in other parts of the world, different models are being developed.

Brazil, paradoxically, continues to be the recipient of considerable foreign investment, despite its long-standing refusal to sign any treaty containing an ISDS mechanism. Recent experience shows attempts to promote a SSDS system with strong elements of mediation. Other EU international agreements specifically provide for voluntary mediation[121] to solve disputes amicably before initiating formal steps for dispute settlement. Comparably, this is not central to the EU approach, which focuses on creating a permanent court. Simply put, once the right to a fair compensation in case of expropriation is recognised, all remaining questions remain unresolved, including when such a right should be recognised, in respect of whom, as well as how and by whom the right to compensation should be quantified.

Whether a stronger mediation model would be more advantageous and more viable to meeting investor state disputes over foreign investments involves, first, addressing whether the idea of a permanent – bilateral or multilateral – investment court compares to using a bazooka to kill a mosquito Second, is mediation under the control of the host state a real alternative, or would the undeniable political interest of the host state in itself prejudice such mediation from the outset, rendering mediation an 'empty cartridge' in ISDS?

Neither model is settled in practice, making definitive answers difficult. Both approaches highlight national and supranational considerations when taking account of public opinion before venturing into complex international negotiations. Directly or indirectly, these negotiations affect fundamental rights and national sovereignty issues, and will impact on the way people live and interact. Analysis of the origin of these models and their historical evolution, reveals differing underlying ideologies. The historical reluctance of Brazil or other Latin American countries towards ISDS is more than the rhetoric of recent left-wing governments. By trying to introduce a compulsory mediation step, even if under state control, the state maintains full control over private litigation on investments. The same can be said of the EU's idea of a permanent court, based on other ideological and historical reasons, especially given the limited number of investor disputes and the western countries' jurisdictions involved.

The ongoing process is rushing towards providing partial and supplementary answers to questions arising. Incidental factors seem to have dictated the process of reforming ISDS, rather than any long-term vision. The problems already started with the Treaty of Lisbon, which raised a further barrage of questions that the

[121] Relevant CETA Provisions: Art 8.20 'Mediation'; Art 8.19.3, Art 8.23.5 'Submission of a Claim to the Tribunal'; Art 8.39.6 'Final award'.

Singapore judgment has not laid to rest, and for which the Belgian state requested the Opinion recently delivered by the CJEU. Is investment protection exclusive or mixed? What should one do with existing intra-Member States Bilateral Investment Treaties? Should Member States be allowed to continue to negotiate BITs? Should there be a presumption of inheritance of existing BITs containing ISDS rather than continuing with SSDS? And if so, how should criticisms of existing ISDS systems be addressed?

The saga turned epic first of all with TTIP, providing more transparency concerning arbitrators' choices, and then with the push to create a bilateral permanent court. CETA remains silent on this, as do other recent agreements. The arbitrators are to become 'quasi-permanent' judges adhering to a code of conduct, and rules on their independence before, during and after their appointment. Still, in the CETA situation, the Belgian region of Wallonia pressed for more, securing a new 'code of conduct' for the judges before the creation of the tribunal itself. Judges not respecting the rules would be subject to sanction, forced to reveal their activities prior to their appointment, and banned from professions and specific duties for a certain amount of time after the end of their mandate. The provisional entry into force of CETA (without ISDS) was finally concluded but the definitive entry into force with ISDS must traverse 38 unforeseeable national and regional ratifications and/or referendums. Meanwhile, public opinion protests against the threat to states' right to regulate, with the risk that US companies or even EU companies will have access to the ISDS via their Canadian companies. New rules or declarations have been drafted, but the system as such is not a public court: the court has no staff, is open only to investors' claims against the States, and is extremely costly in spite of measures to make access easier for SMEs.

With this said, why go the whole hog and set up a multilateral investment court? It would seem logical in the case of a failure of the current bilateral negotiations, to save, the idea of a permanent court in a multilateral context: but how many cases should justify the creation of the 'bazooka' MIC? Would it be enough to inflate continuous 'improvements' in what seems to be a fragile big balloon, the 'explosion' of which would put at risk not only the EU's trade policy under the common commercial policy, but might also be hijacked for the purposes of anti-Europeanism spreading all over Europe?

Consequently, there are still many open questions, both on core and minor issues. Contrary to what the CJEU affirmed in its Opinion, 'mutual trust' is not only a principle of EU law to be applied only between Member States. Certainly, this is legally correct, but legal principles should be the only engine of international relations. We have just celebrated the centenary of the end of the first world conflict. A new 'war' is underway, certainly a very different one from the global conflicts that have bloodied the planet, without direct casualties, either military or civilian, and without armies fighting one against the other. A global trade war is underway, and it sees old and new 'enemies' in a search of keeping control over raw resources, trade flows, juicy markets, fertile lands and water resources. Refusing to find solutions together, for example by rejecting the Paris Agreement on

Climate Change or by unilaterally imposing protectionist measures in the name of a national 'preference', are hostile acts. Economic refugees are the first indirect victims of this war.

It is probably idealistic, but to pursue common values as opposed to common economic interests may well be the way to establish strategic alliances between countries – not merely a geographic or economic union but a model based on values and principles, a last defence against terrorism, dictatorship and undemocratic regimes.

A community of values founded on mutual trust does not require an extra-national jurisdiction for its own nationals, whether they are investors or not.

17

The Rise of the RCEP: Regional Multilateralism and its Impact on the EU–China BIT

OLGA BOLTENKO

It is impossible to predict the time and progress of revolution. It is governed by its own laws.

– Vladimir Lenin

Those who have knowledge, do not predict. Those who predict, do not have knowledge.

– Lao Tzu

I. Introduction

China has eyed investment treaties with suspicion and caution for many decades. By the end of 2017 however, the Middle Kingdom had reached a stage at which it was ready to release to the public one of the largest bilateral investment treaties the world has ever known. The China–EU bilateral investment treaty (BIT) is likely to emerge as a pioneer of a new generation of Chinese investment treaties, in a radical change from China's successive generations of treaties that have shaped China's inbound and outbound foreign direct investment (FDI) since March 1982, when China concluded its first BIT (with Sweden).

Still in the dark ages of the pre-China–EU BIT, the EU Member States maintain a network of 25 bilateral investment treaties with China. This treaty patchwork covers all EU Member States excluding Ireland. The existing treaties were concluded at different stages of China's economic outlook, and thus offer different levels of substantive protections to the EU investors.[1] This treaty patchwork does not make sustainable trade and investment easy between the world's largest trading blocks. It is for that reason that the China–EU BIT was conceived.

The China–EU Bilateral Investment Treaty (Treaty, or the BIT) is indeed monumental in coverage. Once ratified, it will affect the livelihoods of over

[1] See, EU's Impact Assessment, http://ec.europa.eu/smart-regulation/impact/ia_carried_out/docs/ia_2013/swd_2013_0185_en.pdf,.

two billion people, cover 13.6 million square km of territory, and redefine the China–EU trade that averages over EUR one billion a day in volume. This magnitude is comparable to a number of regional multilateral free trade agreements that have enjoyed the generous attention of the wider public for a number of years. The Trans-Pacific Partnership (TPP) Agreement – as initially envisaged with the US participation – would have affected over 819 million people, and covered over 25 per cent of the world trade.[2] The Regional Comprehensive Economic Partnership Agreement (RCEP) is designed to cover over 45 per cent of the world population (three billion people), with a combined GDP of about USD 17.23 trillion.[3] The ASEAN Comprehensive Investment Agreement affects approximately 625 million people with a gross domestic product of USD 2.3 trillion.[4]

The negotiations of the China–EU BIT have been conducted under an impenetrable wall of confidentiality. In 2013, it transpired largely through brief notices by the relevant governmental departments,[5] that China and the EU had opened the Treaty negotiations. These notices have sparked excitement within the global economic community and academia, to which the present volume is a testament. Ironically, the academic interest in the negotiations process, while insatiable, must confine itself to something in which the academic community historically excels – guess work – for a simple reason that no data is available on the Treaty negotiations.

The secrecy that covers the negotiations of the China–EU BIT is controversial. It fuels the same backlash that emerged as a result of the TPP negotiations. While the Treaty will affect over two billion people in China and the European Union, that very same population has no access to what is being negotiated, and has no influence as to what the negotiators are shaping the Treaty to be.

This level of confidentiality is taking the secrecy that traditionally covers treaty negotiations to a new level. The China–EU BIT confidentiality is different from the TPP, the RCEP, and from the other regional multilateral negotiations. For example, several iterations of the TPP had been released to the public before the TPP was finalised.[6] A number of drafts of RCEP's investment chapter are circulating in the public domain, with annotations by the negotiating Member States.[7] The China–EU BIT drafts have remained largely in the confines of the negotiators.

[2] See, for example, http://dfat.gov.au/trade/agreements/tpp/pages/trans-pacific-partnership-agreement-tpp.aspx.

[3] See, for example, www.mti.gov.sg/MTIInsights/SiteAssets/Pages/FACTSHEET-WHAT-YOU-NEED-TO-KNOW-ABOUT/Factsheet%20on%20RCEP%20(June%202014).pdf.

[4] See, J Chaisse and S Jusoh, *The ASEAN Comprehensive Investment Agreement* (Cheltenham, Edward Elgar Publishing, 2016) 1.

[5] See, http://ec.europa.eu/trade/policy/countries-and-regions/countries/china/.

[6] See, one of the iterations of the TPP investment chapter of 2015, available on Wikileaks at https://wikileaks.org/tpp-investment/WikiLeaks-TPP-Investment-Chapter.pdf.

[7] See, for example, RCEP's draft investment chapter of October 2015 at www.keionline.org/23065/. See also Julien Chaisse and Richard Pomfret 'The RCEP and the Changing Landscape of World Trade--Assessing Asia-Pacific Investment Regionalism Next Stage' (2018) 12(1) *Law and Development Review* 151–90.

This extraordinary secrecy, worthy in the discipline of its keeping perhaps only of the well-guarded secrets of the USSR, has achieved a number of outcomes, both positive and negative. First, it has given ammunition to the call for transparency of treaty negotiations, which is undeniably positive.[8] Second, it has inflamed the backlash that has been plaguing the investor-state dispute settlement mechanism that is often a part of such treaties.[9] Third, and importantly, one of the unfortunate results of this secrecy is that the author of this chapter is forced to delve into an intricate game of guesswork trying to predict the contents of the Treaty without the benefits of having seen any of the drafts. This might seem like an exercise in futility. Indeed, why not wait with the analysis until after the final text of the Treaty is released? This question has no doubt plagued the minds of Wenhua Shan and Lu Wang, when they published their paper on the embryos of data available back in 2015 on the China–EU BIT.[10] The readership of this volume will sooner or later be able to test the accuracy of the author's predictions against the final text of the Treaty once it is released to the public.

One upside of the academic guesswork is certain though: it drives the analytical effort at analysing China and EU's treaty-making policy and, hopefully, it will inform the minds of the decision-makers to a certain extent, and inspire the investment and trade community to take an active stance on their Governments' treaty-making policy.

With this long introduction, the chapter proposes what the author predicts will be the contents of the Treaty on the basis of the trends that are reflected in the latest regional multilateral treaties, in particular in the TPP and in the RCEP. These trends include environmental carve-outs, safeguards of the States' regulatory space in the area of public health and security, links to customary international law when it comes to guarantees of fair and equitable treatment of investments and full protection and security standards, expanded scope of the dispute resolution clause, transparency provisions, possibilities of a standing bilateral investment tribunal, and a number of other forward-looking trends.

The obvious caveat to the predictions is that, while China is the negotiator of the Treaty, it was not involved in the negotiations of the TPP. Thus, many of the TPP traces that are visible in the RCEP drafts – such as the environmental carve-outs in particular – might not be present in the China–EU BIT. One of the most obvious reasons for that is that China – unlike a number of the TPP Member States – appears less environmentally cautious, or in any event less prepared to cripple its heavy industries by an international environmentally friendly treaty.

[8] See, for example, Esme Shirlow, 'A step towards Greater Transparency: The UN Transparency Convention', *Kluwer Arbitration Blog* (2015) http://arbitrationblog.kluwerarbitration.com/2015/03/30/a-step-toward-greater-transparency-the-un-transparency-convention/.

[9] See, for example, P Stothard and S Bruce, 'Unconventional Opinions: The Backlash Against TTIP, TPP and Investment Arbitration' (Lexology 2014) www.lexology.com/library/detail.aspx?g=523b5ce5-8849-4046-aaa7-4232782ed95d.

[10] Wenhua Shan and Lu Wang, 'The China-EU BIT and the Emerging "Global BIT 2.0"' (2015) 30 *ICSID Review* 260–67.

Indeed, China has been trying to find the fine balance between its international environmental obligations and its often environmentally insensitive industries. Despite these attempts, a China-led treaty is unlikely to be as environmentally friendly as the TPP or a number of other treaties.

To see the final predictions and analysis, the readers will have to bear with the author for a few pages until the end of the chapter.

II. Negotiations History and Key Data

A. The China–EU BIT

In 2012, at the outset of the EU's and China's 'great leap forward' in their trade relationship, the parties jointly announced their desire to open the Treaty negotiations in their 'Strategic Agenda for Cooperation for 2020'. As the document title suggests, the agenda set out ambitious goals for China and EU to achieve by 2020. The China–EU Investment Treaty was given particular prominence in the agenda:

> Negotiate and conclude a comprehensive EU–China Investment Agreement that covers issues of interest to either side, including investment protection and market access. The EU–China Investment Agreement will provide for progressive liberalisation of investment and the elimination of restrictions for investors to each other's market. It will provide a simpler and more secure legal framework to investors of both sides by securing predictable long-term access to EU and Chinese markets respectively and providing for strong protection to investors and their investments. It should replace the existing bilateral investment treaties between China and EU Member States with one single comprehensive agreement covering all EU Member States.[11]

As the wording of this ambitious goal suggests, the initial idea for the Treaty foresaw not only investment protection mechanisms but also market access mechanisms, which would transform the Treaty from a typical bilateral investment agreement to a hybrid treaty akin to a free trade agreement.

In the implementation of the 2020 agenda, in May 2010, the European Trade Commissioner Karel De Gucht and the Chinese Minister for Trade, Chen Deming, agreed to launch a Joint EU–China Investment Taskforce to study the options for enhancing bilateral investment and evaluate the desirability and feasibility of potential negotiations of an EU–China investment agreement.[12]

On 20 September 2012, the EU and China held its 15th Summit in Brussels. Jose Manuel Barroso (then President of the European Commission) and Herman Van Rompuy (then President of the European Council), represented the European

[11] See, http://eeas.europa.eu/archives/docs/china/docs/eu-china_2020_strategic_agenda_en.pdf.
[12] See, EU-China Investment Relations – impact assessment, http://ec.europa.eu/smart-regulation/impact/ia_carried_out/docs/ia_2013/swd_2013_0185_en.pdf.

Union. Premier Wen Jiabao of the State Council of the People's Republic of China represented China at the Summit. The Summit leaders announced that the EU and China reconfirmed its commitment to launching negotiations of the EU–China Bilateral Investment treaty.

B. Economy, Trade and Investment Summit Leaders

> 10. Reconfirmed both sides' commitment to launching negotiations of an EU–China Investment Agreement as soon as possible to promote and facilitate investment in both directions, thus resulting in an additional source of growth and employment. Negotiations towards this agreement would include all issues of interest to either side, without prejudice to the final outcome. They agreed to intensify discussions at a technical level in preparation for future negotiations.[13]

In early 2013, the European Commission published a document entitled 'EU-China Investment Relationship – draft impact assessment'.[14] In that document, the EU–China Investment Task Force concluded that the existing bilateral relationships between China and a number of EU Member States do not facilitate trans-boundary FDI flows and disadvantage the trade relationship between China and EU as trading blocks:

> despite the growing attraction and strategic importance of China as an FDI destination, the lack of a predictable and secure environment both for prospective and existing investors negatively affects EU outwards FDI flows to China. The result is not only an untapped potential, but also a growing imbalance, given the relative absence of barriers in the EU towards increasing Chinese inward investment. In the OECD FDI Restrictiveness Index 2010, China appears as the most restrictive of the countries examined, with an FDI restrictiveness index of 0.457 (0 being totally open, 1 being totally closed). Moreover, this restrictiveness index has worsened since 2006, where China ranked 3rd, behind India and Iceland, with an index of 0.405.
>
> The current bilateral and multilateral framework for investment between the EU and China does not offer the possibility to comprehensively address this situation which is unsatisfactory for the future competitiveness of European investors.[15]

In October 2013, the Council adopted the negotiating mandate for the Commission and in November 2013, the launch of negotiations was announced at the 16th EU-China Summit. The first round of talks was held in January 2014.[16]

[13] www.consilium.europa.eu/uedocs/cms_Data/docs/pressdata/en/ec/132507.pdf.

[14] http://ec.europa.eu/smart-regulation/impact/ia_carried_out/docs/ia_2013/swd_2013_0185_en.pdf,.

[15] http://ec.europa.eu/smart-regulation/impact/ia_carried_out/docs/ia_2013/swd_2013_0185_en.pdf, 11.

[16] www.europarl.europa.eu/legislative-train/theme-a-balanced-and-progressive-trade-policy-to-harness-globalisation/file-eu-china-investment-agreement.

Fast track forward, in September 2016, the EU and China held its twelfth round of negotiations of the Treaty. The discussions centred on the Treaty's definitions, fair and equitable treatment standard, the minimum standard of treatment requirement and expropriation. Other challenging topics included domestic regulation, sustainable development, the EU proposals on State-owned Enterprises, and on the Treaty's dispute settlement mechanism.[17]

In October 2017, at the fifteenth round of Treaty negotiations (held in Beijing), the parties' discussions focused on transparency of domestic regulations, licensing and authorisation qualifications for FDI, definition of expropriation, the content of the national treatment standard, and, importantly, on regulation of State-owned Enterprises and sustainable development:

> (i) Transparency: The EU and China discussed a number of provisions that relate to publication and consultation of laws and regulations, requests for information and proceedings taking place before administrative or judicial authorities. Agreement was reached on most of the matters covered, while the few outstanding issues will be revisited at the next round of negotiations.
>
> (ii) Domestic regulation: Exchanges on provisions relating to licensing and authorization qualifications and procedures allowed the EU and China to agree on all core issues covered by the talks.
>
> (iii) Provisions that relate to national treatment: The EU and China had in depth exchanges on a number of provisions and exceptions that relate to the obligation not to discriminate between domestic and foreign investors.
>
> (iv) Expropriation: The discussions focused primarily on the modalities of payment of compensation in case of unlawful takings of investors' property by the host state of the investment. Exchanges facilitated a better understanding of the Parties' respective positions.
>
> (v) Sustainable development: The EU and China agreed on the way discussions on matters that relate to investment-related aspects of environment and labour are to be organized in the coming months. Both sides took note of their respective sensitivities and key requests.
>
> (vi) Financial services: Talks on this point focused primarily on the definition of financial services and the possibility for the EU and China to rely on prudential exceptions in order to adopt measures aiming to ensure the stability and integrity of their domestic financial systems.
>
> (vii) State owned enterprises (SOEs): During this session, the EU presented its approach regarding the principles that should govern the commercial activities of SOEs and responded to China's questions for clarifications.[18]

From 12–15 December 2017, again in Brussels, China and the EU held the sixteenth round of the Treaty negotiations. According to the joint report, that round of negotiations centred around the definition of expropriation, the content

[17] See, generally, www.europarl.europa.eu/legislative-train/theme-a-balanced-and-progressive-trade-policy-to-harness-globalisation/file-eu-china-investment-agreement.

[18] See, http://trade.ec.europa.eu/doclib/docs/2017/october/tradoc_156353.pdf.

of the umbrella clause provision, the national treatment-related exceptions, transparency, sustainable development and financial services.[19]

With a focus on the dispute settlement mechanism, it is important to note that despite their evolving positions of a number of challenging issues such as the environment and the regulation of the State-owned Enterprises, the negotiating parties' positions on the need for investor-state dispute settlement mechanism in the Treaty appears to have remained unchanged throughout the negotiation rounds. In 2010, the EU concluded, in its impact assessment, that

> [EU] investors feel that recourse to judicial remedies in China is not sufficient. In the public consultation, 80% of the respondents who expressed an opinion on the Chinese legal system said that they did not have confidence in it to protect their rights as investors. They explained that the Chinese legal system lacked transparency and consistency, both in the decisions and in the judicial process itself.[20]

Again, no Treaty drafts have been leaked to the public domain, which makes the guesswork of what the Treaty will be even more challenging. Professor Wenhua Shan and Lu Wang predict, in their note on the China–EU BIT, that:

> the substantive rules are likely to be 'recalibrated' by the China–EU BIT. As a result, the traditional issues – such as post-establishment national treatment, standards of compensation and transfer – might cause little difficulty, as both sides have already adopted the fairly standardized formats in their recent treaty practices. It might nevertheless be unlikely to include express reference to the 'Hull Formula' in the BIT, given that China has been strongly opposed to it, and that the BIT would do just as well without such express reference.[21]

There is no reason to deviate from the informed predictions of Professor Shan who advocates that the substantive provisions of the emerging Treaty will be recalibrated. The question is how the substantive protections will be framed by the negotiating parties, and, more fundamentally, what position China will eventually be able to accept with respect to its heavily subsidised State-owned Enterprises and other market access issues.

A foray into China's negotiations position in the context of more visible treaty negotiations, such as those of RCEP, might help make those predictions more precise.

C. The RCEP

The RCEP is a free trade agreement between the 10 ASEAN Member States (Brunei, Cambodia, Indonesia, Laos, Malaysia, Myanmar, the Philippines, Singapore,

[19] See, http://trade.ec.europa.eu/doclib/docs/2017/december/tradoc_156520.pdf.

[20] See, http://ec.europa.eu/smart-regulation/impact/ia_carried_out/docs/ia_2013/swd_2013_0185_en.pdf, 14.

[21] See Shan and Wang (n 10).

Thailand, Vietnam) and the six states with which ASEAN has existing free trade agreements (Australia, China, India, Japan, South Korea and New Zealand).

The RCEP, once it enters into force, will become one of the world's largest and most sophisticated free trade agreements. In its scope, it will exceed the TPP magnitude in a wide range of indicators. RCEP will expand the ASEAN market from 600 million people to 3.5 billion.

While RCEP is at the advanced negotiations stages at the time of writing, it is far from being finalised. The RCEP negotiations are an important indication of what China views to be a modern, balanced investment treaty. The RCEP negotiations are also an important indicator of what China will be prepared to accept in the China–EU BIT.

A number of iterations of RCEP's investment chapter have been leaked to the public over the past few years, including with China's annotations on the drafts. Thus, the RCEP – where China's negotiations position is much more visible – is the only credible source at predicting what the China–EU BIT might be like.

In August 2012, the 16 RCEP Economic Ministers endorsed the Guiding Principles and Objectives for Negotiating the Regional Comprehensive Economic Partnership:

> the objective of launching RCEP negotiations is to achieve a modern, comprehensive, high-quality and mutually beneficial economic partnership agreement among the ASEAN Member States and ASEAN's FTA Partners. RCEP will cover trade in goods, trade in services, investment, economic and technical cooperation, intellectual property, competition, dispute settlement and other issues.[22]

The formal RCEP negotiations were launched in November 2012. Following rounds of intense debates and a number of iterations of the drafts of the treaty,[23] in November 2015, the RCEP Member States issued a joint statement hoping to conclude the negotiations by the end of 2016.

The RCEP was not finalised by 2016 as expected. In November 2016, the RCEP Ministers provided strategic policy guidance to advance negotiations, especially in the core areas of trade in goods, trade in services and investment.

It was expected in early 2016, that the US withdrawal from the TPP would accelerate the RCEP negotiations, and that the RCEP Member States would release the final text of the Treaty by the end of 2017. However, the TPP revival towards the end of 2016 interfered with those plans. In addition to that, the RCEP negotiators must balance the interests of mature, developed economies such as Australia and Japan, with the interests of emerging markets such as Cambodia and Laos, with powerful hybrid economies (both capital exporting and capital importing) China and India thrown into the mix.

[22] See, guiding Principles and Objectives for Negotiating the Regional Comprehensive Economic Partnership, http://dfat.gov.au/trade/agreements/rcep/documents/guiding-principles-rcep.pdf.

[23] See information on the multiple negotiations rounds at http://wtocenter.vn/other-agreement/regional-comprehensive-economic-partnership-rcep.

Navigating through those often conflicting interests takes time. On the other hand, the TPP as initially conceived went beyond the standard free trade agreement ambit and covered intellectual property, labour rights and State-owned Enterprises. The RCEP's substantive scope is less ambitious – with its more traditional focus on tariffs on goods, and services. One would have assumed that the less ambitious scope of the RCEP would have made the negotiations easier. However, RCEP's largest economies – China, Japan and India – are locked in a number of territorial disputes that are hindering the progress of the negotiations.[24]

Given the extreme complexity of political, economic and territorial issues involved, by the end of 2017, the RCEP negotiations were far from concluded. No official text of the treaty (or of any of its drafts) has been released to the wider public for comments. However, importantly, in October 2015, several drafts of the RCEP investment chapter were leaked and appeared on Wikileaks and subsequently on other specialised websites.[25]

These leaked drafts, in particular China's position paper of October 2015 on the RCEP investment chapter, informs the views, at least partially, on China's contemporary treaty-making practice.

D. RCEP: Trends in Treaty-making

RCEP will no doubt cover many of the trade liberalisation aspects that are covered in the TPP, and in a number of other regional multilateral treaties, such as trade in goods and services, investment, economic and technical cooperation, intellectual property, competition, environment and dispute settlement.

Again, RCEP is particularly interesting in the context of the China–EU predictions because China is one of the driving forces in the RCEP negotiations. Chances are that the China-led RCEP provisions will find their way to the drafts of the China–EU BIT. It is for the sake of accuracy of these predictions that this chapter focuses on China's position paper of October 2015 on the RCEP's investment texts.

It is understood that the RCEP Investment Chapter is largely based on the corresponding chapter of the TPP, including its environmental carve-outs and the ISDS mechanism.

A number of RCEP negotiating states appear to have proposed additional safeguards to guarantee that the Member States will have the freedom to regulate matters of environment, health and public safety, within their territory, without exposing the host governments to the risks of treaty claims.

[24] See, for example, www.japantimes.co.jp/news/2017/11/14/business/agreeing-rcep-chinas-favorite-trade-deal-set-drag-2018/#.WmlMNbyWb7E.

[25] See, for example, a consolidated October 2015 version at https://rceplegal.files.wordpress.com/2016/08/03-rcep-wgi10-draftconsolidated-investmenttext.pdf; see also, December 2016 draft at www.bilaterals.org/IMG/pdf/rcep-invesment-temporarysafeguardmeasures.pdf; see the negotiations positions of China, India, New Zealand and South Korea on the RCEP investment chapter at https://rceplegal.wordpress.com/2016/08/02/first-blog-post/.

E. TPP-inspired FET and FPS Standards in the RCEP and Potentially in the China–EU BIT

The Fair and Equitable Treatment (FET) standard in investment treaties has been a controversial issue in investment law for decades. The typically sparse wording of the standard in most treaties does not allow for other means to interpret what this standard means than have recourse to the rules of treaty interpretation, and thus, inevitably, Articles 31 and 32 of the Vienna Convention on the Law of Treaties.

The frequency with which foreign investors attempt to engage the host State's liability under investment treaties with reference to the breaches of the FET standard is as astounding as the success rate of the claimants' FET claims.[26] The FET standard is the most frequently invoked standard in investment disputes.[27] Tribunals have interpreted the capacious wording of the FET standard in the treaties to include the host State's obligations to act consistently, transparently, reasonably, without ambiguity, arbitrariness or discrimination, in an evenhanded manner, to ensure due process in decision-making and respect investors' legitimate expectations, at time with an additional obligation to ensure that no denial of justices occurs.[28] In essence, the FET standard is designed to cover everything that does not fall under the auspices of more precise treaty standards, such as expropriation.[29]

This generous coverage has resulted in the States' greater exposure and vulnerability vis-à-vis treaty claims, which is particularly taxing on developing and least-developed states. The backlash against the generous interpretative practices of the FET standard has generated a more balanced wording in contemporary investment treaties. This balanced wording links the FET standard to customary international law and, more specifically, to the minimum standard of treatment of aliens, thus reducing the State's exposure to liability under investment treaties for FET breaches only to those acts that are 'shocking' and 'egregious'.[30]

The FET standard of the TPP is located at Article 9.6(1) of the TPP Investment Chapter. It is part of a wider section titled 'Minimum Standard of Treatment' (Article 9.6). Article 9.6(2) of the TPP clarifies that the applicable standard of FET for covered investments is the 'customary international law minimum standard of treatment of aliens', thus limiting the TPP states exposure to FET claims.

The TPP's approach to FET and its explicit link to customary international law has found its way to the October 2015 iteration of RCEP's investment chapter, which provides, in article 12.1, that: '[t]he concepts of "fair and equitable treatment"

[26] See, UNCTAD report on FET, http://unctad.org/en/Docs/unctaddiaeia2011d5_en.pdf.

[27] See, Rudolf Dolzer and Christoph Schreuer, *Principles of International Investment Law* 2nd edn (Oxford, Oxford University Press, 2012) 130.

[28] See, UNCTAD report on FET, (2012) 1, http://unctad.org/en/Docs/unctaddiaeia2011d5_en.pdf.

[29] See, Dolzer and Schreuer (n 27) 132.

[30] See, J Paulsson and G Petrochilos, 'Neer-ly Misled' (2007) 22 *ICSID Review* 146.

and "full protection and security" [FPS] do not require treatment in addition to or beyond that which is required under customary international law'. China's annotated version of the RCEP investment chapter goes beyond a simple reference to the customary international law. It clarifies, in detail, what the FET standard in the RCEP is intended to mean:

> 3. The concept of 'fair and equitable treatment' and 'full protection and security' do not require treatment in addition to or beyond that which is required by that standard [customary international law], and do not create additional substantive rights. The obligation in paragraph 1 to provide:
>
> (a) Fair and equitable treatment refers to the obligation not to deny justice in criminal, civil, or administrative adjudicatory proceedings in accordance with the principle of due process of law and;
>
> (b) Full protection and security refers to the requirements one each/a Party to provide the level of police protection required under customary international law.

With a fair degree of probability one may assume that this limited standard of FET, with a clear linkage to customary international law, will find its way to the EU–China BIT.

F. TPP-inspired Expropriation Provisions in the RCEP and Potentially in the China–EU BIT

Protection from illegal expropriation is by far the main substantive protection that is awarded to foreign investors under investment treaties. On the basis of expropriation provisions of investment treaties, foreign investors are entitled to bring treaty claims against their host States for conduct attributable to the States that constitutes either direct taking of property, or has the effect of substantially depriving the investment of its value, or depriving the investor if its ability to manage use, or control its investment in a meaningful way.[31]

While direct expropriation appears relatively straightforward, indirect expropriation has posed a number of conceptual issues in the investment community. The latest controversy has arisen out of the concept of the States' right to regulate matters of public concern, such as environment, health and security, within their own territories. Such regulatory measures often negatively affect foreign investment and thus expose the host States to treaty claims.[32]

At the inception of the treaty-making practice, around the time when the first Bilateral Investment Treaty was concluded (Germany–Pakistan BIT, 1958),

[31] See L Yves Fortier and Stephen L Drymer, 'Indirect Expropriation in the Law of International Investment: I Know It When I See It, or Caveat Investor' (2004) 19(2) *ICSID Review – Foreign Investment Law Journal* 293–327. See also Julien Chaisse, 'Promises and Pitfalls of the European Union Policy on Foreign Investment' (2012) 15(1) *Journal of International Economic Law* 51–84.

[32] See, UNCTAD Series: Expropriation – a sequel, http://unctad.org/en/Docs/unctaddiaeia2011d7_en.pdf.

the driving force behind the treaty negotiations was with the powerful capital exporting states. It was in their interest to negotiate and promote investor-friendly treaties. Thus, the expropriation provisions of such first generation of investment treaties tend to be wide and all-encompassing, and inherently investor-friendly.

The economic reality has changed since then. Contemporary investment treaties, and in particular regional free trade agreements such as the TPP, contain carefully-drafted carve-outs that exclude the States' regulatory measures intended to regulate matters of public concern from the scope of expropriation provisions.

Item 3 of the TPP Expropriation Annex does just that: '[n]on-discriminatory regulatory actions that are designed to protect legitimate public welfare objectives … do not constitute indirect expropriations, except in rare circumstances'. Expropriation Annex of RCEP's Investment Chapter (October 2015) traces that wording and excludes regulatory measures from the scope of its expropriation provisions:

> non-discriminatory regulatory measures by a Party or measures or awards by judicial bodies of a Party that are designed and applied interest or public welfare objectives, such as public health, safety, and the environment, shall not constitute expropriation/s under this Article.

The Chinese annotated version of the RCEP draft goes beyond that simple carve-out and provides that: '[expropriation] is intended to reflect customary international law concerning the obligation of States with respect to expropriation'. Chances are that China, a heavily regulated jurisdiction, will continue the trend of regulatory carve-outs and insist on including a qualified carve-out in the China–EU BIT, as well as a clear link to the expropriation standard to customary international law.

G. TPP-inspired Balancing Provision in the RCEP and Potentially in the China–EU BIT

The latest generation of investment treaties and free trade agreements, in their attempts to safeguard the States' regulatory space, have conceived what is known to be a 'balancing provision' that specifically allows the States to regulate matters of environment and health within their territory without being exposed to the risks of expropriation claims.

Article 9.16 of the TPP's Investment Chapter provides that:

> Nothing in this Chapter shall be construed to prevent a Party from adopting, maintaining or enforcing any measure otherwise consistent with this Chapter that it considers appropriate to ensure that investment activity in its territory is undertaken in a manner sensitive to environmental, health or other regulatory objectives.

The RCEP Investment Chapter 2.1.3 (October 2015) reproduces this wording almost verbatim, with a number of variations:

> Nothing in this Chapter shall be interpreted to restrict the rights of a Party to formulate, modify, amend, apply or revoke its laws, regulations and policies. Each Party retains

> the right to exercise discretion with respect to regulatory, compliance, investigatory, and prosecutorial matters, including discretion regarding allocation of resources and establishment of penalties.

Interestingly, the Chinese annotated version of the RCEP Investment Chapter does not contain a similarly worded balancing provision. It remains to be seen whether the RCEP balancing provision will negotiate its way to the final version of the China–EU BIT.

III. Conclusions

In 2013, in its Impact Assessment Report on the EU–China Investment Relations, the European Commission outlined five possible scenarios according to which the parties' trade relationship might evolve:

> No policy change; China and the EU will continue to operate on the patchwork of individual bilateral investment treaties between China and the European Union Member States;
> China and EU will implement a stand-alone Bilateral Investment Treaty;
> China and EU will implement a separate agreement combining investment protection with market access;
> China and EU will integrate investment protection and market access regimes into the currently ongoing negotiations of the Partnership and Cooperation Agreement; or
> China and EU will sign a comprehensive free trade agreement.

Numerous policy and negotiation rounds later, towards the end of 2017, it is apparent that the second option – a China–EU Bilateral Investment Treaty – is the only option that survived.

The first option – continuing operations under the current framework of bilateral agreements and policy dialogues – no longer attends to the needs of the parties' trade and cross-border investment.[33]

The third option – an agreement combining investment protection and market access regulations – seems to be a complementary approach rather than an alternative to a BIT, and is tangibly still on the agenda, but less so than the almost completed China–EU BIT.

The fourth option – a comprehensive Partnership and Cooperation Agreement that would incorporate investment protection and market access, is labelled by the European Commission as 'highly unrealistic'. As the European Commission recorded in its Impact Assessment Report, 'it seems unlikely that the overall stalemate in the PCA negotiations could be overcome since the gap does not seem

[33] See, Impact Assessment Report on the EU–China Investment Relations, 22.

bridgeable at this stage on other key trade chapters including services, sustainable development, IPR and procurement'.[34]

The fifth option – a China–EU FTA – is not even on the parties' agenda as there is no interest on the part of China to open FTA negotiations with the European Union in the near future.

Thus, in the years to come, having discarded the remaining four scenarios in accordance with which a China–EU trade relationship may have developed, the world will see one of its largest bilateral investment treaties – the China–EU BIT. The Treaty emerges as an example of intricate, elaborate, complex negotiations and drafting process run by two equally powerful negotiators.

Professors Shan and Wang predicted in their note at the outset of the China–EU negotiations:

> the substantive rules are likely to be 'recalibrated' by the China–EU BIT. As a result, the traditional issues – such as post-establishment national treatment, standards of compensation and transfer – might cause little difficulty, as both sides have already adopted the fairly standardized formats in their recent treaty practices.[35]

Having studied China's latest positions on these 'traditional issues that might cause little difficulty', in particular in the context of RCEP negotiations, a safer prediction appears to be that China will move away from its traditional treaty practice and negotiate a treaty that will inform a new generation of BITs. The more detailed textual predictions are that the China–EU BIT will contain at the very least:

1. An RCEP-inspired expropriation provision that links the standard of expropriation to customary international law and carves out from the scope of the expropriation provision the parties' regulatory measures intended to protect matters of public policy such as environment, health, and public safety and security;
   A RCEP-inspired FET standard that is linked to customary international law and is described as limited to the obligation not to deny justice in criminal, civil, or administrative adjudicatory proceedings in accordance with the principle of due process of law; and
   Potentially a balancing provision that safeguards the states' regulatory space.

I wish I could say, like Winston Churchill did at a conference in Cairo on 1 February 1943, that 'I always avoid prophesying beforehand, because it is a much better policy to prophesy after the event has already taken place'. And yet, several pages later, I have made a few possibly ill-informed predictions of what the BIT will look like. Only time will tell.

[34] ibid 23.
[35] See Shan and Wang (n 10).

18

The Comprehensive and Progressive Agreement for Trans-Pacific Partnership: Intellectual Property Chapter, Research in Biotechnology and Price of Medicine with Lessons from the European Union

SUFIAN JUSOH

I. Introduction

The last decades brought large progress in improving and using both science and technology, putting forward a lot of possibilities for developing countries to fight difficulties they are facing in many important sectors, for example health, food security, environment and human development generally. Between 2006 and 2016, there were 131,349 patents applied for in biotechnology fields worldwide with an average annual increase of 5.2 per cent; and 249,744 applications for pharmaceutical patents, with an annual increase of 4.1 per cent. Most of the applications are dominated by developed countries, with the exception of China, with the top two countries being the United Kingdom and Switzerland.[1]

Among the major concerns of developing countries in using biotechnology are enhancing their economic growth; and addressing pressing domestic issues such as disease eradication, addressing environmental concerns and increasing food production. Many developing countries continue to rely on imported patented and generic medicine, vaccines and food which affect domestic food security and economy including balance of trade and balance of payment.

Many developing countries would like to progress in science and technology by promoting research and development, either to create new technologies or to

[1] World Intellectual Property Organisation (WIPO), *World Intellectual Property Indicators 2018* (Geneva, WIPO, 2018).

work on existing technologies, which includes patented ones. Nevertheless, they have to grapple with constraints that affect the advancement of local science and technology. The constraints include lack of domestic direct investment and capital, technology advancement and research and development.

Developing countries have a choice of either developing their own research and development capabilities both in the private and the public sector; or contracting through partners either locally or abroad; or to purchase technologies either by way of outright purchase or by paying licence fees and royalty. Developing one's own research and development capability will require heavy expenses, including setting-up infrastructure and facilities and making sure to have the right number of experts and support staff.

This is where research exemption provision in a patent law will play its role as researchers may inadvertently or unknowingly breach someone else's patent in the course of conducting research. It is not an easy task as there is an ongoing process of expansion and straightening of intellectual property rights and privatisation of research goals and priorities[2] which lead to the increase in the demand for higher protection of intellectual property by private research organisations.

When combined with other factors distinctive for developing countries such as inadequate investment in research, it leads to the conclusion that intellectual property rights (IPR) might actually create obstacles for development and access to innovations and that certain measures are necessary in order to balance the expansion of IP and circumvent the problems these processes are causing.[3] The obstacles come in the form of the requirement to obtain consent from the original patent owner in order to work on or with the patent and approvals can be in the form of royalty or licence fee which can be expensive for developing country researchers to pay. Thus, a research exemption provision in a patent law (hereinafter referred to as 'the research exemption') may provide an avenue to overcome these obstacles which then are able to contribute to a wide variety of objectives such as funding cures for healthcare and agriculture issues in developing countries.

The following pages will elaborate the research exemptions in the legal frameworks of Malaysia and Singapore, being two of the ASEAN Member States which have major biotechnology activities and being part of the Comprehensive and Progressive Agreement for Trans-Pacific Partnership (CPTPP). The CPTPP is a trade and investment agreement between 11 countries in the Asia-Pacific region. Those countries are New Zealand, Australia, Brunei Darussalam, Canada, Chile, Japan, Malaysia, Mexico, Peru, Singapore and Viet Nam. The CPTPP is based on

[2] ITC Background Paper on Accessing Patented Knowledge for Innovation, The Innovation, Technology and Society, a call for proposal on how developing countries may access patented knowledge, 2007. For a more recent discussion see B Mercurio and D Kim, *Contemporary Issues in Pharmaceutical Patent Law: Setting the Framework and Exploring Policy Options* (Abingdon, Routledge, 2017).

[3] ITC Background Paper, ibid.

the Trans-Pacific Partnership Agreement (TPP) signed by the same countries, as well as the United States, on 4 February 2016. In January 2017 the US withdrew from the TPP. The resulting CPTPP was signed on 8 March 2018.

In Article 2.29, CPTPP Parties confirm the importance of transparency, cooperation and exchanging information related to the trade of 'products of modern biotechnology', as defined in CPTPP. The text specifically acknowledges that it does not require any changes to CPTPP Parties' existing laws, regulations and policies. The chapter will outline the scope of research exemptions in several developing countries including Malaysia and Singapore. The chapter will then discuss whether the CPTPP Intellectual Property (IP) Chapter restricts any research and development activities in the pharmaceutical and biotechnology sectors in Malaysia and Singapore. The chapter will also make comparisons with the research exemption provisions in the European Union (EU).

II. Research Exemptions Defined

Biotechnology appears to be the area where developing countries could benefit the most from implementing research exemptions in their legal framework, considering the potential that certain end results may have within health-related issues or agriculture. Taking the example of agricultural biotechnology and its implication in improving agricultural capacity of developing countries, research exemptions can be considered in these countries as a tool to reduce poverty and provide more food security on sustainable level.

It is in this light that the World Health Assembly in its adopted strategy explicitly recognises the power of research exemption to solve the problems of neglecting disease in developing countries. The governments of these countries were encouraged to consider research exemptions as an effective tool to improve health related research. It reduces the costs of research in relation to neglected disease by saving resources that would in other ways be spent on licences and have the potential to induce other research activities as well that might not otherwise occur. Most countries did not have any guidance as to how to formulate research exemptions.

The scope of the research exemption is discussed in Article 30, read together with Article 27 of the Agreement on the Trade Related Intellectual Property Rights (TRIPs) of the World Trade Organization. Article 30 does not offer legal security to what extent commercial aspect of research exemption would be allowed. Article 27 of TRIPs requires no discrimination as to the field of technology. whereas Article 30 allows exceptions granted to the patent holder's rights in as far as they are to be which introduces the three steps test, namely that the activities *(1) do not unreasonably conflict with a normal exploitation of the patent; (2) do not unreasonably prejudice the legitimate interests of the patent owner; and (3) take into account the legitimate interests of third parties.*

Given the increasing pace of the tendency to straighten and enforce IP rights, in particular favouring adherence to stringent IPRs beyond the TRIPs minimum standards, as contained in many preferential trade agreements (PTA) such as the CPTPP, countries undertaking domestic technological development will have to design the national law and PTA template to suit their national research and development and technology advancement agenda. For example, research in the pharmaceutical sector is important as a means to creating a sustainable public health policy. For example, the Academies of Sciences of combined select developed and developing countries have issued a joint declaration to 'work with developing countries to build systems of science, technology and innovation for economic and social development, and to promote the education and training of their future leaders particularly in science, engineering, technology and medicine'.[4]

Research exemption provision is an indispensable tool for facilitating access to existing knowledge. When more countries promote and foster innovations, either in the form of basic and fundamental research, or in the case of many developing countries to conduct follow-on research on existing innovation, the more space should be available for research exemptions. This would leave enough liberty for local inventors to use disclosed information and contribute with incremental developments, mostly for the purpose of adopting the innovation for a better use locally. In general, the research exemption allows for the use of a patented invention without the patent holder's authorisation and without financial compensation.[5] However, it only does so in as far as this use is conducted for research or for experimental purposes and this always depends on the exact nature and scope of research and experimental purposes, and to delineate them from commercial activities. Research exemption normally refers to the research or experimental purposes, either academic research or private research which excludes any acts done with a commercial intent. However, it is unclear whether the exemption is limited to acts done on the protected invention or if it also exempts acts done with the patented product or process, using it as a tool.

The main function of the research exemption is to allow research on (or with) protected subject matter. Researchers working on a particular research are still required to abide by the terms of the law of patents, be it the need to obtain the necessary licence to use any patented tools; and not to infringe any third-party patents in conducting the research. Research exemption provision is no longer applicable after a particular product of the research is produced and introduced into the market. Research exemption is only practically relevant where the protected invention that is needed for one's research can be reproduced or purchased by the

[4] Joint science academies' statement on growth and responsibility: the promotion and protection of innovation, in May 2007, https://royalsociety.org/-/media/Royal_Society_Content/policy/publications/2007/8046.pdf (last accessed 20 May 2019).

[5] Michelangelo Temmerman, Patent Research Exemption Defined, unpublished text, file with author.

researcher claiming the exemption. In addition, the research exemption does not imply an obligation of the patent holder to deliver the protected invention for the planned research.[6]

Research exemption is also closely linked with the private use exemption, generally known as the Bolar exemption. The Bolar exemption[7] is limited to research and pre-marketing activities related to pharmaceuticals.[8] It allows acts undertaken with a view to obtain regulatory approval for generic drugs and a similar exemption is also established under European Union law, under the Directive 2004/27/EC.[9]

Research exemptions will need to be linked with the issue of competition policy. This is because intellectual property does not actually consider any impact that an invention may have on competition before granting patent protection.[10] Patent law and patent offices do not normally consider competition issues in granting patents or whether such patents will restrict any future research. In examining innovation, patent granting authorities exclusively focus on legal and scientific conditions of patentability and the 'prior art'. On the other hand, there is a widely accepted perception in antitrust policy of the patent right as a form of monopoly.[11] Although a patent holder is conferred rights to exclude others from exploiting the patent, it does not actually generate a monopoly in the antitrust sense as these rights do not in fact offer significant market power on their own.[12]

Competition issue may also play a role in the case of broad patents, which will then restrict the potential further research in the same field of science and technology. For example, after obtaining a broad patent, the owner may decide

[6] ibid.

[7] The term Bolar exemption is based on the case of *Roche Products, Inc v Bolar Pharmaceutical Co, Inc*, 733 F.2d 858 (1984). In that case the Federal Circuit held that the traditional experimental use exemption to patent infringement (35 USC § 271(a)) did not apply to pre-market testing done by a generic manufacturer and submitted to a regulatory agency. However, the United States Congress introduced the Hatch-Waxman Act which states that 'it shall not be an act of infringement to make, use, offer to sell, or sell within the United States or import into the United States a patented invention … solely for uses reasonably related to the development and submission of information under a Federal law which regulates the manufacture, use, or sale of drugs or veterinary biological products'. 35 U.S.C. § 271(e)(1) ('Bolar exemption').

[8] The World Intellectual Property Organisation (WIPO) has issued a draft reference document on the exceptions regarding acts for obtaining regulatory approval from authorities under the Bolar Exception. See WIPO, Draft Reference Document on Exception Regarding Acts for Obtaining Regulatory Approval from Authorities, Standing Committee on the Law of Patents, Twenty Seventh Session, SCP/27/3, 20 November 2017.

[9] Directive 2004/27/EC Of The European Parliament And Of The Council of 31 March 2004 amending Directive 2001/83/EC on the Community code relating to medicinal products for human use, Official Journal of the European Union, L136/34, 30.4.2004.

[10] Prepared Remarks of James E Rogan under Secretary of Commerce for Intellectual Property and Director of the United States Patent and Trademark Office at the Hearings on Competition and Intellectual Property Law and Policy in the Knowledge-Based Economy, February 6, 2002, US Federal Trade Commission (USFTC).

[11] ibid.

[12] ibid.

not to conduct further research; being satisfied with the power of his patent. Excessive protection allows patent holders to be relaxed, slowing down considerably the innovation process. After obtaining patent protection, the invention can become an idle innovation, if the patent owner does not have any intention to complete the research process and transform its invention into a product suitable for commercialisation. Depending on the significance of the innovation, the patent owner without doubt is in a position to slow down technological progress, given the fact that his patent would not allow others to find a substitutable product either.[13]

Broad patents are not unusual in the biotechnology field. Claims in biotechnology are actually broadly formulated by their very nature.[14] The most obvious example is an invention related to a process of setting a particular gene into a particular organism with a specific method. If the claim would have been limited to a specific gene, organism or process, the invention could be utilised without infringement by simply using another gene, organism or processing method. Expectedly, as a consequence of a narrowly defined claim, the patent potentially is of very limited commercial value.[15] This is the main reason why applications relating to the biotechnology area are as broadly formulated as possible, seeking patent protection covering more than the invention to which it actually relates. Given the trend of patent authorities awarding broad patents to biotechnology related claims, we have to be aware of the consequence that exclusive rights are not only conferred on the unique invention, but they are extending to a development that is only supposed to have equal effect or a purpose.[16]

These problems are accelerated as patent protection is of great importance to biotechnology. The majority of biotechnology companies are small in size, with rather limited technologies available to dispose with, as opposed to technologies available to large companies.[17] In addition, developing a biotechnology product requires a long period of time, and extensive time is needed before these companies are able to commercialise their inventions. Thus, conferring a patent to biotech companies in the early stage of ongoing development is essential to secure sufficient investment required to continue research that may lead to the development of either final or an intermediate product.

[13] Thomas Cottier and Ana Jevtic, Competition, Patents and Innovation – An interdependent relation, unpublished text, file with author.

[14] ibid.

[15] HJ Barton, 'Patent Scope in Biotechnology' (1995) 26 *International Review of Intellectual Property and Competition Law* 605–18. For example, the biological effectiveness of a transformation technique on strains other than those used in inventor's disclosure may not be known at the time of patenting. A later researcher who finds it impossible to make the technique work for a new strain is ipso facto demonstrating that the technique was not enabled for that strain. (The case, however, give only limited comfort to those considering action that might infringe a broad claim that they suspect is invalid.)

[16] JK West, 'Intellectual Property Rights and Competition Policy with a Focus on Biotechnology', in *Best Practice Roundtables in Competition Policy Working Paper No 50* (OECD Paper, 2005).

[17] ibid.

III. The Scope of Research Exemptions in the USA, the EU and Select Developing Countries

A. The USA

Research exemption provisions exist in patent laws, both in developed and developing countries. The United States appears to provide research exemptions in biotechnology, in particular in drug discovery through written law ie the Hatch-Waxman Act 1983,[18] which sets up a system to 'balance the need to stimulate innovation against the goal of furthering the public interest' and judge-made laws (case law). However, there are arguments that court decisions such as in *Helsinn Healthcare SA v Teva Pharmaceuticals USA, Inc*[19] in the United States under the America Invents Act[20] has further narrowed the scope of the experimental research exemption in the country.[21]

B. The European Union

Research exemptions in the European Union (EU) are contained in the European Directive 2004/27/EC,[22] particularly Article 10. This directive amended the earlier European Directive 2001/83/EC on the Community Code relating to medicinal products for human use. Article 10 (6) excludes from infringement of patent rights or supplementary protection certificates (SPCs): 'Conducting the necessary studies and trials with a view to the application of paragraphs 1, 2, 3 and 4'. In addition, the EU Community Patent Conventions (CPC) provide that the rights conferred by a community patent shall not extend to 'acts done for experimental purposes relating to the subject matter of the patented invention'.[23]

However, the EU Directive fails to provide an explanation on what amounts to 'conducting the necessary studies and trials'. The CPC Article 27 has also been incorporated into the national patent laws of many EU Member States. Hence, the meaning of 'conducting necessary studies and trials' as in the EU Directive

[18] The Drug Price Competition and Patent Term Restoration Act (Hatch–Waxman Act), Pub Law No 98-417, 98 Stat 1585 (1984) (codified in relevant part at 35 USC §271(e)). See discussion in A Russo and J Johnson (2015), 'Research Use Exemptions to Patent Infringement for Drug Discovery and Development in the United States' (2015) Feb 5(2) *Cold. Spring Harb Perpect Med* a 020933.

[19] *Helsinn Healthcare SA v Teva Pharmaceuticals USA, Inc*, 855 F.3d 1356 (Fed Cir 2017).

[20] Pub L No 112-29, 125 Stat 284 (codified at 35 USC §§ 100 et seq).

[21] For discussion see K Kostolanksy and D Salgado, 'Does the Experimental Use Exception in Patent Law Have a Future?' (2018) *The Colorado Lawyer* 32–40.

[22] Directive 2004/27/EC Of The European Parliament And Of The Council of 31 March 2004 amending Directive 2001/83/EC on the Community code relating to medicinal products for human use, Official Journal of the European Union, L136/34, 30.4.2004.

[23] Council Agreement relating to Community Patents No 89/695/EEC, 15 December 1989, OJ L 401/01. See Art 27.

and the meaning of 'experimental purposes' in CPC depend on the interpretation provided by the national law of each Member State.

For example, the German Patent Act (GPA), §11 No 2 states that the effects of a patent shall not extend to 'acts done for experimental purposes relating to the subject matter of the patented invention'. The law is to provide for a broad range of allowed uses, for example, producing, importing, possessing and using the protected product or process as a subject of research. The scope of the experimental use in Germany has also been decided in the German Federal Court of Justice (FCJ) decisions in *Klinische Versuche I* (*Clinical Trials I*) of 11 July 1995 and *Klinische Versuche II* (*Clinical Trials II*) on 17 April 1997.

According to Jaenichen and Pitz, the German FCJ in its decisions *Clinical Trials I* and *II* refers to a case-by-case evaluation where both the form of the tested substance and above all the intentions of the persons and companies involved must also be taken into account.[24] They further state that 'experiments are permissible that relate to the constitution of the patented substance, for example, experiments for investigating its composition, producibility, technical usability, and effects. Also allowed are experiments for testing the functionality of the patented invention'.[25]

Germany applies the Bolar-type exemption in §11 No 2b GPA. The law provides that the effects of a granted patent do not extend to studies and trials, including their practical requirements, necessary for obtaining drug approval for the marketing of a drug within the EU or drug approval in a Member State of the EU or abroad. This Bolar-type exemption is not limited to research on the subject matter of a protected product or process but also allows research with a patent-protected product or process. It is also argued that use of a patented research tool falls under the Bolar exemption of §11 No 2b GPA if the use of the tool is necessary for obtaining approval data or if it is explicitly required by the approval authority, either for generic or other innovative products that covers clinical trial activities for the purpose of obtaining regulatory approval.[26]

The United Kingdom on the other hand provides for the research exemption in Section 60 of the United Kingdom Patents Act, which has been modelled on the European Patent Convention. Section 60 (5) (b) of the UK Patents Act exempts an act that is done for experimental purposes relating to the subject matter of the invention.

The term 'experimental purposes' has been clarified in the case of *Monsanto Co v Stauffer Chemical Co*.[27] In this case it was held that 'experimental use' exemption covers activities that seek to generate genuinely new information but not those that seek to verify existing knowledge. It was further held that field trials carried out in order to (1) discover something unknown, (2) test a hypothesis,

[24] Hans-Rainer Jaenichen and Johann Pitz, 'Research Exemption/Experimental Use in the European Union: Patents Do Not Block the Progress of Science' (2015) 5 *Cold Spring Harb Perspect Med* a020941.

[25] ibid, 3.

[26] ibid, 6.

[27] *Monsanto Co v Stauffer Chemical Co* (1985) RPC 515.

(3) find out whether something that is known to work in specific conditions would work in different conditions, or (4) see if the experimenter could manufacture commercially in accordance with the patent could 'fairly be regarded as experiments'. However, trials to demonstrate to a third party or to amass information to satisfy a third party such as a regulatory body or customer that a product works as its maker claims are not to be regarded as acts done for experimental purposes.[28]

The UK Patents Act provides for Bolar exemption in Section 60 (5) (i). The section exempts from infringement 'an act done in conducting a study, test, or trial which is required for the purpose of regulatory approval of generic medicinal products'. Hence, the provision is narrower than the German provision. The UK provision applies only to studies, tests or trials conducted in the context of abridged, hybrid and biosimilar applications for regulatory approval of generic or similar biological to patented pharmaceuticals either in the UK or any other EU Member State.

C. Developing Countries

Many developing countries have introduced research exemption provisions in their national patent laws, using the WIPO Model Patent Law for Developing Countries. Article 23 of the Model Patent Law indicated that the 'use of the patented invention for strictly private or experimental purposes is not to be deemed to be use for industrial or commercial purposes'. Implemented provisions are however not uniform and are based on different criteria.[29]

The diversity in the way developing countries and economies in transition have stipulated experimentation or research exceptions can be roughly summarised in three groups. Many countries provide for exceptions of 'experimentation' or 'experimental purposes' where in some cases the law requires that the act is done only and exclusively for experimental purposes.[30] Other countries limit patent exception for research conducted for scientific purposes exclusively or extend exceptions in a way to include both experimental and scientific purposes.[31] In these countries, if not explicitly defined, either formulation implies non-commercial nature of the exception.

[28] See judgment of Dillon LJ, ibid at 538.

[29] Christopher Garrison, Exceptions to Patent Rights in Developing Countries, UNCTAD-ICTSD Project on IPRs and Sustainable Development, August 2006.

[30] For example Belize, Bhutan, Botswana, Cambodia, Chile, Mongolia, Guatemala, Pakistan, Philipines, Singapore, South Korea, Turkey.

[31] Reference to scientific research is provided in Algeria, Barbados, Cuba, Egypt, Malaysia and so on, while the reference to both scientific research and experimental purposes may be found in countries like Panama, the Republic of China, Costa Rica, Guatemala, Mongolia, Nicaragua and Paraguay.

Some countries like Albania,[32] Antigua and Barbuda,[33] Kyrgyz Republic,[34] Lithuania[35] and Moldova[36] opted for a modern language of exemptions, in the same way as accepted in the EU. These countries limit exception only to the acts related to subject matter of the patent.

Only a few developing countries do not have research exemptions. In these countries, exceptions would be allowed to the extent that such activity is not included in the scope of exclusive rights conferred in the patents owner which implies that the possibility to use the patent in this case would be certainly insignificant.

IV. Emerging Biotechnology Sectors in Malaysia and Singapore

A. Malaysia

This part analyses the impact of research exemption provision in the Malaysian patent law on biotechnology research and development and commercialisation activities in Malaysia. Malaysia is ambitious in developing its biotechnology sector to build up its economy into a knowledge economy in order to compete with its neighbours, China and India in the Asia Pacific region. Malaysia's National Biotechnology Policy[37] aims to give impetus to developing the biotechnology sector into a new economic engine enhancing prosperity and wellness of

[32] See Albanian Law No 9947 on Industrial Property, including as the limitation of the patent rights, among others, 'acts performed merely for experimental purposes relating to the subject matter of the invention'.

[33] Patent Act No 23, stating that the rights under the patents shall not extend to acts done only for experimental purposes relating to patent invention.

[34] Patent Law of the Kyrgyz Republic No 8, 14 January 1998, as amended by the Laws of Kyrgyz Republic No 130 as of 25 July 2002, and No 46 as of 27 February 2003, in its Arti 13 states that the following is not recognized as an infringement of the exclusive rights of the patent owner: (2) conducting scientific research or an experiment with an article containing an object of industrial property.

[35] Patent Law No I-372 of January 18, 1994, as amended by the Law No IX-118 of December 21, 2000 in its Article 21 provides that the patent owner shall have no rights to prevent third parties from performing acts referred to in para 1 and 2 provided that (2) the act is done for purely experimental purposes or for scientific research.

[36] The Law of Patents for Inventions No 461-XIII of 18 May 1995, as amended by the Law No 1079-XIV as of 23 June 2000. Art 24 goes: The use of an invention protected by the patent shall not constitute an infringement of the patent owner's exclusive right: (b) for the performance of research work or scientific experimentation for assessing the application of the subject matter of the invention or for non commercial purposes.

[37] This Policy was launched on 28th April 2005. It encompasses three phases, namely capacity building (2005–10), creating business out of science (2011–15) and turning Malaysia into a global player (2016–20). The 9th Malaysia Plan says that 'biotechnology is poised to be the next wave of knowledge based industries that will contribute to growth and wealth creation, new investment and employment opportunities as well as deliver social and environmental benefits'. See Government of Malaysia, the 9th Malaysia Plan 2006–10, 2006, Ch 6.

the nation by 2020. Under this policy, Malaysia intends to concentrate on all aspects of biotechnology such as agriculture biotechnology, healthcare biotechnology development and industrial biotechnology. At the same time Malaysia plans to conduct research and academic development activities into seven areas: molecular biology, plant biotechnology, animal biotechnology, medical biotechnology, environmental and industrial biotechnology, bio-pharmacy and food biotechnology.

Malaysia also intends to increase its research and development capacity by establishing Centres of Excellence, such as the National Pharmaceutical Institute, the Agriculture Biotechnology Institute and the Malaysia Genome Institute. By establishing these Centres of Excellence, Malaysia hopes to bring together multidisciplinary research teams to co-ordinated research and commercialisation initiatives. These Centres of Excellence are set up in addition to the existing universities and research institutions such as Malaysian Agriculture Research and Development Institute (MARDI), Malaysian Palm Oil Board, Malaysian Rubber Board, Institute of Medical Research and Forest Research Institute of Malaysia (FRIM).

Many of the Malaysian biotechnology companies concentrate on agriculture biotechnology such as tissue culture and cross breeding but none is involved in the commercialisation of genetic modification. Several companies are involved in healthcare biotechnology such as creating stem cell banks, production of nutraceuticals and health and functional food especially from local biodiversity and herbs and at the early stage of biopharmaceuticals.[38] None of the biopharmaceutical companies are capable of producing patented drugs. Malaysia still has to make considerable efforts in the field of pharmaceutical production.

The experimental use exemption in Malaysia is provided for in Section 37 (1) of the Patents Act 1983, and the Bolar type exemption is introduced in Section 37 (1A) of the same Act. Section 37 (1) exempts the rights under the patent for acts done only for scientific research. In addition, Section 37 (1A) exempts the scope of the rights to the patent 'acts done to make, use, offer to sell or sell a patented invention solely for uses reasonably related to the development and submission of information to the relevant authority which regulates the manufacture, use or sale of drugs'. This provision only limits the application of the Bolar type exemption to pharmaceutical drugs only.

The issue now is whether the progress in the indigenous biotechnology activities may also result in the increase in the domestic technology and innovation and whether Malaysia requires a stronger patent regime or a more flexible approach in allowing research and development hence a higher degree of flexibility in the patent research exemption. The answer lies with the number of patented

[38] For a discussion on the challenges faced by biotechnology sector in Malaysia, see G Abuduxike and SM Al junid, 'Health Biotechnology in Malaysia: Issues and Challenges Faced by the Innovative Biotechnology Firms' in A Tsetkova et al (eds), *Innovation in Transition and Developing Countries* (Cheltenham, Edward Elgar, 2017).

indigenous innovation and patent applications. It is submitted that a higher number of locally owned patents will mean Malaysia will tilt towards a higher degree of patent protections in order to encourage more local patents and at the same time to have a less flexible research exemption due to protect local innovation and a higher degree of enforcement of patent rights by the patent owners.

However, Malaysia's patent registry shows that most patents are foreign-owned. In the latest data which is of 2016, out of 2636 registered patents, only 281 were from Malaysian applicants, compared to 2355 patents approved to foreign applicants.[39] The WIPO World Intellectual Property Indicators 2018 show that of all the patents granted in 2017 in Malaysia, 91.4 per cent were approved to non-residents.[40] This is a high proportion compared to the European Patent Office (at 52 per cent to non-residents); the USA (52.7 per cent). Compared to other developing countries, China has a low percentage of non-resident approved patents at 22.2 per cent, India at 86.2 per cent. Singapore however, has a higher percentage of non-resident patents at 93.3 per cent.[41]

In the author's interviews with local researchers from 10 biotechnology companies and research institutes, the researchers and biotechnology companies are aware of the need to conduct research within the parameter of the patent, not to infringe any patents in conducting research using patented research tools and, although many are not aware of the exact existence of the research exemption provision, many are aware of the implications of the research exemption provision in Malaysian patent law.

For example, a senior researcher at the Malaysian Agriculture Research and Development Institute (MARDI), admits that researchers at MARDI are aware of the possible infringement of patented markers, such as in the development of new traits of high nutrient rice, which were used as research tools. MARDI would invest in buying markers or arranging for a royalty-based payment to the patent owner in conducting such research. However, MARDI is worried about the implication of royalties on the final price of commercialised products, as they need to factor in the royalty payable to third party technology providers.

In the healthcare sector, Malaysia does not have the capability of producing patented and novel drugs yet. Pharmaniaga and CCM Duopharma are the largest local pharmaceutical manufacturers that produce generic drugs and conduct contract manufacturing for international pharmaceutical companies. The research and development activities of these companies do not have the capability of producing new patented drugs or novel drugs in Malaysia hence there is little need for research exemption to be applicable to this company.

To generate products, Malaysia's biotechnology companies mainly rely on technology transfer and technology collaboration with foreign technology

[39] Malaysian Intellectual Property Corporation, 2016 Patents Statistics, www.myipo.gov.my/en/patent-statistic/#toggle-id-1, accessed 18 March 2019.

[40] WIPO (n 1) 44 (Chart A.15).

[41] ibid.

partners. The move from relying on the foreign technologies to the development of indigenous and locally researched products may mean that Malaysia will require a flexible approach towards research exemption whilst trying to achieve a balance in the high degree of protection of patented biotechnology products.

In conclusion, a clear research exemption policy is important if Malaysia wants to encourage more indigenous research in the field as at the moment Malaysia has little research and development including in biotechnology.

B. Singapore

Singapore has the most developed biotechnology industry in ASEAN. One of the efforts is building a physical infrastructure, such as '*Biopolis*', an 18 million square foot biomedical sciences hub, housing public research institutes, corporate research and development centres and start-ups, where Singapore prioritises developing pharmaceutics and diagnostics that were expected to yield high value. Singapore has also established the Biomedical Research Council and a Biomedical Grid, a high-security network enabling the biomedical research information to be shared and distributed between interested parties.

Singapore's effort to become the manufacturing and research hub for major multinational biotechnology companies has shown some success where more than 30 leading biomedical sciences companies, such as Takeda and Quintiles, have set up regional and international headquarters in the country. Multinational biotechnology companies in Singapore do not serve Singapore's market alone as it is very small, but their main market is the whole of Southeast Asia which has a population of around 625 million. These operations have also set up their research and development activities either on their own or in collaboration with Singapore's research institutes, for example the Institute of Chemical Engineering and Sciences and Bioprocessing Technology Institute.[42] The main purpose of the research and development collaboration is mainly to optimise manufacturing processes and the formulation of new products.

In relation to research and development, it could be assumed that Singapore will impose a high level of IP protection which means a narrow approach towards research exemption. This is because biotechnology is fast gaining foothold in the country. It is reported that patenting data shows Singapore innovators having a higher interest in the field of biotechnology than the rest of the world, with a total of 350 inventions and a further 180 inventions in pharmaceuticals in 2016.[43] Singapore's policy is to offer a high level of IP protection as a strategy to attract investment in the biotechnology fields. In addition to using IP protection to

[42] Singapore Economic Development Board, 'Overview of Singapore's Pharmaceutical and Biotechnology Industry', *Singapore Biotech Guide 2010/2011* (Singapore, 2011) 13–20.

[43] Intellectual Property Office of Singapore (2016), Singapore Patents Landscape 2016.

attract foreign multinational companies to invest in Singapore the country also has a policy of attracting global talent in biomedical science and biotechnology. Complementing Singapore's strengths in early innovation and translational research, the city-state has also established a core base of 20 leading contract research organisations (CROs) and pharmaceutical companies that manage regional clinical trials from Singapore.

The issue whether there should be broad or narrow application of research exemption should be looked at from two different angles, one from the perspective of attracting foreign researchers and multinational companies; and another from the perspective of local or rather indigenous Singaporean researchers and investors. Multinational companies form part of an important component for Singapore's goal to grow the biomedical sciences sector which comprises pharmaceuticals, medical technology, biotechnology and healthcare services to become the fourth pillar of its manufacturing sector, offering world-class capabilities across the whole value chain of activities.

It could be argued that foreign researchers attached to multinational companies and multinational companies with special funding for research and development and that own high degree of patents would prefer narrow interpretation of research exemption and Singapore would likely entertain this view in order to continuously import foreign capital and foreign researchers. On the other hand, Singapore's indigenous researchers and companies may prefer a broader interpretation of research exemption as this group of people would need to work within the constraint of budgets and the patent rights in order to develop their innovations.

Research exemptions are provided for under Section 66 of the Singapore Patent Act 1994. Section 66 (2) exempts an infringement of a patent for an act (a) done privately and for purposes which are not commercial; or (b) done for experimental purposes relating to the subject matter of the invention. To comply with Singapore's obligations under the US–Singapore Free Trade Agreement, the Patents Act was amended on July 1 2004 to introduce a Bolar-type exemption to patent infringement under Section 66 (2) (h). Under this provision, any acts to support an application for marketing approval for a pharmaceutical product in Singapore will be exempt from infringing a Singapore patent if such acts are in support of an application for marketing approval. Before the Bolar-type exemption provision came into force, the Patents Act provided statutory exemptions from infringement for acts done 'privately and for purposes which are not commercial' and 'for experimental purposes relating to the subject matter of the invention'.

It was uncertain then if clinical trials of patented drugs would fall within these exemptions since there was no case law in Singapore that has dealt with this aspect of patent infringement. However, Singapore Courts will often treat decisions made in other Commonwealth Courts as persuasive on judges. In the UK case of *Monsanto Co v Stauffer Chemical Co*[44] and *Auchincloss v Agricultural and*

[44] *Monsanto Co v Stauffer Chemical Co* [1984] FSR 669.

Veterinary Supplies,[45] it was found that acts done to support an application for marketing approval would fall outside of the experimental use provisions. This is because such acts are considered to ultimately be for commercial purposes.

The inclusion of the Bolar-type exemption provision in the Patents Act, which explicitly excludes from patent infringement clinical trials of patented drugs for the purpose of seeking regulatory approval, clarifies Singapore's position on this aspect of infringement. Accordingly, drug companies are now able to engage in activities seeking to obtain marketing approval for a pharmaceutical product without infringing any Singapore patent rights. Thus, Bolar-type exemption is an important provision in the patent law which allows pharmaceutical companies seeking marketing approvals prior to expiry of patents and this would encourage more investment and commercial activities especially from companies producing generic or competing drugs.

Singapore's position can also be compared to the position of Korea. As Korea advances in biotechnology, there have been concerns about access to technology and negative impact of patents on innovation in Korea's small and medium enterprises. It was found SMEs in Korea faced restricted access when dealing with patented research tools where about 30 per cent of respondents actually made their own tools, and another 30 per cent acknowledged that they used research tools without licence.[46] It was found that most of the respondents believed that the research exemption under the Korean Patent Law should be applied more broadly.[47] Thus, Singapore's indigenous small and medium enterprises may face similar problems as in Korea where they may face difficulties in accessing research tools especially in biomedical field, as those tools may have been patented and owned by foreign multinationals.

V. CPTPP IP Chapter and Research Exemptions

Article 18 of the CPTPP addresses the protection of intellectual property in the Parties to the agreement, which adopts many TRIPs Plus measures including patent extension term and marketing arrangement for generic pharmaceuticals. In analysing the agreement, Article 18 of the CPTPP does not seem to prohibits or restricts patent research exemptions as provided for in the existing patent laws of the Parties. Article 18.2 states that the objectives of the CPTPP is not only to protect and enforce intellectual property rights, but also to contribute to the promotion of technological innovation and to the transfer and dissemination of technology.[48]

[45] *Auchincloss v Agricultural and Veterinary Supplies* [1997] RPC 662.
[46] K Kang and others, 'Effects of Research Tools Patents on Biotechnology Patents in a Developing Country: A Case Study of South Korea' (2009) 9 *BMC Biotechnology* 25.
[47] ibid.
[48] CPTPP, Art 18.2.

It could be implied that the above provision allows the Parties to adopt provisions in the national IP that promote research and development through research exemption provision. This argument is further supported by the fact that Parties to the CPTPP are given the flexibility to adopt measures necessary to protect public health and nutrition and to promote the public interest in sectors of vital importance to their socio-economic and technological development.[49] The Parties also recognise the need to promote innovation and creativity; facilitate the diffusion of information, knowledge, technology, culture and the arts; and foster competition and open and efficient markets, through their respective intellectual property systems.[50]

The argument that CPTPP allows Parties to retain the flexibility for research or research exemption lies in the provision of Article 18.40, that

> A Party may provide limited exceptions to the exclusive rights conferred by a patent, provided that such exceptions do not unreasonably conflict with a normal exploitation of the patent and do not unreasonably prejudice the legitimate interests of the patent owner, taking account of the legitimate interests of third parties.

This provision is consistent with Article 30 of the TRIPS Agreement as discussed above.

The provision on the patent research exemption is subject to provision to allow protection of new usage of existing pharmaceuticals (generally known as 'ever-greening') as long as they meet the requirement of patentability outlined by the national laws of the Parties. Article 18.37 allows for patents to be available for 'inventions new uses of a known product, new methods of using a known product, or new processes of using a known product'. This allows certain pharmaceutical products to obtain new patents if it could be shown that they have new uses. The ever-greening provision allows patent holders to extend the use and terms of the patent for further protection, to the exclusion of third parties who could have conducted research and development in the same field.

The term ever-greening has been defined as 'in the absence of any apparent additional therapeutic benefits, patent-holders use various strategies to extend the length of their exclusivity beyond the 20-year patent term'.[51] There are concerns that product ever-greening could lead to the higher pharmaceutical price and lead to the constraint on the public health spending as they could lead to continues purchase of follow-on or improved products by hospitals or doctors and/or the blocking of the generic products of the original patented and approved pharmaceuticals. The Trilateral Study by the WHO, WTO and WIPO raises concern

[49] CPTPP, Art 18.3.

[50] CPTPP, Art 18.4.

[51] World Health Org, *Public Health, Innovation And Intellectual Property Rights: Report Of The Commission On Intellectual Property Rights, Innovation And Public Health* (2006) 131. See also discussion on the issue in Roma Patel, 'A Public Health Imperative: The Need for Meaningful Change in the Trans-Pacific Partnership's Intellectual Property Chapter' (2015) 16(1) *Minnesota Journal of Law, Science & Technology* Article 10.

that ever-greening could be used to prolong patents protection in an appropriate manner, thus creating negative impact on access to medicine.

It is submitted that new use refers to the scientifically proven use and meets the requirement of patentability of the relevant patents law in the CPTPP member countries. Patentability criteria are still important and being applied by the national patent offices. In applying the requirement of industrial application, one of the important criteria for patentability, some national patent offices may prevent the patenting of pharmaceutical compounds in a situation in which the inventor synthesises compounds 'without knowing how they can be applied to reach a result'.[52] Thus, it is very important for a national patent office to develop a set of criteria to examine any application for new patent relating to ever-greening.

Commercialisation of new products resulting from the research and development activities, especially in the new of usage of pharmaceuticals with expiring patents, also faces obstacles caused by the provision on the Undisclosed Test or Other Data for marketing approvals for new chemical entities and biologics.[53] Under Article 18.49, undisclosed data for new chemical entities are protected for a minimum period of five years from the date of the marketing approval of the new pharmaceutical product. The period of protection for biologics is divided into two options, namely for eight years from the date of first marketing approval or five years for a new pharmaceutical product that is or contains a biologic, that is a product that is a protein or contains a protein produced using biotechnology processes, for use in human beings for the prevention, treatment or cure of a disease or condition.

However, the data protection for new chemical entities and biologics are only applicable to a situation where the regulators require the submission of undisclosed test or other data concerning: (a) only the safety of the product, (b) only the efficacy of the product or (c) both, that has not been previously disclosed. Recognising that international and domestic regulation of biologics is in a formative stage, parties agree to hold consultation after 10 years from the date of entry into force of the CPTPP.

Under Annex 18-C, in order to obtain protection for Undisclosed Test and Other Data for new chemical entity and biologics in Malaysia, an applicant is required to commence the process of obtaining marketing approval for pharmaceutical products within 18 months from the date that the product is first granted marketing approval in any country. The periods of protections for both new chemical entities and biologics begin on the date of marketing approval of the pharmaceutical product in Malaysia.

[52] WIPO, According to the WIPO's *Study on the Role of Patent Systems in Promoting Innovative Medicines, and in Fostering the Technology Transfer Necessary to Make Generic and Patented Medicines Available In Developing Countries And Least Developed Countries*, Standing Committee on the Law of Patents Twenty-First Session Geneva, November 3 to 7, 2014, SCP/21/8, 10 October 2014. See also Ellen T' Hoen, *Private Patents and Public Health, Changing Intellectual Property Rules for Access to Medicines* (Amsterdam, Health Action International, 2016).

[53] CPTPP, Art 18.49.

Article 18.53 provides that, in the event of a third person seeking a marketing approval for a pharmaceutical product using information on safety and efficacy from a previously approved product, the government is required to provide a system to provide a notice to a patent holder linked to the previously approved product about the new marketing approval application during the term of the patent; and adequate time and opportunity for such a patent holder to seek, prior to the marketing of an allegedly infringing product, available remedies through

> certain procedures, such as judicial or administrative proceedings, and expeditious remedies, such as preliminary injunctions or equivalent effective provisional measures, for the timely resolution of disputes concerning the validity or infringement of an applicable patent claiming an approved pharmaceutical product or its approved method of use.

In the alternative, Malaysian may have to adopt a system to preclude the issuance of marketing approval to any third person seeking to market a pharmaceutical product subject to a patent claiming that product, without the consent or acquiescence of the patent holder.

VI. CPTPP, Research Exemption and the Price of Medicine

Generally, the CPTPP IP Chapter allows a party to continue to adopt measures necessary to protect public health and nutrition as long as the measures are consistent with the provisions in the chapter. Importantly the IP Chapter allows Parties the flexibility in implementing the World Trade Organisation's Declaration on TRIPS and Public Health adopted on 14 November 2001[54] including the right to continue with the compulsory licences of certain types of medicines for public health purposes and the utilisation of the WTO's TRIPs health solution.[55]

Parties to the CPTPP agree that the IP Chapter 'can and should be interpreted and implemented in a manner supportive of each Party's right to protect public health and, in particular, to promote access to medicines for all'. The IP Chapter also states that Parties have the right to determine what constitutes a national emergency or other circumstances of extreme constituting public health crises, including those relating to HIV/AIDS, tuberculosis, malaria and other epidemics. Hence the CPTPP parties are allowed to address the issue of access and price to

[54] WT/MIN(01)/DEC/2.

[55] This includes the commitment to access to medicines that are supplied in accordance with the Decision of the WTO General Council of August 30, 2003 on the Implementation of Paragraph Six of the Doha Declaration on the TRIPS Agreement and Public Health (WT/L/540) and the WTO General Council Chairman's Statement Accompanying the Decision (JOB(03)/177, WT/GC/M/82), as well as the Decision of the WTO General Council of December 6, 2005 on the Amendment of the TRIPS Agreement, (WT/L/641) and the WTO General Council Chairperson's Statement Accompanying the Decision (JOB(05)/319 and Corr 1,WT/GC/M/100).

medicine through the compulsory licence and government usage in the national patents laws. However, in the long run, the CPTPP countries should be encouraged to developed their own pharmaceutical industry capacity and capability through the better use of research exemptions.

For example, India and Brazil have managed to develop their own pharmaceutical industry by utilising the flexibility in the research exemptions. The continued usage of compulsory licence to reduce the price of medicine may discourage foreign direct investment and the transfer of advanced technologies in the future. While prices may be reduced and access to medicines may be enhanced in the short-run, the future detrimental consequences may outweigh those benefits.[56] The success of any compulsory licence depends on whether a country has the capability to produce the generic version, and whether the generic manufacturer is interested to produce the pharmaceutical under the compulsory licence.[57] This shows that research exemption is more important that compulsory licences.

In the CPTPP countries, Malaysia became the first country in the world to issue a compulsory licence using under the Doha Declaration on TRIPs and Public Health, paragraph 6 in 2004, which allowed compulsory licence to allow importations of four anti-retroviral HIV/AIDS formulation to Indian drug makers Cipla. The compulsory licences relate to patents of Didanosine owned by Bristol-Myers Squibb and Lamivudine and Zidovudine, owned by GlaxoSmithKline (GSK). The compulsory licences were issued under Section 84 of the Patents Act 1983 (Act 291), under the Rights of the Government.[58] In 2017, Malaysia issued another compulsory licence for sofosbuvir which is for the hepatitis-C treatment. In addition to Malaysia, another party to the CPTPP, Chile has also recently endorsed the issuance of compulsory licences for hepatitis-C.

The price of medicine has also been linked with ever-greening approach undertaken by pharmaceutical companies. There is at least one study relating to ever-greening and the price of medicine by Vernaz et al based on pharmacy invoice data in a hospital in the Canton of Geneva, Switzerland, over a period between the years 2000 and 2008.[59] The study concludes that branded drug manufacturers

[56] Kristina M Lybecker and Elisabeth Fowler, 'Compulsory Licensing in Canada and Thailand: Comparing Regimes to Ensure Legitimate Use of the WTO Rules' (2009) *Journal of Law, Medicine & Ethics, Pharmaceutical Regulations* 222–39. See also Daniel Benoliel and Bruno Salama, (2010) Towards An Intellectual Property Bargaining Theory: The Post-WTO Era' (2010) 32 *University of Pennsylvania Journal of International Law* 265.

[57] Beatrice Stirner and Harry Thangaraj, 'Learning from Practice: Compulsory Licensing Cases and Access to Medicines' (2013) 2(2) *Pharmaceutical Patent Analyst* 195–213.

[58] S 84(1) provides for the 'Rights of Government': 'Nothwithstanding anything contained in [this] Act – where there is national emergency or where the public interest, in particular, national security, nutrition, health or the development of other vital sectors of the national economy as determined by the Government, so requires; or where a judicial or relevant authority has determined that the manner of exploitation by the owner of the patent or his licensee is anti-competitive, the Minister may decide that, even without the agreement of the owner of the patent, a Government agency or third person designated by the Minister may exploit a patented invention'.

[59] N Vernaz and others, 'Patented Drug Extension Strategies on Healthcare Spending: A Cost-Evaluation Analysis' (2013) 10(6) *PLoS Med* e1001460, doi:10.1371/journal.pmed.1001460.

have successfully used the ever-greening strategy to keep the market share and to contribute to the increase in cost at the hospital subject to the study in Geneva. However, the study does not implicitly show that the patenting of new use contributes to the increase in cost. The study recognises that ever-greening strategies take many forms. According to Kesselheim, ever-greening strategy, also known as life-cycle management, includes slight changes in formulation protected by later-issued patents, marketing tools such as drug coupons that reduce patients' out-of-pocket spending on brand-name drugs, negotiating settlements with generic companies to prevent challenges to potentially weak or invalid patents and developing extended-release versions or combination products.[60]

On the other hand, Vernaz et al's study also recognises several limitations such as patient preference for certain brands over generics, and the purchasing policy such as 'by taking an exclusive payer perspective when selecting follow-on drugs' and the management of the hospital initiated prescription. One notable finding of Vernaz et al. is that the Canton of Geneva could have saved about EUR 30 million between 2001 and 2008 if doctors had prescribed generics instead of the follow-on products of the original versions of the drugs. Vernaz et al also recognise that excessive pressure on pharmaceutical companies may also lead to the unintended consequence of reduced investment in innovation.

In some parts of the CPTPP, the price of medicine is also linked with the government procurement method which creates monopoly and rent-seeking activities. Vietnam also uses centralised economic management and this may affect decisions on the price of medicine. In Malaysia, the available records show that Ministry of Health (MOH) of Malaysia purchases about 50 per cent of all medical products from one company, Pharmaniaga Berhad, a State-owned enterprise controlled by Boustead Holdings Berhad, which is controlled by the Lembaga Tabung Angkatan Tentera (Armed Forces Provident Fund). Pharmaniaga has exclusive rights through a Concession Agreement, which is valid for 10 years (expiring in 2024) with the Ministry of Health, to purchase a set range of medical products and distribute them to medical institutions under the Ministry's jurisdiction.[61] The Concession Agreement covers a set range of Approved Medical products from supplies selected by MOH, and Pharmaniaga distributes those products to government medical institutions, including 140 public hospitals and 2856 clinics throughout Malaysia. Under the Concession Agreement, Pharmaniaga procures medical products at prices determined by the MOH, and re-sells those products to MOH at a fixed marked-up price.

The Concession Agreement is anti-competitive as it provides a monopoly to a supplier for about 50 per cent of all medical products required by the government. This means that the government is held captive by the monopoly supplier

[60] AS Kesselheim, 'Rising Health Care Costs and Life-Cycle Management in the Pharmaceutical Market' (2013) 10(5) *PLoS Med* e1001461, doi:10.1371/journal.pmed.1001461.

[61] CIMB, Malaysia's Biggest Pharma Play, http://cdn1.i3investor.com/my/files/dfgs88n/2014/04/24/1480249153-1217043407.pdf.

over the cost of medicine. The government could save more money by having a more transparent and competitive supply system for medical products in the government institutions in Malaysia. Although one cannot speculate the price, it can be assumed that in any monopolistic arrangement, the monopoly is able to control the price at the expense of the consumers. This shows that, in Malaysia, the design of the procurement system could contribute to the higher price of pharmaceuticals.

In Vietnam, there is a study showing that pharmaceutical distributions are still dominated by the State-owned enterprises, which rely on imports and monopolistic practices. Foreign pharmaceutical companies are not allowed to distribute pharmaceuticals directly to hospitals and they have to deal through domestic companies and in not an efficient manner.[62]

The developing CPTPP members may learn from the more developed vertical and horizontal distribution channels of pharmaceuticals in the EU, which leaves much to the free-market system with little intervention from the States. In addition, there is a public service obligation imposed by the EU Directive 2001/83/EC on the Community Code Relating to Medicinal Products for Human Use.[63] Aricle 81 states that

> 'with regard to the supply of medicinal products to pharmacists and persons authorised or entitled to supply medicinal products to the public, Member States shall not impose upon the holder of a distribution authorisation which has been granted by another Member State any obligation, in particular public service obligations, more stringent than those they impose on persons whom they have themselves authorised to engage in equivalent activities.

In addition, to ensure the needs of patients are covered, the EU imposes an obligation upon the holder of a marketing authorisation for a medicinal product and the distributors of medicinal product to ensure appropriate and continued supplies of product to pharmacies and persons authorised to supply medicinal products.

VII. Conclusions

The above discussion shows that research exemption in the CPTPP preserves the same flexibility as contained in the TRIPS Agreement. The implementation of the flexibility in research exemption depends on the policy needs of the CPTPP member. Analysing the position of Malaysia and Singapore, it is safe to state that Malaysia and Singapore may take different approaches in utilising the provision of research exemption in biotechnology. Singapore's biotechnology development

[62] See A Angelino et al, 'Pharmaceutical Industry in Vietnam: Sluggish Sector in a Growing Market' (2017) 14 *International Journal of Environmental Research and Public Health* 976.

[63] Official Journal L – 311/67, 28.11.2001.

is due to investment made by foreign multinationals. Thus, Singapore will have to work on a policy that meets the need and the expectations of foreign multinationals and this will normally involve a narrow interpretation of research exemption in the patent law in order to protect the interest and investment made by the multinational companies.

On the other hand, Malaysia could adopt a broader approach towards research exemption as the country does not have a strong pharmaceutical and healthcare biotechnology sector. Malaysia's focus is to gather its own strength, like biodiversity-based biotechnology such as production of biopharmaceuticals and nutraceuticals, fermented products, agriculture biotechnology and environmental biotechnology. This requires local technology development, either through locally based research and development or through joint research and development with foreign based commercial and foreign organisations.

The provision of the research exemption may not have any impact on the decision to set-up prices of medicine, mainly because Malaysia and Singapore do not major capacity to produce novel drugs or own generic. The higher level of protections and the data protections afforded to the pharmaceuticals and biologics could have an impact on the research and development and production of bio-similar and generic products. The higher level of protection could lead to a higher level of constraint on researchers to conduct research and development whilst generic manufacturers will have to wait longer to have access to protected data and to start the necessary approval process for generic products.

The CPTPP parties could also take some lessons from similar provisions and practice in the EU. Parties to the CPTPP could look to harmonise the research exemption provisions in order to allow more research and development which could lead to the higher level of local technology and capacity development in biotechnology and pharmaceutical fields. At the same time, parties to the CPTPP should look at improving their internal administrative and procurement procedures to allow for free market to assist the distribution of medicine as in the EU. This will assist in reducing monopolistic or anti-competitive practice which in return contributes to the high retail price of medicines.

19

Geographical Indications in the EU, China and Australia

WTO Case Bottling Up Over Prosecco

DANNY FRIEDMANN*

I. Introduction

The genealogy of Geographical Indications (GIs) for wine can be traced back to ancient Greece, where for example wine from Thasos with its distinctive taste had established a reputation.[1] In an effort to protect themselves against false and misleading use, the Thasian wine producers used different shapes of and inscriptions on respective amphorae,[2] which indicated the geographical origin of these wines; linking their quality, reputation and geographical area.

Professor Hughes distinguishes three purposes for geographical words in product names: 1 to communicate geographic sources; 2 to communicate non-geographic product qualities; and 3 to create evocative value.[3] This chapter builds upon Hughes' tripartite distinction and distinguishes the latter category into evocation plus qualifiers, which provides consumer information but makes deception highly unlikely, and evocation that at leastcould be used in a deceptive way. This results in the following quadripartite distinction of geographical words used:

> As a geographical designation of products: this can still lead to confusing scenarios, since many people from Old World countries immigrated to the New World where they gave Old World names to New World places.

* Dr. Danny Friedmann is Visiting Assistant Professor of Peking University, School of Transnational Law in Shenzhen.

[1] In an Athenian comedy by Hermippus, Thasian wine is described as wine 'over which the scent of apples plays'. Fragment 82, quoted in the Epitome of Athenaeus 29e. Andrew Dalby, *Bacchus: A Biography* (Los Angeles CA, Getty Publications, 2004) 133.

[2] Greek jar or vase with a large oval body, narrow cylindrical neck, and two handles that rise almost to the level of the mouth.

[3] Justin Hughes, 'Champagne, Feta, and Bourbon – the Spirited Debate About Geographical Indications' (2006) 58 *Hastings Law Journal* 299, 303–04.

To refer to non-geographical qualities of products: for example the method of production; in French fries, 'French' refers to sliced potatoes that are fried.
To translate, imitate or 'usurp' the geographical word. This category consists of a mixture of two purposes: on the one hand to evoke the GI, but by the very fact of its translation or use of qualifiers, such as 'kind', 'type', 'style', 'imitation' or the like, manifesting that it refers to non-geographical qualities of the product. In other words using the geographical word to describe similarity to the original in some way, but not necessarily in a confusing or deceptive way. Opponents of the use of a geographical name by anybody other than someone from that region, call any such use usurpation ('using someone's reputation by force'). France was the first country who initiated a prohibition against translation, imitation and usurpation, via its *Appellation d'Origine Contrôlée* system, followed by the Lisbon Agreement, Geneva Act of the Lisbon Agreement, TRIPS in regard to wines and spirits, and EU Regulations. In addition, the EU has been pushing internationally for strong-form GIs; no producer from outside the designated region may use the protected name, not even with qualifiers.
To evoke a geographical word: to bring up certain associations or sense of aesthetics of a geographic name; for example Unilever, the UK producer of Viennetta ice-cream, tries to evoke the elegance and luxury of the Austrian city of Vienna. The EU has a non-evocation standard for its GIs.

Since *Scandecor*, normal trademarks have developed, from source indicators of a particular origin with a personal guarantee of satisfaction to an anonymous source and impersonal guaranty, to a constant source and consistent level of quality.[4] In contrast to this trend, certification and collective trademarks and *sui generis* GIs have tried to forge and manifest the link between quality, reputation and geographical area. The argument for certifiers of quality, especially for experience goods such as wine, whereby one has to first purchase a bottle and consume it in order to find out the quality, is cogent. In the contemporary world, GIs are established as a separate intellectual property rights category. There are eight categories in the Agreement on Trade-related Aspects of Intellectual Property Rights (TRIPS). GIs can be found in Part II;[5] just after trademarks, which makes sense, since its subspecies certification or collective trademarks can distinguish the mark to conform to particular standards, such as quality, reputation and origin,[6] and can be used as GI.

Sections II and III provide the Old World approach: Appellations of Origin, and the New World approach: protection of wine GIs via Trademarks and *sui generis* systems; section IV covers international treaties; section V deals with the

[4] *Scandecor Developments AB v Scandecor Marketing AB and Others* (2001) UKHL 21; (2001) ETMR 74; (2001) FSR 22.

[5] Agreement on Trade-Related Aspects of Intellectual Property Rights (TRIPS) 15 April 1994, Marrakesh Agreement Establishing the World Trade Organization, Annex 1C, 1869 UNTS 299, 33 ILM 1197 (1994).

[6] Danny Friedmann, *In Marks We Trust* (2018) 13:7 JIPLP 593–594.

People's Republic of China (China)'s GI system; section VI discusses the bilateral GI treaties between the EU and China; section VII uses *Prosecco* as a case study to see how Italy and the EU are trying to 'transubstantiate' a grape into a GI; section VIII introduces the *pars pro toto* strategy; and section IX provides the conclusion.

II. Old World Approach

Two events provided impetuses for creating specific protection for GIs: first the Great Wine Blight and second plans to abolish the Common Agricultural Policy (CAP) subsidies. The lobby groups of French vintners successfully pushed for the founding of the Institute national des appellations d'origine et de qualité (INAO), that promoted their common interests. And when France and its wine market integrated into the EU, they exerted their power via INAO to promote the interests of the EU wine producers. At the end of this section the different 'identification signs and quality of origin' in the EU will be dealt with.

The Great Wine Blight raged between 1850 and 1870. It destroyed around 40 per cent of the vineyards in France, but also affected vineyards in Germany, Luxemburg and Switzerland. The blight was caused by the gall-forming grapevine parasite *phylloxera*, a venom that attacks the vine roots, which originally originated from North America.[7] Because of the blight, imports, mainly from Italy and Spain, increased tenfold between the late 1860s and late 1870s. Then, from 1871 to 1900, around 50,000 families, many vintners that were hit by the blight, fled to Algeria, where they cultivated 700,000 hectares for wine. Almost all wine, high-strength and cheap, was shipped back to France. Since Algeria was a French département and thus an integral part of France, the Algerian wine could be sold as *vin français* and no tariff could be imposed to protect the vintners in France. French vintners, especially from Bordeaux, Burgundy and Champagne, pressured the French government for protection against the wine glut from Italy, Spain and Algeria. In the 1930s, Algeria, together with Morocco and Tunisia, produced 21 million hectolitres: two-thirds of the international wine production.[8]

In 1905, the French government enacted laws to protect against counterfeit wine. Also, the boundaries of the wine regions were delimitated, each prescribed with permissible grape varieties and viticultural methods. In 1935, these statutes were codified in a law that established the INAO, which issued appellations

[7] Ágoston Haraszthy, who is known as the 'father of California viticulture' where he especially developed the viticulture of Sonoma County, is also known for introducing more than three hundred varieties of European grapes in California: https://en.wikipedia.org/wiki/Agoston_Haraszthy.

It is thought that when some of these grapes were exported to France, and some of them were exposed to phylloxera, it inadvertently set the blight into motion. In contrast to the North American vines, the European vine roots could not protect themselves against the blight. The solution was to graft the European *vitis vinifera* branch on the underpart of American grapevine varieties *vitis riparia* and *vitis rotundifolia*.

[8] Algerian wine: https://en.wikipedia.org/wiki/Algerian_wine.

d'origine contrôlées (AOC) for viticultural regions in France, to debase cheap wine from Algeria.[9]

France also tried to rein in the overproduction of wine in France and Algeria, by taxing vineyards in France and Algeria for overproduction[10] and forcing large-scale producers to uproot their vines or distil wine into alcohol. These measures would later also be implemented in the EU as part of the CAP, especially after 1976, when INAO started to push for an interventionist policy to stop the flood of Italian wine: the EU implemented quality, quantity and price regulations for its wine market. Besides geographical delimitations, precise restrictions were given in regard to the wine growing methods, grape variety, maximum vineyard yield and production practice, minimum and maximum alcohol content and the amount of sugar/additives. First, the GI could only be put on the label and not the grape varieties that were used. Since 2008, the latter is also allowed. To reduce quantity, planting rights were reduced and vineyard grubbing-up schemes were subsidised. Another way was to distil wine into alcohol. In the last 30 years, every year on average 20 to 40 million hectolitres of wine have been destroyed through distillation, which represents 12 to 22 per cent of EU wine production.[11] The enormously expensive CAP,[12] which was prone to abuse and led to unintended consequences,[13] was not sustainable. A Judge of the Court of Justice of the European Union described CAP thus:

> The EU's agricultural markets consist of butter mountains, wine and milk lakes and olive oil pools, surrounded by happy, lazy, over-subsidised EU farmers who are kept in idle luxury by the EU's policy of keeping out all agricultural produce from third countries including Australia.[14]

INAO regulates the classification of wines, their identification signs and quality of origin (SIQO) in France, the determination and demarcation of sections of land where SIQO products are processed, and protects these sections of land, local development and cultural heritage. INAO qualified the highest ranking wine

[9] Giulia Meloni and Johan Swinnen, 'The Political Economy of European Wine Regulations', *LICOS Discussion Paper* 320/2012 (17 October 2012). https://papers.ssrn.com/sol3/papers.cfm?abstract_id=2279338.

[10] In 1962, the year that Algeria became independent, its wine production was 15 million hectolitres. In 2009 this was reduced to 600,000 hectolitres, the same as it produced in 1882. Moreover, the incompatibility of wine with the Islamic dietary laws was not conducive for the wine production.

[11] Above n 9, at 3.

[12] In 1985, CAP was 73 per cent of the EU's total budget; in 2015, this was still 39 per cent of the EU's total budget. CAP expenditure: European Commission, DG Agriculture and Rural Development (Financial Report). https://ec.europa.eu/agriculture/sites/agriculture/files/cap-post-2013/graphs/graph1_en.pdf.

[13] When the EU tried to reduce the production of low quality wine, by subsidising producers of low quality wine to distil the wine into alcohol, some started to maximise the production, since they were guaranteed that their wine, no matter how bad the quality, was purchased.

[14] Eleanor Sharpston, 'The Common Agricultural Policy' in Cheryl Saunders and Gillian Triggs (eds), *Trade and Cooperation with the European Union in the New Millennium* (Alphen aan den Rijn, Kluwer Law International, 2009) 29, 29.

quality as AOC. As of 2009, AOC wines with their high standards for origin, quality and reputation, and strict procedures and use of certain grape varieties and ingredients, were also protected by the Protected Designation of Origin (PDO) sign, which the EU initiated. For a PDO, there should be a link, based on complex interactions of the *terroir*, between the natural environment and human factors. Between 1949 and 2011, the second highest category for wine quality was the Vin délimité de qualité supérieure (VDQS). However, the French Ministry of Agriculture accepted the recommendation of Bernard Pomel's 'viticultural revolution' report to eliminate the VDQS category to simplify the classification system.[15] Legislation for the Vin de Pays terminology was proposed in 1973 and passed in 1979. It allowed producers to distinguish wines that were made using grape varieties or procedures other than those required by the AOC rules and still designate the geographical origin. In 2009, the Vin de Pays was substituted by the Indication Géographique Protégée or in English: Protected Geographical Indication (PGI). For a PGI, the link is usually based on a striking feature of the characteristics of the geographical area.

The EU implemented more protectionist measures. For example: if one imports grapes from outside the EU and makes them into wine in the EU, one cannot call the result 'wine':

> Poured from the bottle, the ruby-colored liquid looks like wine. Swirled around a glass, it smells like wine. Sure enough, it tastes like wine, too. But, at least within the confines of the European Union, the closest it may come to be being called wine is 'fruit-based alcoholic beverage'.[16]

GIs have been used as way to protect first the French wine and, once the EU was established, the wine produced within the EU, against overproduction and perceived unfair competition. When the decision was made to phase-out the CAP, GIs were also offered as a compensation to the farmers that would help increase rural development. In addition the claim was made that the market was willing to pay premium prices for authentic wine if it was protected by GIs. To protect its GIs, the EU established a *sui generis* system for agricultural products, foodstuffs and wines and spirits, well-coordinated, without overlap, in contrast to the Chinese system (see section V). The most important EU legislation can be found in Regulation 1308/2013 of 17 December 2013, which established a common organisation of the markets in agricultural products,[17] including wine, and

[15] The report recommended also to allow the inclusion of names of grapes on wine labels above the Vin de Pays level; and to artificially lower alcohol levels in wine; and use oak chips to flavour wine.

[16] Stephen Castle, 'When Is a Wine Not a Wine? When European Regulations Say It's Not', *New York Times*, 29 May 2012) www.nytimes.com/2012/05/30/world/europe/when-is-a-wine-not-a-wine-when-european-regulations-say-its-not.html.

[17] Regulation (EU) No 1308/2013 of the European Parliament and of the Council of 17 December 2013 establishing a common organisation of the markets in agricultural products and repealing Council Regulations (EEC) No 922/72, (EEC) No 234/79, (EC) No 1037/2001 and (EC) No 1234/2007, OJ L 347, 20 December 2013, 671–854. https://eur-lex.europa.eu/legal-content/EN/ALL/?uri=CELEX:32013R1308.

Regulation 607/2009, which laid down certain detailed rules for the implementation of Regulation 479/2008 as regards PDOs and PGIs, traditional terms, labelling and presentation of certain wine sector products.[18] In the EU, GIs can be protected via EU collective marks,[19] but not via EU certification marks,[20] since the EU insists on the exclusive use of its *sui generis* system of PDOs and PGIs which guarantee a certain quality, origin and reputation.

III. New World Approach

In New World countries, such as Australia, United States, South Africa and Chile, immigrants from the Old World started to cultivate the new land for viticulture. In the 1970s, the New World produced ripe, fruity and sweet wine which met a popular demand. The Old World considered that the most important qualities of wine were derived from the *terroir*: the unique combination of soil and climate; a particular geographical area manifested. The particular mixture of grape varieties, alcohol level and the production methods were more or less fixed. Improvements of or innovations upon authentic wine were frowned upon. In contrast, the concept in the New World countries for making a good wine, was primarily focused on mixing certain grape varieties, alcohol level and on improving the methods of producing wine. Using innovation, the New World countries experimented with wine production at places that were considered difficult. *Terroir* was considered of secondary importance. However, the concepts of New and Old World countries are converging: New World vintners have started to apply some of their innovations in the Old World. The Old World countries are now also allowing to put grape varieties on the label and not just the GIs. Some vintners in the New World countries have also started to use *terroir* as a concept to explain the distinctive character of their wines.[21]

Where the Old World's preferred method to protect GIs is to use a *sui generis* system, the New World's preferred method is using their existing system of trademark law; via certification or collective trademarks. The advantage is that jurisdictions have a wealth of experience with their trademark systems, and no new legislation is needed nor an elaborate and costly international registration system. Besides, the protection of a GI using a trademark can be more innovative: non-traditional trademarks can be used: including three-dimensional, colour or

[18] Commission regulation (EC) No 607/2009 of 14 July 2009 laying down certain detailed rules for the implementation of Council Regulation (EC) No 479/2008 as regards protected designations of origin and geographical indications, traditional terms, labelling and presentation of certain wine sector products, OJ L 193, 24 July 2009, 60–139. http://eur-lex.europa.eu/legal-content/EN/ALL/?uri=CELEX:32009R0607.

[19] Art 74(2) Regulation (EU) 2017/1001 of the European Parliament and of the Council of 14 June 2017 on the European Union trade mark (Text with EEA relevance) OJ L 154, 16 June 2017, 1–99.

[20] Art 83(1) ibid.

[21] Chile's Vina Undurraga promotes its Terroir Hunter wines, which is based on micro-terroirs; each less than five hectares, with distinctive tastes. www.undurraga.cl/.

sound trademarks, while this is not possible with the *sui generis* systems. An additional disadvantage of the *sui generis* system is that if a GI has become generic it is hard to get it removed from the international register. Belson defines certification marks as 'principally indicia of conformity of goods or services to particular standards, stipulated by the proprietor of the mark',[22] and collective marks as 'mark[s] owned by an association or "collectivité" for the use of its members'.[23] Despite the New World countries' preference for the trademark system protection of GIs, in the case of wine most New World countries also use a *sui generis* system.

Australia has been alternately influenced by the Old World and New World approaches. First, Australia could not export wine to the EU, because the wine did not have any formal GIs. The *de facto* GI 'Australia' was not recognised in practice as such by the EU. Therefore, in 1993, Australia amended its Australian Wine and Brandy Corporation Act 1980 (Act 1980).[24] The Act 1980 only controlled and promoted the export of wine, but the Australian Wine and Brandy Corporation Amendment Act 1993 included the establishment of a GI Committee, whose function was to make determinations of GI for wine in relation to zones, regions and sub-regions in Australia.[25] The Australian Wine and Brandy Corporation (Exports) Regulations 1993 (Amendment), regulated Australian GIs.[26] If an Australian wine claims a single GI, at least 85 per cent should be sourced from that geographical area. Multiple GI claims are also possible, but must be each at least five per cent with a maximum of three GIs and a minimum of 95 per cent of the GIs, listed in a descending order.[27] EU labelling focused on GIs. It even prohibited the inclusion of the grape varieties on the labels in the EU until 2008. This gave Australia, and other New World countries, an edge in consumer information. According to

[22] Jeffrey Belson, *Certification and Collective Marks* (Cheltenham, Edward Elgar Publishing, 2017) 30.

[23] ibid, 36.

[24] Australian Wine and Brandy Corporation Act 1980, Act No 161 of 1980, 10 December 1980. www.legislation.gov.au/Details/C2004A02362/.

[25] Australian Wine and Brandy Corporation Amendment Act 1993, Act No 93 of 1993, 16 December 1993. www.wipo.int/edocs/lexdocs/laws/en/au/au014en.pdf.

[26] Australian Wine and Brandy Corporation (Exports) Regulations (Amendment), Statutory Rules 1993 No 374, 22 December 1993. www.legislation.gov.au/Details/F1996B00497. The Amendment included a three-part schedule: Part 1 exempted the protection of a list of GIs or traditional expression until the end of 31 December 1993; Part 2 until the end of 31 December 1997 and Part 3 indefinitely. Also vine varieties were exempted from GI protection, such as 'Hermitage' if the name was used as a synonym for the grape variety 'Shiraz'; and the wine originated in Australia; and the wine was sold in a country other than an EC country. And also 'Riesling' and 'Lambrusco', if the name was used to describe a style of wine traditionally made and marketed under that name; and the name was not used to describe a variety of grapes from which the wine is made; and the wine originated in Australia; and the wine was sold in a country other than an EC country.

[27] Single claim vintage requires 85 per cent of the wine originates from one vintage; multiple claims vintage requires that all claims add up to 100 per cent. Single claim variety requires that 85 per cent of the wine originates from one variety; multiple claims variety requires that all the claims add up to 85 per cent. One can only leave a variety off the label unless you have listed all varieties that appear in greater proportions on that label. Australian Grape and Wine Authority Act 2013, No 161, 1980 as amended, Compilation start date: 1 July 2014. www.legislation.gov.au/Details/C2014C00371. See also: *The Blending Rules*, Wine Australia, www.wineaustralia.com/labelling/further-information/the-blending-rules.

Tony Battaglene, Chief Executive of the Winemakers' Federation of Australia, this consumer information sold the wine, not any GIs.[28]

After Australia had its own *sui generis* GI system, it signed an agreement with the European Community in 1994 to acknowledge lists of each other's GIs and traditional expressions to promote the export of its wine to the EU.[29] Professor Drahos noted that 'unlike in the case of a preferential trade deal that covers many industries and therefore sets up many possible trade-offs and complexities, the negotiations focused solely on the wine industry'.[30] Article 6(4) EC/Australia Agreement 1994, prohibits the registration of a trademark of a protected GI, but lacks the prohibition of the registration of GIs in case of pre-existing trademarks. Australia issued the Australian Wine and Brandy Corporation (Exports) Regulations 1993, and signed the abovementioned EC/Australia Agreement 1994 to anticipate its entry into the WTO and concomitant obligations under TRIPS in regard to GIs.[31] Beside, Australia, the EU and the EU Member States in their own right, became members of the WTO, as of 1 January 1995.

In the EC/Australia Agreement 1994, GI was defined as an indication as specified in Annex 2 (which consists of the lists of the GIs and traditional expressions of EU members and Australia), including an 'Appellation of Origin':

> which is recognised in the laws and regulation of a Contracting Party for the purpose of the description and presentation of a wine originating in the territory of a Contracting Party, or in a region or locality in that territory, where a given quality, reputation or other characteristic of the wine is essentially attributable to its geographical origin.

The New World Country US, which also has a *sui generis* system next to its trademark system since 1979; the American Viticultural Areas (AVA), nevertheless favours its trademark system. After the US and Australia signed the Australia United States Free Trade Agreement (AUSFTA) in 2004,[32] Australia had to change its GI system to allow for cancellation procedures of GIs if they conflict with pre-existing trademarks, according to the 'first in time, first in right' principle,[33] and to

[28] *The Australian wine industry position on Geographical Indications*, Tony Battaglene, Presentation to the Worldwide Symposium on Geographical Indications, WIPO, Ministry of Productive Activities of Italy, Ministry of Foreign Affairs of Italy, Parma (Italy), 27–29 June 2005. http://yucita.org/uploads/yayinlar/diger/makale/The_Australian_wine_industry_position_on_Geographical_Indications.doc.

[29] Agreement between the European Community and Australia, OJ L 86/3, 31 March 1994. https://ec.europa.eu/agriculture/sites/agriculture/files/wine/third-countries/documents/australia-1994_en.pdf.

[30] Peter Drahos, 'Sunshine in a Bottle? Geographical Indications, the Australian Wine Industry, and the Promise of Rural Development' in Irene Calboli and Wee Loon Ng-Loy (eds), *Geographical Indications At The Crossroads Of Trade, Development, And Culture: Focus On Asia-Pacific* (Cambridge, Cambridge University Press, 2017) 259–80, 278.

[31] Above n 5.

[32] Art 17.2 (12)(b)(v)(A) and (B) AUSFTA. AUSFTA was signed on 18 May 2004 and came into effect on 1 January 2005. http://dfat.gov.au/about-us/publications/trade-investment/australia-united-states-free-trade-agreement/Pages/chapter-seventeen-intellectual-property-rights.aspx.

[33] Read more on conflicts between trademarks and appellations of origin, PDOs/PGIs in Danny Friedmann, 'TPP Coup de Grâce: How the Trademark System Prevailed as Geographical Indication System' in Julien Chaisse and others (eds), *Paradigm Shift In International Economic Law Rule-Making* (Singapore, Springer, 2017) 281.

allow co-existence between GIs and trademarks.[34] In 2009, the European Community and Australia signed a new agreement on trade in wine, which explicitly refers to TRIPS to define a GI: '"GI" shall mean an indication as defined in Article 22(1) of the TRIPs Agreement'.[35] Also in 2009, the EU, at the request of Italy, had unilaterally decided to rename the grape variety Prosecco into Glera. The objective was to make Prosecco into a GI, so that other countries could not use the name on their label any longer. Instead of building up support for the name change and 'transubstantiation' from grape variety to GI, via Free Trade Agreements, the European Commission requested on 1 April 2010, by letter, that the term Prosecco be listed on the Australian Register of Protected GI and Other Terms as a GI for Italy. Then the European Commission applied for this change to the Australian Registrar of Trade Marks on 15 March 2012. On 3 April 2012 an objection was received from the Winemakers' Federation of Australia. On 13 April 2012 a second objection was received from the US wine industry, but it did not proceed. On 22 November 2013, the Registrar of Trade Marks held the word Prosecco to have been used in Australia as the name of a grape variety.[36] According to Regulation 58(5)(b) this is a ground of objection to determination of foreign GI or translation of foreign GI.[37]

IV. International Treaties

International treaties have introduced three incarnations of protections of GIs: indications of source on goods; GIs as such; and appellations of origin. Waye and Stern place these GIs along a continuum from regionality to typicality.[38] Typicality or *typicité* are the sensory perceivable characteristics of a wine, derived from the *terroir*, viticultural techniques, varieties of grapes, vintage and local oenological practices.[39] Regionality or régionalité can be defined as the social constructed narrative between wine and place: 'perceptions and experiences of regional gastronomy, social and commercial networks, culture, heritage and the surrounding built environment'.[40]

[34] These changes were implemented through Regulation 17A Australian Grape and Wine Authority Regulations 1981, Statutory Rules No 156, 1981 as amended, in force on 1 July 2014. www.legislation.gov.au/Details/F2014C00910.

[35] Art 3(b) Agreement between the European Community and Australia on trade in wine 2009. OJ L 28/3, 30 January 2009. http://eur-lex.europa.eu/LexUriServ/LexUriServ.do?uri=OJ:L:2009:028:0003:0087:en:PDF.

[36] *Winemakers' Federation of Australia v European Commission* [2013] ATMOGI 1 (22 November 2013). www8.austlii.edu.au/cgi-bin/viewdoc/au/cases/cth/ATMOGI/2013/1.html.

[37] Australian Grape and Wine Authority Regulations 1981, Statutory Rules No 156, 1981 as amended made under the Australian Grape and Wine Authority Act 2013, Compilation start date: 1 July 2014. www.wipo.int/edocs/lexdocs/laws/en/au/au394en.pdf.

[38] Vicky Waye and Stephen Stern, 'The Next Steps Forward for Protecting Australia's Wine Regions' (2016) 42(2) *Monash Law Review* 461–62.

[39] ibid, 461.

[40] ibid, 461–62.

In 1891, the Madrid Agreement for the Repression of False or Deceptive Indications of Source on Goods was signed.[41] Article 1(1) Madrid Agreement protects against the false or deceptive indication, directly or indirectly, as being the country or place of origin. One can place this treaty on the extremity of regionality. The Paris Convention for the Protection of Industrial Property of 1883 was silent about GIs,[42] but in 1925, The Hague Act of the Paris Convention introduced the obligation to protect appellations of origin.[43] Article 1(3) Paris Convention clarifies that the protectable subject matter industrial property shall be understood in the broadest sense and applies not only to industry and commerce proper, but to natural products such as wine as well. Members of the Union could decide on the method of how to do this. However, in 1958, the Lisbon Agreement for the Protection of Appellations of Origin,[44] a Special Union under the Paris Convention, prescribed a *sui generis* regime for appellations of origin which made use of an international register. Article 3 Lisbon Agreement:

> Protection shall be ensured against any usurpation or imitation, even if the true origin of the product is indicated or if the appellation is used in translated form or accompanied by terms such as 'kind,' 'type,' 'make,' 'imitation,' or the like.

According to Article 2(1) Lisbon Agreement, the appellation of origin has a nexus between quality or characteristics and the geographical environment. This quality or these characteristics are due exclusively or essentially to the geographical environment, which includes natural and human factors. The emphasis of this definition is on typicality, although one could argue that human factors not only take into account viticultural techniques, varieties of grapes, vintage and local oenological practices, but also social networks and cultural heritage, and thus is this definition also affected by regionality.

The 1947 General Agreement on Tariffs and Trade (GATT),[45] the predecessor treaty to the World Trade Organization, provided Article IX:6, which urged contracting parties to cooperate to prevent the misrepresentation of the true origin of a product to the detriment of such distinctive regional or geographical names of products of the territory of a contracting party. GATT seems to be all the way to the side of regionality. In 1994, the Agreement on Trade-related Aspects of Intellectual Property Rights (TRIPS) was signed,[46] as integral part of the Marrakesh

[41] Madrid Agreement for the Repression of False or Deceptive Indications of Source on Goods of 14 April 1891, reg no 11848, UNTS 828 (163). https://treaties.un.org/doc/Publication/UNTS/Volume%20828/volume-828-I-11848-English.pdf.

[42] Paris Convention for the protection of industrial property of March 20, 1883, reg no 11851, UNTS 828 (305). https://treaties.un.org/doc/Publication/UNTS/Volume%20828/volume-828-I-11851-English.pdf.

[43] Art 1(2) ibid, The Hague Act on 6 November 1925.

[44] Lisbon Agreement for the Protection of Appellations of Origin and Their International Registration, 31 October 1958, Reg no 923 UNTS 205. www.wipo.int/lisbon/en/legal_texts/lisbon_agreement.html.

[45] General Agreement on Tariffs and Trade (GATT), 1 January 1948, reg no 814, UNTS 55 (187). https://treaties.un.org/doc/Publication/UNTS/Volume%2055/volume-55-I-814-English.pdf.

[46] Above n 5.

Agreement Establishing the World Trade Agreement. TRIPS allows for the protection of GIs via a *sui generis* or trademark system. In 1989, the EU proposed the following draft for the protection of GIs to be included in TRIPS:

> GIs shall be protected against any use which constitutes an act of unfair competition, including use which is susceptible to mislead the public as to the true origin of the product. Shall notably be considered to constitute such:
>
> any direct or indirect use in trade in respect of products not coming from the place indicated or evoked by the GI in question;
>
> any usurpation, imitation or evocation, even where the true appellation or designation is used in translation or accompanied by expressions such as 'kind', 'type', 'style', 'imitation' or the like;
>
> the use of any means in the designation or presentation of the product likely to suggest a link between the product and any geographical area other than the true place of origin.

The New World countries did not like protection for all products against imitation, translation, usurpation and evocation, even with qualifiers. Therefore, the EU had to 'add water to the wine'.[47] The compromise was that only wines and spirits would get additional protection against imitation, translation, even with qualifiers such as 'kind', 'type', 'style', 'imitation'.[48] The protection against evocation without qualifiers was not included in TRIPS. According to Article 22(1) TRIPS, there is a nexus between quality, reputation or other characteristic of the good and the geographical origin. The Lisbon Agreement's nexus was limited to quality or other characteristics and the geographical environment, but TRIPS' nexus is broadened with reputation. The inclusion of reputation shifts the definition a little towards regionality away from typicality.

TRIPS' agnosticism in regard to the question of how to protect a GI, via trademark or *sui generis* system was retained, but Article 23(4) TRIPS prescribes negotiations at the TRIPS Council to establish a multilateral system of notification and registration of GIs for wines. These negotiations have taken place, but have not led to any concrete results, so far.

In 2015, in an effort to appeal more to Old World and New World countries alike, the Geneva Act of the Lisbon Agreement was signed to protect not only Appellations of Origin but also GIs.[49] It also allows intergovernmental organisations, such as the EU, to become member. Beside the translations, or 'kind', 'type', 'make', 'imitation' qualifiers the Lisbon Agreement of 1958 is prohibiting, the Geneva Act 2015 is expanding these with other examples of qualifiers: 'style' (also mentioned in TRIPS), 'method', 'as produced in' and 'similar'. In case new qualifiers are being used, the Geneva Act 2015, just as the Lisbon Agreement uses the open term: 'or

[47] 'Water bij de wijn doen' is a Dutch idiom expression for: 'to compromise'.

[48] Art 23(1), above n 5.

[49] Geneva Act of the Lisbon Agreement on Appellations of Origin and Geographical Indications, WIPO Document LI/DC/19 (20 May 2015). www.wipo.int/edocs/lexdocs/treaties/en/lisbon/trt_lisbon_009en.pdf.

the like'. Article 2(1)(ii) Geneva Act 2015 provides a definition of GI very similar to TRIPS' definition. The definition of appellation of origin, according to Article 2(1)i Geneva Act 2015 has the same wording as the Lisbon Agreement of 1958, except for an interesting addition at the end: 'where the quality or characteristics of the good are due exclusively or essentially to the geographical environment, including natural and human factors, and which has given the good its reputation'. This 'and which has given the good its reputation', refers to the geographical environment, and in contrast to Article 2(1)ii Geneva Act 2015, narrows down the scope of the subject matter a bit, excluding quality or characteristics of the good that are due exclusively or essentially to the geographical environment but which has not given the good its reputation. In other words, one can interpret it as a way to link the typicality of geographical environment to the regionality of reputation.

The Comprehensive and Progressive Agreement for Trans-Pacific Partnership (CPTPP)[50] protects GIs against translations and transliterations (the conversion of one script to another),[51] and provides grounds of opposition of cancellation of GIs, including pre-existing trademarks.[52] However, in case of GIs for wines and spirits TPP members are not required to provide procedures for opposition and cancellation. This treaty seems to be positioned at the same place as TRIPS between regionality and typicality.

V. China's GI System

In China, GIs can be accepted, registered and protected by three government institutions: 43.79 per cent of the GIs are protected by the State Administration for Industry and Commerce (SAIC),[53] via the Trademark Law;[54] 25.66 per cent by the Ministry of Agriculture (MOA), via the Measures for Administration of GIs of Agricultural Products,[55] and 21.16 per cent by the General Administration of Quality Supervision, Inspection and Quarantine (AQSIQ), via the Provisions on the Protection of GIs.[56]

[50] Comprehensive and Progressive Agreement for Trans-Pacific Partnership, the legally verified text was released on 21 February 2018, and was signed on 8 March 2018. www.trungtamwto.vn/sites/default/files/tpp/18.-intellectual-property.pdf.

[51] Art 18.32(5) ibid.

[52] Art 18.32(1)(b) ibid.

[53] Zhu Yuanhua and others, 'The Legal Protection of China's Geographical Indications in the Context of TRIPS Agreement' (2016) 7(2) *International Journal of Business and Social Science* 102.

[54] Trademark Law 1982 adopted by the NPC Standing Committee on 23 August 1982, amended in 1993, 2001, and on 30 August 2013 by the NPC Standing Committee. www.wipo.int/wipolex/en/text.jsp?file_id=341321.

[55] Measures for the Administration of GIs of Agricultural Products, promulgated by the Ministry of Agriculture, Order of the Ministry of Agriculture, No 11, on 25 December 2007 and entered into force on 1 February 2008. http://jiuban.moa.gov.cn/zwllm/nybz/200808/t20080825_1168527.htm.

[56] Provisions for the Protection of Products of GI Promulgated by the General Administration of Quality Supervision, Inspection and Quarantine, promulgated on 16 May 2005, entered in effect on 15 July 2005. www.wipo.int/edocs/lexdocs/laws/en/cn/cn041en.pdf.

The objectives of the Trademark Law and two administrative *sui generis* regulations are: Article 1 Trademark Law 2013;[57] protecting consumers and producers; Article 1 Measures for the Administration of GIs of Agricultural Products[58] and Article 1 Provisions for the Protection of Products of GI;[59] both protecting quality and characteristics of products with GIs. Although the Measures for the Administration of GIs of Agricultural Products are exclusively for domestic agricultural products, the objectives of the three methods of protecting GIs have a significant overlap in the scope of subject matter: 4.82 per cent of GIs are protected by both SAIC and AQSIQ; 3.79 per cent by SAIC and MOA; 0.52 per cent by MOA and AQSIQ; and 0.27 per cent by SAIC, MOA and AQSIQ.[60]

In 2005, AQSIQ announced in Article 26 Provisions for the Protection of Products of GI, that measures would be drafted which would make it possible for foreign GI owners to apply for and register their GIs in China. But only in March 2016, AQSIQ actually issued these measures.[61]

VI. Bilateral GI Agreements between EU and China

In its push for international acceptance of its GIs, the EU is on an offensive to make this happen primarily via bilateral agreements on GIs, whereby the non-usurpation and non-evocation standard is imposed and a strategy of awareness-raising campaigns. Another strategy could be to promote the Lisbon Agreement, and ascend to the Geneva Act of the Lisbon Agreement 2015, although both lack the standard to protection against evocation. Another option for the EU is to mix the recognition of GIs into trade packages within Free Trade Agreements.

In 2003, on 28 August 2003, the EU issued a list of 41 geographical names, which have become generic, but that it wants to internationally re-propertise.[62] This 'claw back' list consists for about one half wines, such as Chablis, Champagne and Chianti, and the other half foodstuffs. The EU has signed special standalone agreements on GIs with China: in 2012, the EU–China GIs for '10 plus 10' was signed.[63] Each entity agreed to recognise and protect each other's GIs, which were all foodstuffs. Here, the EU made the mistake to not protect Chinese translations and transliterations of its GIs.

[57] Above n 54.
[58] Above n 55.
[59] Above n 56.
[60] Above n 53, 102.
[61] Notice on the Protection of Foreign Geographical Indication Products, AQSIQ, 28 March 2016. Art 7 states that the original applicant for the protection of a GI in the country of origin or region where the product is located can apply at AQSIQ. http://kjs.aqsiq.gov.cn/dlbzcpbhwz/zcfg/zxzcxx/201604/t20160413_464279.htm (Chinese).
[62] *WTO talks: EU steps up bid for better protection of regional quality products*, European Commission, Press Release, IP/03/1178, 28 August 2003. http://europa.eu/rapid/press-release_IP-03-1178_en.htm?locale=en.
[63] *EU-China Geographical Indications – '10 plus 10' project is now complete*, European Commission, Press Release, IP/12/1297, 30 November 2012. http://europa.eu/rapid/press-release_IP-12-1297_en.htm.

In 2013, China and the EU drafted a broader list of EU GIs that were to be included in a bilateral agreement on GIs. However, Wang and Kireeva argued that during the latest round of negotiation in December 2013, it was confirmed by the EU, that it perceived the Chinese GIs to have a lower standard, and therefore could not grant them PDO or PGI status.[64] However, finally in 2017, the negotiations came to a close and the EU and China agreed to recognise and protect 100 GIs of each other. This '100 plus 100' bilateral agreement on GIs was signed on 2 June 2017.[65] This time the EU did also protect the translation/transliteration of its GIs in Chinese, including: Conegliano-Valdobbiadene-Prosecco 科内利亚诺瓦尔多比亚德尼 – 普罗塞克.[66]

VII. *Prosecco* Case: 'Transubstantiation' from Grape to GI

The potential adverse effects on consumer information and innovation of the inclusion of a name as a GI can be illustrated by the '*Prosecco*' case. Historically, 'Prosecco' is the name of a grape variety and also a geographical location in the north-east of Italy on the border with Slovenia. To have a grape variety that coincides with the name of a geographical location where the Prosecco grape is not really produced did not sit well with the Italian government and European Commission, who wished that the name Prosecco be exclusively used as a GI. However, products of the vine are excluded from being registered as GIs in many international treaties that deal with GIs.[67] The rationale is that other vintners need to be able to use any grape variety to make wine.[68]

The Vatican teaches that in the Eucharist wine can be changed into the blood of Christ. This so-called transubstantiation is hard to explain. Italy and the EU are faced with a similar challenge: to explain that a grape variety has changed into a GI. The first step for this 'transubstantiation' was for the EU Commission to unilaterally rename the grape variety in 2009 by decree, from 'Prosecco' to 'Glera'.[69]

[64] Wang Xiaobing and Irina Kireeva, 'The Protection of Geographical Indication in the EU and China: Tracing Causes of Delays in the Ongoing Negotiation on the Co-operative Agreement on Geographical Indications' (2014) 2 *Intellectual Property Quarterly* 141.

[65] *100 European geographical indications set to be protected in China*, European Commission Press Release, IP/17/1507, 2 June 2017. http://europa.eu/rapid/press-release_IP-17-1507_en.htm.

[66] Translation/transliteration of Conegliano-Valdobbiadene-Prosecco is 科Ke1内Nei4利Li4亚Ya3诺Nuo瓦Wa3尔Er3多Duo1比Bi3亚Ya3德De2尼Ni2– 普Pu3罗Luo1塞Sai1 克 Ke4.

[67] Products of the vine (names of grapes) are excluded from protection as GI in most international treaties that deal with GIs. See Art 4 Madrid Agreement, Art 5(1) Lisbon Agreement; Art 24(6) TRIPS; Agreed Statement Concerning Article 12 Geneva Act of the Lisbon Agreement; Art 18.32(1) TPP.

[68] Compare this with the *Freihaltebedürfnis*; the general interest in ensuring that the availability of certain signs is not unduly restricted for other traders who offer the goods or services concerned. Opinion of Advocate General Ruiz-Jarabo Colomer, Case C-102/07, *Adidas AG v Marca Mode CV*, ECLI:EU:C:2008:14, 6 January 2008. http://eur-lex.europa.eu/legal-content/EN/TXT/?uri=CELEX:62007CC0102.

[69] Commission Regulation (EC) No 1166/2009 of 30 November 2009 amending and correcting Commission Regulation (EC) No 606/2009 laying down certain detailed rules for implementing Council Regulation (EC) No. 479/2008 as regards the categories of grapevine products, oenological practices and the applicable restrictions. In 2009, the geographical area for Prosecco was also substantially

The sparkling wine 'Prosecco' does not actually originate from Prosecco, which is a suburb of Trieste. Instead, it originates from the hectares of land between Conegliano and Valdobbiadene. In 2009, Italy also expanded the boundaries of the geographical area for Prosecco to four Veneto provinces and five Friuli-Venezia Giulia provinces. Here is Prosecco protected as Denominazione di Origine Controllata (DOC), which is the equivalent of the French Appellation d'origine controlee (AOC) and EU's PDO. Between the cities Conegliano and Valdobbiadene, the Prosecco is protected by the *Denominazione di Origine Controllata e Garantita* (DOCG); guaranteed and sealed by the government.

Interestingly, in the Agreement between Australia and the European Community on Trade in Wine of 1994, 'Prosecco di Conegliano (Valdobbiadene), whether or not accompanied by the GI superiore di Cartizze' was listed as a GI.[70] However, in the 2009 version of the Agreement, the word Prosecco was removed, so that 'Conegliano-Valdobbiadene, whether or not followed by Cartizze',[71] was listed as a GI. Australia was not convinced that Prosecco is a GI. As the last paragraph of Section 3 mentioned, in 2013, the European Commission's request and application to get Prosecco recognised as an Italian GI in Australia fell on deaf ears. According to the Australian Registrar of Trade Marks the word Prosecco is still a grape variety and therefore cannot be used as a GI in Australia.

According to Article 24(6) TRIPS,[72] WTO members are under no obligation to protect as GI 'products of the vine for which the relevant indication is identical with the customary name of a grape variety existing in the territory of that Member as of the date of entry into force of the WTO Agreement'. The WTO Agreement went into force on 1 January 1995, therefore the name change that was unilaterally initiated in 2009 came much too late. Nevertheless, in the EU, 'Prosecco' is only allowed to be used as a GI.

Strictly speaking, one can argue that the use of the name 'Prosecco' as a GI is overbearing: GI's function as a geographical source-indicator does not apply. Also, the prohibition of the name as a grape variety is making it cloudy instead of clear for consumers to learn about the ingredients of the wine they would like to drink, and is not conducive for competition. It also stifles innovation, since producers that are allowed to use the 'Prosecco' name according to the EU, are put in a strait-jacket in regard to the rigid manufacturing process.

Despite the adverse effects on consumer information, product innovation and competition, the Italian government and the EU pursue the acceptance of

expanded. OJ L 314, 1 December 2009, 27–28. https://eur-lex.europa.eu/legal-content/EN/TXT/?uri=uriserv:OJ.L_.2009.314.01.0027.01.ENG.

[70] Agreement between Australia and the European Community on Trade in Wine of 1994, OJ L 86/65, 31 March 1994. https://ec.europa.eu/agriculture/sites/agriculture/files/wine/third-countries/documents/australia-1994_en.pdf.

[71] Agreement between Australia and the European Community on Trade in Wine of 2009, 30 January 2009, OJ L 28/41. http://eur-lex.europa.eu/LexUriServ/LexUriServ.do?uri=OJ:L:2009:028:0003:0087:en:PDF.

[72] Above n 5.

'Prosecco' as a GI. Encouraged by the successes of the *Comité Champagne*, which is protecting the GI 'Champagne', a Consortium was founded for the GI 'Prosecco'.[73] Following in the footsteps of the *Comité Champagne*, which got the 'Champagne Hillsides, Houses and Cellars' recognised as a UNESCO World Heritage Site in 2015, the Consortium applied for the inclusion of the 'Prosecco Hills of Conegliano and Valdobbiadene', in 2010.[74] The strategy here is to link the source of origin of the sparkling wine, namely the *region* between Conegliano and Valdobbiadene, with the name 'Prosecco'. This could facilitate the recognition of the name of the latter as a GI in China. However, even though the EU had unilaterally renamed the Prosecco grape into the Glera grape in 2009, in the 2010 submission for the World Heritage List, the Permanent Delegation of Italy to UNESCO still used the following description: 'The Prosecco vine has been cultivated on these hills for over two hundred years',[75] thereby shooting themselves in the foot over their claim that Prosecco is not a grape but a geographical area. The drafters of the EC/Australia Agreement 2009 did not make this coordination error. While in the EC/Australia Agreement of 1994, Prosecco was described as a vine variety for the GI 'Montello e Colli Asolani',[76] this is no longer the case in the 2009 Agreement.

VIII. Multi-component Term Versus *Pars Pro Toto* Strategy

The EU and China negotiated an agreement to recognise 100 GIs of each other. This '100 plus 100' bilateral agreement was signed on 2 June 2017. It includes the name Conegliano-Valdobbiadene-Prosecco. This suggests that Italy's strategy is to combine a term that could be held generic ('Prosecco') with the non-generic term 'Conegliano-Valdobbiadene': resulting in a Multi-component Term.[77] However, in accordance with the *Napa Valley v Screw Kappa Napa* case in China,[78] one can expect that a Chinese court comes to a similar conclusion in the case of Conegliano-Valdobbiadene-Prosecco. In 2016, the Beijing High People's Court decided that although the name Screw Kappa Napa is not very similar to Napa Valley, 'Napa' is the essential part of the name 'Screw Kappa Napa'. This is what I call the *pars pro toto* (the part becomes the whole) strategy and one can anticipate

[73] *Consorzio di Tutela Prosecco* DOC (Consortium).

[74] On 13 May 2017, the Prosecco Hills of Conegliano and Valdobbiadene are still a candidate for the UNESCO World Heritage list.

[75] *The Prosecco Hills of Conegliano and Valdobbiadene*. (Le Colline del Prosecco di Conegliano e Valdobbiadene submission for the World Heritage List by the Permanent Delegation of Italy to UNESCO, 5 October 2010. http://whc.unesco.org/?cid=326&l=en&id=5566&&&action=doc.

[76] Above n 70, L 86/64.

[77] For the first time an international treaty, the CPTPP, explains what a multi-component term is. Art 18.34(b), above n 50.

[78] Zhuan Ti, 'Napa Valley wins trademark wins legal battle', *China Daily* (21 September 2016). www.chinadaily.com.cn/cndy/2016-09/21/content_26847685.htm.

that a Chinese court will perceive 'Prosecco' to be the essential part of the Multi-component Term Conegliano-Valdobbiadene-Prosecco.

IX. Conclusion

The Old World and New World countries are converging in regard to regionality and typicality. The EU is pursuing its dream to provide its PDOs and PGIs with the strongest international protection possible: promoting additional protection for all GIs, not just wines and spirits, and on top of this enforcing a non-evocation standard.

Bilateral Agreements on GIs and FTAs that include GIs, application for UNESCO World Heritage List, and awareness raising activities, are all strategies to get GIs recognised internationally. However, most international treaties that deal with GIs exclude grape varieties from GI protection. Therefore, it is imaginable that if the EU will be successful in excluding Prosecco wine from China that originates from Australia and other New World countries, this could lead to a dispute at the WTO between Australia, joined by other New World countries, and China joined by the EU.

20

Indian Pharma Sector's Journey for the Innovation Panacea: Lessons from Negotiations with EU and RCEP

DEBASHIS CHAKRABORTY AND NILANJAN BANIK*

I. Introduction

Health is an important component of development, with the positive influence of improved health achievements on labour productivity and economic growth well documented.[1] Conversely, the existing literature reports a strong causative effect of income on infant mortality, demonstrating that if the developing world's growth rate had been 1.5 percentage points higher during the 1980s, half a million infant deaths would have been averted.[2] The causality between health and income runs both ways in many regions across the world, creating room for possible policy interventions.[3] This causal relation, however, is not that strong in the case of India, a densely populated developing country. In spite of being the fastest growing large economy in the world,[4] India ranks quite modestly in the world in terms of key health indicators. For instance, controlling for level of per-capita income, ie, comparing India with other similar regional neighbours, it is revealed that the country has a lower life expectancy and higher infant mortality rate (Figures 1–3). India presently stands at a crucial juncture in its journey towards socio-economic transformation, with the majority population (over 60 per cent) still being young

* The views expressed by the authors are personal, and do not reflect that of their respective institutes. The research assistance of Ms Poulomi Ghosh is gratefully acknowledged.

[1] D Bloom and others, 'The Effect of Health on Economic Growth: A Production Function Approach' (2004) 32(1) *World Development* 1–13.

[2] L Pritchett and L Summers, 'Wealthier is Healthier' (1996) 31(4) *Journal of Human Resources* 841–68.

[3] M Marmot, 'The Influence Of Income On Health: Views Of An Epidemiologist' (2002) 21(2) *Health Policy* 31–46.

[4] In February 2019, in terms of GDP figure, India stands at sixth, after USA, China, Japan, Germany and UK. This depicts a sharp growth for a country, which in 1991 had to go for Structural Adjustment Programme (SAP), following IMF recommendation.

and of working-age in the country.[5] However, there exists significant scope to improve the quality of the Indian labour force in terms of their education, skill and health level, to exploit the demographic dividends.[6] Apart from expansion of existing health infrastructure, improving the performance of pharmaceutical sector in the country would therefore be a crucial development.

The task of improving the health level is particularly important for India, as the country is planning to turn itself in a global manufacturing hub through the 'Make-in-India' initiative launched in 2014. The Indian pharmaceutical sector, which is third largest in terms of volume and tenth largest in terms of value, is a crucial piece in the policy. The sector stood at USD 16.4 billion in 2016–17, contributing to six per cent of the country's total exports.[7] India over the years has emerged as an exporter of both bulk drugs and formulations. It has also evolved as a major player in research and development (R&D) services for global corporates, either through contracts or collaborative programmes.[8] However, presence of a modest innovation policy, affecting the competitiveness of the domestic producers in general and hurting the access of consumers to medicines at an affordable price in particular, have slowed the growth of the process in the past.

The debate on a stronger intellectual property rights (IPR) protection regime in India has become topical in this context. The most common and often misleading perception is that a stronger patent regime will increase the prices of medicines, hitting the poor harder as they spend a larger proportion of their disposable income towards out-of-pocket medical treatment. This argument is based on the premise that IP protection will grant the originator market power for an excessive period, resulting in inefficiency, whereby the innovative medicines are not accessible to the patients. Evidence suggests the vast majority of treatments prescribed in both developing and developed countries are off-patent and therefore unaffected by IP rules.[9] In fact, for developing countries it is the IPR-plus factors such as tariffs and non-tariffs barriers, inefficient supply chains, a lack of proper healthcare service management and cartelisation of domestic pharmaceutical companies, which may collectively influence price of medicines. On the contrary a stricter IPR regime has related benefits – accessibility to cutting edge technology and more foreign direct investment (FDI) inflow.[10] It is to be noted, as per the National Sample Survey

[5] Government of India, Press Information Bureau, 'Optimal Utilization of Demographic Dividend in India, both a Challenge and an Opportunity for India's Economic Growth', 3 December 2018, http://pib.nic.in/newsite/PrintRelease.aspx?relid=186080, accessed 10 March 2019.

[6] AK Singh, 'India's Demographic Dividend: A Sceptical Look' (2016) 10(1) *Indian Journal of Human Development* 10–26.

[7] India Brand Equity Foundation, 'Indian Pharmaceuticals Industry Analysis' (2018), www.ibef.org/industry/pharmaceutical-india.aspx, accessed 12 March 2019.

[8] PricewaterhouseCoopers, *Global Pharma Looks to India: Prospects for Growth* (London, PWC, 2010).

[9] P Stevens and N Banik, 'WHO's new leadership on the Wrong Track', *The Business Times* (2018), www.businesstimes.com.sg/opinion/whos-new-leadership-on-the-wrong-track, accessed 30 April 2019.

[10] R Cavazos Cepeda, D Lippoldt and J Senft, 'Policy Complements to the Strengthening of IPRS in Developing Countries', OECD Trade Policy Papers, No 104, (2010) OECD Publishing, Paris www.oecd-ilibrary.org/docserver/5km7fmwz85d4-en.pdf?expires=1556516819&id=id&accname=guest&checksum=7517E3C9BB97CF33C9F7A4076D35A1B, accessed 30 April 2019.

Organization (NSSO) survey, 70 per cent of India's rural population has to borrow more (25 per cent) in comparison to their urban counterparts (18 per cent) to meet healthcare needs.[11]

In general, the developed countries such as the EU members, Japan and the USA follow a stricter IPR regime. For instance, a reason behind high quality pharmaceutical research and a competitive pharmaceutical industry in the EU has to do with the stringent IPR law.[12] The EU in particular has undertaken many efforts to stimulate innovation, through IPR legislation, co-financing of initiatives and the creation of clear rules of conduct in development processes, such as the legislation related to clinical trials. A key element in promoting innovation has been the elaboration of substantive law on IPR applied in the EU. Since the period that elapses between the filing of an application for a patent for a new medicinal product and its marketing authorisation may make the period of effective protection under the patent rules insufficient to cover the investment put into the research, a supplementary protection certificate (SPC) may be granted according to Regulation (EC) 469/2009.[13] However, in recent years the EU has granted manufacturing export waiver for SPC, with their judgement recommending that generic and biosimilar companies be allowed to build a two-year stockpile of medicine prior to SPC expiry. This could reduce competitiveness in Europe in the field of clinical research and have a negative impact on the development of innovative treatments and medicinal products.[14] The EU in the recent period has been trying to include a stronger IPR provisions in its RTA negotiations, with the bloc enjoying significant bargaining power over the developing country partners.[15] It is to be noted that the disagreement over IPR provisions is a major reason behind the delays in conclusion of the EU–India Bilateral Trade and Investment Agreement (BTIA) negotiations.[16]

The present chapter intends to analyse the scenario in India on IPR protection, the evolving policy orientations and competitiveness reflected through the

[11] N Banik, 'India must move beyond IPR-Protection to Focus on Better Health Outcomes', *The Wire* (2018), https://thewire.in/economy/india-must-move-beyond-ipr-protection-to-focus-on-better-health-outcomes, accessed 30 April 2019.

[12] Lieven Annemans, Irina Cleemput, Frank Hulstaert and Steven Simoens, 'Stimulating Pharmaceutical Innovation in the EU' (2011) 11(3) *Expert Review of Pharmacoeconomics and Outcomes Research* 235–39.

[13] European Commission. Regulation (EC) No 469/2009 of the European Parliament and of the council of 6 May 2009 concerning the supplementary protection certificate for medicinal products. www.deti.ie/science/ipr/pubcodver.pdf, accessed 30 April 2019.

[14] Torstensson, D. 'Does the EU Commission really think weakening IP incentives for biopharmaceutical innovation in Europe is going to create more jobs and economic activity?', Pugatch Consilium www.pugatch-consilium.com/?p=2551, accessed 30 April 2019.

[15] A Moerland, 'Do Developing Countries Have a Say? Bilateral and Regional Intellectual Property Negotiations with the EU' (2017) 48(7) *International Review of Intellectual Property and Competition Law* 760–83.

[16] J Chaisse and D Chakraborty, 'The Evolving and Multilayered EU-India Investment Relations: Policy Conjectures and Regulatory Issues' (2014) 20(3) *European Law Journal* 385–422.

emerging trade patterns, with respect to the pharmaceutical sector. The chapter is arranged along the following lines. First, the health outcomes in India are briefly noted. The orientation towards innovation and IPR is noted next. India's recent policy framework towards pharmaceutical sector is analysed next. Finally, the country's recent participation in mega-regionals like the Regional Comprehensive Economic Partnership (RCEP) is commented upon next, with India's possibilities judged therein through select indices. Based on the discussions, the analysis finally attempts to draw policy conclusions.

II. Health Scenario in India

The following figures, constructed from the World Development Indicators data,[17] outline the prevailing economic and health-related scenario in India compared to the regional neighbours (Bangladesh, China, Pakistan and Sri Lanka). Figure 1 compares the rise in per capita income in India and select neighbouring countries, which displays a modest performance even with respect to South Asian neighbours like Sri Lanka. This observation, despite India's graduation to the sixth spot in global economic ladder in terms of GDP, underlines the persisting inequality. Figure 2 shows the life expectancy at birth (in years) for these countries, depicting India's relatively modest performance on this front as well. Figure 3 shows the number of infant deaths, and the performance of the country is not enviable here either.

The modest performance of India on health front can be explained by several possible underlying factors. First, around 85 per cent of the primary care spending in India is usually directed towards curative services, while the rest is allocated to preventive service.[18] Second, while in the Indian federal structure health happens to be a state subject,[19] the central government also spends money on health through several centrally sponsored schemes, such as National Health Mission and National Health Insurance Schemes (Rashtriya Swasthya Bima Yojana). However, as reflected from Figure 4, given India's large population base, per capita spending on health is abysmally low, when compared to China and Sri Lanka. Third, poorer health achievements on communicable diseases, prenatal and nutrition grounds, part explained by lower income levels, is also evident in India (Figure 5).

[17] World Bank (undated), 'World Development Indicators' <https://datacatalog.worldbank.org/dataset/world-development-indicators, accessed 14 March 2019.

[18] R Srinivisan, 'Health Care in India – Vision 2020: Issues and Prospects', http://planningcommission.gov.in/reports/genrep/bkpap2020/26_bg2020.pdf, accessed 7 March 2019.

[19] According to Art 12 of the Constitution of India, the term 'state' can be used to define both the union and the state governments. India has 29 states and seven union territories.

Figure 1 Per Capita Income in Current USD

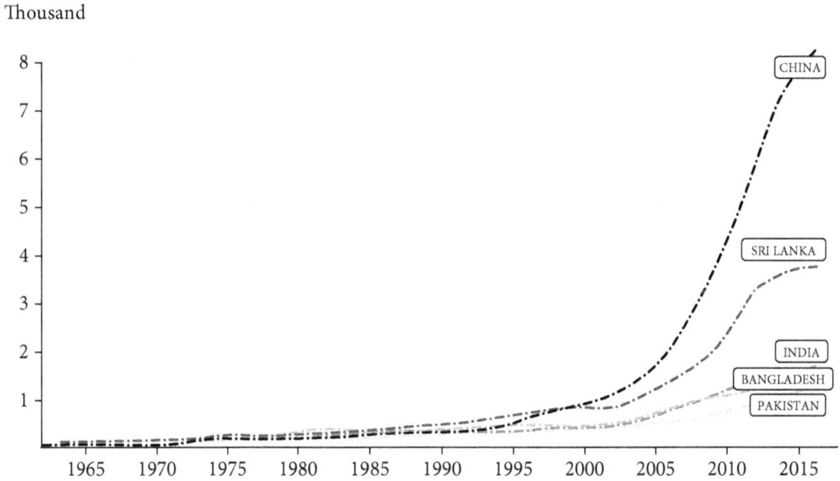

Source: World Development Indicators, World Bank (undated).

Figure 2 Total Life Expectancy at Birth (in Years)

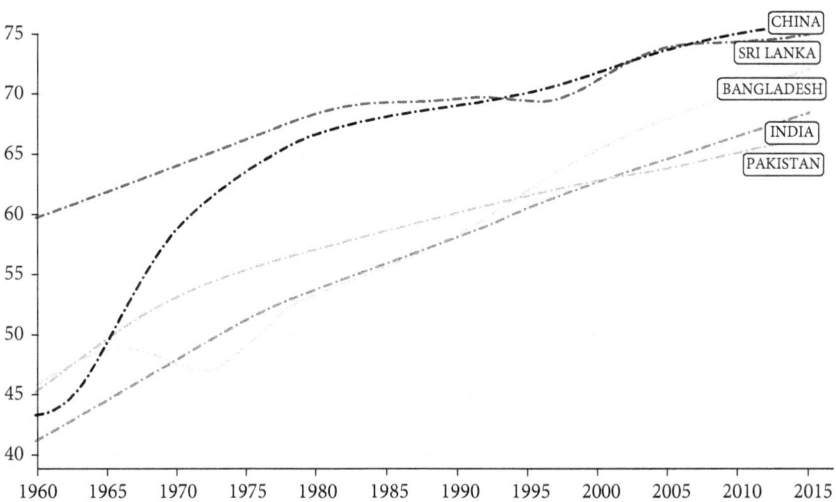

Source: World Development Indicators, World Bank (undated).

Figure 3 Number of Infants Dying before Reaching One-year of Age in 2015

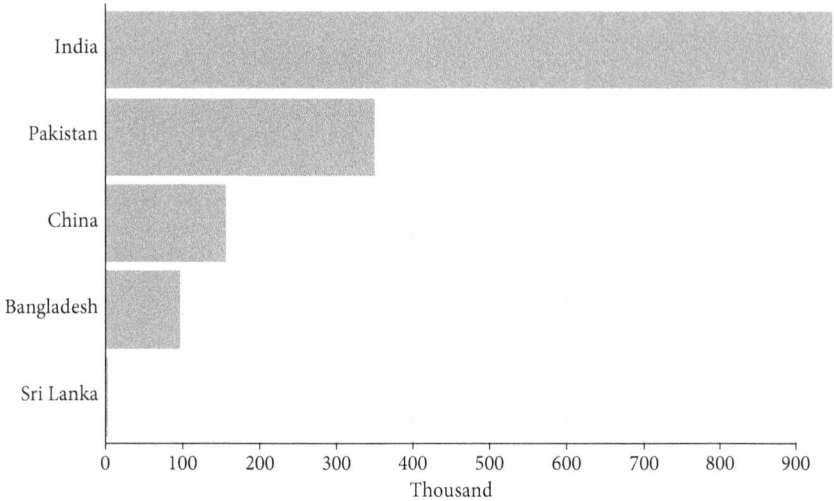

Source: World Development Indicators, World Bank (undated).

Figure 4 Health Expenditure, Public (% of Government Expenditure)

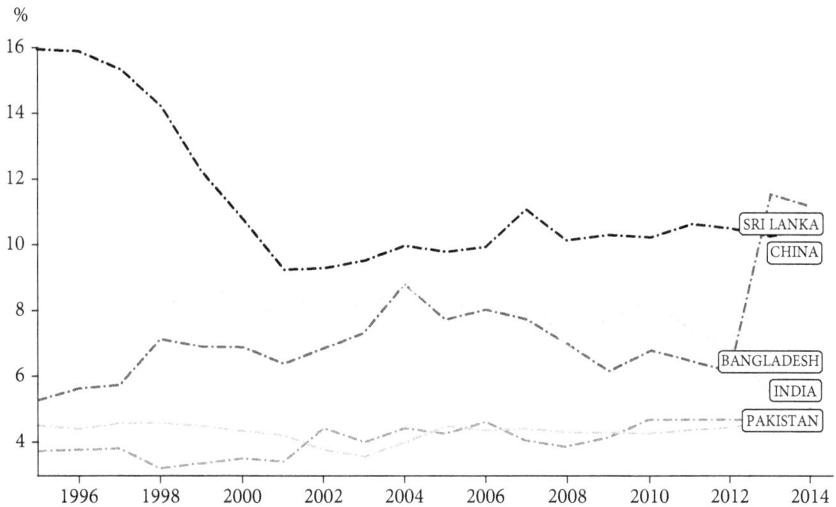

Source: World Development Indicators, World Bank (undated).

Figure 5 Cause of Deaths by Communicable Diseases and Maternal, Prenatal and Nutrition Conditions in 2015 (% of total)

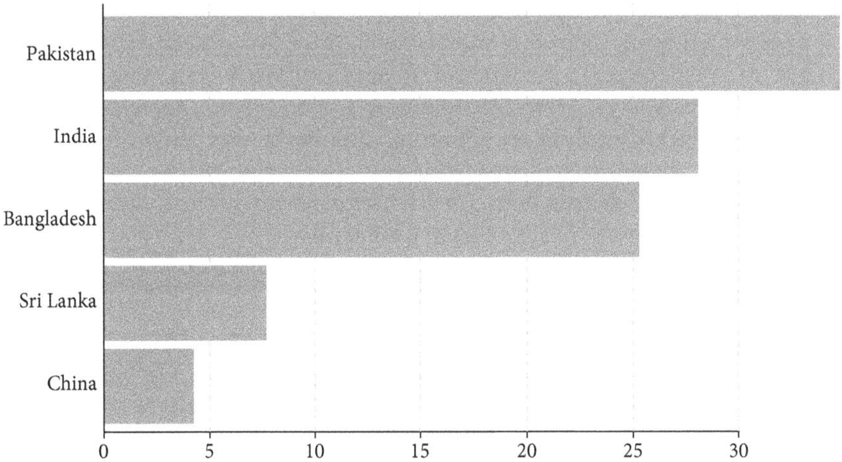

Source: World Development Indicators, World Bank (undated).

At around four per cent of national income, India's expenditure on health front is much lesser compared to China, Sri Lanka and Bangladesh (Figure 4). When measured in per capita terms, India ranks 154th out of 195 countries in terms of access to healthcare, which is worse than South Asian neighbours Bangladesh and Nepal, and even West African countries like Ghana and Liberia.[20] Chronic diseases are the biggest causes of death and disability in India. They account for more than 30 per cent of deaths, with cardiovascular diseases and diabetes, respiratory conditions and cancers (Figure 5). The rise of these diseases is explained by growing air pollution, evolving lifestyle, burning of solid fuels and so on.[21]

Given the lower level of public expenditure on health, in India out-of-pocket (OOP) expenses are increasingly forming a large share of household budget, accounting for about one-third of total household expenditure. In rural India, almost 80 per cent of the OOP expenditure is on medicines, whereas in urban areas, the corresponding figure stands at around 75 per cent.[22] The insurance coverage in India for both indoor and outdoor treatments continues to be narrow, despite a recent rise in the public-private partnerships (PPP) in health insurance, explaining why people have to rely on OOP.[23] Therefore it is imperative that the country keeps

[20] India is placed in the medium Human Development category, and over 1990–2017, the Human Development Index (HDI) composite score of the country increased from 0.427 to 0.640. In 2018, the country was placed at 130th position out of 189 countries. Source: UNDP Human Development Reports.

[21] S Mishra, 'Is Smog Innocuous? Air Pollution and Cardiovascular Disease' (2017) 69(4) *Indian Heart Journal* 425–29.

[22] For details, see 'Prices of Essential Medicines cut by 30-50%' *Economic Times* (New Delhi 2017).

[23] S Razvi, 'Scope of Public Private Partnerships for Healthcare in India: An Analysis of Health Insurance for the Poor', Doctoral Thesis submitted to Indian Institute of Foreign Trade (New Delhi 2018).

the price of medicines in check. The lower price of medicines can be secured in three ways. First, by creating a strong IPR policy to secure innovation, either by domestic firms or by foreign pharma companies, where competition among the key players maintains a downward pressure on price. Second, the import duties, either the Most Favoured Nation (MFN) tariff on World Trade Organization's (WTO) Members or the preferential tariff on Regional Trade Agreement (RTA) partners, can be kept at lower level. Third, control can be imposed on drug prices, which despite short run implementation ease, would compromise the long run innovation among domestic firms. The choices emerging through the evolutions in Indian policy framework are noted in the following.

III. Price of Medicines: Select Drivers

With modest devolution of state support in healthcare (in terms of social security payment or provision of healthcare services), a check on price of medicines emerges as a crucial policy instrument. Price of medicines can change through multiple channels, namely – weak IPR regime, trade barriers (tariff and non-tariff barriers), domestic tax, cumbersome trade procedures, regulatory and administrative hassles, hidden taxes, congestion fee, prevalence of sub-optimal trade infrastructure and so on. The cumulative effects of these barriers increase the price of domestic as well as imported products, which in turn, escalate the final market price. This issue is particularly important in the context of medicines, which are imported in huge volumes, and therefore, has relevance in determining health outcomes for a developing country like India. These factors also impact the functioning of 'supply chains' and affects the participation of pharma companies in the global value chain (GVC) network.[24] 'Barriers at the border and behind the borders' is found to be one of the major obstacles in facilitating cross-border trade, which also increase the cost of doing business.[25] In the following, some of the crucial factors in the Indian context are briefly mentioned.

A. Cost of Doing Business

Although India has implemented several reforms to facilitate business operations,[26] companies still face a maze of government orders, regulations, rules and procedures,

[24] S Ray and S Miglani, *Global Value Chains and the Missing Links: Cases from Indian Industry* (London, Routledge, 2018).

[25] N Banik and J Gilbert, 'Trade Cost and Regional Integration in South Asia', *Asian Development Bank Institute Working Paper No 127* (Tokyo 2008).

[26] For details, see Department for Promotion of Industry and Internal Trade, Ministry of Commerce and Industry, 'Reform Update in India 2019', https://dipp.gov.in/ease-doing-business-reforms/reform-update-india, accessed 11 March 2019.

which raise the cost of doing business in the country. The scenario is clearly visible from the annual Ease of Doing Business Reports, which document how easy it is to do business within a country, taking into account trading regulations, property rights, contract enforcement, investment laws, the availability of credit and a number of other factors. In the Ease of Doing Business Report 2019,[27] the World Bank has placed India in the 77th position, which is a marked improvement from its 134th position out of a sample of 190 countries, five years back in 2014. The rise in composite ranking however hides certain sectoral 'unease' effects. For instance, in the pharma sector a major problem comes from the government-introduced revision of prices of essential medications, which functions with retrospective effects, ie, affecting price of even the medicines which were manufactured previously and available in the market. So, the recall from chemist and re-labelling of the revised lower price forms part of the administrative expenses.[28]

To facilitate the ease of doing business in the pharma sector, a number of steps have been undertaken by the government in the recent period. First, the decision was taken to increase the validity of the WHO Good Manufacturing Practices (GMP) certificate from two to three years.[29] Second, the FDI limit has been allowed up to 100 per cent (under automatic route) for manufacturing of medical devices, thereby facilitating entry of global majors in the domestic market.[30] Third, the Medical Devices Rules (2017) has been framed and notified in line of Global Harmonization Task Force framework.[31]

B. Logistics Cost

The logistics cost in India, at 14 per cent of GDP, is among one of the highest in the world. India's logistics sector is quite complex with more than 20 government agencies, 40 partnering government agencies, 37 export promotion councils, 200 shipping agencies, 36 logistics service and 168 container freight stations. Further coordination between 81 authorities and 500 certifications are required to trade across borders.[32] The Indian Government is currently planning to bring down the logistics cost to 10 per cent of GDP by 2022. For that to happen there is

[27] World Bank, 'Ease of Doing Business in India' (2019), www.doingbusiness.org/content/dam/doingBusiness/country/i/india/IND.pdf, accessed 19 March 2019.

[28] S Shankar, 'How India trips on the ease of doing business in pharma industry', *Hindustan Times* (New Delhi 2016).

[29] P Raghavan, 'CDSCO increases WHO GMP certificate to three years for ease of doing business', *Economic Times* (New Delhi 2018).

[30] Government of India, Press Information Bureau, 'Endeavour of Government is to provide Affordable Quality Healthcare for All and boost Indigenous Pharma Sector through "Make-in-India"' (2019), http://pib.nic.in/newsite/PrintRelease.aspx?relid=187104, accessed 15 March 2019.

[31] Government of India, Make-in-India, 'Sector Survey: Pharmaceuticals', www.makeinindia.com/article/-/v/sector-survey-pharmaceuticals, accessed 17 March 2019.

[32] Business Standard, 'India Aiming To Reduce Logistics Cost To Less Than 10% Of GDP By 2022' (New Delhi 2018).

a need to improve the last mile connectivity by enhancing capacity in port related infrastructure and deployment of multimodal hubs to augment trade while reducing logistics cost.[33]

As approximately 35 and 75 per cent of finished and bulk drugs from India are exported, having an efficient logistic supply chain is crucial for the country.[34] However, the inefficiencies in the Indian pharma sector's inbound and outbound supply chain has been well-documented. It is noted that there is significant scope to improve the supply chain of Indian pharma players in all stages of operations – integrating enterprise software, increasing automation, reconfiguring and using analytics.[35] In addition, given the dominance of generic medicines in India's export basket, the need to reduce the logistic cost to five to six per cent to remain competitive in the world market has been repeatedly underlined by the Pharmaceutical Export Promotion Council.[36]

C. Taxes: Reforms and Beyond

India has recently introduced Goods and Services Tax (GST) which creates a common and integrated market (across various states in India) by subsuming various indirect taxes, such as excise duty, service tax, countervailing duty, valued added tax and also state levies, octroi, entry tax, local taxes and luxury tax.[37] The GST is an indirect tax on the supply of goods and services from the manufacturer to the end consumer. It is a tax which is levied on the basis of value addition in the supply chain and credit of inputs taxes will be refunded at each stage and subsequent stages of value addition. The final consumer will pay the GST levied by the last supplier in the supply chain, and will not have to pay any other indirect tax. As the cascading effect of the earlier tax regime would be avoided, the GST framework is expected to reduce the price of medicines. Under the current GST regime, imported life-saving drugs are GST exempt, whereas most of the medicines are charged at five per cent vis-à-vis the earlier level of 12 per cent (pre-GST rate).[38]

The pre-GST tax regime forced pharmaceutical players to maintain a decentralised supply chain model, ie, maintain multiple warehouses across Indian states

[33] ibid.

[34] Organisation of Pharmaceutical Producers of India, 'Life Sciences Logistics in India' (Mumbai 2014).

[35] ATKearney, 'India's Pharma Supply Chain: Does the Industry Have What It Takes to Win?' (New Delhi 2016).

[36] 'Pharma sector must cut logistics costs to stay in race: Pharmexcil Chief' *Times of India* (New Delhi 2017).

[37] S Mukherjee, 'Inter-Governmental Fiscal Transfers in the Presence of Revenue Uncertainty: The Case of Goods and Services Tax (GST) in India', *NIPFP Working Paper No 255* (New Delhi, National Institute of Public Finance and Policy, 2019).

[38] GST Council (2017), 'Changes in GST Rate for Certain Goods and IGST Rate on Imports of Certain Goods', available at: http://gstcouncil.gov.in/sites/default/files/gst%20rates/GST%20RATE%20APPROVED%20BY%20GST%20Council-%206.10.2017.pdf, accessed 5 May 2019.

in recognition of tax burden from the interstate sale of goods.[39] The reformed tax framework provides them an option to improve the supply chain inefficiencies. Though certain grey areas (eg, issue of promotional free samples)[40] in the tax code still remain, the 9.4 per cent growth of the Indian pharma sector in 2018, recorded in the aftermath of GST introduction, underlines the positive benefits of the long-awaited tax reforms.[41]

D. Procedural Bottleneck

Regulatory measures and non-tariff barriers often affect the price of medicines. It has been noted that extra-tariff factors, such as sales taxes including value-added tax (VAT), mark-ups and other charges have a higher impact on price of medicines than tariffs do.[42] As an imported pharmaceutical product moves along the distribution chain, it undergoes many mark-ups: port charges, warehouse costs, local government levies, distribution costs and retailer mark-ups, to name a few. A diverse range of policies and procedures apply at different stages of the supply chain and any cost associated with these procedures escalate trade costs along the supply stage at each juncture and produce erratic effects on the function of global supply chains.[43]

To understand how these extra-tariff regulatory measures add up to cost, IMS Institute for Healthcare Informatics undertook a study covering five different genres of drugs in India.[44] These medicines fall under five therapeutic areas, namely antibiotics, anti-diabetics, anti-epileptics, anti-hypertension and respiratory agents. This study revealed that in India, the maximum margin for distributors can vary between eight and 10 per cent. The retail drug sellers keep a margin of around 15 per cent. And all these margins have implications in raising the final price of medicines.[45]

E. Productivity Scenario

An increase in per-capita income may happen because of increase in labour participation, technological breakthrough, and/or a combination of both these factors.[46]

[39] S Nair, 'India's looming Goods and Services Tax (GST): considerations for the pharmaceutical industry', *Ernst Young India* (New Delhi 2016).

[40] D Sikarwar, 'Free pharma samples come under GST lens', *Economic Times* (New Delhi 2018).

[41] S Das and S Phadnis, 'Indian pharma industry records 9.4% growth in 2018, dispels GST gloom', *Business Standard* (New Delhi 2019).

[42] M Olcay and R Laing, 'Pharmaceutical Tariffs: What is their effect on Prices, Protection of Local Industry and Revenue Generation?' *Report Prepared for The Commission on Intellectual Property Rights* (Innovation and Public Health 2005).

[43] MJ Ferrantino, 'Using Supply Chain Analysis to Examine the Costs of Non-Tariff Measures (NTMs) and the Benefits of Trade Facilitation' (Geneva, World Trade Organization, 2012).

[44] IMS Institute for Healthcare Informatics, 'Understanding the pharmaceutical value chain' (Montreal, IMS Institute for Healthcare Informatics, 2014).

[45] ibid.

[46] United Nations, 'The impact of the technological revolution on labour markets and income distribution', *Frontier Issues* (Department of Economic & Social Affairs, Geneva 2017).

Similarly, a stronger IPR regime may also motivate the foreign players to invest in India and the associated technology transfer may boost productivity. If population growth in the labour force happens to be exogenous, then labour productivity can be increased by improvement in human capital (education, skills, etc), availability of physical capital (machinery, equipment) and increase in the overall efficiency of production embodied in total factor productivity (TFP). According to the Asian Productivity Organization (APO) productivity database, average TFP growth in India rose from two per cent in 2000–05 to 4.7 per cent during 2005–10, but decelerated to 4.3 per cent in 2017.[47] The pharma sector on the other hand, despite increased export earnings, had not necessarily witnessed higher efficiency in the first decade of the new millennium.[48]

The recent rise in both-way merger and acquisitions in Indian pharma sector is resulting from multiple drivers, namely: improving global competitiveness, rising upward in the GVC, creating newer market, obtaining market intelligence, consolidation of market shares and so on.[49] In the global scale, the application of Advanced Analytics (AA), facilitated by technological change, resulted in a significant rise in clinical trial and output productivity. Application of AA in leading Indian pharma companies since 2017 has shown promising results, which is expected to drive the growth engine further.[50]

IV. Pharma Sector in India: The Policy Framework

A. The Policy Regime: Effective in Facilitating Innovation?

During colonial period, the Patents and Designs Act (1911) enabled India to adopt a strong product patent regime involving all inventions. After independence, India introduced the Scientific Policy Resolution (SPR) (1958), which however performed poorly due to multiple constraints prevailing at that juncture (eg, nascent stage of scientific orientation).[51] Since the mid-1960s, therefore, a debate surfaced in the country on the efficacy of the existing patent system to facilitate

[47] See, P Priya and A Agarwal, 'Exports Need a Make-In-India push', *Financial Express* (New Delhi 2015); S Chakraborty, 'Why investment and productivity is key to India's GDP growth', *Financial Express* (New Delhi 2018).

[48] M Mazumdar and M Rajeev, 'A Comparative Analysis of Efficiency and Productivity of the Indian Pharmaceutical Firms: A Malmquist-Meta-Frontier Approach' (Bangalore, The Institute for Social and Economic Change, 2009).

[49] V Vyas and others, 'Determinants of Mergers and Acquisitions in Indian Pharmaceutical Industry' (2012) 5(9) *Eurasian Journal of Business and Economics* 79–102.

[50] Federation of Indian Chambers of Commerce and Industry (FICCI), 'Trends & Opportunities for Indian Pharma', *White Paper* (New Delhi 2018).

[51] D Sharma, 'Growth and Failures of India's Science Policy' (1976) 11(51) *Economic and Political Weekly* 1969–71.

competitive R&D and manufacture of essential drugs and medicines for affordable access to consumers, particularly in light of the monopoly right enjoyed by foreign pharmaceuticals on their invented molecules (eg, anti-diabetes drugs).[52] Resulting from the dynamics of the debate, the Indian Patent Act (1970) was introduced, putting the pharmaceuticals sector under the process patent regime. In other words, the Indian corporates were allowed to reverse engineer and produce the drugs invented in other countries through a different process. This intervention was considered crucial for reducing the import dependence of the country for bulk drugs and formulations on one hand and encourage domestic pharmaceutical sector on the other.[53] As a result, while the domestic generic drugs production flourished, foreign firms started leaving the Indian market to protect their IPR.[54]

As expected, the R&D scenario in India did not improve. The Technology Policy Statement (TPS) (1983) attempted to facilitate development of indigenous technology through R&D as well as efficient absorption and adaptation of imported technology.[55] However, the impact of the TPS on pharmaceutical sector performance was not highly significant.

As per negotiations under the WTO, India agreed to introduce the product patent regime from 1 January 2005, graduating from the then system of process patent. Apart from the protection given to product patent, the protection of test and other data required to be submitted for marketing approval was also covered.[56] The pace of initial reforms were challenged by the USA[57] and EC[58] at the WTO dispute settlement body and India had to ensure compliance in the subsequent period. It was acknowledged that a collaborative strategy with global multinationals, rather than confrontation, might benefit the local players.[59] It was further hoped that the transition to the product patent regime would enhance the level of R&D expenses among Indian pharma corporates.[60] The period also witnessed

[52] 'No Room for Product Patents', *The Economic Weekly* (Mumbai 1965) 108–09.

[53] N Zacharias and S Farias, 'Patents and the Indian Pharmaceutical Industry', *Report by Nishith Desai Associates* (Mumbai 2002).

[54] AR Khanna and HK Singh, 'India's IPR Regime: Reconciling Affordable Access with Patent Protection' (Strategic Studies Programme, Indian Council for Research on International Economic Relations, New Delhi 2015).

[55] KG Senapathy and J Dasgupta, 'Policies to Drive Innovation in India', www.wipo.int/edocs/pubdocs/en/wipo_pub_gii_2012-chapter8.pdf, accessed 13 March 2019.

[56] B Dhar and KM Gopakumar, 'Effect of Product Patents on the Indian Pharmaceutical Industry', www.wipo.int/edocs/pubdocs/en/wipo_pub_gii_2012-chapter8.pdf, accessed 18 March 2019.

[57] DS50: India – Patent Protection for Pharmaceutical and Agricultural Chemical Products (Complainant USA). For details, see J Chaisse and D Chakraborty, 'Dispute Resolution in the WTO: The Experience of India' in D Sengupta and others (eds), *Beyond the Transition Phase of the WTO: An Indian Perspective on the Emerging Issues* (New Delhi, Academic Foundation, 2006) 507–40.

[58] DS79: India – Patent Protection for Pharmaceutical and Agricultural Chemical Products (Complainant EC). For details, see Chaisse and Chakraborty, ibid.

[59] N Lalitha, 'A SWOT Analysis: Indian Pharmaceutical Industry in WTO Regime' (2002) 37(34) *Economic and Political Weekly* 3542–55.

[60] PS Mehtas, 'TRIPS and Pharmaceuticals: Implications for India' (1998) 17 *Schweizerisches Jahrbuch für Entwicklungspolitik* 97–106.

the entry into force of the Science and Technology Policy (STP) (2003), the aim of which was to follow a coherent approach in converting national R&D efforts into innovations. Promoting international science and technology cooperation, and formulating strategies for attracting higher levels of both public and private investments in scientific research were among the major features of the policy.[61]

The introduction of product patent regime indeed benefited the Indian pharma sector in terms of consolidation, increased R&D spending among market leaders, development of improved generics, increase in approvals in both US and UK markets and so on.[62] However, new drug discovery was understandably not observed immediately after 2005. As the introduction of the product patent regime resulted in re-entry of foreign players, in the subsequent period development of new products by Indian players led to expansion of the retail formulations market.[63] However, growing R&D intensity of a section of the industry resulted in rising market concentration, with consequent influence on drug pricing.[64]

Taking note of the evolving dynamics and modest achievements in the post-2005 period, the National Knowledge Commission (2006–09) recommended creation of an effective innovation ecosystem through various policies, including reinvigorating knowledge-imparting institutions and creation of a world class environment for knowledge creation.[65] India subsequently declared 2010–20 as the decade of innovation, and to facilitate R&D and innovation in the country further in a concerted manner, the Science, Technology and Innovation Policy (STIP) was introduced in 2013. The policy focuses on development of appropriate skill level among the young, creation of world class R&D infrastructure, facilitation of greater private sector participation in R&D activities, establishment of a national innovation system, among other goals.[66] Finally, in order to promote traditional India medicines and other modes of treatment, namely Ayurveda, Siddha and Unani & Homoeopathy (ASU&H), the National AYUSH Mission (NAM) was launched in 2014.[67]

While all the past policies in principle provided a positive thrust for R&D and innovation, in practice the conversion of them to tangible benefits remained modest owing to a number of reasons.[68] First, despite various attempts, the

[61] N Sen, 'Science and Technology Policy–2003' (2003) 84(1) *Current Science* 13.

[62] Dhar and Gopakumar (n 56).

[63] K Bharadwaj, 'Five Years into the Product Patent Regime: India's Response' (New York, United Nations Development Programme, 2010).

[64] ibid.

[65] National Knowledge Commission, 'Recommendations of the National Knowledge Commission', *Academic Foundation* (New Delhi 2009).

[66] Government of India, Ministry of Science and Technology, 'Science, Technology and Innovation Policy 2013' (New Delhi 2013).

[67] Government of India, Ministry of Health & Family Welfare, Department of AYUSH, 'National AYUSH Mission: Framework for Implementation' (New Delhi 2014).

[68] For a detailed analysis, see B Dhar and S Saha, 'An Assessment of India's Innovation Policies', *RIS Discussion Paper No 189* (New Delhi 2014); Confederation of Indian Industry and Deloitte, 'Innovation Ecosystem in India; (New Delhi 2014).

university-industry interface in India remained weak, given the wide quality diversity in the former and scepticism in the mind of the latter. Second, the Indian pharma market has largely been unsuccessful in bringing together public and private sectors to nurture learning and innovation. Third, political economic undercurrents often remained a strong force. Fourth, while the size of the high-skilled scientist group increased in India, the number of mid-skilled research professionals, another crucial element of research ecosystem, remained at a modest level. On the other hand, the working IPR infrastructure (eg, functioning examiners in patent offices) in the country is still inadequate.

Table 1 provides summary statistics of Indian pharmaceutical sector's external, research and operational orientations over the last two decades with help of CMIE PROWESS data reported on financial performance of the corporate sector units.[69] For understanding the temporal changes in the behavioural pattern, the time period has been divided in three periods, namely – 2001–05 (primarily process patent period), 2006–10 (introduction of product patent period) and 2011–17 (India's increasing involvement in regional agreements). The figures reported in the table indicate the composite industrial average during that year. From the top panel, it is observed that the outward orientation of Indian pharma sector is largely increasing.[70] The outward orientation is reflected both in growing export (ie, revenue earning from export sales) and import (ie, import of raw materials and components from abroad) inclinations. The middle panel on the other hand shows a rise in domestic R&D expense as well as in royalties and other technical know-how fees payments to foreign firms, indicating a growing recognition of undertaking new product developments. The R&D scenario prevailing in the pharma sector in the post-2005 period initially remained modest in comparison to the corresponding figure for developed countries.[71] Only in the recent period, R&D is showing an increasing trend, given the growing popularity of the co-development arrangements between Indian and multinational pharmaceutical companies.[72] The relative rise in pollution abatement cost, noted from the bottom panel, underlines the growing urge to comply with global standards to prevent rejections of export consignments.[73]

[69] Centre for Monitoring Indian Economy (undated), 'PROWESS database', Mumbai.

[70] The decline in some variables in the last column can be attributed to the fact that data collection process in the last reported year is still in progress.

[71] RK Joseph, 'The R&D Scenario in Indian Pharmaceutical Industry', *RIS Discussion Paper No 176* (New Delhi, Research and Information System for Developing Countries (RIS), 2011).

[72] Nishith Desai Associates, 'The Indian Pharmaceutical Industry: Business, Legal & Tax Perspective' (Mumbai 2019).

[73] 'In 6 years, US FDA rejected 13,000 Indian products', *Economic Times* (New Delhi 2016).

Table 1 Pharmaceuticals Sector–Key Industry characteristics in India (%)

Industry Characteristics	2001–05	2006–10	2011–17
External Orientation			
Export (as % of Sales)	30.623	37.295	35.701
Import of raw materials (as % of Cost)	12.993	14.407	10.871
Import of capital goods (as % of Cost)	1.309	1.766	1.074
Imported raw materials consumed (as % of Cost)	13.465	1.074	8.470
Raw material imports (as % of Raw material purchases)	53.838	88.524	79.882
Research Orientation			
R&D Expense (as % of Cost)	2.737	3.915	4.529
Royalty Payment (as % of Cost)	0.047	0.041	0.060
Royalties, technical know-how fees (as % of Cost)	0.064	0.053	0.068
Licence fees (as % of Cost)	0.011	0.010	0.005
Operational Orientation			
Packaging and packing expenses (as % of Cost)	3.445	3.097	0.023
Environment and pollution control related expenses (as % of Cost)	0.031	0.036	0.046
Income from carbon credits (as % of Sales)	0.00	0.00	0.00

Source: Computed by authors from PROWESS data.

Given the modest rise in R&D expenses, and the consequent development of new drugs at competitive price, the urge for controlling prices of essential drugs in India and monitoring their availability/shortage is still strong. The National Pharma Pricing Authority (NPPA) has been entrusted to regulate the prices of essential drugs under the National Pharmaceutical Pricing Policy (NPPP), and as of 15 December 2016, 853 formulations were placed under price control.[74] Apart from medicines, the components for surgeries considered as essentials, eg, bare metal stents (BMS) and drug eluting stents (DES), are now covered under the aegis of NPPA.[75] Interestingly, it deserves mention that the USA has cited the price control mechanism on pharma sector in India in its bid to suspend the Generalized System of Preferences (GSP) benefits on Indian exports.[76]

[74] Government of India, Make-in-India, 'Sector Survey: Pharmaceuticals' (n 31).

[75] Government of India, Department of Pharmaceuticals, 'Notification for including Coronary Stents in Schedule 1 of DPCO 2013', http://pharmaceuticals.gov.in/sites/default/files/Notification_2.pdf, accessed 2 March 2019.

[76] Press Trust of India, 'India requests US to maintain GSP beneficiary status', *Businessworld* (New Delhi 2018).

B. Drug Price Control Order: Facilitating R&D?

Presently, there is an existing list of 72 formulations and 355 brands of drugs (around 1000 drugs in number) which are under price control by the National Pharmaceutical Pricing Authority (NPPA).[77] While the optimality of drug pricing control for making life-saving drugs available for the public in a low-income country is noted, excessive control is not good for pharma industry. Such a policy reduces the expected profitability from innovations and dampens the growth prospects of drug manufacturing companies. In the Indian context, the drug manufacturing companies like Roche, Bayer, Novartis, Glen mark and Pfizer have lost market share and now face cost constraints. This is because they have lost patent fights and now domestic drug manufacturers produce generic drugs which are much cheaper than the specific version.[78] Conversely the domestic pharma companies mostly manufacture generic drugs with little or no investment in R&D.

C. Compulsory Licensing Debate in India

To soothe the perception of developing countries that MNCs may charge higher prices for medicine, the 2001 'Doha Declaration' clarified several public health aspects of the TRIPS Agreement. In particular, the declaration reaffirms the rights of all WTO members to 'grant compulsory licences, and the freedom to determine the grounds upon which such licences are granted (paragraph 5(b))',[79] wherein the governments are allowed to give a third-party authorisation to override a patent. In 2005, India under the new Patent Act implemented strong clauses in favour of inventors (for example, product patents replacing the earlier process patents). Under this regime of TRIPS-Plus flexibilities, the country retained the right to use compulsory licence. The use of compulsory licence is seen as a way to reduce the price of patented medicines. Since 2001, several lower and middle-income countries including India have issued compulsory licences (the majority for HIV medicines), generally citing high prices as a justification. India has positioned itself as pharmacy of the developing world, with 85 per cent of the HIV/AIDS patients treated by Médecins Sans Frontières (MSF) in over 30 countries, sourcing medicines from India.[80] Additionally, MSF buys more than 25 per cent of the drugs

[77] Press Trust of India, 'Government brings 42 non-scheduled cancer drugs under price control', *Economic Times* (New Delhi 2019).

[78] N Mahajan, 'Case Study On Government's Drug Pricing Control And Strategies By Pharma Companies for Retailing' (2018) 7(2) *International Journal of Business and Management Invention* 16–22.

[79] For details, see WTO Doha Declaration on TRIPS, www.wto.org/english/thewto_e/minist_e/min01_e/mindecl_trips_e.htm, accessed 5 March 2019.

[80] Popularly known as Doctors Without Borders, MSF is an international humanitarian medical non-governmental organisation (NGO) of French origin.

for malaria, tuberculosis and antibiotics from India. Moreover, approximately fifty per cent of essential medicines that UNICEF distributes in developing countries come from India, 'while 75–80 percent of medicines distributed by International Dispensary Association are made in India'.[81] Therefore the use of compulsory licence in India will have an effect on price of medicines in other countries as well.

In March 2012, India granted its first ever compulsory licence. The licence was granted to Indian generic drug manufacturer Natco Pharma Ltd for Soafenib Tosylate, a drug used for treating liver and kidney cancer, patented by Bayer.[82] Bayer sought injunction against NATCO at the Intellectual Property Appellate Board (IPAB), which however upheld the decision to grant the licence.[83] Ever since, there was a series of applications for granting compulsory licence which were rejected by the patent office in India.[84] During February 2016, while reviewing Special 301, the US–India Business Council (USIBC) observed that the Government of India has privately reassured that it would not use a commercial licence for commercial purposes.[85] In fact, as has been documented through an extensive survey in Bond and Saggi (2012), compulsory licences are used more as a barrier for innovations, often failing to reduce price of medicines, the original intention with which it had been included in the TRIPS Agreement.[86]

D. Make-in-India: Active Push for Innovation

In recognition of the growing competition in general and the impending challenges to the domestic pharmaceutical sector in the aftermath of introducing product patent regime in particular, India established the National Manufacturing Competitiveness Council (NMCC) in 2004. The 'National Manufacturing Policy' was formulated in 2011, which identified a number of key sectors for augmenting competitiveness, including pharma.[87] The 'Make-in-India' scheme was subsequently introduced in 2014 to attract leading global majors to relocate their production units in India.[88] Pharma and biotechnology sectors were included in

[81] P Golikeri, 'EU Firm on Strong IP Provisions in Free Trade', *Daily News and Analysis* (2010).

[82] Bayers sold this drug at exorbitant rates, with one month's worth of dosage costing around Rs 2.8 Lakh. Natco Pharma offered to sell it around for Rs 9000, making it affordable for people belonging to every stratum. For details, see N Shukla, 'Compulsory Licensing in India' (2019), www.mondaq.com/india/x/772644/Patent/Compulsory+Licensing+In+India, accessed 24 March 2019.

[83] Khanna and Singh (n 54).

[84] P Saha and A Mukherjee, 'Compulsory Licensing of Pharmaceutical Patents in India: A Policy Shift', (2019) 54(5) *Economic and Political Weekly*.

[85] USIBC, 'USIBC Hearing Statement to the Office of the USTR Concerning the 2016 Special 301 Review' (2016), http://freepdfhosting.com/6dd037b8b4.pdf, accessed 24 March 2019.

[86] E Bond and K Saggi, 'Compulsory licensing, price controls, and access to patented foreign products' (2012), www.wipo.int/edocs/mdocs/mdocs/en/wipo_ip_econ_ge_4_12/wipo_ip_econ_ge_4_12_ref_saggi.pdf, accessed 23 March 2019.

[87] Government of India, Ministry of Commerce and Industry, Department of Industrial Policy and Promotion, 'National Manufacturing Policy' (New Delhi 2011).

[88] Government of India, 'Make-in-India', www.makeinindia.com/home/, accessed 12 March 2019.

the focus sectors, in recognition of their significant roles in domestic value addition and exports.

To improve product quality, innovation and trade, a set of policies has been introduced in India since 2014. First, for fuelling R&D activities on priority basis approval of 11 National Institutes of Pharmaceutical Education & Research (NIPERs) has been granted.[89] Second, to facilitate technology transfer from developed countries, FDI in pharma sector has been allowed up to 100 per cent through the automatic route for manufacturing of medical devices. Third, 'Pharma Vision 2020' has been introduced to make India a global leader in end-to-end drug manufacture,[90] to make India a drug discovery and innovation powerhouse through capacity creation at home. Fourth, while generic drug exports from India is increasing, the country's reliance on China for import of raw materials is also on the rise.[91] Hence, encouragement has been provided to facilitate indigenisation of Active Pharmaceutical Ingredients (APIs) with a goal to lower imports of these products from China.[92]

E. Foreign Investment in India

Tie-ups between several Indian domestic drug manufacturers and foreign multinationals – Piramal Healthcare with Abbott Laboratories; Ranbaxy Laboratories with Daiichi Sankyo; Dr Reddy's Laboratories with GlaxoSmithKline; Shanta Biotechnics with Sanofi Aventis; and Biocon with Bristol Myers Squibb – have allowed India to move up the value chain, with formulations and packaging moving in the country.

The success of STIP (2013) and the Make-in-India (2014) policy in attracting foreign investment can be observed from the Department of Industrial Policy and Promotion (DIPP) data on FDI implemented over the last six years.[93] It is observed from Table 2 that the number of projects receiving foreign investment in the pharma sector since 2013 are showing a rising trend, along with the absolute value of investment in the segment. Notably, FDI propensity in the pharma sector (shown as per cent of investment within aggregate industry sector) has increased from 2.91 per cent in 2013 to 7.12 per cent in 2017. A relative decline is noted in 2018, despite a rise in FDI in pharma sector in absolute scale.

[89] Government of India, 'Progress Under "Make-in-India" Programme', *Unstarred Question No 1631* (Rajya Sabha 2018), http://dipp.nic.in/sites/default/files/ru_1631.pdf, accessed 4 March 2019.

[90] IBEF (n 7).

[91] M Kallummal and K Bugalya, 'Trends in India's Trade in Pharmaceutical Sector: Some Insights' (2012), http://wtocentre.iift.ac.in/workingpaper/Working%20Paper2.pdf, accessed 10 March 2019.

[92] ASSOCHAM, 'IPR in pharmaceuticals: Balancing, innovation and access' (2016), www.assocham.org/newsdetail.php?id=5886, accessed 15 March 2019.

[93] Department for Promotion of Industry and Internal Trade, Ministry of Commerce and Industry, 'Secretariat of Industrial Assistance (SIA) Statistics', https://dipp.gov.in/publication/sia-statistics, accessed 22 March 2019.

Table 2 Investment implemented in Drug and Pharmaceuticals segment

Year	Number of Projects in the Pharma Sector	Investment in the Pharma Sector (Rs Crore)	Total Investment in all Industries (Rs Crore)	FDI in the Pharma Sector (% of total investment)
2013	18	2282	78497	2.91
2014	17	1190	78747	1.51
2015	19	1356	77972	1.74
2016	28	2041	100537	2.03
2017	44	5085	71396	7.12
2018	40	7072	255783	2.76

Source: Obtained from SIA Statistics, DIPP (undated).

An analysis of FDI inflows in India reveals that foreign players are now eager to increase their stakes in Indian firms. Data reveals that the FDI inflows are growing because foreign investors are claiming more and more stakes in the Indian start-ups and brownfield ventures.[94] Unlike in the case of a greenfield investment, where the parent company constructs new production facilities and builds distribution hubs, in brownfield investment the foreign company or government entity purchases or leases existing production facilities to launch new production activity in the host country. This is partly due to the fact that over the last few years, the FDI limit in the brownfield projects in various sectors has sharply increased. The government has allowed up to 74 per cent FDI in brownfield pharmaceutical companies through automatic route, and 100 per cent in brownfield pharmaceutical projects through approval route. The start-up space is no exception.[95] The other reason might be that players from the 'West' are apprehensive that in the absence of stronger data exclusivity provisions in India, the results of their clinical trials might be accessed by competitors.[96]

V. Trade in Pharmaceuticals Sector

A. Trade with World

After formation of the WTO, India initially relied more on multilateral trade reform process for export promotion until the Cancun Ministerial (2003), after

[94] CH Unnikrishnan, 'Hold of foreign firms on Indian pharma market gradually rising', *Livemint* (Mumbai 2010).

[95] N Banik and K Das, 'As India's Economic Indicators Slump, FDI Inflows Have Never Looked Better. Why?', *The Wire* (2017), https://thewire.in/business/indias-economic-indicators-slump-fdi-inflows-never-looked-better, accessed 24 March 2019.

[96] Khanna and Singh (n 54).

the failure of which the country gradually started engaging in RTAs.[97] Though the India–Singapore Comprehensive Economic Cooperation Agreement (CECA) was signed in 2005, the RTA participation deepened in particular from 2010 onwards, with the country entering into the India–ASEAN FTA (2010), followed by the India–South Korea Comprehensive Economic Partnership Agreement (CEPA) (2010), India–Japan CEPA (2011) and Indo–Malaysia CECA (2011).

Over the years, India has emerged as a major exporter of pharma products in the world. Table 3 shows the position of India in the global pharmaceutical (HS 30) exports in the new millennium in terms of average market share, as computed from Trade Map data.[98] The analysis has been divided in three periods, namely 2001–05 (process patent/reliance on WTO for exports), 2006–10 (initial days of product patent/engagement with RTAs) and 2011–17 (increasing involvement in RTAs). It is observed that India has witnessed a sharp rise in its average export share in world market from 0.88 per cent in 2001–05 to 2.30 per cent in 2011–17. The observed results indicate two possibilities. First, the preferential access in RTA partner markets might have helped the pharma sector in line with other merchandise export categories. Second, the Indian pharmaceutical exports is likely to be gaining competitiveness in the world markets.[99] It has been recommended that India's global presence in pharmaceutical exports can be deepened further through certain coordinated policy efforts, namely: upgradation of quality systems, infrastructure creation, capability enhancement, move to create a brand for reliable, high-quality medicine supply, improving transparency and predictability of regulations and so on.[100]

Table 3 India's Share in World Exports of Pharmaceuticals (in %)

Exporting Countries	2001–05	2006–10	2011–17
Germany	13.16	15.12	15.39
Switzerland	8.9	9.8	12.34
USA	9.12	8.96	8.71
Belgium	12.38	12.14	9.33
UK	9.96	7.92	6.94

(continued)

[97] J Chaisse and others, 'The Three-pronged Strategy of India's Preferential Trade Policy – A Contribution to the Study of Modern Economic Treaties' (2011) 26(2) *Connecticut Journal of International Law* 415–55.

[98] International Trade Centre (undated), 'Trade Map Database', www.trademap.org/, accessed 11 March 2019.

[99] The pharma exports from India received supports from the Foreign Trade Policy (2015–20), which introduced Merchandise Exports from India Scheme (MEIS) to enhance competitiveness in partner countries through incentives in terms of duty credit scrip. For details, see Government of India, 'India's Foreign Trade Policy 2015–2020' (2015), http://dgft.gov.in/policies/foreign-trade-policy, accessed 2 March 2019.

[100] FICCI, 'Realising "Make-in-India" – Journey to become the most preferred manufacturer of high quality affordable medicines' (2015), http://ficci.in/spdocument/20712/Final-Realizing-Make-in-India-Vision.pdf, accessed 16 March 2019.

Table 3 *(Continued)*

Exporting Countries	2001–05	2006–10	2011–17
Ireland	7.50	6.18	6.23
France	9.38	8.00	6.74
Italy	5.00	3.94	4.47
Netherlands	3.94	5.36	4.47
India	0.88	1.20	2.30

Source: Computed by authors from Trade Map data.

Table 4 shows the composition of India's pharmaceutical exports at HS six-digit level, by showing the top six products over two time periods. It is observed that over 2008–12 to 2013–17, the share of these six product groups have increased, presently accounting for 94.02 per cent of total pharma exports. Nevertheless, medicaments consisting of mixed or unmixed products (HS 300490) explains a significant proportion of Indian pharma exports.

Table 4 Composition of India's Pharmaceuticals Trade Basket (%)

HS Code	Product Description	Share in India's Pharmaceutical Exports	
		2008–12	2013–17
300490	Medicaments consisting of mixed or unmixed products for therapeutic or prophylactic purposes	61.67	73.38
300420	Medicaments containing antibiotics, put up in measured doses	11.09	7.45
300220	Vaccines for human medicine	3.38	4.88
300410	Medicaments containing penicillins or derivatives thereof with a penicillanic acid structure	4.26	4.00
300450	Medicaments containing pro-vitamins, vitamins, including natural concentrates and derivatives thereof	4.14	2.01
300390	Medicaments consisting of two or more constituents mixed together for therapeutic or prophylactic purposes	4.42	2.29
Total		88.95	94.02

Source: Computed by authors from Trade Map data.

Table 5 illustrates the directional flow of India's pharmaceutical exports, by showing the top 13 destination markets over the three periods noted earlier. It is observed that India's major export markets are spread across continents, though the West, particularly USA, accounts for a much larger share in India's export basket (33.84 per cent during 2011–17). In Europe, a number of EU member countries (UK, Germany) and Russia are among the major partners. Africa (South Africa, Nigeria, Kenya), Asia and the Pacific (Australia, Sri Lanka, Philippines, Nepal, Myanmar) and Latin America (Brazil) are among the other prominent export destinations. The increase in absolute export volume and rising market share of Indian pharma products has tilted the trade balance is several markets. In recent times, India's pharma trade balance with Europe and USA has become positive,[101] despite massive rejections on quality grounds.[102] It also deserves mention that actual competitiveness of Indian pharma exports in US market has improved only moderately.[103] In several markets including Africa, export of herbal and other traditional Indian medicines are gaining ground, part owing to the AYUSH initiative.[104]

Table 5 India's Export Direction – Leading Partners (in %)

Countries	2001–05	2006–10	2011–17
USA	14.32	21.62	33.84
UK	3.98	4.48	3.71
South Africa	1.58	3.40	3.74
Nigeria	5.30	3.48	3.03
Russia	8.36	6.62	4.16
Kenya	1.36	2.02	2.17
Australia	0.72	1.00	1.56
Sri Lanka	2.72	2.00	1.47
Brazil	2.74	2.26	1.57
Philippines	0.94	0.82	1.24
Nepal	2.30	1.42	1.23
Myanmar	0.96	1.04	1.23
Germany	2.78	2.38	1.76

Source: Computed by authors from Trade Map data.

[101] N Banik and J Singh, 'Demystifying the Role of "Barriers at and behind the Borders" in India: A Case Study of Pharmaceutical Products', *CUTS International Working Paper* (Jaipur 2017).

[102] *Economic Times* (n 73).

[103] D Chakraborty and others, 'Recent US-China Tariff War: Opportunities for Indian Pharmaceutical Exports?' (2018) 5(4) *Journal of Economic Bibliography* 209–22.

[104] Pharmexcil, 'Sudan Pharma Market Report', Hyderabad, https://pharmexcil.com/uploadfile/ufiles/1390922514_Sudan%20market%20report.pdf.

B. Trade Barriers

The real competitiveness of a sector can be part gauged by the protection accorded by the domestic government towards it. The pharma sector in India is protected through tariffs, which are essentially regressive taxes as they take a higher proportion of income from the poor vis-à-vis their richer counterparts. A study by Banik and Stevens analysed the impact of tariffs on pharma products in emerging economies.[105] One of the major findings of the study is that the total volume of trade in pharma products has increased during 2006–13 for countries outside the WTO's 'zero-for-zero initiative'.[106] Trade in pharma products grew at a compounded annual growth rate (CAGR) of 20.7 per cent over this period. This implies that tariffs impeded access to a large proportion of marketed pharmaceuticals and medicines.

India (tariff rate of 10 per cent) is among the major five countries, levying high tariffs on imported medicines and vaccines. Only Nepal, Pakistan, DR Congo (11 per cent) and Russia (10.2 per cent) charge a relatively higher tariff on this sector. Other countries charging high pharma tariffs are Uruguay (9.9 per cent), Argentina (9.8 per cent), Brazil (9.8 per cent) and Thailand (9.3 per cent).[107] All the countries outside the WTO Pharmaceutical Agreement are increasing their consumption of medicines as they grow wealthier. As per the data from the WTO Tariff Database,[108] a number of pharma products falling under tariffs coverage have not fallen over 2006–16. During 2016, under HS-3004 category, India has imposed tariffs on 137 products. It was found that the product category with the highest number of tariff lines is HS-300490 (other medicaments, in packaging for retail sale), which contains, among others, anaesthetics, anti-retrovirals, antimalarials and a number of antiseptic product categories. Import tariffs can be a major determinant of final price, as they can significantly increase the price of imported goods before they embark on the journey down the distribution chain.

The degree of protection to the pharma sector in India can be explained with the help of Table 6, which compares the average tariff in the country with the USA since 1995 with help of World Integrated Trade Solution (WITS) data.[109] It is seen from the table that while the trade-weighted average tariff in USA during 2011–16 has been near zero, the corresponding number for India is 9.97 per cent. The

[105] N Banik and P Stevens, 'Pharmaceutical tariffs, trade flows and emerging economies', *Geneva-Network Working Paper* (United Kingdom 2015).

[106] Under 'Zero-for zero initiative' USA and 21 of its trading partners, agreed in 1995 to the reciprocal elimination of import duties on approximately 7,000 pharmaceutical products under the WTO Pharmaceutical Agreement.

[107] Banik and Stevens (n 105).

[108] World Trade Organization, 'WTO Download Facility', http://tariffdata.wto.org/, accessed 8 March 2019.

[109] World Bank, 'World Integrated Trade Solution', https://wits.worldbank.org/, accessed 3 March 2019.

number of imported tariff lines are also found to be much lesser as compared to the USA. Finally, free imports as percent of total imports under pharma sector in USA is nearly 100 per cent, signifying a high degree of trade openness. However, in case of India the corresponding number is around 0.31 per cent, underlining that almost every pharma import is covered by some degree of tariff barrier. While the trade policy can be part justified by the domestic consolidation exercise in the form of the 'Make-in-India' initiative, the moderate competitiveness level can also be comprehended.

Table 6 Effective Applied Tariff in Pharmaceutical Sector – Comparing India and US

Year	Simple Average	Weighted Average	Total Number of Tariff Lines	Number of Free Lines expressed as Percent of Free Lines	Free Imports as a Percent of Total Imports
USA					
1995–2000	0.24	0.11	863	99.50	99.65
2001–2005	0.06	0.00	1023	99.46	100.00
2006–2010	0.06	0.00	1043	99.14	99.94
2011–2016	0.12	0.00	1089	98.33	99.96
India					
1995–2000	34.75	35.31	30	3.34	0.69
2001–2005	25.71	26.86	140	3.56	0.52
2006–2010	10.65	10.97	215	1.40	0.27
2011–2016	9.74	9.97	214	1.12	0.31

Source: Computed by authors from WITS data.

Apart from tariff barriers, the country takes recourse to certain forms of Non-Tariff Measures (NTMs) on the imports as well. As per the *Macmap database*, India imposes a large number of NTMs on pharmaceutical imports, which were quite significant in 2016.[110] The most frequent NTMs used in India include: labelling requirement (21.4 per cent); packaging requirement (12.99 per cent); authorisation requirement (9.83 per cent); registration requirement (8.34 per cent) and traceability requirement (6.39 per cent) respectively. For India to have a meaningful collaboration with RTA partners, eg, Regional Comprehensive Economic Partnership (RCEP) members, there is a need to reduce such regulatory constraints.

[110] International Trade Centre, 'Market Access Map Database', www.macmap.org/, accessed 9 March 2019.

C. India's Act East: Trade with RCEP Partners

It is often argued that the future of India's trade lies in the 'East', ie, Asia and the Pacific, which forms a sizable market for Indian merchandise as well as services exports. The country has already taken the plunge in that direction by launching the 'Act East Policy' in 2014. India is presently busy in the RCEP negotiations, which began in May 2013. RCEP involves ASEAN countries and its six FTA partners, namely – Australia, China, India, Japan, New Zealand and South Korea. India already has RTAs with ASEAN, Japan and South Korea, while negotiations with Australia and New Zealand are on. With China however the country has no effective comprehensive trade agreement at present. The RCEP negotiations are however moving slowly and India has taken a cautious approach so far.[111]

For pharma exports, the 'East' can provide an opportune market, as the 'West' countries, as members of Anti-Counterfeiting Trade Agreement (ACTA), have in the past stopped Indian generic medicine export consignments in transit.[112] Though the EU later agreed to stop such confiscations, the potential future threat still looms large.[113] It is therefore important to note whether Indian pharma exports erect some form of trade barriers while trading with RCEP and the country's competitiveness in the RCEP markets.

Table 7 shows the emerging trade balance scenario for India in the pharma trade (Harmonized System classification 30) with the RCEP partners. India enjoys an overall positive average trade balance with RCEP during the recent (2011–17) period. The trade balance is however negative and worsening in three partners, namely China, Indonesia and South Korea. Given the fact that India maintain a higher tariff on pharma products (around 10 per cent), after the RCEP-led reforms, which is likely to reduce the tariff towards zero per cent, the trade balance may change. It may be remembered that China in particular enters the Indian market with positive tariff at present.

Table 7 India's Pharmaceutical Sector (HS 30) Trade with RCEP Partners

	Export			Import			Trade Balance		
Countries	2001–05	2006–10	2011–17	2001–05	2006–10	2011–17	2001–05	2006–10	2011–17
Australia	11.91	47.48	178.19	2.95	4.03	12.15	8.96	43.45	166.04
Brunei Darussalam	0.09	0.07	0.04	0.00	0.00	0.00	0.09	0.07	0.04

(continued)

[111] D Chakraborty and others, 'Is It Finally Time for India's Free Trade Agreements? The ASEAN "Present" and the RCEP "Future"' (2019) 9(2) *Asian Journal of International Law* 359–91.

[112] See, DS 408 – European Union and a Member State – Seizure of Generic Drugs in Transit (Complainant: India); E Bonadio and CM Cantore, 'Seizures of In Transit Generics at the EU Borders: India and Brazil v the EU' (2010) 1(4) *European Journal of Risk Regulation* 404–08.

[113] 'EU agrees to stop confiscation of Indian generic drugs', *Economic Times* (New Delhi 2011).

Table 7 ***(Continued)***

	Export			Import			Trade Balance		
Countries	2001–05	2006–10	2011–17	2001–05	2006–10	2011–17	2001–05	2006–10	2011–17
Cambodia	7.29	16.82	32.48	0.00	0.01	0.00	7.29	16.81	32.48
China	25.20	25.25	40.77	7.90	41.57	128.81	17.30	−16.32	−88.04
Indonesia	4.03	9.61	22.26	4.80	16.20	97.25	−0.77	−6.59	−74.99
Japan	8.40	9.37	45.05	4.66	12.29	19.50	3.74	−2.92	25.56
Lao PDR	0.20	0.96	2.50	0.00	0.01	0.02	0.20	0.95	2.48
Malaysia	11.08	23.80	44.70	2.03	3.03	4.09	9.04	20.78	40.61
Myanmar	15.75	47.26	143.02	0.00	0.08	0.00	15.75	47.17	143.02
New Zealand	3.70	14.06	37.07	0.11	0.60	0.86	3.59	13.47	36.21
Philippines	14.92	38.02	142.91	0.34	1.48	0.19	14.57	36.54	142.72
Singapore	14.42	19.37	59.07	0.94	4.77	13.67	13.49	14.60	45.40
South Korea	8.40	9.31	11.77	5.73	11.05	36.63	2.68	−1.74	−24.87
Thailand	11.30	31.82	75.80	0.54	1.36	1.74	10.76	30.46	74.07
Viet Nam	39.42	81.56	143.71	0.27	0.50	0.42	39.16	81.06	143.29
Total	176.10	374.76	979.34	30.26	96.96	315.32	145.84	277.80	664.02

Source: Computed by authors from Trade Map data.

The extent of the incomplete tariff reforms in India against the ASEAN partners, vis-à-vis China can be understood with help of Figure 6. China entered into FTA with ASEAN in 2005, as compared to India's entry into FTA with the bloc in 2010. Figure 6 shows the movement of average tariff barrier in the pharma sector on Malaysia (a representative ASEAN partner) by China and India. Since 1990, India maintained a high level of tariff barrier against Malaysia, while the tariff imposed by China has been relatively lower. In the aftermath of the Sino–ASEAN FTA, from 2010 onwards, China imposes a zero per cent tariff on imports from Malaysia. India on the other hand increased average tariff on pharma products after entry of the Indo–ASEAN FTA in 2010 and only after 2015 the same has come down. The tariff trend indicates that during RCEP negotiations the onus of tariff reform will be more on India. The saving grace is that during negotiations India has been able to secure a gradual tariff reform plan with RCEP partners, who presently are not linked with the country through a pre-dating RTA (ie, Australia, China and New Zealand).[114]

[114] Transnational Institute (undated), 'RCEP: A secret deal', www.tni.org/files/publication-downloads/foe-rcep-secret-deal-2-web.pdf, accessed 11 March 2019.

Figure 6 Effective Applied Tariff on Malaysia – Comparing India and China in Pharmaceuticals (HS 30)

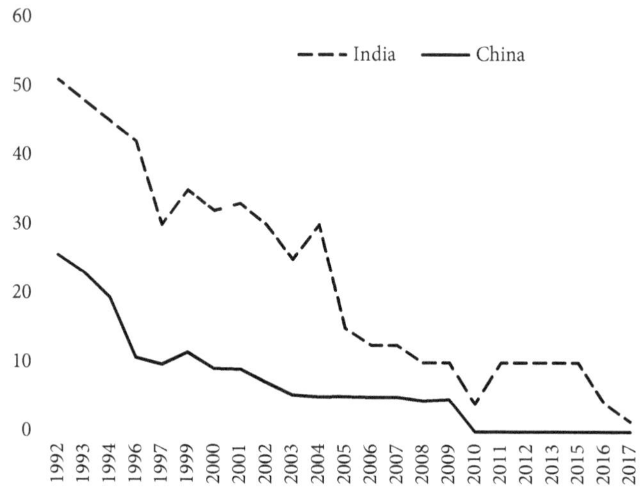

Source: Constructed by authors from WITS data.

D. Competitiveness in RCEP Market

One underlying reason behind India's decent pharma export performance in the RCEP market can be explained through the matching inclinations in trade pattern or *complementarity*; ie, whether India's export supply orientation might actually be in line with the import demand pattern of RCEP partners. The complementarity in the trade pattern of the partners can be judged from the *Trade Complementarity Index* (TCI), using the following formula:

$$TCI_{ij} = 100\ X \left[1 - \frac{(\Sigma\ |M_{jk} - X_{ik}|)}{2} \right]$$

where, X_{ik} is share of pharmaceutical export *k* (at HS 4-digit) in India's total exports (within the corresponding HS 2-digit, ie, HS 30), and M_{jk} is share of the same product in partner's (say, Australia) import. The X_{ik} and M_{jk} are considered over the HS 4-digit level, ie, HS 3001 (Dried glands and other organs etc) to HS 3006 (Pharmaceutical preparations and products etc). Higher values of TCI in exports over time indicate increasing similarities between sectoral export basket of a country (India) and import basket of its partner (ie, RCEP countries) and vice versa. Increasing TCI values underlines the possibility of increase in export of country *i* to country *j*. As trade is not symmetric, given the difference in domestic factor and demand conditions, a country's export and import complementarities with the same partners can be different.

Table 8 summarises the bilateral *Trade Complementarity Index* (TCI) in the pharmaceutical sector between exports from India and imports by RCEP countries (ie, India's export complementarity) for three periods, 2008, 2012 and 2017. It is observed from the table that while India's average export TCI values have increased for several countries (Brunei, Indonesia, South Korea), underlining possible export opportunities, decline in the same for a number of big RCEP economies (Australia, China, Japan, New Zealand, Thailand) is not a good sign. On the other hand, India's import complementarity has increased considerably from Australia, China and South Korea, indicating possible import growth from these sources. It may be noted that India is already suffering from a trade deficit in pharma sector against China and South Korea.

Table 8 India's Trade Complementarity Index with RCEP Partners

	India Export – Partner Import			**Partner Export – India Import**		
Country	**2008**	**2012**	**2017**	**2008**	**2012**	**2017**
Australia	87.06	88.44	77.25	77.73	74.20	90.13
Brunei Darussalam	89.57	87.31	96.01	73.66	69.46	76.24
Cambodia	85.92	89.55	86.14	67.91	63.60	43.90
China	88.39	84.27	76.64	45.75	53.07	60.84
Indonesia	72.03	77.57	74.14	90.08	90.47	78.33
Japan	78.30	79.89	75.60	87.34	85.55	84.32
Lao PDR	76.93	73.99	70.10	78.27	84.23	66.42
Malaysia	–	74.02	50.22	–	–	31.89
Myanmar	92.09	92.70	93.46	81.94	73.08	69.36
New Zealand		92.01	88.88		63.36	62.05
Philippines	86.04	84.33	75.71	89.01	95.40	83.88
Singapore	88.65	88.74	85.50	70.30	69.24	65.87
South Korea	73.15	59.83	69.98	74.11	73.95	85.87
Thailand	86.01	83.61	78.50	71.32	75.56	73.92
Viet Nam	87.70	94.15	94.11	84.34	70.70	67.49

Source: Computed by authors from Trade Map data.

Finally, the intensity with which a country is able to enter a partner market compared to the benchmark of the rest of the world, can be understood through the Export Intensity Index (EII). EII can be calculated by the following formulation:

$$EII = \frac{x_{ij}/X_{iw}}{x_{wj}/X_{ww}}$$

In the numerator, X_{ij} refers to the bilateral sectoral export of a given country pair (say, India's pharmaceutical export to Myanmar), while X_{iw} indicates India's global exports (ie, total pharmaceuticals export to all countries). In the denominator, X_{wj} and X_{ww} represents world's pharmaceuticals export to the importing country (ie, Myanmar in this case) and to the world respectively. The value of EII above one for any given country-pair (say, India and Myanmar) indicates that the export penetration from India is 'intense', while a value less than 'one' indicates otherwise. It is argued that with trade integration the index is expected to increase, eventually exceeding one.

In the current context, the EII indices has been computed for the RCEP market for the six major pharma products (shown in Table 4 earlier) noted in Table 9. The average EII figures are shown for two periods, 2009–12 and 2014–17, for each individual RCEP partner market. It is observed from the table that for not a single product India enjoys 'intensiveness' advantage in all RCEP markets. In particular, medicaments consisting of mixed or unmixed products (HS 300490), which is a major export item from India, is having intensive relation during both periods only in Cambodia, Malaysia, New Zealand, Philippines, Thailand and Vietnam. Countries where India enjoys intensive relation for more than three pharma exports for both periods include: Cambodia, Laos, Malaysia, Philippines, Singapore, Thailand and Vietnam. This puts a question mark on India's real competitiveness in RCEP partners and the potential benefits in the post-bloc period.

Table 9 India's Export Intensity Index with RCEP Partners

RCEP Partners	300490		300420		300220		300410		300450		300390	
	2009–12	2014–17	2009–12	2014–17	2009–12	2014–17	2009–12	2014–17	2009–12	2014–17	2009–12	2014–17
Australia	0.56	1.00	0.54	0.82	0.01	0.00	2.78	4.46	0.88	0.14	5.10	3.44
Brunei Darussalam	0.04	0.04	0.00	0.00	0.00	0.00	0.39	0.00	0.00	0.00	0.02	0.00
Cambodia	8.04	5.40	55.68	31.80	1.04	12.56	19.14	18.44	16.14	12.55	97.26	26.32
China	0.11	0.04	0.01	0.04	0.18	0.63	0.01	0.02	0.01	0.01	3.91	1.49
Indonesia	1.59	0.76	1.37	0.14	1.32	5.06	1.68	0.03	0.68	0.01	7.27	18.57
Japan	0.10	0.08	0.02	0.05	0.00	0.01	0.01	0.01	0.31	0.00	0.50	0.27
South Korea	0.17	0.06	0.28	0.24	0.16	0.00	0.37	0.26	0.06	0.06	0.58	1.51
Laos	–	5.03	–	10.75	10.01	55.14	0.01	0.00	0.83	4.47	0.31	0.17
Malaysia	2.10	1.25	3.80	2.39	0.58	0.71	3.05	2.01	0.45	0.30	8.61	6.39
Myanmar	–	13.11	–	45.32	–	61.99	–	38.48	4.44	16.59	–	13.62
New Zealand	2.52	1.96	0.57	1.18	0.00	0.00	2.00	0.74	1.93	0.11	1.02	0.95
Philippines	4.26	3.94	6.06	4.34	7.60	7.32	2.67	2.51	0.99	1.42	12.43	20.80
Singapore	0.76	0.79	7.38	8.28	2.29	0.74	26.85	4.12	3.90	3.83	30.76	19.71
Thailand	1.62	1.55	0.68	0.46	1.15	1.60	3.99	2.22	2.05	0.62	1.89	2.53
Viet Nam	4.06	1.83	2.20	1.51	1.00	4.32	2.91	0.64	1.91	0.81	5.74	1.45

Source: Computed by authors from Trade Map data.

E. IPR Negotiations under RCEP: Comfort Zone for India?

In the recent past, the mega-regional trade negotiations have focused on strengthening of the IPR regime in constituent partners, often moving towards TRIPS-Plus provisions. Protecting patent rights of corporates as well as maintaining data exclusivity has been two major focus areas in these negotiations. For instance, the data exclusivity provisions discussed in Trans-Pacific Partnership (TPP) may potentially delay the entry of generic drugs in the market on one hand and increase their price for the consumers on the other.[115] RCEP negotiations on IPR front on the other hand started with a discussion only to reduce IPR-related obstacles to trade and investment among members, much to India's comfort.[116] However, an evolving perspective from RCEP partners is being witnessed in the recent period, when Japan and South Korea stressed the need to keep IPR provisions of the bloc business-friendly, which raised potential concerns over access to medicines and public health policy choices, a major focus area for Indian policymakers given the current domestic scenario.[117]

The importance of data exclusivity provisions are not new for India, as they have already emerged as a major bone of contention during the India–EU Bilateral Trade and Investment Agreement (BTIA) negotiations.[118] The Satwant Reddy Committee in India (2007) earlier analysed the compliance of domestic provisions with Article 39.3 of TRIPS (relating to data protection requirements) and concluded that the existing Indian legal framework offer sufficient protection against unauthorised use or disclosure of confidential data.[119] However, in the recent period, a number of Indian firms characterised by higher research-orientation (eg, Biocon, Glenmark, Dr Reddy's, Lupin, Bharat Biotech) are calling for, 'stronger data protection laws to protect their investments in global clinical trials … regulatory data protection (RDP) in order to promote innovation and investment in the development of new medicines'.[120] Given the deepening research intensity of Indian pharma majors and the co-development arrangements between Indian and multinational pharma companies, a re-look into the existing policies is in order.

It deserves mention that five ACTA member countries, the group which is very particular about treatment of generic medicines, have become part of RCEP negotiations. They are Australia, Japan, New Zealand, Singapore and South Korea.

[115] P Agarwal, 'Impact of TPP on International, Regional and other Plurilateral IP Norm Setting' (2017) 22 *Journal of Intellectual Property Rights* 7–15.

[116] Y-C Kim, 'RCEP vs TPP: The Pursuit of Eastern Dominance' in Y-C Kim (ed), *Chinese Global Production Networks in ASEAN, Understanding China* (Geneva, Springer, 2016) 19–37.

[117] Japan's stance might be guided by perspectives from business groups like Keidanren, whose members include pharma majors from both Japan (eg, Takeda and Astellas Pharma) and the global theatre (eg, Pfizer and Sanofi). For details, see Transnational Institute 'RCEP: A secret deal', www.tni.org/files/publication-downloads/foe-rcep-secret-deal-2-web.pdf, accessed 16 March 2019.

[118] Chaisse and Chakraborty (n 19).

[119] For details on Satwant Reddy Committee recommendations, see Khanna and Singh (n 54).

[120] ibid.

The proposal by Japan and South Korea to make RCEP IPR provisions 'business-friendly' therefore needs to be viewed in this light. The point might be underlined with two examples. First, the proposed RCEP text on border enforcement is TRIPS-Plus in nature, as instead of using the provisions against trademark counterfeiting and copyrights piracy (in line with WTO code), goods (particularly generic medicines) in transit are being targeted instead in the RTA negotiations.[121] Second, for border enforcement TRIPS provisions under WTO requires countries to come up with 'adequate evidence of infringement' and 'sufficiently detailed description of the goods in dispute'.[122] RCEP draft text on IPR negotiations instead requires simply 'any information', which may facilitate rampant misuse of the provision.[123] Understandably in the recently concluded 25th Round of RCEP negotiations (2019) in Bali, India moved very cautiously on the IPR front, as it is not inclined to accommodate any TRIPS-Plus provisions in RCEP. From an Indian standpoint such an event might deter competition in the market by strengthening the position of global majors on one hand and potentially hurt the exports of generic medicines on the other.

VI. Conclusion

Nations that have not implemented, or do not enforce, robust IPRs protections end up harming their economic development in at least three possible ways. First, they dis-incentivise and deter future innovative activity. Second, they discourage trade and FDI flows, which only hurts their own consumers and businesses, by both limiting their choices and inhibiting their enterprises' ability to access best-of-breed technologies that are vital to boosting domestic productivity. Third, in countries with weak IPR protections, firms are forced to invest undue amounts of resources in protection rather than invention. On the contrary, stronger IPR provisions put the domestic sector on stronger footing and steadier growth path. The evidences from the pharma sectors in EU and other developed countries underline this fact and may be taken into account by Indian policymakers.

The current discussion indicates that given the policy framework, for a sizable period of time, R&D expenses was not a necessary condition for pharma companies for survival in the Indian market. Thanks to the process patent regime, while the domestic firms specialised in generic medicines and flourished, it also limited their long-term growth prospects. The modest competitiveness pattern of Indian pharma exports, as seen from the Export Intensity Index in RCEP partners, is

[121] Medecins Sans Frontiers, 'Regional Comprehensive Economic Partnership: Intellectual Property Chapter and the Impact on Access to Medicines', *Access Campaign, MSF RCEP IP Chapter Technical Analysis* (Geneva 2016).

[122] World Trade Organization, 'Part III – Enforcement of Intellectual Property Rights' (1995), www.wto.org/english/docs_e/legal_e/27-trips_05_e.htm, accessed 23 March 2019.

[123] MSF (n 121).

an indication of the same. On the other hand, the policy-induced supply side inefficiencies helped little to augment affordable access to medicines for domestic consumers, which prompted authorities to take recourse to price control mechanisms.

For a developing country like India, with a majority of the population meeting their health expense need from their own pocket, it is easy to blame a stringent IPR regime as an area of concern. However, it is observed that other beyond-IPR factors, such as, tariffs and NTMs, inefficient supply chains, incomplete reforms on ease of doing business etc also contribute significantly to increase the price of medicines. Lack of a strong IPR regime simultaneously with a drug price control in effect may delay innovation and the advent of cutting-edge medicines, which are much required for securing a better health outcome.

Adoption of a dual policy approach is therefore crucial for India. First, on the domestic front an ecosystem for facilitating innovation and R&D orientation needs to be facilitated through a series of systemic reforms, primarily reducing the transaction cost of doing business. Second, given the complementarity of RCEP market for India's pharma exports, it makes economic sense for India to join the bloc, but only with TRIPS-compliant provisions. Given the domestic dynamics in Indian pharma sector, it is unlikely that the country would be able to comply with the negotiating stance adopted by Japan and South Korea (eg, on border measures) in the short run. It has been acknowledged that if RCEP finally agree on stringent TRIPS-Plus IPR provisions, it would end up hurting consumers by denying them cheaper access to essential medicines.[124] Other RCEP partners therefore need to acknowledge India's domestic compulsions and shelve the TRIPS-Plus reforms for long run. Meanwhile for India, lateral learning from the policy frameworks of the EU and other countries are crucial to usher in the much-required firm-level innovations.

[124] PK Yu, 'The RCEP and Trans-Pacific Intellectual Property Norms' (2017) 50 *Vanderbilt Journal of Transnational Law* 673–740.

INDEX

Note: Alphabetical arrangement is word-by-word, where a group of letters followed by a space is filed before the same group of letters followed by a letter, eg 'legal systems' will appear before 'legalisation'. In determining alphabetical arrangement, initial articles and prepositions are ignored.

www.ingramcontent.com/pod-product-compliance
Ingram Content Group UK Ltd.
Pitfield, Milton Keynes, MK11 3LW, UK
UKHW021911150926
475560UK00003B/322